HC
467
.E266
1991

Economic development
in the Republic of
Korea.

$49.50

DATE			

DISCARD

© THE BAKER & TAYLOR CO.

ECONOMIC DEVELOPMENT
IN THE
REPUBLIC OF KOREA

126°E   128°E   130°E

DEMOCRATIC PEOPLE'S
REPUBLIC OF KOREA
(North Korea)

38°N   38°N

KANGWŎN

East Sea
(Sea of Japan)

Seoul

Inch'ŏn

KYŎNGGI

NORTH
CH'UNGCH'ŎNG

REPUBLIC OF KOREA

W—E

SOUTH
CH'UNGCH'ŎNG   Taejŏn

NORTH
KYŎNGSANG

36°N   36°N

Yellow Sea

Taegu

NORTH
CHŎLLA

SOUTH KYŎNGSANG

Kwangju

Pusan

SOUTH CHŎLLA

Korea   Strait

TSUSHIMA

34°N   34°N

Cheju   Strait

USSR

NORTH KOREA
(DPRK)

East Sea

CHEJU

JAPAN

CHINA   SOUTH KOREA
(ROK)

East
China
Sea   Pacific
Ocean

0   50   100   150 miles
0   50   100   150   200 kilometers

TAIWAN

126°E

ECONOMIC DEVELOPMENT IN THE REPUBLIC OF KOREA
A Policy Perspective

Edited by
Lee-Jay Cho and Yoon Hyung Kim

An East–West Center Book
Distributed by the University of Hawaii Press

Library of Congress Cataloging-in-Publication Data

Economic development in the Republic of Korea / edited by Lee-Jay Cho
and Yoon Hyung Kim.
    p.   cm.
  Includes bibliographical references and index.
  ISBN 0-86638-131-7 : $49.50
  1. Korea (South)—Economic policy—1960- 2. Korea (South)—Social
policy. 3. Industry and state—Korea (South) I. Cho, Lee-Jay.
II. Kim, Yoon Hyung.
HC467.E266 1991
338.95195—dc20   90-20706
                                                                  CIP

Published in 1991 by the East-West Center
1777 East-West Road, Honolulu, Hawaii 96848

Distributed by the University of Hawaii Press
2840 Kolowalu Street, Honolulu, Hawaii 96822

Contents

PART I: POLITICAL AND ECONOMIC BACKGROUND

PART II: ECONOMIC POLICIES, 1961–80

MONETARY AND PRICE POLICIES

AGRICULTURAL POLICIES

INDUSTRIAL POLICIES

PART III: CULTURE, EDUCATION, AND SOCIAL CHANGE

PART IV: EPILOGUE

List of Figures

List of Tables

Contributors

Editors

Lee-Jay Cho is vice president for academic affairs at the East–West Center, and director of the East–West Population Institute in Honolulu, Hawaii. Dr. Cho was an advisor to the government of the Republic of Korea on population, human resources, and urban issues in the 1960s and 1970s. Recently, he has led and participated in many studies on China's population and economic development policy. Dr. Cho has a Ph.D. in sociology from the University of Chicago, a doctorate in economics from Keio University, and a doctorate in demography from Tokyo University.

Yoon Hyung Kim is professor of economics at Hankuk University of Foreign Studies in Seoul, and research associate at the East–West Population Institute, East–West Center, Honolulu, Hawaii. Dr. Kim was director-general of the Planning Bureau of the Ministry of Energy and Resources of the Republic of Korea from 1977 to 1980 and chief of the Development Planning Office of the Korea Development Institute from 1973 to 1978. From 1971 to 1973, Dr. Kim was an economist in the Development Research Center of the World Bank in Washington, D.C. Dr. Kim received his Ph.D. in economics from Stanford University.

Authors

Kennon Breazeale is a research associate at the East–West Center, Honolulu, Hawaii, serving jointly in the institutes of Culture and Communication, Resource Systems, and Population. Dr. Breazeale has a doctorate (D.Phil) in oriental studies from the University of Oxford.

Kwang Choi is professor of economics at Hankuk University of Foreign Studies in Seoul, and a member of the Budget System Review Committee, Economic Planning Board, and the Tax Review Commission, Ministry of Finance, Republic of Korea. He is also on the Board of Directors of the Korea Development Bank. Dr. Choi was a senior fellow of the Korea Development Institute during 1981–85. He has a Ph.D. in economics from the University of Maryland.

Sung Hwan Jo is professor of economics and dean of the College of Economics at Sogang University in Seoul. Dr. Jo has a Ph.D. in economics from Yale University.

Kwang Suk Kim is professor of economics at Kyung Hee University in Seoul. Dr. Kim was an economic advisor to the U.S. Agency for International Development mission in Korea from 1958 to 1970. He was a research director and vice president of Korea Development Institute during 1972–82. From 1986 to 1989 he was dean of the Graduate School of Business Administration, Kyung Hee University. Dr. Kim has a Ph.D. in economics from Korea University.

Wan-Soon Kim is professor of international economics at the College of Business Administration, Korea University, and concurrently chairs the Korean Trade Commission, Ministry of Trade and Industry, Republic of Korea. Since 1975 Dr. Kim has been a member of several advisory committees for the government of the Republic of Korea, including the Tax Advisory Committee of the Finance Ministry. During 1967–71, he was an economist at the International Monetary Fund, and subsequently spent about two years as a senior fellow at the Korea Development Institute. He has a Ph.D. in economics from Harvard University.

Won Bae Kim is research associate at the East–West Population Institute, East–West Center, Honolulu, Hawaii. Dr. Kim has taught at the University of Hawaii and Dong-A University in Pusan, Korea. He has a Ph.D. in urban and regional planning from the University of Wisconsin-Madison.

Chung Hoon Lee is professor of economics at the University of Hawaii, and research associate, Resource Systems Institute, East–West Center, Honolulu, Hawaii. Dr. Lee has a Ph.D. in economics from the University of California at Berkeley.

Kyung Tae Lee is a senior fellow at the Korea Institute for Economics and Technology and counselor to the minister of trade and industry, Republic of Korea. Dr. Lee served as deputy division director of the Banking Bureau of the Ministry of Finance, Republic of Korea, from 1974 to 1977. Dr. Lee has a Ph.D. in economics from George Washington University.

Suk-Chae Lee is an economic secretary (assistant minister rank) with the Office of the President of the Republic of Korea, where he has served since 1984. During this period he was involved in many key economic policy decisions and has been in charge of macroeconomic policy, international economic policy, agricultural policy, and recently regional development policy. Dr. Lee was with the Economic Planning Board during 1970–84 and worked at various bureaus including service as assistant director and director of the Economic Planning Bureau. Dr. Lee has a Ph.D. in economics from Boston University.

Andrew Mason is professor of economics at the University of Hawaii, and research associate, Population Institute, East-West Center, Honolulu, Hawaii. Dr. Mason has a Ph.D. in economics from the University of Michigan.

Pal Yong Moon is professor of economics at Konkuk University in Seoul. He has also been a member of the Agricultural Imports Committee, Ministry of Agriculture and Fisheries, Republic of Korea, since 1980. Previously Dr. Moon was a member of the Agricultural Policy Advisory Committee, Ministry of Agriculture and Fisheries (1976–82) and senior fellow, Korea Development Institute (1972–76). Dr. Moon has a Ph.D. in economics from Oregon State University.

Sang-Woo Nam is senior fellow at the Korea Development Institute where he has been actively involved in macroeconomic policymaking since 1977. Dr. Nam served as counselor to the deputy prime minister of the Republic of Korea in the early 1980s. He was an economist at the World Bank during 1986–88 in the Macroeconomic Division of the Development Research Department and the Asia Regional Office. Dr. Nam has a Ph.D. in management from the Massachusetts Institute of Technology.

Chong Kee Park is professor of economics at Inha University, Inch'ŏn, Korea. He also is a member of the Board of Directors, Citizens National Bank; Budget System Review Committee, Economic Planning Board; Tax Advisory Committee, Ministry of Finance, Republic of Korea; and Research Advisory Committee, Korea Development Institute. He was a senior fellow and research director of Korea Development Institute during 1971–73 and dean of the College of Business and Economics at Inha University during 1985–87. Dr. Park has a Ph.D. in economics from George Washington University.

Yung Chul Park is professor of economics at Korea University. Professor Park has served as advisor to the Korea Research Institute for Human Settlements, the Bank of Korea, and the Ministry of Finance, Republic of Korea. He has a Ph.D. in economics from the University of Minnesota.

Acknowledgments

The editors would like to express their profound gratitude to the Economic Planning Board of the Republic of Korea, the Korea Development Institute, the Korean Research Foundation, the Korean Traders' Association, and the Korea Institute of Industrial Economics and Technology for their generous financial support which, together with the expertise contributed by many of their senior staff members, has ensured the successful completion and publication of this book.

We want to acknowledge the invaluable contributions made by Mr. Chung Yum Kim, formerly Korea's ambassador to Japan and chief of staff, Office of the President of the Republic of Korea. Our sincere thanks also to the many former and current government officials who provided access to unpublished government data and were a unique resource for background material on the policymaking process during the Park years.

We are grateful to Dr. Daniel B. Suits of the University of Michigan and Dr. Kwang Suk Kim of Kyung Hee University in Seoul for their valuable contributions to the substantive editing of the government policy measures. Appreciation is also due to Dr. Chung Hoon Lee, Dr. Burnham Campbell, and Dr. Kennon Breazeale for their helpful suggestions. Dr. Ki-Jun Rhee, director cf the Asia–Pacific Institute in Seoul and Dr. Shinichi Ichimura of Kyoto University provided useful comments on an earlier draft. Anne Stewart, who served as manuscript editor of this volume, has done so much in the preparation of this work that without her valuable contributions we would not have seen its publication.

We are indebted to many people who helped bring this book to completion. The Graphics and Production Services Unit of the East–West Center brought the book to a camera-ready state. We are especially indebted to Jacqueline D'Orazio for production coordination, Russell Fujita for the book's design, and Lois Bender for typesetting. We are also grateful to Corinne Holland, editorial assistant at the East–West Population Institute, for proofreading the manuscript and Allison Greenspan for preparing the index. We also thank Janet Heavenridge, production manager at the University of Hawaii Press, for her assistance with the project.

Lee-Jay Cho
Yoon Hyung Kim

Preface

During the 18 years of President Park Chung Hee's leadership, from 1961 to 1979, the Republic of Korea underwent dramatic economic development, maintained relative domestic political stability, and achieved major economic and political advances in the international arena. A salient feature of this period of rapid growth was the close and extensive cooperation between government and business in pursuit of national development objectives. This cooperation is reminiscent of Japan, where policy reflects a fairly good consensus of opinion among the principal elements of the Japanese industrial community. In Korea[1] the government and its development policymakers took much more assertive leadership and set policies, with the business community cooperating in their implementation.

By any economic criteria, the South Korean economy registered outstanding material performance in the 1960s and 1970s. The gross national product (GNP) increased in real terms more than thirteenfold when measured at 1980 constant prices (from 3.00 trillion won in 1961 to 39.25 trillion won in 1979). Comparing South Korea with North Korea, the South did not overtake the North in per capita GNP until the late 1960s. In 1987, however, the South exceeded the North by more than sixfold in GNP and more than threefold in per capita GNP. From one of the poorest developing countries in 1961, South Korea was transformed into a semi-industrial, middle-income nation by the final year of the Park era, and during that period per capita income rose from a mere US $82 to US $1,644.

The rapid development was led by export-oriented industrial expansion and was achieved in spite of poor natural resource endowments. Korean exports, which remained stagnant at a low level in the 1950s, increased rapidly at an average annual rate of 39.1 percent when measured in constant 1980 dollars (from US $40.9 million in 1961 to $15.1 billion in 1979), with manufactured goods accounting for the majority of total exports. As the rapid expansion of exports stimulated the domestic economy, real GNP grew by an average annual rate of 9 percent during 1961–79, compared with only about 4 percent in the immediate postwar period 1954–61. The manufacturing sector, in particular, expanded at an average annual rate of 17.5 percent during 1961–79, thereby increasing its share of GNP from 13.5 percent to 26.9 percent. Over the same period, the share of agriculture,

---

1. Throughout this volume, "Korea" refers to the undivided peninsula up to 1945 and to South Korea—the Republic of Korea—after World War II. Likewise, "Koreans" refers to the entire Korean populace up to 1945 and thereafter specifically to South Koreans. References to modern North Korea should be clear from the context of the discussion. This terminology has been adopted for simplicity of style and does not imply any cultural or political judgment.

forestry, and fishing declined from 38.7 percent to 20.5 percent (BOK, *Economic Statistics Yearbook,* 1986).

What caused this transformation? The rapid economic growth that characterizes the Park era can be attributed to many factors, including investment and rapid capital growth, expansion of industrial productive capacity, and the development of human resources and labor productivity. Other contributing factors were the favorable worldwide economic conditions prevailing during the 1960s, Korea's political stability, the commitment of the country's leaders to economic development (as illustrated by the launching of the First Five-Year Economic Development Plan), the outward-looking strategy of industrialization, the vitality and entrepreneurship of the emerging corporate leaders, the grassroots support and participation in rural transformation, and the close government-business interplay in Korean economic development. It can also be argued that the cultural values shared in common among the Koreans, Chinese, and Japanese contributed to the quality of the labor force, principally through education.

Manufacturing output expanded dramatically during the 1960s and 1970s, thereby leading the rapid growth of an economy that had been shattered by the Korean War (1950-53). As Korea shifted from the import-substitution strategy of the postwar 1953-61 period to an export-led industrialization strategy during 1962-79, exports (principally manufactured goods) rose sharply. Along with the dramatic increase in the proportion of the manufacturing sector in GNP, the share of this sector in total employment nearly tripled during the high-growth period under President Park. In particular, the output share of heavy and chemical industries nearly doubled (to almost 55 percent) by 1979.

The Park era is also characterized by a dramatic increase in capital formation. The average proportion of GNP devoted annually to gross domestic capital formation increased sharply (from about 15 percent in 1962-64 to about 32 percent in 1977-79). During 1953-63 Korea financed up to two-thirds of total investment requirements from foreign sources, most of which was economic aid from the United States. When the major fiscal and financial reforms were set in motion in the mid-1960s, however, the government successfully mobilized domestic resources. The gross domestic savings rate, which was about 3-5 percent until the early 1960s, rapidly increased to 28 percent on average during 1977-79. Moreover, the sectoral savings pattern underwent drastic changes. Government saving was negative up to 1963 but rapidly increased in the late 1960s and 1970s. Household saving also remained negative during 1961-63 but increased remarkably to 12.6 percent of GNP in 1977-79. More than 80 percent of GNP was expended on private consumption until the early 1960s, but Korea successfully reduced its average propensity to consume to 62 percent in 1977-79. Throughout the entire 1953-89 period, however, it was the business sector that made the greatest contribution to the rapid increase in gross domestic saving. As a result of the sharp increase in domestic saving over the past three decades, Korea's national economic capacity has expanded to such an extent that the country is now able to finance more than its entire gross domestic capital formation.

The labor force required for expansion of manufacturing production during the high-speed growth period was provided by the existing unemployed urban population and the abundant human resources in the rural sector already available in the early 1960s. Rapid industrialization was thus not restrained by shortages of labor and skills. From the early 1960s, concurrent with the industrialization drive, the government embarked on a bold family planning program and successfully reduced the population growth rate. The sharp growth in per capita GNP in real terms led to a commensurate substantial increase in per capita private consumption, greatly improving the living standard of the Korean people as a whole.

Prior to the 1960s, about two-thirds of the Korean labor force resided in rural areas. Even though total population grew at about 2 percent on average per year between 1963 and 1979, the "baby boom" after the Korean War resulted in an increase on average of 3.4 percent per year in the total labor force. Rapid industrialization, led by the expansion of labor-intensive manufacturing for export, nonetheless absorbed the existing unemployed population as well as the newly participating labor force. The growth rate of urban employment far outstripped that of the rural areas, reducing the urban unemployment rate by about two-thirds (from 16.0 percent in 1963 to 5.6 percent in 1979). This rapid increase in urban employment substantially alleviated unemployment throughout the economy. In the meantime, the proportion of urban employment in the total employed population rose sharply (from 35.6 percent in 1963 to 58.5 percent in 1979). The rising demand for labor in the industrial and urban sectors led to heavy migration from rural areas. But, although rural employment was declining, value added in agriculture in real terms was growing at a fairly respectable rate. Labor productivity in the manufacturing sector also rose at a healthy rate, and real wages increased even more rapidly.

High-speed growth could not have materialized without Korea's abundant human resources and continuous investment in education. Over the two decades from 1960 to 1980, the average number of years that the employed population spent in school nearly doubled (from 4.2 years to 8 years). The improvements in education not only enabled urban employment to increase quickly without significant shortages of skilled workers until early in the 1980s, but also contributed to increased labor productivity and wage levels.

Rapid growth and structural change in such a brief span of time was not achieved without sacrifices. The tempo of inflation accelerated at an annual rate of about 19 percent throughout the period 1962–79. This inflation can be attributed mainly to the approximately 29 percent average annual growth rate of the money supply, caused by the accumulation of fiscal deficits, expansion of preferential policy loans, grain-price subsidies, and the low level of the domestic savings rate at the outset of industrialization. Inflation was regarded by the Korean government as the inevitable price for high-speed economic growth. Although an economic stabilization program was initiated in the last year of the Park administration, inflationary pressure was not brought under control until the mid-1980s, by which time Korea was faced with yet another crunch in the form of mounting foreign debt.

This book examines the major economic policies of the 1960s and 1970s. The measures examined in this work, which were formulated and implemented during the administration of President Park, played a critical role in transforming the structure of the Korean economy and in moving it to a higher growth path. The conceptual framework underlying the appraisals in this book is also based on the broader premise that Korea's economic performance during the 1960s and 1970s was an outcome of the interactions among environment (defined to include resources, technology, and international markets), the economic system, government policy, and the public. The success stories and hard lessons of recent Korean experiences will serve, moreover, as a valuable set of materials for future socioeconomic development planning and implementation by both Korea and other developing countries.

This research project was planned and coordinated by the East–West Center on a cost-sharing and cooperative basis with the Korean Traders Association, the Korea Development Institute, and the Korea Institute of Industrial Economics and Technology. Comprehensive and detailed case studies of 18 major economic policy measures constitute the core of the book. Additional chapters have been designed to place these policies in the broader perspective of cultural values, the development of human resources, and modern political change in Korea. The final chapter summarizes the political, economic, and social development of Korea during the 1980s.

The case studies have a common structure, thereby providing a basis for tracing patterns of economic policy, interactions, the Korean model of economic development, and the lessons for the future. Each examines the main features of a particular policy measure, its theoretical appropriateness and effects, and the interaction of government, business, and the public in its formulation and implementation.

Prominent Korean scholars were invited by the East–West Center to write specific modules in their respective areas of expertise. Active participation by Korean institutions was an important feature of the project. Subsequent amendments resulted from information and criticism obtained at consultative meetings. At those meetings, former senior economic policymakers from Korea, prominent Korean business leaders, and U.S. scholars engaged in intensive discussions to clarify the historical background of each policy study and to provide supplementary unpublished data and information. This book attempts to describe economic policymaking during the Park years as accurately as possible through the contributions of Korean scholars and policymakers who were involved directly and indirectly in the economic modernization of Korea during the last three decades.

Lee-Jay Cho
Vice President for Academic Affairs
East-West Center
  and
Director
East-West Population Institute
East-West Center, Honolulu, Hawaii

Yoon Hyung Kim
Professor of Economics
Hankuk University of Foreign Studies
Seoul, Korea
  and
Research Associate
East-West Population Institute
East-West Center, Honolulu, Hawaii

PART I
POLITICAL AND
ECONOMIC BACKGROUND

1 Political and Economic Antecedents to the 1960s

by Lee-Jay Cho and Yoon Hyung Kim

Remarkable changes were forced on the Korean people during a relatively brief time span, not only after World War II but also earlier in this century. For a better understanding of Korea's present-day social and economic institutions, it will be useful to examine first some of the broad historical patterns of the country's transition from kingdom to colony and finally to republic.

Korea has always been surrounded by harsh political reality and forced to tackle the challenges thrust upon it by its powerful neighbors, particularly China and Manchuria. In response, nevertheless, Koreans absorbed and benefited from the invaders' culture and know-how. Despite many foreign intrusions during its long history, including Japanese incursions on the mainland in the sixteenth century, Korea was able to maintain its political independence until the turn of the twentieth century. The ancient Korean monarchy survived until 1910 partly because the kingdom remained a tributary under the protection of the Chinese imperial system. By the end of the nineteenth century, however, the great Chinese empire was crumbling under misrule and was no longer capable of meeting its traditional obligation to ensure the defense of its tributaries. Korea became a bone of contention among its three large neighbors and was soon overwhelmed by the emerging power of Japan.

The Meiji revolution in Japan swept away the Tokugawa *bakufu* (military regime) in 1868, launching a new stage of development by bringing in Western technology and ideas. The resultant modernization touched upon almost every aspect of Japanese society—from clothing to the constitution and from the legal system to the education system. For some time after the Meiji revolution, the Japanese followed the policy of *tatsuaron* ("getting away from Asia"), which meant the avoidance of "continental Asian" influences in general. Viewing China and Korea as technologically backward, Japan turned to the West for its technology and scientific ideas. By no means, however, did Japan abandon the values with which it had been imbued for centuries. On the contrary, its blending of East Asian values together with Western technology and science greatly expedited modernization and economic development in Japan. Thus, by the turn of the twentieth century, within one generation after the Meiji revolution, Japan became the only modern power in Asia that was able to challenge the Western powers.

In contrast to the outward-looking Japanese attitude, Korea continued to turn inward, maintaining its overly Sinified political system and upholding its traditional tributary relationship with Beijing. Continuing to view China as the center of the world, while not realizing that the world was passing it by, Korea was dubbed the "Hermit Kingdom" (Griffis 1897).

Korea's long history of seclusion ended partly as a result of Japanese gunboat diplomacy, which forcibly opened the country to trade under the 1876 Korean-Japanese treaty of commerce. During the following several decades, Japanese immigrants began to arrive in Korea to develop businesses. Starting with their monopoly on foreign trade, they gradually established complete control over the Korean economy. The Korean branch of the Japanese Dai Ichi Bank was opened in 1878 and assumed the role of central banking in 1905, linking the currencies of the two countries. In October 1909, the central bank of Korea was established. Thus, for the first time, a modern financial system was introduced to all of Korea, together with a modern currency system. (For further discussion, see Palais 1975; Griffis 1897; and K. Z. Cho 1977.)

ANNEXATION BY JAPAN

Korea was unable to meet the external challenges confronting it at the end of the century—whether military aggression or international politics—and could not defend its sovereignty. Rival imperial ambitions brought Japan into two wars for control of Korea—with China in 1894–95 and with Russia in 1904–05. Subsequently, the Japanese virtually ruled Korea through the advisory system *(kumon kaiji)* and supervisors *(tokanfu)*. In 1910 the Korean peninsula became part of the Japanese empire through annexation.

Prior to the Meiji revolution, the Japanese had always regarded China as the origin of superior culture and Korea as the transmitter of that culture to the archipelago. The Japanese, therefore, had looked upon China and Korea with profound respect. While the Meiji revolution was making great advances, however, China and Korea were unable to break away from their political and technological backwardness. In spite of the tradition of cultural superiority and heritage from continental Asia, Japan began to regard the Chinese and Koreans as second-class nationalities, giving rise to the Japanese sense of national as well as racial superiority. Thus, the Korean peninsula was not regarded after annexation as equivalent to the provinces within Japan, but rather as a colony governed by the *Sotokufu* (Office of the Governor-General)—an institution imposed by the Japanese government and officially headed by a high-ranking general in the Japanese army. Traditional Korean administration was swept away.

Basically, the Japanese aim was to structure Korean economic expansion to meet the overall needs of the Japanese economy. In the beginning, the Japanese tried to develop the Korean economy as a major source of food for Japan and as a market for Japanese manufactured products. Thus from annexation through the 1920s, the Japanese made a major effort to raise agricultural productivity, especially in the production of rice, by transferring Japanese technology to increase productivity per unit of land in Korea. As the Japanese developed the industrial sector in Korea, ownership in this sector became almost wholly Japanese, and most of this sector's leadership consisted of Japanese immigrants. The Japanese share of total paid-in capital in the industrial sector increased from 32 percent in 1911, to 80 percent in 1917, and to 90 percent in 1921 (Suh 1978:10).

After annexation, Japan developed plans not only to make Korea permanent Japanese territory, but also to use the peninsula as a base for further territorial expansion. The vast northeastern part of China (Manchuria) offered an enticing abundance of the natural resources that Japan lacked. Its coal reserves were almost comparable to those of the United States; it also had other important mineral resources, petroleum, and forests. In 1932 Japan established a puppet state in Manchuria that was administered, for all political and economic purposes, by the Japanese imperial government. Japan could be best provisioned with the products of this resource-rich territory by way of the Korean peninsula, and this link soon became known as "the lifeline of the great Japanese empire."

The availability in Korea of mineral resources, hydroelectric power potential, and cheap labor were advantages for developing the industries needed to provision both Japan and Japan's forces in Manchuria. The quality of the Korean labor force was almost comparable to that of Japan, with the advantages that some of the work force spoke Japanese and had received a Japanese-style education. After 1932, when the Japanese-controlled government was established in Manchuria, the geographical position of Korea gave it increased strategic importance for further development of these industries in Korea, which in turn enabled further Japanese expansion in East Asia. Thus, from the early 1930s to 1941, the initial emphasis on rice production was replaced by promotion of large-scale industries. This shift was primarily to meet the growing need of the arms build-up as Japanese military power expanded: beginning with the creation of the new state in Manchuria and followed by the occupation of major coastal cities in China in 1937, the extension of Japanese power into Vietnam in 1940, and finally the Japanese attacks throughout Southeast Asia at the end of 1941.

During the period of Japanese colonial rule in Korea the agricultural sector continued to grow at a low but fairly steady rate, but the manufacturing sector was growing several times faster, especially during the late 1930s. Indicators of economic growth, such as annual growth rates in the production of commodities (Table 1.1), demonstrate that fairly rapid development did take place in Korea. The overall growth rate of the economy during this period was about 3 percent, whereas the population was increasing at a net rate of only around 1 percent, showing that Korea experienced substantial economic growth under Japanese colonial rule.

Table 1.1. Annual growth rates of commodity products by industrial origin: 1910–39 (%)

Period	Agricultural sector	Manufacturing sector	Overall growth
1910–15 to 1916–21	3.2	7.0	3.4
1916–21 to 1922–27	1.3	8.9	1.9
1922–27 to 1928–33	2.7	8.2	3.2
1928–33 to 1934–39	1.0	15.0	3.4
1910–15 to 1934–39	2.0	9.7	3.0

Source: Suh (1978).

The rapid growth of the Korean industrial sector was an outcome of Japanese capital investment. It was imposed on the Koreans from outside and was unconnected to the traditional sectors of the Korean economy. The linkage effect, in which both traditional and modern sectors grow simultaneously while complementing and benefiting each other, did not take place in Korea. Some sectors of the Korean economy thus remained relatively backward, whereas others were as advanced as their counterparts in Japan.

The Japanese favored capital-intensive development in certain military industries, and introduced the latest technology. This resulted in further imbalance and sharper wage differentials between the agricultural and manufacturing sectors. The productivity gap also became wider, as agricultural workers became progressively less productive when compared with those in manufacturing. The productivities were nearly equal in 1920, when the real product per worker in agriculture was 91 percent of that in manufacturing; by 1940 the ratio had fallen to a mere 24 percent. This unbalanced dualistic growth in the Korean economy sufficed, from the Japanese viewpoint, so long as the growth met the needs of the Japanese economy.

ECONOMIC LEGACY OF COLONIAL RULE

In terms of technical and economic development, the 36 years of Japanese occupation were not entirely disadvantageous to Korea. In carrying out its imperialistic expansion, Japan provided the Korean peninsula with substantial infrastructure, including:

- the railway traversing the peninsula from Pusan to Seoul to Shinyiju, providing a strategic link across the peninsula with major towns in Manchuria

- major investments in branch railway lines, roads linking the major cities of the peninsula, and major harbor facilities at Pusan and Inch'ŏn to facilitate the trade in commodities between Korea and Japan

- a modern communications system, including telephone and telegraph networks

- the European-style Japanese educational system in which, however, the medium of education was strictly the Japanese language
- Keijo Imperial University, which later became Seoul National University
- medical studies and the modern medical profession
- factories for textiles and other manufactures
- the modernization of the mining industry
- the modernization of agriculture
- the centralized administrative structure

While under Japanese rule, Koreans did gain some social and economic benefits, even if confined to only some segments of society. Many of these were conducive to later economic growth—in particular, the lasting benefits of technical education, acquisition of new skills and technical know-how, experience in working with entrepreneurs and in large-scale industries, and changing habits of consumption. Despite the colonial policy of extracting from Korea both natural and human resources, manufactured goods, and agricultural products to help meet the needs of Japan, despite the relative backwardness of the traditional sector (as opposed to the large-scale, Japanese-led industrial sector), despite the fact that Koreans could not play a leadership role in either the agricultural or the manufacturing sector, they were nonetheless brought into a development scheme for higher agricultural and industrial productivity. High-yielding varieties of rice were introduced, not for the benefit of Koreans but as a secure source of supply for Japan. To accelerate this plan, the Japanese built agricultural training centers and agricultural high schools throughout the peninsula. The independent-minded Koreans were resentful of such programs, despite their long-term benefits, because these modernizations were forced on them by a foreign power.

When the Japanese left Korea in 1945, they could not take with them the physical plant, and they also left behind the people who had helped them to manage their plants. Their assistants, who had never played an executive role before, had acquired enough skills and knowledge from technology transfer to assume control immediately and did not have to start building these sectors all over again.

Given the conditions prevailing at the time, the economic development of Korea was remarkable. The Japanese, of course, never expected to lose control of Korea; if they had hedged their policies around the possibility of being dislodged, they would never have invested so heavily to provide the peninsula with so much infrastructure. But because the Japanese-controlled Korean economy was designed and structured primarily to benefit the Japanese, the material benefits to the Koreans were less than what might appear superficially to be the case in view of such rapid growth.

There was a transmigration of several million Japanese from Japan to the

Korean peninsula. Large numbers of Koreans also migrated to Japan, where they supplied cheap labor for the construction of roads, munition works, and the textile industry, and to Manchuria for frontier development, particularly agriculture and mining. The Koreans were compelled to migrate at first. Later, because of Japanese agricultural and land policies in Korea, many farmers and other Koreans felt that they could make a better living in Japan or Manchuria, and they therefore migrated voluntarily.

Japanese nationals were always given priority in the new settlements, in educational institutions, in occupations, and of course in the government hierarchy. Koreans were denied a leadership role in their own government because Japan (unlike some colonial powers, such as Great Britain) did not bring the colonized people into their own local civil service.

During World War II enormous sacrifices were forced upon Koreans through military conscription and the compulsory mobilization for paramilitary service in Japan and throughout the war zones of the Pacific and Southeast Asia.

In the years immediately following the war, after almost four decades of Japanese rule, anti-Japanese sentiment led Koreans to eliminate virtually everything readily identifiable as Japanese in origin. In retrospect, this seems an unfortunate process. By phasing out or eliminating what was perceived to be Japanese, the Koreans did away with certain positive Japanese accomplishments, but ended up by retaining some negative qualities that were to hamper subsequent development. At one extreme, even some useful public equipment was destroyed because it was Japanese-made.

Koreans could straightforwardly reject the tangible manifestations of Japanese influence, but found it less easy to cast off institutions and habits developed during the Japanese occupation. The highly centralized Korean bureaucracy was modeled after the tightly controlled Japanese colonial apparatus, although not perceived as such. Even after the Japanese bureaucracy had departed, therefore, some of its more undesirable structural elements were retained, for the sake of convenience. One example is the military police (the much-feared *kampeitai* of the war years) with its secretive monitoring and control. Whereas in Japan the postwar American military administration helped to eliminate the vestiges of the old military machine, the postwar Korean bureaucracy was actually drawn from the remnants of the Japanese military organization.

Japanese influence was brought strongly to bear on the Korean character most widely through the Japanese system of universal primary education. The *shu-shin* (self-refinement) system of education was a Japanese adaptation of Confucian ethics; it was taught in all Korean elementary schools, principally for the purpose of assimilating Koreans as Japanese imperial subjects. With modifications suited to Korean national identity and national values, the substance could have been useful to the modern Korean education system. Unfortunately, because it had been instituted by the imperial Japanese government, Koreans insisted on its elimination. Yet by 1945 the Japanese-style school system had already had its effect on Korean education, not least because it was Korea's initial experience with genuinely universal education.

The South Koreans were still able to employ the Japanese legacy of skills and technology. Although Korean managers had never been trained to perform by themselves without Japanese supervision, those with a three-quarters grasp of their enterprises' operations were quickly able to close the remaining gap in their knowledge. South Korea's greatest resource was its people. It initially had the larger share of the divided country's population. It also gained about two million emigrants from the North during the Korean War, many of whom had achieved high levels of education and economic status, further increasing the quality of human resources. The postwar return of Koreans from Japan and Manchuria likewise brought valuable skills to Korea.

Because Korea had long been part of the Japanese economic system, Koreans were able to acquire postwar technological innovations from Japan, to take advantage of Japanese methods of conducting business, trade, and manufacturing, and to understand Japanese ways of thinking that could be profitably utilized by Koreans. These types of interchanges were not possible for most of the other countries, such as Indonesia and the Philippines, that had been under the Japanese imperial system only briefly. Added to this was the massive direct contact with U.S. technology and interchange that would later contribute to Korean economic development. Although Koreans had no say in or control over the economic, educational, and other policies imposed on them for 36 years, the experience gained under the Japanese and the economic infrastructure forced on Korea contributed in numerous ways to subsequent Korean economic growth.

NATIONAL LIBERATION AND ALLIED OCCUPATION, 1945–48

The modern history of independent Korea begins in 1945, when the peninsula was emancipated from Japanese colonial rule. Through an unfortunate sequence of events at the end of the war, the peninsula became divided. The American leaders' and policymakers' lack of understanding of East Asian history, politics, and cultures brought about this arbitrary division, which was not intended to be permanent. The Russians had long held territorial ambitions in East Asia, and the situation at the war's end provided the Soviet Union with the opportunity to advance in the wake of the crumbling Japanese empire. The American delegation to the Yalta Conference in February 1945 was unable to resist Soviet pressure for the division of the Korean peninsula and agreed in principle to joint occupation. The 38th parallel was subsequently proposed by the Pentagon and accepted by the Soviet command as the limit of military operations by their respective occupation forces. American troops occupied the southern part of Korea up to the 38th parallel, and Soviet troops occupied the remainder of the peninsula. Thus the Soviet Union, for its negligible involvement in the Far Eastern Theater during the final ten days of the war, was able to form a strategic alliance with leaders in the North, thereby gaining greater access to the Pacific Basin through the northern half of the Korean peninsula.

The years from 1945 to 1948 were a period of political instability and economic turmoil, which precluded any orderly movement toward development. With the withdrawal of nearly 70,000 Japanese administrators, who had governed Korea for 36 years, the political and economic apparatus of the nation was virtually paralyzed. The political division diverted most of the energies of Korean leaders to the political questions affecting the divided country.

The lack of seriousness with which American leaders regarded the commitment of the United States to establish a free and independent Korea resulted in the overall failure to install an effective Korean government. One reason was that the United States Army Military Government in Korea (created in January 1946) received instructions from Washington through General MacArthur's staff in Tokyo, who were concerned primarily with the occupation of Japan and took little interest in Korean affairs. Whereas Japan benefited in the long run from some of the changes instituted by the occupation forces, the U.S. military government in Seoul was unprepared, erratic, and almost totally ignorant of Korean culture and the economic situation. The artificial division of the country had a devastating impact on the Korean economy, because the industrial base was in the North and the South was predominantly agricultural. To alleviate mutual difficulties in Korea and Japan, the U.S. staff in Seoul and Tokyo could have allowed some economic cooperation between the two countries, including barter trade (Meade 1951). But little thought was given to the economic welfare of the Korean nation and its populace, although the U.S. military government made a significant contribution by initiating discussion of land reform. The politically and economically chaotic period of occupation by U.S. troops lasted for three years. (For a detailed discussion of the U.S. military government in Korea, see Meade 1951.)

The elements for launching postwar economic development were all still in place at the end of World War II: the benefits of the physical plant, Korean experience in participating in the modern sectors of the economy, the education system, and technology gained from Japan. Also, fairly rapid urbanization had taken place during the later colonial period, and by around 1940 about 20 percent of the population was urban. Thus Korea had a relatively large urban workforce, much of which had received at least a primary Japanese-style education. Given the necessary capital input from abroad, Koreans could have embarked on their postwar development almost immediately after the Japanese departure—if they had had the benefit of political stability and a peaceful international climate.

Unfortunately, as indicated earlier, the peninsula was divided in 1945 by arbitrary, external, political decisions. Because the country's natural resources and large-scale industrial plants were mostly in the North, whereas the South was primarily agricultural, the complementarity between North and South was lost. Even worse, much of the physical plant, in both the North and South, was destroyed during the Korean War.

FIRST REPUBLIC AND THE KOREAN WAR, 1948–60

Syngman Rhee, a prominent Korean independence leader, energetically pressed the United States to establish a unified and independent country by all possible diplomatic means. However, North Korean leaders refused to allow the proposed general election under the supervision of the United Nations Commission for Korea. When all efforts failed to achieve a unified government through a general election, no alternative remained except the formation of a government in the South alone. In May 1948 a general election was held in South Korea, under United Nations supervision, and Syngman Rhee was elected president. The Republic of Korea was proclaimed in the South on 15 August 1948; the Soviet command was instrumental in forming the Democratic People's Republic in the North. The nation was effectively divided under two politically incompatible and mutually hostile regimes. The Rhee government eliminated the remnants of Communist activity in South Korea and helped diminish considerably whatever sympathy there was for Communist institutions and practices.

The charismatic first president successfully defended South Korea, with direct involvement by United Nations forces, against the North Korean invasion that began on 25 June 1950. The bloody Korean War lasted three years, destroyed a quarter of the wealth of South Korea, and inflicted the loss of over a million lives. As a condition for agreeing to accept the Korean Armistice signed on 27 July 1953, Syngman Rhee concluded a mutual defense treaty with the United States. This treaty, which has subsequently served as the cornerstone of security relations between the two countries, stipulates that an armed attack on either country would cause each to "act to meet the common danger in accordance with its constitutional process." To ensure the survival of the Republic of Korea against North Korean aggression, the Rhee government also systematically expanded the Korean armed forces into the largest formal organization in Korean society, thereby laying the foundations for South Korea as a viable independent nation-state. (For further details on the Rhee period, see Oliver 1954, 1978.)

Syngman Rhee helped lay the political foundations of an independent, modern country and some of the groundwork for later rapid economic development. Although the idea of land reform came from the United States, the program was pursued by the Korean government, partly out of political necessity in view of the land reform taking place in the North. President Rhee sought land reform as a right that was justly due to the peasantry and fought for it against political reactionaries. The program also coincided with the president's intention to cripple his political opposition, which was based on the landlord *(yangban)* class.

Land reform was implemented in two stages. Initially land that was formerly under Japanese ownership or control was distributed to farmers. Under Rhee's leadership, the government broke up large Korean-owned estates and set a limit of three hectares per owner. Land reform probably lowered crop production during a brief initial period, because the government could not immediately replace the inputs (notably seed, fertilizers, and credit) formerly supplied by the landowning class. In the longer term the reform succeeded in raising productivity, and politically it placated the rural population.

The reform helped to bring about a more equitable distribution of assets and income in at least two ways. First, poor farmers received a share of the assets formerly exploited by the Japanese and the landlord class. Second, the landowners were partly compensated in the form of government bonds. The rapid decline in the value of these bonds because of inflation contributed to the redistribution of income.

Syngman Rhee maintained democratic ideals and allowed some of the basic elements of democratic institutions to operate. Reflecting on the past four decades of Korean history, the Rhee period was perhaps the most liberal in terms of freedom of expression, freedom of the press, and direct elections of both parliamentary representatives and the president. This period also witnessed experiments with local autonomy.

The president's political subordinates and other bureaucrats, who made and implemented many administrative decisions without the president's knowledge, were responsible for the corruption that spread during the last years of the Rhee government. Contrary to accusations made at that time, none of the corruption can be attributed to the president himself. Syngman Rhee was personally not ostentatious, nor did he accumulate wealth. In the end, he lost his grip on the country by refusing to obey the dictates of public opinion which yearned for a more democratic process. He had simply become too old (he was age 85 in 1960) and too conservative in his outlook to assess the changing political and social realities of the republic. He established some bad precedents, which have left a blot upon Korean constitutional history, notably by forcing an amendment to the constitution in 1952 (to ensure his own re-election) and again in 1957 (to enhance his personal authoritarianism). His March 1960 landslide victory for a fourth term in office was marred by accusations of election-rigging and violence toward the opposition. As a result of mounting political discontent, corruption in government, despair over lack of opportunities for the younger generation, and the economic hardships endured since the Korean War,

Rhee's increasingly personal authoritarian government was overturned by a student uprising in April 1960.

SECOND REPUBLIC, 1960–61

Out of the ensuing chaotic period emerged a revised constitution, fresh elections, and a new government formed in August 1960 by Prime Minister Chang Myon, thereby shifting from an authoritarian regime toward a more democratic one. The "democracy" of 1960–61, however, encouraged and widened splits, aggravated the power free-for-all, and projected an image of weakness and hesitation where chaotic conditions demanded strength and resolution (Henderson 1968).

Although the military remained politically neutral until 1961, largely because of Syngman Rhee's strong political leadership and skills, the Chang government was too weak to maintain civilian supremacy over the military. In view of the fact that the military had emerged as the strongest organization in Korean society since the Korean War, the possibility of military intervention in government was quite high. In retrospect, it seems regrettable that the Chang regime was overturned within nine months of assuming office. Given adequate time, the parliamentary system might have survived, strengthening the foundations for the democratic process in Korea.

Thus far, efforts toward postwar reconstruction in Korea, which began after the ceasefire in 1953, had left the economy stagnant and at the subsistence level. The Rhee government had embarked on reconstructing infrastructure and industrial facilities and stabilizing prices, with American aid as the major financial resource. Recovery from the Korean War was slow, and during the period 1953–61 the economy was kept alive largely by massive economic and military assistance from the United States. Between 1953 and 1961 the average annual growth rate of GNP in real terms was merely 3.9 percent. However, because the population was growing at an average annual rate of 2.9 percent, per capita GNP in real terms increased by no more than 1 percent on average each year.

The subsequent growth process was doubtless made easier by the massive influx of foreign exchange during this critical period of development, which held the country together and prevented massive starvation and economic dislocation. During the entire period 1945–83, aid or assistance from all sources to Korea is estimated at over US $26 billion (AID, U.S., 1985). Much of this was in the form of grants or concessions. About one-third of the total was military assistance, much of which was given during and just after the Korean War. By expediting postwar reconstruction and the recovery of the economy, these forms of assistance helped to lay the foundations for subsequent development during the 1960s. As discussed in the following chapter, economic modernization was one of the most urgent challenges facing the government that came to power in 1961.

2 Major Economic Policies of the Park Administration

by Lee-Jay Cho and Yoon Hyung Kim

MILITARY GOVERNMENT, 1961–63

The coup d'etat of May 1961, headed by General Park Chung Hee, dramatically increased the influence of the military in Korean society and marked the beginning of political involvement by the military, which continued for the next 27 years. The justifications given for the military takeover were the pervasive corruption in government, inefficient bureaucracy, social disorder, degenerated national spirit, lagging economic development, and prevailing poverty. Under the encompassing ideology of "modernizing the fatherland," the new military regime set out to implement political reform, bring back social discipline and order, and re-educate or "reform" individuals by placing greater emphasis on traditional cultural values and by generating a national spirit of independence.[1]

When the new military government began to formulate policies for economic development, capital was scarce. The domestic savings rate was extremely low. Foreign aid was rapidly declining, both in quantity and variety. Business enjoyed little public confidence, and entrepreneurial talent was deficient. Under these circumstances, the government asserted its leadership by setting the stage for formulating policies for national development. During the period 1961–63, the military government established the institutional framework for industrial development.

The Economic Planning Board (EPB), established in July 1961, was headed by a senior minister for economic planning, who was given the title of deputy prime minister. The EPB has subsequently developed into a powerful bureaucratic organization responsible for development planning and policymaking. In this capacity, it coordinates the functions of the Ministries of Finance, Commerce and Trade, Transportation, Agriculture, Health and Social Affairs, and Science and Technology.

---

1. To demonstrate that these goals were not just rhetoric, the new regime rounded up gangsters and syndicate leaders and paraded them in the streets. To exemplify the seriousness of their actions, a gangster leader was executed. Housewives caught in secret dance halls were paraded in the streets as examples of persons violating the Confucian norms of family harmony. Several scores of generals in the armed forces were arrested and jailed for corruption. A few of the largest capitalists were "pointed at" for dishonest accumulation of wealth.

Government Control Over the National Economy (1961–62)

The First Five-Year Economic Development Plan (1962–66) was formulated by the EPB. To implement it, the government embarked on investment planning. The major issue was how to finance major industrial investment projects. Under the conditions prevailing in the early 1960s—the extremely low domestic savings rate, the absence of a well-functioning financial and capital market, and the decline of foreign aid—the military government had to develop a means for providing long-term capital to industry. Thus, the supply of capital for the needs of industrialization led to the government's control of access to domestic credit and foreign borrowing (see Chapter 3). This measure was aimed not only at increasing government influence in the allocation of financial resources but also at expanding the availability of loanable funds, particularly from foreign sources. In fact, the system of foreign-loan repayment guarantees (which required EPB approvals to loan seekers) contributed substantially to increasing the inflow of foreign capital.

Recognizing its role as the predominant source of capital for industry in the early 1960s, the government resorted to the practice of "overloaning" by the central bank (Bank of Korea), which helped to forge close links between commercial banks and industry. Through the device of formally short-term but in reality long-term current-account credits (the so-called "rollover" of commercial bank loans), commercial banks could play the role of industrial investment banks designed to finance the long-term investment needs of the economy. Korean enterprises willing to conform to the government's development priorities were entitled to borrow from a commercial bank amounts well in excess of the individual companies' net worth. The commercial banks, in turn, overborrowed from the central bank. The Bank of Korea was the ultimate guarantor of the financing system and the minister of finance served as chairman of the Monetary Board. Thus, the government gained detailed control over the policies and lending decisions of commercial banks. This so-called "indirect" financing reduced the financial risks associated with the high-debt levels of Korean enterprises because the central bank had a major role in deciding the fate of a defaulting company. By thus reducing the risks for foreign lenders, the government opened the door to massive foreign borrowing. During the early industrialization period, therefore, the Korean government not only selected strategic industries to be nurtured and provided with industrial financing, but also assumed the major risk for large-scale investment ventures undertaken by private enterprises.

In the meantime, the printing of money as an expedient to mobilize domestic resources for growth and employment resulted in rapid expansion of the money supply and contributed to inflation. To cope with inflation, the government resorted to an incomes policy (see Chapter 4). The first policy measure enacted by the military regime in 1961 was the imposition of a complete price freeze. Although the price freeze was lifted after two months, the government continued to rely on a system of selective price controls to alleviate the burden of the high rate of inflation on low-income families and to restrain price inflation. Some of the long-term consequences of government intervention in both the factor market (through interest and wage controls) and the commodity market (through price controls) resulted in distortions of resource allocation. The failure of the first two policy measures thus necessitated the 1964–65 exchange-rate reform, export-promotion policy, and import-liberalization measures (see Chapter 5), which were formulated after President Park achieved a popular mandate through his victory in the October 1963 general election. With aggregate demand policies directed to promoting growth and employment, the government continued to rely extensively on price-control measures to stabilize the price level.

Population Policy

Prior to the military takeover of the government, no discussion of population control was possible. The traditional Confucian value of the large extended family was shared by Korea's leaders. In particular, Syngman Rhee's government was not receptive to policy dialogue concerned with population control, despite the fact that the Korean population was growing far more rapidly than at any previous time.

Debate on the implications of Korean population growth and the wisdom of establishing a nationwide program to encourage low fertility became possible only upon the overthrow of the Rhee regime in 1960. President Park Chung Hee as a nationalist and Confucianist was initially reluctant to introduce family planning to Korea, but arguments by Korea's technocrats that rapid population growth would impede Korea's development were convincing. A decrease in the birthrate was adopted as one of the goals of Korea's First Five-Year Economic Development Plan (see Chapter 12). Funds were provided through the Ministry of Health and Social Affairs to establish government-sponsored family planning in Korea.

The Korean family planning program accomplished its primary objective. Korean women are bearing only two children each on average compared with six children each in 1960. Given this fertility level, Korea's population should stop growing in the twenty-first century and stabilize at about 60 million—approximately 18 million more than in 1987. Among the positive structural results, the success in the rapid reduction in fertility and the consequent reduction in childbearing responsibilities have contributed to increased labor-force participation by Korean women. Also, the increase in labor-force quality resulting from the higher education attainment of children from small families has contributed to the rise in labor productivity. Moreover, a significant proportion of the increase in the domestic savings rate, which is essential for continued capital accumulation, can also be attributed to the decline in the number of young dependents.[2]

THIRD REPUBLIC, 1963–72

In accordance with the military regime's commitment to transfer the powers of government to a civilian administration through a national election, there was a constitutionally legitimate and peaceful transition to the Third Republic in late 1963. Under the new constitution, General Park Chung Hee was elected president through popular election in October 1963, and a civilian government was formed.

President Park came from a very poor farming village and acquired a strong sense of social justice and egalitarianism, having suffered from poverty and having been influenced as a young adult by socialist ideas (*Time Magazine*, May 1961). He also demonstrated a strong predilection toward authoritarianism for the sake of efficiency and order. His early attraction to socialism, combined with the need for rapid economic development and the lessons learned from the Japanese for mobilizing the populace to expedite rapid development, enabled him to combine many positive elements of capitalism, socialism, and military discipline. Park possessed many of the qualities of the traditional (Confucian) authoritarian leader whose actions were "for the good of the masses" (in the sense used by the Confucian scholar, Mencius), and was very effective in this role.

The president had a strong commitment to eradicating the prevailing extreme poverty in the rural areas, which he himself had suffered during his childhood and youth. Having lived as a poor farmer himself, he understood the situation of Korean farmers. His New Community (Saemaul) Movement was started for the purpose of transferring the benefits of development to the backward rural villages (see Chapter 16). The movement mobilized local labor for local improvements, providing poor villages with basic infrastructure—paved roads, bridges, better housing, schools, and training facilities. Some aspects of the Saemaul training program resem-

---

2. No consistent and general theory of demographic transition has yet been developed, but the rapid transition process in Korea has clearly helped to promote and expedite economic growth (L. J. Cho 1984; Cho and Togashi 1985). The demographic transition in Europe began in the eighteenth century and was completed in the twentieth. As high birth rates and death rates were reversed, and birth rates continued to be low, the age structures became similar in most European countries. Japan was the first Asian country to pass through this transition, completing it in the 1960s. Korea was already in the midst of transition in the 1970s, whereas the transition has barely begun in most of the Southeast Asian countries. As economies such as Korea's and Taiwan's pass through the newly industrialized stage, and export their own capital and technology, similar benefits may be shifted to the lower-wage Southeast Asian economies. For economic planning in the latter region, Korea's recent experiences may thus provide valuable insights.

bled the Chinese May 7 Cadre Schools,[3] with their training centers to re-educate leaders for national revival, and recalled the Chinese slogan "With self-reliance you survive." The program also reflected the "group solution" to a problem frequently found in Chinese, Japanese, and Korean traditional culture and history. By providing incentives with training, technology, and construction materials, the Saemaul movement was fairly successful in motivating farmers to participate in projects for the common good, and it fostered a sense of national spirit.

Another factor contributing to President Park's popularity was his handling of business leaders. The leaders of the conglomerates were told in essence that their property was not their own but really belonged to the nation. Under the president's influence, they curbed their lavish spending and extravagant life-styles and were also encouraged to invest not merely in ways that were best for their own corporate profits but in ways that the government regarded as best for long-term national economic development goals.

President Park acquired a great following among the masses—especially among the poor rural people, whom he understood very well. As far as they were concerned, his leadership during the first 15 years of his presidency was a success, partly because it provided Koreans with a sense of national pride and renewed their sense of national identity through development.

To President Park, economic development was "an integral part of a nationalistic vision of a more independent Korea to come—more independent of U.S. aid and influence and as an economically stronger and independent entity, more able to deal with North Korea" (C. H. Park 1963:19–20). Under the slogan of "Eradicating Poverty through Rapid Economic Growth," the military regime gave first priority to the promotion of economic growth. This strongly appealed to the country in the early 1960s and became a nationally supported goal of the Third Republic. One objective of the Park regime was to catch up first with Taiwan, a rapidly industrializing country, and to follow closely Japan, an economic superpower. Having passed through the prewar Japanese-style education system, Park had learned a great deal about the role of the Meiji revolution in modernizing the Japanese economy. He also realized that only through economic growth could a country earn international respect. He thought that democratic institutions could not prosper without a strong economy, and his philosophy was, therefore, "economic development first, democracy later."

---

3. The May 7 Cadre Schools got their name from a letter by Mao Zedong, dated 7 May 1966, addressed to Marshall Lin Piao stating that all Chinese should do physical labor combined with an educational program ("physical work and study program") to raise their political consciousness. During the later part of the Chinese Cultural Revolution, all cadres were sent to re-education farms organized in the spirit outlined in the letter.

Economic Liberalization and Reforms (1964–67)

One of the principal reasons for the tightening of economic control in the early 1960s was that Korea was still a major recipient of U.S. aid. The United States, through its Office of Economic Coordinator, wielded considerable influence over Korean economic policy, to the extent that assistance funds were linked with development policies. The 1961 coup was not welcomed by the United States which, therefore, tried to pressure the new government to loosen its political grip by various means, such as withholding the delivery of goods until certain conditions were met. The incomplete flow of assistance in commodities and raw materials created difficulties for the Korean government, and measures were taken through government control of credit and foreign borrowing to limit imports and stabilize the markets. These measures exacerbated the situation, requiring additional policy measures as correctives.

Imports of raw materials and industrial machinery increased dramatically, however, because the government was trying to stimulate industrial activities by pumping money into large-scale projects. By the end of 1963 Korea's foreign exchange holdings had shrunk to no more than $90 million. The prospects of a severe foreign exchange deficit for 1964 were even more serious. The fragility of postwar Korea's economic health and its consequent poor credit standing in international financial markets, combined with the political turmoil resulting from rapid changes of government, made it extremely difficult for Korea to attract foreign capital. Faced with a severe foreign exchange crunch, the construction of some large-scale industrial plants was interrupted. Worse yet, because of the shortages of imported raw materials, some of the existing plants faced a slowdown in operation. Under these circumstances, and in view of the rapid reduction of foreign aid, the government decided to promote exports to earn foreign exchange. From this point in time, the importance of "export promotion" was equated with that of "national defense" and was frequently referred to as the means for national survival.

Korea had little experience in dealing with large-scale manufactured exports. In the past they had dealt only with exports of raw materials such as tungsten and some agricultural products. The government had to rethink its organizational structure to deal with the new task of expanding trade. A convenient model for Korea was provided by Japan's Ministry of Commerce and Industry (subsequently transformed into the Ministry of International Trade and Industry, or MITI). In 1965 Korea's Ministry of Commerce and Industry, patterned after its Japanese counterpart, was reorganized to create an export component in each of its industrial bureaus, supplementing the existing Bureau of Foreign Trade. The main function of each export component was to set annual export targets by commodity, as well as by region and country of destination, and to monitor the export performance of the firms that were under the purview of each bureau. The immediate task was to enable factories to operate by making raw materials available. Then the government curtailed domestic sales of exportable commodities as a means of promoting their export.

One of the major issues the government was confronted with was how to deal with the possible losses that firms would incur by exporting commodities that thus far had not been tested or accepted in world markets. To be competitive these commodities would have to be marketed below prevailing world prices. The government recognized the need for substantial financial support and subsidies for the exporting companies to expand exports. To achieve this objective, the government launched its 1964–65 exchange-rate reform, export-promotion measures, and import-liberalization program. In 1964–65, as discussed in Chapter 5, the won was devalued and the system of multiple exchange rates was replaced by a unitary, floating exchange rate designed to maintain a realistic effective exchange rate. The exchange reform was combined with export-promotion measures (in the form of tax concessions, preferential credits, and export subsidies), and with the import-liberalization program that was designed and implemented during 1964–67.

The ideas for these comprehensive export-promotion policies were generated at the Monthly Export Promotion Meeting, which was initiated in 1965. The meeting served as a forum for business and government and was chaired by President Park and attended by trade-related ministers, business association leaders, heads of major financial institutions, and representatives of major export firms. Institutional arrangements, legal and procedural issues, and other policy matters for promoting exports were discussed, and fairly concrete policy recommendations and determinations were made on the spot. This forum contributed greatly to the elimination of innumerable bottlenecks that had impeded the promotion of exports.

Subsequently exports expanded rapidly. In June 1964, the government had set its export target for the end of that year at US $120 million. On 30 November 1964 Korea's exports passed the $100-million mark for the first time within a single year, and the last day of November has been commemorated annually ever since as Export Day. This remarkable achievement provided both government and business with such self-confidence that the old Korean saying equivalent to "He who tries will succeed" was frequently heard in business circles. The expansion of exports resulted in corresponding increases in production, and therefore the government framed export promotion and industrialization into a coherent strategy of export-led industrialization. Measures were also taken to liberalize imports, with the aim of reducing various domestic distortions resulting mainly from quantitative restrictions on imports. The implementation of the import-liberalization program, however, was not completely satisfactory, as discussed in Chapter 5.

Along with these policy measures, the Park government initiated the interest-rate reform in 1965 (see Chapter 6). Sustained rapid economic growth required a continuous rapid increase in investment. Yet limits had already been reached for financing the required capital investment by means of domestic saving and the mobilization of financial resources through commercial banks. The government's industrial financing policy resulted in excessive monetary expansion and inflation. During 1961–65 a high inflation rate prevailed, despite the government's efforts at direct price controls, and the highest bank deposit rate became negative in real terms for a number of years. The time and savings deposits of the financial institutions did not increase in real terms between 1962 and 1965, despite the nationwide savings campaign launched by both the government and financial institutions. An overriding issue for rapid industrialization then was how to mobilize private savings through financial intermediaries. The principal aims of the interest-rate reform of 1965, which sharply raised interest rates on both time deposits and loans of banking institutions, were to attract private savings through financial intermediaries for ultimate increases in aggregate domestic saving and investment, as well as to improve the effectiveness of interest-rate policy for resource allocation and monetary control.

On 30 September 1965 the Monetary Board raised the ceiling on savings deposits from 15 to 30 percent per annum; the ceiling on ordinary bank loans was raised from 16 to 26 percent per annum (see Chapter 6). At the same time, the central bank introduced a new system of subsidizing the deposit-money banks to compensate them for losses incurred as a result of the negative margins between the deposit and loan rates. Patterned after the Taiwan success story of 1957–58, the 1965 interest-rate reform in Korea was mainly designed to increase the attractiveness of financial saving rather than to improve the financial soundness of the banking institutions. At that time, there was an incalculable amount of currency floating in the unofficial "curb market." The government tried to encourage the transfer of these funds to the regulated banking institutions by trying to inculcate the general public with an appreciation of dependable, stable, institutionalized interest on their money. The high-interest-rate strategy, which was maintained for almost seven years until August 1972, did affect the savings behavior of the general public and succeeded in achieving an increase in saving.

During 1966–67 major tax reform measures were undertaken to increase tax revenues and aggregate domestic savings. The reform measures entailed the reorganization and upgrading of tax administration in 1966 and the subsequent enactment of a comprehensive revision of tax law in 1967 (see Chapter 10). The establishment of the Office of National Tax Administration in 1966 was a turning point in Korea's development financing. The revamping and restructuring of tax administration contributed significantly to the efficiency of tax collection and more than doubled revenue within a year by eliminating corruption, tax evasion, and arbitrary tax assessment procedures. At the same time, there was no apparent public resistance to the measures.

Agricultural Policy and the Saemaul Movement (1969–71)

It is apparent that the government put utmost emphasis on policy measures for promoting export-oriented industrialization by mobilizing available capital resources. Yet President Park, as mentioned earlier, had experienced the misery of the poor farmer's life, and his lifelong desire was to promote rural development and to improve the quality of village life. However, in the first few years of his government, the president's freedom of policy action was constrained by the scarcity of capital resources.

Immediately after the military takeover, the government advocated agricultural reform. This involved rearranging and eliminating some exploitive elements of the moneylending system that were then operating to the detriment of agricultural communities. The system was especially oppressive for poor farmers, who had to borrow money during the growing season and repay at exorbitant interest rates after disposing of their crops.

The government also tried to rearrange some landholdings to consolidate small plots of arable land, as a means of increasing productivity. Another project attempted to improve the exploitation of underground water resources. Most important of all, shortly after assuming leadership, President Park initiated the National Reconstruction Movement, which was aimed especially at the rural sector and focused on arousing a spirit of revival for modernizing the villages. This movement can perhaps be regarded as the precursor of the Saemaul (new community) movement discussed below. Although some progress was made in the rural sector, it was inevitably overshadowed by the rapid growth of the industrial sector up to 1969, because of the scarcity of resources available to agriculture.

Moreover, up until 1969 the government had maintained low grain prices to hold urban wages at a relatively low level. This may have been one of the major factors responsible for slow growth in the agricultural sector, which eventually led to food shortages and a growing disparity between urban and farm household income. By the end of the 1960s, as a result of sustained industrial growth, the government felt that sufficient (although still limited) capital resources were available for modernizing the agricultural sector. The government launched a two-pronged reform to stimulate food-grain production, raise farm incomes, and promote rural development: adoption of the two-tier price system for rice and barley in 1969, and the launching of the Saemaul movement in 1970 (discussed in Chapters 15 and 16, respectively).

Under the two-tier price system that took effect with the 1969 harvest, the government procured grain from farmers at a price higher than what urban consumers had to pay when it was resold to them. This system provided price incentives for an increase in farm production and at the same time held down urban consumers' food costs. The implementation of such a two-tier price system conflicted in several ways with the objectives of financial and monetary stability. Nevertheless, it significantly contributed to the increase in farm income and grain production, in that the measure encouraged the expanded cultivation of high-yielding varieties as well as the improvement of farming techniques.

The Saemaul movement launched in 1970 was a bold stroke in the government's policy toward rural development. This movement not only embodied President Park's ideals about modernizing the rural sector but also represented his strong personal mission to upgrade the village life of the poor. It was conceptualized and designed to revitalize and rebuild rural communities by inculcating the "will to work" among villagers and by organizing rural human resources so that they could be channeled into productive activities. In some ways, it recalls the "will to economize" depicted by Nobel laureate Sir Arthur Lewis as a prerequisite of Western economic development.

The movement involved close cooperation among government agencies at all levels in the effort to introduce more rational thinking in the management of farm production and village life, to inculcate a national revival spirit, and to promote diligence, self-help, and mutual cooperation. Numerous small-scale investment projects were undertaken with government support and assistance for the improvement of rural infrastructure (such as building farm access roads, bridges, washing facilities, toilets, and wells), as well as improving farm income. The basic principle of the Saemaul movement was that the government provided the necessary construction materials (such as cement and steel) free of charge; other goods (such as fertilizers and roofing materials) were provided at subsidized rates. The villagers in turn supplied the organized human resources for the construction projects. Work was performed collectively on village projects (such as bridges) but individually on others (such as house improvements). The movement thereby mobilized rural residents, insofar as the villagers' own resources would permit, for the common goal of improving rural infrastructure.

This movement contributed remarkably to the improvement of the rural infrastructure and environment, and consequently to better average farm income. By the mid-1970s rural household income had increased so dramatically that it had caught up with and, in one year, even surpassed urban household income. The Saemaul movement was instrumental in developing and modernizing rural communities. These poor villages had been a symbol of poverty in the Korean peninsula for many centuries. The movement helped to extract poor farmers from a situation of low morale and frequent despair and to inspire them with a development-oriented mentality and make them good citizens. After it had been in existence for about ten years, however, the movement came under some criticism, mainly for its authoritarian approach, which discouraged voluntary participation by the rural people and even led to some misallocation of resources.

Promotion of Science and Technology

About the time the plans for the Saemaul movement were being implemented, the government launched a major effort to upgrade science, technology, and professional skills. In 1968 the government founded the Korean Institute for Science and Technology (KIST). KIST's objective was not only to import advanced science and technology but also to introduce and disseminate advanced industrial technology. It was designed as an institute for research and applied science (operating in part under contracts from big industries) to provide innovations in manufactured commodities, especially in the field of electronics. KIST sought to bring leading Korean scientists and technicians residing abroad back to Korea, and to do so offered these expatriates international-level salaries. As a result, many high-level Korean scientists returned and joined Korea's scientific research efforts. These scientists and technicians also worked on industrial applications, thereby contributing to the quality of Korean manufacturing.

The government also founded the Institute of Advanced Science and Technology as a teaching institution—it was combined with KIST in the early 1980s to form the Korea Advanced Institute of Science and Technology (KAIST).

The government placed great emphasis on promoting and upgrading skills in the fields of craftsmanship and services (such as mechanical skills, metal work, tailoring, and carpentry), which were important to industrial development. The emphasis placed on the acquisition of scientific and technical skills resulted in the founding of the Professional Skills and Craftsmanship Training Center, which has had long-term beneficial effects on the economy. Pilot projects were started in Seoul by the president and, once in successful operation, were spread to other provinces of the country. A national testing center was also established for certifying craftsmanship and services skills.

Along the same lines but on the economic front, the government established the Korea Development Institute (KDI) in 1972, to attract leading economists and social scientists to study and provide recommendations on long-range development issues and macroeconomic directions. KDI recruited most of its staff among Koreans abroad, offering salaries on an international scale. Such innovative measures to bring in talent, advanced technology, and scientific knowledge—not only to promote industrial growth but also to upgrade the country's level of science and technology—contributed to the rapid industrialization that followed in the 1970s.

External Affairs and National Security

A fairly bold step taken during the Third Republic, which provided a boost to economic development, was the normalization of diplomatic relations with Japan in 1965. Syngman Rhee, having devoted most of his life to the movement of liberation and national independence from the Japanese empire, had a tremendous hatred toward Japan. During his presidency, the government tried to eradicate everything manifestly Japanese by banning, for example, Japanese songs, Japanese movies, and the use of the Japanese language. This policy was implemented even though the Korean leaders themselves had been trained by and had served in the Japanese bureaucracy and military. In 1965, when the treaty with Japan was concluded, strong anti-Japanese sentiments were still widespread and were manifested principally through student demonstrations.

In seeking to establish closer ties between the two countries, President Park had political and economic objectives. The geographical proximity of Korea and Japan, and their common bond in the alliance of free nations against the common threat of communism, made it inconvenient and somewhat absurd not to have diplomatic relations. Furthermore, Korea could benefit from Japanese investment and technology by fostering economic cooperation through diplomatic relations. Under the reparations terms of the treaty, Japan transferred US $300 million to Korea as a grant-in-aid and arranged for a long-term development loan of US $200 million at 3.5 percent interest. These funds were used to develop the Pohang Steel Company and for irrigation, farm mechanization, and other works designed to increase productivity in the agricultural and fisheries sectors. The payment of reparations not only facilitated technology transfer from Japan but also provided Korea with considerable foreign exchange, which was useful for the development of the country. In this regard, it is important to note also that between 1962 and 1981 roughly $42 billion in foreign lending and grants was received by Korea—one-third from public and two-thirds from commercial sources—further facilitating economic growth during this period (AID, U.S., 1985). The move to normalize diplomatic relations thus contributed directly to international economic cooperation as well as to subsequent growth at home.

The drive to meet the foreign exchange requirements of the expanding economy likewise benefited from Korea's participation in the protracted Vietnam War, from 1965 until the withdrawal of American troops from South Vietnam in 1973. The war had important ramifications for the Korean economy. It provided both the military and business sector with invaluable technical skills and experience. Korean business firms were offered lucrative opportunities to market their manufactured goods, the Korean service sector identified numerous openings to provide services to both American and Korean troops stationed in Vietnam, and Korean construction companies took advantage of highly profitable construction projects in Vietnam. Moreover, two divisions of the Korean armed forces were stationed in Vietnam, and their military pay and allowances were provided in U.S. dollars under international arrangements. The influx of foreign exchange earnings from these war-related activities was especially valuable to the Korean economy, which was just taking off during this period.

A few unfavorable international events had serious consequences for political and economic development in Korea. In 1968 scores of North Korean armed infiltrators reached Seoul in an attempt to assassinate President Park. Other guerilla groups struck at villages in the mountainous areas of South Korea. These actions, combined with the international events that followed, changed the political and military situation, and the country took a definite turn toward tighter military security. Then, with the 1969 Guam Doctrine, the United States emphasized that its Asian allies would henceforth have to bear the primary responsibility for their own conventional defense. Subsequently, in 1971 the Nixon administration removed one of the two U.S. divisions from Korea. In July 1971 the United States unveiled its basic shift in policy toward the People's Republic of China. As Mason argues, "Widespread doubt existed in Korea as to the willingness of the U.S. to support its allies in East Asia and this emphasized the necessity of rallying around a strong leader" (Mason et al. 1980:53). Under these circumstances, it was clear that Koreans would have to make greater efforts to achieve self-reliance and self-defense.

The earlier part of the Third Republic witnessed a more democratic process with great emphasis on economic development. In the later period, the international political and military security situation was changing, and there was greater concern about national security issues, thereby causing a movement towards greater regimentation and national mobilization. Political development was perceived to have stalled, therefore, students and intellectuals in urban centers began to express a sense of uneasiness and dissatisfaction.

FOURTH REPUBLIC, 1972–80

The Fourth Republic can be viewed as an "emergency regime" in the sense that the existing regime was structurally transformed to make way for arbitrary rule by the executive authority for as long as it claimed that a period of crisis prevailed (Das Gupta 1978). The national security crisis brought on by the turmoil of superpower politics and the perceived threat of a North Korean invasion provided the justification for amending the constitution to enable President Park to issue emergency decrees, dissolve the national assembly, and perpetuate his tenure indefinitely. The proposed constitution was submitted to popular referendum, and was supported by the majority of the voters.

Once President Park had successfully met his major challenges of launching economic development and modernization and reviving the national spirit, he felt a great need to maintain the momentum of change and thereby consolidate the achievements of the previous decade. Having nurtured this process from the start, the president felt that no one other than himself could accomplish this task. Because his grand scheme for the nation was working well at the time, it is understandable that he did not want to leave office in the midst of a process that had not yet reached the successful conclusion that he envisaged. However, the constitutional limitation on his tenure was a stumbling block. The constitution was amended in 1969 to allow him to be elected for a third term. Finally, under the 1972 constitution, all limitations on Park's future re-election were removed.

The 1972 constitution was given the title *Yushin* (Revitalizing), a term that was used to label the Meiji revolution (called in Japanese the Meiji *Yishin*). President Park had begun the work of laying the foundations of a nation-state that could survive on its own, internationally as well as against the threat of North Korea, without being totally dependent on the United States and other allies. He also wanted to complete the task of modernizing Korea in the way that Japan had modernized during the Meiji era (1868–1912). Through the initiation of state capitalism, Japan had developed enterprises as well as entrepreneurs by mobilizing warriors (the samurai class). The state initiated the development of textile mills, mining activities, shipbuilding, and other enterprises, and later transferred ownership at low prices to private hands, thus giving rise to the family-owned conglomerates of the twentieth century. The Japanese modernized education, taking Western technology and combining it with Japanese thought derived from Confucianism and Legalism.[4] They also achieved social order and harmony by encouraging development of individual discipline through adherence to the values of Confucian ethics, loyalty to the state, filial piety toward parents and family, and loyalty to the organization (government or private) to which they belonged. It took more than 40 years in the Meiji period to accomplish this, thus laying the foundations for Japan's subsequent development.

Clearly, numerous parallels emerge when these changes of the late nineteenth century in Japan are compared to those that began in Korea just

---

4. Legalism, which was synthesized by Han-fei-tzu (d. 233 B.C.), advocated the enforcement of law with liberal rewards and heavy punishment, the manipulation of statecraft, and the exercise of power by the ruler. The Legalist school shared certain concepts with other schools—such as the equality of all men—but rejected the Taoist natural standard of the Way, the Confucian moral standard of *jen*, and the religious standard of heaven advocated by Mo-tzu. The philosophy of the Legalist school was put into strict practice during the Ch'in dynasty (221–206 B.C.), but soon thereafter Confucianism began to gain ground and within less than a century became the state doctrine (W. T. Chan 1979:417). Nonetheless, Legalism's influence remained and its precepts served as the basis for the establishment of the Chinese bureaucracy.

a little more than a century later under the *Yushin* Constitution. To the mind of President Park, a mere eight or ten years in office were not sufficient to build the modern state that he envisaged, nor sufficient even for some of the most basic achievements of the Meiji revolution. He set himself the task of replicating in Korea what was done during the Meiji reforms in Japan. In essence, the objectives in modernizing the two countries were basically similar: economic development, a strong defense, and a cohesive society based on the Confucian ethics of harmony and loyalty. President Park made explicit efforts to inculcate in the Korean populace the Confucian value of *chung hyo* (loyalty to state, filial piety, and harmony). In this respect, the Japanese and Korean techniques for achieving national goals also appear similar, notably in terms of education and mobilization of the population. The *Yushin* measures, for example, included institutionalization of student military training, and establishment of hometown militias and a civil defense corps. Great emphasis was placed on social cohesion and national integration.

From 1972 onward, the Park regime became more authoritarian, moving toward increasing limitation of civil liberties and participation in the political process. The government created a weak national assembly and sought to counterbalance it with a strong bureaucracy. President Park did attempt, however, to decrease military influence in political and economic affairs.

Emergency Decree and Policy Measures for Industry (1972–74)

As Korea entered the 1970s, a few signs in the world economy boded ill for Korea's export-led industrialization. Economic recession in major industrialized countries, the increase of protectionism in world trade, and international monetary disturbances in the early 1970s generated uncertainty in the Korean business community about the short-term prospects for sustaining Korea's export growth. When the growth of exports slowed in 1971, the economy started to cool off and slid into economic recession in 1971 and 1972. In the process, it was realized that the capital structure of many Korean firms was neither stable nor healthy. By the early 1970s many companies had grown into large-scale enterprises in terms of sales, assets, and employment. These companies, however, started their businesses with little equity; although they grew very large, they subsequently became heavily dependent on loans from domestic commercial banks and on foreign loans. For their working capital they had to resort to the unorganized curb market. When the economic slowdown arrived and the 1971 devaluation of the Korean won reduced their current earnings, at the same time increasing the won-costs of servicing their foreign debts, these large enterprises faced severe short-term cash-flow problems and the possibility of defaulting on their foreign loans. Such short-term, high-cost financing forced some of the companies into bankruptcy or to come under bank control. In this situation economic growth stagnated.

To stave off massive bankruptcies and to stimulate the economy, the Presidential Emergency Decree for Economic Stability and Growth was announced on 3 August 1972. This measure, discussed in detail in Chapter 7, was taken essentially to relieve the financial strain on business firms, to improve corporate financial structures, and to curb inflationary pressures. Under this decree, loans from unorganized money markets (which charged extremely high interest rates) were forcibly converted into "new debt claims" with lower interest rates and rescheduled payments. A credit-guarantee fund was established for small and medium-size businesses. Bank interest rates were reduced for both borrowers and depositors. Many in the business community were cognizant of the extremely serious implications of massive bankruptcies and also of rampant usury. Business leaders were convinced that their enterprises could not survive under such a climate and that the short-term curb market profiteers rather than the institutionalized banks were running the show. The president finally came to share their view and announced this drastic measure to eliminate the tyranny of usury. It is arguable that, had business not been saved from bankruptcy, those who contributed in major ways to rapid economic expansion in the decade that followed would not have been able to make such a contribution. Some argue, however, that the emergency decree, while giving immediate and substantial assistance to debt-ridden firms, provided only temporary relief but no long-term financial solutions to industry.[5]

The emergency decree of 1972 went side by side with a policy measure to open private companies to public shareholding, with emphasis on the gradual separation of ownership and management. In 1972 the government enacted the Law on Opening of Closed Corporations to induce large family-owned enterprises to sell a portion of their equity to the public. President Park did not have a liking for large capitalists, which is understandable, considering his own background. He personally examined the results of this measure by requiring a monthly report on the progress of opening up the family-held companies. The large corporations found various means to avoid opening up from the beginning; therefore, on 29 May 1974 the presi-

---

5. An interesting commentary by Professor Shinichi Ichimura of Kyoto University on Chapter 7 of this book is noted here:

[An assessment of the 1972 emergency decree] requires a view on history rather than an economist's analytical mind. The late President Park may have been a historic figure who played the role that Korea needed just at that time. He reminds me, as a Japanese scholar, of Oda Nobunaga who achieved an end to the Medieval Age and started a period of rationalization and secularization [in Japan] and was assassinated by his subordinate. Leave the evaluation of President Park to an outstanding Korea historian some decade later (Ichimura 1985).

dent issued a special directive to force recalcitrant companies to comply (Chapter 18). By 1979 publicly held shares were supposed to be 49 percent of total shares in 355 of the largest 500 companies in Korea. The ultimate design for reducing family holdings to only 10 percent of shares was already in the planning stages, but it was never actually implemented. Moreover, during the same period, the total value added of the top 20 conglomerates, as a percentage of gross domestic product, increased significantly, from 7 percent in 1973 to 14 percent in 1978.

The government under President Park made a consistent effort up to 1979 to regulate the excess concentration of economic power in the hands of a small number of large corporations. Since 1979, however, not much progress has been made in opening up the family-held companies. Looking at the situation in the late 1980s, some would argue that efforts along these lines have met with limited success. However, if the policy intentions of the Park government had been implemented continuously over a longer span of time and had not been interrupted by the president's death in 1979, it is conceivable that public shareholding in the larger corporations might have increased to a greater extent than it has.

Another policy measure sought to promote heavy and chemical industries as envisaged in the Heavy and Chemical Industries Promotion Plan announced by the government in 1973 (Chapter 17). It was an ambitious scheme to foster the growth of heavy engineering and petrochemical-process industries, including iron and steel, nonferrous metals, shipbuilding, industrial machinery, electronics, and petrochemicals. This plan was seemingly motivated by two arguments. First, the development of defense-related industries was considered a necessity, in view of the signals from the United States regarding the eventual withdrawal of U.S. ground forces from Korea. Second, the increase of heavy industrial goods in the commodity composition of Korean exports was necessary to increase the value added in its exports (such goods represent higher value added) and also to cope with increasing protectionism against labor-intensive light manufactures in world markets (particularly in view of rapidly rising wage levels in Korea). The government provided a variety of incentives to the enterprises investing in the designated heavy and chemical industries, which ranged from preferential loans and tax concessions to protection through restrictions on commodity production. The government's big push succeeded in developing a nucleus of heavy and chemical industries in Korea. But the concentration of scarce capital in this sector had an adverse effect on the economic stability and export competitiveness of other sectors of the economy (agriculture, light manufacturing, and nontradable goods). The financial insolvency of many of the latter firms in the early 1980s may be attributable to the lopsided allocation of financial resources in favor of the heavy and chemical industries.

The rapidly changing international political scene in the early 1970s—in particular the visits of the American president and other top leaders to China (viewed in Korea and elsewhere as the "Nixon Shock") and the opening of the dialogue between Japan and China—made it extremely difficult for Korean leaders to assess the implications and future consequences of such changes for Korea's national security. The sense of insecurity and instability resulting from not knowing what was going to happen must have strongly motivated President Park and his economic policymakers to place stronger emphasis on heavy and chemical industries, which would enable Korea to become more self-reliant in national defense. A question arose as to whether the United States would be trustworthy and reliable in time of desperate need for military hardware and other direct support for the defense of Korea. Unbalanced investment in the heavy and chemical industries caused distortions in the country's industrial structure, in income distribution, and in other dimensions of the economy. Nevertheless, the concern for national security, especially vis-à-vis the increasing belligerence of North Korea, was the overriding issue facing the Korean leadership. The threat from North Korea was exemplified by a 1976 incident when North Korean soldiers ruthlessly hacked to death two American officers who were attempting to trim the branches of a tree in the demilitarized zone. Joint U.S. and Korean military plans for possible counteraction were subsequently formulated and approved by the presidents of both countries. Another work crew was sent to continue the trimming. South Korean and U.S. air and ground forces were on alert and prepared, if they too were attacked, to strike across the demilitarized zone to recapture territory up to the 38th parallel that had been lost during the Korean War. This time, the North Koreans took no action, but under such tense circumstances verging on war, national security overrode all other concerns as the focus of South Korean policymaking.

As the government implemented the policy measures to expand heavy and chemical industries, their will was further intensified by President Carter's platform for the complete withdrawal of all U.S. troops from Korea by 1982. The Korean government thus set 1980 as the target date for fulfilling the basic requirements of self-reliance in the defense industry.

Having relieved business firms of severe financial restraints through the 1972 emergency decree, the subsequent massive investment in heavy and chemical industries spurred industrial growth through the 1970s. Such rapid industrial expansion entailed significant changes in industrial structure and market organization. There was also noticeable change in the distribution of industrial and economic power, and a sizable number of large-scale corporations (perceived as associated with family fortunes) emerged. The emergence of the *jaebul* (family-connected corporations) was beginning to change the public's perception of the benefits of the development-first strategy, in that rapid economic growth was perceived to have resulted in distortions in the distribution of income and wealth. In this context, the freezing of the curb market was regarded by many as financial relief to help large businesses at the expense of the middle-income people who had invested in the curb markets.

Policy Reponse to the Oil Crisis (1974)

The Middle East war of October 1973 and the ensuing oil crisis caused a sudden panic in Korean economic circles. The Arab oil embargo led to a quadrupling of the world oil price in 1973–74, followed by recession in the Japanese and U.S. economies. Korea depended on imported oil for about 55 percent of its total energy requirements, and the situation was serious. The Presidential Emergency Decree for National Economic Security was announced in January 1974 (Chapter 8). The essence of the decree was: (1) to secure the welfare of the majority of the population by minimizing the impact of oil price increases on low-income groups, (2) to discourage luxury expenditures and promote frugality among high-income groups and corporations, and (3) to minimize the deterioration in the balance of payments. The decree's energy-specific measures aimed to promote energy conservation and reduce dependence on imported oil, and were later consolidated into an integrated policy that became the centerpiece of Korea's energy policy.

On the macroeconomic side, the government attempted to sustain a high rate of economic growth by borrowing from abroad. In a sense, the policy response to the oil crisis was a success in the short run, in that the country was able to maintain a relatively high rate of growth during 1974–75. The real rate of GNP growth in 1974 was 7.7 percent, which compares favorably with those of the major industrialized countries as well as with some of Korea's major trade competitors such as Singapore and Taiwan. Nevertheless, this policy measure may have contributed in subsequent years to increasing Korea's foreign debt-service burden and to inflationary pressure. The negative impact of the policy measure on the balance of payments was so serious that net foreign exchange reserves declined nearly to half a month's imports at the end of 1974. The deteriorating balance-of-payments situation was a portent that continued economic growth might not be possible.

Promotion of General Trading Companies and Construction Exports (1975)

Changes in the international economic environment immediately following the 1973–74 oil shock dampened the prospects for continuous expansion of Korea's commodity exports. At the same time, the prospects for exporting construction services to the oil-rich Middle East countries appeared promising. Against this background, the government undertook two specific policy measures in 1975 to promote the creation of general trading companies and exports of construction services.

The measure to designate specific companies to function as "general trading companies" (GTCs) was taken in early 1975 by presidential decree (see Chapter 19). Prior to formulating the policy measure, numerous consultations among some of the major Japanese conglomerates and Korean policymakers resulted in recommendations containing principally the ideas of Ryuzo Sejima[6] of the Japanese conglomerate Itohchu. The top ten companies were designated as GTCs. The principal objectives of the establishment of the GTCs were to strengthen Korea's export marketing activities by using the extensive network of the GTCs' overseas branches to perform the role of "windows" or export agents for small and medium-size firms producing export commodities and to reduce excessive competition among Korean firms. The small and medium-size industries' share of export commodities constituted about 50 percent of the GTCs export trade a few years after the initial designation of the GTCs.

Patterned after the Japanese model of general trading companies *(shogogaisha)*, Korea's GTCs contributed substantially to revived export expansion. But unlike their Japanese counterparts, the Korean GTCs were much more competitive among themselves (to the extent of cutthroat competition) rather than complementary (as is the case of the Japanese GTCs) in delimiting functional markets. The Korean GTCs did increase exports but were perceived as having used their financial resources, obtained through preferential bank loans, for real-estate speculation and the acquisition of existing medium-size firms and small export firms. For example, the large conglomerates experienced a dramatic increase in earnings from overseas construction contracts. Many of the construction companies were using those funds to buy real estate, either for speculation or for later domestic development projects. Because these construction companies were generally associated with the GTCs, it looked as though the conglomerates were buying up real estate, whereas it may be that only the construction companies were involved in the real estate dealings. In any case, the positive impact of the GTCs for the long term was the recruitment of a new generation of young, competent, well-trained managers both in the home offices and abroad, whose subsequent experience and training have contributed to the quality of corporate entrepreneurship.

The Overseas Construction Promotion Act was promulgated in December 1975 to provide a legal basis for government support to and supervision of the export of construction services, and to promote the international

---

6. Ryuzo Sejima, who graduated from the Japanese military academy at around the same time as Park Chung Hee, is still an active business leader and remains influential in political circles in Japan.

sion of the export of construction services, and to promote the international competitiveness of the Korean construction industry (see Chapter 20). The Park government saw salvation for the heavy industrialization strategy in the export of construction services to the Middle East. The act required that a company obtain a license from the Ministry of Construction to engage in the overseas construction business. Construction companies licensed by the ministry were provided with performance bonding by Korean banks and were insured against exchange fluctuations and other risks of foreign trade. They also received tax benefits on income derived from foreign construction.

The implementation of this policy measure was not entirely a success. The more profitable activities of the contractors—building harbor facilities and industrial plants, for example—were very successful in earning foreign exchange. A few major companies encountered serious losses, however, notably in the construction of housing, mainly because of a lack of understanding of the culture and behavior of Islamic people. The Middle Eastern countries complained at first about Korean government control over and interference in free competition among competing companies. Despite government efforts to manage construction export services to the Middle East, some destructive competition took place to the detriment of the overall industry, and some Middle East governments later complained about "dumping" of construction services because some companies were grasping for any opportunity to obtain contracts regardless of their capabilities to fulfill them.

Korea's balance of payments improved substantially during 1976–77, thanks to the boom in Middle East construction activities, but the overexpansion of construction service exports was threatening to disrupt the stability of the economy. The surplus balance was an entirely new phenomenon for Korea's economic policymakers. The influx of foreign exchange earnings from the Middle East contributed to the dramatic increase in the money supply and fanned inflation. Because of the lack of both experience and insight with respect to the surplus balance, the distortion in the finance sector was not properly handled and the negative impact lingered, exacerbating later difficulties. In the early 1980s, after the boom had ended, the financial insolvency of many construction firms became evident. In retrospect the government should have taken more decisive action in streamlining and curtailing the overseas construction service industry when the demand for these services began to decline.

Policy Measures for Social Development and Urban Growth (1976–77)

While Korea was emerging as a newly industrializing country and eliminating absolute poverty, concern about social welfare received increasing attention. As a result of the heavy emphasis on economic growth, efforts toward social development and welfare were lagging in the mid-1970s. The Park government was able to launch only a limited social welfare program, which included the enactment of the Medical Insurance Law at the end of 1976 (see Chapter 13).

Since the law's implementation in July 1977, the health insurance program has played an important role in making medical services more accessible to the working population. Although the number of persons covered by the program has increased steadily, many problems remain to be solved in order to achieve an adequate level of service for the population at large. The medical insurance system has not received the level of investment needed to fulfill its function.

During the 1960s, 1970s, and 1980s, the spatial structure of human settlements in Korea was drastically transformed. As discussed in Chapter 14, rapid industrialization was accompanied by massive rural-to-urban migration. As a result, the proportion of the total population residing in urban areas increased from 28 percent in 1962 to almost 60 percent in 1980. The principal problems in Korean urban growth have been the persistent primacy of the capital city and regional imbalance. This is partly a result of the government's development strategy, which stressed economies of scale and agglomeration.

Although the Korean government began taking some policy initiatives in the late 1960s to grapple with these problems, the 1977 Population Redistribution Plan was the most ambitious government effort to guide the pattern of urbanization. The 1977 measure was prompted by the increasing belligerence of North Korea, in that the economic and industrial predominance of the capital city made South Korea precariously vulnerable to easy attack or sabotage from the North. The plan was comprehensive in the sense that it employed almost every conceivable means and strategy to achieve the planning objectives.

The Korean population redistribution policy achieved limited success initially. The predominance of the capital city in economic, financial, educational, and other aspects still seems to be increasing. The ineffectiveness of the plan can be attributed to its lack of integration with economic development policies, the control-oriented nature of its policy measures, and the lack of a firm political commitment for population dispersal. The redistribution policy should have been formulated in the early 1970s, when the country was at the take-off point in industrial development. An effective and comprehensive policy could then have had a greater impact. Nevertheless, the Korean experience in population redistribution provides a valuable lesson for other countries that are considering the formulation or implementation of a national urban policy.

Value-Added Tax (1977)

The Fourth Five-Year Economic and Social Development Plan emphasized the promotion of heavy and chemical industries to strengthen national defense, and social development projects to enhance the people's welfare. The government was painfully aware of the need for increased revenues as well as other sources of capital.

Up until 1977 Korea maintained a complicated structure of domestic indirect taxes. Then in July 1977 the value-added tax (VAT) was formally introduced (see Chapter 11). The principal objectives of VAT were, on the one hand, to simplify the existing tax structure and, on the other, to increase revenues. Some economic policymakers at that time were greatly attracted to the VAT system already operating in some of the countries of the European Economic Community. When the basic idea was first brought forth for discussion, an Irish tax expert who was a strong advocate of the merits of the system was consulted. Subsequently, a study team was formed to review and evaluate the VAT system operating in European countries; the study results were formulated into recommendations for adopting the system in Korea. The principal proponent of this system was an economist who had recently returned to Korea from an American university. The VAT as implemented in advanced industrial countries was theoretically neat and persuasive both from the tax administration viewpoint and in the context of rational behavior. However, the noneconomic aspects of human behavior based on traditional values, customs, and habits were lacking in this "pure" frame of thinking. If the majority of the populace are not educated or persuaded to cooperate willingly in the implementation of a tax reform, the costs of enforcement may ultimately outweigh its advantages and merits.

There has been heated argument as to whether VAT caused price increases, thereby contributing to inflation. It has been argued that the policymakers, by intentionally placing emphasis on the heavy and chemical industries, were prepared to live with a certain level of inflation in any case to meet the target of national security self-reliance by 1980. In addition to revenues generated under the VAT system, the dramatic increase in Middle East construction earnings was also fanning inflation. It has also been argued that the rate of price increases in the first half of 1977 was greater than in the second half (that is, after the introduction of VAT). However, a proper evaluation of the impact of the new tax system would have to be carried out over a much longer time frame. The Korean experience has demonstrated that the VAT system, although simple in principle and neat theoretically, created voluminous paperwork and procedures that were, at that time, not consonant with the habits and behavior of the populace, thereby causing irritation, annoyance, and complaints which were, in the end, manifested in political consequences. The public's perception of the tax was that it would benefit big business but would hurt smaller businesses. The implementation of VAT contributed to the decrease in popular support for the government during the general election of 1978 and was the beginning of serious political trouble for the regime. The VAT reform can thus be regarded as a political-economic foible. In the Korean cultural setting one has to conclude that VAT was some years ahead of its time.

Comprehensive Economic Stabilization Program (1979)

During the 1961–79 period, the Park government accepted inflation as an inevitable price for sustained economic growth. The policy response to the first oil shock in 1974, the massive injection of capital into the heavy industrialization projects in 1976–78, and the sudden increase in money supply resulting from the influx of foreign exchange earnings from the Middle East added to the inflationary pressure in the latter half of the 1970s. As inflation accelerated, however, it became clear that sustained economic growth would be difficult unless inflation was curbed. The weakening of export competitiveness, inflationary distortions in resource allocation, and the growing frustration of workers who were increasingly aware of the widening disparity in the distribution of wealth and income pointed to chronic inflation as a principal factor undermining economic health.

The government announced the Integrated Economic Stabilization Program in April 1979 (see Chapter 9). The essence of this policy package was to control aggregate demand through restrictive fiscal and monetary management and investment adjustment in the heavy and chemical industries. Subsequently, with the change of government in 1980 as a result of President Park's assassination, the new team of policymakers modified the policy package more into controlling costs and prices—for example, by reducing interest rates and freezing wages. However, before the program produced any signs of price stability, the economy was hit by the second oil price increase and the worldwide economic recession. The assassination of President Park and ensuing political turmoil caused a drastic setback in economic activity. The numerous policy measures taken during 1980–86 to stimulate the economy were, in most cases, cautious and sensitive so as not to jeopardize price stability. Nonetheless, the stabilization effort initiated by the 1979 measures was not abandoned—not even during the difficult period of the oil shock and recession. It has been continued and, as a result, there has been a fairly sharp deceleration in inflation since 1981.

ASSASSINATION OF PRESIDENT PARK
AND TRANSITION TO THE FIFTH REPUBLIC

A serious political disturbance began in September 1979 when the head of the major opposition party was dismissed from the National Assembly and his followers resigned in protest. This disturbance was severely repressed. Then, in October 1979, President Park Chung Hee was assassinated by the head of the Korean CIA, abruptly ending his 18-year term of state control.[7]

The assassination of President Park was followed by serious civil disturbances and economic disruptions during the final year of the Fourth Republic. President Park's prime minister, Choi Kyu Hah, was sworn in as interim president, and a new cabinet was formed. During the next six months, the government was basically trying to cope with the chaotic disruptions in the wake of the assassination, including political activism among the opposition early in 1980 and student rioting in the universities. The business community became demoralized, and the military grew increasingly uneasy. Although the government did what it could to stabilize the economy from the political shocks, the Korean economy for the first time in two decades experienced negative growth (-3.7 percent in GNP in 1980).

President Choi, who rose to the presidency as a docile bureaucrat, was never groomed for a role that demanded forceful and effective political leadership. During the critical transitional period in late 1979 and early 1980, President Choi demonstrated no leadership ability or courage in managing the political vacuum created by the assassination. In December 1979 a power struggle within the military culminated in an internal leadership takeover by a group of officers around General Chun Doo Hwan. This group then began playing an increasing political role. In May 1980, when the government was confronted by the Kwangju civil uprising for "democratization," the military took control of the country, extended martial law, and restored order in Kwangju (although at the cost of about 190 lives). General Chun formally retired from the army to head the government and promised a general election under a new constitution within a year.

This chapter has attempted to paint only a broad backdrop to introduce the main features of the Park administration's policy measures in historical perspective. The following chapters will review 18 major policy initiatives that were developed to further the government's rapid economic development strategy from 1961 to 1979. Each author provides an analytical assessment of the impact of a particular measure and a detailed examination of how government and business interacted and cooperated in its implementation. These policy measures and reforms in some instances played a critical role in transforming the structure of the Korean economy and helped put it on a rapid growth path. Some policies, however, not only failed to

---

7. The assassin was Kim Jae-Kyu, a long-time friend of President Park. He was about to be removed from his powerful position as head of the Korean Central Intelligence Agency and was locked in a rivalry struggle with the president's bodyguard, Cha Jae-Chul. Kim actually planned to shoot only Cha, but having done so, he assassinated the president as well.

achieve the intended results but also led to circumstances in which another corrective measure was needed. The policy measures included in this book are by no means exhaustive, and it might be argued that some measures excluded from this study are equally important. The editors believe, however, that the measures selected for this study represent the critical policy events underlying the rapid economic development of the 1960s and 1970s.

PART II
ECONOMIC POLICIES, 1961–80

MONETARY AND
PRICE POLICIES

TAXATION POLICIES

POPULATION AND
PUBLIC HEALTH POLICIES

AGRICULTURAL POLICIES

INDUSTRIAL POLICIES

MONETARY AND
PRICE POLICIES

3 The Development of Financial Institutions and the Role of Government in Credit Allocation

by Yung Chul Park

In 1961 Korea's financial institutions were largely composed of the Bank of Korea, the Korea Development Bank (KDB), the Korea Agricultural Bank (KAB), and a few nationwide commercial banks.

The KDB was established in 1954 with the primary mission of providing medium- and long-term loans to industry. It was placed directly under the authority of the Ministry of Finance and so was not subject to the control of the central bank, the Bank of Korea. However, because of its inability to attract funds from the public, the KDB had to rely heavily on the central bank for its supply of funds. The inflationary condition, small private savings, and low ceilings on interest rates discouraged the public from purchasing long-term debt instruments from the KDB.

The KAB was set up at about the same time, as a bank for the farmers' associations. Like the KDB, and for the same reasons, it had difficulty in raising funds from the public and thus had to rely for funds on the government and the central bank.

Until 1957 the commercial banks, with the exception of the Choheung Bank, were largely owned by the government. The government of Korea received the shares in the banks from the U.S. military government, which had confiscated them from Japanese owners at the end of World War II. In 1957 the government denationalized the banks by selling its shares to private individuals. A stigma was, however, attached to this denationalization as many of these individuals (mainly owners of conglomerates) had become wealthy by reaping high profits, tainted with corruption, in the importing business controlled by government licenses. This later provided a rationale for the military government in repossessing the shares held by large private investors in the commercial banks.

The financial market that existed in Korea just before the military takeover in 1961 was not, therefore, a single homogeneous market but contained a dual structure: the KDB and KAB, established and controlled directly by the government, and the commercial banks, most of which had been denationalized only a few years before. Of the two, the former exercised a dominant influence in the allocation of funds, accounting for 71 percent of total lending in 1960. The latter's share, which was 45 percent in 1955, declined to 29 percent in 1960. Thus, contrary to what one would have

45

expected, the denationalization expanded the influence of the government in the financial market. When the military government expropriated the privately held shares in the commercial banks in 1961, it was not, therefore, converting a free market into a controlled market but merely increasing the degree of control.

The military leaders who took over the government in May 1961 were committed to a mixed economy in which the government and the public sector would play a dominant role in economic development. They pledged themselves to powerful government programs aimed at overcoming the country's underdevelopment.

As a first step toward achieving financial control, the new leaders, within three months after their takeover of the government, reorganized the agricultural financing and marketing institutions by combining the agricultural cooperatives and the KAB into one entity known as the National Agricultural Cooperatives Federation (NACF). The NACF was responsible for providing credit to farmers, supplying them with agricultural inputs, and marketing their output, as well as purchasing grain on government account to help stabilize grain prices and ensure supplies for government needs.

The second major innovation of the military government was the establishment of the Medium Industry Bank (MIB), also in August 1961, for the purpose of providing loans to medium and small enterprises. The functions of the MIB (now the Small and Medium Industry Bank) were similar to those of the commercial banks in that it accepted deposits and made mainly short-term loans, but its loans had to go only to enterprises with fewer than a certain prescribed number of employees and whose total assets were less than a certain amount.

Both of these initial ventures—the NACF and the MIB—were manifestations of the government's desire and commitment to improve the lot of small farmers and businessmen. The rapid expansion of loans through these institutions in 1961 resulted in a significant shift in the allocation of credit. The share of these two banks in total bank credit jumped from 32 to 38 percent during 1961, largely at the expense of the commercial bank share, which dropped from 29 to 24 percent.

In October 1961 the government repossessed the shares of the commercial banks that were held by large stockholders on the grounds that these were illegally hoarded properties. Furthermore, the voting interest of any single stockholder was restricted, under the Temporary Act on Bank Administration, to no more than 10 percent of the total shares, regardless of actual holdings. As a result, the government became the dominant stockholder with comprehensive controls over the banks ranging from the appointment of senior officers to issuing directives on banking operations. The government was responding to concerns that the privately owned banks would contribute to the concentration of economic power along the lines experienced in Japan (B. Kim 1965:66).

The next step in the financial reform program of the military government was the revision of the KDB charter to increase its capital, authorize it to borrow funds from abroad, and guarantee foreign loans obtained by Korean enterprises. This guarantee procedure was subsequently extended to the other commercial and special banks and proved to be a major factor inducing the inflow of foreign capital.

These institutional changes culminated in May 1962 when the Bank of Korea Law was revised to bring the central bank unequivocally under the control of the minister of finance. The minister of finance had wielded de facto authority over the Bank of Korea from its inception, in part because of the need for financing the Korean War and postwar reconstruction. There was continual debate from 1950 to 1962 between those who supported the autonomy of the central bank as provided in its charter and those who believed that monetary policy should be one of several coordinated elements of economic policy with the minister of finance, as chairman of the Monetary Board, providing the focal point of that coordination (B. Kim 1965).

In late 1962 the government consolidated a number of small mutual financing companies into the Citizens National Bank, which was to concentrate on small loans to businesses and households. Also in 1962, the Central Federation of Fisheries Cooperatives was created to provide credit and marketing services to the fishing industry comparable to those the NACF provided to agriculture.

The legislative changes of 1962 were a manifestation of the orientation of the new government toward development of a core of centrally managed, powerful institutions and instruments for carrying out the First Five-Year Development Plan (1962–66).

MAIN FEATURES OF THE POLICY MEASURES

Guaranteeing Repayment of Foreign Loans: A New Role for Korean Banks

As the main instrument for promoting the inflow of foreign loans, the government devised, during the 1960s, a system of bank guarantees for the repayment of loans. The impetus for this appears to have come mainly from the prospective normalization of relations with Japan. The Korean government preferred to have the resulting capital inflow in the form of loans rather than equity shares so as to minimize Japanese ownership and control of Korean business. Furthermore, although the arrangement for a loan was to be worked out directly between the borrower and the lender, it required government approval. The government, therefore, had ultimate control over the volume of foreign financing and its allocation among competing sectors.

Korean enterprises wishing to borrow abroad first had to obtain the approval of the Economic Planning Board (EPB), which in turn sought approval of the National Assembly for the issuance of a guarantee covering repayment of the foreign borrowings. Once the guarantee had been authorized, the Bank of Korea (and subsequently the Korean Exchange Bank) issued the guarantee to the foreign lender, while the KDB (and subsequently the commercial banks) issued guarantees to the Bank of Korea. The ultimate borrower was committed to repay the loan, but he had the backing of both the KDB and the Bank of Korea that, in the event of his default, the loan would be repaid. Thus the risk of default for the lender was negligible, and the Korean borrower had assurances of support not only from the domestic banking institutions but also from the central bank and the EPB.

The foreign loan guarantee operations became significant in 1963 when KDB acceptances (time drafts and bills of exchange) went up from 2.2 billion won in the previous year to 18.1 billion (Cole and Park 1983). Over the next two years, the total guarantees increased by over 25 billion won each year and then jumped by nearly 70 billion won in 1966, at which time they were nearly equal to the total of outstanding bank loans. Also in 1966 the commercial banks assumed a significant role in the guarantee activity, accounting for nearly 30 billion of the 70 billion increase in that year. Thus the Korean banking system, while not actually intermediating between foreign lenders and domestic borrowers, was facilitating such lending activity, without committing much of its own financial or human resources. From 1963 to 1966 foreign guaranteed loans were the major source of new financing for Korean businesses.

Because the banks played a very limited role in the decision-making process in regard to these loans and issued the guarantees on instruction from the government, they took little responsibility for evaluating either the economic or financial feasibility of a project. Eventually when some of the projects proved unsound, the government had little basis for holding the banks accountable and therefore had to take extraordinary measures to relieve the banks of the bad debts.

The Interest-Rate Reform

The interest-rate reform of September 1965 (see also chapter 6), though sometimes viewed as a revamping of the whole interest-rate structure, was essentially a major increase in the interest rate paid on time deposits designed to mobilize private savings through the nationalized financial institutions. There were some increases in the rates charged on loans, but these had little impact on the volume of lending or lending practices because the new rates were still not high enough to affect the demand for loans. The increase in the time-deposit rate from 15 to 30 percent per year, however, did result in a quantum jump in the financial resources of the commercial and special banks and substantially changed their institutional role. All the banks (except the KDB, which did not raise its deposit rate) became important mobilizers of financial savings and for the first time began to give some attention to this role. They were also partly relieved from their total dependence on central bank credit or government budgetary allocations of aid counterpart funds as primary sources for their lending.

Between 1965 and 1969 total bank deposits rose from 10 percent to 30 percent of GNP. During this period, real GNP increased by 57 percent and nominal GNP by 158 percent, whereas total deposits rose by nearly 700 percent. Total bank loans increased by an amount almost exactly equal to the deposits between 1965 and 1969 (Cole and Park 1983). A substantial excess of deposits over loans in the commercial banks was offset by a loan surplus at the KDB.

The interest-rate reform contributed to mobilizing real private savings and put vast financial resources at the command of the government. Clearly the role of the banking system had changed dramatically from the early 1960s when it was mainly engaged in rationing a limited supply of credit. Although the banks had not acquired any greater degree of independence in decision making as to the allocation of credit—decisions on all the guarantees and many of the larger loans were made by the government—they did have a greatly expanded managerial role over a system that exerted a major influence on the allocation of resources.

New Banking Institutions in the Late 1960s

Specialized banking institutions were established in 1967 and the doors were opened to the creation of new private banking ventures. The Korea Exchange Bank (KEB) was created as a separate entity from the personnel, facilities, and financial resources of the foreign-exchange and foreign-operations departments of the Bank of Korea. The KEB's stock was wholly owned by the Bank of Korea, and it had functioned largely as an extension of the central bank since its inception. Thus the change was mainly one of form rather than substance.

Much the same can be said for the Korea Trust Bank, a consolidation of the trust departments of the five national commercial banks, also established in 1967. Trust accounts in Korea are fairly close substitutes for time deposits and the Korea Trust Bank had held substantial amounts of demand deposits since its inception. Thus it functioned much like a commercial bank and had been treated as such by both the central bank and the financial authorities until it was merged with the Seoul Bank in 1976 to become the Bank of Seoul and Trust Company.

The Korea Housing Bank was also created in 1967 "to finance housing funds for low-income families" (BOK, *Financial System*, 1983:47). Its purpose was to extend loans for construction and purchasing of houses and to firms producing housing construction materials. By 1978 the Korea Housing Bank was raising roughly one-third of its funds through the sale of debentures, and 55 percent through demand and time deposits. Depositors received preferential treatment in the granting of loans, which provided an incentive, in addition to the interest rate, for holding its deposits.

Nevertheless, in 1978 the Korea Housing Bank's share of total bank deposits was only about 4 percent.

Of greater significance was the action by the government in 1967 authorizing the chartering of *local banks* to conduct commercial banking business principally within limited geographic areas. The objectives of the government were to achieve greater dispersion of banking services and to see that the banks would concentrate on meeting the needs of local enterprises. The local banks engage in branch banking with their head offices in the provincial capitals and branches confined to the same province. Initially they were prohibited from engaging in foreign-exchange operations, but as they became better established that prohibition was relaxed. Also the local banks were authorized to charge interest rates on loans up to 2.5 percentage points higher than the national commercial banks and to pay higher interest rates on time deposits. These banks are privately owned and less closely regulated and controlled than the government-owned banks.

A final institutional innovation of 1967 was the granting of permission to a limited number of foreign banks to open branch offices in Korea. In the first year, five banks (three American and two Japanese) established branches; by the end of 1974, four more were permitted. Since then the number of foreign bank branches has risen rapidly, reflecting the growing volume of external transactions. The kinds of activities in which these branches can participate are, however, quite circumscribed, and they rely mainly on funds borrowed from their head offices to make loans in foreign currency, especially to importers.

Development of Nonbank Financial Institutions and the Capital Market

Banking and traditional financial institutions had accounted for most of the financial intermediation during the postwar years (1948–53). Throughout the 1950s and 1960s, life insurance, postal savings, and the trust business of commercial banks had a commanding share of the nonbanking financial sector, although money in trust was actually time and savings deposits at the deposit-money banks with longer maturities.

The restructuring of the financial system in the 1960s, which gave the control of financial institutions to the government, was followed by policy measures in the 1970s aimed at developing nonbank financial intermediaries and the capital market. This financial policy had its major objectives in diversifying financial assets and institutions and also creating financial intermediaries that could compete effectively with and eventually eliminate the unregulated money market. As a result of the government's efforts, a variety of new nonbanking institutions came into existence, and their assets and liabilities grew rapidly in the 1970s. Considering the nature of their operations, it also appears that some of these institutions, such as the investment finance companies and mutual savings and finance companies, were instrumental in attracting private savings from the unregulated money markets into the regulated financial sector.

Most of the nonbank financial intermediaries are privately owned, major exceptions being the KDB and the Export–Import Bank of Korea. Although the government regulates their financial operations, these institutions, unlike deposit-money banks, have been left relatively free in their asset management.

The Export–Import Bank of Korea was created primarily for the promotion of exports of heavy and chemical products. It was legally established in 1969, but its operations were handled by the KEB for the next seven years. Since becoming a separate entity in 1976, the size of its loan portfolio has increased markedly. The bank provides medium- and long-term credit for foreign trade and overseas investment with its own resources and with funds borrowed from the government and the National Investment Fund.

A stock exchange was established in 1956, but for more than a decade thereafter the securities market was plagued by speculation and stock price manipulation. The "stock exchange" was really a market for government bonds and did not function as a stock market until the 1960s. By the mid-1960s it had become evident that heavy reliance on bank loans and foreign loans for the financing of corporate investment was leading to high debt–equity ratios dominated by short-term loans for many businesses. With this realization and the government's desire for greater diffusion of corporate ownership and diversification of financing sources, the government renewed its efforts to develop a modern capital market and began to implement a series of reform measures.

In September 1968 the Law for Fostering the Capital Market was enacted. This law was aimed at encouraging major corporations to go public. In December 1972 the government was entrusted with powers to designate a corporation as eligible to go public and to issue ordinances for it to do so. The Securities and Exchange Commission and its executive body, the Securities Supervisory Board, were established in February 1977 to carry out various functions related to the supervision of the securities market and institutions.

Efforts to improve the efficiency of the capital market continued into the 1980s. Repurchase agreements were introduced to enlarge the scope of the bond issue market. As a first step toward liberalizing the capital market to foreign investors, US $30 million in beneficiary certificates were sold in the United States and Europe in January 1981.

The rapid growth of nonbank financial intermediaries and the capital market beginning in the early 1970s brought about a significant change in the role of the government in resource allocation. The expansion reduced the scope of government intervention in the allocation of resources. The numerous measures undertaken to develop the nonbank financial institutions and the capital market also reflected the government's desire to gradually liberalize the financial system in the 1970s.

Recent Liberalization Measures

By the mid-1970s it was apparent to both the government and the business community that the development strategy that relied on extensive government intervention was becoming increasingly counterproductive. After a decade of rapid growth fueled by the expansion of exports, Korea had developed a complex and sophisticated economy with a large external sector.

The sheer size and complexity of the economy inevitably reduced the scope of government control and diminished the government's ability to administer a system of rigid controls. Doubts were raised as to whether the government could effect an efficient allocation of real resources through the credit allocations it controlled.

Although the need for a greater reliance on market mechanisms as an alternative to the system of control was clearly recognized, government planners continued to resist relinquishing economic decision-making power to the private sector. They, in fact, intensified their interference with the allocation of resources in the process of promoting the heavy and chemical industries as the future export sector. To divert a large share of the nation's investment resources to these industries, the government tightened its grip on the financial system.

The government took further steps to divert more resources to the heavy and chemical industries as evidenced by the creation of the National Investment Fund (NIF) in 1974. The KDB had played a dominant role as the long-term credit bank in the 1950s and 1960s, though other special banks had increased in importance as suppliers of long-term funds in the 1960s. In the early 1970s, when the Third Five-Year Development Plan was prepared, it was clear that the deposit-money banks (including the KDB) could not be expected to provide sufficient financing for the development of heavy and chemical industries—one of the major objectives of the third plan. A new financing channel, the NIF, was established to augment the flow of domestic savings to investment in the heavy and chemical industries.

The major sources of NIF loanable funds consisted of: (1) the proceeds from the sales of NIF bonds; (2) contributions in the form of deposits made by the deposit-money banks (exclusive of foreign bank branches and fisheries cooperatives), the members of the National Savings Association, money in trust, insurance premiums of nonlife insurance companies, and various public funds managed by the central and local governments and other public entities; and (3) transfers (or deposits) from the various government budgetary accounts. As for the contributions, the deposit-money banks were, for instance, required to deposit 15 percent of the increase in their savings deposits at the NIF and the nonlife insurance companies had to deposit 50 percent of their insurance premiums and other revenues.

The Ministry of Finance was responsible for the administration of the fund, but its actual management was entrusted to the Bank of Korea. The NIF made loans for both fixed investment and working capital to the heavy, chemical, and other major industries with the deposit-money banks, the KDB, and the Export–Import Bank of Korea acting as intermediaries.

The NIF loans were made at subsidized rates. In 1978 the lending rates varied from 6 percent for export suppliers credit to 16 percent for the loans to the heavy and chemical industries with three- to eight-year maturities, whereas the interest rates on NIF deposits ranged from 6 percent per annum (for three-month deposits) to 18.6 percent (for one year and over deposits and NIF bonds). The losses resulting from the negative margin between the deposit and lending rates were fully compensated for by the government.

Because of a lack of coordination in the development of the heavy and chemical industries, there was excessive investment and duplication of similar projects in many subsectors of these industries. The setback in the development of heavy and chemical industries and the associated drain on domestic resources, more than anything else, renewed the debate on the need for financial liberalization toward the end of the 1970s. Since then it has been frequently pointed out that such a misallocation of resources could have been avoided had the management of the financial system been left in the hands of the private sector.

Government planners and financial specialists agreed that government control of the financial institutions and interest rates should be relaxed and eventually eliminated in order to increase competition in the financial industry. What they disagreed on was the pace at which financial liberalization should be pursued and the proper role of the government in a liberalized financial regime.

The new regime that came into power in 1980 was strongly committed to financial liberalization as a major policy objective. The government divested itself of the ownership of one of the five commercial banks, the Hanil Bank, in June 1981. The denationalization was preceded and followed by abolishing various government directives that had regulated personnel management, budgets, and other operational matters of commercial banks. In the same month the monetary authorities established a commercial paper market that was not subject to government control. This market was expected to serve as a bridge between the curb market and the organized financial system and to provide a reference point for setting official interest rates. This move was widely regarded as a first step toward freeing the interest rates from government control. In line with this policy direction, the yields on new corporate debentures were allowed to fluctuate within an upper and lower limit of 1 percent of the banks' reference rate.

After the privatization of the Hanil Bank, the government also announced a plan to charter three joint-venture commercial banks with Korean and foreign partners to promote competition in the banking industry and to establish a linkage with international financial markets. One of these banks began operation in 1982, and another in 1983. In late 1981 two investment funds worth US $30 million were floated to let foreigners buy Korean shares.

At the end of November 1979, the average required reserves were 23 percent of deposits at the deposit-money banks. The ratio was gradually reduced to 3.5 percent in November 1981, before it was raised again to 5.5 percent in May 1982. The substantial reduction was aimed at giving more freedom to the banks in their management of lendable resources and easing the strain on bank profits.

In January 1982 the monetary authorities abolished the direct control over bank lending through credit ceilings and quotas in preference to an indirect reserve control. This change also signaled the government's intention to refrain from interfering with bank credit allocation.

These reform measures were significant and refreshing developments in a country that had long suffered from financial repression. Most of all, they reflected the government's determination to develop a freer financial system where the price mechanism reigns and to open the financial industry to foreign competition.

For almost a year after denationalization of the Hanil Bank, however, little visible progress toward financial liberalization had been made. For a while in the early months of 1982 there was a growing feeling that the government was stalling the reform. The lack of progress could largely be attributed to the disagreement among the policymakers on the pace of liberalization. On the one hand, there were those who believed that gradual liberalization was nothing but a code word for the continuation of financial repression and argued for an overhauling of the entire financial system within a short period of time. On the other hand, there were the moderates; they were concerned about the possible adverse effects of premature and swift reform. In particular, these "detractors" argued that financial liberalization conflicted with the government's overall as well as sectoral allocation of investment through the implementation of the consecutive five-year development plans. According to the moderates, financial control is a means for effecting the allocation of real resources. As long as the government attempts to influence resource allocation, it is argued, it cannot deprive itself of the most important means of control. More realistically, those who subscribed to gradual liberalization pointed out the extremely high leverage of Korean firms. Few could have survived the scrutiny of privatized commercial banks, and in the absence of the government's allocational interference in the form of relief financing, they believed, most of the firms that had borrowed heavily from the banks would have gone bankrupt. Until their balance sheets improved substantially, as the argument went, freeing the financial markets could not be implemented.

For a while, the gradualists appeared to have prevailed, but the curb market scandal that broke out in May 1982 changed the financial and political environment and eclipsed their influence. The swindle, ostensibly engineered by a couple extensively involved in curb-market lending, tarnished the image of a regime committed to building a just society. It jolted an economy already deep in recession, clouding further the prospects of an early recovery. It paralyzed the financial markets, severely curtailing the availability of credit. Under the circumstances, the government had to do something quickly to stop any further hemorrhaging of the economy. The monetary authorities began an infusion of fresh credit (created by printing money) into the economy to supplement the informal credit that had dried up overnight. The government also had to find a scapegoat for the scandal, which it found conveniently in the curb market. The root cause of the scandal, however, was the structural deficiencies in Korea's financial system that provided room for the expansion of the informal credit market. Nonetheless, the swindle set the stage for a complete reversal of the government's macroeconomic policy, quickened the pace of financial reform, and led to two radical measures on June 28 and July 3, along with other reform actions. The measures lowered the bank deposit and lending rates by more than 4 percentage points (June 28) and introduced an identification system in which depositors at banks and holders of other financial assets were required to reveal their real names (July 3). The July 3 measure was strongly opposed and was subsequently indefinitely postponed.

THEORETICAL APPROPRIATENESS

Government Intervention

Allocation of credit is one of the key functions of finance. Whereas financial growth may not necessarily stimulate private savings and may take place even when private savings as a proportion of income remains unchanged or declines, it is widely believed to contribute to efficient allocation of physical resources. The underlying assumption is that financial intermediaries, because of their scale economies and specialization, are more efficient in resource allocation than individual savers. Financial intermediaries are often able to allocate more resources than they mobilize from private savers because a major share of funding from the government and foreign sector is channeled to borrowers through the financial institutions.

Few governments in developing countries seem to believe in the allocational efficiency of either the financial markets or the financial institutions. As documented by Shaw (1973) and McKinnon (1973), the financial sector is perhaps the most heavily regulated industry in developing countries. The governments of these countries intervene extensively in credit allocation in the belief that without their intervention credit allocation would not reflect social and economic priorities—priorities that are often set by these governments. The Korean government has been no exception in this regard. It has behaved as if in the absence of its interference some sectors would receive more credit than socially and economically desirable while other sectors would receive too little.

Government intervention in the allocation of credit is often justified when: (1) the financial markets are imperfect so that these markets cannot allocate resources to the sectors with the highest private rates of return, and (2) a market allocation of resources conflicts with government objectives and therefore does not achieve the greatest social benefits as perceived by the government. The latter case does not, however, necessarily call forth government intervention in the allocation of credit. If, for instance, greater output than a competitive market outcome is desired, a direct subsidy to production is superior to government allocation of credit as a policy instrument. But, on the grounds that a direct subsidy may be politically undesirable, government intervention in credit allocation instead of a subsidy may be justifiable as a second-best solution.

To allocate financial resources in a manner that is perceived to be desirable on social and economic grounds, the government authorities first have to control the interest rates on loans to keep them below a market-clearing level. Low interest rates generate an excess demand for credit supplied by the regulated financial institutions. The excess demand, in turn, requires either the government or the management of the financial institutions to ration the available supply of institutional credit to borrowers according to a set of loan allocation criteria. Second, the government authorities will have to exercise the credit-rationing power to effect a desired allocation of resources. This exercise often necessitates government ownership (or control over the management) of banks and nonbank financial institutions. Third, the government will have to institutionalize a system of credit rationing.

Pattern of Credit Allocation by the Government

If government intervention in credit allocation could be justified on economic and social grounds in the context of the Korean economy, what are the allocational criteria that have guided it? And how rational are they? In any economy, government allocational criteria will be influenced by economic and social objectives as well as by economic efficiency, and these factors will change over time. Governments also attempt to achieve multiple, often conflicting objectives. For these reasons, there are no simple standards for evaluating the rationality or optimality of government allocational criteria.

Guidelines on allocation of credit are set forth in the Regulations Pertaining to the Use of Funds in the Financial Sector. These regulations have been amended since their passage in 1958, and their scope and emphasis on the preferred industries and sectors modified from time to time by government directives (W. Hong 1980:110–45). When a set of allocational criteria is pieced together from the regulations, directives, annual financial stabilization plans, and five-year development plans, it becomes clear that economic efficiency has seldom been the major criterion in the allocation of credit. Instead, government credit allocation policy was dictated by, and carried out to accommodate, the development strategies and investment policies set forth in the four successive five-year development plans. Thus, one sees that in the 1950s the thrust of government allocational policy was directed to channeling more resources to support import-substitution activities and for the production of daily necessities in order to stabilize the economy and to ease the burden of the balance-of-payment deficits.

Since the launching of an export-led development strategy in the mid-1960s, the basic allocational objective of the government was to support the development of export-oriented sectors in preference to the import-substitution and nontradable goods sectors, in particular the manufacturing sector. Throughout the 1960s and in the early 1970s (which encompasses the first two five-year development plans and part of the third), there was a clear emphasis on allocating more resources to labor-intensive, light manufacturing industries. During subsequent years, the allocational objective was shifted to the promotion of heavy and chemical industries as latent export sectors.

Financial needs will vary from industry to industry depending upon differences in factor intensity, capital–output ratio, investment-gestation period, and cash-flow requirements. For instance, agriculture will, in general, need less financing per unit of output than will the manufacturing industries. Given the possibility of credit fungibility—that is, the inability to track the flow of credit to a specific use—there is no reason to believe that credit rationing will necessarily influence real investment in different sectors in the intended directions. For these reasons, one could argue that information for previous periods on loan distribution primarily reflects differences in industrial characteristics with regard to financial requirements, rather than the consequences of government allocational policy. The ratio of bank loans to nominal output presented in Table 3.1, however, shows that the ratios of the manufacturing and social overhead sectors rose markedly between 1955 and 1960. This evidence, considered in conjunction with the strict credit rationing exercised by the government, suggests that a large portion of bank loans was, in fact, allocated according to a loan-priority ranking consistent with the policy direction of the 1950s with its emphasis on import substitution. It is difficult, however, to determine the extent to which credit rationing contributed to the realization of the changes in the industrial structure envisioned by the government.

During 1960–69, Korea's period of most rapid financial growth, the manufacturing sector, which accounted for the bulk of exports and registered the highest rate of growth, was accorded a growing share of bank loans. More than 70 percent (on average) of private foreign borrowings was allocated to the manufacturing sector during 1962–67 (Table 3.2; W. Hong 1980:168–69). Over the next five years, there was little change in this lopsided allocation.

Table 3.1. Ratios of bank loans to output by sector: 1955–80 (%)

Year	Total	Agriculture, forestry, hunting, and fishing	Mining and quarrying	Manufacturing		Social overhead	Services and other
				Light	Heavy and chemical		
1955	6	3	26	17	41	14	2
1960	16	14	33	34	90	23	5
1962	18	14	30	41	82	35	7
1965	13	6	18	25	48	25	6
1967	17	8	31	35	59	26	8
1970	30	14	51	54	90	36	17
1971	38	15	83	59	89	41	15
1972	34	15	96	58	101	59	12
1973	35	16	61	69	82	52	13
1974	38	15	51	98	68	59	13
1975	35	13	36	71	74	55	13
1976	33	13	43	63	70	52	11
1977	33	14	28	65	71	46	12
1978	34	13	30	56	81	44	15
1979	37	14	43	60	91	47	15
1980	43	19	32	63	101	53	17

Sources: BOK, National Income (1982); BOK, Economic Statistics Yearbook (1960–86).

Table 3.2. Commercial foreign loans, sector share as a percentage of total loans: 1962–80

Year	Total (10⁶ US $)	Agriculture, forestry, hunting, and fishing (%)	Mining and quarrying (%)	Manufacturing		Social overhead (%)	Services (%)	Other (%)
				Heavy and chemical (%)	Light (%)			
1962	0.1				100			
1965	27.9	38		23	36	3		7
1967	137.8	7	1	28	36	20	3	
1970	283.2	2	3	38	21	34	5	
1972	306.6	3		64	11	18	5	
1974	614.7	4		28	39	22	5	2
1976	841.0	2		48	27	12	11	
1978	1,929.8	*		55	13	26	6	
1980	1,415.3	1	*	39	5	45	10	*

Source: BOK, Financial System (1983).
*Less than 1 percent.

Although self-sufficiency in grain (rice in particular) remained a major policy objective, agriculture's domestic loan share declined gradually from 35 percent in 1960 to about 12 percent at the end of 1969, reflecting the relative slowdown of growth in this sector. The social overhead sector remained one of the priority sectors in the 1960s and received a large share of bank loans relative to its output as it had in the 1950s, although less in terms of loans per unit of output (Table 3.1). The government also allocated a large share of its foreign borrowings to the social overhead sector during the period (Table 3.3). In the 1960s the total loan share of services and other industries almost doubled compared with the figure in the 1950s, mostly at the expense of agriculture (Table 3.4). This was not necessarily the result of relaxation of credit rationing by the government, but was due to the fact that more financial resources became available after the interest-rate reform.

Heavy industries in the manufacturing sector received a growing share of bank credit in the 1970s (Table 3.4). This development reflected the change in Korea's development strategy that promoted heavy and chemical industries for both import substitution and export production. Along with the investment expansion in heavy and chemical industries, there was a noticeable shift in the allocation of financial resources to them. As presented in Table 3.4, their proportion of total bank loans rose from less than 20 percent during 1970–74 to over 29 percent by 1980. Throughout the 1970s the majority of foreign loans whose payments were guaranteed by domestic banking institutions were channeled to the heavy and chemical industries. From 1977 to 1980 this sector accounted for more than 80 percent of the total foreign loans to manufacturing (Table 3.2; Table 3.3). Because a large portion of these loans were rationed by government authorities, the changes in the sectoral loan shares reflected the government's efforts to direct resources to the targeted industries. The decline in agriculture's loan share continued into the 1970s. This trend can be explained by the relative decline in the size of the agricultural sector together with the institution in 1969 of a price-support program in place of a credit-support program for agriculture.

Conflict with Stability and Long-Term Growth

Although government control of finance is often denounced as the cause of inefficient allocation of resources and as contributing to a high rate of inflation and discouraging private savings, none of these negative effects were visible in Korea during the 1960s. On the contrary, the performance of the economy was spectacular during the 1965–69 period. The economy grew by more than 10 percent per annum on average, while the average annual rate of inflation was moderate at less than 9 percent. Indeed, government intervention in the allocation of resources in favor of export-oriented sectors and other strategic industries appears to have been an appropriate policy.

Table 3.3. Public foreign loans, sector share as a percentage of total loans: 1962–80

Year	Total (10⁶ US $)	Agriculture, forestry, hunting, and fishing (%)	Mining and quarrying (%)	Manufacturing		Social overhead (%)	Services (%)	Other (%)
				Heavy and chemical (%)	Light (%)			
1962	6.3				40	57	3	
1965	11.2		22			68	9	
1967	79.6		3	8	9	54	25	1
1970	147.1	29		19	1	31	21	*
1972	432.4	9		10		24	13	44
1974	373.6	22		6		40	33	*
1976	712.1	15		2		35	48	*
1978	817.7	20	*	3		47	30	*
1980	1,518.4	11	*	3		74	12	*

Source: BOK, Financial System (1983).

*Less than 1 percent.

Table 3.4. Loans and discounts of deposit-money banks, sector share as a percentage of total loans: 1955–80

Year	Total (10⁹ won)	Agriculture, forestry, hunting, and fishing (%)	Mining and quarrying (%)	Manufacturing		Social overhead (%)	Services (%)	Other (%)
				Heavy and chemical (%)	Light (%)			
1955[a]	3.8	25	7	13	33	7	13	2
1957	10.9	45	1	11	27	1	13	2
1960	24.3	49	1	10	20	3	14	3
1965	72.1	27	2	15	25	3	19	9
1967	178.0	17	2	19	27	8	20	7
1970	722.4	14	2	20	25	11	20	9
1971	919.5	14	2	18	28	13	16	9
1972	1,198.0	13	3	19	30	14	13	8
1973	1,587.5	13	1	20	34	13	11	8
1974	2,427.8	11	1	20	37	13	11	7
1975	2,905.3	10	1	23	34	13	11	7
1976	3,724.9	10	1	25	32	13	11	7
1977	4,709.0	11	1	26	31	13	11	8
1978	6,609.0	10	1	27	28	13	13	8
1979	8,977.8	9	1	28	27	15	11	9
1980	12,204.4	9	1	29	26	16	13	7

Source: BOK, Economic Statistics Yearbook (1960–86).

Note: Deposit-money banks are commercial and specialized banks. Rows may not sum to totals because of rounding.

a. Commercial banks and the KAB.

During the Third Five-Year Development Plan (1972–76), however, the negative effects associated with repressive financial policies began to surface and could no longer be ignored, as they increasingly undermined the government's ability to stabilize the economy and to mobilize domestic resources (Shaw 1973).

First, financial growth, which had begun increasing rapidly in the middle of the 1960s, slowed considerably, barely keeping up with economic growth. The slowdown was accompanied by an appreciable fall in the domestic savings ratio, adding a still greater burden to savings mobilization efforts and the nation's resource management problems.

Second, the problems of maintaining the internal and external stability of the economy were magnified and became more difficult to manage in the course of pursuing the export-led growth strategy, yet continued financial control left the economic authorities with no effective anticyclical policy instruments at their disposal. As the export sector expanded rapidly and accounted for an increasingly large share of output, domestic business fluctuations were influenced and often led by changes in world market conditions. Monetary policy loses much of its effectiveness as an anticyclical weapon in a small open economy under a fixed exchange-rate system. This would be the case even if the economy had a sophisticated financial system; however, such a system did not exist in Korea during the 1970s and adoption of a more flexible exchange-rate system was opposed because it was viewed as destabilizing, among other reasons. Therefore, with monetary and financial policies directed toward the growth objective, the authorities had no effective short-run stabilization policy instruments and the existing ones were largely inoperative.

Third, continued government domination of the financial system, from the viewpoint of the proper role of finance, was in the long-run likely to interfere with successful implementation of the outward-looking strategy. Repressive monetary and financial policies resulted in an increasingly rigid financial system and artificially segmented financial markets. Financial institutions grew large in number and variety, but had no incentives to improve or expand their role as intermediaries and became unresponsive to changing financial conditions and the needs of the economy. These institutions were cut off from the international financial community and, in their isolation, perpetuated financial practices that were outdated and suitable only to a closed economy. In contrast, private firms, in particular those that were export-oriented, aggressively penetrated world markets where they established a firm foothold and succeeded in enlarging their market share. The private firms upgraded their production processes and management practices to international standards and accumulated considerable marketing expertise.

Isolated from the international financial centers, however, domestic financial institutions were unable to provide adequate and efficient international financial services to these world-market-oriented firms. Nor were they effective or active in channeling much needed foreign credit with favorable terms and conditions to these firms. This discrepancy between the real sector, which was rapidly opening up, and the closed financial sector was ultimately detrimental to the overall growth of the economy.

Finally, it became apparent that government control of finance was one of the major causes of the concentration of economic power and the worsening inequality in income distribution. According to SaKong (1980:2–13), preferential credit allocation that favored large and established borrowers with a subsidized rate was the major cause of the growth of business conglomerates during the 1970s in Korea.

Faced with these disturbing problems arising largely from continuing financial repression, many economists in Korea and abroad began to advocate a fundamental change in monetary and financial policies aimed toward gradually building a more liberalized financial system. That financial liberalization should be the ultimate goal of the authorities was generally accepted. Like any other economic policy, however, liberalization was not without problems. These problems produced strong opposition, in particular from policymakers and the business community. Financial liberalization was opposed because: (1) it could result in a very high and unstable interest-rate structure that would produce a cost-push effect on inflation and put an enormous burden on a large number of highly leveraged firms; (2) it was in conflict with what some economic authorities saw as the proper role of the government in a mixed economy; and most important, (3) liberalization would not allow for the successful implementation of the new industrial development strategy that emphasized the development of skill- and technology-intensive heavy and chemical industries.

The first problem was the least important. Liberalization would certainly result in high interest rates, but there was no evidence it would bring about an unstable interest-rate structure or accelerate inflation.

The second problem was related to the paradox that the Korean economy depended in a large measure on private enterprises operating under highly centralized government guidance, and it was therefore in part a political issue. With the rapid growth of the external sector, the sphere of government influence and scope of government control over the conduct of economic affairs had diminished. Export-oriented growth strategy, to be successful, also required gradual relaxation of import-control and foreign-exchange regulations. The economic authorities were aware of the need for such external liberalization and took steps to institute the required policy changes. At the same time, however, the government felt the need for (and attempted to obtain) a tighter grip on the economy for political, social, and to some extent economic reasons. The problem was not so much the government's direct involvement but rather the means by which it attempted to influence the economy, namely, through direct control over the financial system. This would certainly necessitate and perpetuate financial repression.

The third problem did indeed pose a serious dilemma. As early as the preparation stage of the Third Five-Year Development Plan, it became apparent that the high-growth objective could not be achieved by following the same industrial development strategy pursued during the first and second plans. The third plan thus called for major shifts in production and export through the expansion of heavy and chemical industries. This shift in strategy, which signaled the entering of the secondary import substitution and export promotion stage of development, was made public in late 1972 and was fully reflected in the Fourth Five-Year Plan (1977–81).

Although the new strategy was viable and perhaps the only alternative consistent with the high-growth objective, it also presented a number of formidable problems. One of these problems was that the strategy would require the intensification, rather than relaxation, of government intervention in the financial system. The strategy required that enormous foreign as well as domestic resources be invested in industries with relatively high capital–output ratios, long investment-gestation periods, and uncertain rates of return on capital. Its success was dependent on unpredictable foreign demand at a time when trade protectionism was increasing and the prospects for any substantial increase in domestic savings were not favorable. It was, of course, theoretically possible to overcome the shortage of domestic savings by foreign borrowings over and above what was necessary to meet the need for foreign exchange. But Korea's external requirements were already large enough to preclude this as a viable option for any extended period of time.

Fungibility and the Effectiveness of Government Intervention

The ultimate objective of government controls over credit allocation is to bring about an allocation of physical resources that furthers the government's overall objectives for the country, even if the allocation is not the most efficient use of resources. To what extent has the Korean government since 1961 succeeded in attaining this objective? This is a difficult question to answer, even at a theoretical level, and one that requires reliable microdata for an empirical examination.

There is little or no reliable data on Korea that could be used to investigate the causal relationship between credit allocation and physical resource allocation. The task is further complicated by the unanswered question on the causality between finance and economic development. The key to the answer lies in the fungibility of credit. If credit fungibility is of a high degree, the government cannot expect to be successful in effecting what it considers to be an optimal allocation of physical resources.

It is often alleged that when the financial markets are imperfect and the financial sector is in an infant industry stage, government intervention may be warranted and effective. The effectiveness stems from the fact that financial market imperfections reduce credit fungibility. That is, when financial markets are fragmented among regions and different classes and groups of borrowers, funds do not flow freely from one separated and artificially segmented market to another. In such a financial regime, government intervention has a better chance of success in channeling bank credit to the ultimate use of physical resources.

Financial market fragmentation exists in Korea perhaps because the financial markets have not had enough time to develop into a unified national market. The financial markets are, however, segmented largely because of government controls over the interest rates and management of the financial institutions. Therefore, the fragmentation may be viewed as a result of a deliberate effort on the part of the government to facilitate its directed credit allocation. The growth of the unregulated money market could, in part, be attributed to the financial market fragmentation engineered by the government. One of the major functions of the unregulated money market has been to facilitate the flow of funds among markets that are geographically separated and artificially segmented by interest rates, sectors, and borrowers. The existence of the huge unregulated money market, therefore, suggests a strong possibility of credit fungibility in Korea, which would in turn reduce the effectiveness of government intervention in resource allocation.

The fungibility issue could be examined at the two stages of the credit allocation process. At the first stage, which is related to the lending behavior of the financial institutions, it is quite possible that the financial intermediaries may simply evade or ignore the credit guidelines and directives and, therefore, may themselves be guilty of credit diversion. This problem does not appear to have been serious in Korea because of the government's close supervision of the day-to-day operations of the deposit-money banks and other financial intermediaries. It is widely suspected, however, that the financial institutions have consistently evaded government guidelines for the allocation of credit to medium- and small-scale enterprises. For a period of time during the latter part of the 1970s, the deposit-money banks were required to make available a minimum of 30 percent of their total loans to small- and medium-scale industries. No one believed that the actual allocation of these institutions was anywhere close to the guideline quota. Because of the ambiguities in the definition of small and medium enterprises, the banks were easily able to meet the quota without necessarily lending the required amount to small-scale businesses. Given their traditional aversion to small borrowers, the banks may have taken advantage of the vagueness in the regulations and thereby facilitated credit diversion.

At the second stage of credit allocation, which is related to the behavior of borrowers, it is quite conceivable that a large part of bank credit was diverted to uses other than those predesignated by the government. This diversion would be possible because the deposit-money banks and the KDB do not have an effective system of credit-use supervision. Even if they did have an effective system, the management of these financial institutions would not be much concerned about (and hence would not actively supervise) the actual use of bank credits, because the management is not responsible for the provision of directed and policy loans. The lack of autonomy in bank management may thus have aggravated credit diversion.

The fact that business firms invest heavily in real assets is evidence of credit fungibilty. A special measure, issued in September 1980, required 1,217 large firms to report their holdings of land and buildings, classified into those used for business operations and others presumably held for real asset speculation. The responses showed that business groups and corporations held a large share of their total assets in the form of real assets such as land and buildings. According to the government, the holdings of these assets were far greater than the level normally required for the firms' business operations. The presumptions are that businesses invest in real assets as a hedge against inflation and as a source of collateral for bank loans and that the majority of their holdings were financed by bank loans in the first place. One large business group, formerly a ranking exporter, was so heavily involved in real estate speculation with export loans that it went bankrupt in 1978 when its export earnings fell sharply and the real estate boom cooled off. Undoubtedly, there have been numerous similar cases involving smaller businesses.

As noted before, a more important reason to suspect a considerable degree of credit fungibility was the existence of and the important role played by the unregulated money market, particularly prior to the curb-market freeze measure of 3 August 1972. These unregulated markets acted as a short-term money market for large business borrowers and as a retail credit market for consumers and small businesses. In so doing, they provided a linkage among the segmented markets and hence a channel for diverting government-controlled credit from the intended uses. As shown in Cole and Park (1983:119–20), large businesses often borrowed their working capital from and lent their idle funds through the unregulated money market. In doing so, the large businesses assumed the role of financial intermediaries, in addition to their normal business activities. They did so largely because there was no active short-term money market, and the government-dominated financial institutions could not provide adequate short-term credit facilities.

Financial requirements for investment and production activities and seasonality in the demand for loans will vary according to the industry and will change over time. The major requirement of some sectors is long-term external financing, whereas others need short-term loans. The processing of a bank loan, with the exception of overdrafts, takes a long time from application to an actual loan disbursement. No matter how sophisticated and detailed a credit-guideline system the government devises, it cannot expect to account for all the factors that determine the sectoral demand for loans in formulating its control system. Indeed, if the credit-allocation guidelines and directives were enforced to the letter, the financial system would be paralyzed. The unregulated money markets have complemented an otherwise extremely rigid financial system and thereby facilitated smooth flows of funds between the different markets in Korea.

Inflationary Implication

Monetary accommodation—that is, easy credit to export industries resulting in a rapid expansion of the money supply—was a logical consequence of the government's use of the financial system and policy as a means of intervening in the allocation of resources. As a result, the scope of monetary policy as an instrument of anti-inflationary policy was severely restricted. The majority of subsidies to preferred industries had been financed by borrowings from the central bank, and these borrowings were immune to stabilization policy. In addition, a large fraction of bank credit had been earmarked in the form of "policy" or "directed" loans for strategic industries and uses. These loans thus escaped from monetary tightening.

Government control over financial institutions also complicated the effective management of monetary policy. With government control, deposit-money banks, which dominate Korea's financial system, have been no more than a banking bureau of the government. Their main role was to allocate deposits and new credit supplied by the central bank to the sectors and industries and often to individual borrowers designated by the government. Under these circumstances the portion of lendable resources the banks could allocate under their own discretion was greatly limited. In recent years more than 50 percent of the deposit-money banks total loans could be classified as "directed" policy loans whose volume and allocation were determined by the government itself, often independently of monetary stabilization. To the extent that the government attempts to mobilize domestic resources by means of excessive credit creation and inflation, it becomes logical and perhaps unavoidable to allow continuous rollovers of short-term loans and the accumulation of overdue loans when the deposit-money banks are confronted with a huge chronic excess demand for loans.

The large share of "directed" loans and the practice of rollovers have made deposit-money banks' portfolios extremely illiquid. This illiquidity has made it difficult for the banks to adjust their asset portfolios in response to changes in financial market conditions or monetary policy. Thus, credit tightening has elicited little response from the banks in the short run and has become ineffective as an anti-inflationary measure.

EFFECTS OF THE POLICY MEASURES

Before discussing the effects of the financial policies during 1961–80, we need first to address the issue of credit fungibility. If the degree of credit fungibility were high, the pattern of real-resource allocation would not correspond to the pattern of credit allocation planned by the government. In the extreme case of perfect fungibility, the government would find itself incapable of influencing real-resource allocation with its control of credit allocation. Clearly, then, if the government's development strategy relying on credit allocation were to succeed, the degree of credit fungibility would have to be tolerably low.

What was the degree of credit fungibility in the two decades after the military takeover of the government in 1961? Our attempt at empirical estimation has led to a tentative finding that anywhere from 50 to 70 percent of each dollar of government funds allocated to a particular sector was diverted to other sectors. Although this seems to be a high degree of "slippage," it cannot be denied that in the case of Korea the government did have some influence on real-resource allocation through its control over credit.

Even though there is no firm evidence to support the hypothesis, it seems reasonable to argue that the degree of credit fungibility has increased over time in Korea. In the early 1960s it was probably low because the economy was simple, the financial market segmented and underdeveloped, and the number of enterprises receiving preferential credit small. In such a situation, the recipients of credit would have found few alternative ventures to divert funds to and also might have felt that they were under close scrutiny by the government.

With rapid economic growth, the degree of credit fungibility probably increased. There were now more enterprises and more alternative ventures to which funds could be diverted. To an individual recipient, the expected rate of return from diverting funds from their designated use may have increased, whereas the expected cost from being caught and penalized may have decreased. The increasing degree of credit fungibility must then have reduced the government's ability to control real-resource allocation via credit control.

A more fundamental issue relating to the use of financial policies as an instrument for economic development is the question of whether or not the real-resource allocation engineered through credit allocation has promoted Korea's economic development. This is not an easy question to answer and is part of the controversy over the use of industrial policy as an instrument for promoting economic development or a high rate of economic growth. Chalmers Johnson (1982), for instance, has argued in his *MITI and the Japanese Miracle* that the industrial policy of the Ministry of International Trade and Industry (MITI) had been critically instrumental in the rapid economic growth of postwar Japan. Despite his persuasive argument, supported with well-documented research, the question of the role of MITI has yet to be answered to the satisfaction of many economists.

If the positive effects of the financial policies on economic development are in dispute, there seems to be no disagreement on their negative effects. As noted earlier, monetary accommodation and the control over financial institutions had reduced the scope and effectiveness of monetary policy as an anti-inflation instrument. Lacking monetary policy as a stabilization policy, the government had to rely on price controls and incomes policy. The distortionary effect on resource allocation resulting from these measures must, therefore, be ultimately traced back to the financial policies that rendered monetary policy ineffective as a stabilization policy.

Another negative effect is the socially and politically undesirable concentration of economic power and the resulting inequities in income distribution. As SaKong (1980) has shown, the preferential credit allocation favoring large and established borrowers contributed to the growth of business conglomerates during the 1970s. Even if these firms had the advantage of large-scale economies, there was no compelling reason for subsidizing their growth.

In the final analysis, if there is one lasting effect of the financial policies of 1961–80 that has been beneficial to Korea's economic development, it may be the growth and development of a variety of financial institutions. Their growth, which was initiated by the government, has gradually increased their role as true financial intermediaries, has reduced the scope of government intervention in the financial market, and thus has brought about its gradual liberalization.

CRITICISM AND LESSONS

In the early 1960s Korea's financial sector was dominated by a few nationwide commercial banks mostly supplying short-term working capital to large businesses. The securities market was moribund, and the financial needs of medium- and small-size firms and consumers were served by unregulated money markets or curb markets, which were fragmented and scattered throughout the country. Under these circumstances, the government probably had no alternative to controlling the financial institutions for mobilizing domestic savings and for guiding the resources in the desired directions.

Beginning in the early 1970s, the government moved toward diversifying financial assets and institutions. With the promulgation of the August 3rd (1972) measures, the government established several nonbank financial intermediaries and subsequently encouraged new types to come into the financial system to compete with commercial banks. The government was determined to develop a modern capital market, and this determination led to a series of measures that culminated in a partial opening of the market to foreign investors.

The growth of the nonbank financial intermediaries and the expansion of the securities market brought about a noticeable change in the role of the government in the allocation of the economy's investable resources. Because the government did not, or could not, intervene in the asset management of nonbank intermediaries and dictate the allocation of funds through the capital market, the share of domestic financial resources controllable by the government declined. More important, this development coincided with the realization of the need for gradual financial liberalization in the mid-1970s.

The government was indeed prepared to loosen its tight grip on financial institutions and conduct a more flexible interest-rate policy after the 1970-71 recession. These liberalization efforts were thwarted, however, by the first oil crisis and, more important, by the shift in development strategy toward the promotion of heavy and chemical industries. Given the high rate of inflation triggered by the first oil crisis and the subsequent investment and export boom, the government found it extremely difficult to pursue a flexible interest-rate policy. Also, given the enormous amount of resources required for the development of heavy and chemical industries, the government did not expect that the necessary funding could be raised in the private market without government intervention. The government decided it could not relinquish control of, or make any major changes in the financial system, though it was certainly in need of a serious reform.

For a number of reasons that include the second oil price increase in 1979 and the worldwide recession that followed, the promotion of heavy and chemical industries as the future export sector was far from successful. The promotion effort resulted in a considerable drain on the economy's investment resources, a slowdown in growth with rampant inflation, and a growing current-account deficit beginning in 1979. The worsening economic situation was further aggravated by the assassination of President Park in October 1979, followed by a renewed debate on the needs for greater reliance on price mechanisms and the private sector for the management of the economy. As a first step toward laying the foundation for a market- and private-sector oriented economy, many within and outside Korea began to advocate financial liberalization. Some people believed that the repressive financial system was primarily responsible for the massive investment in heavy and chemical industries.

The new government that came into power was strongly committed to a free-market economy and financial liberalization measures, including the transfer of the government-owned shares of four nationwide commercial banks to private owners. However, the government authorities have yet to show any indication of floating interest rates, which is the crucial prerequisite for liberalization. Although the five nationwide commercial banks are now fully owned by private shareholders, the government continues to appoint all the senior bank officials and to interfere with their asset management in the form of "relief financing" set up to bail out troubled firms. Despite the strong commitment and numerous liberalization measures, one cannot but feel that it is business as usual as far as Korea's finance is concerned.

Can we say, with the benefit of hindsight, that events warranted the interruption of the process of financial liberalization? If the survival of the established firms was at stake, why couldn't the government subsidize them directly? Also, if the government thought it necessary to promote heavy and chemical industries, why didn't it make direct subsidies to the production of output of these industries? Direct subsidies would have accomplished the same objectives, but without distorting relative prices as did credit control.

Some might argue that Korea's limited fiscal capacity would have made tax-cum-subsidy measures impracticable, if not impossible. Given the success in building financial institutions, it is, however, difficult to believe that the government would not have succeeded in building an effective fiscal system if it had tried to do so.

The answer to the questions above may lie in the characteristics inherent in the economic system. In a mixed economic system where the role of government is more direct than that of setting broad rules and policies, the government regards it as imperative to take quick administrative action in response to a disturbance to the system. To the government, then, credit control is an important policy instrument that is relatively easy to use administratively and highly visible in terms of its apparent effectiveness. In other words, credit control is a policy instrument that the government can ill afford to give up unless it is intent on changing the basic features of the system.

A fundamental reform that is needed, therefore, is a move toward an economic system where the role of government is less direct and is largely confined to setting broad rules and policies. To a government committed to carrying out such a reform, financial liberalization should be only one in a series of policy changes that need to be carried out to achieve its long-term objectives.

4 Price Control and Stabilization Measures

by Yung Chul Park

Growth and stability have been the two most important economic policy objectives in Korea since 1961. The nearly 9 percent annual economic growth rate that Korea experienced during 1961–80 was remarkable by international standards; the same could hardly be said about the stability record. The rate of inflation, as measured by the wholesale price index (WPI), was more than 16 percent per year on average for the same period—almost three times as high as the inflation rates of Korea's major trading partners (the United States and Japan)—and ranged from a low of 6.4 percent to a high of 42 percent. Calculated using the GNP deflator, the rate of inflation was higher still, at 18 percent per year on average for the 1961–80 period (Table 4.1). The high rate of inflation, coupled with an overvalued exchange rate, was largely responsible for the persistent balance-of-payments problem. Despite the rapid growth of exports, Korea consistently recorded a deficit in its current account throughout the period (except for 1965 and 1977). The deficit fluctuated between 1 and 11 percent of GNP.

To facilitate a better understanding of the environment in which the policies were designed and implemented, it will be instructive to first review the history and analyze the causes of inflation in Korea since 1961.

INFLATIONARY TRENDS IN KOREA

There were periods of relatively moderate annual rates of inflation (less than 10 percent) in the latter part of both the 1950s and the 1960s, alternating with periods of relatively high rates in the early 1960s and throughout the 1970s. For the purpose of this study, it is convenient to divide the period 1961–80 into three subperiods: (1) resurgence of inflation during 1961–64 (after a period of relative price stability in the latter part of the 1950s), which resulted from numerous government measures to stimulate economic growth and was exacerbated by poor agricultural harvests; (2) rapid growth and relative internal and external stability from 1965 to 1973; and (3) the period of 1974–80 during which abrupt swings in the external sector buffeted a more open economy, and attempts at maintaining high rates of growth resulted in high rates of inflation and external imbalances as part of the adjustment process.

Table 4.1. Price indexes: 1961–80

Year	Wholesale price index		GNP deflator	
------	Index (1975=100)	Change (%)	Index (1975=100)	Change (%)
1961	14.8	13.8	9.8	14.0
1962	16.1	8.8	11.6	18.4
1963	19.4	20.5	15.0	29.3
1964	26.2	35.1	19.5	30.0
1965	28.8	9.9	20.7	6.2
1966	31.4	9.0	23.7	14.5
1967	33.4	6.4	27.4	15.6
1968	36.2	8.4	31.8	16.1
1969	38.5	6.4	36.5	14.8
1970	42.0	9.1	42.2	15.6
1971	45.7	8.8	47.3	12.1
1972	52.0	13.8	54.7	15.6
1973	55.6	6.9	61.9	13.1
1974	79.0	42.1	80.2	30.0
1975	100.0	26.6	100.0	24.7
1976	112.1	12.1	117.7	17.7
1977	122.2	9.0	136.9	16.3
1978	136.5	11.7	165.1	20.6
1979	162.1	18.8	197.0	19.3
1980	225.2	38.9	247.9	25.8

Sources: BOK, *National Income* (1982); BOK, *Economic Statistics Yearbook* (1965, 1970, 1980, 1982); EPB, ROK, *Major Statistics* (1982).

Development Financing and Inflation, 1961–64

One of the main reasons given by the military leaders for their coup d'etat in May 1961 was the economic stagnation under the previous two regimes. It was, therefore, not surprising that the military government initiated a series of measures to stimulate economic growth. Finding meager tax revenues and declining foreign aid, the government had to run substantial budgetary deficits to carry out the stimulative measures. The deficits, which were financed by printing money, led to a rapid expansion of domestic liquidity. After a negative rate of expansion in 1960, the supply of money had grown by almost 58 percent by the end of 1961 (Table 4.2).

Concerned about the rapid liquidity expansion and believing that money-lenders and businessmen were hoarding their wealth in currency and deposits, the government undertook a currency reform in June 1962. The reform succeeded in slowing down the rate of growth of money to below 10 percent per year for the next two years, but failed to channel hoarded wealth into productive investment. Instead, its more pervasive effect was

Table 4.2. Money supply and reserve base: 1961–80

Year	Money (M_1) Amount (10⁹ won)	Change (%)	Total money (M_2) Amount (10⁹ won)	Change (%)	Total reserve base Amount (10⁹ won)	Change (%)
1961	35.8	57.7	41.3	60.7	25.4	51.2
1962	39.4	10.1	51.6	24.9	29.8	17.3
1963	41.9	6.3	55.4	7.4	27.9	–6.4
1964	48.5	16.7	63.6	14.8	32.7	17.2
1965	65.6	34.2	97.1	52.7	48.4	48.0
1966	85.1	29.7	157.0	61.7	80.2	65.7
1967	123.0	44.5	253.8	61.7	110.9	38.3
1968	177.9	44.6	436.6	72.0	156.2	40.8
1969	252.0	41.7	704.6	61.4	216.0	38.3
1970	307.6	22.1	897.8	27.4	299.7	38.8
1971	358.0	16.4	1,084.9	20.8	288.2	–3.8
1972	519.4	45.1	1,451.8	33.8	427.5	48.3
1973	730.3	40.6	1,980.5	36.4	624.1	46.0
1974	945.7	29.5	2,456.5	24.0	775.0	24.2
1975	1,181.7	25.0	3,150.0	28.2	1,077.0	39.0
1976	1,544.0	30.7	4,204.8	33.5	1,437.7	33.5
1977	2,172.6	40.7	5,874.3	39.7	2,071.6	44.1
1978	2,713.8	24.9	7,928.7	35.0	2,802.0	35.3
1979	3,274.5	20.7	9,877.8	24.6	3,468.0	23.8
1980	3,807.0	16.3	12,534.5	26.9	3,243.9	–6.5

Source: BOK, *Economic Statistics Yearbook* (1982).

Note: Total reserve base = currency issued + bankers' deposits.

to undermine confidence in financial institutions and assets, thus encouraging the holding of real assets and expansion of unregulated money-market transactions.

The 1962 financial debacle was aggravated by a rice crop failure in the same year and by a severe decline in the barley harvest the following spring. The liquidity expansion in 1962, caused by the currency reform and a poor grain harvest, built up strong inflationary pressures in the economy.

In 1964 the government devalued the won by almost 100 percent. Although that measure helped to improve Korea's export competitiveness, it had a devastating effect on prices. A sharp decline in imports, along with higher import prices, set off the a surge of inflation of over 35 percent in 1964.

The estimated effect of currency devaluation on prices in Korea varies from study to study. The simulation results of S. W. Nam (1981) and the Bank of Korea quarterly economic model (unpublished) show that a 1 percent devaluation in the won exchange rate to the U.S. dollar would raise domestic prices (WPI) by 0.3 to 0.4 percent in one year.

Rapid Growth and Relative Price Stability, 1965–73

The years between 1965 and 1973 were a period of outstanding performance for the Korean economy. Output grew at an average annual rate of 10 percent and price increases were relatively modest at an average of about 8 percent as measured by the WPI (15 percent on the GNP deflator). The current account was in deficit throughout the period, but the continuous expansion of exports and large inflows of foreign capital, induced by the monetary reform in 1965, helped to reduce anxiety over the growing current-account deficits. The deficit remained at a level of over 8 percent of GNP between 1968 and 1971 before falling to about 3 percent in 1972 and 1973. The stimulus for industrial growth came mainly from the export sector and the government's successful campaign to promote exports.

The period of 1965–73 was a kind of "golden age" in Korea's economy, characterized by relative price stability and high growth. What factors and developments could explain the exceptional performance? On the demand side, export expansion was undoubtedly the engine of growth. Exports, consisting mostly of labor-intensive manufactures, increased annually at a rate of 37 percent in real terms during the period, thereby increasing the exports-to-GNP ratio to 30 percent in 1973, compared with less than 6 percent in the early 1960s. The increase in fixed-capital formation was equally impressive. Between 1965 and 1973, fixed investments in real terms increased sevenfold. As a result the proportion of investment in GNP more than doubled, from 11 percent in 1964 to 24 percent in 1973. Largely because of an overall balance surplus caused by large capital inflows, the supply of money (M_1) expanded by 35.4 percent and M_2 (M_1 plus saving deposits with commercial banks) increased by 41.7 percent a year on average from 1965 to 1973 (Table 4.2).

These developments in aggregate expenditures and domestic liquidity would normally generate strong inflationary pressures. There were, however, other favorable developments on the demand side that moderated price increases. The financial reform in 1965 raised the interest-rate ceiling on bank time deposits from 15 percent to 30 percent per year. This readjustment increased the real interest rate (the nominal interest rate adjusted for inflation) to a positive 19 percent in 1966, from a negative 15 percent in 1964, and maintained the rates at a level of 12 to 22 percent for the following four years (Table 4.3). The sharp increase in interest rates induced savers to substitute financial assets for real assets such as real estate, household durables, and inventory. These portfolio substitutions dampened increases in land and housing prices and subsequently lowered housing rents. The interest-rate readjustment also encouraged households to save more. As a percentage of GNP, domestic savings more than tripled between 1965 and 1973 (Table 4.4). More important, the large interest-rate differential between the domestic and foreign capital markets, together with the government repayment guarantee (which eliminated any risk of default and

Table 4.3. Interest rates: 1961–80

Year	Nominal interest rate on time and savings deposits (%)	Real interest rates (A)[a] (%)	Real interest rates (B)[b] (%)	Curb market interest rate (%)	Seoul land values Index (1963=100)	Seoul land values Change (%)
1961	12.5	–1.1	–1.3	u	u	u
1962	15.0	5.7	–2.9	u	u	u
1963	15.0	–4.6	–11.1	52.4	100	u
1964	15.0	–14.9	–11.5	61.4	168	68.0
1965	18.8	8.1	11.9	58.8	225	33.9
1966	30.0	19.3	13.5	58.7	u	u
1967	30.0	22.2	12.5	56.4	495	u
1968	27.6	17.7	9.9	55.9	755	52.5
1969	24.0	16.6	8.0	51.2	1,390	84.1
1970	22.8	12.6	6.2	50.8	1,445	4.0
1971	22.2	12.3	9.0	46.3	1,860	28.7
1972	15.7	1.7	0.1	38.9	1,966	5.7
1973	12.6	5.3	0.5	39.2	1,997	1.6
1974	14.8	–19.2	–11.4	37.6	2,610	30.7
1975	15.0	–9.2	–7.8	41.3	3,315	27.0
1976	15.5	3.0	–1.9	40.5	4,196	26.6
1977	16.2	6.6	–0.1	38.1	5,606	33.6
1978	16.7	4.5	–3.2	41.7	8,354	49.0
1979	18.6	0.2	–0.6	42.4	9,740	16.6
1980	22.4	–11.9	–2.7	45.0	10,879	11.7

Sources: BOK, *Economic Statistics Yearbook* (1965, 1970, 1975, 1982); Mills and Song (1979); unpublished data obtained from the Ministry of Construction, ROK.

u—data unavailable.

a. $(1 + \text{col. 1}) \dfrac{\text{WPI}_{t-1}}{\text{WPI}_t} - 1$

b. $(1 + \text{col. 1}) \dfrac{\text{GNP deflator}_{t-1}}{\text{GNP deflator}_t} - 1$

exchange-rate depreciation on foreign loans), caused a massive inflow of foreign capital in the form of trade credits, cash loans, and direct investment, thereby enlarging Korea's capacity of importing much-needed capital goods and raw materials.

On the supply side, the high interest rates raised the cost of production. This cost-push effect was partially offset, however, by other developments. The unit labor cost (nominal wages adjusted for labor productivity) rose by less than 4 percent on average per year, though it displayed considerable year-to-year fluctuations (Table 4.5). Import prices of food grains,

Table 4.4. Savings, investment, and balance of payments as percentages of
GNP: 1961–80 (current prices)

Year	National savings	Gross fixed investment	Current account
1961	2.8	11.7	1.4
1962	3.3	13.7	−2.0
1963	8.7	13.5	−3.7
1964	8.7	11.3	−0.7
1965	7.4	14.8	0.3
1966	11.8	20.2	−2.7
1967	11.4	21.4	−4.1
1968	15.1	25.0	−7.4
1969	18.8	25.8	−7.3
1970	17.3	24.4	−7.2
1971	15.4	22.5	−8.9
1972	15.7	20.6	−3.6
1973	23.5	24.0	−2.4
1974	20.5	25.5	−11.2
1975	18.6	26.0	−9.3
1976	23.1	23.8	−1.1
1977	25.1	26.0	0.0
1978	26.4	30.6	−2.3
1979	26.6	32.5	−6.9
1980	19.9	32.7	−9.4

Source: BOK, *National Income* (1982).

energy, and other raw materials remained virtually unchanged between 1966
and 1969, though thereafter they climbed sharply.

Despite these favorable demand and supply developments, the monetary authorities were concerned about the rapid growth of money supply and domestic credit and took measures to restrain liquidity growth. Reserve requirements were raised to unprecedented levels—a marginal rate of 50 percent on demand deposits from October 1966 through March 1967—but the credit expansion continued unabated. That it was possible to have such a rapid expansion of credit without causing inflation could be attributed in part to the lagged effect of monetary growth. But it was mostly the result of the matching growth in the demand for bank time deposits with the substantial increase in savings.

After five years of uninterrupted high growth it looked as though the economy was finally cooling off in 1970. Export growth declined from its previous high levels largely owing to the economic slowdown affecting Korea's major trading partners and rising trade protectionism. The rate of growth of exports fell for three consecutive years beginning in 1969. This

Table 4.5. Wages, productivity, and unit labor cost in manufacturing: 1961–80

Year	Nominal wages			Labor productivity			
	Amount (won)	Index (A) (1975=100)	Change (%)	Index (B) (1975=100)	Change (%)	Unit labor cost (A/B) (1975=100)	Change (%)
1961	2,840	8.7	9.2	23.2	12.1	37.5	-2.8
1962	2,990	9.2	5.3	24.0	3.4	38.3	2.1
1963	3,310	10.2	10.7	25.4	5.8	40.2	5.0
1964	4,010	12.3	21.1	27.6	8.7	44.6	0.9
1965	4,680	14.4	16.7	32.0	15.9	45.0	0.8
1966	5,480	16.9	17.1	33.3	4.1	50.8	12.8
1967	6,640	20.4	21.2	39.2	17.7	52.0	2.4
1968	8,400	25.8	26.5	46.2	17.6	55.8	7.3
1969	11,270	34.7	34.2	56.9	23.4	61.0	9.3
1970	11,515	35.4	2.2	64.4	13.2	55.0	-10.0
1971	15,040	46.2	30.6	70.1	8.9	66.0	20.0
1972	16,127	49.6	7.2	75.5	7.7	62.0	-6.0
1973	18,994	58.4	17.8	81.8	8.3	71.4	15.0
1974	25,253	77.7	33.0	90.1	10.1	86.2	20.7
1975	32,521	100.0	28.8	100.0	11.0	100.0	16.0
1976	43,376	133.4	33.4	106.8	6.8	124.9	24.9
1977	54,340	167.1	25.3	117.7	10.2	142.0	13.7
1978	73,348	225.5	35.0	131.2	11.5	171.9	21.1
1979	94,565	290.8	28.9	151.5	15.5	191.9	11.6
1980	119,139	366.3	26.0	167.2	10.4	219.1	14.2

Source: Professor M. K. Bae of Seoul National University.

slowdown was accompanied by an appreciable drop in investment demand.

Tight monetary policy pursued over the preceding three years (1967–69) began to pay off. Together with a fall in export demand, which automatically reduced domestic credit expansion, the tightening managed to reduce the rate of expansion of M_1 from more than 40 percent in 1969 to 22 percent in 1970 and to 16 percent in 1971. That curtailment in domestic liquidity might have accounted in part for the sluggishness in investment demand. In 1970 the economy registered a relatively low rate of growth (7.3 percent), but the sharp deceleration was caused mainly by a poor rice harvest. The economic slowdown in manufacturing activities did not begin until the first quarter of 1971 and lasted less than a year. In retrospect, the downturn did not call for any expansionary measures, given the accelerating consumer-price increases. This was not, however, the course the policymakers took.

To revive export demand the government devalued the currency by 17 percent in June 1971. The devaluation raised the prices of imported goods and (with a lag) domestically produced goods. More important, it caused a corresponding increase in the cost of servicing foreign loans, which had grown dramatically since 1963. In the scramble for funds to meet foreign obligations, businesses had three major potential sources: domestic banks, foreign lenders, and the unregulated financial markets. The tight monetary policy markedly reduced the availability of bank credit. Foreign loan guarantees by government-owned banks went up sharply in 1971, but about half of the increase was a reflection of the devaluation. In 1972 the loan guarantees actually declined, and businesses were forced to turn to the unregulated money-market lenders.

After considering various measures to relieve the financial pressure on business, the government implemented the Presidential Decree for Economic Stability and Growth on 3 August 1972. The decree reduced official interest rates to the pre-1965 reform levels; more important, all the curb-market, high-interest, short-term loans were converted into low-interest, long-term loans with a grace period of several years. These measures relieved the financial burden of firms with large foreign borrowings, but they also resulted in a substantial expansion of M_1. The rate of increase of M_1 jumped to 45 percent in 1972, then declined to 40 percent in 1973. As a result of the reduction in interest rates, real interest rates (adjusted in terms of the GNP deflator) fell to 0.1 in 1972 and rose to 0.7 percent in 1973.

The slowdown and financial distress of 1972 were moderated by the export and investment boom of 1973. Korea's devaluation, followed by Japan's appreciation of the yen in late 1972, resulted in a doubling of Korea's total exports. The spectacular growth of exports, the liquidity expansion by more than 40 percent for two years in row, and negative real interest rates all contributed to a large excess demand for goods and services. That excess demand, ignited by the oil price increase of late 1973, erupted into violent inflation.

Oil Crisis and Suppressed Inflation, 1974–80

The oil price increases of late 1973 dealt a severe blow to the Korean economy. The crisis suddenly dampened Korea's growth prospects and, together with the excessive credit expansion of the previous two years, provoked a steep increase in the rate of inflation for the next several years. Because Korea was (and still is) heavily dependent on imported oil, the oil price increases caused more than a 20 percent deterioration in Korea's terms of trade during the 1976–79 period (Table 4.6); and the subsequent world recession led to a sharp drop in world demand for Korea's exports.

Korea's response to the oil crisis was to impose heavy taxes on oil products to minimize their use, and to borrow heavily abroad to finance the imports needed to sustain production and investment. These measures were designed to mitigate the worst effects of the price increases and to maintain overall growth. Little effort was made, however, to hold down domestic price increases. Assuming that Korea's competitors (Taiwan, Hong Kong, and Singapore) would equally suffer the harshness of the oil crisis, the policymakers opted to fully accommodate the price increases. Bank credit

Table 4.6. Terms of trade: 1963–80

| | Unit value index | | Net barter |
Year	Exports (A)	Imports (B)	term of trade (A/B) × 100
1963	54.4	45.0	121.0
1964	55.6	45.5	122.3
1965	57.7	46.3	124.7
1966	63.0	45.3	139.2
1967	65.9	45.7	144.2
1968	67.9	45.3	149.9
1969	64.5	44.6	144.7
1970	67.4	46.2	145.7
1971	66.5	46.0	144.5
1972	67.3	46.8	143.7
1973	85.2	62.5	136.4
1974	107.9	97.2	111.0
1975	100.0	100.0	100.0
1976	111.7	98.0	114.0
1977	122.3	100.2	122.0
1978	135.4	105.8	128.0
1979	161.8	129.2	125.3
1980	170.3	163.9	103.9

Source: BOK, *Economic Statistics Yearbook* (1965, 1970, 1975, 1982).

was expanded by nearly 50 percent to help finance needed imports. As a result of this accommodation policy, wholesale prices rose by 42 percent in 1974. About a year after the oil price increases, in an effort to improve Korea's export competitiveness, the policymakers undertook a 21.8 percent devaluation to stabilize the real exchange rate, which had been appreciating with the growing differential between domestic and foreign inflation rates (Table 4.7). This devaluation was partly responsible for another 26 percent in inflation in 1975. There was a sharp deterioration in the current account but, through heavy borrowing abroad, the government managed to produce a substantial overall balance surplus by 1975. On the positive side, GNP continued to grow by 8 percent in real terms during 1974 and 1975. This gambler's approach to the external shock seemed to have paid off handsomely as far as growth and employment were concerned, but at a high price. The growth-first response to the oil crisis seriously undermined economic stability and made it increasingly difficult to restore price stability in subsequent years. The task of restraining price inflation was further exacerbated by the upturn of the world economy, which contributed to another boom year for Korea's exports in 1976.

Alarmed by the two years of high inflation following the oil crisis, the authorities began to pay more attention to restoring price stability. Starting in 1976 they tightened the supply of credit and money, but given the automatic credit expansion associated with export growth, there was a limit on their ability to squeeze the credit supply. To complement the restrictive monetary policy, a comprehensive incomes policy was put into effect that included strong price-control measures covering a wide range of consumer and producer goods. In 1976 and 1977 inflation showed a sharp deceleration, but beginning in 1978 prices began to soar again and by the end of the year had risen by more than 20 percent in terms of the GNP deflator. This sudden upsurge was to be expected. In fact, a close examination of developments since the early 1970s indicated that several inflationary factors had been lurking behind the scene for some time.

In the midst of strong inflationary pressures, Korea was hit by the second oil crisis in 1979; as in 1974 the cost increase resulting from the external shock was accommodated by credit expansion. For the next three years prices measured by the WPI continued to climb at a high rate. The average annual rate of inflation during this period was close to 27 percent. Along with high rates of inflation, a substantial divergence between price increases of tradable and nontradable goods occurred. The inability of the government to control domestic credit was (as in earlier periods) one of the greatest contributors to rampant inflation after the second oil crisis.

On the demand side, the inflationary impact of the oil crisis was further aggravated by the promotion of heavy and chemical industries that began in the early 1970s. Low nominal interest rates, which drove down real interest rates to a negative level, induced savers to move out of financial

Table 4.7. Indexes of nominal and real exchange rates: 1969–80 (1975 = 100 won per US $)

Index	1969	1970	1971	1972	1973	1974	1975	1976	1977	1978	1979	1980
Nominal exchange rate[a]	167.8 (288.42)[b]	155.6 (311.13)	138.0 (350.80)	122.9 (393.97)	121.5 (398.32)	119.2 (405.97)	100.0 (484.00)	100.0 (484.00)	100.0 (484.00)	100.0 (484.00)	100.0 (484.00)	79.7 (607.43)
Effective nominal exchange rate[c]	60.2	72.0	79.5	83.5	79.4	83.4	100.0	101.1	96.6	86.6	87.0	110.0
Purchasing power parity[d]	113.3	117.1	107.0	104.9	122.5	118.2	100.0	90.4	90.0	91.8	84.1	74.6
Real effective exchange rate (REER)[e]	125.9 (384.49)[b]	132.9 (364.30)	128.9 (376.50)	117.1 (413.16)	99.2 (487.82)	100.9 (479.78)	100.0 (484.00)	110.7 (437.28)	111.1 (435.68)	108.9 (444.39)	118.9 (407.10)	106.8 (453.20)

Source: BOK, *Economic Statistics Yearbook* (1970, 1975, 1980, 1982).

a. Monthly average.

b. Figures in parentheses are the levels of nominal and real exchange rates.

c. Effective nominal exchange rate is calculated as a weighted average of the won prices of the currencies of Korea's four major trading partners, where the weights are given by the four countries' trade shares. The respective weights are: U.S. = 0.4569; Japan = 0.4281; West Germany = 0.0727; and U.K. = 0.0422.

d. Trade-weighted.

e. REER $= e_k \cdot \sum_{i=1} w_i \cdot \mathrm{WPI}_i \cdot e_i / \mathrm{CPI}_k$ where e_k is the won-dollar exchange rate, w_i is the trade weight for country i, WPI_i is the WPI for country i, e_i is the ith country currency–dollar exchange rate, and CPI_k is the CPI for Korea.

assets and into real assets. The subsequent real-estate speculation hiked the prices of housing and land and thereby raised inflationary expectations.

On the supply side, real wages shot up and so did unit labor costs. The rice price-support program, which had been in effect since 1968, added to the inflation problem. The price-control measures introduced in 1975 distorted the relative price structure and, as expected, resulted in black markets for a number of commodities. With the realization of the adverse consequences of price and wage controls, the government reduced the number of controlled goods from 148 to 35 in 1979. That relaxation led to a realignment of relative prices and a subsequent high rate of inflation. One favorable development was that prices of imported goods remained stable between 1976 and 1978, before rising again in 1979 with the second oil crisis.

CAUSES OF INFLATION

In Korea's inflation history, one can see that every inflationary upsurge, one way or another, had a monetary connection. The annual rate of money growth (M_1) averaged 31.7 percent in the 1960s and 29.6 percent in the 1970s. Given a real income elasticity of the demand for money (M_1) of less than 1.0, those rates were too high, even when the economy was growing at almost 10 percent a year on average, to achieve the government's annual target rate of inflation below 10 percent. The corresponding growth rates of M_2 were 46.4 percent and 30.3 percent respectively. Although much of the M_2 expansion was associated with the increase in real savings, this measure of money with its income elasticity of 1.2 also indicated a substantial excess supply of money (elasticity figures are from S. W. Nam 1981).

From an analytical point of view, such a monetary connection is neither surprising nor interesting. What is necessary, and in fact crucial, is to ascertain why monetary expansion was occurring. From 1945 through the mid-1960s, money growth was an autonomous policy instrument. Monetary expansion during that period resulted from the government's effort to reconstruct the war-ravaged economy and to develop industry by extracting savings from households through the inflation tax and channeling these resources to strategic industries.

Since the launching of the First Five-Year Development Plan in 1962, monetary expansion has by and large been accommodated to factors other than stabilization goals. For example, the government's response to the oil crisis was to accommodate fully the cost-push effects of the oil price increases through a monetary expansion. Other policy measures that rendered monetary policy passive and accommodating were the export-led growth strategy, the grain price-support program, and the promotion of heavy and chemical industries. This section focuses on these policies as the major causes of inflation in the 1970s.

Export Promotion and Inflation

From 1965 and throughout the 1970s, the deposit-money banks provided loans through the central bank rediscount facilities at very favorable interest rates to all exporters and to producers supplying intermediate goods to be used in export goods production. These loans were granted automatically on the basis of valid letters of credit or similar evidence of export orders. In the early years of the export-financing system, the loan amounts granted were set at 80 percent of the domestic costs of export production for terms ranging from 90 to 120 days at an annual interest rate of 6.5 percent. Through the use of a domestic letter of credit covering orders of exporters from their domestic suppliers, these suppliers also shared in the favorable bank loan schemes.

The main defect of the automatic credit system is that it results in considerable loss of control over credit expansion by the monetary authorities. This was not a serious problem when exports were a small fraction of GNP, but as they rose to over 40 percent of GNP, the importance of this continuing outflow of credit became more serious. Initially, the monetary authorities attempted to compensate for the expansion of export credit by restricting the supply of other types of bank lending, but that was not easy to do. Squeezing other types of credit meant that nonexporters and producers in the nontradable sector had to obtain financing through the unregulated financial markets at higher interest rates. This differential effect of tight monetary policy biased against nonexporters and its implications for inflation through the relative contraction of the nontradable sector clearly limited the extent to which the credit squeeze could be enforced.

In the 1970s actual exports frequently exceeded expected levels. When that happened, there was a double expansionary effect on money supply. Not only was there an automatic increase in bank credit, but there was also a related increase in foreign-exchange reserves through an improvement in the overall balance that added to the supply of money. An increase in export demand is expansionary and, other things being equal, generates inflationary pressure. In Korea this expansionary effect has been exacerbated by the monetary expansion associated with the export credit and a fixed or managed floating exchange-rate system.

The quantitative effects of the export-credit system on money supply and prices are difficult to measure, because the system directly affects the level of output and balance of payments, as well as prices. Using regression equations, S. Kim (1980) estimates that between 1962 and 1978 automatic export credit contributed to 6.2 percent of the outstanding reserve base each year on average. Although this figure was low, its variability was high. The contribution ratio, which is defined as the increment due to the export credit extension to the actual level of reserve base, ranged from a high of 27.5 percent to minus 9 percent in 1977. The standard deviation of this ratio for the period was 9.23. The high variability may explain in part the equally high variability of the reserve base and money supply. Again using single regression equations, S. Kim (1980:122–25) shows that the additional reserve base increase was accountable on average for about 1 percentage point of the annual rate of increase of the gross domestic product (GDP) deflator during the sample period. The inflationary effect of the export credit was not important for any given year; its cumulative effect over time, however, was substantial. According to S. Kim (1980), termination of the export credit could have lowered the base-year rate of inflation by 2 to 3 percentage points within two or three years.

Grain Price-Support Program

After World War II the American military government in Korea imposed a rice price-control system that strictly enforced rice collections from farmers and a complete rationing system for urban consumers. The control system was partially relaxed by the new government established in 1948. In 1950 the government enacted the Grain Management Law, which remains to this day the basic legal authority for food grain policy. The primary objective of the system was to enable the government to secure sufficient grain from farmers so as to stabilize the rice price and the economy by exercising control over grain distribution and consumption through manipulation of government stocks (Ban, Moon, and Perkins 1980:234–59).

The grain market in Korea is characterized by a dualistic system that combines free market transactions and government control. Free market transactions exist by tacit assent of the government, which has the sole right to import and export grain. During the First Five-Year Development Plan (1962–66), the government pursued a low grain-price policy in an effort to stabilize prices and wages in the urban industrial sector. That policy discouraged grain production and encouraged rice consumption, widening the food gap and imposing a burden on the balance of payments. From 1952 through 1962 the government purchase price continued to be lower than the estimated cost of production (Ban, Moon, and Perkins 1980:240).

With the increasing food shortage and the growing income disparity between urban and rural households, the policymakers reversed the low grain-price policy and adopted a two-tier price system beginning with the 1968 crop. For the next seven years the terms of trade between agricultural products and nonfarm products improved considerably, although thereafter they deteriorated. The two-tier price system, which was intended to pay a higher price to farmers and charge a low price to urban wage earners, posed a serious problem for economic stability in Korea in the 1970s.

There are no strict formulas for determining the government purchase and selling prices, but these controlled prices have been influenced largely by price movements and grain market conditions. Past experience shows that determination of the rice purchase price (the most important grain price with a CPI weight of more than 200) has taken into consideration increases in the general price level and prices paid by farmers to maintain a stable farm parity ratio. Setting the rice price has always been a political issue and as such has often been dictated by political considerations.

The selling price has also been determined in consideration of stability objectives and financial problems that arise when it is set below the purchase price plus handling costs. Free-market prices of rice have fluctuated depending upon supply availabilities and the government selling price; owing to the difficulties of estimating rice production, however, the manipulation of government stocks has not been effective in keeping the free-market prices in line with the government selling prices. Overall, it appears that under the two-tier price system the rice price has been partially indexed to the movements in the general price level. This indexation feature has contributed to high inflation in Korea. When the purchase and selling prices of rice are set toward the end of each year, the new prices cause an upward adjustment of prices of other goods and services and raise nominal wages. In a highly inflationary environment, purchase and selling prices have had to rise in step with other price increases, and then with a lag the announcement of new rice prices leads to high prices of other commodities. This process has been under way since the late 1960s.

Partial indexation has been only a part of the problem with the two-tier price system. Since 1970 the selling price plus intermediate handling costs has always been lower than the purchase price, with the exception of 1972. The difference, or deficit, arising from the grain-management program has been financed mostly by borrowing from the central bank. At the end of 1982 the accumulated deficit financed by printing money was 1.5 trillion won, equivalent to 26 percent of the money supply (M_1). The expansion of the grain management deficit has been one of the major sources of credit expansion and of reducing the scope and flexibility of monetary policy in Korea.

Dynamics of Development Strategy, Exchange-Rate Policy, and Inflation in the 1970s

After a decade of export promotion of labor-intensive manufactures, the Korean authorities began, in the early 1970s, to develop skill- and technology-intensive industries (known in Korea as "heavy and chemical industries") as the export sector of the future. A massive investment program in these industries, financed largely by foreign loans and central bank credit, was put into effect in 1973 and pursued vigorously until 1979. To the dismay of the policymakers who conceived this industrial restructuring, the development strategy ran into a host of financing, engineering, quality, and marketing difficulties. Except for shipbuilding and iron and steel, these industries have yet to become efficient exporters.

Much of the investment in the heavy and chemical industries, which was by and large induced by distorted incentives, took place during the 1977-79 period, when the economy was already experiencing a high rate of inflation. As a result of the large investment, the ratio of fixed investment to GNP shot up from a historic average of about 25 percent to 33 percent in 1979. Given a stable domestic savings-to-GNP ratio, a high rate of investment expands aggregate demand (total spending for goods and services) and, other things being equal, causes the external position of the economy to deteriorate. To make matters worse, the investment program entailed serious supply-side problems that intensified inflationary pressures emanating from the demand side. During 1977-79 more than 70 percent of manufacturing investment was undertaken in heavy and chemical industries. This lopsided allocation of investment resources generated severe sectoral imbalances between the tradable and nontradable sectors and within the tradable sector. The lack of investment in light manufacturing—the traditional export sector—had an adverse effect on Korea's export performance, while the sluggish investment in the nontradable sector created a supply shortage and rapid price increases in this sector.

After the one-shot devaluation in 1974 the nominal exchange rate was kept at 480 won per U.S. dollar. The high rate of domestic inflation relative to the rates experienced by Korea's major trading partners resulted in an 18 percent real appreciation of the won between 1974 and 1979 (Table 4.7). Other things being equal, such a real appreciation results in a shift of national aggregate demand in favor of traded goods that include exportables and importables whose prices in a small open economy are greatly influenced by the conditions prevailing in the world markets. The real appreciation, on the supply side, induces a shift of domestic resources to the more profitable nontraded-goods sector. These demand and supply shifts would, in general, slow price increases and would be reflected in a deterioration in the current account. In Korea the expected resource shift did not, however, take place as a large share of resources was channeled to the tradable-goods sector (heavy and chemical industries, in particular) through the government's directed resource allocation. As a consequence, the excess demand for nontradables remained unabated and their prices went up further. To complicate matters even more, this forced allocation of resources to heavy and chemical industries did not help meet the domestic demand for tradables. One reason for this was that a large increase in the domestic demand for tradables consisted of consumer goods such as high-quality and processed food products and consumer durables. Because the majority of investment resources were allocated to the capital-goods producing sector, the excess demand for consumer tradables had to be satisfied by imports. Another reason was that Korean firms continued to import machinery and petrochemicals, because of suspected low quality and the difficulty of securing domestic finance for the purchase of the domestic import substitutes.

Although most of the heavy and chemical industries (shipbuilding, basic metals, and power-generating equipment, in particular) were from the beginning developed for export markets, the results were less than expected. Thus, while the tradable-goods sector was saddled with huge idle capacity, the import demand for tradables rose sharply. The combined effects of these developments were reflected in a widening trade deficit and rampant inflation. Available evidence bears out the causal relationship between inflation and a current account deficit. From 1975 to 1978 the price of imports increased on average less than 1 percent a year and export prices, about 8 percent; in contrast, the deflator for social overhead capital and services (which may be used as a proxy for a price index for nontradables) rose by 23 percent on average per annum. The current account deficit rose to 9.4 percent of GNP in 1980 from a small surplus in 1977.

The heavy and chemical industry investment program also produced a cost-push effect. The production inefficiencies and underutilized capacities considerably reduced labor productivity. Despite declining productivity, nominal wages (and hence the unit labor cost) soared as skilled workers, who were in short supply, were bid up by firms in heavy and chemical industries and as construction workers were sent to the Middle East. This cost-push effect was accommodated through money expansion and subsequently undermined Korea's international competitiveness.

Finally, the inflationary environment built up high price expectations, which in turn began to accelerate the rate of price increases. At the same time, the official interest rates, which were adjusted downward in 1972, were kept well below a market-clearing level. The negative real interest rates induced household savers to shift out of financial assets and into real assets and commodity inventories. The surge in the demand for houses, land, jewelry, antiques, and art objects pushed up prices of these assets markedly. As shown in Table 4.3, the land-price index almost quadrupled over the five-year period of 1974–79.

Although the data do not show it, partly because of price control and estimation problems, such a steep rise in land prices must have increased housing rents. It certainly brought about a housing and construction boom. Under normal circumstances, the speculation would have been moderated through an increase in housing supply; the export of construction services and materials, however, reduced the supply capacity of new housing and commercial buildings. Real-asset speculation in the latter part of the 1970s provoked a further increase in expected inflation, which in turn added to the inflationary pressure.[1]

---

1. It is not surprising, therefore, that S. W. Nam (1981) finds that the coefficient of the expected rate of inflation is close to 1 in an expectation-augmented Phillips curve estimated by using quarterly data for 1972–81 in Korea.

Ineffectiveness of Demand-Management Policy

The poor stability record in Korea has been largely the result of the combination of the lack of effective policy instruments and the unwillingness of government to sacrifice growth for price stability. Among the various demand-management policy instruments, monetary policy stands out as the most effective and flexible in developing economies. Monetary policy has been extensively relied upon in Korea and has served as almost the sole tool for controlling aggregate demand. The annual financial stabilization program, which focuses on monetary management, specifies year-end money supply targets and coordinates short-run stabilization policies. The targets of M_1 and M_2 growth rates have been the most publicized aspects of the stabilization programs, but have seldom been attained.

Monetary policy cannot be blamed entirely for the poor stability record. After all, it is no more than one of many instruments that must be coordinated in any serious effort to control inflation. There has been a glaring lack of such coordination as evidenced by mounting fiscal deficits when a contractionary credit policy was pursued.

On the institutional side, some traditional instruments such as open-market operations (buying and selling of government securities on the open market) could not be utilized because of the absence of well-developed money and capital markets in which the price mechanism functions. For that reason, the monetary authorities have had to rely on direct control measures—control of ceilings and quotas on these banks' loan expansion, changes in required reserve ratios, manipulation of the deposit-money banks' stabilization accounts with the central bank, and forced sales of stabilization bonds to these banks and institutional investors. These direct control measures have been affected and to some extent offset by Korea's growing access to international financial markets and a large unregulated financial market that has met a considerable portion of business needs for working-capital finance. With the growth of the external sector in both size and importance, the increased foreign-capital transactions have weakened the effectiveness of monetary policy. Despite supposedly strict government control of capital movements, businesses somehow have managed to borrow from abroad when domestic financial markets have become tight, though the reverse phenomenon of lending abroad has been rather rare.

The control over official interest rates resulted in fragmented and artificially segmented markets for a large number of financial assets and an uneven flow of funds among these markets. As long as the prices of these assets were controlled by the government, an equilibrium in these markets could be maintained only through quantity rather than price adjustments. As a result, exogenous changes in the rates of return to any assets, or the expectation of change, triggered sizable asset substitutions in the aggregate wealth portfolios, thereby making financial-asset markets highly unstable. In the absence of price adjustments that could abate the large and frequent movements of funds between asset markets, the effects of monetary policy were unpredictable.

The absence of well-functioning financial markets and the lack of policy coordination were only part of the monetary policy dilemma in Korea. Monetary accommodation severely restricted the scope of monetary policy as an anti-inflationary instrument. The main cause of monetary accommodation was the government's use of the financial system and policy as a means of intervening in the allocation of resources. The bulk of subsidies to preferred industries and fiscal deficits were financed by borrowing from the central bank. These borrowings were relatively immune to stabilization policy. The export-credit system, with its automatic credit expansion feature, and the grain price-support program, whose deficits were almost entirely financed by printing money, in fact worked as built-in destabilizers in the Korean economy and made monetary policy procyclical rather than anticyclical (Cole and Park 1983:248–52). Together with the grain-management deficits and export subsidies, the types of central bank credit that could not be controlled through the manipulation of traditional policy instruments accounted for anywhere from 30 percent to 45 percent of the reserve base in the 1970s (Table 4.8). In addition, a large fraction of bank credit was earmarked in the form of "policy" or "directed" loans for strategic industries and uses. These loans always escaped monetary tightening.

MAIN FEATURES OF PRICE CONTROL MEASURES

Complete Freeze and Relaxation, 1960–63

One of the first economic policy measures announced by the military council that succeeded the Chang Myon government in May 1961 was an across-the-board freeze on prices of goods and services. Ever since, some type of price control has been maintained as a means of slowing inflation in Korea. The various control programs have differed mainly in the number of commodities subject to price control.

Two months later, the complete freeze was lifted with the exclusion of the prices of the main staples—rice and barley. The relaxation in July was followed by the enactment of a law on price controls in November of the same year. The law, which provided the legal basis for direct price controls, gave the government the authority to select the commodities to be controlled and to determine the maximum level of their prices.

For the next two years the government managed a limited system in which five commodities—rice, barley, coal briquettes, coal, and fertilizer—were subject to price controls. Subsequently 13 additional major commodities and raw materials including flour, soybeans, beef, pork, steel plates and bars, cotton fiber, and cloth were added to the list.

It was not long before the authorities realized that the control system was not working. Shortages of some controlled items (and inevitably black

Table 4.8. Bank of Korea lending: Selected years, 1975–81

Type of lending	1975	1978	1980	1981
Directed loans (10⁹ won)				
Export financing	3,797	7,751	12,915	16,279
Energy conservation loans			5	711
Long-term export financing				1,266
Agriculture loans	260		711	661
Fisheries loans	55	284	500	619
Defense industry support loans		90	167	119
Other	41	1,140	253	4
Subtotal (A)	4,153	9,265	14,511	19,659
Total BOK lending (B) (10⁹ won)	7,961	11,785	24,450	33,711
(A/B) (%)	52.2	78.6	59.3	58.3
Reserve base (C) (10⁹ won)	10,770	28,020	32,439	28,016
(A/C) (%)	38.6	33.1	44.7	70.2

Source: BOK, *Economic Statistics Yearbook* (1985).

markets for them) developed. Even the prices of those products whose supplies were adequate went up along with other prices because of hoarding
and the spread of inflationary expectations.

With the realization of these classical problems associated with price controls, the government shifted the thrust of its stabilization policy to demand
management in June 1963, confining direct intervention to those items
whose prices could be controlled administratively. In addition, to complement monetary and fiscal policy, the government began to manage the supply of and demand for daily necessities and important raw materials, instead
of controlling their prices directly. This change in stabilization policy was
reflected in an overall policy measure issued in January 1964.

As noted before, the period from 1965 to 1969 witnessed spectacular
growth in a stable environment and a clear movement away from market
intervention and toward greater reliance on price mechanisms. Beginning
with the adoption of a unified and floating exchange-rate system in March
1965, the government took a number of measures for raising interest rates
to a more realistic level and liberalizing imports. Aided by these policies,
which stimulated domestic savings, supported export expansion, and
brought in a large amount of foreign capital, the economy could grow
without provoking another round of inflation. As a result, the need and
political demand for price controls greatly diminished.

Imposition of a Comprehensive Control System, 1972–73

Toward the latter part of the 1960s, several symptoms appeared that indicated a rapid build-up of inflationary pressure. The most noticeable was
the acceleration of liquidity expansion. The rates of price increases during

the first two years of the 1970s were moderate in retrospect, but higher than the target rates and thus a serious policy issue. The relatively high rate of inflation was accompanied by a mild recession. The setback in the performance of the economy was attributed to "structural problems" accumulated during the period of rapid growth and led to the enactment of the Presidential Decree for Economic Stability and Growth on 3 August 1972. The decree signaled an end to liberalization efforts and a return to control-oriented economic management.

One of the policy objectives specified by the decree was to reduce the rate of inflation to 3 percent per annum. To attain this target rate of inflation, the government announced, in February 1973, a comprehensive policy package for stabilization that included 16 measures. The most important element of this package was the imposition of a rather comprehensive price-control system that had been discarded in the mid-1960s. The system was geared to control nearly all prices that mattered. To administer the control program, the Economic Planning Board (EPB) revived the functions of the governmental committee for price stability, which had been dormant since its inception in 1963. The committee reviewed price developments for major product items monthly and issued specific measures for restraining price increases product by product.

A month later the government promulgated the Law of Price Stability, which was designed to strengthen the government's ability to control prices. Before the enactment of this law, the concerned ministries primarily had relied on the cooperation of business in following government guidelines, because they did not have the legal authority to set and alter prices directly. If a firm did not comply with the government's guidelines, it was threatened with an audit of its tax return or a revocation of its business license. Under the new law the government could control practically all prices including rents, real estate, and services, and could prosecute those engaged in unfair trading activities (for instance, charging a price higher than the ceiling) for excessive profit taking. For essential products such as foodstuffs, medical supplies, and building materials, the law required businesses to post their prices.

The onset of the first oil crisis produced insistent demands for controls and administrative solutions as inflation erupted with new force, and under pressure the government issued its third special measure of the year for price stability in December. The measure was aimed at minimizing the impact of oil price increases on domestic prices. Predictably, the main feature of the special measure was the direct control of prices of about 60 products consisting mostly of daily necessities and important raw materials.

The hope of achieving the 3 percent price-increase target was shattered toward the end of 1973 as the prices of oil and other primary commodities began to skyrocket. The target was raised to a more realistic level of 10 percent. Together with this change, the EPB (which was in charge of price-control administration) allowed some prices—in particular those of petro-leum products—to be adjusted upward to reflect the sharp oil price increase in December 1973.

Back to Partial Relaxation

In a country that depends entirely on imported oil, the quadrupling of oil prices was bound to inflict severe damage on the economy. It was also real-ized that the stabilization attempt through price controls in the face of ra-pidly rising prices of imported commodities was simply not possible. Nor was it efficient from the standpoint of resource allocation. The selective price controls also produced supply shortages and black markets in the controlled items.

In recognition of these problems and to lessen the adverse impact of the oil crisis, the government issued an emergency measure in January 1974 for restoring economic stability. This measure was followed by a compre-hensive policy package for price stability three weeks later (5 February 1974). One of the significant aspects of the package was the introduction of a mild form of wage control.

The new stability measures emphasized increased reliance on demand management and a relaxation of price-control measures. In an effort to im-prove the archaic distribution system, which was one of the causes of sup-ply shortages, higher prices, and black markets for many important products, the government implemented a number of measures designed to encourage the establishment of corporate retail chains, stores specializ-ing in daily necessities, and distribution outlets for the goods produced by small and medium-size firms.

Most of all, the two stability measures issued early in 1974 recognized that external-supply shocks could not be depreciated away and had to be reflected in domestic prices to whatever extent possible. While there was a clear departure in anti-inflation policy from direct intervention in com-modity markets to classical demand management and building up of the distribution infrastructure, price controls continued to be imposed during the latter part of the 1970s, though somewhat less stringently than before.

Antitrust Legislation

Government efforts to legislate antitrust laws in Korea date back to 1963, when excess profits amassed by a monopoly firm erupted into a political issue. The government continued to press its case for the legislation dur-ing subsequent years, but on each occasion the government proposals were opposed and postponed. In December 1975 the government finally suc-ceeded in pushing through the National Assembly its Law on Price Stabil-ity and Fair Trade, the forerunner of the Fair Trade Law promulgated in 1981.

The major objective of the legislation was twofold. First, it attempted to regulate unjustifiable price-setting practices by monopolies and oligopolies. Second, it aimed at developing an environment for orderly and fair competition among businesses, which is generally the spirit of any antitrust law. But in Korea the legislation was primarily motivated by the desire to establish a more effective and stronger administrative authority for price controls.

According to the law, a firm was classified as a monopoly if its market share was greater than 30 percent in an industry and it had total annual sales of 2 billion won or more. Three firms could be regarded as forming an oligopolistic market structure if, together, they accounted for more than 60 percent of the market as a whole and if each firm had a 20 percent market share or more. Even when their market shares were not dominant, firms could be placed in the category of either monopoly or oligopoly if they were powerful enough to set prices. In implementing the law, the EPB identified 127 products and 203 business concerns and placed them under the regulation of monopoly and oligopoly.

Real-Asset Price Regulation and Value-Added Tax

Inflation showed little sign of abating during 1977-78. High and continuing inflation inevitably induced the public to form high inflationary expectations, which in turn led to rampant speculation in real assets as a hedge against inflation. For a while it seemed that prices of land sites, housing, antiques, and even consumer durables would rise without limit. Price controls on building materials, electronics, and other products were aggravating the situation further. To worsen an already serious situation, the government introduced a value-added tax (VAT) system in July 1977, which necessitated an across-the-board adjustment of the entire price structure. The adjustment, it was feared, could accelerate inflation further. Consequently, the number of products subjected to the fair trade law increased, maximum prices of many products were set, and fees and charges of various services had to be posted. In general, the range of administrative price controls was greatly expanded.

Despite the reinforcement of the administrative price controls, the implementation of the VAT raised many prices. Real-asset speculation intensified further and was getting out of control. Something had to be done to reverse the dangerous trend, and in August 1978 comprehensive measures for stabilizing land prices and curbing real estate speculation were put into effect. One of the measures required that all future land transactions be reported to and approved by the government. Another measure expanded the areas subject to the government standard land price. These measures were complemented by heavier taxes on capital gains realized through land transactions and on idle land sites.

Greater Relaxation of Price Controls

Inflation continued to be the most serious economic problem and understandably became the focus of intense policy discussions within the government. These discussions, together with public concern, led to the formulation and implementation of various measures for economic stability in April 1979. The measures marked an important change in economic policy management, signaling a move toward overall economic liberalization. First, the comprehensive policy package left little doubt that economic stability was placed ahead of growth as a policy objective. Second, it emphasized the need to restore market mechanisms to guide the allocation of resources and the need for a greater private-sector role in the management of the economy. In line with this market-oriented economic philosophy, the government relaxed price controls and reduced the number of products regulated under the Law of Price Stability and Fair Trade. To lessen the burden on low-income families caused by the high rate of inflation, the government identified 25 products whose prices were to be monitored and kept stable by augmenting their supplies through imports and provision of tax incentives to the producers.

THEORETICAL APPROPRIATENESS AND EFFECTS

Price Controls as an Anti-inflation Measure

In its attempt to achieve and maintain price stability, the Korean government has, since 1961, administered price controls extensively and intensively—oscillating between a comprehensive and a limited system of controls and guidelines. The "permanency" and oscillation of the administrative price controls make it difficult to analyze their effectiveness empirically.

Were price controls effective in slowing inflation? Were they a theoretically appropriate instrument for controlling inflation in a Korea bent on rapid economic development? These questions are difficult to answer in a rigorous manner, and little help is available from the theoretical and empirical studies that have been carried out for other countries.

Proponents of incomes policy argue that "temporary" wage-price controls could speed up the decline in inflationary expectations by providing a period of relative price stability and indicating to the public that the government was serious about pursuing an anti-inflationary program. This argument essentially rests on the assumption that price controls could induce economic agents to adjust their inflationary expectations downward. If inflationary expectations are adaptive in formation and hence depend on past rates of inflation, price controls would break expectations. If, however, expectations are formed rationally, price controls would have no effect on inflationary expectations as long as other policies affecting the rate of inflation remained the same. To the extent that the controls were keeping prices below the equilibrium level, business firms and workers would surely expect renewed inflation at the end of the control period. In such a case the termination of controls would cause a rebound in the price level.

Korea's experience with incomes policy as an anti-inflation instrument casts serious doubt on whether price controls indeed lowered the rate of inflation below what it might have been in the absence of the controls. Several reasons can be suggested for this skepticism. Some prices have been controlled consistently since 1961; the numerous special, emergency, and regular measures aimed at combating inflation have always included price controls. These measures have differed, as far as the controls are concerned, mainly in their coverage of controlled-price products. Since price controls have become a way of life in Korea, an announcement of new ones could not have produced a strong effect. After so many impositions of price controls, people have become callous about what the government has been saying about the control measures.

Another reason to doubt the effectiveness of price controls as a stabilization instrument is that enforcement has been uneven. Despite the efforts of a strong government, price controls have frequently been evaded by business firms and have created black-market prices, lowered quality, and led to shortages of the controlled products. As a result, people have seldom sensed any actual decline in the rate of inflation and have begun to distrust official price statistics that dutifully record official prices. Under these circumstances, it is difficult to believe that people would adjust their inflation expectations downward in response to an imposition of price controls.

There is another reason why expectations have failed to adjust. As noted before, in administering incomes policy the government has moved back and forth between a comprehensive and a limited control system. On each occasion a comprehensive system has been discontinued and replaced by a relatively limited one. As a consequence people have come to expect failure from comprehensive controls because of the harm they inflict on the economy by interfering with the allocative function of the market.

The fourth factor responsible for the ineffectiveness of the control measures may have been that expansionary aggregate demand policies have been used to sustain rapid growth while price controls have been imposed to stabilize prices. Experiences of other countries clearly show that incomes policies cannot be a substitute for restrictive aggregate demand policies as a cure for inflation.

Price Controls as a Distributional Device

Although the primary objective of price controls may have been to lower the rate of inflation, price controls have also served other purposes, such as the redistribution of income. The goods and services that have been selected for price control are what may be called basic necessities and their prices have a significant effect on the real income of low-income households. By controlling those prices the government has been able to raise the real income of this group. The price of rice, for instance, has been controlled, regardless of the size of harvest, in order to supply it at low prices to urban consumers whose welfare is critical for political stability. It has been controlled also to provide favorable terms of trade to rice farmers.

During the 1960s and 1970s the government relied more or less on credit control and on credit expansion by the central bank to mobilize domestic resources for rapid economic development. This development strategy led to inflation, with an inordinate share of the inflationary tax burden falling on low-income wage earners. Price controls may be viewed as the government's attempt to attenuate the burden by providing basic necessities to this group. If and when the resulting shortages were acute enough, they could easily be blamed on profiteering businesses. Price controls have thus served the government well by helping maintain political stability and allowing it to stay with its development strategy.

Were price controls necessary as a distributional device? In the case of rice, for example, the price could have been freely determined in the market, and people below a certain level of income, whether farmers or urban wage-earners, could have received an income subsidy. Whether or not the Korean economy had the fiscal capability to carry out such a scheme is a difficult question to answer.

Whatever the situation may have been in the past, there seems to be no reason for continuing with price controls as a distributional device. Their adverse effects on allocative efficiency and equity are too well known to be repeated here. In their place the government should find measures that would bring about an equitable distribution of income but would not at the same time load the economy with an excess burden from price distortion.

Price Controls as an Antimonopoly Measure

As noted earlier, price controls have been used as an antimonopoly or antioligopoly measure. If price controls are used as a bona fide measure for regulating monopoly because of its anticompetitive conduct, they should be judged by their effect on allocative efficiency and not by their effect on inflation.

Whatever merit there may be in regulating monopolies with price controls, it is hard to overlook the fact that monopolies are to a large extent the products of government policies. Credit control, for example, has favored large, established firms at the expense of small, new ones. It is ironic that having created monopolies with one set of policies the government is now compelled to regulate them with another set of policies.

With the exception of those in the nontraded-goods sector, monopolies or oligopolies can operate as such in a small open economy because of government protection from import competition. Their protection may be warranted in their "infant" stage, but if the government is concerned with their monopoly conduct, they are no longer in need of protection from import competition. Instead of regulating monopolies with price control, the government should go directly to the root cause of the problem and eliminate protection from import competition and government-created barriers to entry.

CRITICISM AND LESSONS

During 1945–80 Korea experienced erratic and relatively high inflation (in comparison, that is, with its export competitors and major trading partners). Until 1964 the inflation was attributable to war, political instability, periodic mismanagement of a shallow and small financial system, and printing money as an expedient to mobilize resources for growth and employment. During that period monetary factors certainly played an initiative role.

In the 1965–80 period, which was characterized by successful export promotion and rapid growth, the role of monetary factors was more accommodative than initiative. The efforts to allocate a large share of the nation's limited resources to the sectors producing exports (intensive in labor beginning in the mid-1960s and in skill and technology after the first oil crisis) and to the farm price-support system contributed to excessive monetary expansion. The oil price increases were largely accommodated to minimize their disruptive effects on growth and employment.

During the period under review, Korean planners might have felt that the cost of reducing inflation through a restrictive aggregate-demand policy, when measured in terms of foregone output and a higher unemployment rate, was too large for a labor-abundant developing economy like Korea's to bear. So long as rapid growth was the prime objective, restrictive aggregate-demand policies predictably ran into strong resistance from the most affected group—the business community that had grown in power and influence—and were soon reversed, even if the prevailing economic conditions called for a continuation of restrictive policies. Thus, when the economy was sluggish, an expansionary credit policy could be implemented with little objection. Unfortunately, the converse has not been the case, and inevitably monetary policy has become procyclical.

With aggregate-demand policies directed to promoting growth and employment, the planners have had no choice but to rely extensively and continuously on incomes policy—mostly in the form of price controls—to stabilize inflation. That is, the government has assigned incomes policy to combating inflation and aggregate-demand policy to sustaining rapid growth.

Price controls do not have any measurable effect on the long-run rate of inflation. Even in the short-run, unless employed as a means of buying time to prepare a more flexible policy, price controls do not seem to work because they do not induce people to lower their inflationary expectations, especially in an economy where price controls have become a permanent fixture.

One more lesson from Korea's experience with price controls is that incomes policy cannot be used to control inflation while expansionary demand policies are used to stimulate employment. As a tool for controlling inflation, price controls cannot be a substitute for restrictive demand-management policies.

The Korean planners must have been aware of the nonsubstitutability between the two policy instruments. An important question, then, is why the government made monetary policy accommodating and procyclical. One answer may be that the government chose a development strategy that necessitated continuation of repressive financial policies—mobilization of domestic resources through printing money and allocating these resources through credit rationing based on a set of criteria that made monetary policy passive and accommodating. Another answer may be that, given the choice between stagnation and inflation, the government saw inflation as the lesser evil.

5 The 1964–65 Exchange Rate Reform, Export-Promotion Measures, and Import-Liberalization Program

by Kwang Suk Kim

Industrial policy during the postwar reconstruction period (1953–60) was inward-looking. The government controlled imports not only for balance-of-payments reasons but also to promote import-substitution industries. The government used both high tariffs and various quantitative restrictions to control imports, while maintaining an overvalued exchange rate in the face of rapid domestic inflation. A complex structure of multiple exchange rates was also developed to avoid balance-of-payments difficulties. These measures, in effect, encouraged import substitution mainly in the consumer-goods industries. Although some minor attempts were made to increase exports, the structure of incentives during the period was, on balance, biased against exports.

After the frustrating economic performance in the late 1950s and the collapse in 1961 of the Chang Myon government, the military government began to shift economic policy from reconstruction and inward-looking industrialization to a program of rapid industrialization based on exports. Since this shift in industrialization policy called for changes in many existing policies, the government committed itself to a variety of reforms. The military government first attempted to complete the task of unifying the exchange rate begun by the preceding civilian government. In 1962 the government undertook reforms of the exchange controls, the national currency, the government budget system, and the tax system. It also took necessary measures to encourage the introduction of foreign capital in the face of declining foreign assistance. Some of these measures, however, turned out to be ineffective or detrimental to economic growth due mainly to the expansionary policy of the government.

The military government devised several measures to promote exports during 1961–63. It made direct subsidy payments to selected categories of export commodities. Preferential loans for exports became an important instrument of export promotion beginning in 1963 because the interest rate on such export credit was gradually reduced from nearly 14 percent per annum in 1961 to 8 percent in 1963 while other loan rates were unchanged at the 14 percent level. In addition to tariff exemptions on imports of raw materials for exports, which had been instituted in 1959, the government formalized the exemptions of domestic indirect taxes on exports and intermediate inputs used in export production by making the necessary legal provisions in 1961. The government also granted a 50 percent reduction in income tax on earnings from exports and sales to United Nations forces in Korea and from tourism in 1962. In addition, the Export Promotion Law enacted in 1962 included a provision that licenses for imports using Korea's foreign exchange should be limited in any year to those traders who, during the previous year, had achieved a certain export minimum. This export minimum-value requirement for obtaining an import license was set at US $10,000 in 1962 and then gradually raised to $30,000 in 1964.

What was really important for export promotion during this period, however, was the export–import link system adopted in 1963, under which exporters could use the import rights linked to their export earnings for importing or could sell them on the free market at a premium rate of exchange. This indicates that most of the export promotion measures adopted during 1961–63 had the characteristic of ad hoc measures to offset the disincentive effect of an overvalued official exchange rate on exports. Even on the import side, the export–import link system played an important role in restricting imports, since the value of non-aid commercial imports for any year could be automatically limited to the amount of Korea's annual export proceeds. In addition, the government tightened import controls by means of quantitative restrictions in 1963, while maintaining the structure of highly differentiated tariffs by commodity groups that had been established originally in 1949 and revised in 1957.

As a result of the ad hoc export-promotion measures, commodity exports increased rapidly during 1961–63 from a very low base. However, imports also increased rapidly, despite government measures to control them. Although commercial imports were effectively controlled by the export–import link system as well as by quantitative restriction, total imports increased fairly rapidly during the same period, due mainly to increased imports of food grain and capital goods as separately recommended by the government. For this reason, Korea's foreign exchange reserves declined rapidly from US $207 million at the end of 1961 to $132 million by the end of 1963 (at which time foreign reserves were not even adequate to cover import requirements for three months on the basis of actual imports for that year). A rapid decline in foreign assistance also contributed to creating foreign exchange shortages. In any case, due to this foreign exchange shortage, the new civilian government that succeeded the military government around the end of 1963 had to focus its attention increasingly on the problems of foreign exchange shortages and inflation.

The 1964–65 exchange-rate reform, export-promotion measures, and import-liberalization program were designed and implemented as a package of reform measures to unify the exchange rate and to establish a system of incentives consistent with an export-oriented industrialization strategy for growth. In the process of formulating and implementing the reform package, there was much opposition from interested business groups, particularly against the exchange-rate reform and import liberalization. Despite the internal opposition, the government did implement the reform measures, some of which were considered drastic by many observers. It seems, in retrospect, that the government was able to resist opposition to the reform measures and to follow through on their implementation because it considered them indispensable for achievement of high economic growth through export-oriented industrialization.

MAIN FEATURES AND IMPLEMENTATION OF THE POLICY MEASURES

The Exchange-Rate Reform (1964-65)

For over a decade, from the end of the Korean War until early 1964, Korea maintained a system of multiple exchange rates. Under the regime of multiple exchange rates, the official exchange rate was almost always overvalued despite large periodic devaluations to offset the progressive inflation of the won. The official exchange rate was not really important, however, because practically all trade and other commercial activities were conducted at exchange rates that were significantly higher than the official rate in terms of won per U.S. dollar. For instance, during the late 1950s the official exchange rate was fixed at 50 won to the dollar (Table 5.1). Because exporters and others with foreign exchange earnings were generally given transferable rights to use their foreign exchange earnings (or proceeds) for importing, free-market exchange rates on export dollars, differentiated according to the source of earnings, developed in Korea. In the 1950s and the early 1960s, the free-market exchange rates on export dollars from Japan were in general much higher than the rates on export dollars from other countries, mainly because the foreign exchange earnings from exports to Japan could be used only for importing from that particular country. Separate exchange rates also applied to foreign exchange obtained by remittances from religious organizations and by selling services to United Nations forces in Korea between September 1954 and January 1961. In addition, the U.S. military payment certificate was transacted at market-exchange rates that differed from those for the U.S. greenback.

Multiple rates were also applied in the allocation of both government-owned foreign exchange and U.S. aid dollars because government allocations of such foreign exchange were made under a system of foreign exchange bidding, by imposing a foreign exchange tax, or other methods to increase the de facto exchange rate to a level higher than the official rate (Frank, Kim, and Westphal 1975:29-36).

After the large devaluation in early 1961, the government attempted to unify the exchange rate. That attempt failed, mainly owing to high inflation caused by the expansionary policy of the military government. A

Table 5.1. Nominal exchange rate movements, won to U.S. dollar: August 1955 to March 1965

| Time period | Official exchange rate | Free-market exchange rates[a] | | | | U.S. MPC | Korean WPI (1965=100) |
		Export earnings from Japan	Earnings from other countries	Other import dollars[b]	U.S. greenback		
8/15/55	50.0	95.0	82.0	75.0	80.2	66.2	32.3
1956[c]	50.0	107.0	100.8	84.7	96.6	81.0	36.6
1957[c]	50.0	112.3	105.7	84.5	103.3	84.5	42.5
1958[c]	50.0	122.5	101.5	89.3	118.1	102.9	39.9
1959[c]	50.0	139.9	124.7	113.5	125.5	114.9	40.8
2/23/60	65.0	171.8	138.7	129.3	144.9	129.2	43.2
1/01/61	100.0	156.3	141.6	132.0	139.8	120.6	48.2
2/01/61	130.0	147.9	145.4		148.3	128.9	50.6
1962[c]	130.0	nt	nt		134.0	126.5	56.0
1963[c]	130.0	169.8[d]			174.5	147.8	67.5
5/03/64	256.53	314.0[d]			285.6	236.2	95.0
3/22/65	256.53	279.0[d]			316.0	263.0	97.0

Source: Kim and Westphal (1976:35–36).

MPC—military payment certificate.

nt—no transaction.

a. Except for the annual averages, free-market rates normally represent the average rate for the months indicated, not the rate for the date indicated.

b. Separate rates on religious dollars (remittances) and services earnings, which existed between September 1954 and January 1961.

c. Annual average for year.

d. Indicates an effective exchange rate—the official rate plus market premium per export dollar.

system of multiple exchange rates reappeared in early 1963 due to the adoption in that year of the export–import link system under which exporters were given the right to use their export earnings for imports. In 1963 the average market premium on foreign exchange earned by exporting was about 30 percent of the official exchange rate (Table 5.1).

A significant step in the unification of the foreign exchange rate as well as in the transition to an export-oriented industrialization policy was the exchange-rate reform of 1964–65. In May 1964 the government devalued the official exchange rate from 130 to 256 won per U.S. dollar and announced that the existing fixed exchange-rate system would be changed to a unitary floating exchange-rate system. According to Gilbert Brown, who participated in the Korean exchange-rate reform as a USAID (United States Agency for International Development) adviser, the new exchange rate was based on a median value of the purchasing-power-parity (PPP) ratio calculated at the end of 1963 (Brown 1973:139). Because there was no reliable benchmark with which to work, the PPP ratio was calculated for those domestic goods for which the prices of comparable foreign goods were available.

It was not until March 1965, however, that the government allowed the actual floating of foreign exchange. It feared that the floating might set off foreign exchange speculation, resulting in further devaluation of the won and higher inflation. The first stage of the exchange-rate reform was, therefore, nothing more than a simple, large devaluation. The new exchange rate based on the PPP ratio was considered by many to have undervalued the won slightly at the time of devaluation. As a result, Korean exports of goods and services increased rapidly in 1964 while the absolute level of imports declined. Contrary to the situation in the early 1960s, the government continued the tight fiscal and monetary policy it had started during the latter part of 1963. Thanks to that effort, the domestic price level was relatively stabilized beginning in the second half of 1964, despite the large devaluation.

Following the exchange-rate reform, the government gradually abolished the full-scale export–import link system and lessened nontariff barriers on imports by increasing the number of importable items in the Ministry of Commerce and Industry's semiannual trade programs. The government, however, announced the implementation of special tariffs beginning in 1964 for the restriction of nonessential imports. The special tariffs, which were to be levied on top of the regular tariffs, were introduced to soak up excess profits accruing to importers of selected commodities. The tariffs were levied at the rate of either 70 or 90 percent of any profit in excess of the normal profit, or the spread (assumed to be 30 percent) between the c.i.f. import price[1] of goods plus regular tariffs, domestic indirect taxes, and the estimated resale price of the same goods. These tariffs were actually imposed on the basis of market surveys on domestic wholesale prices of imported

---

1. The c.i.f. import price includes cost of merchandise, shipping insurance, and freight charges.

items, as well as the import prices. Initially about 2,200 commodity items were selected for the imposition of these special tariffs.

The government also suspended direct subsidy payments to exporters immediately following the devaluation but reintroduced the system in the fourth quarter of 1964. Export dollars were still transacted on the gray market at premium rates of exchange. The premium rates showed some fluctuation but generally declined after May 1964 because the government gradually increased the proportion of export earnings that traders could use for commercial imports.[2] During the first quarter of 1965 (until March 22), premiums on export dollars ranged from 23 to 29 won per dollar, or from about 9 to 11 percent of the official exchange rate.

On 22 March 1965 the government announced that the unitary floating exchange-rate system was being put into effect from that date. Domestic price levels were becoming relatively stabilized beginning in the latter half of 1964 owing to the strong implementation of financial stabilization programs during the previous year. The International Monetary Fund (IMF) provided a stand-by credit in the amount of US $9.3 million for the purpose of exchange-rate stabilization. That enabled the Korean government to feel more confident about maintaining a stable rate of foreign exchange. The unitary floating exchange rate system was to operate in the following manner:

1. All foreign exchange earned by exporting and by sales to United Nations forces in Korea were supposed to be converted into foreign exchange certificates to be issued by foreign exchange banks (except in cases of amounts less than US $50). The foreign exchange certificates were to be effective for 45 days after the date of issuance[3], and could be freely transacted on exchange markets during that period. When the certificates expired, they were to be surrendered to the exchange bank for conversion into domestic currency.

2. All those who required foreign exchange for imports, including imports financed by USAID (but excluding PL 480 funds), were to submit exchange certificates at the time of issuance of import licenses by the exchange banks.

3. The Bank of Korea (the central bank) was to announce the daily foreign exchange buying and selling rates of both the central bank and the foreign exchange banks on the basis of free-market prices on exchange certificates during the previous day.

---

2. Although the full-scale export–import link system was abolished in May 1964, the premium on export dollars existed because the traders whose export record did not meet the minimum requirement had to buy export dollars on the gray market to maintain the status of licensed traders and to maintain their imports for commercial activities.

3. The exchange certificates were originally (from March 1965) effective only for 15 days, but the effective period was gradually extended to 45 days by June of the same year (Kim and Westphal 1976:82).

4. The foreign exchange department of each commercial bank was to play an exchange bank role by buying and selling the exchange certificates.

5. The Bank of Korea was given the right to intervene in the exchange market for prevention of any large fluctuations in exchange certificate prices that could result from seasonal and speculative factors.

Following the adoption of the new system, the market price on the exchange certificates was first formed at 270 won per U.S. dollar. The market-exchange rate then gradually declined to 256 won to the dollar in April. Beginning in early May, however, the market-exchange rate gradually increased to reach 280 won per dollar by the end of the same month, as demand for imports increased. In June the central bank began to intervene in the exchange markets by increasing the supply of exchange certificates. From 22 August 1965 until 1967 the central bank could actually peg the market-exchange rate at around 270 won to the dollar by continuously increasing the supply of exchange certificates. That indicates that the Korean monetary authorities (the Ministry of Finance and the central bank) actually transformed the system of the unitary floating exchange rate into a fixed-rate system, after some initial floating.

When the exchange-rate reform was announced in 1964, some in the business community, particularly powerful, large business groups, expressed opposition to the reform. Although both export and import-substitute industries could gain by the devaluation, the large business groups opposed it because they preferred to operate under extensive controls rather than under a realistic exchange rate and relatively free-market situation. Some of the business groups that were highly dependent on imported raw materials also opposed the devaluation. The business groups' opposition to devaluation was, however, not so strong during 1964–65, mainly because the business sector's foreign debts were still relatively small.

It seems, therefore, that the exchange-rate peg at around 270 won to the dollar in 1966 and 1967 was more attributable to the rapid accumulation of foreign reserves than to the business community's opposition to further depreciation of the won. The increase in foreign reserves during this period was mainly the result of the rapid increase in foreign borrowing after the interest-rate reform of 1965, which widened the interest-rate gap between domestic and foreign financial markets. The rapid expansion of exports might also have contributed to the accumulation of foreign reserves. In any case, the Korean monetary authorities were faced with the difficult job of sterilizing the monetary expansion caused by the accumulation of foreign reserves. Because further depreciation of the won would make it more difficult to control the money supply, the Korean monetary authorities left the exchange rate pegged for over two years.

Between 1968 and 1974, a gradual depreciation of the won was allowed by the government, mainly to offset a widening inflation-rate gap between Korea and its major trading partners. In many cases the government used the method of periodic devaluation rather than allowing a clean floating on the foreign exchange markets. Although most exporters were urging more rapid depreciation, at least to maintain a PPP-adjusted exchange rate constant at the 1965 level, the depreciation of the won proceeded more slowly, mainly because of strong pressure from the huge business firms that had borrowed heavily from abroad. The business firms with large foreign debts opposed devaluation because it would increase the won cost of the foreign debt-service burden proportionately. These firms had become an influential group opposing devaluation in Korea by the late 1960s.

After December 1974 Korea actually maintained a fixed exchange rate of 484 won to the dollar until the early 1980s, despite the gradual overvaluation of the won and the resulting deterioration in the country's balance of payments. The delay in devaluing the currency in the late 1970s was partly attributable to political instability, in addition to the usual opposition from the business group with large foreign debts. The government of the late President Park could not take the unpopular policy of devaluation in 1978 and 1979, although the need for some devaluation was well understood by many policymakers.

Export-Promotion Measures

The Korean government employed various ad hoc measures to promote exports, even before the exchange reform of 1964–65. The price competitiveness of Korean exports was greatly enhanced after the devaluation in 1964, which was proportionally quite substantial. For that reason, the government reduced the direct subsidy payments to exporters in 1964 and abolished such payments beginning in 1965. The export–import link system was also gradually eliminated except for a small number of unprofitable export items. At the same time, however, the government not only maintained many of the export-incentive measures that had been adopted before 1964, but also introduced new schemes resulting in an overall increase in export incentives after the exchange-rate reform.

Immediately following the announcement of the exchange-rate reform in May 1964, the Ministry of Commerce and Industry (MCI) was asked to prepare a comprehensive plan for export promotion, consistent with the new exchange-rate system. The ministry drew up a list of export-promotion incentives for discussion with the business community, as well as with other government agencies. The MCI's list included tax concessions, preferential loans for exports, local letters of credit, wastage allowances, minimum export requirements for licensed traders, and government support for overseas marketing activities. In addition, the MCI recommended an increase in the amount of preferential export credit per dollar value of exports to match the increased need for domestic funds for exports under the new, realistic exchange rate. The MCI's list also included some new recommendations, such as subsidies for export firms suffering losses, assigning commercial attachés to Korean embassies abroad, sending other export promotion teams abroad, and removing restrictions on foreign travel related to the export business. The additional recommendations were formally adopted by the government in 1964–65, although the incentive effects of those measures appear not to have been as important as those discussed below.

Tax concessions. The 50 percent reduction in income tax on earnings from exports and other foreign-exchange earning activities was continued in 1964–66, as was the exemption of domestic indirect taxes on export products and intermediate inputs into export production. Accelerated depreciation was allowed in 1966 for export industries. The government extended the scope of tariff exemptions to the import of machinery and equipment for export industries in 1966, in addition to the tariff exemptions on imports of raw materials for exports (which had been granted since 1959).

Preferential loans for exports. The preferential interest rate on export loans was further reduced from 8 percent per annum to 6.5 percent in early 1965. Because the interest-rate reform of 1965 sharply raised the interest rate on ordinary bank loans from 16 percent per annum to 26 percent, while leaving the preferential rate on export credit unchanged, the subsidies implicit in the preferential loans for exports increased greatly beginning in 1965. These preferential loans were mostly financed by the rediscount of export bills at the central bank.

Local letter of credit and standby credit. Two credit systems to support export industries were put into effect in 1965 through a revision of the foreign exchange control regulation. Under the local letter of credit system, an exporter who had received an export letter of credit from a foreign buyer could issue a "local letter of credit" to the domestic producers of export products and raw materials for export on the basis of the export letter of credit. The local letter of credit issued by the domestic exporter was to be settled by foreign exchange certificates when the export shipment was made. That indicates that all production activities supported by the local letter of credit could be subject to preferential export credit, and to the tax and tariff concessions usually granted to export activities. The system was, in fact, meant to encourage the use of domestic raw materials for export production. At the same time, the standby credit system was intended to assist in the overseas marketing activities of Korean exporters. Standby credit, a type of clean letter of credit, was normally issued by the Bank of Korea for an exporter on the basis of a foreign exchange payment guarantee from any foreign exchange bank. The credit could be used as guarantee money for the overseas branch's opening of an export letter of credit to the head company and for other contracts related to foreign exchange earning activities.

Wastage allowances. Beginning in 1965, the government formally introduced a system of wastage allowances on raw materials imported for the manufacture of exports. The system allowed for technical and other handling losses of imported raw materials, in addition to the actual requirements for export production. The ratios of wastage allowances to total imports, which varied by type of export commodity, were determined by the MCI on the basis of technologically set requirements. However, because neither tariffs nor indirect taxes were levied on imports of such raw materials, those exporters who were able to conserve on raw materials could greatly profit by using them for production for the home market or by selling them in the market. In fact, the government gave generous wastage allowances to exporters in the latter half of the 1960s to increase export incentives.

Minimum export requirement to maintain the status of licensed trader. The minimum export requirement for licensed traders, established in 1962, was continued simply by gradually increasing the minimum export performance from US $30,000 in 1964 to $100,000 by late 1966.

Government support for overseas marketing activities. The government intensified its support for overseas marketing activities of Korean exporters through the expansion of the overseas network of the Korea Trade Promotion Corporation (KOTRA) beginning in 1964.

From this summary, it becomes clear that the system of export incentives was well established by the end of 1965, with some minor exceptions. The system that remained in effect into the early 1980s was generally established by 1965. Although some modifications to the system have been made since then, they were mainly to accommodate changing economic conditions in Korea. Probably one exception was the scheme of discounted prices for such overhead inputs as electricity and railway transport, which was authorized for bulky mineral and other exports during the late 1960s and the first half of the 1970s. The value of overhead price reduction was, however, quite small in relative terms.

The government abolished direct tax reduction on income earned from export and other foreign exchange earning activities effective from 1973, partly because of pressure from such international organizations as the General Agreement on Tariffs and Trade (GATT) and the IMF and partly because such a measure was no longer required for export promotion. The government did, however, provide some tax concessions to facilitate the overseas activities of Korean exporters in the same year. In 1975 the system of outright tariff exemptions on imports of raw materials for exports was changed to a drawback system, under which exporters were, in principle, required to pay tariffs on imports but refunded the payments when exports were actually shipped out. This drawback system was intended primarily to improve tariff administration because the annual volume of such imports for the manufacture of export commodities had, by the mid-1970s, increased substantially.

Turning to the implementation aspect of the measures, it should be emphasized that each of the export-promotion measures was actually implemented to meet its purpose and was applied indiscriminately to all exporters who could satisfy the criteria specified in the regulations. In other words, the government agencies did not, in general, have much discretionary power in the implementation of export-promotion measures. For instance, preferential export credit could be obtained by any exporter who could present to a foreign exchange bank an export letter of credit from foreign importers. It seems that this aspect of the export-promotion measures has been very important in increasing exports since the mid-1960s.

Finally, in the formulation and implementation of Korea's export-promotion policies, we should not overlook the important role played by the export-targeting system and the Monthly Export Promotion Conference. The export-targeting system in early 1962 was originally used to set the annual target of total commodity exports. But by the latter half of the 1960s, the export-targeting system was well instituted in the government as a regular instrument of export promotion. The annual export target was broken down by major commodity group and by destination (major countries and regions). The target was usually established in the early part of each year by accepting the MCI's export projections, which were based on past performance and the forecasts of related industrial associations for the year. The targets by major commodity group were allocated to related industrial associations, while the targets by destination were allocated to Korean embassies in respective countries or regions for implementation. The MCI maintained a "situation room" to monitor export performance, comparing it with the annual targets, which were broken down by quarters. The status of export performance was then reported to the Monthly Export Promotion Conference, which was regularly attended by the president.

The Monthly Export Promotion Conference, initiated in early 1966, was renamed the Monthly Trade Promotion Conference in the early 1970s to avoid any friction with countries that were export competitors. The conference was usually attended by all cabinet members, heads of major financial institutions, business association leaders, and representatives of major export firms. The people attending the conference were asked to give their opinions on the MCI's report on the status of export performance and its recommendations to solve any expected shortfall from the targets. Businessmen, in particular, were asked to present their problems, difficulties, and opportunities. Government officials had to respond to businessmen's criticisms of past government performance and their recommendations for improvement in the presence of the president. In essence, the conference served to disseminate the president's emphasis on export promotion and also contributed to quickly solving many problems encountered by exporters, particularly in the early stages of export expansion, through the final decisions of the president. Most of the export-incentive measures described above actually took their final form through deliberations of this conference.

Import-Liberalization Program

Although tariff barriers against imports were, in effect, increased by the enforcement of special tariffs after the 1964 devaluation, nontariff trade barriers were gradually lessened. The main instrument of import control, other than tariffs, has been the semiannual trade program of the MCI. The program usually classified and listed the commodity items by automatically approved items, restricted items, and prohibited items until the first half of 1967, although there were some additional classifications from time to time (Table 5.2). The automatic approval items could be imported without prior approval from the MCI or other ministries, whereas the import of restricted items required prior approval from the government ministries. The prohibited items were not, of course, eligible for import licenses. There was a gradual lessening of import restriction by the semiannual trade program between 1964 and 1967 (Table 5.2), as evidenced by the gradual increase

Table 5.2. Import restrictions by semiannual trade program: 1961–67

Period	Automatic approval (A)	Restricted (B)	Import permissible (C=A+B)	Prohibited (D)	Total (E=C+D)
1961 I	1,546[a]	35	1,581	305	1,886
II	1,015	117	1,132	355	1,487
1962 I	1,195	119	1,314	366	1,680
II	1,377	121	1,498	433	1,931
1963 I	776	713	1,489	442	1,931
II	109	924	1,033	414	1,447
1964 I	u	u	1,124	617	1,741
II	u	u	496	631	1,127
1965 I	1,447	111[b]	1,558	624	2,182
II	1,495	138[b]	1,633	620	2,253
1966 I	2,104	136[b]	2,240	583	2,823
II	2,307	139[b]	2,446	386	2,832
1967 I	2,950	132	3,082	362	3,444

Source: Kim and Westphal (1976:72, 89).
u—unavailable.
a. Includes the 309 items that could be imported only with export earnings.
b. Includes both the ''partially restricted'' and ''restricted'' items that were distinguished in the trade programs for these periods.

in the number of automatic approval items as well as the decline in the number of prohibited items.

In 1967 an important step was taken in the direction of import liberalization. Between 1964 and 1967, Korea's foreign reserves accumulated rapidly due to several factors: a rapid expansion of exports, an increase in foreign exchange remittances from Korean workers in Vietnam and West Germany, and the increased inflow of foreign capital (including cash loans), which was strongly attracted by high interest rates in Korea. For those reasons, the government initiated a program of import liberalization in the middle of 1967.

An ad hoc working committee was created within the MCI in early July 1967 to prepare an import-liberalization program. The committee, which consisted mainly of officials of division-chief level from related government ministries, was chaired by a director-general level official from MCI. The committee agreed to adopt a negative-list system for future trade control, instead of the positive-list system that had been in use until that time. Under the new system, the trade program listed only those commodity items whose import was prohibited or restricted—implying that all items not listed were automatic approval items.

The committee agreed that commodity items to be prohibited or restricted would include: (1) items already under import restriction in accordance with existing laws, (2) items hazardous to public health, (3) items considered harmful to national security and public safety, (4) items deleterious to sound public morals or violating social norms, and (5) items considered too luxurious in proportion to the country's current stage of economic growth. In addition, the committee decided that the import items to be liberalized would include: (1) items that had already been liberalized, (2) items on which basic tariffs exceeded 50 percent, and (3) items with a ratio of domestic wholesale price to c.i.f. import price exceeding 500 won to the dollar.

On the basis of those criteria, the committee examined each of the 30,000 commodity items classified in the 1963 edition of the United Nations *Standard Industrial Trade Classification (SITC) Manual*. The criteria could not, however, be strictly observed due mainly to strong pressure from related industrial associations and the government organizations dealing with the problems of industrial development. The number of automatic approval items was increased substantially by the import-liberalization program of 1967. The real effect of that program on domestic industries was, however, considered very small because it did not liberalize items for which imports were expected to increase rapidly. For this reason, the effect of the program on imports was not very significant.

Table 5.3 compares the old and new programs in terms of the number of commodity items by control category. The number of automatic approval items for imports increased considerably with the adoption of the negative-list system. For instance, more than half of the total 30,000 commodity items

Table 5.3. Comparison of the old and new trade programs, by number of export and import items and control category: 1967

Control category	Trade program effective until July 24, 1967	New program effective from July 25, 1967[a]
Export items		
Prohibited	57	579
Restricted		2,465
Automatic approval	610	26,956
Total	667	30,000
Import items		
Prohibited	244	2,617
Restricted	92	10,255
Automatic approval	3,760	17,128
Total	4,096	30,000

Source: Kim and Westphal (1976:96).

a. The classification of commodity items is based on the highest digit classification given in the 1963 edition of the United Nations *Standard International Trade Classification (SITC) Manual*. This classification is roughly equivalent to the level of commodity classification used in the old trade program.

classified in the *SITC Manual* could be considered automatic approval items, because they were not listed in the new trade program. It is not, however, actually possible to compare the numbers of restricted and prohibited items in the new program with those in the old program, because under the old system those items not listed in the trade program were the restricted or prohibited items. In any case, we can say that the adoption of the negative-list system in the second half of 1967 was an important mark of progress toward import liberalization in Korea.

Together with the adoption of the negative-list system for nontariff import restrictions, the government worked out a tariff-reform proposal in the second half of 1967, which was to be effective from early 1968. The main purpose of the tariff reform was to reduce the import tariff barriers in compliance with the basic direction of trade liberalization. Ronald McKinnon, who was invited to Korea to advise on the tariff reform, recommended that a uniform tariff rate of 20 percent be applied across the board to most commodities, and an exceptionally high tariff rate of 90 percent be applied to the limited number of industrial products that Korea wanted to protect as infant industries and on other grounds (McKinnon 1967). Although some initial work was done by the Ministry of Finance along the lines suggested by McKinnon, the basic structure of the new tariff rates finally approved by the National Assembly turned out to be not much different from the original. This reflects the fact that the original reform proposal prepared by the ministry underwent many changes because of pressure from various industrial associations and strong opposition from other ministries. The tariff reform actually reduced the maximum rate from 250 to 150 percent but raised the simple average of tariffs for a majority of the commodity groups classified by the two-digit Brussels Tariff Nomenclature (BTN) groups (Kim and Westphal 1976:101).

Although the government had originally announced in mid-1967 that it would continue to promote import liberalization, it was not able to increase the rate of import liberalization after the first half of 1968, measured in terms of the ratio of automatic approval items to total tradable commodities (Table 5.4). As the balance of payments situation deteriorated due to accelerating domestic inflation and to an increase in foreign debt service burdens beginning in that year, the government generally tightened import controls. For that reason, the rate of import liberalization showed a declining trend from 62 percent in the first half of 1968 to 49 percent by the second half of 1975. The rate of import liberalization gradually increased thereafter, but it was still around 69 percent in 1980. Although the rate increased to 77 and 80 percent in 1982 and 1983, respectively, it seems that these increases were partly attributable to the change in the system of commodity classification (Table 5.4).

Similarly, the government was not able to make much progress in effectively reducing the level of tariff protection on domestic industries after 1967, although tariff reforms have taken place a few times since then. At the time of the 1973 tariff reform, the government abolished the special tariffs that had been imposed on top of the regular tariffs since 1964. The government reduced the tariff rates on 1,067 items, while increasing the rates on 440 items, thus resulting in a reduction of average tariff rates from 38.8 to 31.3 percent. A far-reaching tariff reform, effective from early 1977, increased the number of commodity items subject to the (approximately) 20 percent tariff from 35.7 percent of total tradable items to 52.8 percent, while the number of high-tariff items was reduced (MOF, ROK, 1978:297–98). Despite these reforms, the basic structure of tariffs remained a "cascade" type throughout the period, because tariff rates generally escalated from a lowest level on unprocessed raw materials to the highest level on consumer luxuries until 1983. A new reform was undertaken to revise the tariffs effective from 1984.

THEORETICAL APPROPRIATENESS

It seems clear that the package of policy reform measures was undertaken by the Korean government with the following basic objectives: (1) to unify the exchange rate through a large devaluation and then to maintain a realistic rate by floating on the foreign exchange market; (2) to adjust the system of export incentives so as to make it consistent with the new exchange-rate system; and finally, (3) to liberalize imports and thereby reduce various

Table 5.4. Import restrictions by semiannual trade program: 1967–83

Period	Prohibited	Restricted	Automatic approval (A)	Total (B)	Rate of import liberalization (A/B) (%)
			Number of commodity items		
1967 II	118	402	792	1,312	60.4
1968 I	116	386	810	1,312	61.7
II	71	479	756	1,312	57.6
1969 I	71	508	728	1,312	55.5
II	75	514	723	1,312	55.1
1970 I	74	530	708	1,312	54.0
II	73	526	713	1,312	54.3
1971 I	73	524	715	1,312	54.5
II	73	518	721	1,312	55.0
1972 I	73	570	669	1,312	51.0
II	73	571	668	1,312	50.9
1973 I	73	569	670	1,312	51.1
II	73	556	683	1,312	52.1
1974 I	73	570	669	1,312	51.0
II	73	574	665	1,312	50.7
1975 I	71	592	649	1,312	49.5
II	66	602	644	1,312	49.1
1976 I	66	584	662	1,312	50.5
II	64	579	669	1,312	51.0
1977 I	63	580	669	1,312	51.0
II	54	496	547	1,097	49.9
1978 I	50	458	589	1,097	53.7
II		424	673	1,097	61.3
1979 II		327	683	1,010	67.6
1980 II		312	693	1,010	68.6
1981 II		1,886	5,579	7,465	74.7
1982 II		1,769	5,791	7,560	76.6
1983 II		1,482	6,078	7,560	80.4

Source: MCI, ROK (1967–83).

Note: The classification of import items is based on the four-digit SITC codes through the first half of 1977, on the four-digit codes of the Customs Cooperation Council's Nomenclature (CCCN) from the second half of 1977 to the same period of 1980, and on the eight-digit CCCN codes thereafter.

domestic distortions arising from high tariffs and quantitative restrictions. As already suggested, the government attained the first two objectives to a certain extent but was not quite successful in attaining the third one. This indicates that the actual achievements of the policy measures did not in fact reach the levels necessary to meet all the basic objectives of the measures. We are, however, attempting to examine the theoretical appropriateness of the policy measures in terms of the intended objectives, rather than in terms of actual achievements.

We will first consider whether or not it was theoretically appropriate for Korea to shift its industrialization strategy from import substitution to export promotion in the early 1960s. The industrialization experiences of other developing countries generally support the policy shift made by the Korean government, particularly in view of that country's small land size and limited natural resources.

Many developing countries in the postwar period adopted a policy of import substitution as an industrialization strategy. In countries where this policy was emphasized, the domestic production of manufactured goods was protected by high tariffs, quantitative restrictions of imports, and other controls. Exports were usually discouraged by an overvalued exchange rate, the prevalence of inefficient industries, and the higher profitability of domestic sales relative to exports. The countries that emphasized import substitution made rapid progress in industrialization during the early stage of easy import substitution when domestic production replaced the imports of nondurable consumer goods and intermediate goods used in their manufacture. Once the stage of easy import substitution was over, however, the production of nondurable consumer goods and their inputs could not be expanded rapidly because of the limited domestic market. These countries then turned to import substitution in durable consumer goods and machinery and in the intermediate inputs used in their production. Because the industries producing these types of goods are generally more capital- and technology-intensive than the nondurable consumer goods industries, and usually require high levels of output for efficient operation, many countries encountered difficulties in this stage because of the small size of the domestic market and the technological and capital requirements of such industries (Balassa and Associates 1982; Balassa 1971; Little, Scitovsky, and Scott 1970).

By the early 1960s Korea had completed the stage of easy import substitution and was faced with slow growth of output due to the limitations of the domestic market. Instead of emphasizing further import substitution in durable consumer goods, machinery, and their intermediate inputs, Korea started to promote the export of consumer goods and other light industry products that could be more efficiently produced by labor-intensive methods. Because Korea had been one of the typical developing countries following the path of import-substitution-oriented industrialization, it might have encountered the same difficulties experienced by other countries had it pursued further import substitution in durable consumer goods and machinery. Korea not only lacked economically important natural resources but also faced shortages of capital and high-level technologies in the early 1960s. It was a poor country with only an abundant supply of relatively well-educated labor. For this reason, the shift to an export-oriented strategy in the early 1960s was an appropriate policy choice and led to the rapid growth of the labor-intensive exports for which Korea had comparative advantages.

It is generally understood that export-oriented industrialization brings economic efficiency and increased resource productivity to a small economy that could not be expected under a regime of import-substitution-oriented industrialization. First, increased productivity of resources can result from economies of scale in production, which can be realized by expanding production for exports. If a small developing country pursues an import-substitution-oriented policy, economies of large-scale production cannot be expected, because the protected domestic market is usually limited, and inefficient domestic industries cannot expand their production beyond that market. Second, increased efficiency and productivity of resources may come about because export-oriented industries generally undertake more rapid technological innovation for improving product quality to meet international standards, and usually face greater pressure to find ways to lower costs than do firms producing for protected domestic markets. Finally, increased efficiency and productivity can be realized through import liberalization and the increased availability of imports, which are usually possible only in a country following an export-oriented strategy.

Once it is accepted that the shift to an export-oriented industrialization strategy in the early 1960s was the right policy choice for Korea, the theoretical appropriateness of the package of policy measures can be dealt with in terms of international trade theory. If a country is pursuing an export-oriented strategy, a free-trade regime will provide an ideal or optimal situation, as conventional trade theory teaches us. An assumption in the static theory of trade and development is that world prices of tradable commodities reflect the true opportunity costs of production of those commodities. Thus the tariffs, import controls, and multiple exchange rates that distort world-market prices are considered to result in economic inefficiencies and loss of welfare for the country in question, as well as for the world. To achieve external balance under this situation, a country has to maintain a unified exchange rate at an equilibrium level so that the demand for and supply of foreign exchange can be equated, without any price-distorting policy.

There are only two exceptional cases where we may justify some divergence between world-market prices and domestic prices. One is the case of an infant industry requiring protection for a limited period of time. The other is the case of optimal tariffs that can improve the terms of trade for the country imposing the tariffs. The latter case is, however, relevant only for those products in which a country can enjoy some monopoly in world trade and is applicable only on the assumption that there is no retaliation by other countries.

This kind of free-trade situation does not actually exist in the real world. Practically all national states use tariffs and other price-distorting measures to protect their industries from imports and to attain an equilibrium in their balance of payments, although the degree of price distortion from the norm of world market prices may vary widely by country. We cannot, therefore, expect that any country will, in the near future, dismantle all the price-distorting measures that have been in use. Likewise, it is quite unrealistic to expect that Korea will abolish all tariffs and nontariff barriers to trade and maintain its external balance only on the basis of a unified exchange rate. The theoretical appropriateness of the Korean reform package should be considered in this perspective. That is, although the reform package could not remove much of the price distortion that had existed prior to the reforms, it did represent an advance in the direction of removing various price-distorting measures.

The exchange-rate reform of 1964–65 was able to eliminate the multiple exchange rates that had existed prior to the reform and succeeded in unifying the exchange rate, thereby reducing the deviations of exchange rates from a unified equilibrium rate. The adjustment of export-promotion measures following the exchange-rate reform and the program of import liberalization were carried out for the purpose of reducing the divergence between world prices and domestic prices resulting from various government interventions.

Regarding the export promotion measures, it was thought that Korean exporters deserved government subsidies even under the unified floating exchange-rate system. The main reason was that they were new entrants to the international markets and would not be well accepted there unless they could trim their prices below quoted world prices—in addition to the fact that many other countries were giving direct and indirect subsidies to exporters. The subsidies implicit in the government promotion measures for exports have therefore been gradually reduced since the mid-1960s.

EFFECTS OF THE POLICY MEASURES

The exchange-rate reform of 1964–65, the export-promotion measures, and the import-liberalization program were designed and implemented as a package over a four-year period. Because the three policy measures are all interrelated, the effect of an individual reform or policy measure on the economy cannot be easily isolated from that of the other individual measures. For this reason, we will consider the effects of the entire package of policy measures on the economy rather than dealing with the measures separately.

Effects on Relative Incentives

A quantitative assessment of the effects of the policy package is attempted here by making time-series estimates of three indicators of relative incentives: (1) export subsidies per U.S. dollar export, (2) tariffs and tariff equivalents per dollar import, and (3) effective exchange rates for exports and imports.

Table 5.5 presents estimates of net and gross export subsidies per U.S. dollar export for Korea during the period 1962–80. The net export subsidies include direct cash subsidies, the export dollar premium, direct tax reduction, and interest-rate preferences, whereas the gross export subsidies include the exemptions of both domestic indirect taxes and tariffs on top of the net export subsidies.[4]

The net export subsidies can be called genuine subsidies in the sense that they directly affect the profitability of exporting. Since domestic indirect tax and tariff exemptions do not add to exporters' revenues and do not affect the profit rate on export sales, these are included not in the net export subsidies but only in the gross subsidies. These indirect tax and tariff exemptions, however, make domestic production for exports using existing capacity more attractive than production for domestic sales, because they reduce production costs of exports below those for domestic markets. In this sense, we suggest that the gross export subsidies give the level of incentive to exporting, relative to selling domestically, while the net subsidies indicate the level of export incentives compared with a free-trade situation (Westphal and Kim 1982).

The net and gross export subsidies per dollar of export are examined in terms of their ratios to the official exchange rates. As shown in Table 5.5, both the net and gross export subsidies per dollar accounted for a much higher percentage of the official exchange rate in 1963–64 than in later years. A major reason was that the export dollar premium was quite substantial during 1963–64 because of the use of the export–import link system, whereas the official exchange rate was still quite unrealistic. In 1965, the year in which the exchange rate was completely adjusted by the reform, net export subsidies per dollar dropped to 3.7 percent of the new official exchange rate but gradually increased to around 6.4–7.4 percent of the exchange rate during 1966–71. After 1971, however, the ratio of net export subsidies to the exchange rate further declined to a range of 1.9–3.2 percent, owing to the abolishment of direct tax reduction beginning in early 1973 and to the reduction of the gap in interest rates between preferential export credit and

---

4. Because of the lack of consistency in time-series data, it was not possible to estimate subsidies implicit in excessive wastage allowances for export production, accelerated depreciation allowances, discounts on the prices of overhead inputs, or the effect of the limited export–import bank system in use after 1964. According to Westphal and Kim (1982), the subsidy implicit in the wastage allowance alone was equivalent to 2.4 percent of total merchandise exports in 1968, but subsidies resulting from other measures were much smaller in relative terms.

Table 5.5. Estimates of net and gross export subsidies per dollar of export, annual averages: 1962–80

Year	Official exchange rate (won to US $) (A)	Various export subsidies per U.S. dollar of export (won)								Ratio to exchange rate (%)	
		Direct cash subsidies (B)	Export dollar premium (C)	Direct tax reduction (D)	Interest rate preference (E)	Net export subsidies[a] (F = B+C+D+E)	Indirect tax exemption (G)	Tariff exemption (H)	Gross export subsidies[a] (I = F+G+H)	Net export subsidies (J = F/A)	Gross export subsidies (K = I/A)
1962	130.0	10.3		0.6	0.9	11.8	5.1	4.7	21.6	9.1	16.6
1963	130.0	4.1	39.8	0.8	2.9	47.6	5.3	6.6	59.5	36.6	45.8
1964	214.3	2.9	39.7	0.7	6.0	49.3	7.6	10.1	67.0	23.0	31.3
1965	265.4			2.3	7.6	9.9	13.9	15.4	39.2	3.7	14.8
1966	271.3			2.3	10.3	12.5	17.8	21.3	51.6	4.6	19.0
1967	270.7			5.2	14.7	20.0	17.8	24.6	62.4	7.4	23.1
1968	276.6			3.0	15.2	18.2	19.9	39.6	77.7	6.6	28.1
1969	288.2			3.7	14.7	18.4	27.4	34.3	80.1	6.4	27.8
1970	310.7			3.5	17.3	20.8	27.0	40.4	88.1	6.7	28.4
1971	347.7			4.8	18.1	22.8	32.2	48.0	103.0	6.6	29.6
1972	391.8			1.9	10.5	12.5	26.4	66.3	105.2	3.2	26.9
1973	398.3			1.4	7.4	8.7	21.0	64.4	94.2	2.2	23.7
1974	407.0				8.6	8.6	22.5	55.1	86.3	2.1	21.2
1975	484.0				12.9	12.9	33.8	34.3	81.0	2.7	16.7
1976	484.0				12.3	12.3	33.6	35.9	81.8	2.5	16.9
1977	484.0				9.4	9.4	53.1	30.6	93.1	1.9	19.2
1978	484.0				11.0	11.0	53.6	30.0	94.6	2.3	19.5
1979	484.0				11.0	11.0	56.6	30.3	97.9	2.3	20.2
1980	618.5				20.6	20.6	74.6	36.4	131.6	3.3	21.3

Source: Westphal and Kim (1977) for 1962–77 data; C. H. Nam (1981) for 1976–78 data; and the author's estimates for 1979–80.
a. Totals may not sum due to rounding errors.

ordinary bank loans beginning in 1972. The gross export subsidies per dollar showed a similar pattern of change over time, but maintained a much greater percentage of the exchange rate than the case of net export subsidies, implying that the relative incentive to export vis-à-vis domestic sales was much greater than the net export incentives.

Table 5.6 shows the estimates of actual and legal tariffs and tariff equivalents per dollar of imports for the period 1962–80. The actual tariffs and tariff equivalents are much lower than the legal tariffs and tariff equivalents, reflecting the fact that significant tariff exemptions were granted for export and other purposes during the period. If we calculate the ratio of these tariffs and tariff equivalents per dollar of imports to the official exchange rate, as in the case of export subsidies, the results are the average actual and legal tariff rates weighted by the amount of imports. According to the data (Table 5.6), the average actual tariff rate generally showed a gradual decline from about 14–15 percent in 1963–64 to the 5–6 percent range in the first half of the 1970s. The average legal tariff rate generally remained over 20 percent until 1973, although there were a few exceptions. Beginning in 1974, however, the legal tariff rate declined significantly, owing mainly to the reduction to a zero rate of legal tariffs on oil imports which had increased rapidly in nominal terms after the first world oil crisis (1973–74). In any case, the actual and legal tariff rates do not really reflect changes in the degree of domestic protection over time because they do not include the impact of quantitative restrictions on imports. This is even truer for the period after 1964 during which time the quantitative restrictions were significantly lessened compared with earlier years.

Despite the limitations in the estimated export subsidies per dollar of export, and the estimated tariffs and tariff equivalents per dollar of import, some of these estimates are used to derive the nominal effective exchange rates for exports and imports, as shown in Table 5.7. In other words, the net export subsidies per dollar were added to the official exchange rate to obtain the nominal effective exchange rate for exports, while the actual tariffs and tariff equivalents per dollar were added to obtain the effective rate for imports. This implies that the effective exchange rate for exports gives an index of net export incentives compared with a free-trade situation, whereas the effective rate for imports gives an index of actual trade protection on domestic industries. These estimates of nominal effective exchange rates are then adjusted by a PPP index to correct for changes in domestic prices and in the prices of Korea's major trading partners. The results are the PPP-adjusted effective exchange rates for exports and imports shown in Table 5.7.

The PPP-adjusted (real) effective exchange rate for exports increased in terms of the number of won per dollar between 1962 and 1964, indicating that the exchange-rate reform of 1964–65 increased the net incentive to export. Another important point was that the exchange-rate reform substantially reduced the gap between the official and the effective exchange rates

Table 5.6. Estimates of actual and legal tariffs and tariff equivalents per dollar of import, annual averages: 1962–80

Year	Official exchange rate (won to US $) (A)	Tariffs and tariff equivalents per U.S. dollar of import (won)					Ratio to exchange rate (%)	
		Actual tariffs (B)	Export dollar premium (C)	Sub-total (D=B+C)	Tariff exemptions (E)	Legal tariffs (F=D+E)	Actual tariff rate (G=D/A)	Legal tariff rate (H=F/A)
1962	130.0	16.4[a]	0.0	16.4	6.9	23.3	12.6	17.9
1963	130.0	12.0	6.2	18.2	9.7	27.9	14.0	21.5
1964	214.3	21.0	11.7	32.7	17.9	50.6	15.3	23.6
1965	265.4	27.7		27.7	20.9	48.6	10.4	18.3
1966	271.3	25.1		25.1	28.3	53.5	9.3	19.7
1967	270.7	25.5		25.5	32.5	58.0	9.4	21.4
1968	276.6	25.9		25.9	45.4	71.3	9.4	25.8
1969	288.2	24.5		24.5	47.3	71.8	8.5	24.9
1970	310.7	25.7		25.7	54.1	79.8	8.3	25.7
1971	347.7	21.8		21.8	59.7	81.5	6.3	23.4
1972	391.8	23.4		23.4	85.1	108.5	6.0	27.7
1973	398.3	19.4		19.4	75.4	94.8	4.9	23.8
1974	407.0	18.5		18.5	44.2	62.7	4.5	15.4
1975	484.0	24.9		24.9	30.6	55.5	5.1	11.5
1976	484.0	31.4		31.4	37.6	69.0	6.5	14.3
1977	484.0	35.7		35.7	38.2	73.9	7.4	15.3
1978	484.0	42.9		42.9	37.0	79.9	8.9	16.5
1979	484.0	36.0		36.0	33.5	69.5	7.4	14.4
1980	618.5	34.4		34.4	34.7	69.1	5.6	11.2

Source: Westphal and Kim (1977) for 1962–75 data; C. H. Nam (1981) for 1976–78 data; and the author's estimates for 1979–80.
a. 1962 figure includes a small amount of foreign exchange tax collected from U.S. aid imports.

Table 5.7. Nominal and PPP-adjusted effective exchange rates for exports and imports, annual average basis: 1962–80

Year	Nominal exchange rate (won to US $) Official rate (A)	Effective rate for Exports[a] (B)	Effective rate for Imports[b] (C)	WPI, Korea (D)	WPI, major trade partners[c] (E)	PPP index (F=E/D)	PPP-adjusted exchange rate (won to US $) Official rate (G=A×F)	Effective rate for Exports (H=B×F)	Effective rate for Imports (I=C×F)
1962	130.0	141.8	146.4	56.0	97.7	174.5	226.9	247.4	255.5
1963	130.0	177.6	148.2	67.5	98.4	145.8	189.5	258.9	216.1
1964	214.3	263.6	247.0	90.9	98.6	108.5	232.5	286.0	268.0
1965	265.4	275.3	293.1	100.0	100.0	100.0	265.4	275.3	293.1
1966	271.3	283.8	296.4	108.8	102.8	94.5	256.4	268.2	280.1
1967	270.7	290.7	296.2	115.8	103.9	89.7	242.8	260.8	265.7
1968	276.6	294.8	302.5	125.2	105.6	84.3	233.2	248.5	255.0
1969	288.2	306.6	312.7	133.7	108.7	81.3	234.3	249.3	254.2
1970	310.7	331.5	336.4	145.9	112.8	77.3	240.2	256.2	260.0
1971	347.7	370.5	369.5	158.5	115.4	72.8	253.1	269.7	269.0
1972	391.8	404.3	415.2	180.7	126.8	70.2	275.0	283.8	291.5
1973	398.3	407.0	417.7	193.3	155.6	80.5	320.6	327.6	336.2
1974	407.0	415.6	425.5	274.7	188.4	68.6	279.2	285.1	291.9
1975	484.0	496.9	508.9	347.4	197.0	56.7	274.4	281.7	288.5
1976	484.0	496.3	515.4	389.4	206.7	53.1	257.0	263.5	273.7
1977	484.0	493.4	519.7	424.5	226.8	53.4	258.5	263.5	277.5
1978	484.0	495.0	526.9	473.4	266.1	56.2	272.0	278.2	296.1
1979	484.0	495.0	520.0	562.5	284.1	50.5	244.4	250.0	262.6
1980	618.5	639.1	652.9	781.3	323.7	41.4	256.1	264.6	270.3

Sources: Tables 5.5 and 5.6; EPB, ROK, Major Statistics (1983).

a. Official exchange rate plus the net export subsidies per U.S. dollar of export given under column (F) of Table 5.5.

b. Official exchange rate plus the actual tariffs and tariff equivalents per U.S. dollar of import given under column (D) of Table 5.6.

c. An average of WPIs for the U.S. and Japan, weighted by the average shares of the U.S. and Japan in Korea's total trade volumes (exports and imports) with the two countries during 1963–80. The Japanese WPI was, however, adjusted by the index of exchange rate of yen to the dollar.

by largely replacing the market premium on foreign exchange earned by exporting with the official devaluation of the won. The reform, therefore, stabilized export incentives by superseding the ad hoc administrative measures that had been frequently changed by the government. The real effective exchange rate for export, however, gradually declined in the latter half of the 1960s mainly because the government failed to maintain the real official rate constant in the face of domestic inflation. For this reason, the 1965 level of the real export rate could not be regained until 1972. Between 1972 and 1975, Korea was able to maintain a realistic real effective rate for export, despite a decline in net export subsidies during the period. That accomplishment was partly attributable to the readjustment of the dollar value in relation to other major currencies that took place in 1972–73 and partly to the more rapid adjustment of the exchange rate in Korea during the period. In the second half of the 1970s, some overvaluation of the won was again allowed by the government.

The real effective exchange rate for imports, which was also increased by the exchange-rate reform, generally moved in parallel with the export rate between 1965 and 1980, although the former was slightly higher than the latter throughout the period. That indicates that the real effective rate for imports could have been somewhat unrealistic in the second half of the 1960s and again during the same period of the 1970s, as in the case of the export rate.

In summary, the package of reform measures that was undertaken during 1964–67 did bring about some increases in the measurable incentive to export, as well as in the level of protection for domestic industry. What was more important than these increases was that the reform package replaced a complicated, largely ad hoc system of export incentives based on multiple exchange rates and direct cash subsidies with a simplified and more stable system. The reform package may therefore be credited with having laid the foundation for continued rapid growth of exports by ensuring more stable profit margins for exporters than in the past (Westphal and Kim 1977:120). The government could not, however, completely succeed in maintaining the stable levels of incentives to export and import substitution after 1965, as evidenced by the won overvaluation in the latter half of both the 1960s and 1970s.

Effects on Export Growth and the Balance of Payments

The package of policy reforms discussed above should have had a great impact on Korea's export growth and balance of payments. In fact, Korea's rapid export growth began in the early 1960s starting from a very small base. Between 1960 and 1965 the nominal value of commodity exports increased by an average annual rate of about 40 percent from US $33 million to $175 million. Even after 1965 the rapid rate of export growth continued despite the expansion of the base figures, thanks to the effect of the reform package.

During the following 15 years, the nominal value of exports grew by about 35 percent annually to reach approximately $17.5 billion, or 35 percent of nominal GNP, by 1980. The total value of exports for 1980 was roughly equivalent to 1 percent of world exports.

The rapid growth of exports was accompanied by a substantial change in the commodity composition of exports. Korean exports in the early 1960s were mostly primary products, such as tungsten, iron ore, raw silk, agar-agar, and fish. Manufactured exports accounted for a small fraction of total exports in the early 1960s but increased more rapidly than the exports of primary products thereafter. Manufactured goods—principally clothing, electrical machinery, textile yarns and fabrics, footwear, transport equipment (mainly ships), iron and steel sheets, and plywood—accounted for about 90 percent of total exports by 1980. Accompanying this structural change in export commodities was significant diversification of export markets. In 1965 about 60 percent of Korean exports went to two countries—the United States and Japan. By 1980 the percentage declined to about 44 percent as sales to the Middle East, Europe, and other areas outside Asia expanded. The diversifiction of export markets can also be shown by the number of countries to which Korea exported: 163 countries in 1980, compared with only 24 countries in 1965 (BOK, *Economic Statistics Yearbook*, 1960–80).

The reform package of 1964–67 also brought about a rapid increase in imports, although the direct impact of the import-liberalization program was relatively small. The nominal values of commodity imports, which had remained almost constant during the period 1953–60, increased by an average annual rate of 6 percent during the following five years, despite a gradual reduction in foreign assistance. Between 1965 and 1980 the nominal value of imports increased at an average annual rate of about 30 percent to reach US $21.6 billion by 1980. Thus the ratio of imports to GNP rose from about 15 to 39 percent during the same period. The increase in imports directly caused by the import-liberalization program of 1967 was estimated by the MCI to have amounted to only US $27 million in the final five months of 1967 and $68 million in 1968, therefore, most of the import growth cannot be explained by import liberalization alone. The rapid growth of imports depended upon several other factors as well.

First, the rapid expansion of exports during 1965–80 not only increased the availability of foreign exchange for imports but also necessitated a corresponding increase of imports for export production. Second, external finance, such as foreign loans, direct investment, and properties and claims funds from Japan, increased continuously during the same period, more than offsetting the decline in U.S. assistance. Third, the world-market prices of important resources, including crude oil, increased rapidly in the 1970s and the early 1980s. Fourth, the rapid export-oriented industrialization and growth created an ever-increasing real demand for imports. Finally, it should be emphasized that the won was overvalued from time to time due to the more rapid rise in domestic prices than in the prices of Korea's major trading partners.

Because the rapid growth of exports was matched by growth in imports, Korea could not significantly improve its trade balance during 1965–80. The trade deficits actually increased in absolute level between 1965 and 1980, although there were some fluctuations in the interim years (Table 5.8). The net balance on goods and services in the country's balance of payments also showed a similar trend during the period. The current balance in the balance-of-payments account, which is equivalent to the net balance in goods and services plus net transfer receipts from abroad, also showed a deficit in most of the years under observation, implying that Korea's external debts should have accumulated to a considerable magnitude by 1980.[5]

To explain some basic causes of these continuous balance-of-payments deficits, an attempt was made to correlate the current balance with both the PPP-adjusted official exchange rate and the index of net barter terms of trade for Korea (Figure 5.1). The figure presents the ratio of the current balance to total imports of goods and services, so that the relative magnitudes (rather than absolute levels) of the current-account deficits can be shown for respective years. The real exchange rate is shown in an index with the base year 1965 equal to 100, as in the case of the terms of trade index.

What we can observe from Figure 5.1 is that the relative size of the current balance is generally positively correlated with the index of the PPP-adjusted official exchange rate (measured in terms of won to the U.S. dollar), except for a few years (1974–75 and 1980) during which the terms of trade index for Korea declined sharply because of the world oil shocks. That observation seems to indicate that Korea could have avoided the continuous large deficits in its current balance, had it maintained the 1965 level of the real exchange rate unchanged throughout the whole period 1965 to 1980. Maintaining the real exchange rate at the 1965 constant level, however, was made difficult by Korea's high rate of domestic inflation as compared to that in major industrialized countries throughout the period. It is suggested therefore that domestic demand management, which allowed high inflation in the economy during the period, was ultimately responsible for the chronic deficits in the balance of payments.

Effects on Industrialization

The package of policy reforms had a significant impact on the pattern and sources of industrialization in Korea. Because the reform package resulted

---

5. Korea's foreign debt outstanding actually increased to US $37.3 billion by the end of 1982 and to approximately $40 billion by the end of 1983.

Table 5.8. Major trends in Korea's balance of payments: 1960-80

Year	Trade balance (10⁶ US $) Exports	Imports	Balance	Total imports of goods and services (10⁶ US $)	Net goods and services (10⁶ US $)	Current balance (10⁶ US $)	Ratio to total imports of goods and services (%) Net goods and services (%)	Current balance (%)
1960	33	365	-332	379	-262	14	-69.1	3.7
1965	175	416	-240	484	-194	9	-40.1	1.9
1966	250	680	-430	777	-323	-103	-41.6	-13.3
1967	335	909	-574	1,060	-417	-192	-39.3	-18.1
1968	486	1,322	-836	1,547	-670	-440	-43.3	-28.4
1969	658	1,650	-992	1,945	-794	-549	-40.8	-28.2
1970	882	1,804	-922	2,182	-803	-623	-36.8	-28.6
1971	1,132	2,178	-1,046	2,634	-1,018	-848	-38.6	-32.2
1972	1,676	2,250	-574	2,768	-541	-371	-19.5	-13.4
1973	3,271	3,837	-566	4,620	-499	-309	-10.8	-6.7
1974	4,515	6,452	-1,937	7,598	-2,305	-2,023	-30.3	-26.6
1975	5,003	6,674	-1,671	7,997	-2,114	-1,887	-26.4	-23.6
1976	7,815	8,405	-591	10,120	-663	-314	-6.6	-3.1
1977	10,047	10,523	-477	13,284	-211	12	-1.6	0.1
1978	12,711	14,491	-1,781	18,718	-1,557	-1,085	-8.3	-5.8
1979	14,705	19,100	-4,396	24,121	-4,590	-4,151	-19.0	-17.2
1980	17,214	21,598	-4,384	28,347	-5,770	-5,321	-20.4	-18.8

Source: BOK, Economic Statistics Yearbook (1960-80).

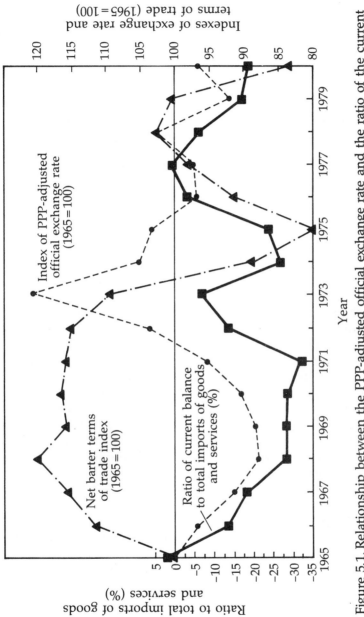

Figure 5.1. Relationship between the PPP-adjusted official exchange rate and the ratio of the current balance to total imports of goods and services: 1965–80

Source: Tables 5.7 and 5.8; EPB, ROK, *Major Statistics* (1983).

in rapid growth of manufactured exports as described above, value added in the manufacturing sector grew very rapidly after the early 1960s. For instance, the growth rate of the manufacturing sector, which had averaged about 11 percent annually during 1953–62, accelerated to 16 percent in the following two decades. Although the growth rate of GNP also accelerated from 3.6 percent during the earlier period to 8.4 percent during the later period, the share of the manufacturing sector in GNP more than doubled from about 14 percent in the early 1960s to 29 percent by 1980.

This rapid growth of manufacturing was accompanied by a considerable structural change within the same sector. The light industries, mainly food processing and textile industries, which had accounted for 70 percent of total value added in manufacturing until 1963, gradually declined to 47 percent by 1980. During the same period, however, the share of heavy and chemical industries in total manufacturing value added rose rapidly from 30 to 53 percent.

How did the major sources of industrialization shift because of the reform package undertaken in the mid-1960s? To deal with this question, we compare the sources of growth of manufacturing output between the two periods, 1955–63 and 1963–75, on the basis of the author's previous work (Kim and Roemer 1979:99–124; Mason et al. 1980:149–54). In contrast to the usual method of decomposing the sources of growth in terms of changes in the amount and productivity of broadly defined primary factors, the sources of manufacturing output growth are analyzed here in terms of the relative contributions of domestic demand expansion, export expansion, import substitution, and technological change to the output growth.[6]

The analysis of the sources of industrialization is based on the input-output tables for 1955, 1963, 1970, and 1975, which have been consistently deflated into 1968 constant world prices to eliminate the effects of domestic price distortions arising from tariffs, domestic indirect taxes, and quantitative restrictions on imports. The tables were also adjusted to make them consistent for comparison. The sources of industrial growth were decomposed for three time intervals (1955–63, 1963–70, and 1970–75), and then the results for the last two periods were linked to give a single estimate for the period from 1963 to 1975. Although the decompositions were made for the whole economy, including the primary and the social overhead and services sectors, only the result for manufacturing is summarized in Table 5.9. It should also be noted that the table presents both direct and total measures of the sources of growth; the difference should be taken to reflect the backward linkage effects of direct change in various autonomous factors on the expansion of output.

---

6. The analysis of sources of industrial growth was made by using the Syrquin method (Syrquin 1976), which is a modification to the pioneering work of Chenery, Shishido, and Watanabe (1962). This approach essentially starts from the basic demand-supply balance and attributes change in the structure of production to various demand factors.

Table 5.9. Sources of manufacturing output growth: 1955–63 and 1963–75 (%)

Sources of growth	1955–63	1963–75
Domestic demand expansion		
Direct	68.3	71.1
Total	57.9	51.5
Export expansion		
Direct	6.1	24.7
Total	8.7	38.8
Import substitution		
Direct	25.6	4.2
Total	34.9	7.0
Technological change		
Direct		
Total	–1.5	2.7
Total output increase	100.0	100.0
Total output increase in billion won	241.2	3,283.3

Source: Mason et al. (1980:152–53).

Note: By Syrquin's method—first difference (Syrquin 1976).

The relative sizes of both the direct and total contributions of various autonomous factors to total manufacturing output growth varied considerably from 1955–63 to 1963–75 (Table 5.9). The direct contribution of export expansion (EE), for instance, was about 6 percent of total manufacturing output growth in the earlier period, but it increased to 25 percent in the later period, while the direct contribution of import substitution (IS) declined from 26 to 4 percent between the two periods. Similarly, the total contribution of EE increased sharply from around 9 percent in 1955–63 to 39 percent during the later period, while the total IS contribution declined from 38 to 7 percent. The direct contribution of domestic demand expansion (DDE) increased between the two periods, while the total contribution (including indirect effects) of the same factor showed a decline. The contribution of technological change (TC), or more specifically changes in input–output coefficients, showed a small increase during the later period.

This indicates that the growth of manufacturing output was mainly attributable to DDE and IS in the early period and to DDE and EE in the later period. DDE was the most important factor for the growth of manufacturing output in both periods, as would usually be expected. Trade effects, however, shifted significantly between the two periods. These results support the conclusion that import substitution was much more important to Korea's industrialization during the period 1955–63 than was export growth, but that situation reversed itself during the later period. This conclusion partially corroborates the hypothesis that the reform package of the mid-1960s was quite effective in altering the pattern of industrialization in Korea.

CRITICISM AND LESSONS

The objectives of the reform package could not all be accomplished owing partly to the unsatisfactory implementation of the policy measures by the government and partly to changes in the economic environment after the initiation of the policy measures. For instance, the government was able to succeed in completely unifying the exchange rate but was not quite able to maintain the realistic 1965 level of the PPP-adjusted exchange rate after the exchange rate unification in 1965. We can say that the government succeeded in almost completely institutionalizing the system of export incentives, consistent with the new exchange rate and the export-oriented industrialization strategy. With regard to the import-liberalization program, however, no significant progress could be observed after the initiation of that program in 1967. It seems that this failure to make progress in import liberalization was at least partially attributable to the unsatisfactory performance of exchange-rate management by the government.

The limited success in the implementation of the reform package is reflected in the effects of that package on the economy. The reform package, on the whole, greatly increased the relative incentive to export vis-à-vis domestic sales, although the level of net export incentives compared with a free-trade situation was relatively low and was gradually reduced after the reform. As a result, commodity exports continued to increase rapidly in the late 1960s and 1970s, thereby making possible a rapid industrialization and growth of GNP during that period. The reform package was also effective in changing the pattern of industrialization in Korea. That is, it made the major sources of manufacturing output growth shift from domestic demand expansion and import substitution to domestic demand expansion and export expansion. Despite the rapid growth of exports and the rapid progress in industrialization, however, Korea could not significantly improve her balance of payments following the reform package. The main reason is that imports also expanded very rapidly after the reform measures, not because of progress in import liberalization but for other reasons. Although one can give many reasons why the imports expanded so rapidly as to cause a chronic deficit in the trade balance, the overvaluation of the won from time to time was certainly a major factor.

The first lesson we can draw from the Korean experience seems rather obvious. That is, it is critical to maintain a realistic effective exchange rate if a country is to achieve rapid export growth and an external balance simultaneously. Korea was able to achieve a rapid growth of exports by increasing direct and indirect subsidies to exports whenever the exchange rate became unrealistic, because of the higher inflation in Korea than in its major trading partners, but failed to attain an equilibrium in its balance of payments. Consequently Korea's external debts accumulated to a high of US $40 billion by the end of 1983, equivalent to nearly 50 percent of GNP. If Korea had maintained the 1965 level of the PPP-adjusted exchange rate through the 1970s, the country could have avoided the chronic deficits in its current balance on external transactions.

The second lesson is that although maintaining a realistic exchange rate is as critical as suggested above, it is not easy to succeed in the face of chronic high domestic inflation. Because devaluation usually raises the relative prices of imports, it causes a further increase in the rate of domestic inflation. For this reason, policymakers tend to delay devaluation for fear of its effects on domestic price levels. Once they have started to delay, the Korean experience indicates that it becomes more difficult to change the exchange rate because the margin of change would be much greater than the adjustment originally avoided. The adjustment then waits until the adverse effects of the currency overvaluation become intolerable in light of the country's balance of payments. I would therefore suggest that domestic price stabilization is very important in maintaining a realistic effective exchange rate.

The third lesson is that in the early stage of export promotion by a developing country, a big push by the government may be helpful for export expansion since products of new entrants into the world market are not well accepted and have to be offered at prices lower than prevailing world prices. The level of net export incentives, however, should be gradually reduced so that domestic industry becomes efficient and able to compete with foreign industries without much government support. Because the continuous expansion of exports and national product depends upon the development of efficient and competitive domestic industry, technological innovations should be promoted to enhance industrial productivity, mainly by means of gradual reductions in protection and government subsidies after a certain stage.

Fourth, the Korean experience suggests that it is a difficult task for a small, open developing country to attain its internal and external balances simultaneously. When world market conditions are favorable for Korean exports, Korea's external balance may be improved by the rapid expansion of exports. This improvement, however, causes rapid expansion of the money supply from the foreign-exchange sector, thereby creating a new problem in the country's demand management. During a period of recession in advanced industrial countries, however, the country experiences a recession and a deterioration in its balance of payments, caused not only by a decline in foreign demand for the country's exports but also by the contraction of liquidity by the foreign sector. The small, open developing country is also vulnerable to external shocks, as shown by the experience of Korea during the two worldwide oil shocks (1974–75 and 1979–80). In those circumstances the effects of external disturbances on the balance of payments could be reduced if the country had adopted a fluctuating exchange rate. But then the country's policymakers lose their ability to control domestic prices by means of fiscal and monetary policy. Any small developing country adopting an export-oriented development strategy should, therefore, take into account the problem of increasing vulnerability to external disturbances and prepare appropriate countermeasures.

Finally, it is suggested that devaluation becomes increasingly difficult to undertake as a country's external debts increase. Development theory suggests that the introduction of foreign capital is desirable for a capital-scarce developing country with a relatively high rate of return on capital. The inflow of foreign capital then augments the shortage of domestic capital and contributes to an acceleration of economic growth rate in the country. Although this theory might be correct, we should not neglect the fact that once the external debts accumulate to a substantial level, the government may lose its ability to adjust the exchange rate freely when required for attainment of an external equilibrium, because of strong pressure from large business groups with foreign debts. There is a danger, when a country cannot devalue its currency to achieve an external balance, that external debts may continuously increase to a level unmanageable by the economy. It is therefore emphasized that a developing country should first try to increase domestic saving before trying to borrow from abroad. In this way, the level of foreign debt could be restricted to a manageable level to retain the country's ability to freely adjust its exchange rate.

6 The Interest-Rate Reform of 1965 and Domestic Saving

by Kwang Suk Kim

During 1960–65 the level of gross domestic investment was less than 15 percent of GNP, except in 1963 when it was 18.1 percent. Inasmuch as gross domestic savings ranged only from 0.8 to 8.7 percent of GNP during that period, the larger part of the gross domestic investment still had to be financed by foreign grants and loans. Despite the low ratio of investment to GNP, the growth rate of GNP started to accelerate in 1963. The average annual growth rate of GNP during 1963–65 was about 8.2 percent, which was more than double the 3.6 percent average annual growth rate of the preceding nine years (1954–62). The high growth during 1963–65 seems to have resulted from both increased utilization of existing industrial capacity to meet rapidly increasing demand, and increased agricultural production because of favorable weather conditions (ROK 1966:22).

To make up for the shortage of domestic capital and to activate the sluggish domestic economy, the government resorted to fiscal deficit financing and monetary expansion in 1961–63. The result was a return to high inflation after a period of price stability in 1958–60, which had been attained by strong implementation of the financial stabilization program. A new stabilization program had to be instituted in late 1963. The rate of price inflation measured by the national WPI declined from an annual average of about 20 percent during 1960–64 to about 10 percent a year beginning in 1965. However, because Korea had experienced a long period of inflation, a general expectation of price inflation still existed.

The economic environment that existed in 1965 was not favorable for the country's financial development. Korea's organized financial market as of 1965 consisted mainly of the central bank, five commercial banks, and four special banks—the National Agricultural Cooperatives Federation (NACF), the Medium Industry Bank, the Korea Development Bank (KDB), and the Citizens National Bank. Each of the commercial banks maintained a large network of branches throughout the country, and offered not only checking accounts but also various savings deposits with different terms. Special banks, excluding the KDB, offered similar savings accounts. The general public, however, avoided depositing their savings in these financial institutions; time and savings deposits did not increase in real terms between 1962 and September 1965, despite strong savings campaigns by both the government and the financial institutions (Table 6.1 and Table 6.2).

Table 6.1. Trend in financial savings before and after the interest-rate reform: 1962–72 (in 10^9 current won)

Month/year	Time deposits	Installment savings	Mutual installments	Notice deposits	Saving associations	Other savings[a]	Money in trust	Total[b]
12/62	6.7	2.2	0.9	2.2	0.2	0.0	2.3	14.5
12/63	4.9	3.7	1.6	2.3	0.3	0.0	5.0	17.8
12/64	4.4	4.2	2.2	3.2	0.4	0.0	5.6	20.1
06/65	5.4	4.6	2.8	3.9	0.5	0.0	6.6	23.8
09/65	5.9	4.9	3.1	4.4	0.6	0.0	7.3	26.2
10/65	12.9	5.1	3.2	3.7	0.6	0.0	7.3	32.8
11/65	15.2	5.4	3.3	3.9	0.6	0.0	7.3	35.7
12/65	17.5	5.9	3.5	2.9	0.7	0.1	7.6	38.2
03/66	21.8	8.0	3.8	4.3	0.7	0.1	9.2	47.9
06/66	27.5	11.0	4.3	4.5	0.8	0.1	10.7	58.8
09/66	34.7	15.3	4.8	4.7	1.0	0.1	13.6	74.1
12/66	37.0	19.9	5.3	6.7	1.0	0.1	15.5	85.6
06/67	54.2	28.6	5.8	9.5	1.2	0.1	22.0	121.3
12/67	72.4	36.0	7.0	11.2	1.4	0.8	30.0	158.9
12/68	147.6	71.8	11.1	11.8	2.0	11.3	51.7	307.2
12/69	249.8	144.2	17.1	12.5	2.9	25.1	67.2	518.7
12/70	318.0	176.3	25.1	17.5	4.1	35.3	79.3	655.6
12/71	395.8	221.3	31.5	11.1	5.8	43.2	124.8	833.5
12/72	486.4	294.5	36.6	20.1	7.4	66.5	158.4	1,070.0

Source: BOK, Economic Statistics Yearbook (1962–73).

a. Includes the new household deposits and the housing installment deposits established in 1967.

b. Amounts may not sum to totals because of rounding errors.

The deposit rates offered by the financial institutions were unfavorable in the light of people's price expectations. Interest rates on bank deposits and loans were maintained at low levels owing to the artificial ceiling rates imposed by the monetary authorities (the Ministry of Finance and the central bank). For many years during the period 1960–65, the highest bank deposit rate (equal to a ceiling rate) was actually negative in real terms, if the annual rate of inflation is taken into account. It was natural, therefore, to expect that demand for loans from the financial institutions would chronically exceed the supply of loanable funds generated by deposits into the financial institutions. The government or the monetary authorities had to intervene directly in the allocation of scarce loanable funds, because the rate of interest could not bring about an equilibrium in the financial market. Although the government well understood the need to increase saving through financial institutions, it was more concerned about the negative effect of high interest rates on investment and, as a result, was slow in moving toward raising the interest rates on bank deposits and loans.

Under such conditions, investment in equities would be attractive to individual savers. There was, however, little opportunity for average individual savers to invest in such equities in an economy where the predominant form of enterprise was a closely held or family corporation. As of 1965 the stocks of only 17 corporations were listed in the Korea Stock Exchange, and most of these stocks were actually issued by public corporations. It is not surprising that the lack of financial investment opportunities resulted in reduced personal savings and the use of savings for real estate speculation and for lending out in the unorganized financial markets that operated outside the domain of the monetary authorities' regulations.

The unregulated or unorganized financial markets flourished notoriously in Korea during 1960–65. One estimate put outstanding assets and liabilities in the unorganized markets on the order of 40–45 billion won in 1964 (Gurley, Patrick, and Shaw 1965:81). That figure was equivalent to almost one-quarter of private-sector liabilities in primary securities and one-third of the private sector's portfolio assets in primary securities. The size of outstanding assets and liabilities in the unorganized market ranged from 56 to 63 percent of total domestic credit at the end of 1964. Interest rates on loans from the unorganized money markets varied widely, depending upon the credit standing of borrowers and the amount of the loans involved. The interest rate most frequently quoted in the unorganized market was about 48–60 percent per annum in 1964–65 (before the reform), whereas the highest bank rates on time deposits and loans were only 15 and 16 percent, respectively.

MAIN FEATURES OF THE REFORM

The Democratic Republican government that came into power in December 1963, succeeding the military government, started in early 1964 to

Table 6.2. Trends in money supply, quasi-money loans of deposit-money (in 10^9 won, unless otherwise stated)

End of year	In current prices				GNP deflator[b] (1975=100) (E)
	Money supply (M_1) (A)	Quasi-money (B)	Money supply (M_2) (C=A+B)	Loans of DMB[a] (D)	
1962	39	13	52	43	11.6 (18.4)
1963	42	13	55	49	15.0 (29.3)
1964	49	15	64	53	19.5 (30.0)
1965	66	31	97	72	20.7 (6.2)
1966	85	72	157	103	23.7 (14.5)
1967	123	131	254	178	27.4 (15.6)
1968	178	259	437	331	31.8 (16.1)
1969	252	453	705	563	36.5 (14.8)
1970	308	590	898	722	42.2 (15.6)
1971	358	727	1,085	920	47.3 (12.1)
1972	519	933	1,452	1,198	54.7 (15.6)
1973	730	1,251	1,981	1,588	61.9 (13.2)
1974	946	1,511	2,457	2,428	80.2 (29.6)
1975	1,182	1,968	3,150	2,906	100.0 (24.7)
1976	1,544	2,661	4,205	3,725	117.7 (17.7)
1977	2,173	3,703	5,874	4,709	136.9 (16.3)
1978	2,714	5,215	7,929	6,609	165.1 (20.6)
1979	3,275	6,604	9,878	8,978	197.0 (19.3)
1980	3,807	8,728	12,535	12,204	247.9 (25.8)

Source: BOK, *Economic Statistics Yearbook* (1962–81).

a. Deposit-money banks (DMB) include all commercial and special banks except the Korean Development Bank.

b. Figures in parentheses indicate annual percentage change in the GNP deflator.

promote various economic policy reforms for attaining the basic goal of export-oriented industrialization and growth. The exchange-rate reform was carried out in May 1964. The second target of the policy reform was to change the structure of bank interest rates. Tax reform and trade liberalization were on the agenda for future action.

To prepare for the interest-rate reform, the Korean government and the Bank of Korea began, in early 1965, to study the complicated structure of interest rates. At that time, interest rates in the organized financial market were not only unrealistically low compared with the average market yield on national bonds and interest rates in unorganized markets, but also showed wide variation by source of funds and by lending institution. On the basis of their study, the government prepared a reform proposal recom-

banks, and ceiling deposit rate, in both nominal and real values: 1962–80

In 1975 constant prices				Ceiling deposit rate (%)	
Money supply (M_1) (F=A/E)	Quasi-money (G=B/E)	Money supply (M_2) (H=C/E)	Loans of DMB[a] (I=D/E)	Nominal[c] (J)	Real[d] (K)
336	112	448	371	15.0	1.0
280	86	366	327	15.0	–3.4
251	77	328	272	15.0	–14.3
319	149	468	348	18.8	–11.2
359	303	662	435	30.0	23.8
448	478	927	650	30.8	15.5
560	814	1,374	1,040	27.6	12.0
690	1,241	1,931	1,542	23.8	7.7
729	1,398	2,127	1,711	22.8	8.0
757	1,536	2,293	1,945	22.1	6.5
949	1,705	2,654	2,190	15.8	3.7
1,179	2,021	3,200	2,565	12.6	–3.0
1,179	1,884	3,063	3,027	15.0	1.8
1,182	1,968	3,150	2,906	15.0	–14.6
1,312	2,260	3,572	3,165	15.5	–9.2
1,587	2,705	4,290	3,440	15.8	–1.9
1,644	3,158	4,802	4,003	16.5	0.2
1,662	3,352	5,014	4,557	18.6	–2.0
1,536	3,520	5,056	4,923	22.9	3.6

c. Average nominal rate for each year estimated, weighting by the number of months.
d. Column (J) minus the annual percentage increase in column (E) lagged one year.

mending that the high interest-rate strategy be implemented by the second quarter of the same year. The actual implementation of the reform proposal was delayed, however, until the end of September owing partly to some opposition within the government and partly to the National Assembly's slow action in amending the Interest Rate Limitation Law, which prescribed the upper ceiling on interest rates at 20 percent per annum. The National Assembly amended the law on 14 September, raising the upper ceiling from 20 to 40 percent per annum. The interest-rate reform was finally announced and put into effect on 30 September 1965. Cole and Park (1983:201) suggest that the interest-rate reform was announced on that date because there was a provision in the annual stabilization program for 1965, jointly agreed upon by the Korean and American governments as the basis for the annual U.S. aid program to Korea, that such reform would be implemented by the third quarter of that year.

It seems that the monetary authorities designed the high interest-rate strategy for Korea mainly on the basis of the successful experience of Taiwan's high interest-rate policy during 1950–58. The Bank of Korea had sent its research staff to Taiwan in early 1965 to study the design, implementation, and results of Taiwan's high interest-rate policy. (For details on the Taiwanese experience, see Irvine and Emery 1966.) In addition, recommendations made by John Gurley, Hugh Patrick, and Edward Shaw—renowned experts on money and finance—provided valuable guidance to Korean policymakers. These American professors collaborated on a study of the Korean financial system, commissioned by the USAID program. Recommendations in their report of July 1965 covered a wide range of necessary policy measures for improvement of the Korean financial system, including the suggestion that the interest rates on both bank deposits and loans be raised by removing artificial ceilings (Cole and Park 1983: 298–303). It seems that the authors played an important role in the formulation of the reform package, not only because they provided technical advice but also because they were influential in persuading high-level government officials and politicians who had been reluctant to accept the high interest-rate policy.

When the government announced the reform measure, the Korean business sector, particularly large enterprises, expressed considerable displeasure. The reason for their complaints was the expected increase in the cost of bank loans, and therefore that the high interest-rate strategy would lead to a high rate of domestic inflation due to the cost-push effect of the higher interest rates on the price level. Some business leaders also expressed concern that the high interest rates might reduce domestic investment and consequently result in a recession. The government responded with an advertisement campaign for the reform. It seems, however, that the government considered the complaints of large businesses when it raised the interest rates on special bank loans financed from government funds in October 1965.

The purpose of the reform was to sharply raise both deposit and loan rates of financial institutions in order to attract private savings into the organized financial markets and at the same time to discourage bank loans for unproductive purposes. The Monetary Board of Korea, a committee within the central bank, announced that the ceiling rate on saving deposits was being raised from 15 percent per annum to a high 30 percent, while the ceiling rate on ordinary bank loans (unspecified short-term loans) was being raised from 16 to 26 percent per annum (Table 6.3).

The Monetary Board set the maximum interest rate on savings deposits at 2.5 percent per month so that each bank could adjust its deposit rates by term structure within the ceiling rate. All banking institutions, however, adopted a uniform schedule of deposit and loan rates (Table 6.3), by an agreement of the Korean Bankers' Association, thus avoiding severe interbank competition. The reform measure not only sharply raised the interest

Table 6.3. Changes in principal interest rates of banking institutions as of 30 September 1965 (% per annum)

Interest rates	Old rate	New rate[a]
Rates on deposits		
Time deposits		
3 months maturity	9.0	18.0 (1.4)
6 months maturity	12.0	24.0 (1.8)
12 months maturity	15.0	26.4 (2.0)
18 months maturity		30.0 (2.2)
Notice deposits	3.65	5.0
Savings deposits	3.6	7.2
Installment savings deposits	10.0	30.0
Passbook deposits	1.8	1.8
Demand deposits	0.0	0.0
Rates on loans		
Discount on commercial bills	14.0	24.0
Loans on other bills (unspecified)	15.0	26.0
Overdraft	18.5	26.0
Overdue loans	20.0	36.5
Call loans	12.0	22.0
Credits for exports and supply of goods to U.S. armed forces[b]	6.5	6.5

Source: BOK, *Economic Statistics Yearbook* (1967).

a. Indicates the actual rates agreed upon by the Korean Bankers Association. The rates given in parentheses are the monthly interest rates corresponding to the annual rates indicated. (No compounding of the monthly rate is formally permitted by financial institutions.)

b. In the case of unperformed export or supply of U.S. offshore procurement, the rate on other bills is applied.

rate on time deposits but also set the interest rate on a monthly basis, following the general practice in unorganized money markets during the period. That meant that, for time deposits, depositors could take interest earnings at the end of each month. An automatic compounding of interest earning by month was not permitted by the banking institutions, but depositors could have the interest earning compounded monthly by contracting to deposit it into installment savings accounts.

Interest rates on various types of bank loans were also raised after the ceiling rate set by the monetary authorities was raised to 26 percent. But one of the special features of the reform was that the ceiling loan rate was set lower than the maximum deposit rate. The purpose of this "reverse margin" between the deposit and loan rates was, of course, to place emphasis on increasing financial saving, while not raising the cost of loans so high as to discourage sound business borrowing. To make up the possible reduction of bank earnings resulting from the reverse margin between the deposit and loan rates, a new system of subsidizing deposit banks was introduced. That system required the central bank to pay interest on the bank reserves against time and savings deposits deposited at the central bank. The interest rate that the central bank would pay on bank reserves was not fixed, but was to be adjusted according to the size of reduction in bank earnings.[1] A higher rate of 36.5 percent was set, however, for overdue loans to prevent loans from being overdue because of the deposit rate being higher than the loan rate.

To determine how realistic the new interest rates on deposits and loans were in the Korean context, it might be helpful to give some indications of the market rate of interest and the rate of return on capital in the country. As already suggested, the interest rates in unorganized money markets generally ranged between 4 and 5 percent per month. This unorganized market rate could not be accepted as the market rate of interest that would bring about an equilibrium in the organized financial markets, because, as Bottomley (1963:637–47) suggested, it included an additional premium for risk. An average yield on national bonds floated in the market was around 1.9 to 2.0 percent in 1964 and during the first nine months of 1965. The monthly yield on national bonds provided an important indicator of the market rate of interest because it was generally determined by market demand for and supply of such bonds without much intervention by the monetary authorities. Therefore, even though the ceiling deposit rate of 2.5 percent per month was about half the interest rate in unorganized money markets, it was much more attractive than the market yield on public bonds.

As regards the bank loan rate, the government originally announced that even if it were sharply raised to 26 percent, the average interest burden of industries might not increase. The government announcement indicated that if business borrowing from unorganized markets at a higher interest rate were reduced by the increased supply of bank loans at an annual interest rate of 26 percent, a weighted average interest burden on industries might be unaffected or reduced in the long run. In any case, the new ceiling loan rate was not considered too high to discourage business borrowing from the financial institutions, in view of the rate of return on capital in Korea, and also the lending rate in unorganized markets. A study of capital costs based on the survey of selected industrial establishments suggested that an average annual rate of return in Korean manufacturing industries was 13.5 percent in real terms in the mid-1960s (KEDI 1967:79). The Bank of Korea's analysis, however, disclosed that the ratios of net profit to net worth in Korean manufacturing in 1963 and 1964 were 19 and 15 percent,

---

1. This system of paying interest on reserves was originally suggested by Gurley, Patrick, and Shaw (1965:30–36), as was the establishment of a stabilization account in the central bank as a monetary control technique.

respectively. The same source also indicated that the ratio of payable interest and net profit to gross capital was about 12 to 13 percent in 1963–64 (BOK, *Economic Statistics Yearbook*, 1966:210–11). Because of the general practice of statistical underreporting on profits during this period, however, it was generally believed that the marginal product of capital in Korea was as high as 20 percent in real terms.[2]

There was no explicit aim to set the real rate of interest equal to the average rate of return on capital. The government, however, tended to compare the implicit real rate of bank loans with the various indicators of capital profitability, assuming an annual inflation rate of about 10 percent as in 1965. Inasmuch as the interest elasticity of investment demand was unknown in Korea, the maximum loan rate that would not discourage investment could be found by such a comparison.

It must be made clear that the loan rates described above were to be applied only to loans from banking funds. Although rates on loans from government funds were also raised, they were much lower than those for bank funds. The rates on long-term, government-fund loans generally ranged from 7.5 to 12.0 percent per annum depending upon the government budgetary source, with the exception of long-term loans for irrigation and housing, which ranged only from 3.5 to 4.0 percent per year. These government-fund loans at lower interest rates were supplied mainly through the KDB and the NACF for long-term investment in key industries and in the agricultural sector.

Because the changes in interest rates on government-fund loans were small, the interest-rate reform resulted in a widening of the gap between the loan rate on banking funds and that on government funds. This was a major point of criticism at the time of reform. The government, however, argued that the preferential rate on loans from government funds was needed to attract private investment in certain sectors or industries that the government wanted to promote. Another argument was that the rate on long-term loans should be based on a long-run expectation of interest-rate movements. That argument shows that the Korean policymakers who had designed the reform considered the high interest-rate strategy to be a temporary measure to cope with the problems of low savings and high demand for investable funds under inflationary conditions. The Korean policymakers seemed to have thought that price stability could be attained in the near future and that the interest rates would decline in the long run.

The interest rate on export credit was maintained at its pre-reform level of 6.5 percent per annum (Table 6.3), thus widening the interest-rate gap between export credit and other commercial loans. As a result, the lower

2. Brown (1973:203–06) attempted to estimate the real rate of return on capital in Korea using national income account data for 1962–67. His results indicate that the real rate of return on new investment was somewhat higher than 20 percent during that period.

rate on export credit further intensified incentives to exporters. This favorable export credit was made available to all exporters who could present export letters of credit as collateral. Despite the lower interest rate on their export credit, it was quite profitable for the banking institutions that extended such credit, because they could obtain financial resources through the central bank's rediscount of export bills at an annual interest rate of only 3.5 percent.

The interest-rate reform of 1965 was accompanied by a shift in monetary control techniques from the previous reliance on a direct method to the use of indirect instruments. Before the interest-rate reform, domestic credit had been controlled by imposing ceilings on bank loans. During the reform these ceilings were removed, thereby allowing the banking institutions to expand loans within the limits of their excess reserves. At the same time, the Bank of Korea introduced the stabilization account proposed by Gurley, Patrick, and Shaw (1965) and also decided to use the method of forced sales of the central bank's stabilization bonds to the financial institutions for the purpose of monetary control through manipulation of bank reserves. These two instruments were to be used to complement the instrument of legal reserve requirements.

The interest-rate reform resulted in a rapid increase in bank savings deposits beginning in the fourth quarter of 1965. Bank loans also expanded rapidly as savings deposits increased, because the loan ceilings that had been imposed by the government before the reform were completely abolished. In addition, the inflow of foreign capital started to increase rapidly in 1966, partly because of the signing of a diplomatic normalization agreement between Korea and Japan in 1965 and partly owing to the increased differential between domestic and foreign interest rates. The system of bank guarantees for the repayment of foreign loans, instituted in 1962, began to be actively used immediately after the interest-rate reform as an instrument to facilitate borrowing from abroad by Korean enterprises.[3] In any case, the rapid increase in foreign capital inflow, together with the continued expansion of Korean exports, caused a sudden jump in the growth of foreign exchange reserves, thereby creating a new source of excessive monetary expansion. The main issue of the monetary policy was, therefore, how to control excessive liquidity arising from the increased foreign capital inflow, as well as the expansion of domestic bank loans.

To control the money supply for price stabilization, the monetary authorities had to raise the legal reserve requirements for loans drastically in February 1966. Between October 1966 and March 1967 a high marginal reserve requirement of 45–50 percent was imposed on incremental deposits on top

---

3. The system of bank guarantees for repayment of foreign loans might have increased the interest rate differential between domestic and foreign loans by lowering interest rates on foreign loans more than would have been the case without such a system.

of the basic reserve requirements, which were 35 percent for demand deposits, 20 percent for short-term savings deposits, and 15 percent for long-term savings deposits. In addition to this method of increasing reserve requirements, the Bank of Korea attempted to sterilize the excess reserves of deposit-money banks by forcing the banks to purchase its stabilization bonds and to deposit bank reserves in the central bank's stabilization account. That action indicates that the sharp increase in banks' time and savings deposits that was made possible by the higher interest rate was used largely for sterilizing the excessive expansion of bank reserves coming mainly from the explosive inflows of foreign capital, including cash loans. These developments contradicted the original purpose of the interest-rate reform.

Under the situation, the government could adopt one of three policies, consistent with the basic goal of export-oriented industrialization and growth. The first policy option was to restrict foreign capital inflows by means of direct control or by the imposition of an interest-equalization tax on imported foreign capital. This policy option was suggested by many economists but was not accepted by the government, out of fear that such action might shut off foreign finance, which had just begun to increase. The second alternative was to increase imports through trade liberalization so that foreign exchange reserves would not accumulate too rapidly. That policy alternative could not be undertaken because of strong business pressure to protect domestic industries. The third option was to accumulate foreign reserves, squeeze the supply of domestic credit, and gradually reduce domestic interest rates, particularly bank deposit rates. The third option was the one the government adopted. (These points are also discussed in Cole and Park 1983:208–09.)

The high deposit and loan rates of banking institutions, which became effective in September 1965, were maintained without change until April 1968, when the monetary authorities started gradually to reduce the bank rates (Table 6.4). By June 1969 the maximum interest rates on deposits and loans were reduced to 22.8 and 24 percent, respectively, thereby completely eliminating the reverse margin between the deposit and loan rates that had been hurting the profitability of financial institutions. The high interest-rate strategy ended on 3 August 1972, when the government announced the Presidential Emergency Decree for Stabilization and Growth, which included a drastic reduction in interest rates of banking institutions among other important policy measures. After the August 3rd measure of 1972, the high interest-rate strategy was not adopted again except for a short period in the early 1980s when the economy was under a high inflationary condition due to a sharp rise in world oil prices and to a domestic excess demand situation. Thus, the high interest-rate strategy was applied in Korea for about seven years after its adoption in late 1965.

Table 6.4. Changes in the ceiling deposit and loan interest rates of banking
institutions: 30 September 1965 to 28 June 1982 (% per annum)

Effective from	Ceiling deposit rate	Ceiling loan rate[a]
09/30/65	30.0	26.0
04/01/68	27.6	26.0
10/01/68	25.2	25.2[b]
06/01/69	22.8	24.0
06/28/71	21.3	22.0
01/17/72	17.4	19.0
08/03/72	12.6	15.5
01/24/74	15.0	15.5
08/02/76	16.2	18.0
10/04/77	14.4	16.0
06/13/78	18.6	19.0
01/12/80	24.0	25.0
09/16/80	21.9	22.0
11/08/80	19.5	20.0
11/09/81	18.6	19.0
11/30/81	17.4	18.0
12/29/81	16.2	17.0
01/14/82	15.0	16.0
03/29/82	12.6	14.0
06/28/82	8.0	10.0

Source: BOK, *Economic Statistics Yearbook* (1965–83).

a. Indicates short-term rate on ordinary loans (loans on other bills) for other than "superior enterprises." Local banks, however, could charge a slightly higher rate than the rate reported here.

b. End of reverse margin.

THEORETICAL APPROPRIATENESS OF THE REFORM

The primary objective of the 1965 reform was to increase private saving through financial institutions, and the secondary objective was to enhance the role of interest rates in resource allocation and monetary control. Here I consider only the theoretical appropriateness of the reform in relation to its primary objective. The theoretical appropriateness is expected to be more controversial in relation to the primary objective than to the secondary objective.

As previously stated, financial saving in the form of bank deposits were not increasing in real terms during the first half of the 1960s, but the demand for such saving was growing rapidly for financing domestic investment. The most probable reason for the sluggish growth of financial saving during that period was the low real interest rates offered by financial institutions, which were, in fact, negative in some years when the annual rate of inflation was taken into account. In that respect, the interest-rate reform of 1965 was an appropriate policy choice of the government for an increase in financial saving.

It is generally believed that economic development is accompanied by rapid growth of financial assets, because the financing of economic development in a market economy necessitates the accumulation of debt and financial assets, as explained by Gurley and Shaw (1956:257–76; 1955:515–38; 1967:257–68). The process of financing economic development through the accumulation of debt and financial assets is generally divided into two types—direct finance and indirect finance. In the mid-1960s, when the interest-rate reform was undertaken, the technique of direct finance was still underdeveloped in Korea. Indirect finance, therefore, played a far greater role in mobilizing savings and directing them to productive investment in Korea than it did in developed countries where the technique of direct finance was well developed.

In economies where the capital markets are highly developed, saving deposits in banking institutions is only one of the saving instruments available to individuals. An increase in the bank savings deposits may therefore represent only a shift between savings deposits and other financial assets. In that case, raising the interest rate on bank time deposits may not contribute to increasing financial saving even if the higher interest rate brings about an increase in bank savings deposits. The situation of Korea in 1965, however, was quite different from that of developed countries. In Korea, where the bond and equities market was still underdeveloped, financial saving through banking institutions was the most important savings instrument available to the majority of the population, if savings through unorganized money markets were excluded. Life insurance and postal savings could be important in attracting small savers, although savings through such nonbank financial intermediaries had been relatively small until 1965. The interest rates applied in such savings schemes were usually adjusted in response to the change in the bank interest rates, without much time lag.

The rate adjustments indicate that a sharp increase in bank deposit rates, which could increase savings deposits, may contribute to increasing the flow of savings into the organized financial market of Korea. An important question, then, is whether this increase in financial saving will ultimately contribute to increasing aggregate domestic saving. This question is actually equivalent to asking whether the high interest rates of banking institutions contribute to increasing aggregate real saving and investment.

Conventional theory does not seem to support the hypothesis that higher interest rates will increase aggregate domestic saving. According to the Keynesian view, aggregate saving is a function of income level in an economy. Some development economists have taught that aggregate saving is determined primarily by the growth of a modern business sector in an economy. For that reason, the saving strategies suggested for developing countries during the 1960s usually emphasized forced saving through taxation and credit expansion while often neglecting the possible strategies for increasing voluntary saving. As pointed out in a report published by the Economic Commission for Asia and the Far East (ECAFE 1962), many developing countries in Asia deliberately designed monetary and fiscal policies to maintain interest rates in organized money markets at low levels. An immediate objective of such policies was the reduction of the interest burden on government borrowing. Aside from that purpose, the policies were based on the Keynesian view that aggregate saving is a function of income and that there is a strong inverse relationship between the level of the interest rate and the volume of investment (ECAFE 1962:22).[4] That kind of low interest-rate policy was not a unique case for developing countries in the Asian region but a general phenomenon for most developing countries in all regions, as suggested by Tun Wai (1956:249–78). That it was so indicates that there were no strong theoretical and empirical supports for adopting the high interest-rate strategy as a means of mobilizing voluntary private savings. Despite the weak support on both theoretical and empirical grounds, Korean policymakers announced that the high interest-rate policy would greatly contribute to increasing aggregate domestic saving. Justifications for this view were not made clear at the time of the reform. Nevertheless, the high interest-rate policy was an appropriate policy choice for increasing domestic savings in Korea.

First, bank deposits in Korea played a far greater role in the mobilization of savings than in many developed countries. The higher interest rate on bank time deposits may have resulted in some shift of savings from other forms to bank deposits. But, because the capital market was still underdeveloped, it was not expected that any substantial amount of savings could be shifted from the capital market to the financial market. It was expected that an increase in time deposits would come mainly from the reduction of household current consumption and the shift in savings from unorganized money markets. Because savings in the form of unorganized money market assets not only were risky for savers but also were used largely for unproductive purposes, such as the purchase of consumer durables and family ritual expenses, the shift of savings from the unorganized market to the organized market was considered beneficial in that aggregate savings were increased and directed into productive investment.

Second, it was expected that domestic investment would increase despite the higher interest rate on bank loans, because the rate of return on investment was thought to be higher than the new loan rate. In the mid-1960s the shortage of domestic savings was considered to be a major constraint

---

4. Along this line, Jain (1965:29–40) even suggested that a zero (or nearly zero) rate of interest should be maintained for a higher level of savings and high growth of GNP.

on economic growth because intended investment far exceeded the supply of savings, unlike the situation in advanced countries. Therefore, if higher interest rates could initially induce people to save a larger share of their incomes, this increase in saving would in turn contribute to an increase in investment and consequently to the growth of national income. The growth of national income induced by the initial increase in saving would again positively affect the saving propensity of the nation. This process of increasing domestic saving would be repeated and domestic saving would continue to grow after the interest-rate reform. (This point was also suggested by Brown 1973:199–202.)

EFFECTS OF THE REFORM

The interest-rate reform of 1965 had been expected to have wide-ranging effects on the economy, including both direct and indirect effects on financial markets, aggregate saving and investment, and the pattern of resource allocation in the country. The discussion here is limited to the direct effects of the reform on financial saving, aggregate real saving and investment, organized financial market operations, and unorganized money market conditions.

Rapid Increase in Financial Savings

Contrary to conventional expectations regarding public responses to changes in interest rates in developing countries, the people's response to the sharp rise in interest rates was both rapid and substantial. The rise in bank deposit rates was followed by a rapid increase in financial savings, defined to include the time and savings deposits of banking institutions as well as commercial banks' trust accounts. Some of the rapid response was also due partly to an intensified savings campaign staged by the government immediately after the interest-rate reform.

Total financial saving (time and savings deposits plus money in trust) increased by about 25 percent within one month of enactment of the interest-rate reform. The rate of increase in time deposits was much greater than the rate of increase for total financial saving (Table 6.3). Other types of savings deposits remained almost unchanged, whereas time deposits more than doubled during the first month after the reform.[5] This pattern of increase in financial saving was expected because the interest rate on time deposits was more favorable than that on short-term savings deposits such as notice deposits, or installment savings deposits (including mutual installment deposits). Installment savings could not be increased within a short period of time because under these savings schemes individual savers

---

5. A small shift from demand deposits to time deposits was observed immediately after the reform. The shift was relatively small and temporary, however. Demand deposits also increased after the reform. See BOK, *Economic Statistics Yearbook* (1966:table 26) and the Bank of Korea yearbooks for later years.

would usually deposit a small sum of money each month (by installment) until the contracted deposit target amount was reached. In any case, that pattern of increase in financial saving generally continued until December 1965 (Table 6.1).

To compare such a sharp increase in financial saving after the interest-rate reform with other financial indicators over a longer period, the data in Table 6.4 are helpful. To highlight some of the major changes after the reform, the total quasi-money (which is roughly equivalent to time and savings deposits of banking institutions) more than doubled in real terms between December 1965 and December 1966. It increased more than ten times in real terms in the six years from December 1965 until the end of 1971. Such a rapid increase was in marked contrast to the negative growth of real quasi-money between 1962 and 1964, during which time the ceiling deposit rate was held constant at 15 percent per annum despite a much higher rate of inflation in the country. The increase in real quasi-money was initially due to the rapid saving response by households and individuals. According to the flow of fund data published by the Bank of Korea, about 81 percent of the small increase in time and savings deposits in 1964 was contributed by individuals (BOK, *Economic Statistics Yearbook*, 1966, 1972). The share of contributions by individuals increased to 88 percent in 1966—that is, after the reform. The individual sector share in the increase of time and savings deposits, however, gradually declined thereafter to reach around 70 percent by 1971.

The increase in real quasi-money was very sharp as already explained, but the total level of money supply (M_1) was kept under control through a stabilization program. Real money supply increased by about 13 percent in 1966 and by about 137 percent between 1965 and 1971. In contrast, the broadly defined money supply (M_2) increased at a much more rapid rate than the narrowly defined money supply, because real quasi-money expanded sharply after the reform. Real M_2 increased nearly five times between 1965 and 1971. As a result, quasi-money, which had been roughly less than a quarter of the broadly defined money supply before the interest-rate reform, increased to 46 percent of M_2 by the end of 1966 and to 67 percent by the end of 1971. The nominal value of quasi-money expanded sharply from a mere 2 percent of money GNP in 1964 to nearly 7 percent in 1966 and then to 22 percent by 1971, but the narrowly defined money supply increased only from 6.8 percent of money GNP to roughly 11 percent between 1964 and 1971. Loans of deposit-money banks were also able to expand rapidly after the reform as the rapid increase in quasi-money made possible a rapid expansion of loanable funds.

Although the quasi-money expanded rapidly in relation to M_1, M_2, and GNP during the period of high interest rates, the rate of increase in quasi-money seems to have slowed considerably after 1972, the year in which the bank interest rates were sharply reduced by the monetary authorities.

After 1972 real deposit interest rates often became negative. Reflecting the decline in incentives to financial savers, real quasi-money increased by only 106 percent during the eight-year period from 1972 to 1980, though the narrowly defined money supply increased by about 62 percent during the same period. The nominal value of quasi-money barely increased from 23 to 25 percent of nominal GNP between 1972 and 1980.

Effect on Aggregate Saving and Investment

One who expects a rapid increase in savings through financial institutions after a rise in interest rates may not necessarily agree that the change in interest rates affects the aggregate levels of real saving and investment. Although this chapter has emphasized the important role of financial saving through banking institutions in the mobilization of domestic saving in Korea, it is still unclear whether the high interest-rate strategy actually caused a sharp increase in the aggregate levels of real saving and investment.

Two previous studies on the effect of the Korean interest-rate reform on aggregate domestic saving give somewhat different results. One by Brown (1973) attempted a regression analysis mainly to measure the effect of the 1965 reform on aggregate private saving. For that analysis Brown generally assumed that annual domestic private saving was a function of private disposable income, a nominal or real interest rate, and the domestic private savings lagged a year. Most of his regression results indicated that the regression coefficient of the interest rate variable was not only positive as expected but also statistically significant in explaining the ratio of private saving to private disposable income. Brown therefore concluded that the interest-rate reform of 1965 "caused the saving function to shift upward as people desired to save a larger share of their incomes" (Brown 1973:200). A more recent study by Cole and Park (1983), however, which did not undertake a regression analysis as in Brown's study, suggested that "the effect of the financial reform on domestic savings is ambiguous, because it was only one of many changes that contributed to the upward shift in the saving function" (Cole and Park 1983:211).

To examine the effect of the 1965 reform on aggregate domestic saving, I first prepared a statistical table showing the trends in the ratio of sectoral gross savings to GNP for Korea during 1962–82. Table 6.5 shows that the ratio of gross domestic saving to GNP increased rapidly after 1965. A close look at the data, however, indicates that the rapid increase in the gross domestic saving rate was mainly due to the increase in government saving—which could not have been affected by the higher interest rates of banking institutions.

During the period of high interest rates (1965–71), gross domestic saving increased from 7.4 to 15.4 percent of GNP. Only government savings showed a sharp increase, from 1.7 to 5.4 percent of GNP, during the same period, while business-sector savings remained almost unchanged at 7.5

Table 6.5. Trend in the ratio of sectoral gross savings to GNP: 1962–82 (%)

Year	Gross domestic saving rate				Foreign saving rate	Statistical discrepancy	Gross saving= gross investment
	Government	Business	Household	Subtotal			
1962	–1.5	7.1	–2.3	3.3	10.7	–1.1	12.8
1963	–0.4	7.1	2.0	8.7	10.4	–1.0	18.1
1964	0.5	6.5	1.8	8.7	6.9	–1.6	14.0
1965	1.7	7.7	–2.1	7.4	6.4	1.2	15.0
1966	2.8	7.5	1.6	11.8	8.4	1.3	21.6
1967	4.1	7.9	–0.6	11.4	8.8	1.7	21.9
1968	6.1	7.8	1.1	15.1	11.2	–0.4	25.9
1969	5.9	7.7	5.2	18.8	10.6	–0.6	28.8
1970	6.5	7.5	3.4	17.3	9.3	0.2	26.8
1971	5.4	7.5	2.5	15.4	10.7	–0.8	25.2
1972	3.6	9.1	3.0	15.7	5.2	0.7	21.7
1973	4.2	11.4	7.9	23.5	3.8	–1.7	25.6
1974	2.3	12.1	6.1	20.5	12.4	–1.9	31.0
1975	4.0	11.3	3.4	18.6	10.4	0.4	29.4
1976	6.2	10.9	6.0	23.1	2.4	–0.0	25.5
1977	5.6	10.9	8.6	25.1	0.6	1.6	27.3
1978	6.5	9.9	10.0	26.4	3.3	1.5	31.1
1979	7.2	9.7	9.7	26.6	7.6	1.2	35.4
1980	6.2	8.2	5.5	19.9	10.2	1.4	31.5
1981	6.7	8.3	4.6	19.6	7.9	0.9	28.4
1982	6.7	9.7	5.1	21.5	4.8	–0.1	26.2

Source: BOK, *National Income* (1982).

Note: Ratios are based on current price series. Percentages may not sum to totals because of rounding errors.

to 7.7 percent of GNP. In contrast, household savings, which should have been most affected by the high interest-rate policy, increased from –2.1 to 2.5 percent of GNP between 1965 and 1971. But the base year 1965 was an unusual year. The household saving rate even in 1963 and 1964 was 1.8 to 2.0 percent. Thus it might be more correct to say that the household saving rate simply showed a wide fluctuation by year during the period of high interest rates, rather than a notable increase.

Such a yearly fluctuation in the household saving rate may be an artifact resulting from the inclusion of "changes in agricultural inventories" in household saving. Although the changes in agricultural inventories directly affect the level of gross capital formation and therefore the level of domestic saving, they are primarily determined by the level of agricultural production in the current year because the major crop, rice, is harvested near the end of the calendar year in Korea. That implies that household saving in the form of increases in agricultural inventories is determined independently from the household propensity to save out of the current income. To eliminate the yearly fluctuation in the household saving rate caused by the fluctuation in agricultural inventories, one can easily adjust the income and saving data by subtracting the increases in agricultural inventories from both household disposable income and savings (Table 6.6). Apart from that adjustment, the adjusted household saving rate given in Table 6.6 is a better indicator of the household saving propensity than that given in Table 6.5 because it measures that sector's saving propensity out of all current disposable income—including transfers from abroad. The household sector's

Table 6.6. Trend in household saving rate, adjusted for change in agricultural inventories: 1962–81

Year	Disposable income (10^9 won) (A)	Savings (10^9 won) (B)	Change in agricultural inventories (%) (C)	Adjusted disposable income (10^9 won) (D=A–C)	Adjusted savings (10^9 won) (E=B–C)	Adjusted household saving rate (%) (F=E/D)
1962	291.0	–3.4	–5.6	296.6	2.2	0.7
1963	421.3	16.9	17.7	403.6	–0.8	–0.2
1964	617.8	25.2	20.8	597.0	4.4	0.7
1965	673.0	1.5	–0.1	673.1	1.6	0.2
1966	853.7	42.9	8.3	845.4	34.6	4.1
1967	1,022.4	17.1	–18.3	1,040.7	35.4	3.4
1968	1,279.3	48.3	–16.7	1,296.0	65.0	5.0
1969	1,681.1	152.4	47.7	1,633.4	104.7	6.4
1970	2,058.7	119.6	50.3	2,008.4	69.3	3.5
1971	2,554.0	118.1	62.3	2,491.7	55.8	2.2
1972	3,126.4	169.3	72.9	3,053.5	96.4	3.2
1973	4,000.6	477.2	44.7	3,955.9	432.5	10.9
1974	5,597.8	511.1	80.7	5,517.1	430.4	7.8
1975	7,350.0	405.1	115.4	7,234.6	289.7	4.0
1976	9,601.8	890.2	143.1	9,458.7	747.1	7.9
1977	12,308.2	1,553.7	198.6	12,109.6	1,355.1	11.2
1978	16,748.2	2,509.4	75.8	16,672.4	2,433.6	14.6
1979	21,108.0	3,001.1	261.6	20,846.4	2,739.5	13.1
1980	25,173.5	2,130.9	–458.2	24,715.3	2,589.1	10.5
1981	30,791.2	2,258.3	588.8	30,202.4	1,669.5	5.5

Source: BOK, *National Income* (1982).

Note: Amounts are expressed in current won.

domestic saving rate in Table 6.5 does not include saving out of such transfers from abroad.

In any case, the adjusted household saving rate showed a large increase after the interest-rate reform of 1965. As shown in Table 6.6, adjusted household saving, which had been less than 1 percent of disposable income until 1965, increased to 4.1 percent in 1966 and remained at least higher than 3.4 percent of disposable income until 1970. The adjusted household saving, however, declined to 2.2 percent of disposable income in 1971. It is normally expected that the higher interest rates would mainly affect household saving. There is no good reason to expect that government and business savings would be positively affected by the higher interest rates. In this respect, one may argue that the sudden jump in the adjusted household saving rate after 1965 reflected the positive effect of the interest-rate reform on domestic saving. There may be some truth in such an argument because the adjusted saving rate after 1965 became consistently higher than that prior to the 1965 reform.

The adjusted household saving rate, however, remained at a relatively high level even after 1972, when bank interest rates (both nominal and real) were again arbitrarily reduced by the government, although household saving had been fluctuating widely between 3 and 11 percent of disposable income. The fact that the household savings propensity was sustained at the higher levels after 1972 may reflect a habit-forming effect on saving. That is, the households that were induced to save a greater share of their income by the rise in interest rates were continuing to save a similar or even higher share of their increased income, even though the incentives to savers were largely removed by the reduction of interest rates. The higher saving rate after 1972 may also reflect the effect of average disposable income per household in the 1970s being higher than in the 1960s. In view of these developments after 1972, it is doubtful whether the sharp increase in the household saving rate (adjusted) after 1965 only reflected the effect of the high interest-rate policy adopted in 1965 and continued until early August 1972. As suggested by Cole and Park (1983), the higher ratio of household saving to disposable income after 1965 could have been made possible not only by the higher interest rates but also by many other factors, including the higher growth rate of income, better investment environment, and the relative price stability attained during 1965–73.

After the interest-rate reform of 1965, gross domestic investment expanded continuously in relation to GNP. As already suggested, gross domestic investment, which had been generally less than 15 percent of GNP until 1965, increased to 22 percent in 1966 and continuously expanded to reach about 29 percent by 1969. Even after 1969, the gross domestic investment rate was generally maintained at a level higher than 25 percent of GNP (22 percent in 1972 being the only exception). The large increase in gross domestic investment was made possible not only by the rapid increase in domestic saving but also by the continuous inflow of foreign saving. In any case, the growth of domestic investment after 1965 indicates that the higher interest rates of banking institutions did not discourage domestic investment, as expected by some people, but rather contributed to increasing such investment by increasing the supply of both domestic and foreign loans.

Effect on Organized Financial Markets

Because bank deposits, particularly time and savings deposits, increased rapidly after the interest-rate reform, the monetary authorities could expect to improve the techniques of monetary control as originally planned at the time of the reform. The monetary authorities therefore abolished the loan ceiling system and attempted to control the money supply through the indirect techniques of bank reserve manipulations. In early 1966 the monetary authorities began to experiment with all the indirect techniques of monetary control available in Korea. The inflow of foreign capital, mainly in the form of foreign loans, greatly accelerated in early 1966, because of the increased gap in interest rates between domestic and foreign financial markets after the 1965 reform. The increased inflow of foreign capital, together with the rapid expansion of Korean exports, caused a rapid accumulation of foreign reserves. To contract the monetary expansion coming from the rapid accumulation of foreign reserves, the central bank had not only to increase legal reserve requirements for banking institutions but also to freeze a substantial portion of bank deposits by means of forced sales of stabilization bonds and compulsory deposits in the central bank's stabilization account.

As a result, bank loans declined in relation to deposits until around the end of 1967, although the absolute level of bank loans expanded rapidly. The relative decline in bank loans, in addition to the profit squeeze caused by the reverse margin between the bank deposit and loan rates, contributed to a further deterioration of profitability in banking operations after the interest-rate reform.

Table 6.7 provides data on the profitability of banking operations before and after the 1965 reform. The weighted average annual rate of interest due for all commercial bank deposits increased from 2.7 percent in the first half of 1965 to 11.1 percent during the same period of 1966. The average interest rate on commercial bank loans also increased from 16.1 to 25.0 percent during the same period. The difference between the earning and cost ratios to all available funds, however, declined from 1.5 to –0.7 percentage points between the first half of 1965 and the same period of 1966. That is, the ratio of earnings (interest and other income) to total available funds was 9.5 percent, which was 1.5 percentage points higher than the ratio of costs (interest and operating costs) to total funds in the first half of 1965. The ratio of earnings to total available funds, however, became lower than the cost ratio in the first half of 1966. This was partly because the ratio of loans to

Table 6.7. Changes in the costs of funds and earnings of commercial banks before and after the interest-rate reform

Description	First half	
	1965	1966
Average interest rate on deposits		
(A) Interest accrued during the period (10^6 won)	504	3,606
(B) Average balance of deposits for the period (10^6 won)	36,933	65,052
(C) Annual average rate on deposits [2(A)/(B)] (%)	2.7	11.1
Average interest rate on loans		
(D) Interest accrued during the period (10^6 won)	2,180	5,769
(E) Average balance of loans for the period (10^6 won)	27,157	46,230
(F) Annual average rate on loans [2(D)/(E)] (%)	16.1	25.0
Annual ratio of costs and earnings		
(G) Annual ratio of costs to available funds (%)	8.0	13.6
(H) Annual ratio of earnings to working funds (%)	9.5	12.9
(I) Difference between the cost and earning ratio [(H) – (G)] (%)	1.5	–0.7

Source: BOK, *Economic Statistics Yearbook* (1967).

deposits was reduced from 73.5 to 71.1 percent between the two periods and because the ceiling rate on loans was lower than on deposits.

To provide some compensation for the reduction in the rate of banking funds utilization and for the reverse margin between the deposit and loan rates, the central bank paid a 5 percent rate of interest on bank reserves against time and savings deposits during 1966–67. But banking institutions actually started to benefit from the system of bank guarantees for the repayment of foreign loans as the inflow of foreign loans accelerated beginning in 1966. The banks could then collect about 1.0 to 1.5 percent on the face value of foreign loans as guarantee fees without really committing their own resources. Beginning in early 1968, the banks were able to gradually expand their loans in relation to deposits because monetary control had been relaxed somewhat.

Although a substantial portion of the increased financial savings was sterilized for the purpose of monetary control, particularly in the early period of the reform, bank loans to the private sector expanded sharply after September 1965. The higher interest rates on loans did not become a factor restricting loan activities in Korea. The banking funds derived from the increased financial savings were lent out to the business sector mostly for working capital; only about 10 percent of commercial bank loans was used for the purchase of industrial equipment. Even though the loans of banking institutions expanded rapidly after the reform, the supply of loanable funds remained as a scarce factor in the sense that demand for loanable funds exceeded the supply of such funds at the new rate of interest. This was probably due to the complementary relationship between domestic bank loans and foreign financing. Since the introduction of foreign capital was authorized mainly for fixed investment purposes, the domestic enterprises borrowing from abroad had to borrow also from domestic financial markets for working capital requirements. Of course, the restriction of bank loans for stabilization purposes also contributed to the continuous scarcity of bank loans in Korea.

Even so, the increased supply of bank loans at the higher rate of interest made it easier for the average business person to obtain a bank loan. Bank loans now were no longer the source of easy profits for corporations and individuals, because the loan rates were high enough to discourage unproductive investment. After the reform, it seemed that the bank loans were largely replaced by foreign loans as a source of easy profits since the interest rates on foreign loans were generally much lower than those on domestic loans. Because of the large inflows of foreign loans at rates lower than the domestic bank rate, the monetary authorities had to freeze a significant portion of domestic savings deposits to meet the overall money supply target. If the inflows of foreign capital had been effectively controlled to a reasonable minimum, the organized financial markets could have functioned more effectively in both mobilizing and allocating domestic resources.

Effect on Unorganized Money Markets

The activities of unorganized money markets were widespread in all sectors of the Korean economy before the interest-rate reform. The unorganized money markets were involved not only in money lending for households and small business but also in mobilizing and lending a fairly large amount of funds to big enterprises. It is difficult, however, to evaluate the effect of the interest-rate reform on unorganized money markets. Available data on the unorganized money market activities are not only scant, but also may not be reliable. For instance, a Bank of Korea survey conducted in the first quarter of 1967 indicated that no significant change had occurred in the unorganized market after the reform (BOK, *A Survey on Business Finance*, 1967:5–8). Some businesses still borrowed a portion of their financial requirements from the unorganized markets, where the dominant rate of interest was still about 4 to 5 percent per month as before the reform.

According to Bank of Korea survey data for the previous periods, interest rates in the unorganized market showed an upward trend until about mid-1966. The trend was probably due to a temporary shift of funds from the unorganized markets to bank deposits after the 1965 reform, whereas demand for such nonbank loans was not largely replaced by bank loans. The unorganized market rate, however, returned to the original level thereafter. There are indications that the activities of unorganized money markets continuously expanded in the late 1960s, with some setbacks in the initial period of the reform. In any case, the unorganized markets flourished until August 1972, when the Presidential Emergency Decree was issued to force both private moneylenders and business borrowers to report the outstanding volume of loans to the business sector and the business sector's debts to the unorganized money markets. The size of business enterprises' borrowings from the unorganized markets, reported and confirmed in accordance with the decree, amounted to about 346 billion won, equivalent to 23 percent of total domestic credit in 1972 and 42 percent of all outstanding loans of banking institutions, including the KDB, as of August 1972. But this volume of unorganized money market loans excludes the outstanding loans of the household sector, including farm households, which were not required to be reported by the government decree (Cole and Park 1983:163–65).

That explains why the interest-rate reform could not succeed in reducing unorganized money market activities as originally anticipated. How, then, could the unorganized markets continuously flourish even when the interest rates in the organized markets were substantially raised, and when the sizes of both domestic and foreign credit could be rapidly expanded after the reform? Here are a few points—not answers—related to these questions.

First, a rapid increase in domestic bank loans, together with the increased inflow of foreign capital after the interest-rate reform, made possible the rapid expansion of Korean industries, which in turn necessitated a further increase in external finance. This brought about a continuously increasing demand for domestic bank loans despite the high loan rates. Because of the increasing demand for bank loans and also for foreign loans, domestic bank loans were still allocated to industries on the basis of government guidelines that gave priority to those industries the government wanted to promote. Industries not favored by the government could not easily obtain bank credit or foreign capital even after the reform, and had to turn to unorganized markets for necessary external finance. This situation explains the continuous expansion of demand for unorganized money market loans after the reform.

Second, even if bank loans could be expanded, the unorganized market loans could not be completely replaced by bank credit, partly because of the rigid loan procedures of Korean banking institutions. The Korean banking system tended to place a heavy emphasis on loan securities (particularly real estate collateral), but moneylenders in the unorganized markets put more weight on the credit standings of borrowers. Bank loan procedures usually were also complicated and time-consuming, and therefore, were not a good source of for short-notice funding needs. A formal short-term money market had not yet been established in the late 1960s, so the unorganized money markets provided an economic source of credit for temporary short-term requirements (e.g., daily loans, loans for a month or two), whereas bank loans usually required various incidental expenses including insurance costs, paperwork, and time.

Finally, unorganized money market activities flourished even after the reform because they provided the only source of credit for the average household in Korea. As suggested, Korean banking institutions restricted their loans for household consumption needs (including housing finance) in the late 1960s.

CRITICISM AND LESSONS

The interest-rate reform of 1965 certainly brought about a sharp increase in savings through financial intermediaries, which in turn made possible an increase in the supply of bank loans. After the reform, the household saving propensity adjusted for the increases in agricultural inventories rose substantially, suggesting that the higher interest rates could have positively contributed to the growth of aggregate domestic saving in Korea. However, there is not enough evidence to show that the sudden jump in the household saving rate after 1965 was entirely attributable to the higher interest-rate strategy.

It may be true that the higher interest rates contributed to the upward shift of the household saving propensity in the late 1960s, but many other changes favorable to saving and investment also took place during the period. Investment in industries was not hindered by the higher interest rates but expanded sharply owing to the increased supply of loanable funds from both domestic and foreign sources. Although the interest-rate reform did not succeed in reducing the activities of unorganized money markets, the organized financial markets were substantially expanded by the reform. As bank deposits increased after the reform, the monetary authorities improved the techniques of monetary control by relying more upon the indirect method of controlling the reserve base of the banking system, rather than imposing loan ceilings.

The interest-rate reform, however, widened the gap in interest rates between domestic and foreign financial markets, thereby greatly increasing incentives to borrow from abroad. The system of bank guarantees for the repayment of foreign loans instituted in 1962 could therefore be actively used to facilitate the inflow of foreign capital after the reform. The increased inflow of foreign capital undoubtedly contributed to increasing gross domestic investment in Korea, but it created a difficult problem for monetary stabilization. The increased inflow of foreign capital, together with the rapid expansion of Korean exports, caused a rapid accumulation of foreign reserves, thus creating excessive monetary expansion. To control the money supply for price stabilization, a considerable proportion of the increase in bank deposits had to be frozen. This implies that the higher interest-rate policy, which was originally aimed at mobilizing domestic financial savings for domestic investment, was only helping in the conversion of such savings (after succeeding in creating them) into foreign-reserve assets. Because the supply of domestic credit was continuously squeezed while indirectly encouraging business borrowings from abroad, some sectors of the economy that could not gain access to foreign finance had to rely continuously on credit from unorganized money markets. The increased inflow of foreign capital at a low interest rate contributed to further increasing demand for domestic credit mainly owing to complementarity between foreign finance and domestic credit. As a result, the government could not succeed in balancing demand for and supply of loanable funds even at the higher interest rates and had to intervene continuously in the allocation of loanable funds as it had done before the reform.

Despite the squeeze of domestic supply of loans, which was necessitated by the rapid accumulation of foreign reserves, domestic credit could be expanded much more rapidly during the period of high interest rates than in the earlier years because financial savings had increased rapidly after the reform. On the whole, therefore, the high interest-rate policy adopted in 1965 made a great contribution to the development of financial markets in Korea, although this contribution may be difficult to define in detail. Financial assets and liabilities grew rapidly in relation to GNP during 1965–71. Because the high interest-rate policy was suddenly reversed to one of extremely low interest rates in August 1972, however, the financial development fostered by the interest-rate reform of 1965 came to a halt in 1972. Thereafter, real interest rates in organized financial markets were so often negative that the real growth of financial savings became sluggish despite the rapid growth of GNP in the 1970s. It is the opinion of many economists outside the government that if the abrupt reversal of interest-rate policy had not been made in 1972, Korean financial development could have made rapid progress even during the 1970s. Given the rate of domestic inflation, a policy of gradual reduction in interest rates might have produced a much better result for Korea's financial development than the abrupt policy reversal.

What kind of lessons can be learned from the Korean experience with the high interest-rate policy described? Four lessons may be important for other developing countries and also for Korea's future development.

First, a reasonably high rate of interest should be maintained in developing countries, where insufficient capital is one of the major constraints to economic growth. As the Korean experience suggests, a high interest rate will bring about a rapid increase in saving in the form of financial assets. Saving strategies suggested for developing countries tend to emphasize government saving. It is generally difficult, however, to sharply raise the ratio of government savings to GNP because increasing tax revenues every year is not an easy task for any representative government to undertake. The high interest-rate strategy would be easier to put into effect for increasing voluntary saving in developing countries. Nevertheless, it is widely believed that households in many developing countries have been accumulating a large proportion of their savings in the form of tangible assets such as residential dwellings, noncorporate business structures, and durable consumer goods. A high interest rate could therefore contribute to diverting such savings from unproductive tangible assets into financial intermediaries where the saving could then be channeled to productive investment. Even if one assumes that the high interest rates cannot increase the aggregate level of real saving, their implementation will result in a more "efficient composition of wealth" (Patrick 1966:181). The efficient composition of wealth is expected to have a positive effect on the growth rate of the national economy.

Second, it is important to equalize interest rates on various types of loans available within a country, regardless of sources of funds, except for minor differences in maturity term and credit standing of borrowers. In the Korean case, preferential interest rates were applied to special bank loans from government funds and to export credit financed out of the central bank's rediscount. What was more critical in the Korean experience was that the domestic high interest-rate policy opened up a new source of disturbance to domestic financial markets because no measure was taken to equalize interest rates on foreign loans with the domestic rate. As long as these preferential loans from both domestic and foreign sources were available at an interest rate much lower than the rates on ordinary commercial bank loans, the demand for such loans would continuously expand because the loans represented windfall gains to borrowers. Because of the large expansion of preferential credit, the supply of nonpreferential credit had to be squeezed to meet the money supply target. It is suggested that developing countries that adopt a high interest-rate policy should at least take measures to equalize the interest burden on foreign borrowings with that on domestic loans, if they are to succeed in equilibrating the domestic financial market at the high interest rate.

Third, a consistent interest-rate policy would be much more desirable than an abrupt change in policy direction from a high interest rate to a low one. In the case of Korea, the abrupt change in policy direction in 1972 (and also in 1982) seems to have hurt the general public's confidence in government policy, thus reducing public support for government policy. Instead of suddenly reversing the policy direction, the Korean government should have taken a gradual approach, and at least maintained a positive real rate of interest in the country. The real rate of interest should be estimated by taking into account people's expected rate of inflation, rather than just the current or lagged rate of inflation measured by either the WPI or the CPI. Although it is not easy to exactly measure the expected rate of inflation, it seems that people's price expectations in Korea have been influenced more by rises in real estate prices than by changes in the WPI or CPI in recent years. In any case, the gradual approach to monetary policy would probably have resulted in a much better performance in financial aspects of development than what actually happened after 1972. This is an important lesson, not only for other developing countries but also for future policymaking in Korea. The abrupt reduction of the interest rate in Korea in June 1982 (the so-called June 28 measure) indicated that Korean policymakers had not learned the lesson from the failure of the August 3rd measure in 1972.[6]

Finally, a reverse margin between bank deposit and loan rates should be avoided except for short periods of time. In the Korean case the bank deposit rate was set at a slightly higher level than the loan rate to increase the attractiveness of financial savings compared with returns from alternative forms of saving at the time. Such a reverse margin was probably necessary in the initial stage of the high interest-rate policy to change the attitudes of the general public toward financial saving. The reverse margin of bank interest rates, however, not only made it necessary for the central bank to find other means of compensating for banking institutions' losses arising from the reverse margin, but also contributed to creating excess demand for loans. Inasmuch as the deposit rate was higher than the loan rate, some business enterprises with enough funds of their own still retained bank loans while depositing their idle balances in the form of time deposits. Some pyramiding of deposits on loans might also have taken place as people redeposited bank loans to take advantage of the after-tax interest rate, which was higher on deposits than on loans. These practices are partly attributable to the tax system in Korea but actually increased because of the reverse margin of bank interest rates.

---

6. On 28 June 1982 the government announced a drastic reduction of interest rates on bank deposits and loans. The banks' ceiling deposit rate was reduced by a wide margin, from 12.6 to 8 percent per annum, and the rate on ordinary bank loans was cut from 14 to 10 percent per annum. On 3 July, about a week after the June 28 measure, the government announced that, beginning in 1983, it would enforce the use of real names for the possessors of all financial assets. Although the actual implementation of this measure was later postponed indefinitely, that announcement, combined with the earlier June 28 measure, seems to have had a considerable negative impact on Korea's financial development, probably increasing incentives for capital flight.

7 The President's Emergency Decree for Economic Stability and Growth (1972)

by Wan-Soon Kim

"Enrich the Nation and Strengthen the Army" was perhaps the most popular slogan of the late President Park Chung Hee's inherently authoritarian government. In practical terms, this meant that economic development was the key to the regime's political success and stability, because it was the means for overcoming political and social unrest and frustrations. Having thus enshrined rapid economic growth near the top of its value hierarchy, the Korean government was prepared to intervene directly in economic management whenever it believed that its vigorous pursuit of a high-growth policy was being stifled.

The President's Emergency Decree for Economic Stability and Growth, announced on 3 August 1972, is a classic case in point. In early 1971 the economy appeared to be cooling off. There was an appreciable drop in investment demand, partly caused by the tight credit policy, whereas price increases appeared to be accelerating. With the collapse of the Bretton Woods system as a result of the Nixon price and wage freeze in August 1971, international economic and monetary disturbances generated uncertainty within the Korean business community about the short-term prospects for Korea's renewed export growth. The combination of all these elements led to a definite slowdown in the Korean economy in the latter half of 1971, which continued throughout most of 1972.

In particular, the economic slowdown revealed the chronically unstable and weak financial structures of many business firms, especially the large, highly leveraged ones. Between 1965 and 1969 the total domestic indebtedness of manufacturing industries to financial institutions had increased from 2.6 to 9.2 percent of GNP, and the amount of the curb-market loans was reported to have reached about 190 billion won, or about 28 percent of domestic credit (Cole and Park 1983:126). Likewise, the rate at which the annual volume of external borrowing was expanding was no less than that of domestic indebtedness. From a negligible amount in 1965, gross external borrowing had reached US $1,800 million in 1969, about 189 percent of Korea's total exports, the highest since 1962 (I. C. Kim 1983a:111–17). Over the four-year period 1966–69, foreign saving accounted for, on average, almost 40 percent of total investment and about 10 percent of GNP. In sum, corporate indebtedness was stretched to such an extent that a moderate slowdown in demand could cause a number of firms to experience serious financial difficulties.

Because of the heavy reliance on borrowed capital during the 1966–69 investment boom, the average debt/equity ratio of manufacturing industries almost reached 400 percent by 1971. Furthermore, the 1971 devaluation of the won caused a sudden jump in the cost of foreign-debt servicing, creating severe short-term cash-flow problems. Interest expenses rose from 5.9 percent of net sales in 1968 to 9.9 percent in 1971 (Table 7.1). Consequently, the ratio of net profits to net sales decreased very sharply from about 6 percent to a negligible 1.2 percent over the same period. In the case of firms with high debt leverage, the burden of fixed financial charges was extremely heavy, and the number of business failures increased alarmingly.

Influential business associations reacted quickly to the sagging economy. In the latter part of 1971 the Federation of Korean Industries, representing Korea's major firms, sought a meeting with President Park to convey their ideas for dealing with highly leveraged or bankrupt firms. They called for direct government intervention and made a number of policy recommendations, including the conversion of curb-market loans into bank claims, reduction of the corporate tax burden, and lower interest rates.

Table 7.1. Selected financial ratios in the manufacturing industry: 1963–78

Year	Debt/equity ratio[a]	Interest expenses/ net sales ratio	Net profit/ net sales ratio	Share of securities in corporate investment financing (%)
1963	92.2	3.0	9.1	14.8
1964	100.5	4.9	8.6	11.7
1965	83.7	3.9	7.9	9.3
1966	117.7	5.7	7.7	8.1
1967	151.2	5.2	6.7	3.5
1968	201.3	5.9	6.0	6.4
1969	270.0	7.8	4.3	11.5
1970	328.4	9.2	3.3	14.9
1971	394.2	9.9	1.2	15.1
1972	313.4	7.1	3.9	19.5
1973	272.7	4.6	7.5	21.5
1974	316.0	4.5	4.8	8.2
1975	339.5	4.9	3.4	12.2
1976	364.6	4.9	3.9	16.0
1977	350.7	4.9	3.5	17.7
1978	366.8	4.9	4.0	30.8

Sources: BOK, Financial Statements Analysis (1981); BOK, Flow of Funds Accounts (1980).
a. Total liabilities/net worth.

The Korean government could have allowed the debt-ridden firms to go bankrupt, but it was feared that an increasing number of bankruptcies would seriously undermine the nation's credit rating in the international capital markets. More important, that option would have had adverse political consequences for the Park government, which had identified its political success with the attainment of rapid economic growth (Cole and Park 1983:160–61). For these reasons, the Park government decided to intervene directly in an attempt to relieve the financial strains on business firms, contain inflationary pressures, revive business confidence, and reform corporate financial structures. Until the announcement of the emergency decree in August 1972, a series of meetings between three economic ministers and certain business leaders were held to work out policy tools.

True to his commitment to rapid economic growth, President Park resorted to temporary stopgap measures to alleviate the business slump and to provide relief to debt-ridden firms. The President's Emergency Decree for Economic Stability and Growth placed a moratorium on curb-market loans, stretched commercial bank loans, reduced interest rates, provided rationalization funds to assist key industries in improving productivity, and launched an all-out campaign to stop inflation.

This chapter will examine and evaluate the successes and failures of the emergency decree, which lasted for about one and one-half years, in terms of its intended purposes and apparent effects. This is basically a short-run analysis. Although neither the benefits nor the costs can be calculated, the crucial factor here is to examine the long-run implications of the use of the decree for government economic management during the ensuing years. The principal argument is that the emergency decree had a remarkably small effect on Korea's financial development. As the economy became increasingly complex, the government's use of discretionary command procedures became both limited and inefficient in the face of strong market forces.

This study relies upon three major sources for its approach and information. First, the author is indebted to the theoretical work of Shaw (1973) and McKinnon (1973, 1976), who regard the poor results of savings mobilization in developing countries as a consequence of financial repression. Second, Jones and SaKong (1980), in their in-depth study of the roles of government and of business in Korea's rapid industrialization, illustrate, in particular, how the Korean government made use of discretionary command procedures as a method of policy implementation. Third, for data to support and verify a number of points made here, the author has benefited from the work of Cole and Park (1983) on the evolution of Korea's financial system and its contribution to Korea's economic development.

MAJOR FEATURES OF THE EMERGENCY DECREE

The emergency decree of 3 August 1972 provided for a series of drastic measures that, in the short-run, were intended to revive business confidence and to attack the inflation problem at its roots. The long-run intentions were to achieve a more balanced capital structure and to strengthen the competitiveness of private business firms. Foremost among the measures to improve the financial position of business enterprises was that of freeing major companies from the stranglehold of the high interest rates (about 36 percent per annum on the average) charged by the underground moneylenders. In essence, the decree consisted of the following five measures:

1. All loan agreements between firms with business licenses and lenders in the curb market were nullified as of 2 August 1972, and converted into officially confirmed "new" debt claims. Loans exceeding 3 million won were rescheduled for repayment over a five-year period after a three-year grace period, at 16.2 percent annual interest, or the lenders had the option of converting their loans into equity shares, the latter being mandatory for creditors with substantial ownership interest in the borrowing firms. In other words, the (so-called "disguised") informal money-market loans made by large stockholders or executives to their firms were converted into shares or stocks.

2. Approximately 30 percent of the short-term, high-interest (15.5 percent per annum) commercial bank loans held by business firms, amounting to 200 billion won, were replaced by long-term loans at 8 percent annual interest payable over a five-year period after a three-year grace period. The actual amount of replacement was about 194 billion won.

3. The establishment of a credit guarantee fund for small and medium industries, and for agricultural, forestry, and fishery businesses, amounting to 2 billion won in government funds, allowed the banking system to make loans up to ten times the amount of the fund without collateral requirements.

4. An Industrial Rationalization Fund of 50 billion won was created to provide long-term, low-interest loans to support mergers and modernization of priority industries to improve their efficiency, profitability, and competitiveness. In addition, business firms that could meet the rationalization criteria were granted higher depreciation rates and investment tax credits for investments using domestic resources.

5. In support of anticyclical flexibility in budgetary procedures, the decree abolished the existing pegged revenue sharing with provincial governments and made equalization grants dependent on the budgetary conditions of the central government at a given time.

In addition to these emergency measures, the Economic Planning Board (EPB) was instructed by the president to take five supplementary steps. First, as an explicit digression from the hiking of interest rates in 1965, the commercial banks' annual lending rate was reduced from 19 to 15.5 percent; and time deposit rates, from 16.8 to 12 percent. The reduction in interest rates was intended not only to provide financial relief to debt-ridden enterprises but also to eliminate immediately the cost-push effects of higher interest rates. Second, the exchange rate, which had been eroding since the beginning of 1972, was to be pegged at 400 won to the dollar, with the proviso that the won would not be devalued by more than 3 percent per year. Third, as a direct attack on inflation, the annual increase in wholesale prices was to be controlled within 3 percentage points per annum. Fourth, to keep inflation rates at 3 percent, utility rates were not allowed to increase. Finally, maximum restraint was exercised on the 1973 government budget by reducing increases of wages and salaries of government employees and by restraining increases in public investments.

EFFECTS OF THE EMERGENCY DECREE

Unorganized Money Market and Financial Policies

In an inflationary environment of ample investment opportunities with high rates of return, the government's rapid growth strategy induced larger firms with easy access to bank credit to rely heavily on bank loans for their investment capital. And, as growth was extremely rapid in relation to the existing scale of operations, internal cash generation could not cover an appreciable proportion of the financial requirements for investment and working capital. Interest payments on rapidly accumulating debt, both external and internal, seriously eroded net profits.

In addition, other critical factors supported the continued preference for debt financing against the generation of retained earnings for reinvestment. First, the special tax on retained earnings of closely held family corporations, charged in addition to the applicable corporate income tax, tended to encourage companies to dispose of much of their profits by paying dividends. Second, Korean investors had a general tendency to emphasize current cash yields and to expect a steady annual return from an investment, which resulted in disproportionately high dividend payments to profits—an element of considerable rigidity in corporate dividend policy. Third, depreciation allowances (a tax-deductible business expense item, as well as a source of corporate savings) were permitted in generous amounts but were seldom consistently charged by companies because of their desire to avoid losses. (Tax authorities were said to "penalize" companies showing losses in this manner.) This led to low internal cash generation. Fourth, businessmen were taking advantage of the corporate tax system that allowed interest paid on borrowed funds as a cost in determining profits (subject to a 40 percent tax rate), whereas interest income from high-yielding time deposits was granted a tax-exempt status. In other words, firms earned an interest spread and gained a tax advantage by depositing their own funds and then borrowing them back. Finally, the supply of equity funds from sources external to the companies was limited because of the par-value pricing method and the high financing cost of new issues.

The net effect of those factors was the extremely high debt/equity ratio of manufacturing enterprises—nearly 400 percent on average—prior to the emergency decree (Table 7.1). Therefore, in times of financial stringency, or when they were pressed for cash to make external debt-service payments on schedule or to satisfy short-term working capital needs, the debt-ridden firms (mostly large ones) came to the curb markets to borrow at rates that were generally between 30 and 50 percent per annum.

In developing countries, where financial markets are fragmented and underdeveloped, financing capital needs is generally more difficult for small and medium-size firms than for large ones. Korea was no exception. There were several reasons why the smaller firms and traditional businesses had to rely on the informal financial markets for most of their working capital and for some financing of fixed investment. First, the banking sector was not able to mobilize adequate financial savings to meet the growing demand for bank loans, largely because of the low return on saving deposits. Second, banks and other financial intermediaries tended to refuse credit to small borrowers, who were often unable to offer acceptable collateral. Third, in financing traditional activities, informal lenders could offer greater flexibility and lower transaction costs because of their intimate knowledge of local business conditions. Last, the government allocated a large share of bank credit to the so-called "essential" industries and very little to "small-scale" industries, small farms, or small processing industries (Cole and Park 1983:168–69).

On the supply side, individual savers who would otherwise have deposited their funds in formal financial institutions were encouraged by high interest rates to enter the curb market as lenders. Business firms were also able to maximize profits by channeling temporary excess liquidity into the curb market on a short-term basis (Cole and Park 1983:169).

The curb market served, therefore, as a short-term money market for both large and small business borrowers. But even though the unorganized money market served useful functions, the government attempted to eradicate it, using command procedures instead of trying to eliminate the inefficiencies of the institutional banking system. The government strongly objected to the existence of the informal credit institutions for two valid reasons. First, they wanted to recoup lost tax revenues from the unreported financial transactions and profits of the "underground" institutions. Second, in times of financial stringency they found that their tight monetary policy measures became ineffective because of the capacity of the curb market to reallocate credit and raise the velocity of money (Cole and Park 1983:158).

As an outcome of the emergency decree, reliable information on the size of the informal money markets was revealed by debt-ridden business firms. The total of the curb-market loans declared by them amounted to about 350 billion won, equivalent to 80 percent of the broad money supply and to 34 percent of the outstanding domestic credit of the banking system (Cole and Park 1983:127). Approximately 114 billion won of these borrowings were lent to enterprises by their owners and shareholders.

Although thousands of curb-market lenders went bankrupt, the lower interest rate on the rescheduled debts provided immediate and substantial assistance to heavily indebted firms. According to a rough estimate by the Bank of Korea, the annual savings from the reduction of the interest burden in 1973 reached more than 100 billion won (BOK, *Report on the Results of the August 3, 1972, Presidential Emergency Decree,* 1973:63). As a whole, the emergency decree was believed to have directly caused a 3.2 percent reduction in the average ratio of financial costs to total business costs for all manufacturing, thereby increasing the ratio of profit to net worth for the same industry by about 9 percentage points (K. S. Kim 1972:45–66).

The debt-refunding operations proved, however, to be only a temporary relief to firms in financially difficult positions. In the long run, the measures directed at improving the capital structure of private business firms failed because they were not followed up by basic policies to deal with the institutional and economic factors that led to the emergence of the curb market.

Most crucial, the government failed to eliminate the disparity between interest rates in the formal and the informal markets. The general downward interest-rate revision contained in the emergency decree marked a complete return to financial repression and conveyed clearly the government's message that it would adhere to a policy of low interest rates and credit rationing—the major causes of the continued expansion of the unorganized financial markets and the persistence of financial dualism.

In addition, institutional factors failed to deal with the country's financial market anomalies. It was widely believed that many debtors did not bother to report their debts, despite the apparent inducement to the borrowers for declaration under the emergency decree, because they knew that the curb market crackdown would not last indefinitely and that institutional sources of funds would remain as scarce as ever. Furthermore, the biggest private moneylenders, who were the most important source of capital for the informal money market, were able to take their money out of the market through a sort of information sharing arrangement among ultimate lenders, borrowers, brokers, and dealers. According to Kang Kyong Shik, the minister of finance during 1982–83, the emergency decree failed because the government did not make it impossible for curb-market lenders to hide behind anonymous bank deposits (*Far Eastern Economic Review,* 9 July 1982:48–50). Under the banking laws, technically anyone could deposit an unlimited amount of money just by giving any name and a matching seal for bank registration and withdrawals. Curb-market operators probably took advantage of this protection of anonymity and used banks as conduits for secret lendings.

By requiring a resident registration number to identify depositors, the government might have marginally succeeded in identifying curb-market loans that were secretly advanced to companies or anonymously deposited in banks. However, big private moneylenders were also the owners of large business enterprises and could easily say that such large deposits were for investment in their own companies. "Dummy" names could be used for bank deposits to hide curb-market operations. Minister Kang's proposal to require a "real-name" deposit system, if implemented, could have contributed to a more equitable taxation of capital income. The tax on property income, such as income from bank deposits, is relatively lower than the tax on wage income. By using "anonymous" names, financial transactions can be easily concealed. It would have been an almost impossible task, however, for the proposal to have effectively eliminated the role of the curb market in the nation's economy and business.

The informal money markets were temporarily suppressed but began to revive only one year later. The emergency decree simply resulted in a large-scale capital levy on curb-market lenders and a transfer of capital to borrowers, causing a temporary disruption of the informal money markets in their effective and competitive role of funding the small-scale sector over the limits of formal market intermediaries (Cole and Park 1983:165).

The emergency decree had little impact on the recovery and subsequent expansion of the economy. The major factor in the sharp upturn of economic activity after the emergency decree was an upsurge in export demand and a consequent revival in fixed investment. Merchandise exports rose during 1973 by more than 98 percent (in current dollars) compared to the previous year. An important factor in the almost unprecedented growth in Korean exports was the sharp expansion in total Japanese imports estimated at about 70 percent during 1973. Korea benefited from this expansion because of its traditional trade links with Japan and its improved export competitiveness due to its devaluation of the won. Between 1971 and 1973 the won had been devalued by 18 percent against the dollar and 39 percent against the Japanese yen, which was considerably larger than the increase in the domestic price level.

Similarly, the emergency decree had little impact on Korea's financial development. Within a year most of the indicators measuring the extent of financial development, profitability, and other elements of management efficiency began to deteriorate and then returned to the levels that had prevailed before the emergency decree. The debt-refunding operations might have had more serious repercussions for the economy in the following years if the upsurge in export demand had not more than offset the effects of the disruption of the credit system (Cole and Park 1983:164–65).

Price Stabilization

An ambitious goal of the emergency decree, aimed at paving the way for renewed economic growth, was to limit wholesale price increases to 3 percent annually, beginning in 1973. Because "expectations of inflation" were blamed for propelling the price movement and as inflation had been strongly built into every aspect of economic life in Korea, the gradual attainment of price stabilization seemed almost impossible. It was argued that if the inflation psychology was ever to be eliminated in Korea, it would have to be done within a short period of time by government-imposed, drastic, shock-therapy measures (K. S. Kim 1977).

The Korea Development Institute rendered theoretical, as well as empirical, support to the government's program by substantiating the feasibility of the 3 percent price stabilization target, by applying Song Heeyhon's price equation derived from quarterly data for 1965–71. Song developed a Harberger-type dynamic model of inflation to explain the short-term variations of the wholesale price in Korea. The short-term variations of the wholesale price were explained by changes in money supply, income, the foreign exchange rate, public utility prices, and the price of rice. Having analyzed the factors increasing the WPI, Song (1972:192) forecasted that the 3 percent price stabilization goal might be attained in 1973 if the government could keep the exchange rate at about 400 won per U.S. dollar and hold the annual average rates of increase in the rice price, public utility charges, and money supply within the assumed levels of 5 percent, 3 percent, and 19.9 percent, respectively, while achieving a high annual growth rate of real nonagricultural GNP of 12.3 percent.

In 1972, at the same time that the government was making efforts to restrain undue monetary expansion, improve industrial productivity, and stabilize the exchange rate, rice prices, and public utility charges, it was also creating broad-based, direct measures to control private prices. Direct measures were also being taken to stabilize import prices. For example, when the international prices of scrap iron and lumber shot up, the import predeposit ratios for these commodities were temporarily reduced. Restrictions on the export of some commodities were also imposed when supplies were short in the domestic market.

The government negotiated directly with each industry to persuade them to reduce their prices. The so-called cost-reduction campaign under the Ministry of Commerce and Industry succeeded in suppressing the prices (warehouse delivery) of about 42 industrial goods by 2 to 15 percent in three months (February to April 1973). Also, the Office of National Tax Administration set up 460 "mobile price control patrols" and 80 "price assurance forces" to monitor price increases. Where "gouging" and "cornering" were found, violators were subjected to an immediate tax investigation, a special excess profits tax, and curtailment of bank credit. Moral suasion was also attempted through a major meeting between government and business leaders (Jones and Sakong 1980:125).

The results of the direct price controls were predictable, leading to undesirable developments such as under-the-table payments, supply shortages, poor product quality, and other strategies to circumvent the controls. The government responded with production quotas and daily checks on shipments of major producers. The Law on Price Stability, enacted in March 1973, prohibited both sales at greater than ceiling prices and restricted shipments.

Realizing the inefficiencies and long-term ineffectiveness of such direct price controls, the government lifted the freeze in December 1973. Because prior approval was required for price increases, and some justifiable price increases were long overdue, when allowed, prices tended to leap upward. Finally, on 5 February 1974, in the wake of the 1973 oil shock, direct price controls were abolished and replaced by selective controls on 32 items. That marked the end of the emergency decree as well.

The government's direct price-control measures contributed, in the short run, to preventing some monopolistic price increases, but with massive administrative costs. Besides, certain fundamental factors made government control over prices unworkable. First, the complete elimination of inflation psychology within a short period of time by shock measures was a formidable (if not an impossible) task for the government. Second, price controls encouraged the emergence of black markets. The discrepancy between controlled and black-market prices caused expectations of high future prices that tended to aggravate the prevailing inflation psychology and made the price stabilization effort all the more difficult. Finally, the government's price stabilization efforts were frustrated by the upheaval in world commodity markets and by the acceleration of price pressures in the United States and Japan. Overseas price developments could not have been foreseen when the target of limiting price increases to 3 percent was adopted in 1972 as part of the emergency decree.

Change in Interest-Rate Policy

A policy of high nominal rates of interest is generally unpopular and therefore often politically difficult. The 1965 financial reform in Korea provoked an outcry of protests in business circles and drew dire predictions of inflation, bankruptcies, and a slowdown of growth. None of these happened.

Businessmen and the general public tend to think of inflation in cost-push terms. They see the possible adverse effects of higher interest rates and rising capital costs but fail to see the much more important effect of financialization of household savings and improvement of efficiency of investment, both leading to a higher level of savings, investment, and growth.

The high-interest-rate policy of 1965 was gradually relaxed over the years. With the onset of the business slowdown and the resurgence of inflation in 1971–72, the average debt/equity ratio of Korean firms at 4 to 1 became almost untenable under the high interest rates, in particular the annual average of 36 percent interest charged on curb-market loans. Therefore, quick financial relief to those debt-ridden enterprises was considered imperative. Also, Korean officials argued that if reasonable price stability could be expected through the government's drastic anti-inflationary measures, a positive real rate of interest would be attainable even at relatively low nominal rates. Furthermore, the rising real cost of capital was believed to be an element of cost-push inflation that, if not checked, would weaken Korea's competitiveness in the export markets. For those reasons the emergency decree reduced the commercial bank basic lending and time-deposit rates by 3.5 to 4.5 percentage points. Thus, the government returned to the pre-1965 style of financial repression.

Korean officials have a deep-rooted belief in the efficacy of a low-interest-rate policy. To begin with, there has been an historical antipathy to high interest rates. Second, policymakers thought that market-determined interest rates would rise to very high nominal levels and contribute to inflation. Third, the economic authorities held that the cost of capital should be kept low in order to achieve a high rate of economic growth in line with the government-led development strategy and to cajole reluctant businessmen into taking the risks inherent in the development of the heavy and chemical industries. Fourth, in the 1970s saving was shown to depend on income, the remittances of overseas workers, and other factors more than on changes in interest rates. Finally, even if the policymakers had realized the merits of a positive real interest-rate policy, they were not willing to pursue an unpopular course in the face of strong opposition from the favored borrowers (Cole and Park 1983:138–40).

After the general downward adjustment of nominal interest rates in August 1972, the real interest rates in the banking sector were, on average, close to zero and sometimes negative during 1973–78, because of the higher rates of inflation. In comparison, the curb-loan rates consistently carried annual interest rates at about 36 percent on average, reflecting the nominal rate of return to fixed assets and to capital in the manufacturing sector (Table 7.2). The residential land-value index almost doubled between 1972 and 1975. As a result, the growth of the formal financial sector slowed down, and much of domestic savings shifted back into the curb markets or into other assets. In short, the reduction in the real interest rates on bank deposits drove savers away from the banking institutions to the markets for real assets (land, apartments, and houses) for speculation and to the informal money markets.

The low-interest-rate policy generated an excessive demand for credit and necessitated discretionary allocation of funds, which usually excluded smaller firms because of their inadequate collateral and credit standing. Not surprisingly, priority in credit allocation or "policy" loans was given first to the government-owned or controlled enterprises, then to those industries considered strategic to economic development, such as large export firms. Although Jones and SaKong (1980:109) maintain that resources were generally allocated to qualified users under the Park government, some personal bias and corruption were nevertheless the predictable outcome of discretionary credit rationing.

Table 7.2. Interest rates, rates of return, and real estate prices: 1964–78

Year	Nominal interest rate on time deposits (%)	WPI (1975 = 100)	Real interest rate (%)	Curb market interest rate (%)	Rates of return to fixed assets in manufacturing sector (%)	Housing prices (1965 = 100)	Residential land prices (1965 = 100)
1964	15.0	26.2	-14.9	61.4	32.0		
1965	30.0	28.8	8.1	58.8	43.0	100	100
1966	30.0	31.4	19.2	58.7	40.0	142	165
1967	30.0	33.4	22.2	56.4	37.0	165	200
1968	26.0	36.2	17.7	55.9	28.0	217	303
1969	24.0	38.5	16.6	51.2	28.0	365	675
1970	22.8	42.0	12.6	50.8	25.0	379	676
1971	22.0	45.7	12.3	46.3	23.0	516	993
1972	15.0	52.0	1.7	38.9	27.0	593	1,033
1973	12.6	55.6	5.3	39.2	34.0	683	1,116
1974	15.0	79.0	-19.3	37.6	30.0	802	1,400
1975	15.0	100.0	-9.2	41.3	29.0	1,108	2,009
1976	15.6	112.1	3.0	40.5	33.0	1,414	2,707
1977	15.8	122.2	6.6	38.1		1,759	3,472
1978	16.9	136.5	4.5	41.7		3,055	7,895

Sources: Cole and Park (1983:tables 30 and 49); KNHC, *Handbook of Housing Statistics* (1983:322).

Following the policy of low interest rates and government efforts to foster the capital markets, the demand for stocks and corporate debentures grew significantly, and dependency on them rose from 6 percent of total sources of corporate funds in 1968 to 22 percent in 1973 (Table 7.1). The long-term securities markets, however, neither reduced the heavy reliance on bank and foreign-loan financing nor weakened the direct link between the government and the large corporations. To keep the large industrial groups under effective control, the government could not let the market dictate the allocation of credit. Two additional factors impinged on the adequate supply of securities. First, few firms were willing to raise funds through the equity markets beyond the amounts required by the government because of the par-value pricing method and the high financing cost of new issues (Cole and Park 1983:274). Second, as noted before, the low-interest-rate policy, in combination with inflation and tax deductibility, increased the preference of corporations for debt over equity financing.

Cole and Park (1983) argue that the renewed financial repression after 1972 had no apparent adverse effects on either overall economic growth or aggregate domestic savings, at least until 1978. Indeed, the Korean economy grew at an average annual rate in excess of 10 percent over the period 1973-78. Domestic savings rose from 19 percent of GNP in 1969 to 26 percent in 1978.

Cole and Park (1983) do not discount upward-biased economic growth by allowing for non-national account components, but externalities such as the environmental effects of industrial growth have aroused serious concern in Korea. Water and air pollution and the disposal of wastes are the main environmental problems Korea faces. Wastes discharged into the four main rivers and the coastal waters near the big cities increased rapidly during the 1970s.

Income distribution, however, seems to have deteriorated since the latter half of the 1970s. Soaring prices of real estate may have been responsible for the deterioration in the distribution of wealth. Between 1972 and 1978 average housing prices increased by more than five times and residential land prices increased by more than seven times, whereas wholesale prices rose less than threefold (Table 7.2). As a result, the differences in wealth between those with their own houses and those without have widened markedly.

A highly regressive set of rapid growth strategies, especially preferential low interest credit and tax concessions, generally accorded to large industrial enterprises at the expense of small and medium-size business firms, contributed to the concentration of business in Korea. At present, the level of industrial concentration in Korea is relatively low by historic Asian standards, but it is increasing at a rapid rate.

Moreover, government encouragement of capital-intensive projects has preempted investment funds that might have gone to the small and medium industries, which produce a large part of the country's daily necessities. Consequently, both the shortage of consumption goods and the excess demand for them have become an important source of inflation in recent years.

Finally, some symptoms of inefficiency have been visible. Owing in large part to the government's growth-promotion measures, the rapid expansion of the heavy and chemical industries caused by overinvestment has resulted in some duplication of investment and excess capacity. The rapid increase in the incremental fixed capital output ratio from 2.5 during 1964–73 to 3.7 during 1974–81 was a matter of some concern (BOK, *National Income*, 1982:351–52). This evidence of the deteriorating efficiency of invested capital was a warning note to Korea's long-run debt servicing capacity. Thus, the importance of industrial deepening and technological upgrading for an improvement of productivity of capital cannot be overemphasized.

A high positive interest rate is called for, not because it functions as an unambiguous, direct inducement to save, but because it represents the opportunity cost of holding financial assets. If the growth of the organized financial system is a top policy priority and if the intention is to induce a shift in savings from curb markets, the monetary yield on the latter should at least be comparable to the rate of return on holdings of goods or other tangible assets, as determined by the rate of change in their prices.

Industrial Rationalization

As Korea entered the 1970s its industrial sector had become more oriented toward heavy manufacturing and chemical industries and more dependent on export demand than in the 1960s. It was widely recognized by both government and industry that simply promoting industrialization was not sufficient and that manufacturing industries had to be able to export at competitive prices. Therefore, with the onset of the business slump in 1971–72, the decline in profitability of major industry groups caused serious concern.

Clearly influenced by the experience of the Japanese Ministry of International Trade and Industry in modernizing and rationalizing key industries during the period 1952–60, the Park government decided to create, through the emergency decree, an Industrial Rationalization Fund of 50 billion won to provide long-term, low-interest loans to modernize equipment and machinery, initiate mergers, and improve the capital structure of manufacturing industries. These measures were intended to make Korean industries more productive so that they would contribute to achieving the 3 percent rate of domestic-price stabilization. The government also meant to make priority industries more competitive in the world market, and where appropriate, to force mergers and consolidations that would bring about economies of scale.

The Industrial Rationalization Council was established under the Office of the Prime Minister to determine who would obtain financial privileges under the emergency decree. The council was chaired by the minister of the EPB and its membership included various economic ministers, governors of special banks, and other private members designated by the president. The council examined candidate companies to determine whether they met the eligibility criteria under which they would receive preferential loans, tax allowances, preferred access to loans of banking institutions, and various administrative favors. Final approval, however, rested with the president.

To be eligible to receive financial privileges under the decree, companies had to fit within one of the following categories: (1) industries producing goods or services indispensable to the nation; (2) industries promoting related industries; (3) machine and raw material manufacturing industries; (4) export industries, tourism, and other foreign-exchange earning industries; and (5) farmers' subsidiary businesses or agricultural/fisheries processing industries that would significantly increase the incomes of farmers and fishermen.

Furthermore, companies had to demonstrate that their rationalization and development would make them more productive and profitable and thereby benefit the overall national economy. Rationalization funds were to be used to facilitate mergers and consolidations in order to encourage specialization and vertical affiliation of production, optimum scale and methods of production, and the liquidation and transformation of businesses that were redundant. Funds were also to be used for improvement of the physical plant and equipment, to increase captial and otherwise strengthen the financial structure of an industry, and for development of technology and innovation.

Concerned about the considerable increase in the concentration of Korean industry during the period 1966-71, the Industrial Rationalization Fund endeavored to assist small and medium industries important in textiles. The criteria for rationalization of small and medium industries or enterprises were supposed to be determined on an individual basis, taking into consideration the special position and characteristics of those industries.

In addition to providing favorable loans, the emergency decree set allowable accelerated depreciation at 50 to 80 percent for companies that met the economic eligibility criteria. A further stimulus to the substitution of capital for labor was provided by the tax investment credit for investments using domestic resources. The new credit allowed corporations to deduct 10 percent (the rate had previously been 6 percent) of the cost of new investments using domestic resources from their income and corporate tax liability, until the end of 1974. Accelerating depreciation and the investment tax credit together increased the level of corporate investment. According to one crude estimate, an investment of 14 billion won would have been generated for the manufacturing sector if the maximum depreciation rate of 80 percent had been applied (W. S. Kim 1972:143-52).

Some 36 billion won of the 50 billion fund was released by the end of 1973. Manufacturers of polyvinyl chlorides were one of the first groups to take advantage of the financial assistance offered by the government in their attempt to merge companies and rationalize production facilities and programs by expanding the most efficient units and shutting down the uneconomic ones. The amount of government loans distributed for the expansion of facilities in such key industries as electric power, steel, polyvinyl chlorides, and others supplying raw materials accounted for more than 75 percent of the total, whereas less than 4 percent of the funds were given to small and medium-size industries.

It is apparent that the screening procedures left virtually complete discretion to the Industrial Rationalization Council. Because almost any enterprise could construct an argument for privileges under some provision of the decree, and given the excess demand for preferential credit at a low rate (8 percent per annum), discretion was thus inevitable. The success or failure of the rationalization scheme depended on the government's ability to make the right judgments about trends in international trade and about which Korean industries would have a comparative advantage. Pointing to the considerable difficulties in documenting the manner in which discretion was actually exercised under the Park regime, Jones and SaKong (1980:107–09) conjecture that the government made a genuine effort to ascertain whether the applicant met the economic eligibility criteria, and resources were generally allocated to qualified users. It is more than likely that if a consensus in the council on an industry plan were reached through coercion rather than persuasion, personal bias and wrong judgment would have misallocated the resources.

Tax Revenue Sharing

The principal type of central government grant in Korea is tax revenue sharing. The amount of locally shared revenues is the difference between the amount needed for standard services defined by the central government (calculated on the basis of a system of unit costs) and the amount yielded by 80 percent of the local taxes at the legal or standard rates enumerated in the Local Shared Tax Law. Although this method appeared objectively to recognize inequalities of financial capacity and needs existing at the local level, the total grant disbursed was not the aggregate of the excess of total needs over total revenue. Instead, the grant was pegged at 17.6 percent of the estimated national internal taxes (central government taxes, excluding custom duties and monopoly profits), and actual distribution procedures became subject to political negotiations between the central and local governments.

Still other defects existed. First, the amount needed for standard services was computed only on the basis of the units of services enumerated in the Local Finance Law, which inadequately measured minimum public service levels. Adjustments made to expenditure requirements due to unforeseen factors, such as price increases, were inadequate. Second, a regionally differentiated unit-cost method without due regard to population size, for instance, was discriminatory among provinces. The third defect stemmed from the fact that the local governments had neither their own kinds of tax nor the power to raise or lower tax rates in response to the needs of the local residents. In short, Korea's equalization scheme offered no opportunity for the provinces to exercise their own tax efforts.

The 1972 emergency decree, drawing upon the experience of the previous 20 years, eliminated the legal stipulation of the proportions of revenue sharing in order to reduce the 1973 government budget and to enhance the anticyclical role of future budgets. In other words, the emergency decree made central government financial transfers subject to the policies of the central government at a given time. In the 1973 budget, the funds transferred from the central government to local governments decreased by 0.93 percent to 16.67 percent of national internal taxes.

It was believed at the time that the end to guaranteed earmarking left local governments uncertain that minimum financial requirements could be met, because transfers could fluctuate from year to year depending on national policy demands on the budget. This author has argued that local governments were entitled to revenue growth linked to the growing economy and that transfers should be put on a more stable and objective basis to preserve local autonomy (W. S. Kim 1977:342–46).

Between 1972 and 1980, locally shared tax revenue, measured as a percentage of national internal taxes, declined from 17.6 percent to 10.2 percent (EPB, ROK, *Budget Summary, 1983,* 1985). A precise formula for the determination of the grant amount was restored in July 1982, but with the reduced percentage of shared tax revenue at 13.27 percent of the estimated national internal taxes.

REFLECTIONS ON
AND LESSONS OF KOREAN EXPERIENCES

Although Korea is predominantly a private-enterprise economy, a policy environment exists in which private business firms have been compelled to follow government direction. Given the government's highest policy priority of rapid economic growth and identification of rapid growth with the regime's political success, the Park government could not allow any financial deterioration or constraints to interfere with that objective.

The monetary reform of 1965, although not a consistent financial liberalization, demonstrated the effectiveness of a positive real rate of interest. The measure led to a dramatic rise in household deposit savings, the growth performance of the economy was impressive, and the rate of inflation dropped sharply. In contrast, the thrust of the 1972 economic policies was a major retreat to financial repression.

The abrupt attack on the curb market did not work. Its total elimination turned out to be an impossible task, precisely because the measures enforced did not address the real reasons why the informal money market had flourished. First, to achieve a high rate of economic growth in line with the government-led development strategy, the government deliberately cajoled businessmen into relying heavily on the "policy" loans of the financial institutions under its effective control. Second, the government had a policy of providing preferential low-interest credit, so that priority projects got started right away, but the government failed to institutionalize the informal money market. Furthermore, because the commercial banks failed to supply short-term liquidity and improve their loan operations, the curb market has been a major source of funds, meeting urgent short-term financial requirements for a large number of firms, both big and small. Contrary to what the government argued, the curb money market has not been a constraint to economic growth. It did not inflict harm on the public, especially the small businesses, nor did it impede the efficiency of capital as a whole. In sum, a low-interest-rate policy and consequent credit rationing were the major causes of the continued expansion of the unorganized financial markets in Korea.

Therefore, any rash attempt to close the market that supplements the very deficiencies of the organized financial markets would seriously impair the normal operations of the nation's businesses. Thus, Cole and Park (1983:290–91) conclude that one important lesson to be learned from the Korean experience with the curb markets is that the social costs incurred by the administrative control of the credit market are too great and that it is difficult for the government to destroy a financial system that is fulfilling a useful role. Thus, Cole and Park indict any abrupt attempts to suppress the curb markets, such as the emergency decree, as being contrary to the broader public interest.

The principal short-term target of the decree was price stabilization. According to Jones and SaKong (1980:290–91), however, the government's attempt at broad-based price controls proved to be inefficient and was in fact an aberration. Furthermore, a year after the emergency decree, the outcome of this domestic policy was completely overshadowed by the worldwide recession following the Arab oil embargo (October 1973), the food crisis, and the recession in the United States. In December 1973 alone, wholesale prices jumped by 5.4 percent; and during the first quarter of 1974, the WPI increased by 22.5 percent. Under such a situation approaching hyperinflation, the real interest rates in the banking sector were on an average close to zero or sometimes even negative. And the curb money market appeared to gain its market share once again.

The emergency decree was believed by many policymakers to have brought some improvements. But, at best, they were short-lived and more apparent than real. The recovery and subsequent expansion of the economy were largely due to an upsurge in exports. The decree had no appreciable impact on Korea's financial development. Hence, one conclusion that can be drawn from the Korean experience is that repressive measures require continued intervention to make up for their flaws. The Korean government's failure to enhance financial deepening in subsequent years persuaded the monetary authorities to retreat farther from liberal financial policies. Likewise, any success would only have reinforced the rationale of the repressive measures (Min 1976:56).

Finance had mattered as much as the real-sector variables, such as investment, saving, and export, in explaining growth and development. The sharp increase in the incremental fixed capital–output ratio during 1974–81 raises a serious question as to the efficiency of invested capital during this period. Symptoms of inefficiency are obvious in some industrial sectors, largely brought about by officially directed, subsidized credit, and government coercion that had initiated various industrial projects, in spite of their dubious comparative advantage. As a result, excess capacity emerged in heavy industries, while excess demand in the face of capacity limitations for light industrial goods fueled inflationary pressures. Furthermore, the long gestation periods of heavy industrial investment, creating income gains without immediate output gains, also boosted domestic prices.

One important legacy of the emergency decree is the continuing antipathy to high nominal interest rates. Since 1980 downward adjustments of the interest rate on one-year time deposits continued until the rate reached 8 percent per annum in June 1982. As in the case of the emergency decree, such sharp reductions were justified on the grounds of providing financial relief to debt-ridden enterprises. As usual, the government argued that because of its successful anti-inflationary measures, a positive real rate of interest would be attainable at relatively low nominal interest rates. Obviously, the government used the current rate of inflation in its computation of the real interest rate, but failed to consider whether the yield on monetary savings was at least comparable to the rate of return on holdings of goods or other tangible assets. The currently used price indexes underweigh the rapidly rising housing costs and cannot represent the opportunity cost of holding financial assets.

Another important legacy of the emergency decree is a borrowing profile that business firms in Korea have developed over the years. Since "problem" firms have been rescued so long as they have conformed to government policies and have responded to government suggestions, they are assured that the government is likely to assist them in any future periods of financial stringency. This, in turn, has prompted the new entrepreneurs to incur, even if not recklessly, the risk of overexpansion and excessive corporate indebtedness. In other words, a system of credit allocation based on preferential financing has encouraged Korean enterprises to rely more on debt financing than on internally generated funds. Indeed, it is a moot question if Korean business firms, after having been addicted to borrowing, would be able to overcome their financial difficulties without external assistance.

Some people argue that the authorities "know best" and that they can intervene directly in economic management, enforcing discretionary decisions that will prove, in the end, to be both coherent and desirable. In the past, the combination of persuasion, inducement, and coercion often succeeded under a repressive political system. But as the emergency decree illustrates, even the use of the government's discretionary command procedures was limited in the face of strong private market forces. The curb market has survived many repeated assaults. As the Korean economy becomes more complex, the bureaucracy simply cannot control as many aspects of the economy in as much detail as it would like. On the grounds of reduced complexity and more efficient allocation of resources, the repressive financial system should be dismantled and the discretionary bureaucratic decision making should be withdrawn.

8 Policy Response to the Oil Crisis and the Presidential Emergency Decree (1974)

by Yoon Hyung Kim

The Middle East war of October 1973 and the oil crisis brought home to Korea its extreme vulnerability to external developments. The Arab oil embargo and the quadrupling of the world oil price, coupled with the recession in the Japanese and U.S. economies and the high price of food grains and raw materials, posed a major threat to the future prospects of the Korean economy. When the oil price shock occurred, Korea depended on imported oil for 55 percent of its total energy needs, and was, therefore, hit hard by the sharp increase in the world oil price.

Korea's energy resources are limited to anthracite coal, hydropower, and firewood. Anthracite coal is the main domestic energy resource with total reserves estimated at 1.5 billion tons, of which no more than 545 million tons are recoverable (about 30 years' supply at the 1980 production rate). Anthracite coal deposits are in mountainous areas, which require draft- and shaft-type underground mines and labor-intensive mining with low productivity compared with other methods of mining. The quality of coal is poor (about 3,500–5,500 kcal/kg) and is not suitable for coking coal. Korea's hydroelectric potential is estimated at 2,000 MW and is concentrated on four main river systems—Han, Naktong, Kum, and Sumjin. Most of the sites are small and have a low head, so that costly dams are needed to regulate the river flows.

At the beginning of the industrialization drive of the First Five-Year Economic Development Plan (1962–66), fuelwood was the basic energy source. It could not, however, provide sufficient energy for industrial production and power generation, which were growing at average annual rates of 15 percent and 17 percent, respectively.

Because firewood had been the predominant source of primary energy through the early 1960s, the mountains were denuded. Concerted efforts for reforestation have been pursued since the early 1960s. A law for the preservation of forests was enacted and a reforestation program was undertaken to control erosion and to protect watersheds. Only limited fuelwood was available from the thinning and removal of excess trees and cutting was allowed only by permit.

The government encouraged not only the industrial sector but also the urban residential and commercial sectors to replace firewood with domestic

183

anthracite coal. Most of the limited firewood could then be used by the rural sector. Accordingly, the share of firewood used for industrial energy declined sharply from 71 percent in 1961 to 16 percent in 1966; its share in the residential and commercial sector declined from 58 percent to 52 percent. The share of firewood in the total supply of primary energy declined from 57 percent in 1961 to 43 percent in 1965 (Table 8.1).

The government took a series of steps to encourage domestic coal production. The most impressive policy was the enactment of the Provisional Coal Development Law in December 1961, providing for the amalgamation of small, private coal mines. As a result, the production of anthracite coal increased twofold from less than 6 million tons in 1961 to about 12 million tons in 1966, showing an average annual growth rate of about 15 percent. The share of coal in total primary energy consumption rose from 33 percent in 1961 to 44 percent in 1965 (Table 8.1).

As the economy spurted in the early 1960s, the domestic supply of anthracite coal could not meet the growing demand for fuel by the industrial and power sectors. The growth rate of the manufacturing sector increased from 15 percent per annum in 1962–66 to an average rate of 22 percent per annum in 1967–71; the growth rate of the electric power sector increased from 17 percent to 22 percent per annum.

The urban population (i.e., inhabitants of cities and towns of more than 20,000 persons) rose from 28 percent of total population in 1961 to 34 percent in 1966. The rapid growth of urban areas led to a virtual explosion in the urban residential and commercial demand for fuel and, in late 1966, brought about severe supply shortages of coal briquettes used for household cooking and heating. The 1966 coal shortage was the turning point. The government then adopted a new energy-transition policy to replace oil for anthracite coal as the major fuel.

To restructure consumption patterns, the government took measures ranging from administrative orders and guidelines to publicity campaigns about the greater convenience and cleanliness of oil heat. It made the import of kerosene space heaters duty-free, encouraged the use of other oil-heating appliances, imported large quantities of heating oil to meet immediate needs, and began drawing up plans for future growth in fuel needs to be met from an expanded domestic refinery capacity and direct imports.

The government restricted coal consumption by the nonresidential sector. The Korea Electric Power Company was ordered to use oil instead of coal for all generating plants capable of burning either fuel. This restrictive policy led to inefficiencies and maintenance problems in coal-fired power plants. The government also strongly encouraged industrial plants to replace coal with oil and to install oil-burning equipment.

The substitution of petroleum for coal was successful because of the experience and knowledge in the field of petroleum acquired through joint ventures with foreign oil companies, the comparative technical and

Table 8.1. Structure of the primary energy supply: 1961–80

Energy Source	1961 10³ TOE	%	1965 10³ TOE	%	1969 10³ TOE	%	1973 10³ TOE	%	1979 10³ TOE	%	1980 10³ TOE	%
Domestic												
Coal	3,226	32.9	5,291	43.9	5,647	32.5	7,244	29.2	7,887	20.9	8,602	22.7
Hydroelectric	163	1.7	178	1.5	359	2.1	306	1.2	582	1.5	496	1.3
Firewood	5,636	57.4	5,142	42.7	4,355	25.1	3,672	14.8	2,892	7.7	2,517	6.6
Subtotal	9,025	92.0	10,611	88.1	10,361	59.7	11,222	45.2	11,361	30.1	11,615	30.6
Imports												
Oil	790	8.0	1,439	11.9	6,981	40.3	13,624	54.8	24,690	65.3	24,024	63.2
Nuclear	0	0	0	0	0	0	0	0	788	2.1	869	2.3
Coal	0	0	0	0	0	0	0	0	954	2.5	1,475	3.9
Subtotal	790	8.0	1,439	11.9	6,981	40.3	13,624	54.8	26,432	69.9	26,368	69.4
Total	9,815	100.0	12,050	100.0	17,342	100.0	24,846	100.0	37,793	100.0	37,983	100.0

Source: Ministry of Energy and Resources, ROK, unpublished data.

Note: Coking coal is excluded from the primary energy supply.

TOE—tons of oil equivalent.

economic advantages of petroleum for power generation and industrial use, and the greater convenience and cleanliness of oil heating for middle- and upper-income households and for commercial uses. This comparative advantage lasted, of course, only as long as oil supplies were cheap and abundant.

The increased competition from petroleum fuels led to a decrease in coal production by 17 percent in 1968. It then remained at the lower level until 1969, increasing unemployment and hardship in coal-producing regions. To encourage investment in coal mining and to slow the growth of oil imports, the government increased the import duty on bunker-C fuel oil, from 5 to 10 percent in 1969, using the additional revenue for investment or subsidies in the coal industry.

During the Second Five-Year Development Plan (1967–71), coal's share in industrial use and power generation declined considerably. In 1966 coal accounted for 78 percent of thermal power generation and 40 percent of industrial requirements; in 1971 the respective shares were only 5 percent and 6 percent. This important shift in Korea's energy policy can be better seen in the sharply increased share of oil in total primary energy supplies, from 8 percent in 1961 to 55 percent in 1973 (Table 8.1).

The quadrupling of the world oil price in 1973–74 raised the costs of oil imports to $1.1 billion in 1974 from about $296 million in 1973. In addition to the serious deterioration in its terms of trade resulting from the sharp rise in the price of oil, the attendant world recession led to a weakened world demand for exports, thereby exacerbating the immediate international balance-of-payments position.

In response to the oil crisis, the government assumed four major tasks: a diplomatic mission to the Middle East, a mission to the international financial markets, macroeconomic policy measures, and energy-specific policy measures. The government identified a top-level Korean manager of an oil company with intimate contacts in Saudi Arabia and employed him as an intermediary to contact the Saudi government. In December 1973 the Korean government dispatched a presidential envoy to Saudi Arabia, carrying a letter from President Park. The Saudi government proposed in response that the Korean government issue a statement sympathetic to the position of the Arab countries. While the government was withholding the statement and consulting with the U.S. government, the Japanese prime minister visited Saudi Arabia and issued the same statement. The Korean government then followed suit.

To secure channels of credit, the government made use of three former Korean bankers who had good relations with foreign bankers. The government sent these financial experts to New York, London, and Tokyo to convince foreign bankers of the growth potential and credit-worthiness of the Korean economy.

The government implemented a set of policies in January 1974 designed to deal with the changes in the external environment. The two main policy measures were the energy-specific measures aimed at energy conservation and reduced dependence on imported oil, and the financial policies of relying heavily on external savings. The government thus made little attempt to control inflation, which it viewed as imposed by external factors, and allowed bank credit to expand by nearly 50 percent to finance imports for economic growth (Cole and Park 1983).

In the face of external shocks such as that of 1973–74 a country could respond by: (1) expanding its exports, (2) replacing imports with import substitutes, (3) reducing imports by maintaining a lower economic growth rate, or (4) increasing external debt to sustain a high economic growth rate. Korea's main response was to combine measures (1) and (4), thereby achieving a real GNP growth rate of 8 percent in 1974, an average annual GDP growth rate of 7.2 percent during 1974–82, and an increase in the external trade (exports plus imports) to GDP ratio from 40.3 percent in 1972 to 67.7 percent in 1982. The effectiveness of Korea's response to the external shock must be attributed, in part, to its outward-oriented trade and industrialization policies and market-oriented pricing policies. These contributed to the resilience of the Korean economy to external shocks.

What is unique, however, about Korea's response to the external shock is that, in addition to the policies described above, it undertook certain microeconomic and energy-specific measures to cope with the shock. The Presidential Emergency Decree for National Economic Security is a measure specifically designed to sustain the standard of living for low-income groups, promote consumption restraints, conserve resources, better utilize domestic resources, and maintain the balance-of-payments equilibrium.

This chapter focuses on these microeconomic and energy-specific measures, analyzing how they helped the Korean economy cope with the external shock of 1973–74 and its aftereffects.

MAJOR FEATURES OF THE POLICY MEASURES

In December 1973 the president's Economic Secretariat began an intensive effort to produce a set of policy measures. Their work was confidentially guided by the senior secretary for economic affairs of the Office of the President, mobilizing only selected government bureaucrats and a few economists from the Korea Development Institute. Within one month, the government issued a set of policy measures known as the Presidential Emergency Decree of 14 January 1974, to mitigate the worst effects of the oil price increases and to maintain overall growth.

The Korean government also brought together its then widely dispersed energy experts to formulate energy policy. Their review of the Japanese Heat Management Law and energy conservation legislation in France, Germany, and Scandinavian countries led to formulation of the Heat Management Law, which was enacted in January 1974.

The Presidential Emergency Decree for National Economic Security

The Presidential Emergency Decree of 14 January 1974 was a set of sophisticated policy measures that: reduced the burden of oil-price adjustments on low-income groups, thus sustaining their standard of living; imposed heavy taxes on the incomes of high-income groups and on the consumption of luxury goods; improved working conditions of low-income wage earners; reformed the system of tariff-rate exemptions; and adjusted the 1974 budget.

The decree provided a substantial, one-year temporary cut in business income tax and earned income tax. The cut ranged from 30 to 100 percent, increasing as the level of income decreased. The exemption limit of the acquisition tax and property tax was raised from 30,000 to 60,000 won. In addition, the implementation of the newly enacted National Welfare Pension Program and the Private Schoolteachers Pension Program was postponed for one year in 1974 to relieve the low-income groups of the burden of contributing to pension funds. Moreover, as a price-stabilization measure, the sales prices of rice, barley, and coal briquettes—basic necessities of daily life—were heavily subsidized and administrative guidance was used to secure a balance of their supply and demand. An "unjust-profit" tax was applied to windfall gains made through price manipulations. The government also suspended the travel tax on train, streetcar, city bus, van, and passenger-ship fares, and reduced the travel tax on taxicabs from 20 percent to 10 percent. To maintain the farmers' standard of living, the government increased the purchase price of rice by 500 won per bag (from 10,877 won to 11,377 won per bag) in 1973, with no limit on the quantity of rice purchased. For the urban poor, the government executed public works projects amounting to 10 billion won, which expanded employment opportunities for low-income urban workers. Another measure created a fund totaling 30 billion won to be used as a special credit for small and medium-size firms at the subsidized interest rate of 12 percent, or 3 percent below the normal bank rate. The government compensated the commercial banks for the resulting interest loss. Two billion won from the government budget was also contributed to the Trust Guarantee Fund to enhance the mortgage position of small and medium-size firms.

The government restrained consumption and promoted conservation by raising taxes on certain commodities, thus making up for the revenue losses caused by reduction in the tax burden for the poor. Substantial increases in customs tariffs and commodity taxes were applied to liquors, passenger cars, and luxurious items such as jewels, precious metals, and furs. To further restrain luxury consumption, entertainment-related taxes were increased by 50–200 percent. Acquisition taxes on villas, deluxe cars, and golf courses were raised and corporate real estate used for nonbusiness purposes became subject to the tax. The property tax on residential property, which had been a uniform 0.2 percent, was made progressive with a maximum rate of 5 percent. Taxes on vacant land and land held by corporations for nonbusiness use were raised from 0.2 percent and 0.4 percent, respectively, to a flat rate of 5 percent. The gasoline tax was raised by 50 percent.

The decree specified that priority be given to wage payments and other claims against employers arising from employment service when employers disposed of their properties. Heavy punishments were imposed on entrepreneurs for overdue wages, unjust dismissals, and poor working conditions.

The system of tariff-rate reductions and exemptions was modified to secure the balance between supply and demand and thus maintain price stability by increasing the items eligible for elastic tariff rates from 25 to 70, including rice, salt, raw materials, agricultural chemicals, and assorted feeds. To limit imports and improve the balance-of-payments position, tariff reductions and exemptions were made item-by-item instead of industry-by-industry, as applied earlier, and the range of exemptions was reduced.

Finally, the government modified the budget for 1974 because of the drastic changes in internal tax and tariffs. Although the revenue from the income tax and the travel tax was expected to decline by 39.6 billion won, the revenue from the liquor tax, entrance tax, commodity tax, acquisition tax, property tax, and taxes on petroleum products was expected to increase by 63.8 billion won. Out of the net revenue increase, 32.8 billion won was appropriated for financing the public works projects, the subsidy to farmers, the subsidies to the coal industry and to small and medium-size firms, and a 30 percent increase in salaries of government employees. Moreover, 43 billion won from the general account plus 7 billion from the special account were held in reserve to suppress aggregate demand by controlling government expenditures. Use of this reserved fund required approval from the president.

Energy-Specific Policy Measures

The Korean government's immediate response to the 1973 oil crisis was to introduce emergency measures for energy conservation and nationwide publicity campaigns for voluntary conservation of energy. This first emergency program was consolidated later into a more comprehensive energy program, the main objective of which was to achieve economic growth with less energy consumption and less dependence on oil. Accordingly, several energy-specific policies, which were designed to conserve energy and substitute other fuels for oil, were implemented in 1974.

Energy conservation measures. Some of the most important conservation measures include pricing policies, publicity campaigns, financial and fiscal incentive schemes, regulations for registration, and institutional arrangements.

Subsidized electricity had been used to promote industrial development and coal briquettes were subsidized for the poorest segment of the population. The increase in the price of petroleum in 1974, however, drastically altered that policy. The government increased the domestic prices of petroleum products to fully reflect the increased cost of imported oil. Passing on the sharp rise in the world oil price to final consumers generated strong incentives for conservation. Furthermore, a heavy tax was imposed on gasoline, increasing from 200 percent to 300 percent.

Initially, the government was reluctant to increase abruptly the prices of coal and electricity, especially in the case of coal briquettes, because these were used by the middle- and lower-income groups. Later, when a government study on coal consumption patterns showed that many users of coal briquettes could afford the full cost of coal, the price of coal briquettes in real terms increased sharply from 1977 through 1980. This had the effect of inducing conservation and stimulating coal production. In 1975, after charging subsidized rates for many years, the Korea Electric Company (KECO) obtained substantial rate increases; to encourage energy conservation KECO introduced peak-load pricing in 1977 and increasing block schedules in 1979.

These pricing policies appropriate for energy conservation were further augmented with other conservation programs. The Heat Management Law, enacted on 1 January 1974, was aimed at promoting effective use of energy by industry. The law, which was amended in December 1975, required that every firm using more than 500 tons of anthracite coal (or its equivalent) submit an annual plan for energy conservation and employ a heat manager to supervise the plan's execution.

The Heat Management Law also provided for the establishment of energy consumption standards and the creation in May 1974 of the Korea Energy Management Association (KEMA). The law commissioned KEMA, under the guidance of the Ministry of Commerce and Industry, to perform heat audits, train heat managers, inspect fuel-using equipment, provide technical assistance to large heat users, and recommend methods for improving efficiency in energy use.

During 1975–80 KEMA conducted numerous activities including heat audits of large-scale industrial plants, technical guidance visits to medium-size industrial and large commercial plants, on-site energy conservation reviews, and consultations. It also carried out inspection of boilers and pressure vessels for pressure and safety. If the recommended improvements had been carried out the savings would have been, according to KEMA's estimate, 9.4 percent of industrial energy consumption in 1975–80. KEMA also held energy conservation meetings, seminars, and training workshops for heat managers, engineers, and technicians.

Since 1975 the government has been promoting an annual National Convention on Energy Conservation Promotion and an annual Energy Conservation Exhibition. Case study reports by heat managers, engineers, and technicians are discussed and energy-savings systems, new developments, and models of new concepts are exhibited. The national convention, held in Seoul and presided over by the prime minister, is attended by more than 3,000 participants each year. Commendations are announced for successful conservation cases, and prizes ranging from the President's and Prime Minister's Prizes to the Minister's Prize are awarded.

The efforts of the government to promote energy conservation were also reflected in institutional developments. The Korea Institute of Energy Conservation (KIEC) was established in September 1977 to conduct research on several aspects of conservation, with special emphasis on maximizing the efficiency of fuel-using equipment. KIEC became the Korea Energy Research Institute (KERI) in 1980, performing integrated energy-policy studies. In 1978 the Ministry of Energy and Resources was formed, taking its staff largely from the Ministry of Commerce and Industry. The new ministry assumed responsibility for national energy planning and energy conservation.

In response to the second oil shock of 1979–80 and the doubling of the world oil price, the Ministry of Energy and Resources promulgated the Law Governing Rationalization in the Use of Energy in June 1980, which replaced the Heat Management Law. The objective of the new law was to promote the rational use of energy in all areas and for all users, including residential, commercial, and transportation sectors not previously covered. It has the same strict regulations as the Heat Management Law, but also empowered KEMA to order fuel conversion and to designate uses of fuels. The new law also included provisions for improvement of the total energy supply system and established a fund to assist in rationalizing energy utilization. The fund provided preferential loans for: (1) introduction of energy-saving equipment, (2) installation of combined heat and power supply systems, (3) installation of building insulation, and (4) research on and development of energy-saving equipment.

Within the framework of the above legislative and institutional arrangements, the Korean government introduced several conservation policies specifically aimed at industrial, transportation, residential, commercial, and the power sectors.

The Law Governing Rationalization in the Use of Energy of 1980 introduced fiscal and financial incentives to encourage investment in energy-saving techniques and equipment. Preferential loans for industrial energy savings investment, insulation of buildings, and solar system installation were provided by the Energy Rationalization Fund, the Energy Savings Facilities Fund, and the Solar Energy Promotion Fund. The government also provided tax incentives for energy-saving investment, such as special depreciation allowances (100 percent of investment for the first year) and an investment tax credit of 8–10 percent from corporate or income tax. The government also reduced the tariff rates on imported energy-saving facilities from 15–30 percent to 0–15 percent.

To promote energy conservation in the transportation sector, the government restricted the private ownership of automobiles by imposing high acquisition and quarterly use taxes on cars and a gasoline tax of 300 percent. Since 1977 a special excise tax of 180 percent on gasoline and 7 percent on diesel fuel has been levied, in addition to the general value-added tax of 10 percent. Furthermore, the government enforced temporary conservation restrictions during the first and second oil crises—gas stations were closed on Saturdays and Sundays, limitations were put on the use of official cars, and speed limits were strictly enforced. In the residential and commercial sectors, the government launched various publicity and educational campaigns to encourage voluntary energy conservation, such as using less light and heat at home, limiting the use of private cars, and walking any distance shorter than two kilometers between home and office and school.

During the first and second oil crises, the government imposed many temporary but mandatory restrictions on the use of energy. Air-conditioning was banned except during the period from July 10 to August 20; outdoor signs using electricity were not allowed except for hospitals, pharmacies, and emergency purposes; the number of street lights or the level of lighting was cut in half; restaurants and similar commercial establishments were instructed to close one night per week; elevator operations on floors lower than the third were banned; and surcharges were imposed on individual households using more than 500 kilowatt-hours (kwh) of electricity per month.

Building codes for new homes and buildings were made mandatory. The government also instituted schemes for labeling energy efficiency for a limited number of consumer electric appliances. Finally, preferential loans were made available for home insulation and installation of solar hot-water heaters.

Because the power sector was the largest end-user of primary energy, the government embarked on a coordinated effort to improve overall energy efficiency for power plants and to promote energy conservation at the consumer end. KECO gradually retired old plants with low thermal efficiency and set up mandatory targets of thermal efficiency for each remaining plant. The 345-kV transmission network, commissioned in 1971, became the backbone of the transmission system. KECO also upgraded the distribution voltage from the 100/200V to the 220/330V level. Furthermore, an automatic load-dispatching facility installed in 1979 enables KECO to provide economic dispatch. The most important measure for saving electric energy, however, was the revised tariff structure. Residential and commercial consumers were put on an escalating block schedule so that, as they used more electricity, the average charge per kwh increased. Furthermore, the previous decreasing rate schedule for industrial customers was replaced in 1979 by a flat-rate schedule for all energy consumption. Finally, for load-management purposes, peak-load pricing was introduced in 1977 for large industrial customers. Such revisions of the tariff structure were introduced as an incentive to reduce consumption and shift use to hours when average electricity costs were lower.

Transition away from oil as the dominant source of primary energy. The Korean economy has undergone three energy transitions. The first transition, from firewood to anthracite coal, was made during the period of the First Five-Year Economic Development Plan (1962–66). The second transition was characterized by the replacement of coal by oil during the period of the Second Five-Year Economic Development Plan. Since the oil crisis of 1973–74, a new transition from oil to a different mix of imported fuels has been under way.

The oil crisis of 1973, the steep rises in oil prices in 1974, the prospect of further oil price increases, and the possibility of future shortages led the government to promote the maximum exploitation of domestic energy resources and to diversify imported fuels among oil, coal, and nuclear energy. The government promptly launched an interim program for increased development of domestic energy resources and a nationwide campaign to conserve energy. It also prepared a long-term plan for rationalizing energy supplies and minimizing their costs. To increase production of domestic coal, the government raised the price by 51 percent in 1974 and by another 26 percent in 1975. It also provided a grant of up to 70 percent of the cost of getting a mine into operation and concessionary loans for up to 15 percent of these costs for the coal industry. This subsidy was mainly financed with the proceeds from the special tax levied on bunker-C oil. Although the government had promoted maximum exploitation of hydroelectric resources, hydropower could not meet the sharp increase in fuel demand arising from rapid economic development and industrialization. Consequently, the government looked to other imported fuels, particularly nuclear fuel and coal.

The government strongly encouraged the cement industry to replace oil with imported bituminous coal through subsidized credit measures. It also ordered the power company to burn coal instead of oil in all generating plants capable of burning either fuel. Furthermore, the government switched its major fuel for power generation from oil to a mix of nuclear energy, bituminous coal, and oil by constructing nuclear power plants, coal-fired power plants, as well as oil-fired power plants. Since the first oil crisis, the central feature of the Korean program for power expansion has been a massive shift to nuclear power and coal-fired thermal power. Finally, as domestic coal nearly reached its maximum rate of production, the government began to import anthracite coal to slow down the substitution of petroleum products for coal in the residential and commercial sector.

THEORETICAL APPROPRIATENESS

The Presidential Emergency Decree

The principal objectives of the decree were to bring about an equitable distribution of the burden of the imported inflation and to cushion the effect of the worldwide recession on domestic economic growth. To this end, tax reductions for low-income groups and tax increases for high-income groups were introduced, along with lower controlled prices on basic necessities and higher taxes on luxuries and leisure activities. The decree also included measures preventing the deliberate deterioration of the work environment and established the rights of workers to protect them from abuses by their employers.

Although one of the objectives was to distribute the burden of the imported inflation in an equitable manner, the decree actually sought to reverse the increasing disparity in income distribution of the preceding several years. Earlier economic policies were oriented toward achieving economic growth and little attention was paid to equitable income distribution. The gap between the rich and poor had become, however, a cause for social unrest by the early 1970s and it became necessary for political stability that the government undertake measures to bring about income redistribution. The oil crisis gave the government a timely opportunity for introducing the measures, which under other circumstances would have met with greater resistance from certain segments of the society.

Given the objectives of redistributing income in favor of the poor and restraining the consumption of luxuries by the rich, were the measures in the decree appropriate? Lowering taxes for low-income groups and raising taxes for high-income groups for the purpose of redistribution are measures consistent with efficient allocation of resources, if they have a negligible effect on the work–leisure choice. Also, given the objective of curtailing the consumption of luxuries and leisure activities and what might be called conspicuous consumption, heavy taxation of such activities was an appropriate measure.

Additional measures for income redistribution such as the provision of low-priced basic necessities and the dual-pricing system for rice (selling rice at a low price and buying it at a high price) created a price distortion in the economy. The dual-pricing system—which required government financing—contributed to inflation and inefficient allocation of resources. The low controlled prices of basic necessities brought about occasional shortages in supply and necessitated the provision of subsidies to production to increase their supply. Where subsidies were not offered or were insufficient to increase production to meet the demand, shortages were met with imports. These imports, which were larger than they would have been if prices had not been held artificially low, required additional foreign exchange.

Although heavy taxation of the consumption of luxuries and leisure activities is appropriate to the objective of curtailing these activities, it may not have been needed if the financial institutions had been liberalized. Given the repressed financial regime and low interest rates, there was little incentive for the rich to save for future consumption. The consumption pattern of the rich of overspending on current consumption should be viewed, therefore, as a consequence of the distortion in the financial market.

In Korea the rich and the middle class could lend money in the unorganized money markets, earning rates higher than those offered by the banks. The Presidential Emergency Decree of 3 August 1972, which was intended to relieve the debt burden of large businesses, had a confiscatory effect on moneylenders in the unorganized money markets. After that experience and faced with low interest rates in the organized money market, it would not be too difficult for anyone to decide to spend more now and save less.

The distortion in the financial market and government actions like the decree of 3 August 1972 may have caused the saving ratio of households to be lower than it would have been without such distortion and thereby led to the heavy reliance on foreign savings. Thus, the distortion in the financial market; government actions affecting property rights, consumption of luxuries and leisure activities; and foreign debt should be considered not as separate but as interdependent issues. High taxes on leisure activities and the consumption of luxuries may help restrain such activities, but will do little to increase domestic saving, and thus decrease dependence on foreign savings, without financial liberalization and the security of private property.

The decree made a provision for preferential credit assistance to small and medium-size firms on the verge of bankruptcy. Its objective was to maintain employment and thus ensure the livelihood of low-income wage earners. Although the measure is commendable, one must ask why the small and medium-size firms were more vulnerable than others to bankruptcy. The large firms have been favored customers in the organized money markets whereas small and medium-size firms were the major borrowers in the unorganized money markets. The latter paid higher interest rates than the former and were probably adversely affected by the decree of 3 August 1972, as it had the effect of drying up the credit supply in the unorganized money markets. This is an example of how distortion in one market necessitates the introduction of distortion in another market. The result is "patch-on-patch-up" economic policies where the excess burden of the two policies is additive, not offsetting.

The effectiveness of the decree of 14 January 1974 in coping with the first oil crisis may lie in its moderating influence on wage increases. Tax cuts for low-income groups and lowering the prices of basic necessities cushioned the decrease in real wages caused by oil price increases. These measures, combined with increased taxes on high-income groups and on luxury items, made it possible for the government to hold wage increases to a moderate pace. These moderate wage increases contributed to Korea's ability to increase its exports of services and merchandise, to carry out successful import substitution, and to allow an annual GDP growth rate of 7.2 percent during 1974–82. This was accomplished, in part, by making Korean labor internationally competitive; the decree made this possible without bringing about political instability. Income redistribution and restraints on luxury consumption, which were the principal objectives of the decree, could be thus regarded as intermediate steps toward this end.

Energy-Specific Policy Measures

Broadly speaking, energy-specific policy measures may be broken down into price and nonprice measures. These measures were introduced to achieve energy conservation and substitution of other fuels for oil.

The key to understanding the Korean energy policy and response to the oil crisis lies in recognizing that, throughout the 1960s and into the early 1970s, the use of energy was subsidized for industrial users to promote industrial development and for households because it was a basic necessity. Oil price increases, however, made this cheap energy policy too costly to continue. Adjustments were thus made in the prices of fuels to reflect the increases in the world price of oil which brought about energy conservation and interfuel substitution.

A more fundamental issue is whether or not nonprice measures such as publicity campaigns and the employment of heat managers were necessary. As additional measures to price adjustments they may have contributed to the speed at which energy conservation and interfuel substitution were carried out. The effectiveness of such measures, however, depends on the moral leadership of politicians or the coercive power of the government. The effectiveness of the moral leadership of politicians is short-lived and the coercive power of the government entails enforcements costs and creates room for discontent and corruption. A society must choose, given its historical and political background, an optimum combination of price and nonprice measures to bring about energy conservation and interfuel substitution. Whether or not the combination introduced in the decree was optimal is difficult to say, but the effectiveness of the moral leadership of politicians and of the coercive power of the government is subject to the law of diminishing returns.

EFFECTS OF THE POLICY MEASURES

The Presidential Emergency Decree[1]

In 1974 GNP grew at an annual rate of 8 percent in real terms, and in 1974–82 GDP grew at an annual rate of 7.2 percent. Compared with the rate of 9.7

percent in 1964–73, this was a slight decrease. Relative to other developing countries in Asia and to the rest of the world, Korea fared well during the turbulent period of 1974 through 1982. What accounts for this performance of the economy? How much did the decree contribute to it?

In their study of external shocks and policy responses of Asian countries, Naya, Kim, and James (1984:18) conclude:

> The NICs [newly industrializing countries] were able to withstand the impacts of the external shocks much more successfully than countries in Southeast and South Asia, though the effects on the NICs were greater relative to the size of their economies. The reason for the better performance of the NICs lay in their long-term strategies and policies rather than in their short-term responses. Their outward-looking trade and industrialization policies and market-oriented pricing policies, especially for production inputs, added to the resilience of their economies.

Although we agree with the above conclusion, we believe that the decree as a short-term measure had the effect of stabilizing wages in the face of deteriorating terms of trade. Among the NICs, Korea relied less on import reduction through lower GNP growth as a policy response to the external shocks, but more on export-market penetration and import substitution. The reason for the latter is, we argue, the international competitiveness of Korean labor. The decree contributed to that competitiveness by holding down the rate of wage increase.

In analyzing the factors accounting for Korea's economic growth in 1974–82, the role of external savings cannot be ignored. Table 8.2 shows a close relationship between the imports of petroleum and petroleum products and the increase in foreign debt. There were clear quantum jumps for both items in 1974 and 1979—the years of oil crisis. We also find three distinct phases in the table. In 1968–73 the average annual imports of petroleum and petroleum products was $169 million and the average annual increase in foreign debt was $603 million. These amounts increased, respectively, to $1.7 billion and $2.1 billion in 1974–78, and to $5.8 billion and $5.6 billion in 1979–82. These figures indicate that Korea's foreign debt in effect financed its oil imports. Thus, without having to reduce imports, the country increased its exports and carried out its successful import substitution with a small decrease in its economic growth rate.

In 1982 Korea had an external debt of $37 billion. One could have argued then that its excellent record in 1974–82 was purchased at the price of this huge external debt and that the day of reckoning was due at any moment. Naya, Kim, and James (1984) argued, however, that given its ability to adjust to external shocks, and with continuing excellent export performance, Korea should be able to meet its debt obligations. According to their

---

1. The author is grateful to Dr. Chung H. Lee for contributing this section concerning the effects of the Presidential Emergency Decree.

Table 8.2. External debt and imports of petroleum and petroleum products:
1967–82 (10⁶ US $)

Year	External debt outstanding	Increase in external debt	Imports of petroleum and petroleum products
1967	645		59
1968	1,199	554	73
1969	1,800	601	108
1970	2,245	445	133
1971	2,922	677	187
1972	3,589	667	218
1973	4,260	671	296
1974	5,937	1,677	1,020
1975	8,456	2,519	1,339
1976	10,533	2,077	1,658
1977	12,648	2,115	2,065
1978	14,871	2,223	2,312
1979	20,500	5,629	3,416
1980	27,365	6,865	6,164
1981	32,490	5,125	6,918
1982	37,314	4,824	6,740

Source: Adapted from Table 4 in I. C. Kim (1983b) and BOK, *Economic Statistics Yearbook* (1970–85).

Note:
Average annual increase in external debt
  1968–73: $603 million
  1974–78: $2,122 million
  1979–82: $5,611 million

Average annual imports of petroleum and petroleum products
  1968–73: $169 million
  1974–78: $1,679 million
  1979–82: $5,810 million

calculation, Korea's debt service to GNP ratio was 4.7 in 1973, 4.8 in 1980, and 5.7 in 1982. Their estimates of the debt service to exports ratio during these three years were 15.1, 12.2, and 13.1, respectively. The figures were taken to indicate that Korea's ability to service external debt did not significantly deteriorate during 1974–82. The current account surpluses of recent years have indeed proved their prediction to be correct.

Energy-Specific Policy Measures

Progress in energy conservation. Some conservation measures have already brought about important changes in energy efficiency, particularly in the industrial sector. Although it is difficult to define the exact effect of these measures, the use of macroindicators backed with more disaggregated indicators provides a useful means of monitoring progress in energy efficiency.

Overall energy efficiency and intensity of energy use (measured by energy consumption per unit of real GNP), rose sharply between 1960 and 1973 (Figure 8.1). But since then, this trend has been reversed due to increased conservation efforts and structural changes in the economy.

Inasmuch as the energy/GNP ratio is not an exact measure of energy conservation potential, more detailed analyses are needed to assess gains in energy efficiency. Hence, we estimated an energy-demand equation using time-series data from 1961 to 1980 (see note in Table 8.3). With this equation we estimated the hypothetical energy consumption—the consumption that would have prevailed if there had been no oil crisis—at 43,299 thousand TOE (tons of oil equivalent) in 1980 (Table 8.3). Compared with the actual energy consumption, these hypothetical figures are higher by about 3 to 8.4 percent. These estimates suggest that Korea's energy conservation program was fairly successful.

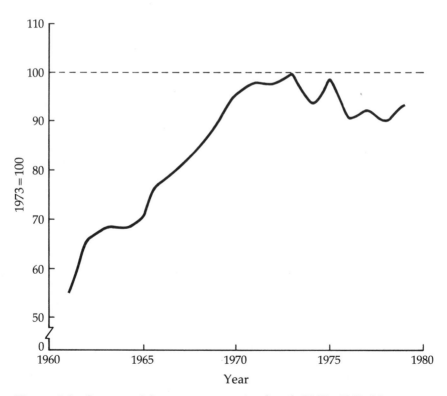

Figure 8.1. Commercial energy per unit of real GNP: 1960–80
Source: EPB, ROK, *Handbook of Korean Economy* (1980).

Table 8.3. Actual versus hypothetical energy: 1974–80

Year	Total primary energy (10³ TOE)		Estimated reduction of energy consumption (%)
	Actual	Hypothetical	
1974	25,510	27,654	8.4
1975	27,076	28,673	5.9
1976	29,805	31,566	5.9
1977	33,074	34,761	5.1
1978	36,157	38,660	6.9
1979	40,503	41,727	3.0
1980	41,103	43,229	5.2

Source: Ministry of Energy and Resources, ROK, unpublished data.

Note:

$$\ln E = 0.5892 + 0.5442 \ln E_{-1} + 0.4518\ Y - 0.0560\ D,$$
$$(2.29)\quad (6.10)\qquad\qquad (5.80)\qquad (-3.03)$$
$$R^2 = 0.998,\ DW = 1.92$$

where E = energy consumption in 10^3 TOE

E_{-1} = lagged energy consumption in 10^3 TOE

Y = GNP in 1975 billion won

D = 0, 1961–73

1, 1974–80

Figures in parentheses are t-values for the estimated coefficients.

The equation is statistically significant, explaining 99.8 percent of the variance in aggregate energy consumption for the period. It was used to estimate hypothetical energy consumption for 1974–80, assuming that $D = 0$. The estimated values were then compared with actual energy consumption, the difference between the two being a rough indicator of the reduction in energy demand obtained in 1974–80.

TOE—tons of oil equivalent.

An accurate estimate of conservation results is hampered by conceptual difficulties and by data limitations. Nevertheless, an econometric model can provide a useful means of monitoring progress in energy efficiency, especially if it is backed up by more disaggregated indicators such as sectoral energy consumption per unit of output. In the case of Korea it is possible to use input–output tables for 1970, 1975, and 1978, and derive physical coefficients of total energy use for the industrial sectors. Table 8.4 shows these fixed-coefficient estimates used for industrial energy savings during 1970–75 and 1975–78, assuming that no technical change in energy use occurred between these periods.

Table 8.4 clearly reveals a large decrease in energy requirements between 1970 and 1978. If technology as represented by the 1970 energy-use coefficients had persisted until 1975, all industries would have required 23 percent more than their actual use. The difference would have been even greater (34 percent) by 1978. If, however, technology as represented by the 1975 energy-use coefficients had persisted until 1978, all industries would have required 8 percent more energy. That is, energy savings of more than 8 percent did occur between 1975 and 1978 over and above those achieved between 1970 and 1975.

Table 8.3 indicates that direct energy coefficients in the manufacturing sector declined more sharply between 1970 and 1975 than between 1975 and 1978. These large changes between 1970 and 1975 happened soon after the petroleum price increases and resulted mostly from short-run, improved energy-conservation management rather than from long-run economies associated with new plant or equipment. They seem to have occurred mainly in light and heavy manufactures where energy is used primarily for processing, materials forming, cutting and handling (e.g., textiles, electrical machinery, transport, and machinery) rather than in the production of basic materials. Savings in energy-intensive manufactures occurred in 1975-78, as energy-saving designs and economies of scale were incorporated into new plants and equipment. Table 8.4 also indicates that an important technical change in energy consumption occurred in rapidly expanding industries that have higher energy costs.

The input–output studies suggest that the heavy industry path of industrialization, adopted in the early 1970s, was accomplished without requiring more energy for a given level of industrial activity. Table 8.4 shows that direct energy-use coefficients of manufacturing, which were expressed in thousand tons of oil equivalent (10^3 TOE) per 1975 billion won of gross output, declined from 1.28 TOE/10^6 in 1970 to 1.02 in 1975 and then to 0.824 in 1978. This was achieved through a greater emphasis on less energy-intensive heavy and chemical manufactures.

Table 8.5 shows the structural changes in the manufacturing sector between 1970 and 1978. The output share of light manufactures declined gradually from 52.6 percent to 44.2 percent, while that of heavy and chemical manufactures rose from 47.4 percent to 55.8 percent. Note, however, that within heavy and chemical manufactures the output share of energy-intensive manufactures decreased from 39.9 percent in 1970 to 34.0 percent in 1978. (For a more detailed study, see Y.H. Kim 1983.)

Progress in energy transition away from oil. Korea has made considerable efforts to decrease its oil dependency mainly through restructuring fuel patterns for power generation away from oil to a mix of nuclear energy, bituminous coal, and oil. Although the main benefits of the restructuring are expected to accrue in the next 5-10 years because power plants have the longest investment gestation period in the economy, some of the decisions made since 1974 have already brought about important changes in energy supply patterns with the oil dependency of the electric-generation sector declining from 81 percent in 1973 to 77 percent in 1980. Korea's oil dependency rose from 53 percent in 1973 to 63 percent in 1979, but declined to 61 percent in 1980 (Kim and Smith 1989).

Table 8.4. Estimates of energy efficiency by sector: 1970–78 (excluding noncommercial energy)

Sector	Gross output (10⁹ won at 1975 prices)			Energy intensity (TOE per 10⁶ won)			Energy savings (10³ TOE)		
	1970	1975	1978	1970	1975	1978	1975[a]	1978 (I)[b]	1978 (II)[c]
Light manufactures	2,052.6	4,859.3	8,483.8	0.653	0.513	0.413	964.0	844.4	2,532.9
Food, beverages, tobacco	1,044.5	1,820.4	3,149.3	0.525	0.482	0.367	78.3	362.2	497.6
Textiles and apparel	554.0	2,532.6	3,600.0	0.886	0.572	0.479	653.9	334.8	1,465.2
Lumber and wood products	176.7	269.3	478.5	0.526	0.451	0.353	20.2	46.9	82.8
Miscellaneous manufactures	277.4	687.0	1,256.0	0.752	0.444	0.364	211.6	100.5	487.3
Heavy manufactures	294.0	1,534.7	4,158.4	1.235	0.483	0.360	1,262.6	496.9	3,791.3
Fabricated metal products	43.2	180.0	494.6	1.795	0.992	0.699	144.5	144.9	542.1
General machinery	63.5	185.7	471.5	0.891	0.816	0.566	13.9	117.9	153.2
Electrical machinery and equipment	96.1	681.6	2,073.4	1.059	0.344	0.278	487.3	136.8	1,619.3
Transport machinery	74.1	423.2	942.9	1.001	0.366	0.267	607.3	93.3	1,446.4
Precision and optical products	17.1	64.2	176.0	0.488	0.339	0.316	9.6	4.0	30.3
Energy-intensive manufactures	1,559.5	3,886.1	6,547.4	2.104	1.866	1.650	814.4	1,661.2	3,068.5
Pulp and paper	88.9	216.4	384.3	1.440	0.997	0.893	95.9	40.0	210.2
Chemicals, coal, petroleum	1,085.2	2,550.7	4,009.4	1.678	1.450	1.359	581.6	364.9	1,279.0
Nonmetallic mineral products	196.0	338.5	573.4	4.230	3.920	3.289	104.9	361.8	539.6
Primary iron and steel	160.4	689.6	1,356.2	2.512	2.705	2.136	-133.1	771.7	509.9
Primary nonferrous metals	29.0	90.9	224.1	3.397	1.581	1.033	165.1	122.8	529.8

Manufacturing (total)	3,906.1	10,280.1	19,189.6	1.280	1.020	0.824	3,041.0	3,002.5	9,392.7
Agriculture	2,301.6	2,629.8	3,097.3	0.067	0.102	0.128	-92.0	-80.5	-188.9
Fishery products	150.5	316.0	328.2	3.245	2.944	4.813	95.1	-613.4	-514.6
Mining	79.5	114.4	159.2	1.373	1.235	1.211	15.8	3.8	25.8
Electricity	147.5	319.3	507.2	15.252	14.544	13.831	226.1	361.6	720.7
Construction and other utilities	1,005.2	1,579.8	2,808.2	0.829	0.554	0.449	434.4	294.9	1,067.1
Transport and storage	572.3	1,044.3	1,728.3	5.240	4.237	3.826	1,047.4	710.3	2,443.8
Commerce and services	2,997.6	4,360.3	6,341.0	0.616	0.460	0.553	680.2	-589.7	-399.5
Grand total	11,160.3	20,644.0	34,159.0	1.226	1.152	1.065	5,448.0	3,089.5	12,547.1

Source: BOK, *Input–Output Tables* (1970, 1975, 1978).

a. 1975 energy savings through the use of 1975 energy coefficients instead of 1970 coefficients.

b. 1978 energy savings through the use of 1978 energy coefficients instead of 1975 coefficients.

c. 1978 energy savings through the use of 1978 energy coefficients instead of 1970 coefficients.

TOE—tons of oil equivalent.

Table 8.5. Composition and growth of the manufacturing sector: 1970–78 (%)

Subsector	Composition			Annual growth rate	
	1970	1975	1978	1970–75	1975–78
Light manufactures	52.6	47.3	44.2	18.8	20.4
Food, beverages, and tobacco	26.8	17.7	16.4	11.8	20.0
Textiles and apparel	14.2	20.3	18.8	30.3	20.0
Lumber and wood products	4.5	2.6	2.5	8.8	21.1
Miscellaneous manufactures	7.1	6.7	6.5	19.9	22.3
Heavy manufactures	7.5	14.9	21.7	39.2	39.4
Fabricated metal products	1.1	1.8	2.6	33.0	40.1
General machinery	1.6	1.8	2.5	23.9	36.4
Electrical machinery and equipment	2.5	6.6	10.8	48.0	44.9
Transport machinery	1.9	4.1	4.9	41.7	30.6
Precision and optical products	0.4	0.6	0.9	30.3	40.0
Energy-intensive manufactures	39.9	37.8	34.1	20.0	19.0
Pulp and paper	2.3	2.1	2.0	19.5	21.1
Chemicals, coal, and petroleum	27.8	24.8	20.9	18.6	16.3
Nonmetallic mineral products	5.0	3.3	3.0	11.5	19.2
Primary iron and steel	4.1	6.7	7.0	33.9	25.3
Primary nonferrous metals	0.7	0.9	1.2	25.7	35.1
Grand total	100.0	100.0	100.0	21.4	23.1

Source: Table 8.4.

CRITICISMS AND LESSONS

The Presidential Emergency Decree

There is no doubt that by most standards we may regard Korea's response to the external shock of 1973–74 (and that of 1979) as a success. One measure of this success is that GDP grew at an average annual rate of 7.2 percent during the turbulent 1974–82 period. This is higher than the rate achieved by any of the other Asian developing countries, except Hong Kong and Singapore.

This success in maintaining a high rate of economic growth was in part due to the fact that the government did not deviate from its basic macroeconomic objectives—rapid economic growth and industrialization—in the face of a severe external shock. Instead of reducing imports by lowering the rate of economic growth and instituting import-substitution, the government continued with its policies of export promotion and external financing. These policies made it possible to pursue macroeconomic objectives without being overly concerned with the balance-of-payments constraint. One consequence of the policies was, however, a rapid increase in Korea's external debt, which rose from $3.6 billion in 1972 to $12.6 billion in 1977 (J. H. Kim 1987). Such a rapid increase in external debt, which eventually reached $40 billion in 1983, raised doubts in some quarters as to the solvency of the Korean economy—but these doubts disappeared by the mid-1980s with the continuing success of the economy and current account surpluses.

The Presidential Emergency Decree of 14 January 1974 played a critical, short-term role complementary to the macroeconomic policies. Given the terms of trade deterioration resulting from the oil price increase, there would have been pressure for wage increases if the burden of the deterioration was not equitably shared. In one sweep the decree brought about income distribution, thus mitigating the effect of the oil shock on the poor and wage earners. The government was thus able to moderate wage increases and maintain the competitive edge of the Korean economy. The decree probably made it easy for the government to stay with its macroeconomic policies and thus achieve its objectives of export expansion and economic growth.

It is obvious that drastic measures such as the decree cannot be undertaken by a weak government or a government subject to pressure from strong interest groups. Such policy instruments may not be easily duplicated in other countries or even in Korea in later years. In other words, we may say that the decree was an economically efficient and effective instrument that was politically feasible at the place and at the time it was implemented. Whether an equally drastic measure would be politically feasible in Korea at a later date is highly questionable.

Energy-Specific Policy Measures

With rapidity and flexibility the Korean economy achieved three energy transitions, and its energy conservation efforts were also successful in reducing the energy growth rate. The energy transitions and energy conservation were accomplished through a set of policy packages that included pricing policies, regulation, fiscal and financial incentives, and institutional reforms. But these various measures were taken in a rather piecemeal fashion lacking an overall coordination that recognized their interdependence.

Korea's indigenous energy resources remain limited and the country will continue to be heavily dependent on imported fuels, especially oil. According to projections of the Korea Development Institute, the contribution of domestic supplies of energy will continue to diminish, from 31 percent in 1980 to 13 percent in 1991. If the projections are correct, 87 percent of the country's total energy requirements will have to be imported. Continuation of the recent rapid economic growth rate—around 8 percent—thus entails acceleration of the third energy transition, from oil to a mix of other imported fuels, and economies in the use of energy.

Because energy pervades all aspects of economic activity and its demand is derived from the structure and growth of the whole economy, the policy goal of achieving an optimal mix of fuels and conservation of energy will be realized only if it is supported by adequate policies of demand management in the consuming sectors—industry, transportation, and residential/commercial. It is, therefore, essential that the energy implications of alternative development policies in all these sectors be properly appraised, and that effective trade-offs be made between energy efficiency and additional capital expenditures, fuel conversion and additional capital expenditures, and technologies that differ in energy intensity and capital cost.

Clearly, maximization of energy efficiency requires changes in the economic structure. The essence of restructuring the sectoral output mix is to redirect final demand and producers' purchases away from energy and energy-intensive goods. Accordingly, the current incentive system should be reformulated to accelerate changes for both the final demand mix and the input proportions of domestic production. Meeting the energy challenge entails a large-scale reallocation of resources and thus calls for bold policy changes covering prices, tariffs, subsidies, tax incentive schemes, and financial policies. Unless Korea realigns its economic policies in this way, before oil becomes scarce and more expensive, its economic security will be endangered.

Critical to such realignment would be further institutional arrangements to make the Ministry of Energy and Resources stronger and more expert. But no matter how good the Ministry of Energy and Resources becomes, much of its work will involve coordination with other ministries as well as with businesses and the public. In formulating and implementing energy policy, the ministry will have to judge political, economic, technical, and other market forces affecting energy choices. Such judgments must be based on support from other key ministries such as finance, industry, transportation, construction, foreign affairs, and defense. This puts a high premium on the political standing of the energy minister and on his skill in interministerial decision making.

The Ministry of Energy and Resources should develop a considerable capacity for negotiating with other ministries and official bodies, cultivating allies, and finding ways to persuade reluctant officials, businessmen, and others about the efficient use of energy and the consequential changes in regard to fuels. Thus a premium is also placed on the kinds of contacts the ministry's experts and policy planning staff have with all other parts of the government. The extent to which these other government bodies participate in the ministry's effort to have close exchanges rests on the power of the minister and on the caliber of his staff.

9 The Comprehensive Stabilization Program (1979)

by Sang-Woo Nam

By the early 1970s Koreans had learned to live with a high rate of inflation—a rate that had averaged well over 10 percent per year since 1960. Korean policymakers and others tended to look at inflation as an inevitable price for high economic growth. After the first oil price shock of 1973, however, there were obvious signs that inflation was accelerating.

During the nine years preceding the energy crisis, the rate of increase in consumer prices had averaged 11.4 percent per year, but during 1974–75 the rate jumped to 25 percent. These high rates were caused by more than just the import price hike; they reflected inflationary pressures that had built up over many years. By 1976–78, the inflation rate was several percentage points higher than it had been before the oil crisis. Even with virtually no import price increase, consumer prices continued to rise at an annual average of 13 percent (Table 9.1).

Table 9.1. Macroeconomic overview: 1976–78

Item	1976	1977	1978
GNP growth (%)	15.1	10.3	11.6
Fixed investment (%)	14.7	26.6	39.4
Exports of goods and services (%)	43.0	26.7	17.5
Employment growth (%)	6.1	3.0	4.3
Unemployment rate (%)	3.9	3.8	3.2
Current account balance (10^6 US $)	–314	12	–1,085
Commodity exports (10^6 US $)	7,815	10,047	12,711
Receipts from overseas construction (10^6 US $)	247	657	1,049
New orders received (10^6 US $)	2,502	3,516	8,145
Inflation rate (%)			
Wholesale prices	12.1	9.0	11.7
Consumer prices	15.3	10.1	14.4
Food and beverages	17.8	11.6	16.7
GNP deflator	17.7	16.3	20.6
Wages	35.5	32.1	35.0

Sources: BOK, *Economic Statistics Yearbook* (1979); Ministry of Construction, ROK, unpublished data.

It is not difficult to trace the sources of the accelerating inflation. One of the main causes was the excessive expansion of the money supply, which grew at an average annual rate of 32.1 percent during the 1976–78 period. That rapid expansion of money was largely a consequence of the growth of net foreign assets, a large deficit in the government's Grain Management Fund, brisk investment demand, and the expansion of preferential policy loans (Table 9.2).

On the supply side, the sectoral imbalance in the allocation of capital for fixed investment aggravated inflationary pressures. During 1976–78 more than 77 percent of all manufacturing equipment investment was undertaken in the heavy and chemical industries. To make the investment possible, an increasing share of bank credit was allocated to these industries, a share that reached 60 percent in 1978 even though heavy and chemical industries accounted for only half of manufacturing production (KDI 1981).

With a disproportionate share of scarce capital being diverted to investment projects that required a long gestation period, the modernization and capacity expansion of other sectors was constrained. These sectors included agriculture, small and medium-size businesses, and the commodity distribution system—sectors that together ensure the smooth supply of daily necessities and other essential commodities. Low productivity in these sectors and the resulting supply shortages were major sources of inflation and threatened to disrupt the stability of the economy.

Government efforts to reduce inflation through price controls did more harm than good. In the course of regulation the government usually deferred justifiable price adjustments for far too long. Once increases were

Table 9.2. Expansion of the money supply: 1971–78 (%)

Item	1971–73	1974–75	1976–77	1978
Money supply (M_1)	34.0	27.3	35.7	24.9
	(33.1)	(24.5)	(34.7)	(32.2)
Sectoral contribution				
Government	7.8	21.0	–2.0	4.5
(Grain and fertilizer management)	(8.9)	(26.4)	(13.6)	(8.5)
Private	17.2	51.0	5.8	46.9
Foreign	10.8	–31.3	41.9	–11.6
Other	–1.8	–13.4	–9.9	–15.0
Quasi-money	28.5	25.6	37.2	40.9
Money supply broadly defined (M_2)	30.3	26.1	36.6	35.0
	(33.6)	(26.6)	(33.1)	(39.3)

Sources: BOK, *Economic Statistics Yearbook* (1979); Ministry of Finance, ROK, unpublished data.

Note: Based on year-end figures except for those in parentheses, which are based on annual averages.

allowed, prices tended to acquire an independent upward momentum. This pattern of "stop–go" price setting also led to such undesirable effects as supply shortages, deteriorating product quality, and inadequate investment.

On the cost side, high inflation was accompanied by a rapid rise in wages. During 1976–78, wages increased at an annual rate of 34.2 percent, far surpassing the growth of labor productivity—an indication that wage increases were a major inflationary factor. With soaring housing and land prices, the rapid wage increases seemed to have produced little improvement in workers' welfare (Table 9.3). Finally, it was frequently alleged that the introduction of the value-added tax (VAT) system in 1977 exacerbated inflation. The VAT system may have indeed contributed to accelerating inflation because of the downward rigidity of prices in the process of price restructuring.

Persistent high inflation threatened the prospects for high growth by eroding the competitiveness of Korean exports in the international market. Weakening export competitiveness means slow growth for the Korean economy, which is dependent on an outward-looking growth strategy. Korean export growth slowed between 1977 and 1979, as export profitability deteriorated with the acceleration of wage and price increases. During 1976–79, Korea's export profits dropped by 32 percent as unit labor costs rose by 137

Table 9.3. Export profitability and export growth, 1976–79

	1976	1977	1978	1979
Nominal wage (manufacturing) (A)	134.7	180.2	242.1	311.4
Labor productivity (manufacturing) (B)				
KPC index[a]	107.2	118.8	133.1	154.1
National income data[b]	101.0	110.5	123.8	131.2
Unit labor cost [(C)=(A/B)]				
KPC index	125.7	151.7	181.9	202.1
National income data	133.4	163.1	195.6	237.3
Unit value of exports (won) (D)	111.7	122.3	135.4	161.8
Export profitability (D/C)				
KPC index	88.9	80.6	74.4	80.1
National income data	83.7	75.0	69.2	68.2
Growth of exports (%)[c]				
Korea	51.8	30.2	26.5	18.4
Taiwan	53.8	14.6	35.5	26.9
Singapore	22.5	25.1	23.0	40.4
Hong Kong	41.9	12.9	19.5	31.7

Sources: BOK, *Economic Statistics Yearbook* (1980); IMF (1982); Directorate General of Budget, Accounting and Statistics, Taiwan, *Monthly Bulletin of Statistics* (1977–80).

a. Korea Productivity Center (KPC) index (1975 = 100).

b. Computed by using national income data (value added per worker, 1975 = 100).

c. Percentages computed on the basis of current US dollars.

percent and the unit value of exports increased only about 62 percent (Table 9.3). Unit labor costs, measured in U.S. dollars, rose only 23 percent in Singapore and 40–45 percent in Taiwan and Hong Kong during the same period.

There was increasingly strong evidence that the potential energy of the nation was being wasted by the high inflationary pressures and diverted from effective concentration on economic development. Korean entrepreneurs, lured by incentives to speculate in real estate and inventories, were distracted from the technological and managerial innovation needed for long-term growth. Businesses were frequently blamed for being preoccupied with borrowing as much money as possible from banks, only to invest it in real estate or to expand unproductive businesses.

The waste of productive resources was also evident in the more diffused atmosphere of society at large, and it was closely related to the widening disparity in income distribution. The rich made speculative fortunes overnight that far outstripped what an honest wage earner could save in a lifetime. Thus, more and more resources, including some of the nation's best managerial talent, were enticed into speculative activities. Finding themselves unrewarded, workers grew frustrated and developed negative attitudes toward their work. Their discontent was occasionally expressed in organized demonstrations.

Although consistent data on income distribution are scant, income distribution seems to have deteriorated in the latter half of the 1970s. Tighter credit rationing in favor of the heavy and chemical industries, which occurred at the expense of small and medium-size businesses, and various government regulations restraining competition among producers contributed to the concentration of economic power. Soaring prices of real estate was probably an even more important cause of the deterioration in the distribution of wealth. Between 1973 and 1978, average housing and residential land prices jumped by factors of 4.5 and 7.1, respectively, while consumer prices and urban household income multiplied only 2.3 and 3.5 times (EPB, ROK, *Annual Report on the Family Income and Expenditure Survey*, 1982; KNHC 1980). Thus the differences in wealth between those with their own houses and those without widened (Table 9.4).

Table 9.4. Household income distribution by class and degree of income concentration: 1965–80

Item	1965	1970	1976	1980
Gini coefficient	0.344	0.332	0.391	0.389
One-tenth distribution ratio (lower 40%/upper 20%)	19.3/41.8	19.6/41.6	16.9/45.3	16.1/45.4

Sources: Figures for 1965, 1970, and 1976 are from KDI (1979), estimated by Dr. Choo Hak Joong. Figures for 1980 are from EPB, ROK, *Social Indicators* (1982).

MAJOR FEATURES
OF THE STABILIZATION PROGRAM

Major Contents of the Program

A consensus within the government that a major policy change was needed had been developing for some time. The newly appointed deputy prime minister, Shin Hyon Whack, was strongly in favor of a stabilization policy. Therefore, in December 1978, President Park asked three institutions—the Economic and Scientific Council, the Bank of Korea, and the Korea Development ment Institute (KDI)—independently to propose policy measures to deal with the problems of the Korean economy. Upon being briefed by each of the these institutions, President Park asked the Economic Planning Board (EPB) to formulate and implement comprehensive stabilization measures based on the three reports.

The result was the Comprehensive Stabilization Program announced on 17 April 1979 by the EPB. The major features of the program were:

- restrictive budget management with expenditure cuts and deferral of some public investment projects;
- restrictive monetary policy with particular attention given to improving the operation of preferential policy loans and interest rates;
- adjustment of investment in the heavy and chemical industries;
- facilitation of the supply and stabilization of the price of daily necessities, including improvements in the commodity distribution system, financial and tax support for producers, elimination of institutional barriers restraining supply capacity, and a deceleration of price controls; and
- reaffirmation of the government's determination, originally announced in the August 1978 Comprehensive Measure, to prevent a recurrence of real estate speculation.

Restrictive Fiscal and Monetary Management

To cool off the overheated economy, the government further limited monetary expansion, which had already been restricted since late 1978. The year-end target of monetary expansion was set at 23–25 percent, a drastic reduction compared with the record of the previous three years, when growth in the broadly defined money supply had ranged from 33 to 40 percent annually. However, the trend of strong private investment and consumption expenditures early in 1979 indicated that the GNP growth rate for 1979 would greatly surpass the original target which had been set at 9 percent. Thus, the government thought that monetary restrictions should be strengthened to make sure that the monetary target would be attained. Because the government had already planned to restrict the foreign sector's contribution to the expansion of the money supply by limiting the increase in net foreign assets to below $300 million, it had to tighten credit in the government and private domestic sector.

The stabilization program included measures to reduce the money supply available to the government sector by about 300 billion won, an amount equal to 7 percent of total government revenue and 15 percent of the total increase in the money supply planned for 1979. The program for the reduction of government expenditures included a 5 percent cut in current spending, a reduction in subsidies to local governments, a postponement of construction plans for government offices and government-backed institutions, and adjustments in other public construction work plans.

Attention was also called to the need for conservative fiscal management for 1980, underscoring the importance of a substantial reduction in the deficits generated by the high grain-price support program. Suggested priority areas for the 1980 budget included stabilizing the livelihood of the people and enhancing the nation's economic growth potential by: (1) sponsoring more diversified and mechanized farming, (2) expanding investment in social infrastructure and manpower development, (3) providing greater support for the modernization of the nation's distribution system and to small and medium-size firms, and (4) promoting the machinery industry.

For more efficient financial management and effective credit control, the program emphasized the need to improve the operation of preferential policy loans, including export-support credit and interest-rate adjustments.

Specifically, the program's sponsors noted that the designated strategic sectors had been given priority in the allocation of bank credit causing an excessive reduction in the availability of funds for less favored sectors. It was also recognized that too many sectors were eligible and that there were no clear rules for selection. These were to be corrected to ensure that preferential financing would be sufficiently sustained to provide adequate future support to such strategic sectors as the heavy and chemical industries, particularly in providing financing for exports on a deferred payment basis. On the basis of this diagnosis, officials in charge of the program suggested that preferential financing be decreased and managed by an investment coordination committee that would not only decide the total size but also determine allocation priorities and the desirability of individual projects.

With regard to the export-financing system, qualification for access to export credit was eased to include exporters with annual exports of over $10 million regardless of their ratios of net foreign exchange earnings content. Procedures for exporters to obtain credit for raw material imports were simplified and made more flexible. Interest-rate adjustments for the mobilization of additional savings were made on some categories of bank deposits, corporate bonds, and short-term finance company paper. Interest rates on bank installment time deposits, for example, were raised from 13.2 to 16.2 percent per annum. Furthermore, a more comprehensive program for improvement of the financial sector, including the operation of preferential policy loans and interest rates, was to be prepared by the end of June 1979.

Readjustment of Investment

Investment in the heavy and chemical industries was disproportionately large; the supply of skilled labor and the capacity to absorb related technology lagged far behind the huge investments in these industries. Thus, the products of those investments could not be expected to compete favorably in international markets. The investment needs of the heavy and chemical industries were beyond the capacity of domestic savings, and served to limit investment and supply capacity in the light manufacturing and related service sectors, which produce consumer goods for domestic consumption.

The picture on the demand side was no brighter. The level of investment in the heavy and chemical industries surpassed potential demand even before the second oil price shock in 1979.

Recognizing these problems, stabilization program authorities outlined the following general directions for the support of the heavy and chemical industries.

1. More attention was to be given to such basic requirements for the successful promotion of the heavy and chemical industries as workforce development, the smooth introduction of foreign technology, and an effective incentive system.

2. The support system for the heavy and chemical industries was to be designed to be more concentrated and selective. Support would be limited to areas in which Korea had a strong international comparative advantage. But the industries selected would be given effective and systematic support until they graduated from the import-substitution stage and became competitive export industries. For industrial sectors other than selected heavy and chemical industries, government protection from foreign imports would be reduced and competition allowed.

3. The scale, content, and timing of investment plans for heavy and chemical industrial projects were to be readjusted. The basic guideline for adjusting investment projects was to postpone or cancel projects that led to excess capacity or duplication of facilities. Projects without a long-term comparative advantage in international markets, or without adequate private financing, were also to be reconsidered.

As proposed in the program, the Investment Coordination Committee was established to oversee investment readjustment. Headed by the deputy prime minister, the committee was composed of the ministers of finance, commerce and industry, and energy and resources, together with the chief economic secretaries to the president, and a few others. The committee was to review and consider postponement of all new investment projects and those already under construction that were using over $5 million in foreign loans or domestic loans in foreign currency.

Price Stabilization for Daily Necessities

Because the high rate of inflation during 1976–78 was largely caused by a demand–supply imbalance in food and some other essential commodities, the program included measures to forestall any recurrence of a rapid rise in prices of those commodities. The measures designed to increase the supply of agricultural and marine products were highly comprehensive. Stability in the prices of daily necessities and other essential commodities was also pursued through financial supports, tariff cuts, and institutional reforms.

Improvement of the commodity distribution system was given continuous attention in the stabilization program. The establishment of specialized wholesale dealers and large-scale retail sales outlets such as supermarkets and chain stores was encouraged, and the drafting of a more comprehensive program for the modernization of the nation's distribution system was planned. Finally, to minimize distortions originating from extensive price controls, the number of monopolistic and oligopolistic products whose prices were under government control was to be reduced from 74 items to the roughly 30 items considered critical to the stable livelihood of the people.

To alleviate the economic burden of people most adversely affected by price decontrol, the government planned to extend direct assistance to the poor. A total of about 30 billion won was appropriated to aid the poor. Tuition subsidies for middle-school children were extended and wages for relief employment in public works were increased. Compensation for rises in coal briquette prices was also provided.

IMPLEMENTATION

Policy Response to the Second Oil Price Shock

Less than three months after the Comprehensive Stabilization Program was launched, the nation was hit by a round of steep increases in international oil prices. The immediate impact of the increases, together with the removal of price controls from a large number of commodities, was a sharp acceleration of domestic inflation. Both wholesale and consumer prices rose by as much as 18 to 19 percent in 1979.

Economic activity also slowed suddenly in the latter half of 1979. The growth of GNP, which had been over 10 percent during the first half of the year, dropped to 6.4 percent for the year as a whole. Owing to the increasing uncertainty resulting from higher oil prices, fixed investment decelerated drastically. Commodity exports, which had been slowly weakening since 1977, registered a negative real growth rate (–2.5 percent) in 1979. The current account deficit rose to $4.2 billion, almost four times as large as that of 1978.

By early 1980 prospects were even more gloomy than they had been in 1979. The oil import bill for 1980 was expected to increase by more than

$3 billion, and there was little hope for a comparable expansion of Korea's exports. Under the circumstances, economic policymakers strongly felt that some action should be taken in response to the unfavorable overseas developments and the economic complications caused by domestic political developments. They seem to have been convinced that a doubling of the number of unemployed, to more than one million, would be a critical threat to social and political stability and that a further deterioration in the balance of payments might lead to serious questioning abroad about the creditworthiness of the Korean economy.

Immediately after the New Year's holiday, Dr. Kim Mahn Je, president of KDI, was asked to prepare a report for President Choi Kyu Hah called "Measures to Cope with Economic Difficulties." The report was the basis for the policy package announced on 12 January 1980 by the minister of finance. The package included two important policy adjustments: devaluation of the won and an increase in interest rates.

Given the accumulated overvaluation of the Korean won since 1975, the exchange-rate adjustment was inevitable. The won was devalued by 20 percent—from 484 to 580 won per U.S. dollar. As a follow-up measure, a floating exchange-rate system based on a basket of major currencies was adopted in late February. The decision to float the won was made to prevent abrupt and excessively large exchange-rate adjustments and also to avoid sudden shifts in the terms of trade vis-à-vis non-U.S. trading partners.

The upward annual interest-rate adjustment averaged 5 to 6 percent for all financial assets in the organized markets. The interest rate on general bank loans, for example, was raised from 19 percent to 25 percent per annum. The interest-rate adjustment was designed mainly to offset part of the newly fueled cost-push effect of the won devaluation by absorbing liquidity. In other words, the interest-rate adjustment could be construed as a continued commitment to the stabilization policy on the part of the government.

Reflationary Policy Packages
in Response to the 1980 Predicament

Several months after the interest-rate adjustment, financial savings increased substantially, helping to absorb excess liquidity. However, as the economic situation continued to deteriorate in the midst of social unrest, the government gradually eased the original restrictive policy stance on three separate occasions—in June, September, and November 1980.

The government announced a set of policies on 5 June 1980 calling for the allocation of additional funds for public works programs and the expansion of loans to small and medium-size enterprises and for housing construction targeted for low-income families. To stimulate investment and boost business confidence, the official interest rates were lowered by 1 to 2 percentage points and a planned upward adjustment of interest rates for short-term export loans was postponed. To accommodate these policy adjustments, the targeted money-supply growth rates were adjusted upward by 5 percentage points to 20 and 25 percent for the narrowly and broadly defined money supply, respectively.

In spite of the June measures, general economic activity remained sluggish except for the export sectors, which reacted favorably to the exchange-rate depreciation in January. Therefore, two more policy packages were prepared—one in September and the other in November—to expand housing construction, to stimulate exports and investments, and to support purchases of selected consumer durables.

The policies included measures to reduce the range of capital gains tax rates on real estate transactions from 50–80 percent to 35–75 percent, and to make more credit available to stimulate residential construction. Measures to promote exports included an upward adjustment of export loans per dollar of letter of credit and strong financial support for exports of heavy industrial products on a deferred payment basis. As a means of stimulating fixed investment by easing the financial burden of businesses, bank and nonbank interest rates were readjusted downward by an average of 2 to 3 percentage points in September and another 2 to 3 percentage points in November. Finally, to encourage purchases of selected consumer durables, easy credit and a 30 percent cut in sales tax rates were offered.

Despite these expansionary measures, monetary management continued to be tight, in part as a result of large deficits in the balance of payments. The annual monetary expansion for 1980 was contained at 16.3 and 26.9 percent for the narrowly and broadly defined money supply, respectively.

The performance of the Korean economy in 1980 was disappointing. In the midst of weak domestic demand, GNP declined to 6.2 percent, while unemployment rose sharply to 5.2 percent. An unusually long spell of cold weather throughout the summer months of 1980 resulted in a crop loss amounting to a quarter of the expected yield. Because of the sharp deterioration in the terms of trade, the current account deficit widened to $5.3 billion. Inflation of wholesale and consumer prices accelerated to record levels of 39 and 29 percent, respectively. The 36 percent exchange-rate depreciation vis-à-vis the U.S. dollar together with the 20 percent rise in unit import prices were the primary causes of the rapid rise in the inflation rate.

Stabilization Efforts and Initial Steps
Toward Structural Improvement in 1981

In spite of a strong surge in export orders, recovery remained elusive, with little sign of any pickup in investment. This situation prompted the announcement of an additional reflationary package in April 1981, which included additional credit for exporters and small and medium-size firms to replace or upgrade their facilities, and expanded fiscal support for purchases of domestic machinery and equipment.

The housing construction industry remained weak despite the reduction in the capital gains tax rate in September 1980. Therefore, another program was drafted in late June 1981 to encourage housing construction. The program included an extension of the temporary tax reduction on capital gains, an increase in the deduction for the annual inflation allowance from 10 to 15 percent in the calculation of capital gains, and additional loans for the purchases of small apartment units.

During the last two months of 1981, the government relaxed its tight monetary policy somewhat by lowering the interest rates three times by a total of about 3 percentage points, in step with a sizable decline in the inflation rate. The rates of money supply growth were 4.6 and 25 percent for the narrowly and broadly defined money supply, respectively. In addition to rather tight monetary management, the government resorted to moral persuasion for wage restraint to prevent the effect of the exchange-rate depreciation from being offset by a corresponding wage-price spiral.

To enhance popular understanding of the difficult economic situation and to build a broad consensus behind the new economic policy direction, economic education was started toward the end of 1980 on a presidential initiative. In December 1981 an economic education task force was formed within the EPB until a formal organization—the Bureau of Economic Education—was established a year later.

Stabilization efforts were also reflected in the exchange-rate policy. Exchange rates were maintained within a narrow range and prices for government-held rice and public utility services were set cautiously.

As a result of these efforts, as well as the relative stability in import prices and domestic food prices, the rate of inflation was substantially reduced to a level slightly over 20 percent.

The GNP growth rate for 1981 was 6.4 percent, representing a substantial recovery from the 6.2 percent decrease in 1980. Commodity exports expanded by more than 18 percent in real terms and led the economic recovery. Consequently, the current account deficit was narrowed to $4.6 billion, a $700 million improvement over the previous year.

The significance of 1981 goes beyond the aggregate economic performance of that year. To enhance the efficiency of the entire economic system, the government took important first steps toward major reforms in at least three areas during 1981: financial liberalization, realignment of the industrial incentive system, and promotion of competition among domestic and foreign firms.

The government divested itself of equity shares in the Hanil Bank, one of the nation's five major commercial banks. An over-the-counter commercial paper market was developed for short-term finance companies and merchant banking corporations. Interest rates on these notes were left to market forces, although a ceiling was later imposed.

In the area of industrial policy, new guidelines for industrial promotion were introduced. The basic idea was to equalize incentives for investment in all industries and to gradually phase out the existing discriminatory system. The new guidelines were geared to benefit industries with a current or potential international competitive edge, and projects related to either manpower and technology development or higher energy efficiency.

The Fair Trade and Anti-Monopoly Act, which has been in effect since April 1981, has minimized the purview of direct price controls. To promote foreign competition, commodity imports and direct foreign investment were further liberalized.

Reflationary Measures in Response to the Delayed Recovery of the World Economy

On 14 January 1982, soon after the cabinet reshuffle in early January, the new economic policymaking team—the so-called "real economy" team headed by Deputy Prime Minister Kim Joon Sung—prepared a policy package designed to stimulate economic recovery. The package included measures to promote exports, encourage housing construction and other domestic investment, and expand support for the agricultural sector.

In May the government implemented another set of policy measures to further stimulate the economy. A large-scale road-paving project with a capital requirement of 200 billion won was announced. Small and medium-size firms were given increased financial support amounting to 220 billion won. Efforts to further stimulate housing construction included sharp reductions or the elimination of capital gains taxes on newly built houses and on land to be used for small housing plots, as well as a reduction of the acquisition and registration taxes on small housing units.

Shortly before the May measure, however, an unfortunate incident in the curb-loan market forced two of the largest corporations into bankruptcy. The shock of the incident led to a sharp curtailment of the curb-loan market and also of the activities of the organized short-term financial market. Consequently, many businesses were suddenly faced with a shortage of operating funds, leading to a brief rash of corporate defaults.

Another policy package, released on 28 June, had as its most important feature the reduction of bank interest rates on both deposits and loans by an average of 4 percentage points. Virtually all bank lending rates were lowered to 10 percent per annum, eliminating special consideration for prime borrowers or preferential policy sectors, such as exporters or small and medium-size firms. In addition, the government planned to reduce the corporate income tax rate, and special consumption taxes on some consumer durables were reduced to promote demand for those products.

Finally, with a view to correcting the structural weaknesses of the Korean financial sector, a banking reform program was incorporated into the package. The reform led to three more major commercial banks being privatized by 1983.

In early July, several days after the June measures, the Ministry of Finance announced a proposal to require all financial transactions to be made in the original names of the persons concerned. This proposal sought to weaken the unregulated curb-loan market and to establish an institutional foundation for more equitable taxation. Implementation of this controversial proposal was repeatedly postponed by the National Assembly on the grounds that its potential disruptive impact on the financial market would be too serious and that more administrative preparation was needed prior to its implementation. Nevertheless, some progress was made toward discouraging people from holding financial assets anonymously or under fictitious names by imposing heavy taxes. The "real-name" requirement for financial transactions is scheduled for implementation in 1991.

Bank credit expanded fairly rapidly in the wake of the curb-loan scandal in May. The growth of the broadly defined money supply reached as high as 32 percent during the 12-month period before the end of the third quarter of 1982, but it decreased to 27 percent by the end of the year.

Inflation rates as measured by wholesale and consumer prices were further stabilized at 4.7 and 7.2 percent, respectively, for 1982.

The real GNP growth rate for 1982 remained at 5.3 percent. Commodity exports rose only 2.5 percent, reflecting a delayed recovery of the world economy, but domestic fixed investment showed a sharp 11.6 percent increase. The 1982 current account deficit decreased to $2.7 billion from $4.6 billion in the previous year, or from 7.5 to 4.5 percent of GNP.

Strong Recovery with Further Reduction of Inflation in 1983

Given the expected recovery of the world economy in 1983, top priority in economic management for 1983 was focused on maintaining continuous price stability while fully exploiting the momentum of economic recovery by strengthening the competitive position of Korean industries.

The rate of monetary expansion in 1983 was originally planned at 18 percent in broadly defined terms, compared with a 27 percent increase in 1982. This target was later revised to 15 percent as prices stabilized more than expected partly because of a cut in oil prices in the spring.

During the fall of 1982, several months after the 4 percentage point drop in bank interest rates, the real estate market started to show signs of heating up. Tentative antispeculation measures implemented in December 1982 included a stepped-up monitoring of real-estate transactions in areas of widespread speculation and improvement in the housing distribution system. As a speculative housing boom reappeared in the early spring and summer of 1983, however, the government took additional measures to stop real estate speculation in April and September 1983.

By 1983 the Korean economy had regained the strong growth momentum of old, registering a GNP growth rate slightly in excess of 9 percent for that year (Table 9.5).

Table 9.5. Economic trends: 1979–83

	1979	1980	1981	1982	1983
GNP growth (%)	6.4	–6.2	6.4	5.3	9.2
Fixed investment (%)	9.7	–12.0	–6.1	11.6	12.3
Exports of goods and services (%)	–3.6	9.9	17.2	4.4	13.3
Employment growth (%)	1.3	0.3	2.5	2.7	1.3
Unemployment rate (%)	3.8	5.2	4.5	4.4	4.2
Current account balance (10^6 US $)	–4,151	–5,321	–4,646	–2,650	–1,619
Trade balance (10^6 US $)	–4,396	–4,384	–3,628	–2,594	–1,649
Exports (10^6 US $)	14,705	17,214	20,671	20,879	23,100
Services and transfers (10^6 US $)	244	–937	–1,018	–55	30
Inflation rate (%)					
Wholesale prices	18.8	38.9	20.4	4.7	0.2
Consumer prices	18.3	28.7	21.3	7.3	3.4
GNP deflator	19.3	25.8	16.2	7.7	2.8
Wages	28.3	23.4	20.7	15.8	12.0
Expansion of money supply[a] (%)					
Narrowly defined (M_1)	20.7	16.2	4.6	45.6	17.2
Broadly defined (M_2)	24.6	26.9	25.0	27.0	15.3
Unified budget deficit (ratio to GNP)	1.5	3.4	5.0	4.6	2.6
Interest rates[a] (%)					
One-year time deposit	18.6	19.5	16.2	8.0	8.0
General loans (one-year)	18.5	19.5	16.5	10.0	10.0
Exchange rate[a] (won/US $)	484.0	659.9	700.5	748.8	795.5

Sources: BOK, *Economic Statistics Yearbook* (1984); Ministry of Finance, ROK, unpublished data.
a. Year-end.

The rapid increase in commodity exports since the latter half of 1983 has mainly been the result of the U.S. economic recovery and its overvalued currency. The current account deficit was reduced to $1.6 billion in 1983.

Prices remained remarkably stable throughout 1983 despite the full-fledged economic recovery and the relatively high increase in wages. On an average annual basis, wholesale prices rose only 0.2 percent, and consumer prices showed a modest rise of 3.4 percent.

Consistent with the efforts to stabilize costs, monetary policy remained rather restrictive. That was a significant achievement in light of the depressing impact on the domestic financial market of two tragedies in 1983—the shooting down of the Korean Airlines aircraft and the terrorist bombing of senior Korean officials in Rangoon. Expansion of the money supply during 1983, narrowly and broadly defined, was contained to 17.2 and 15.3 percent, respectively.

During 1983 significant progress was made toward structural improvement of the economy. In the financial sector, divestiture of government shares of the major commercial banks continued, and the lowering of entry barriers late in 1982 was rewarded with the opening of two joint-venture banks, many short-term finance companies, and mutual savings and finance companies.

Efforts to expose the economy to the bracing effects of foreign competition also continued. New policy measures were released in October 1982 that allowed direct foreign investment in an additional 94 Korean Standard Industrial Classification (KSIC) industries, and simplified administrative procedures surrounding such investment.

Korea's import liberalization ratio was again raised from 74.6 to 80.4 percent as the government liberalized imports of an additional 305 Customs Cooperation Council Nomenclature (CCCN) eight-digit commodities in July 1983.

THEORETICAL BASIS AND EFFECTS OF THE POLICY

Monetary Management

The central policy tool in stabilization efforts after 1979 was the restriction of the money supply. The basic approach to stabilization was to let the tight money policy reduce inflationary pressure and, at the same time, to stabilize all the major cost factors such as wages and interest. One could say that Korea's stabilization efforts were basically based on the monetarist thesis that, in the long run, the quantity of money is the key variable determining inflation, whereas real economic activity is little affected by the money supply.

As already described, the growth of the money supply slowed significantly after 1978 (Table 9.5). The drastic fluctuation of money supply growth during 1981–82 largely reflected changes in the bank-deposit system that included the July 1981 strengthening of interest-rate incentives to expand savings deposits, and the July 1982 abolition of the notice deposit.[1]

A major question in managing monetary policy and monitoring its effects is to decide which monetary aggregate to use as a central indicator. In Korea the pivotal indicator shifted from the narrowly defined money supply (M_1) during most of the 1960s, to domestic credit during 1970–78, and then to the broadly defined money supply (M_2) in 1979. The rationale for relying heavily on the broadly defined money supply is that it is a more comprehensive indicator and thus a more stable one.

---

1. A type of deposit requiring notice prior to withdrawal of funds. Firms were the main depositors.

It is true that a broadly defined monetary aggregate is less vulnerable to a shift of funds among different types of deposits due to changes in the interest-rate structure and the deposit system. The fact that an indicator shows a more stable trend, however, does not necessarily indicate that it is a more reliable monetary aggregate in the sense that it has a closer relationship with economic activity. Quite to the contrary, S. W. Nam (1982) shows that the correlation between the rate of monetary expansion and that of nominal GNP is much higher for the narrowly defined money supply. That is why it is mainly the narrowly defined money supply that is used for the analysis in this paper.

In connection with monetary policy after 1979, one may ask whether there is any significant relation between money supply and the inflation rate and, if so, how is it possible to explain the disparity between the relatively high growth rate of money and the slow rate of nominal GNP growth during 1982–83. To answer these questions, the monetarist approach holds that inflation is determined in the money market with the money supply assumed to be more or less exogenously given. Demand for money will depend not only on income, but also on interest rates and the expected inflation rate. Then, a downward adjustment of interest rates and decelerating inflationary expectations will lower the inflation rate for a given rate of monetary expansion by increasing the demand for money.

A simple money-determined price model, presented in Appendix 9.1, seems to strongly support this thesis. The inflation rate is well fitted with the growth of money supply per unit of production, real interest rates, and a measure of inflationary expectations (Figure 9.1). Viewing the same model from another angle, demand for real-money balances also turns out to be significantly affected by real interest rates and inflationary expectations. The rate of growth of the money supply during 1982–83 was high—25 percent in the narrowly defined money supply and 23.8 percent in the broadly defined money supply on an annual average basis—compared with the 13 percent growth of nominal GNP. To a large extent, the difference between the growth rates of the money supply and nominal GNP seems to be explainable by the large drop in interest rates and the decline in inflationary expectations since late 1981.

In this connection, it is not difficult to find examples of steady and significant drops in inflation and interest rates over the course of several years being followed by a period when prices showed stability even with the relatively rapid expansion of the money supply (Table 9.6). After inflation in consumer prices in Taiwan decreased steadily from 18.5 percent in 1960 to 2.4 percent in 1962, the money supply grew at an annual rate of 23.2 percent during 1963–64. Still, prices remained stable and nominal GNP grew only 15.1 percent a year during that period. Chile is another case in point. There, the rate of consumer price increases dropped from 506 percent in 1974 to 40 percent in 1978, and, as the money supply increased at an aver-

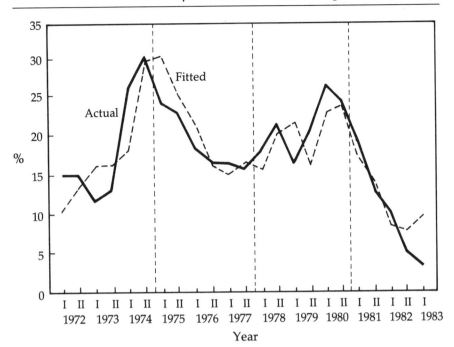

Figure 9.1. The tracking of inflation by money supply growth (annual rate of GNP deflator increase): 1972–83

Note: For the equation from which the fitted values are derived, refer to Appendix 9.1.

age rate of 63 percent a year during 1978–80, the nominal GNP grew at an annual rate of only 48 percent.

Although there is a consensus that a tight money policy is necessary to curb inflation, resistance from business circles has proven to be rather strong. Business leaders have argued for years that Korea's money stock is too small to adequately support economic activity; thus the money supply growth rate should be increased rather than restricted. How erroneous this argument is can easily be seen by comparing countries with differing rates of money supply growth. In the case of Chile, where the money supply grew at a very high annual rate of 125 percent during 1971–81, the M_1/nominal gross domestic product (GDP) ratio dropped from 18.4 percent in 1970 to 5.8 percent in 1981, when the inflation rate went as high as 165 percent. A similar trend was also evident in other Latin American countries suffering from hyperinflation such as Argentina, Uruguay, and Brazil.

Japan and West Germany are the opposite cases in which stable growth of money has led to low inflation and a slight rise in the M_1/nominal GDP ratio. They offer strong evidence that higher levels of money supply growth increase the velocity of money and thus increase the elasticity of nominal GDP (or prices) with respect to the money supply. This is simply because

Table 9.6. Average annual rate of money supply growth and velocity: 1970-81 (%)

Country	Growth of M_1[a] (A)	Growth of nominal GDP[a] (B)	Real GDP[a]	GDP deflator[a]	Change in velocity	Elasticity of nominal GDP with respect to money (B/A)	M_1/Nominal GDP 1970	M_1/Nominal GDP 1981
High-inflation countries[b]								
Chile	124.8	170.2	2.1	164.6	20.2	1.36	18.4	5.8
Argentina	107.8	138.6	1.9	134.2	14.8	1.29	17.0	8.6
Uruguay	53.5	65.2	3.1	60.2	7.6	1.22	14.4	7.8
Brazil	46.7	54.0	8.4	42.1	5.0	1.16	16.5	8.8
Peru	34.3	38.3	3.0	34.3	3.0	1.12	17.0	12.3
Low-inflation countries								
Singapore	14.5	14.1	8.5	5.2	-0.3	0.97	28.1	26.5
Panama[c]	12.4	12.5	4.6	7.6	0.1	1.01	9.6	9.4
Japan	12.3	12.2	4.5	7.4	-0.1	0.99	29.1	30.4
West Germany	7.9	7.7	2.6	5.0	-0.2	0.97	15.4	15.5
Korea	26.2	30.7	9.1	19.8	3.6	1.17	11.5	9.1

Sources: IMF (1983); World Bank (1978-83).

a. Growth rates have been computed by using the least-squares method and are drawn from World Bank (1982).

b. The Latin American countries with the highest inflation rates during 1970-81.

c. The Latin American country with the lowest inflation rate.

GDP—gross domestic product.

expectations of high inflation are produced by rapid monetary expansion and, having these expectations, people become less interested in holding large real-money balances.

Fiscal Policy

The performance of fiscal management in relation to the stabilization efforts may be evaluated by the response to two questions: whether fiscal policy was anticyclical, and how much progress was made toward improving the budget structure and reducing the budget deficit.

Tight fiscal policy was one of the essential elements of the Comprehensive Stabilization Program of April 1979. The program called for a reduction of government expenditures by 100 billion won, the postponement of some public construction projects, and a tight government budget for 1980. Furthermore, in 1979 a surplus of 368 billion won in the general account of 1978 was not appropriated for general budget spending but used to repay borrowings of the Grain Management Fund and the Government Supply Fund. The result was a contraction of the money supply by 129 billion won in the government sector.

As the economy started to plunge into recession in the latter half of 1979, however, fiscal management could no longer serve the stabilization effort single-mindedly. Enacting anticyclical measures, the government expanded construction activity for the purposes of maintaining growth momentum and creating job opportunities, and it augmented its support to low-income households that were badly squeezed by high inflation.

As a result, deficits in the unified budget, which included 16 special accounts and 25 government-managed funds together with the general account, widened sharply to 4.3 percent of GNP during the 1980–82 recessionary period from 2.8 percent of GNP during the overheated period of 1976–78. The public sector's contribution to money supply growth was also substantial. During 1980–82, some 1.8 trillion won of money was created through this sector, accounting for 72 percent of the growth in the narrowly defined money supply (Figure 9.2).

In 1983, when tax revenue increased much faster than had been planned owing to the strong economic recovery, the ratio of the unified budget deficit to GNP dropped to 2.6 percent from 4.6 percent in the previous year, and there was a slight contraction of money through this sector. What is more noteworthy is that the 1984 budget forecasted a surplus of 580 billion won in the general account and its expenditure level was set 30 billion won below that of the 1983 budget. That represented a strong commitment to stabilization efforts on the part of the government. Moreover, the fact that the National Assembly supported the government's budget proposal seemed to indicate that a broad consensus had been reached on the need to improve fiscal management.

The experiences of many developed countries clearly show that sound

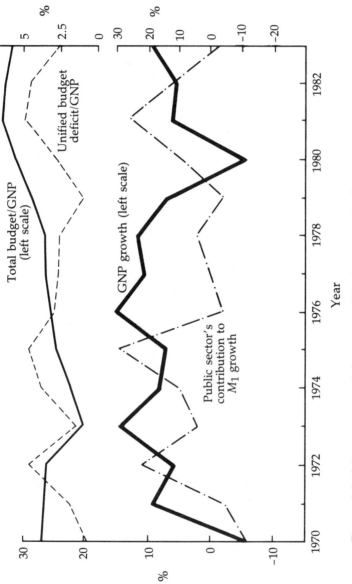

Figure 9.2. Management of the national budget over the business cycle: 1970–83

Source: BOK, *Economic Statistics Yearbook* (various issues).

budget management is essential for maintaining stable prices, avoiding a crowding-out situation in the capital market, promoting a more efficient public sector, and building a healthy reserve. However, the rigidity of the Korean budget structure seriously limits the flexibility of fiscal management.

It is more or less accepted that the minimum defense expenditure will be around 6 percent of GNP or approximately one-third of total spending in the general account. Legally prescribed subsidies to local governments and for education account for another 25 percent. Wages for government employees and the burden of government debts are also nondiscretionary rigid expenditures. These nondiscretionary expenditures, accounting for roughly 70 percent of all general account spending, highlight the importance of reducing the budget deficit.

One of the most critical tasks in the reduction of the budget deficit is improving the operation of government-managed funds. The National Investment Fund and the National Housing Fund could be easily replaced by bank credit. Closing the deficits in the Grain Management Fund and the Fertilizer Account, however, is much tougher.

It took much effort for the government to persuade farmers to accept a lower rate of increase for the government purchase price of rice and barley. Despite a high rate of adjustment for the government's selling price of rice in 1981 and a steady drop in the rate at which purchase prices have increased since 1982, a substantial deficit still remains whose accumulated total at the end of 1983 reached 1.5 trillion won. In 1983 the deficit widened as the government increased purchases and was forced to cut the selling price of rice slightly in situations of stable market prices and growing government stocks (Table 9.7).

The Korean fertilizer industry had been suffering from high production costs because of inefficient facilities, overcapacity, and unprofitable exports. As fertilizer prices were adjusted only once during the 1976–83 period, the deficit in the Fertilizer Account was substantial, leading to an accumulated deficit of 680 billion won at the end of 1983. Borrowings from the Bank of Korea by the Grain Management Fund and the Fertilizer Account together contributed as much as 6.8 percentage points to the 20.9 percent annual growth of the narrowly defined money supply during 1979–83.

Interest and Exchange Rates

After the substantial increase in interest rates in early 1980, the rates were readjusted downward in eight steps. The interest rate on one-year time deposits, for instance, was raised from 18.6 percent to 24 percent per annum in 1980 but was lowered on three occasions and was down to its previous level of 18.6 percent in November 1981. The downward adjustments continued until June 1982 when the rate was lowered from 12.6 to 8 percent per annum (Figure 9.3).

The government considered the interest-rate reductions as justified

Table 9.7. Operation of the Grain Management Fund and Fertilizer Account: 1975–83 (annual averages)

Year	Increase in government rice price		Deficit (10⁹ won)		Borrowings from BOK (10⁹ won)		Contribution to M_1 growth (%)
	Buying (%)	Selling (%)	Grain Management Fund	Fertilizer Account	Grain Management Fund	Fertilizer Account	
1975–78	23.0	18.8	92	22	166	55	15.1
1979	15.4	18.2	209	48	200	0	7.4
1980	22.0	20.8	242	126	130	30	4.9
1981	25.0	37.5	144	162	220	100	8.4
1982	14.0	0.0 (21.2)ª	131	117	200	100	7.5
1983	7.3	–2.3 (–1.9)ª	286	102	250	100	6.0
Accumulated total			1,533	679	1,642	570	

Source: Ministry of Agriculture and Fisheries, ROK, unpublished data.

a. High-grade rice.

BOK—Bank of Korea.

because the anti-inflationary measures were viewed as successful enough to allow positive real interest rates. It also wanted to ease the excessive financial burden of corporations hard-pressed for funds during the recession. Given these policy shifts, one may ask what role the official interest rate was expected to play in Korea and how reasonable was the real interest rate argument?

In the Korean economy, where excess demand for funds has always been a problem, there are limitations on the effectiveness of using interest-rate policies to adjust the demand and supply of funds. Thus monetary policy mainly relied on controls over the money supply in a rather direct way until 1981, but since then it has used a more indirect approach. In practice, interest-rate adjustments have been made with different objectives in mind on each occasion. These included the mobilization of savings, lightening corporate financial burdens in a depressed business environment, and preventing the economy from overheating.

While lowering interest rates in line with decelerating inflation to alleviate the business interest burden, the authorities also attempted to squelch speculative investment in real estate and to lower people's inflationary expectations by stepping up educational efforts to attract financial savings.

When the authorities argued that adequate real interest rates were being given to depositors despite lower nominal interest rates, they were

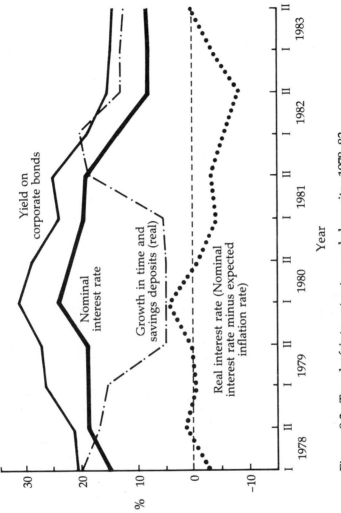

Figure 9.3. Trend of interest rates and deposits: 1978–83

Source: BOK, *Economic Statistics Yearbook* (various issues).

Note: For the calculation of the expected inflation rate, refer to Appendix 9.1.

obviously using the current rate of inflation in their calculation of the real interest rate. When it comes to inflation, however, people usually have long memories and this is particularly the case when they have experienced chronic inflation in the past. The shift of funds from time and savings deposits to demand deposits, the shortening of deposit maturities, and the sporadic speculative movements in the real estate market that followed the June 1982 interest-rate cut seem to indicate that the cut was somewhat larger than justifiable. As time passed and prices remained stable, however, people adjusted to the low interest rate.

Nevertheless, indications are that adjustment is a slow process. The market interest rate, measured by the yield on corporate bonds, was about 5 percentage points higher than the one-year time deposit rate before the June 1982 interest-rate adjustment, but the interest rate differential widened to 7 percentage points in the latter half of 1982 and narrowed only marginally to 6.3 percentage points in 1983. The corporate bond yield was only 27 percent higher than the deposit rate in 1981 but was 78 percent higher in 1983. Time and savings deposits, which grew 19 percent in real terms in the year preceding the June 1982 interest-rate adjustment, increased during 1983–85 at the modest rate of about 10 percent.

In the process of lowering interest rates, important progress was made toward creating a more rational interest-rate structure. By June 1982 the preferential interest rates applied to various policy loans were abolished to make them subject to the same rate as general loans. Until then, the complicated and fairly arbitrary interest-rate structure was believed to be partly responsible for the alleged inefficiency in resource allocation during the 1970s. By eliminating the interest-rate incentive for preferential policy loans, it became easier to scale down or phase out some of the policy loans.

Since early 1980 the exchange rate has been floated against the performance of the currencies of Korea's major trading partners vis-à-vis the U.S. dollar and the differences in the inflation rates between Korea and those countries. This rule enables the exchange rate to be adjusted in such a way as to maintain Korea's overall export competitiveness. The Bank of Korea, which is in charge of managing the exchange rate, seems to have followed this principle fairly closely, even though there has been some deviation.

A look at the degree of exchange rate distortion shows that, during 1981–83, the nominal exchange rate vis-à-vis the U.S. dollar depreciated at a stable 6 to 7 percent a year. Based on a calculation of the real effective exchange rate, the Korean won seems to have been overvalued by about 6 percent during 1981, although that number may vary slightly depending on the composition of the currency basket and the relative weight given to each currency. Since then, owing to the deceleration of the inflation rate, this overvaluation has been essentially corrected (Table 9.8).

Nevertheless, a mechanical calculation of the real effective exchange rate may lead to a misleading conclusion as to the trend of export competitive-

Table 9.8. Real effective exchange rates: 1980–83

End of month	Nominal exchange rate (won/US $)	Nominal exchange rate	Effective exchange rate[a]	Relative price[b]	Real effective exchange rate[c]
		Indexes (end of 1980 = 100)			
12/80	659.9	100.0	100.0	100.0	100.0
6/81	685.1	103.8	96.2	106.1	90.7
12/81	700.5	106.2	100.0	106.5	93.9
6/82	740.8	112.3	97.8	106.3	91.8
12/82	748.8	113.5	102.1	106.9	95.5
6/83	776.7	117.7	103.6	105.9	97.8
9/83	789.3	119.6	105.2	105.6	99.7
12/83	795.5	120.5	105.7		

Sources: BOK, *Economic Statistics Yearbook* (1984); IMF (1983).

a. Effective exchange rate $= \sum_i w_i \left(\dfrac{\text{won per US \$}}{\text{basket currency } i \text{ per US \$}} \right)$.

Basket currencies include those of Korea's seven major trading partners. The weight given to currency $i(w_i)$ is based on its relative trade volume: United States 0.424, Japan 0.397, West Germany 0.067, United Kingdom 0.039, Canada 0.032, France 0.022, and the Netherlands 0.020.

b. Relative price $= \dfrac{\text{WPI (Korea)}}{\sum_i (w_i \text{ WPI}_i)}$.

c. Real effective exchange rate $= \dfrac{\text{effective exchange rate}}{\text{relative price}}$.

ness. For one thing, wholesale price indices may not correctly reflect prices of the goods actually traded. Moreover, the interest rate on export loans was not lowered as much as that on general loans and unit labor costs rose relatively faster than did wholesale prices. Thus export competitiveness after 1982 might have been overestimated because of the difference in interest-rate reductions in the export sector, and to the extent that the export sector is more labor-intensive than the domestic sector.

Wage Policy

Wage guidelines in Korea have a rather short history. They first appeared in a statement by Deputy Prime Minister Nam Duck-Woo in February 1977, when he said, "When a price adjustment is demanded based on wage increases given by monopolistic or oligopolistic producers, the maximum acceptable wage increase will be 15 to 18 percent only." Since the fall of 1981, government announcements of planned pay increases for public servants have served as informal wage guidelines for the private sector. The announced increase rates were 9 percent for 1982, 6 percent for 1983, and a freeze for 1984. Acting through the Bankers' Association of Korea, the government also tried to keep wage increases low by having banks restrict credit to firms that increased wages beyond government guidelines. This move in late 1980, however, faced strong resistance from the Federation of Korean Trade Unions. Whenever there was a more explicit confrontation over this issue, the government would say "There is no official guideline. It is just a suggestion on the part of the government."

That rather insincere and evasive attitude did not help to build a consensus behind the need for wage guidelines. Consequently, workers have become suspicious of any suggestion of wage guidelines, and government efforts to stabilize wages have been ineffective. In spite of a variety of educational programs geared to stabilize wages, the rate of wage increases did not slow as fast as the government had hoped.

Under government influence, negotiated base salary increases in the private sector in 1982 and 1983, which averaged 9.5 and 6.9 percent, respectively, were very close to those for public servants. However, de facto wage increases in the private sector were much higher than the negotiated rates— 15.8 percent in 1982 and about 12 percent in 1983 (Table 9.9)—indicating that effective wage guidelines depend on a broad consensus among labor, management, and the government. Otherwise, businesses can easily circumvent guidelines under the existing complicated wage structure.

Whenever official wage settlements were proposed, the most commonly used formula called for holding wage increases to the rate of inflation plus growth in labor productivity. In practice, ambiguities have always remained, such as which inflation rate (the past or the expected one) should be used and how labor productivity would be measured.

A commonly used labor productivity measure is the productivity index compiled by the Korea Productivity Center (KPC). The KPC productivity

Table 9.9. Increase rates of base salaries and all compensation: 1977–83 (%)

Year	Public servants		Private-sector workers	
	Base salaries	All compensation	Base salaries (negotiated)	All compensation
1977	32.0	25.0	36.0	32.1
1978	20.0	26.0	29.7	35.0
1979	15.0	23.0	26.8	28.3
1980	10.0	22.0	21.5	23.4
1981	10.0	17.0	16.1	20.7
1982	9.0	9.9	9.5	15.8
1983[a]	6.0	8.5	6.9	11.6
1977–83 average	14.6	18.8	20.9	23.8

Sources: Budget Office, EPB, ROK, unpublished data; Korea Employers Federation, unpublished data.

a. Estimated.

index, however, seems to have an upward bias, particularly during recessionary periods. Furthermore, there has been a tendency to apply the rate of labor productivity increase in the manufacturing sector to other sectors, where productivity growth is slower. Measured as value added per worker, labor productivity grew at an annual rate of 5.6 percent during 1976–78, whereas real wages rose as much as 18.5 percent annually. Owing to the stabilization efforts, real wage increases slowed to 2.8 percent a year during 1979–82, although labor productivity declined slightly during the period (Table 9.10).

The rationale for wage restraint was that stable wages were essential for export competitiveness because many of Korea's exports were still labor intensive. Furthermore, because labor costs constitute a large share of total costs of final goods and services, price stability is impossible without stable wages.

As mentioned earlier, Korea's export competitiveness deteriorated sharply during the 1976–79 period because of a sharp increase in unit labor costs. During 1980–82 Korea's unit labor costs in the manufacturing sector rose 50 percent, much faster than in other Asian newly industrializing countries. Nevertheless, because the exchange rate depreciated 51 percent, unit labor costs measured in U.S. dollars did not rise, and they even recovered part of the loss in relative export competitiveness that took place during 1976–79 (Table 9.11).

Misunderstanding and confusion concerning the causal relation between wages and inflation and the contribution of wages to inflation have been frequent. On the basis of regression analysis, some have argued that wage

Table 9.10. Average annual rate of increase in real wages and labor productivity: 1971–82 (%)

Item	1971–73	1974–75	1976–78	1979–80	1981–82
Nominal wages	14.8	30.7	34.2	25.8	18.2
Manufacturing	16.0	31.1	34.3	25.7	17.4
Consumer prices	9.3	24.8	13.3	23.4	14.1
Real wages	5.0	4.7	18.5	2.0	3.6
Manufacturing	6.1	5.0	18.5	1.8	2.9
Labor productivity					
KPC index[a]	8.3	10.5	9.5	12.9	11.8
Manufacturing	9.0	11.4	10.0	13.2	12.7
Value added per worker[b]	7.2	0.9	5.6	–2.4	0.4
Manufacturing	8.2	2.4	7.4	5.0	4.2

Source: BOK, *Economic Statistics Yearbook* (1975, 1980, 1983).

a. Korea Productivity Center (KPC) index.

b. Nonagricultural sector.

Table 9.11. Unit labor costs for manufacturing in Korea, Taiwan, Singapore, and Hong Kong: 1976–82 (1975 = 100)

Item	Korea	Taiwan	Singa-pore[a]	Hong Kong
Nominal wage (A)				
1976	134.7	116.8	104.7	115.9
1979	311.4	188.1	128.6	170.1
1982	526.6	297.0	191.1	240.4
Labor productivity[b] (B)				
1976	101.0	106.9	103.0	107.0[c]
1979	131.2	136.7	114.2	119.6[c]
1982	148.2	157.4	128.9	133.7[c]
Unit labor costs in national currency [(C) = (A/B)]				
1976	133.4	109.3	101.7	108.3
1979	237.3	137.6	112.6	142.2
1982	355.3	188.7	148.3	179.8
Exchange rates per US $ (D)				
1976	100.0	100.0	104.2	99.3
1979	100.0	94.9	91.7	101.3
1982	151.1	103.0	90.2	122.9
Unit labor costs in US $ [(E) = (C/D)]				
1976	133.4	109.3	97.6	109.1
1979	237.3	145.0	122.8	140.4
1982	235.1	183.2	164.4	146.3

Sources: BOK, *Economic Statistics Yearbook* (1980, 1983); Council for Economic Planning and Development, Taiwan (1980, 1983); Directorate General of the Budget, Accounting and Statistics, Taiwan, *Quarterly National Economic Trends* (1977–83); Department of Statistics, Singapore (1980, 1983); Census and Statistics Department, Hong Kong (1977–83); United Nations, *Monthly Bulletin of Statistics* (1977–83).

a. All industries.

b. Value added per worker.

c. GDP/total employment in all but the construction industry.

increases have not had significant responsibility for inflation, although a causal linkage the other way around is fairly strong. However, their price equations usually include the money supply as well as cost variables, combining two independent price models. Thus the claim that wage increases have played only a passive role in the inflationary process seems ill-grounded.

Another erroneous argument based on business accounting data is that the contribution of wages to inflation is very small because wages account for less than 10 percent of total costs in the manufacturing sector. These data are composite income statements aggregated across individual firms at all stages of production. Thus material costs constitute the major share, and they can be decomposed into raw materials, both imported and domestic primary goods, and value added (including wages) in previous stages of processing. The wage share of total costs is therefore much higher than these accounting data indicate.

As for the GNP deflator, a rough estimate of the wage share can be obtained from national income data. Assuming that 70 percent of unincorporated business income consists of wages, and forgetting some minor categories, one can attribute 59 percent of the GNP during the 1970–82 period to wages, 30 percent to return to capital, and the remaining 11 percent to net indirect tax.

By estimating a cost-based price equation utilizing these data, one can decompose the past inflation rate. The explanatory variables in the price equation include composite cost of productive factors calculated by using the above shares, the cost of imports, and a measure of demand pressure in the nonagricultural sector. An agricultural price index is also included, because agricultural prices are, for the most part, determined independently of costs.

According to this analysis, the rise in unit labor costs during 1979–80 was responsible for more than half of the annual inflation rate of 22.6 percent as measured by the GNP deflator (Table 9.12). Although the increase in unit labor costs slowed somewhat during 1981–82, it still contributed more than three-quarters of the 12.2 percent annual inflation rate. Labor costs were not as important in determining wholesale prices as were import costs during the 1979–82 period. They contributed about 9 and 6 percentage points

Table 9.12. Decomposition of inflation by cost factor: GNP deflator, 1971–82 (%)

Item	1971–73	1974–75	1976–78	1979–80	1981–82
Import costs	5.9	15.1	0.5	11.6	4.6
Unit import value	2.7	12.1	0.1	8.3	0.6
Exchange rate	3.2	3.0	0.4	3.3	4.0
Cost of productive factors	5.2	9.2	11.8	14.3	8.2
Wages	5.5	9.0	11.9	12.6	9.5
Demand pressure	–0.3	–0.9	1.7	–4.6	–2.2
Agricultural prices	2.7	3.7	4.2	1.6	1.5
Other	0.0	–0.1	0.0	–0.3	0.1
Actual price increases	13.5	27.0	18.2	22.6	12.2

Sources: BOK, *Economic Statistics Yearbook* (1975, 1980, 1983).

Note: For the equation on which this analysis is based, refer to Appendix 9.1.

to the annual wholesale price increase of 28.4 percent and 13.4 percent, respectively, during the 1979–80 and 1981–82 periods.

Economic Education Program

A policy-related economic education scheme began in Korea in the late 1970s with the efforts of some economic technocrats to persuade top policymakers and other high-ranking officials to deal with the increasing problems with the economy. Their efforts led to the enactment of the Comprehensive Stabilization Program in April 1979. To be successfully implemented, the program needed to secure broad understanding and cooperation from the people. At the initial stage government officials were targeted for education because they were to be the driving force behind the new economic policies.

Since the end of 1980 the economic education program has made rapid strides under presidential sponsorship. In December 1981 an EPB task force, headed by the assistant minister, was established to give the program greater continuity. In November 1982 a regular EPB organization, the Bureau of Economic Education, was established to undertake economic education programs on a more systematic and permanent basis. The target group has been broadened to include all classes of people, and the educational media have been diversified to include lectures, slides, video tapes, newspapers, booklets, radio, and television. The Bureau of Economic Education formulates an annual education program, supports education in other organizations by preparing educational materials and appointing education officers, and sends materials on major economic policies to about 5,000 public opinion leaders in academia, the press, parliament, business, and the army.

Economic education in Korea was started as an attempt to get the broad and active support of the people for the government's economic policies. A good example has been education on economic stabilization, a program in which the government tried to convince people of the gravity of inflation caused by excessive wage demands based on high inflationary expectations.

Not all economic education, however, has been limited to the promotion of government policies. Many programs have given information to economic units to help them rationalize their economic decisions or to enhance people's understanding of the workings of the economy at home and abroad. This approach enables people to plan with greater certainty and to narrow differences in the perception of economic realities that inhibit the domestic consensus needed for effective economic policy-making.

Given the short history of economic education in Korea, it may be too early to evaluate its performance. The nature of the education defies easy evaluation in any case.

LESSONS AND REMAINING TASKS
OF THE STABILIZATION POLICY

Lessons

From the 1960s through the early 1980s Korea had one of the highest inflation rates in the world. Among over a hundred countries included in the World Bank, *World Development Report* (1983) for which inflation data for 1960–81 in terms of the GDP deflator are available, Korea stood in eleventh place, behind only the Latin American countries that had suffered from hyperinflation. By the late 1970s it became obvious that high inflation was undermining the growth potential of the Korean economy. The Comprehensive Stabilization Program of April 1979 was born from the understanding that inflation is not an inevitable product of high growth but something that must be cured to sustain growth.

The Comprehensive Stabilization Program faced rough going in its early stages. The twin blows of the oil price increase and the assassination of President Park several months after the program was launched endangered the program's prospects, requiring constant discipline from the government. In 1980 the Korean economy experienced unprecedented difficulties with political and social unrest, a severe crop failure, a contraction in world trade, and a major exchange-rate depreciation on top of soaring import prices.

In this environment, it was painful and took courage to maintain the restrictive monetary policy stance. To compensate for the weakening of economic activity, a series of reflationary policy measures were enacted during 1980–82. To business circles, the policy packages fell short of expectations and were too weak to boost business activity. To the many academicians who strongly supported the austerity moves, they meant the abandonment of the stabilization policy. In general, the government was cautious in preparing these reflationary packages, with the possible exception of the June 28 measure in 1982 that significantly lowered interest rates. The rate of monetary expansion was substantially reduced, except in 1982 when the relatively rapid growth of money was more or less justified as a response to the weak activity of the financial market in the wake of the curb-loan scandal in the spring.

Around the end of 1982, there was renewed concern over the possibility of reigniting inflation because of the large expansion of the money supply since the early summer, an expected recovery of the economy, and the anticipation of increased raw material import prices in 1983. The government moved quickly after late 1982, however, to tighten its rein over the money supply. The external environment has also been favorable given the cut in oil import prices in the spring of 1983. A lighter financial burden for heavily indebted corporations together with the improving capital utilization ratio partly compensated for the steady rise in unit labor costs. The result was a continued deceleration of inflation to a 3 percent level for 1983.

Inflation rates were low and stable through 1987, but inflation accelerated in 1988 when CPI inflation rose to 7.1 percent from the 1 percent level that had prevailed during 1983–87. From Korea's stabilization efforts and performance, what lessons can one derive that might serve as a reference for other countries?

First, Korea's experience seems to indicate that it takes time—several years—and strong leadership commitment to cure chronic inflation. If a country is to deal with any incidental inflation such as that induced by an oil price shock, the prescription may be a tight money policy for a brief period. However, consistent and uninterrupted care for a considerable time period seems to be required for a country suffering from chronic high inflation. Inflation is fundamentally cured only when the suppliers of productive factors such as workers, capitalists, farmers, and entrepreneurs are satisfied with a low rate of nominal income growth, and this can only be achieved in stages in an inflation-prone country. Therefore, a strong commitment to stabilization policies by the country's leaders is critical. It was apparent that President Chun was serious about curbing inflation; presidential support was the key ingredient responsible for the consistency of the stabilization efforts throughout the prolonged recession.

The second lesson is that for best results stabilization policies should be accompanied by efforts to improve the efficiency of resource allocation. When the allocation of more limited resources is distorted, the supply capacity of some sectors will be constrained and overall industrial efficiency will suffer, resulting in price instability. Korean policymakers were keenly aware of this problem because distorted resource allocation was already an important cause of inflation before the stabilization effort. The Korean approach was to promote more competition not only among domestic suppliers but also with foreign imports, to encourage direct foreign investment in Korea, to realign the industrial incentive system, to allow more autonomy in banking operations, and to check the expansion of the public sector.

Even though the above measures were all appropriate and essential for the long-run efficiency of the economy, Koreans seem to have been less successful in dealing with ongoing resource allocation problems. The process of redressing overinvestment and duplicative investment in some heavy and chemical industries has been slow and ineffective in many cases. Preferential policy loans and credit extended to bail out troubled corporations have restricted credit availability in other sectors. And under a rigid and low-interest-rate regime, banks have had a strong incentive to favor larger corporations in spite of strenuous encouragement by the authorities to give more credit to small and medium-size firms. Moreover, there were some signs of disintermediation (transfer of financial resources when the short-term interest rate exceeds the savings dividend) from financial institutions to the unorganized money market, the real estate market, and consumption.

The third lesson is the importance of a broad consensus on the need for policies to ensure price stability. When relying only on a tight money policy, stabilization efforts may be painful and time consuming. Thus Korean policymakers in recent years have directed much of their efforts to stabilizing the costs of productive factors. These moves have included informal guidelines to restrain wages in the private sector, to keep nominal interest rates low, to discourage high dividend payments, and to stabilize agricultural prices. These efforts cannot be successful without the full support of the parties involved. Such support in turn hinges on convincing them that their relative share of income will not be squeezed by conformity to government guidelines or policies.

The attempt to build a national consensus in Korea and to secure broad cooperation from all sectors often has not been handled very well. Arbitrary and overly ambitious approaches have led to unnecessary resistance and to misunderstandings on the part of groups who feared they were bearing the brunt of the government's efforts to stabilize prices. This reaction is evident from the large wage drifts from negotiated increase rates, instability in the financial market, and widespread distrust among farmers toward government policies. The approach might have been more effective when the income of all factor suppliers was simultaneously dealt with in a more balanced manner.

Finally, for any stabilization effort to be widely appreciated, its primary emphasis should be stabilizing the livelihood of the people. Wage earners are generally observed to have money illusions. Even in situations where their real wage increase is the same, they are more sensitive to price increases when their nominal wage increase is only 10 percent rather than 30 percent. If their shopping basket happens to cost more than the official price index indicates, they are liable to distrust government statistics and are not likely to cooperate with government policies.

Realizing this, the EPB has, since 1981, compiled a separate price index of ten basic daily necessities, including rice, and has tried to stabilize their prices. The government has failed, however, to maintain stable prices in one essential area—the real estate and rental housing market. During 1983, when consumer prices rose only 2 percent on a year-end basis, house rents rose 13 percent. More dramatic was the rise in Seoul's house and land prices, which increased more than 30 percent and 50 percent, respectively, during 1983. As buying homes becomes a more and more remote possibility every year, renters have had to pay an increasing portion of their income for housing. In these circumstances, the government's talk of wage restraint on the basis of stable prices may not sound very convincing.

Remaining Tasks

Although the inflation rate has been reduced much faster than the original target because of restrictive monetary and fiscal management and the favorable trend in import prices, the revised Fifth Five-Year Development Plan (1982–86) concludes that continued efforts to ensure price stability are needed on a more or less permanent basis. More specifically, the plan called for stable monetary expansion at an average annual rate of about 12 percent for the broadly defined money supply, and for the elimination of the unified budget deficit by 1986. (Although this was not achieved, the budget deficit shrank considerably.) Improvement of the commodity distribution system and mobilization of domestic savings were also important objectives of the plan.

Apart from those mentioned, there remain many additional tasks to be undertaken for the successful realization of stabilization goals. An institutional realignment is needed to empower the Bank of Korea with sovereign control over the supply of money. The prime responsibility of the central bank should be in controlling inflation by maintaining a stable money supply; this requires greater independence from the government. As people's inflationary expectations subside, the inflow of savings into the financial market should become more stable and the differential between the free market and official interest rates will narrow. Then, the workings of the financial markets should be improved by gradually liberalizing interest rates. Interest rates should be determined in closer relation to demand and supply conditions in the market as well as by the credit-worthiness of borrowers.

Eliminating the deficit in the government's Grain Management Fund remains a persistent problem. On the assumption that the shift in diet will continue to reduce rice consumption, the agricultural sector may have to undergo a substantial change and the two-tiered price system will no longer be tenable. Farmers will have to be encouraged to switch gradually from major grains to high-value vegetables, stock raising, and fruit. Moreover, in light of the fact that more than two-thirds of farm households own less than one hectare of cultivated land, some institutional changes may have to be made to facilitate the farm mechanization essential for the enhancement of agricultural productivity.

Under the current real estate tax system, large capital gains can be obtained from real estate investments. The incomplete land registration system and the complex regulatory laws on land use make it difficult to establish an effective monitoring system on real estate ownership and transactions. In addition, real estate speculation was, to some extent, the result of the government practice of using taxation on real estate as part of its anticyclical measures. Thus, the antispeculative measures of the government have to be more comprehensive, tackling fundamental problems of supply and demand in the market. The basic approach to the stabilization of real estate prices may include making property and capital gains taxes heavier and more progressive, reforming the housing financing system, and increasing the supply of housing lots and rental houses.

Finally, in an effort to stabilize wages, the government's wage guidelines should try to induce improvements in the wage structure rather than be obsessed with wage restraint alone. In addition to encouraging the larger corporations to restrain the wage increases of highly paid white-collar workers, the government should also consider adoption of a minimum-wage system for production workers. Introduction of a minimum hourly wage will lead to higher productivity, not only by giving workers stronger motivation, but also by inducing firms to become more managerially and technologically innovative. Furthermore, to secure wage stability when substantial changes are taking place in the labor market structure, stepped-up efforts will have to be directed to on-the-job training, retraining programs, and the establishment of an efficient employment information system.

APPENDIX 9.1
Money Demand and Price Equations

The equations presented below were estimated, unless otherwise specified, with semiannual period-averaged data for a sample period of 13.5 years from the first half of 1970 through the first half of 1983. Superscript m in a variable notation denotes the moving average of the current and the previous periods, while $4m$ denotes the moving average of the current and previous three periods. A dot $(\cdot)$ indicates percentage change over the same period of the previous year, and numbers in parentheses below coefficients are t-values.

A. Demand for Money (Ordinary Least Squares [OLS] Estimate)

$$(1) \ \ln(M_1/Pv) = -1.271 + 0.938 \ln \sum_{i=0}^{1} V_{-i} - 2.478 \ln(1 + \dot{P}\dot{v}^e/100)$$
$$\qquad\qquad\quad (25.6) \qquad\qquad\qquad (5.78)$$

$$\qquad\quad - 2.039 \ln[(100 + r_t)/(100 + \dot{P}\dot{v}^e)] - 0.044 \ Df$$
$$\qquad\qquad (7.08) \qquad\qquad\qquad\qquad\qquad (2.67)$$

$$\qquad\quad - 0.214 \ D(81/82) - 0.111 \ D(82/83)$$
$$\qquad\qquad (6.31) \qquad\qquad\quad (2.35)$$

$$\qquad\qquad\qquad\qquad R^2 = 0.9841 \qquad D.W. = 1.43$$

$$(2) \ \ln(M_2/Pv) = -1.877 + 1.038 \ln \sum_{i=0}^{3} V_{-i} - 1.925 \ln(1 + \dot{P}\dot{v}^e/100)$$
$$\qquad\qquad\quad (33.2) \qquad\qquad\qquad (5.07)$$

$$\qquad\quad - 0.799 \ln[(100 + r_t)/(100 + \dot{P}\dot{v}^e)] - 0.034 \ Df$$
$$\qquad\qquad (3.19) \qquad\qquad\qquad\qquad\qquad (2.40)$$

$$\qquad\quad + 0.110 \ D(81/82) + 0.114 \ D(82/83)$$
$$\qquad\qquad (3.75) \qquad\qquad\quad (2.75)$$

$$\qquad\qquad\qquad\qquad R^2 = 0.9918 \qquad D.W. = 1.68$$

where D(81/82): Dummy variable for the second half of 1981 and the first half of 1982

D(82/83): Dummy variable for the second half of 1982 and the first half of 1983

Df: Seasonal dummy variable for the first half of a year

M_1, M_2: Narrowly and broadly defined money supply, respectively

Pv: GNP deflator (1975 = 1.00)

$\dot{Pv}^e$: A measure of the expected inflation rate based on past inflation rates with the weights assumed to show a geometrically declining distribution

$$= \sum_{i=1}^{5} 0.3(1 - 0.3)^{i-1}\, \dot{Pv}_{-i} / \sum_{i=1}^{5} 0.3(1 - 0.3)^{i-1}$$

r_t: Interest rate on one-year time deposits, and

V: Gross national product in 1975 constant prices

B. Money-Determined Price Equations (Estimated with the Cochrane-Orcutt Iterative Technique)

(1) $\ln Pv = 1.746 + 1.045 \sum_{i=0}^{6} w_i \ln(M_1/V)_{-i} + 1.154 \ln(1 + \dot{Pv}^e/100)$
       (7.03)   (4.69)

   $+ 0.691 \ln[(100 + r_t)/(100 + \dot{Pv}^e)]$
     (3.22)

$\varrho = 0.499$ $R^2 = 0.9990$ D.W. = 0.194

where w_i's are polynomially distributed lag coefficients:
$w_0 = 0.092$ $w_1 = 0.122$ $w_2 = 0.144$ $w_3 = 0.159$
$w_4 = 0.165$ $w_5 = 0.163$ $w_6 = 0.154$

(2) $\ln Pw = 6.079 + 1.011 \sum_{i=0}^{6} w_i \ln(M_1/V)_{-i} + 1.509 \ln(1 + \dot{Pw}^e/100)$
       (26.8)   (3.64)

   $+ 0.745 \ln[(100 + r_t)/(100 + \dot{Pw}^e)]$
     (1.90)

$\varrho = 0.642$ $R^2 = 0.9964$ D.W. = 1.87

where Pw: Wholesale price index (1975 = 100)

$\dot{Pw}^e$: A measure of the expected inflation rate in terms of wholesale prices.

$$= \sum_{i=1}^{5} 0.3(1 - 0.3)^{i-1} \dot{P}w_{-i} / \sum_{i=1}^{5} 0.3(1 - 0.3)^{i-1}, \text{ and}$$

$$w_0 = 0.154 \quad w_1 = 0.195 \quad w_2 = 0.209$$
$$w_3 = 0.196 \quad w_4 = 0.156 \quad w_5 = 0.089$$

C. Cost-Based Price Equations (OLS Estimate)

(1) $\ln Pv = -9.358 + 0.336 \ln(Pm \cdot Rex)^m + 0.750[0.59 \ln ULCn^{4m}$
     (10.5)   (8.94)

  $+ 0.30 \ln COC^m + 0.11 \ln(Ti^m / CV_n^m)] + 0.624 \ln Rcu^m$
                                                        (4.00)

  $+ 0.148 \ln Pv,a + 0.022 Df$
     (2.19)   (1.86)

                    $R^2 = 0.9991 \quad D.W. = 1.68$

(2) $\ln Pw = -6.221 + 0.493 \ln(Pm \cdot Rex)^m + 0.443 \ln ULCm^{4m}$
     (17.8)   (16.7)

  $+ 0.203 \ln COC^m + 0.017 Df$
     (2.28)   (1.66)

                    $R^2 = 0.9986 \quad D.W. = 1.64$

where COC: Estimated overall cost of capital

$= DEP/CV + (0.4\ Rb + 0.25\ Rf)\ (1 - Tc) + 0.15\ Rum + 0.2\ Req$

CV: Nominal gross national product

DEP: Capital depreciation allowance

Rb: Bank interest rate on general loans

Req: Dividend yields based on face value of equity stocks

Rf: Approximated effective cost of borrowing from abroad
$= (Reuro + 1.0)\ (1 + RISKex/100) + RISKex$

$Reuro$: Eurodollar rate on three-month maturity loans

$RISKex$: Exchange risk measured as annual rate of exchange rate depreciation during the recent two-year period

Rum: Interest rate on unorganized money market loans, and

Tc: Corporate income tax rate for the highest income bracket

CVn: Value added in the nonagricultural sector in current prices

Pm: Unit price for commodity imports in U.S. dollars

Pv,a: Price deflator for agricultural value added

Rex: Exchange rate in won per U.S. dollar

Rcu: Capital utilization ratio in the nonagricultural sector

$$= (Vn - Vf)/\hat{V}nf$$

Vn: Value added in the nonagricultural sector in 1975 constant prices

Vf: Net factor income from abroad

$\hat{V}nf$: Estimated potential nonagricultural value added excluding *Vf*, which was obtained from the following equation based on quarterly data (1969–82)

$$= - 15.375 + (0.342\ D1 + 0.471\ D2$$
$$(14.1) \qquad (5.85) \qquad\qquad (8.07)$$

$$+ 0.448\ D3 + 0.503\ D4)\ (K_n^m)_{-1}$$
$$(7.69) \qquad\quad (8.68)$$

$$+ 1.702\ \ln\ (K_n^m)_{-1}$$
$$(13.9)$$

$$R^2 = 0.9974 \qquad D.W. = 0.27$$

where *D1, D2, D3, D4:* Seasonal dummy variables for the first, second, third, and fourth quarters, respectively, and

K_n: Capital stock in the nonagricultural sector (period-end)

Ti: Indirect internal tax revenue, and

ULCm, ULCn: Unit labor cost (productivity-adjusted wage cost) in the manufacturing and nonagricultural sectors, respectively, where productivity was measured as value added per employment

TAXATION POLICIES

10 The 1966 Tax Administration Reform, Tax Law Reforms, and Government Saving

by Chong Kee Park

Tax reform is a continuous and sensitive process that promotes the improvement of tax law and administration to ensure they remain responsive to changing economic and social conditions and to the changing priorities and objectives of public policy. There have been numerous tax reforms in Korea since 1961, but the two most important were the reorganization and improvement of tax administration in 1966 and the enactment of a comprehensive tax law revision in 1967. The immediate objectives of these reform measures were to narrow the gap between tax law and practice, and to make the tax structure more responsive to changing rates of inflation and economic growth. The ultimate objectives were to mobilize domestic resources and improve the saving function of the government sector.

Tax revenues increased more rapidly than GNP during 1957–62 (with the exception of 1961), but during 1963–65 failed to keep pace with rising levels of GNP (Table 10.1). Several interrelated factors were responsible for the decline in the tax ratios after 1962, including the rate of growth in GNP

Table 10.1. Tax revenue as a percentage of GNP: 1957–65

Year	Tax revenue as percentage of GNP			Nominal GNP growth rate	GNP price deflator (1965=100)	Inflation rate (% per year)
	National taxes	Local taxes	Total tax revenue			
1957	6.7	0.8	7.5	29.7	37.8	
1958	8.1 (7.3)	0.8	8.9 (8.1)	4.8	37.6	−0.5
1959	11.0 (8.6)	1.0	12.0 (9.6)	6.7	38.4	2.1
1960	11.1 (8.8)	0.9	12.0 (9.7)	11.6	41.9	8.7
1961	8.7	0.9	9.6	20.3	48.4	14.4
1962	9.3	1.5	10.8	17.4	54.9	12.6
1963	7.4	1.5	8.9	40.0	70.4	24.9
1964	6.0	1.2	7.2	42.8	92.9	27.7
1965	7.2	1.4	8.6	15.7	100.0	7.4

Sources: ONTA, ROK, *Statistical Yearbook of National Tax* (1960, 1967); BOK, *Economic Statistics Yearbook* (1967).

Note: Numbers in parentheses are exclusive of education tax, foreign exchange tax, and land income tax levied in 1958, 1959, and 1960.

247

and changes in its composition, changes in price levels, changes in the tax system structure, shifts in the composition of imports, and the altered effectiveness of tax administration. It is important to note that the largest declines in the nation's tax/GNP ratio occurred in 1963–64 when prices were rising most rapidly. The most significant increases in the ratio, however, were recorded in 1958–59 when prices remained relatively stable and the growth in nominal GNP was modest. The big increase in the ratio in 1962 may represent a recovery from the decline in 1961, which was partly attributable to major tax reforms occurring in that year. Thus, the relationship between the tax yield and GNP during 1958–64 suggests that the Korean tax system as a whole was not responsive to changes in nominal GNP, particularly when such changes were accompanied by rapidly rising price levels.

Rapid inflation magnifies the differences in the rates of change among the various economic sectors and types of income. Moreover, in a rapidly developing economy, relatively large structural changes take place within a short time. If these differential rates of growth and structural changes increase the relative importance of sectors subject to lower effective tax rates, total tax revenue would grow less rapidly than GNP, even if revenue yields from taxes increase in proportion to their respective taxable bases. This is what happened in Korea in 1964. The agricultural sector accounted for the unusually large proportion of the growth in GNP in that year, increasing by 15.6 percent in comparison with 9.6 percent for the overall economy. The share of agriculture in GNP rose from 37 percent in 1962 to 47 percent in 1964 (BOK, *National Income,* 1980). Because of the low tax on agricultural income, the total increase in tax yield was small relative to the growth in GNP.

The downward trend in the ratios of tax revenue to GNP since 1962 also reflects unusual increases in prices triggered by a poor harvest in late 1962 and a structural defect in the tax system that prevented the system from responding to increases in prices and money income. The sharp increase in government expenditure and the budget deficit in 1962 further aggravated the inflation that impaired tax collections in the following two years. Over the 1960–62 period total government expenditures increased sharply from 17.0 percent to 25.4 percent of GNP, while total revenues including counterpart funds rose only slightly from 18.8 percent to 20.8 percent of GNP. As a result a huge fiscal deficit, equivalent to 4.5 percent of GNP, was generated in 1962 (Table 10.2). Most of the decline in tax revenues after 1962 was in indirect taxes, the assessment base of which failed to keep up with the soaring inflation of 1963 and 1964. Some of the excise and commodity taxes—such as those on liquor and sugar—were unit taxes (a fixed tax per unit of the commodity) rather than *ad valorem* taxes (a fixed percentage of the value of the commodity), with the result that their tax liabilities fell behind the increase in GNP at current prices. The ratio of liquor tax

Table 10.2. Central general government revenues as a percentage of GNP: 1960–69

Item	1960	1962	1964	1966	1967	1968	1969
	As percentage of GNP						
Internal taxes	8.0	6.1	4.2	6.8	8.3	9.9	10.4
Other taxes[a]	3.0	3.1	1.9	2.4	2.8	3.4	3.4
Other domestic revenue[b]	1.0	3.3	1.4	2.0	1.7	2.0	3.0
Total domestic revenue	12.0	12.6	7.4	11.2	12.9	15.3	16.8
Counterpart fund	6.8	8.2	4.0	3.7	3.1	2.1	0.8
Total revenues	18.8	20.8	11.4	14.9	16.0	17.5	17.6
Total expenditures	17.0	25.4	10.8	13.7	14.5	16.6	17.8
Fiscal balance	1.8	–4.5	0.6	1.2	1.4	0.9	–0.2
	As percentage of total revenues						
Total tax revenues[a]	58.6	44.3	53.0	61.7	69.6	76.3	78.4
Other domestic revenue[b]	5.3	16.0	12.1	13.4	10.8	11.5	17.1
Counterpart fund	36.2	39.6	35.0	24.9	19.6	12.2	4.5
Total revenues	100.0	100.0	100.0	100.0	100.0	100.0	100.0

Sources: BOK, *Economic Statistics Yearbook* (1971); Brown (1973: table 5).

a. Includes customs duties and monopoly profit.

b. Includes trust fund and interest.

revenue to GNP dropped by more than 40 percent between 1962 and 1964, and yields from indirect taxes as a whole declined from 3.1 percent of GNP in 1962 to 1.6 percent in 1964 (C. K. Park 1970).

The decline in the tax ratio after 1962 was also partly due to increased tax exemptions and reductions and because much of the growth in GNP during that period took place in industries enjoying substantial tax benefits. The exemptions and reductions granted under the Corporation Income Tax Law rose sharply from 110 million won in 1961 to 1,046 million won in 1964, representing 6.4 percent and 25.5 percent, respectively, of corporate income taxes actually collected in those years (C. K. Park 1978). Most of these statutory exemptions and reductions were allowed under various provisions of the law to encourage investment in specific industries and to stimulate reinvestment of earnings.

This type of tax concession was not limited to income taxes; tax liabilities of indirect taxes such as customs duties and commodity taxes were also waived for businesses earning foreign exchange. Between 1962 and 1964 customs duties declined from 1.9 percent to 1.2 percent of GNP, while commodity tax revenues dropped from 1.4 percent to 0.5 percent of GNP. Because the share of imports in GNP was at an all-time high in 1962 and 1963, the declining ratios of tax revenues (from customs duties and commodity taxes) to GNP may have resulted from large tax concessions granted on raw materials for manufacture of goods for export and changes in the composition of imports. The decline also is attributable to the unrealistic exchange rate, which understated the won value of imports to which customs rates applied. The large decline in commodity tax revenues during this period was caused by a tightening of import restrictions, forced by the unrealistic exchange rate, that sharply reduced imports of such major revenue-yielding items as radios, TV sets, films, and manufactured textiles (Brown 1973).

The weakening position of tax revenue in the fiscal system was a major cause of concern for fiscal authorities and planners in the government. The implications for future tax and fiscal policies were clear. If the government sector were to provide the necessary share of financial resources to implement the forthcoming Second Five-Year Development Plan, reversal of the declining trend in the tax ratio would be necessary. With the anticipated decrease in counterpart funds and uncertain prospects for private savings, financing from domestic sources, including tax revenues, would have to cover an increasing proportion of total budget requirements.

MAIN FEATURES OF THE POLICY MEASURES

Within certain limits, restoring the tax/GNP ratio could be achieved by improved administration of existing taxes. Lack of tax compliance was still widespread. Strict penalties were not imposed for tax evasion, and tax officials failed to enforce fair and equitable assessments. Bargaining between tax collectors and taxpayers and the resulting payoff were common features of the assessment process. Thus, it was absolutely necessary that tax administration be tightened. Nonetheless, more stringent enforcement of tax laws would not be sufficient; the growth and changing structure of the economy required adjustments in the tax system itself if the government were to play a leading role in financing development. Maintaining required ratios of tax revenue to GNP would necessitate higher tax rates, new tax sources, or both.

Shortly after assuming power in 1961, the military government began to make numerous revisions both in the tax administrative regulations and procedures and in tax laws. To encourage voluntary taxpayer compliance, the Tax Collection Temporary Measures Law and the Tax Delinquent Special Measures Law were enacted, whereby the government gave up all existing claims to penalties for past tax delinquencies but pledged to deal more strictly with future delinquencies. In addition, a tax reduction was provided for voluntary filing of tax returns for personal income tax, corporation tax, and business activity tax. To assist taxpayers in filing voluntary tax returns, a tax accountant system was adopted by enacting the Tax Accountant Law. Additional measures taken during the early phase of the military government to improve tax enforcement included the strengthening of the tax withholding system, reorganization of regional tax offices, and screening and retraining of tax officials.

In December 1961 the government overhauled the entire tax system by making extensive revisions in tax laws. The basic objectives of the tax reform set forth by the new military regime were to: (1) simplify the tax structure to ensure voluntary compliance on the part of taxpayers; (2) improve the income elasticity of the tax system to meet rapidly rising revenue requirements; (3) redesign the tax system to promote savings and investments for economic development; (4) bring about a more equitable distribution of the tax burden; and (5) improve the local tax system to increase the revenues to local governments from their own tax sources (MOF, ROK, 1979b, I:340–41). Although the 1961 tax reform was extensive in nature and coverage, additional revisions and minor changes of tax laws were enacted almost annually to support the implementation of the First Five-Year Development Plan (1962–66).

Tax Administration Reform

Despite strenuous efforts by the military government to improve the revenue productivity of the tax system, the results were disappointing. Various corrections in administrative procedures and in tax laws failed to produce the expected additional revenues. It was not until the president gave his full support to drastic administrative reform and to the tax collection effort that tax revenues began to rise rapidly. The year 1966 marked the beginning of a new era in tax administration in Korea. The Law Amending the Government Organization Law, dated 28 February 1966, provided that "for the purpose of supervising the assessment, exemption, reduction and collection of national domestic tax, as well as all matters pertaining to the management of state-owned property and property vested to the government, the Office of National Tax Administration is hereby created under the direction of the Minister of Finance" (Law No. 1750, Article 26, paragraph 10). Thus, the major function of the Office of National Tax Administration (ONTA), mandated by the law, was to administer all national tax laws in connection with the assessment, exemption, reduction, and collection of taxes and to manage state-owned properties. ONTA consisted of a national office made up of four bureaus and 11 sections, and a field organization consisting of five regional offices located in four cities (Seoul, Taejŏn, Kwangju, and Pusan), each headed by a regional commissioner reporting to the commissioner and deputy commissioner of the national office. Below the regional office level there were originally 77 district tax offices throughout the country, each headed by a district chief reporting to the regional commissioner and the commissioner of the national office. The number of district offices was later increased substantially; by the end of 1982 there were six regional and 105 district offices throughout Korea (ONTA, ROK, 1982).

The organizational reform of national tax administration split the original function of the former Bureau of Taxation in the Ministry of Finance into the semi-autonomous ONTA and the Tax System Bureau (Figure 10.1). While ONTA was responsible only for administration of the national tax laws, the Tax System Bureau in the Ministry of Finance was charged with the primary responsibility for matters related to taxation policy, tax legislation, international tax treaties, and tax analysis and research. In addition to separation of these functions, the reorganization provided for great expansion of the investigation and inspection activities of the tax administration agency. Upgrading of the status of the newly created tax administration agency is shown in Figure 10.1, which compares the organizational structures of the tax administration before and after the 1966 reform. The top tax administrator was raised from bureau director rank (Grade II civil servant) before the reorganization to subcabinet vice minister rank commissioner after the administrative reform. All other positions of tax officials below the commissioner level were also upgraded.

Recognizing that weak tax administration was a source of public discontent, President Park Chung Hee took a strong personal interest in the improvement of tax enforcement, and appointed one of his closest associates in the 1961 military coup as Commissioner of National Tax Administration. The president gave him his full-fledged support against mounting political pressures brought by those who sought relief from higher taxes (Cole and Lyman 1971). Dubbed the "quiet revolution" by President Park, the developments of the last nine months of 1966 thrust the tax administration authority into a position of previously unparalleled prominence. Created during a period of considerable uncertainty, facing an enormous responsibility and burden under the forthcoming Second Five-Year Development Plan, and headed by a relatively unknown individual with no experience in the tax field, ONTA compiled a remarkable record.

The existence of substantial tax evasion and avoidance was at the time widely recognized. In the face of rapidly rising domestic revenue requirements for the economic development programs, it was imperative that this revenue requirement be met first by those who were not paying their fair share of tax imposed by existing law. Unless these people met their tax obligations, additional burdens would have to be placed on those taxpayers who paid their taxes honestly, and the inequity in the distribution of tax burdens would be increased. For these reasons, the commissioner firmly believed that improved enforcement through reduction of evasion and intensification of collection efforts was the most urgent task facing the new tax administration authority.

Accordingly, the initial efforts of the new tax agency concentrated on extensive fraud investigations and internal audits. The new investigation procedure used by ONTA involved a centrally controlled and coordinated information production, processing, and evaluation system. Information

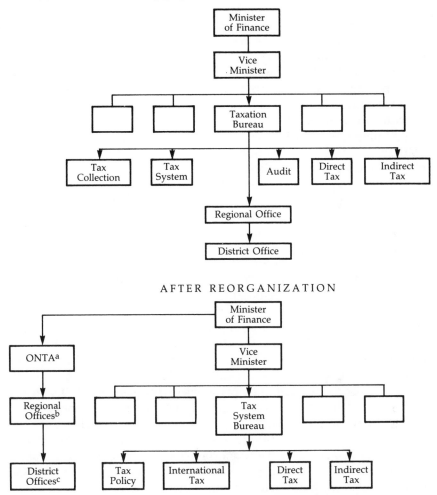

BEFORE REORGANIZATION

AFTER REORGANIZATION

Figure 10.1. Tax administration before and after the reorganization of 1966

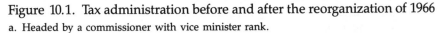

a. Headed by a commissioner with vice minister rank.
b. Headed by a regional commissioner with bureau director rank (Grade II civil servant).
c. Headed by an officer with division chief rank (Grade IV civil servant).

was then channeled to the appropriate field investigation teams for final disposition or referred to regional or district offices for disposition after preliminary investigation. The new procedure was particularly relevant to business conditions and taxpayer practices then existing in Korea. These operations also involved close coordination and cooperation with other pertinent investigative agencies on an unprecedented scale, which in itself was a significant development. Implementation of the improved investigative procedures was impressive, even at the earlier pilot stage.

The number of investigations completed increased sharply from 924 in 1965 to 13,242 in 1966. Additional taxes and penalties collected as a result of implementing new investigation procedures amounted to 2,209 million won in 1966, compared with only 303 million won for 1965. The revenue effect of the improved investigation procedure was manifest in the 1966 figure. The 1966 total amounted to 1,774 million won collected as taxes and 435 million won collected as fines (ONTA, ROK, *An Outline of Korean Taxation,* 1967). The fact that a considerable sum of taxes was collected as a result of fraud investigation suggested that there still existed a great number of tax evaders. The actions of ONTA clearly demonstrated that all citizens and business enterprises were subject to taxation.

Abuse by tax officials was one of the widespread grievances against the government. The Office of Inspector-General was created within ONTA, under the direct supervision of the commissioner (Figure 10.2), to strengthen the internal audit function of ONTA. The new units under the inspector-general were charged with the important tasks of investigating tax officials' misconduct and examining the operations of all segments of ONTA. The significance of the new internal auditing function was its independent status. Previously, internal investigations were staffed on an ad hoc basis with personnel recruited from other divisions of the tax agency; now the reorganized unit had its own permanent staff. Thus, more objective appraisals were possible by the auditing personnel who had no direct ties or allegiance to the activities being audited. As for the other function—internal security—an effective program in that area contributed greatly toward minimizing corruption and improving the public image of the tax administration agency.

During the nine-month period after the inauguration of ONTA on 3 March 1966, a total of 59 district tax offices underwent extensive internal audits. As a result, a total of 350 million won in penalty taxes was collected. According to Table 10.3, which breaks down the sum of penalty tax collection by tax sources, corporate income tax accounted for more than 64 percent of the total penalty taxes collected, followed by personal income tax with 26 percent. Internal audits were conducted on 68 tax offices in 1965, compared with 59 offices in 1966. The incidence of tax delinquencies detected through the audits reached 2,887 in 1965 and 1,237 in 1966, but the sum of penalty tax collected amounted to 18.9 billion won in 1965 and 350.4 billion won in 1966 (ONTA, ROK, *An Outline of Korean Taxation,* 1967:155). Thus the revenue impact of the internal audit was enormous.

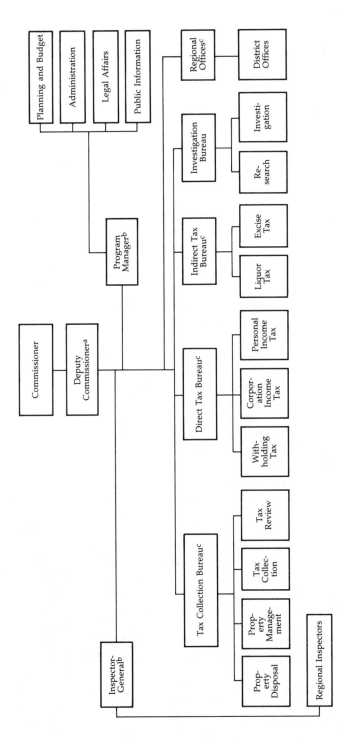

Figure 10.2. Organizational chart of the ONTA
Source: ONTA, ROK, *An Outline of Korean Taxation* (1967).

a. Grade I civil servant.
b. Grade II civil servant.
c. Grade II or III civil servant.

Table 10.3. Result of internal audits, 3 March–31 December 1966

Item	Amount of penalty taxes (10^6 won)	Percentage of total
Personal income tax	89.5	25.6
Corporation income tax	225.6	64.4
Inheritance and gift tax	3.3	0.9
Business activity tax	11.7	3.5
Liquor tax	0.7	0.2
Stamp tax	0.3	0.1
Excise taxes	1.7	0.4
Other	17.5	4.9
Total	350.4	100.0

Source: ONTA, ROK, *An Outline of Korean Taxation* (1967).

ONTA experimented with another application of a new tax compliance procedure: the voluntary disclosure program. Two voluntary disclosure programs of tax evasion were carried out in the last half of 1966. As a new concept adopted in Korea's tax administration policies, these programs encouraged tax violators to confess past evasion in return for immunity from civil and criminal action. Proclaimed as grace periods preceding intensified fraud investigation efforts, the programs achieved noteworthy results. During the first period, which lasted for 45 days between June and July 1966, taxpayers in 771 cases voluntarily disclosed and paid 282 million won in additional taxes. At the beginning, only one period for making disclosures was planned. But, petitions from business associations and the Chamber of Commerce and Industry calling for another chance to disclose past errors led to the scheduling of a second period. During 20 days in September 1966, additional taxpayers in 9,794 cases voluntarily disclosed and paid 1,059 million won in evaded taxes. Voluntary disclosure cases and amounts of tax collection by major regions are presented in Table 10.4.

One of the most important aspects of the improvement in tax administration was the introduction of the "green return" system. Labeled the "green return" simply because of the color of the form used, this system represented a transitional measure taken to encourage individuals and firms to file tax returns on a self-assessment basis rather than under government supervision. Adoption of a voluntary return filing system was thus the first major step toward movement away from the traditional method of having tax officials prepare returns for taxpayers. Under this system, firms that kept satisfactory accounting records and whose accounting books were open to the public were allowed to file their tax returns on a self-assessment basis without interference from tax officials. The pilot operation initially selected 1,574 eligible taxpayers. The number of taxpayers responding totaled 1,359

Table 10.4. Voluntary disclosure program of tax evasion, 1966: Number of cases and amount of tax collected

Region	Cases			Amounts (10^6 won)		
	First period[a]	Second period[b]	Total	First period[a]	Second period[b]	Total
Seoul	204	3,022	3,226	92	717	809
Taejŏn	36	724	760	11	30	41
Kwangju	284	1,975	2,259	23	85	109
Pusan	247	4,073	4,320	156	227	382
Total	771	9,794	10,565	282	1,059	1,341

Source: ONTA, ROK, *An Outline of Korean Taxation* (1967).

a. Refers to 45-day period during June–July 1966.

b. Refers to 20-day period during September 1966.

or about 86 percent of those eligible. There were, however, approximately 2,800 taxpayers actually eligible for this program. To pave the way for expanding the program and bringing all taxpayers under a voluntary system, the government continued to promote voluntary filing and payment by taxpayers through various activities, such as conducting seminars and town meetings, extensive coverage by the mass media, and establishment of taxpayer information and service centers. To stimulate an awareness among the public of the importance of paying taxes and to secure the active support and cooperation of taxpayers, the Ministry of Finance officially designated March 3 as "National Tax Day," to be observed annually.

Tax Law Reform

Subsequent to the large tax law reform of December 1961, there were relatively minor revisions of tax laws between 1962 and 1966 in conjunction with the implementation of the First Five-Year Development Plan. In the 1962 tax revision, for instance, the number of personal income tax brackets was increased from three to four and corporation income tax rates were increased to meet the rising revenue requirements of the government. In 1963–64 the laws relating to corporate income tax, the commodity tax, and the petroleum tax were revised. The corporation income tax was made progressive with two income brackets and rates. The commodity tax base was substantially expanded by adding 24 new taxable commodity items including jewels and precious-metal products, and the tax rates on certain luxury goods were increased. The Petroleum Products Tax Law was also amended to reduce the gasoline tax rate from 300 percent to 100 percent while doubling rates on diesel oil and heavy oil. To provide incentives to invest in certain key industries and to foster foreign exchange earnings by export, the Law Governing Tax Reduction and Exemption was promulgated in 1965. This law in effect consolidated into a single piece of legislation all provisions pertaining to tax concessions to businesses that had previously been included in separate tax laws.

As the government embarked on the Second Five-Year Development Plan (1967–71), another major tax reform was enacted to provide financial support to the economic development plan. The tax reform of 29 November 1967 was the most comprehensive reform since that of 1961. Thirteen existing tax laws were revised and two new tax laws were enacted as an integral part of the government's effort to promote rapid economic growth and industrialization. The major objectives of the tax law reform were to: (1) make the tax structure more conducive to economic development; (2) enlarge the taxable base of the economy; (3) improve equity in the distribution of the tax burden; (4) improve the efficiency of tax administration; and (5) protect the rights and interests of taxpayers (MOF, ROK, 1967:31). Specific measures included in the reform were designed to facilitate the implementation of other policy measures such as avoidance of undue credit expansion, redistribution of income, active promotion of exports, increased private savings, and strengthening of financial institutions.

As a first step toward a gradual transition to a "global" personal income tax system, the 1967 reform introduced a partial globalization of the existing "schedular" system of personal income tax, under which tax rates varied among five schedules (sources) of income: wages and salaries, business income, real estate income, dividends and interest, and other income. If a taxpayer had an annual income in any one of the five categories of the schedular income taxes equal to or greater than the specified amounts, then all of his income was subject to the global tax, provided that total income from all sources exceeded 5 million won. Specified amounts of a minimum annual income were 2.4 million won for wages and salaries, 3 million won for business income, 1.5 million won for real estate income and dividend and interest income, and 1 million won for other income. As tax relief for low-income taxpayers, the exemption for wage and salary earners was raised from 5,957 won to 8,000 won per month. This rise in the exemption amount was accompanied by a partial tax credit system under which a taxpayer was allowed to credit against tax liability an amount equivalent to 3 percent of the difference between 15,000 won and actual monthly income. By means of this credit system, the effective tax rate was reduced on all wage and salary incomes lower than 15,000 won per month. Similar provisions were made for business and real estate income. The statutory rate structure was also revised by increasing the number of income tax rate brackets from five to seven for wage and salary income and from five to six for business and real estate income. Tax rates for each income bracket were adjusted accordingly (Table 10.5).

One of the most important changes in the corporation income tax was an introduction of discriminatory rates for closely held family corporations; for which tax rates were from 5 to 10 percentage points higher than for

Table 10.5. Changes in statutory tax rates for personal income, before and after the 1967 tax law reform

Before the reform		After the reform	

I. Wage and salary income

Monthly income level	Rate (%)	Monthly income level	Rate (%)
20,000 won or less	7	15,000 won or less	7
In excess of 20,000 won	15	In excess of 15,000 won	9
In excess of 40,000 won	25	In excess of 20,000 won	16
In excess of 60,000 won	35	In excess of 30,000 won	18
In excess of 80,000 won	40	In excess of 40,000 won	30
		In excess of 60,000 won	40
		In excess of 80,000 won	50

II. Business and real estate income

Annual income level	Rate (%)	Annual income level	Rate (%)
200,000 won or less	15	200,000 won or less	15
In excess of 200,000 won	20	In excess of 200,000 won	20
In excess of 500,000 won	30	In excess of 500,000 won	30
In excess of 1,200,000 won	40	In excess of 1,200,000 won	40
In excess of 4,000,000 won	50	In excess of 3,000,000 won	50
		In excess of 5,000,000 won	55

Source: MOF, ROK (1967).

"open" corporations. In addition, dividends paid by "open" corporations were tax exempt, while those paid by "closed" corporations were taxable at 15 percent. Also, temporary profit tax exemption or reduction provided under the Corporation Income Tax Law was replaced by the investment tax credit. In another area of direct taxation, the tax reform of 1967 introduced a new land speculation control tax—a capital gains tax levied at 50 percent on profits from transfers of urban real estate.

One of the most significant measures in the area of commodity taxation was the increase in the list of items subject to the tax from 46 to 80. Some of the new items were the result of subdividing previously taxed categories, but many were items that had been removed from the taxable list in the 1961 tax reform but whose sales had subsequently increased. Another major feature of the commodity tax reform in 1967 was the introduction of a system levying the tax at the retail instead of the manufacturing stage on items such as jewels, pearls, and precious metals. Tax rates on luxury commodities and imported items were also increased. To make liquor taxes more responsive to price changes, they were shifted from a unit basis to an *ad valorem* rate schedule. Kerosene and bunker-C oil, which had been previously untaxed, were made subject to rates of 30 percent and 5 percent, respectively; kerosene used for lighting purposes in rural areas was, however, exempt from the new tax. Another new tax introduced in the 1967 tax reform was a 10 percent tax imposed on telephones.

In conjunction with the Third Five-Year Development Plan (1972–76), another major tax law reform took place at the end of 1971 and new tax laws were put into effect beginning 1 January 1972. The 1971 reform was designed to accomplish, among other things, the following specific objectives: (1) to reduce the tax burden of low-income persons, (2) to provide tax inducements to encourage saving by individuals and businesses, (3) to reduce excessively high marginal income tax rates, and (4) to improve horizontal equity so that those with equal ability would be taxed equally (MOF, ROK, 1972:11). In line with these objectives, personal income tax rates on wages and salaries and business income were reduced and the basic tax exemption level was increased. Interest income from bank deposits, which previously had been exempted entirely, became subject to a 5 percent tax. In addition, the minimum income subject to the global income tax was lowered from 5 million won to 3 million won. Corporation income tax rates also were adjusted downward and the application of the investment tax credit system was expanded to cover a wider range of businesses and industries. All told, ten major tax laws were affected by the 1971 reform.

In response to the oil crisis and consequent economic deterioration at home, the Presidential Emergency Decree was declared on 14 January 1974, providing a substantial temporary tax cut for low-income wage and salary workers. The magnitude of tax reduction was 50 percent for annual incomes between 600,000 won and 840,000 won and 30 percent for incomes ranging between 840,000 won and 1,200,000 won. Incomes below 600,000 won were completely exempted from personal income tax for one year (C. K. Park 1978:74).

Until 1974 Korea's personal income tax system consisted of both schedular taxes and a global tax. Under the schedular system, exemptions, deductions, and rate structures varied considerably depending on the type of income. The system was complex and difficult to administer and produced haphazard incidence effects. The primary objective of the 1974 reform was to correct these defects in the personal income tax by replacing the schedular system with one that was almost completely global. Under the new system, virtually all personal incomes (excluding interest and dividend incomes), which were previously included in the five different schedules, are taxed only under the global system. The new system also provided an additional exemption for bonus income, widened the range of deductions to reduce the tax burden on families, increased substantially the maximum levels of deductions, and reduced tax rates over most ranges of taxable income (MOF, ROK, 1975b:9–78). The land speculation control tax, introduced in 1968, was replaced by the capital gains tax. The other nine tax laws were also affected by the tax law reform of 1974.

In July 1975 the Defense Tax Law was enacted for the purpose of providing financial resources required for modernization of the national defense force. Under this law, most taxpayers became subject to a surtax at rates ranging from 0.1 percent to 30 percent. Specifically, the defense surtax covered customs duties, four national internal direct taxes, four national internal indirect taxes, six local tax items, and commercial advertisement (MOF, ROK, 1975a:14–18). The tax, adopted as a temporary measure in 1974, was originally scheduled to expire in 1980, but the expiration was subsequently postponed twice and is now scheduled for 1990.

In a drastic change of the existing indirect tax structure, the 1976 tax law reform adopted a new value-added tax system to replace eight of the 11 existing indirect tax items (the business activity tax, commodity tax, textile products tax, petroleum products tax, electricity and gas tax, transportation tax, admissions tax, and entertainment and restaurant tax). In addition to the value-added tax, special consumption taxes were also levied on luxury consumer goods. The value-added tax law provided for a single basic rate of 13 percent, adjustable within a range of 3 percentage points without legislative approval. Initially, however, a 10 percent rate was applied to minimize inflationary effects of the tax. Exempted from the tax were unprocessed foodstuffs and basic daily necessities such as tap water, coal briquettes for home heating, and medical services. A zero rate was applied to exports (MOF, ROK, 1977).

THEORETICAL APPROPRIATENESS OF THE POLICY MEASURES

Government-sector financing has several objectives. The role of a tax structure is to accomplish the transfer of resources from the private sector of the economy to the government in an efficient and equitable manner. Taxation also has other important economic objectives, such as the promotion of economic growth and adjustments in the distribution of income and wealth (Musgrave 1959). It may be useful to review briefly the appropriateness of the 1966–67 tax reform measures in the light of these overall objectives.

Broadly speaking, the goal of economic development is to improve the general welfare of the people by raising the standard of living. To attain such improvement the economy has to grow not only in terms of total income but also in terms of per capita income. Tax policy has an important bearing on the rate of economic growth, by affecting the rate of investment and other determinants of growth. Over the long term, growth requires increases in investment, whether in manufacturing plant, in the form of infrastructure such as highways and electric power, or in human capital formation such as education and health. To finance the desired rate of growth in a noninflationary manner, savings have to be large enough to pay for the required level of investment. Savings not derived from the private or foreign sectors must, therefore, be provided by the government sector through increased domestic revenue, including taxes.

The fundamental premise underlying the 1966–67 tax reform was that a substantial increase in government domestic revenue was needed to provide for noninflationary financing of the investment requirements of the development plan. The attainment of the required level of domestic savings depended, to a large extent, upon the degree to which the government could continue to increase the ratio of tax revenue to GNP and to restrain the growth in current domestic expenditure. Strengthening the revenue potential of the tax system was thus the major concern of the tax reform. The 1967 tax law reform program was formulated so as to provide for changes estimated to produce a net increase of 6.7 billion won in 1968 national internal tax revenues. Another important source contributing to the growth in tax revenues was the administrative improvement of tax enforcement.

The objective of tax reform is to provide a tax structure compatible with the financing of a desired rate of economic growth. As the required rate of growth increases, so must the necessary level of finance. The issue, however, is not one of total tax revenue only. The way in which a given amount of total tax revenue is raised influences the private savings rate. Certain measures, such as taxes on luxury commodities, are more conducive to household saving than are others, like higher marginal rates under the personal income tax. That was one important reason that the 1967 tax law reform sharply increased the reliance on taxation of luxury items by substantially expanding the base of taxable goods, coupled with increased tax rates. Increased commodity taxation also increased government saving by increasing tax revenues. A savings incentive was provided by exemption of interest income on bank deposits from the personal income tax, even though the provision is objectionable on equity grounds. Similarly, the higher rate of taxation on corporate dividends was designed to encourage the retention of earnings in corporations and to stimulate business saving.

Tax policies affect not only the level but also the pattern of private investment, and it is important to avoid causing serious distortions as a result of tax measures. Distortion often results when tax incentive provisions are implemented without clearly defined objectives. The 1967 tax law reform was designed to minimize distorting effects by limiting future use of incentives to situations where they would be most needed. Provisions dealing with profit tax exemption or reduction under the Corporation Income Tax Law were replaced by the investment tax credit. The investment tax credit is usually preferred because it applies only to investment in depreciable assets, which are the primary source of productivity gains, whereas rate reduction applies to earnings from all physical capital, including inventory investment (Musgrave 1967).

Although economic growth is an important objective of tax policy, equity goals must be considered as well. (For a discussion of equity standards applied by tax theorists, see Bittker 1980.) It is important to consider how tax laws contribute to distribution of income and wealth. In particular, policy should aim at improving the welfare of those segments of the population that have lagged behind and whose standards of living have remained very low. Tax reform should contribute to securing more equitable distribution of income and improved distribution of the tax burden—a distribution that will reduce the share borne by the low-income groups. Adjustments in the distribution of income must be subject to the constraint, however, that they take into account the adverse effects on incentives and economic growth which might arise from them.

The tax law reform program of 1967 presented the improvement of equity in the distribution of the tax burden as an important policy objective. To reduce the tax share borne by low-income taxpayers, the exemption limit was raised, removing a considerable number of low-wage earners from the tax roll. In addition, by means of the newly introduced tax credit system, the effective tax rate was reduced on all salary and wage incomes lower than 15,000 won per month. These two adjustments in the personal income tax law resulted in revenue losses of approximately 4.2 billion won in 1968 (MOF, ROK, 1967:42).

Attainment of the target rate of revenue growth depends to an important degree on increased effectiveness in administration of the tax system. The imposition of new taxes, the increases of tax rates, and the broadening of the base of existing taxes may all be needed to meet rising revenue requirements. But such measures will have only limited effects on the government's ability to meet its responsibilities in financing investment requirements unless the capabilities for tax administration are also strengthened. Improved administration is, therefore, a vital aspect of tax reform. Tax evasion and avoidance were widespread in Korea, especially among the self-employed in commerce and trade and in the professions. The primary objectives of administrative reform were to reduce tax evasion, eliminate unnecessary administrative burdens on the taxpayer, and to secure a more equitable and effective application of the law. Unless taxpayers feel that the tax system is reasonably equitable and efficiently enforced, not much can be done to improve taxpayer cooperation and morale. The tax administration reform of 1966 was a first step toward achieving these broad objectives.

EFFECTS OF THE POLICY MEASURES

One of the major characteristics of Korea's tax system has been the perverse response of tax yields to changing rates of inflation and growth. During periods of relative price stability, 1958–60 for example, tax enforcement was tightened and tax revenue yields increased sharply; but in 1963 and

1964, when inflation accelerated, the increase in tax revenue slowed considerably. The tax reforms of 1966–67 were designed to improve these structural deficiencies and to strengthen the revenue potential of the tax system.

The creation of ONTA brought much more forceful tax enforcement in Korea. The most important administrative improvements introduced by the new tax agency were the reorganization of tax administration, the growing emphasis on investigation and audit, and the promotion of voluntary filing and payment of taxes. The tax law reform enacted late in 1967, effective for fiscal year 1968, included a number of changes in rates, coverage, exemptions, credits, and so forth that affected the yields of some major taxes in the system. These, and subsequent structural and administrative modifications, were reflected in the changes in revenues from 1966 to 1968 as well as from 1962–64 to 1966–68 (Table 10.6).

The increase in tax revenues, both in absolute amounts and relative to GNP, reflects the government's determination to reverse tax trends that partly contributed to the inflationary pressure of the early 1960s. Following the tax reforms of 1966 and 1967, total internal tax revenue rose sharply from 42.1 billion won in 1965 to more than 70 billion won in 1966 and to 156.4 billion won by 1968. The unprecedented tax revenue goal of 70 billion

Table 10.6. Trends in tax revenue and other measures of tax performance: 1962–72

Year	Tax revenue[a] (10^9 won)	Percentage increase in tax revenue	Tax revenue as percentage of GNP	Income elasticity of tax revenue
1962	21.5	20.1	6.2	1.49
1963	24.7	14.9	5.1	0.44
1964	29.2	18.2	4.2	0.49
1965	42.1	44.1	5.2	2.44
1966	70.0	66.5	6.8	1.68
1967	103.8	48.3	8.2	1.44
1968	156.4	50.6	9.8	1.49
Averages				
1962–64	25.1	17.7	5.2	0.81
1966–68	110.1	55.1	8.3	1.54
1969	218.1	39.4	10.5	1.14
1970	283.8	30.1	11.0	1.08
1971	355.5	25.3	11.3	1.04
1972	374.3	5.3	9.7	0.32

Sources: ONTA, ROK, *Statistical Yearbook of National Tax* (1968, 1974); BOK, *National Income* (1974).

a. Refers to national internal tax revenue.

won for 1966, adopted by the new commissioner of taxation upon taking office, was exceeded by 11 million won. This amounted to an annual rate of increase of 66.5 percent in 1966. A hefty increase of more than 66 percent in a single year was the highest growth rate ever recorded in the history of Korea's tax collection. It was obvious that administrative improvements, rather than changes in tax laws, were the key factors in this unprecedented increase in tax revenue in 1966. Minor tax law changes occurred in 1965, but these had little impact on revenue yield. Although both tax law changes and administrative improvements, without even considering economic growth, contribute to the increase in tax revenue, it is difficult to separate the two effects because they usually occur at the same time. One estimate of ONTA shows, however, that the revenue effect of improvement in tax compliance and investigation of tax evasion alone was about 6.5 billion won in 1966, representing more than 9 percent of the total taxes collected in that year (ONTA, ROK, *An Outline of Korean Taxation*, 1967:140).

From 1967 to 1968 total tax revenue rose from 103.8 billion won to 156.4 billion won, an increase of 50.6 percent. However, more than 48 percent of this increase was in the form of personal and corporation income taxes, which together grew by 53.9 percent in 1968. Structural changes in the income taxes contained in the 1967 tax law reform are reflected in these changes in revenues for 1968. The marked increase in revenue from personal income tax appears to have resulted from growth in the number and income of taxpayers, better enforcement and compliance, or a combination of these factors—rather than from changes in tax rates or exemptions. The increase of more than 8.6 billion won in corporation income tax revenue in 1968, however, reflected other factors in addition to the structural changes made in the 1967 tax law reform. With the large increase in corporate net income in 1968, the increase of 54.1 percent in corporation income tax revenue reflected primarily the growth in the tax base.

Table 10.6 also shows several indicators of long-term tax revenue performance after 1962. The rate of increase in tax revenues rose sharply from an annual average of 17.7 percent during the confused 1962–64 period to an average of more than 55 percent during the fiscal push of 1966–68. From 1966 to 1968 tax revenues more than doubled; over the same period GNP, at current prices, increased barely more than 50 percent. The tax effort measured by tax/GNP ratios of these two distinct periods rose from 5.2 percent in the confused period to 8.3 percent in the accelerated tax drive period. While tax revenues increased in absolute amounts in the years between 1962 and 1964, the growth in tax revenues failed to keep pace with the increase in GNP. Reversing this deteriorating trend, the ratio of tax revenue to GNP began to increase rapidly after 1966 when tax collection efforts began to gain momentum. According to the measures of tax elasticity shown in the last column of Table 10.6, the elasticity of total tax yields with respect to GNP averaged 1.54 for the 1966–68 period, as compared with an average of only 0.81 during 1962–64. It should be noted that the income elasticity of tax revenue was only about 0.4 in both 1963 and 1964.

While total tax revenues continued to rise steadily after 1966, increased revenues from improved tax administration reached an upper limit and the high revenue growth rates experienced in the 1966–68 period began to slow in the early 1970s. Three aggregate measures of tax behavior presented in Table 10.6 show some signs of decline in the early 1970s. The sharp decline in growth rate as well as in other measures in 1972 is largely attributable to major tax reforms of 1971 that reduced the personal income and corporation income tax rates. Tax revenues from these two sources actually declined in absolute amounts in 1972, substantially reducing the growth rate of total internal tax revenue to a mere 5 percent and the overall tax/GNP ratio down to less than 10 percent. Moreover, the elasticity of total tax yields with respect to GNP sharply declined to 0.32 in 1972. The tax law reform of 1971 as well as the slowdown in economic growth during 1971–72 had an adverse effect on revenue yields.

Most of the decrease in personal income tax revenue that resulted from the tax law changes was the result of reductions in tax rates and a 50 percent increase in the size of the basic tax exemption. In addition, the President's Emergency Decree for Economic Stability and Growth on 3 August 1972, which provided additional investment tax credits and other incentive provisions to encourage increased investment in industrial plant and equipment, resulted in a sharp decline in the absolute amount of corporation income tax yields in 1973 (I. K. Hong 1974). Corporation income tax revenue declined from 56.7 billion won in 1971 to 54.8 billion won in 1972 and to 49.8 billion won in 1973. Tax collection efforts were again lax in 1977, reflecting substantial changes in the tax structure contained in the tax law reform of 1976. This reform provided for substantial increases in tax exemptions for personal income tax. As a consequence, the annual growth rate of personal income tax revenue abruptly declined from 60.6 percent in 1976 to 10.5 percent in 1977, while that of total internal tax revenue dropped from 35.4 percent to 22.2 percent over the same period.

That the drive to increase tax collection through tax reforms of 1966–67 was successful is also suggested by the improved fiscal position of the general government budget sector. As shown in Table 10.2, central general government domestic revenue increased rapidly from 7.4 percent of GNP in 1964 to 12.9 percent and 16.8 percent of GNP, respectively, in 1967 and 1969. From 1962 to 1964 the relative importance of the general government budget sector including counterpart funds contracted sharply under the impact of rapid inflation. In 1964, for instance, the total revenues of the sector were equivalent to only 11.4 percent of GNP, as compared with 20.8 percent GNP in 1962. From 1964 to 1969, however, total revenues of the general government budget increased considerably, so that the ratio of these revenues to GNP rose from 11.4 percent in 1964 to 17.6 percent in 1969.

Between 1964 and 1969, the composition of general government budget revenues underwent a significant change, as shown in the bottom half of Table 10.2. The increasing share of total revenue derived from internal taxes, customs duties, and profits transferred from the Office of Monopoly after 1966 stands in sharp contrast to the much smaller contributions from these sources in the early 1960s. In 1962, when counterpart funds still accounted for nearly 40 percent of total revenues, national taxes and monopoly profits accounted for 44 percent. But the share of the latter has increased sharply since 1964, reaching nearly 70 percent in 1967 and more than 78 percent of total receipts in 1969. Because the relative importance of counterpart funds as a source of general budget revenue continued to diminish from more than 39 percent in 1962 to less than 5 percent in 1969, the government budget sector had to rely to an ever-increasing degree on tax revenues—the tax reform of 1966–67 made a significant contribution to this effect. The necessity of meeting a rising share of budget revenues from tax sources has undoubtedly served as a constraint on expansion of government expenditures from the budget. The rate of increase in tax revenue was much faster than that in expenditures during the 1964–67 period, and an expanding surplus generated in the budget helped finance the nation's development programs. In 1967 there was a budget surplus equivalent to 1.4 percent of GNP.

The shift in the budget sector from a deficit to a surplus position after 1964 made a major contribution to the growth in domestic savings, which facilitated rapid growth. Given the low level of income and the difficulties involved in bringing about a rapid increase in private savings, the fiscal sector assumed a major share of the task of meeting the national domestic savings requirement during the 1966–68 period.

Domestic savings continued to be dominated by the private sector until about the mid-1960s, but the government sector moved from negative saving to positive saving in 1964. The effect of the 1966–67 tax reform measures is amply demonstrated by sharp increases in the level of government saving through 1970. Table 10.7 shows that government saving increased steadily from dissaving (negative saving) of 1.8 billion won in 1963 to more than 100 billion won in 1968 and to 175 billion won in 1970. As a percentage of GNP, government-sector saving rose from a negative rate of minus 0.4 in 1963 to a positive rate of 6.5 in 1970, raising the total domestic savings rate from 8.7 percent to 17.3 percent. This was accompanied by rapid increases in tax revenues and a growth in the overall tax/GNP ratio from 8.6 percent in 1963 to 14.8 percent in 1970. This progress was possible only by substantially increasing the government's ability to collect more tax revenues and by restraining the growth of government consumption.

From 1963 to 1970 government saving increased by 176.9 billion won, accounting for 42 percent of the increase in domestic savings. As a result, the government saving share in domestic savings rose from less than 6 per-

Table 10.7. Government saving as a percentage of GNP: 1963–72 (10⁹ current won)

Year	Government saving		Domestic saving		Government saving as percentage of domestic saving
	Amount	Rate (%)	Amount	Rate (%)	
1963	−1.84	−0.4	43.72	8.7	−4.6
1964	3.33	0.5	62.64	8.7	5.7
1965	13.79	1.7	59.39	7.4	23.0
1966	28.55	2.8	122.83	11.8	23.7
1967	52.55	4.1	145.76	11.4	36.0
1968	100.87	6.1	249.33	15.1	40.4
1969	127.45	5.9	405.92	18.8	31.4
1970	175.06	6.5	465.21	17.3	37.6
1971	178.30	5.4	506.17	15.4	35.1
1972	143.65	3.6	633.10	15.7	22.9

Source: EPB, ROK, *Major Statistics* (1983).

cent in 1964 to more than 40 percent in 1968 but then slightly declined to 37.6 percent in 1970.

That the increase in tax revenues was accompanied by increased savings in the government sector is quite clear. But what is not clear is the effect of increased government revenues and savings on total domestic savings. It is probable that certain taxes work to reduce private saving by more than the amount that government saves out of the additional revenues. We may speculate that heavy reliance on tax revenues to raise government saving might have had some adverse effects on the growth of private saving, but it is difficult to verify this with existing data. As one observer put it, "as for the effects of taxation on private saving, on the one hand private saving as a percent of income probably would have risen more rapidly if the growth of government revenues (about 30 percent per year in constant prices) had been less. On the other hand, income probably would not have grown as rapidly as it did if it were not for the increase of efforts to expand government revenue and saving" (Brown 1973:192). Out of all this, one may draw the general conclusion that increased tax revenues and government saving made a significant contribution to moving the Korean economy to a high-growth path during the second half of the 1960s (Mason et al. 1980; Johnson 1972).

CRITICISMS AND LESSONS
OF THE KOREAN EXPERIENCE

The rapid expansion of government functions and activities in Korea after 1961 resulted in renewed emphasis on the role of taxation in the promotion of economic growth and welfare. As the economic and social structures of the nation became more complex and interdependent, the concept of the role of taxation also changed. Taxation is no longer considered merely as a device to finance government activities but has been increasingly recognized as an important tool for achieving economic objectives and for bringing about a more equitable distribution of income and wealth.

What can other developing countries learn about taxation and its effects from the Korean experience? Tax policy played only a minor role in the development process of Korea until the early 1960s. Compliance problems were severe, tax collection was lax, and a continuing rapid rate of inflation limited what could be accomplished through structural reform. It was not until the government began to make more conscious and systematic efforts to correct serious deficiencies in the whole tax system that there were dramatic increases in tax collections and in the efficiency of tax administration. A major breakthrough in the tax effort came in 1966–67, when the national tax ratio increased from 7.2 percent of GNP in 1965 to 13.2 percent in 1968. The substantial improvement in tax administration was probably the most important single factor in this breakthrough. Korea was well aware that efficient administration was a crucial aspect of tax policy, and no system could be better than its actual implementation.

It would be less than candid, however, to leave the impression that tax reform and administrative improvement in Korea faced no problems. There were some major difficulties. Resistance from vested interest groups, both public and private, and inertia constituted major barriers. A serious shortage of trained managers and technicians, rigid government employment practices, an unpredictable political climate, and commercial intrigues were some of the other problems.

There was a growing feeling that increased tax revenues through improved administration would soon reach an upper limit and, therefore, that growth in revenues should be more directly related to growth in the tax base and changes in the tax structure. Another view also prevailed—that rapid increases in the ratio of total tax revenues to GNP were constrained by widespread inequities inherent in the tax structure, and that these inequities had become less tolerable as improvements in tax administration pushed assessments to higher levels to meet revenue requirements. Thus, the 1967 tax law reform concentrated on structural improvements of the tax system. There have been numerous tax law changes since 1961, but the 1967 revision can be considered one of the few comprehensive tax law reforms that occurred during these years. The reform broadened the tax base, raised tax rates, and introduced a number of equity and incentive features into the tax system.

The Korean experience provides evidence for the general expectation that the tax structure changes in the course of economic development. During the course of economic development since 1961, the composition of the tax structure in Korea gradually shifted from commodity-oriented indirect taxation to income-based direct taxes and back again to indirect taxation. One of the most important lessons that can be learned from the Korean experience is that, contrary to what has often been widely observed, the income tax has an important role to play even on a limited scale in the revenue system of developing countries. Income taxation was found to be an important source of government revenue in Korea, where revenue yields from both personal and corporation income taxes represented 34 percent of total tax revenue of the central government in 1968, compared with only 15–25 percent in the early 1960s. Despite such inhibitions as the lack of tradition in income tax compliance and enforcement, Korea has made significant progress in developing a system of taxing incomes. Korea's experience clearly shows that income tax is a potentially productive source of tax revenue in the context of rapidly rising revenue requirements of developing countries.

Did Korea pursue appropriate tax goals? Tax reform cannot be adapted to any single goal, such as adequate revenue, economic growth, stability, or equity. Since there are trade-offs among these conflicting objectives, all must be taken into account. The primary concern underlying most of the major tax reforms occurring in Korea during 1960–80 was, however, the stimulation of economic growth. An improved tax treatment of business and investment was common to these reforms. Though the equity objective was mentioned, the major focus of the 1967 reform was "to make the tax structure more conducive to economic growth." One of the greatest deficiencies in Korea's tax system results from the wide range of tax incentives and special tax privileges provided to business, which led to a built-in erosion of the tax base. It is generally agreed that these provisions have been costly, inequitable, and ineffective in achieving their intended objectives. In 1979 the cost of lost revenue was as high as 40 percent of the total corporation income tax that would have been collected in the absence of the tax incentive system. Even more significantly, this relief has been used mainly by the largest corporations (Tait, Faria, and Heller 1979). It is, therefore, important to reassess carefully whether tax incentives are essential to stimulate new investment and thus justify the distortions in resource allocation and the huge revenue loss.

In Korea, where heavy reliance is placed on fiscal incentives to spur economic growth in the private sector, some regressiveness of the tax system is unavoidable. In past tax law reforms only minor emphasis has been placed on the equity aspect of taxation. Although the improvement of equity in the distribution of the tax burden was cited as one of the stated objectives of the 1967 reform, tax policy per se did not have an important equalizing effect on the distribution of income. Some changes in the personal income tax have been enacted to increase tax exemptions for low-income groups and to improve its progressivity in the rate structure. The 1967 reform, for example, provided for an increased tax exemption limit and also introduced the partial tax credit system to provide some progression in the lower income ranges. Another example of a tax relief measure was the Presidential Emergency Decree of 14 January 1974, which provided a substantial temporary tax cut for the low-income wage and salary earners. But major areas of the personal income tax reform in the past have had to do with adjusting the incentive effects inherent in the direct tax system. Some of the fiscal incidence studies on Korea indicate that tax impacts on income distribution have not been substantial in Korea (Bahl, Kim, and Park 1986). Others also pointed out that the redistribution of income and wealth was not a major concern of government economic policy (Cole and Lyman 1971).

The tax law reform of 1967 introduced a partial globalization of the schedular system of personal income tax, and another comprehensive tax reform of 1974 made the personal income tax almost completely a global tax system. In spite of this modernization reform, personal income tax in Korea plays a far less important role than it should. The share of personal income tax in total tax revenue has been declining steadily since the early 1970s. While the principle of the global income tax system has been accepted, the present form of this tax is unsatisfactory. There are several provisions that limit the usefulness of this tax as a means of bringing about more equitable treatment of taxpayers with incomes from different sources. This limited role reflects the fact that a large proportion of personal income, such as dividend and interest income, is only partially taxed. From the standpoint of equity and of raising more revenue for the government, all dividend and interest income must be fully included in the global income tax base.

In another area of direct tax, more vigorous efforts should be made to increase tax revenue from land, financial assets, inheritance, and gifts. Just as income and consumption expenditures are considered an important criterion for taxation under the current income and value-added taxes, wealth should also be treated as an important criterion for taxation under an equitable tax system. Taxation of wealth should form an important element of the overall tax structure of the nation. Improved methods for more vigorous enforcement of inheritance and gift taxes would certainly increase the share of wealth taxes in total tax revenue. Revenues from inheritance and gift taxes currently account for much less than 1 percent of total central government tax revenue. But the tax effort in this area should improve considerably in the future, so that the inheritance and gift tax yield may eventually account for 2–3 percent of total tax revenue.

The value-added tax has been contributing significantly to the increased tax revenue since its introduction in 1977. As a result, indirect taxes (including value-added tax) now account for more than 65 percent of total internal tax revenues. The tax structure needs to be improved to prevent the regressive nature of the value-added tax from having severe adverse effects on the distribution of income and of the tax burden. Special attention needs to be focused on the likely impact of the tax on the expenditure patterns of different household groups, particularly the burden on low-income wage earners.

11 Introduction of the Value-Added Tax (1977)

Trị giá gia tăng

by Kwang Choi

In December 1976 the Korean government passed legislation to bring a value-added tax (VAT) into effect from 1 July 1977. The introduction of VAT in Korea—as a substitute for a complicated system of indirect taxes—was part of a large-scale tax reform in 1976, in which 18 taxes were created or amended. VAT, together with a newly enacted special consumption tax, replaced eight categories of indirect taxes: the business tax, commodity tax, textile tax, petroleum products tax, admissions tax, travel tax, gas and electricity tax, and entertainment and food tax.

Each of the previous indirect taxes replaced by VAT had its own rate structure as well as a different tax base and administrative procedure. The consolidation and incorporation of numerous indirect taxes into VAT was expected to simplify the rate structure, tax base, and administration of the indirect tax system, thereby eliminating the overlapping auditing practices that had plagued the previous system. VAT is also an important instrument against tax evasion by means of the reciprocal controls exercised by taxpayers themselves.

The concurrent introduction of the special consumption tax along with VAT was designed to inject some progressivity into the indirect tax system through increased taxes on goods and services consumed disproportionately by high-income groups.

VAT was also expected to promote exports and capital formation. Under VAT, exports are zero rated at the final stage of production and rebates are available on taxes paid at earlier stages of production. With the previous system the cumulative taxes at earlier stages of transactions in export goods were either not rebatable or only partly refundable. Therefore, it was believed that the introduction of VAT would have a favorable effect on exports, which have been the driving force behind the rapid growth of the Korean economy. Because the previous indirect tax system did not provide credit for the taxes paid on investment goods, and because taxes were not to be imposed on capital investment under the new regime of consumption-type VAT, VAT was expected to encourage capital formation.

The introduction of VAT was strongly recommended because the previous cascade turnover tax system was believed to have several disadvantages resulting in resource misallocation and inefficiency. First, the turnover tax encouraged vertical integration because the reduction of interfirm sales

273

reduced total tax liabilities. Second, it penalized specialization for the same reason. Third, estimates of the tax content of a price at any particular stage of production were perforce arbitrary, which in turn made indirect tax adjustment at country borders arbitrary. All in all, the adoption of VAT was regarded as a reform of an unwieldy and distortionary indirect tax system.

Although the government emphasized that VAT was designed not to increase tax revenue but to remove the negative effects of the previous gross turnover taxes, it must be stated that the government expected VAT to yield the substantial revenue necessary to meet the fiscal demands required for the successful implementation of the Fourth Five-Year Economic Development Plan. The influence of budgetary needs was, if not the only cause, at least an important reason for the decision to establish VAT in Korea.

VAT is superior to a business tax or a sales tax from the viewpoint of revenue security for two reasons. First, under VAT, only buyers at the final stage have an interest in undervaluing their purchases because the deduction system ensures that buyers at earlier stages will be refunded the taxes on their purchases. Therefore, tax losses due to undervaluation should be limited to the value added at the last stage. Under a retail sales tax, however, both retailer and consumer have a mutual interest in underdeclaring the actual purchase price.

Second, under VAT, if payment of tax is successfully avoided at one stage, nothing will be lost if it is picked up at a later stage. Even if the tax is not picked up subsequently, the government will at least have collected VAT paid at stages previous to that at which the tax was avoided. If evasion takes place at the final stage, the state will lose only the tax on the value added at that point. If evasion takes place under a sales tax, however, all the taxes due on the product are lost to the government.

There is a big difference between the theoretical advantages of a hypothetical tax and the actual advantages of a particular form of tax. However simple VAT may be in theory, the Korean experience with VAT makes it clear that it is not simple in practice. It creates a host of problems that give rise to voluminous paperwork, more or less arbitrary distortions in trade and consumption, and inequities in the tax burden. This chapter examines the Korean VAT and draws lessons from its effects since its introduction in 1977.

MAIN FEATURES OF THE KOREAN VAT

The structure and administration of VAT in Korea are basically similar to those of the countries in the European Economic Community (EEC). It is a consumption-type VAT, the variety in use throughout Europe. Under Korean VAT businesses are permitted to deduct immediately from sales not only current inputs but also the full value of capital goods accrued during the taxable period.

VAT is collected by the invoice method—each firm must collect VAT on the value of its sales (unless they are exempt) but is entitled to a credit for taxes invoiced by its suppliers. As credit is allowed only if supported by invoices provided by suppliers, this method of administration is expected to facilitate audits because each firm is required to supply evidence on taxes that should have been paid by its suppliers.

Scope and Tax Base of VAT

The scope of VAT is usually defined with reference to both taxable transactions and taxable persons. The Korean VAT code defines taxable transactions as the supply of goods or services and importation of goods. Supply of goods is the delivery or transfer of goods by contractual or legal action, including the sale of goods on an installment basis and the personal use of business assets, as well as inventory goods when a business closes. Supply of services includes the rendering of services or having a person use or utilize goods, facilities, or rights on any legal or contractual basis. Importation of goods is simply the entry of goods into Korea from abroad.

A taxable person is anyone who independently engages in the supply of goods or services. Taxpayers include individuals, corporations, any organization of persons, foundations, and state and local authorities, regardless of whether the taxable transactions generate profits. The requirement that a taxable person act in an independent capacity excludes employees from an obligation to charge VAT on services provided to their employers.

The taxable amount or tax base is the full amount received for the supply of goods or services. It includes taxes (other than VAT and the defense surtax), duties, and incidental expenses such as packing, transportation, and insurance costs charged to the purchases. For sales on installment or credit, the tax base is the total price of goods supplied. The taxable amount does not include discounts or rebates and the value of goods returned or broken, lost, or damaged before they are delivered to their purchaser.

Tax Rates

Before the introduction of VAT, Korea suffered from a complicated rate structure of indirect taxes. The business tax, which was a major target of the tax reform, had five differentiated rates ranging from 0.5 percent to 3.5 percent of turnover, depending on the category of business. The previous indirect tax system had more than 50 rates ranging from 0.5 percent to 300 percent (Table 11.1). The complicated structure of the indirect tax system had created a strong desire to simplify and consequently to adopt a single VAT rate.

Although Korea has a single-rate VAT system, like those of Denmark and Sweden, the VAT code has allowed the government to adjust the normal rate (13 percent) by as much as 3 points when deemed necessary to improve the general state of the economy or to adjust tax revenue. Since its inception the VAT has been implemented at the minimum level of 10 percent. In 1988 the National Assembly passed legislation fixing the VAT rate

Table 11.1. Pre-VAT and VAT tax rates: 1977

	Pre-VAT regime				VAT regime		
	Tax rates				Tax rates[a]		
Item	Number	Minimum	Maximum	Item	Number	Minimum	Maximum
Business tax	5	0.5	3.5	VAT[b]:			
Commodity tax	17	2.0	100.0	General			
Textile tax	7	10.0	40.0	taxpayers	1	10.0	10.0
Petroleum				Special			
products tax	4	10.0	300.0	taxpayers	2	2.0	3.5
Admissions tax	12	5.0	250.0	Special con-			
Travel tax	3	5.0	20.0	sumption tax[c]	13	10.0	180.0
Gas and							
electricity tax	1	15.0	15.0				
Entertainment							
and food tax	4	2.0	20.0				

Source: MOF, ROK (1980).

a. Rates effective at the time of VAT introduction.

b. Special taxpayers are taxed at 2 percent or 3.5 percent of their turnover, whereas general taxpayers are taxed at a 10 percent rate.

c. The minimum and maximum rates of the special consumption tax as of 1 January 1988 are 5 percent and 100 percent, respectively.

at 10 percent, removing the discretionary power of the government to adjust the tax rate by plus or minus 3 percent.

There are also exceptions to the single 10 percent rate. Businesses whose sales are less than 36 million won a year (24 million won a year prior to July 1988) are taxed at a rate of 2 percent of turnover. Furthermore, individuals engaged in brokerage and intermediary services are subject to a 3.5 percent tax on their turnover unless it exceeds 6 million won.

The Korean VAT system cannot be directly compared to the VAT systems of other countries. Most European countries have multiple-rate VAT structures that apply higher rates to luxuries and lower rates to necessities. But we must look at the indirect tax system as a whole to make a valid comparison of one country with another. For example, although Korea does not have a multiple-rate VAT system, many items are subject to other taxes (such as the special consumption tax, liquor tax, defense tax, and education tax) in addition to VAT, which produces the same effect as a multiple-rate system (Table 11.2).

Zero Rating and Exemption

Korean VAT provides two types of tax exemption: "zero rating" and "exemption." "Zero rated" supplies are technically taxable but at a zero rate.

Table 11.2. Taxes applied to selected goods as a percentage of the producer's price: 1988

Item	Producer price	Special consumption tax or liquor tax	Defense tax	VAT	Education tax	Delivery price	Consumer price
Subject to special consumption tax							
TV (black and white 14")	100.0	5.0	1.5	10.6		117.1	140.4
TV (color 20")	100.0	28.0	8.4	13.6		150.0	175.2
Refrigerator (below 250 l)	100.0	28.0	8.4	13.6		150.0	180.1
Washing machine (w.p. 350B)	100.0	40.0	12.0	15.2		167.2	192.2
Piano	100.0	20.0	6.0	12.6		138.6	162.6
Passenger car (below 2,000 cc)	100.0	15.0	4.5	12.0		131.5	131.5
Coke (355 ml)	100.0	20.0	6.0	12.6		138.6	170.4
Sugar (15 kg)	100.0	30.0	9.0	13.9		152.9	168.9
Coffee (2 kg)	100.0	40.0	12.0	15.2		167.2	195.6
Subject to liquor tax							
Unfiltered liquor (*takju*)	100.0	10.0		11.0		121.0	u
Beer	100.0	150.0	45.0	31.0	15.0	241.0	u
Distilled spirits (*soju*)	100.0	35.0	3.5	13.8		152.3	u
Whisky	100.0	200.0	60.0	38.0	20.0	318.0	u
Wine	100.0	40.0	4.0	14.8	4.0	162.8	u
Vodka	100.0	40.0	4.0	14.8	4.0	162.8	u

Source: MOF, ROK (1983a).
u—unavailable.

The implication is that VAT charged on inputs relating to them can be reclaimed just as were inputs relating to taxable supplies. "Exempt" supplies are outside the scope of VAT altogether so there is no question of reclaiming the relevant input tax.

The zero rate applies to exports from Korea, services rendered outside of Korea, international transportation by ship and aircraft, and other goods or services supplied to earn foreign exchange. Zero rating is applied only to traders who are residents or to domestic corporations; however, for international shipping and aerial navigation, nonresident traders and foreign corporations are subject to zero rating on a reciprocity basis.

For exempted goods or services, tax is charged on purchases from the exempt supplier but not on the value added by the exempt organization. If the exempt firm sells to households and has positive value added, exemption reduces net liabilities. If the exempt firm sells to other firms, its exemption increases their tax burdens, because businesses that purchase exempt inputs have no credits to apply against their own tax liability.

Korean VAT allows a variety of exemptions for social, political, and administrative reasons. Exemptions are applied to basic necessities such as unprocessed foodstuffs and piped water; to certain classes of commodities that would be hard to tax, such as banking and insurance services and owner-occupied housing; and to certain commodities classified as social and cultural goods, such as medical and health services, education, books, newspapers, and artistic works. Goods and services supplied by public enterprises, independent professional services, and duty-exempt goods are exempt from VAT. Monopoly goods, telephone services, postage stamps, and so forth are exempt from VAT because supplementary separate taxes are imposed. Finally, to reduce administrative and compliance problems, small taxpayers whose annual tax liability is less than 20,000 won (10,000 won prior to December 1988) are exempt from VAT.

Administrative Aspects

Registration with the VAT authorities is the initial step in the administrative process. A trader must register at the VAT office in the district in which he resides within 20 days after he commences taxable activities. A record of all registered taxpayers is maintained on a computer file that includes: the VAT registration number, taxpayer's name and residence number, and firm's name and address, telephone number, business code, trade, classification, date of registration, and date of commencement of business.

The Korean VAT law requires an enterprise to register separately at each place it conducts business and to furnish a separate return for each location. This is an unfortunate carryover from earlier business tax laws and deters efficient business administration without increasing the tax yield.

When a registered trader supplies goods or services, he must issue an invoice to the buyer showing the date of supply; the seller's name, address, and VAT registration number; the customer's name and registration number; the value and identity of the goods or services supplied; and the amount of VAT. There are two types of tax invoices. General tax invoices are presented by the taxpayers to the district office and numbered serially. Special taxpayers use simplified tax invoices and are not required to submit any invoices to tax authorities.

Each invoice must be prepared in quadruplicate. One is kept by the seller, another is sent by the seller to the district tax office, and the third copy is kept by the purchaser, who sends the fourth copy to his district tax office. The two copies received at tax offices are forwarded to the computer data processing unit, which carries out a cross-check of sales against purchases.

In the latter half of 1977, 7.2 percent of all invoices (buyer and seller) failed to match; in 1982 the proportion of mismatches decreased to 1.4 percent. Interestingly, output invoices caused fewer difficulties than input invoices. The mismatching ratio for output invoices for each year was about half of that for input invoices. This result is consistent with our expectations since VAT tax liability can be minimized by maximizing input claims. The percentage of mismatched input invoices fell from 12.1 percent in 1977 to 2.4 percent in 1982. Erroneous data, which mean that sales and purchases of invoices match but the details of the invoices do not, decreased from 5.9 percent in 1977 to 0.3 percent in 1982 (MOF, ROK, 1983a).

Initially, all tax invoices in which the value of a transaction exceeded 100,000 won were computerized for auditing, but as of July 1980 computer processing was restricted to tax invoices with a value of 300,000 won or more. As a result, the number of invoices processed by computer dropped from 112 million in 1978 to 33 million in 1982 (MOF, ROK, 1983a).

There are two steps in the tax payment and return procedure. First, taxpayers are required to furnish the tax authorities with preliminary returns stating their tax base and the tax amount payable or refundable within 25 days (50 days for foreign corporations) from the date of termination of each preliminary return period. The first tax period is from January through June and the second is from July through December. Second, taxpayers must file with the tax authorities the tax base and tax amount payable or refundable for each taxable period within 25 days (50 days for foreign corporations) after its expiration. Taxpayers are required to submit tax invoices at the time of the preliminary or final return concerned. This quarterly payment of VAT has proved easier to work with than the more frequent two-month tax period used under the old business tax system.

Traders who are engaged in retail businesses or who operate ordinary restaurants and hotels must install a cash register (with tape for audit purposes) and issue tax invoices showing the value of supply. By such compliance traders are deemed to have fulfilled their obligations of bookkeeping and receive a tax deduction equivalent to 0.5 percent of total sales.

Penalties are imposed for failure to register or apply for inspection, for nonissuance of tax invoices, and for default on tax returns and payments. Penalties equivalent to 1 percent and 2 percent of total sales for individuals and corporations, respectively, apply for the biannual inspection. For failure to issue a tax invoice in transactions between taxable persons or failure to keep proper records, the penalty is 1 percent of the sales amount for individuals and 2 percent for corporations. Where a trader fails to file a return, or does not pay the tax amount due, or files a tax return under-reporting his obligations, he is liable to a penalty equivalent to 10 percent of his tax liability (ROK 1976). Penalties have been imposed mostly on general taxpayers for failing to issue tax invoices, for delaying the submission of invoices to government, or for submitting incorrect returns (MOF, ROK, 1983a).

Transitional measures were necessary to eliminate certain problems of double taxation that otherwise would have arisen when VAT was introduced in Korea. Taxpayers were allowed to take credits for previous taxes that had already been paid on inventories on the date of the changeover. Since the taxes replaced were of a multistage turnover variety, a difficult problem arose in determining the effective tax rate on the many types of goods in inventories, so the government imposed the average rate on each inventory item.

Treatment of Small Businesses

Under any form of sales taxation, small businesses have to be granted special treatment because of their inability to cope with the requirements of keeping adequate records that larger enterprises can handle at a reasonable cost. The purpose of the special treatment is to reduce the administrative burden on small enterprises but not the taxes that normally would be charged on the goods and services they supply.

Small businesses, called "special taxpayers" under Korean VAT, are those whose total sales are less than 36 million won a year. For businesses engaging in transactions through a proxy, agent, intermediary, cosignee, or contractor, any trader whose annual sales are less than 6 million won is treated as a special taxpayer. Unlike general taxpayers whose tax base is value added, a standard 2 percent tax rate is used to calculate the amount of tax due to the government. Small businesses engaged in transactions through a proxy, agent, intermediary, cosignee, or contractor are taxed at a rate of 3.5 percent on their annual sales.

When a business eligible for special taxation has submitted tax invoices to the government, an amount equivalent to 5 percent of the input tax amount is deducted from the tax amount payable. Special taxpayers issue simplified tax invoices and file their tax returns every six months, whereas general taxpayers issue standard tax invoices and file returns and pay taxes every three months. Special taxpayers do not have to file a preliminary tax return but do have to pay half of their taxes to the government during the immediately preceding tax period.

In Korea special taxpayers file about 76–78 percent of all VAT tax returns (MOF, ROK, 1983a). Although general taxpayers are in the minority, they are the more important source of revenue. General taxpayers pay approximately 94–95 percent of the total VAT, whereas the tax amount contributed by special taxpayers comprises only about 5–6 percent of VAT collected (MOF, ROK, 1983a).

IMPLEMENTATION PROCESS

Careful examination and long preparation preceded the introduction of VAT in Korea. Much of the interest in the introduction of VAT was undoubtedly stimulated by the widespread acceptance of VAT in Europe. Although the decision to introduce VAT was made in 1971, the law was not enacted until 22 December 1976, and took effect on 1 July 1977. It is not clear, however, whether the two years or so immediately prior to the adoption of VAT were sufficient to prepare for its implementation.

Extensive studies of the VAT system were conducted before the government's formal VAT announcement on 19 January 1976. To benefit from the experience of European countries, the government sent a small delegation to talk to officials who were administering the tax in the EEC countries where it had already been enacted. The Korean VAT also embodies proposals prepared by such well-known authorities as James D. Duignan, Carl S. Shoup, and Alan A. Tait, all of whom contributed to the development of the new tax law.

The Korean government allowed less than one year for disseminating information and conducting educational programs to explain the new law to taxpayers and the general public before the tax became effective.

To secure the cooperation of the business community, the government set up a special Deliberation Committee for the Implementation of VAT, composed of government officials and representatives of the Chamber of Commerce, the Korean Federation of Industries, the Korean Traders' Association, the Korea Tax Accountants Association, the Korea Institute of Certified Public Accountants, and the Customs Brokers Association.

Nationwide tryout exercises of filing tax returns were carried out on three separate occasions (in March, May, and July 1977) before the changeover to VAT. On average, more than 98 percent of the taxpayers in the groups concerned participated in these trial runs. Important steps taken before the introduction of VAT included the introduction of new invoices for business tax withholdings at the beginning of 1975. This was a good transition process to the invoicing system needed for VAT. The withholding system under the business tax was successfully adapted to the transitional needs of the administrative structure needed for VAT.

Concurrent with the consultation and information program, the Korean government expanded and retrained its tax administration staff. This task was facilitated by a substantial reservoir of trained personnel experienced in administering the complicated business tax and other indirect taxes. The government provided additional training for 32,444 public officials under the auspices of the Ministry of Finance, the Office of National Tax Administration (ONTA), and the Office of Customs. The ONTA staff increased by 1,999 from 9,443 in 1976 to 11,442 in 1977. Most of this increased recruitment was a result of VAT. However, the new recruits did not go directly into VAT work but were assigned to other sections to release more experienced officers for VAT. Because VAT replaced another kind of consumption tax, there were no structural changes in the organization of tax administration.

To introduce the new tax to officials who would be dealing with VAT, the government prepared a staff handbook explaining the tax procedures in detail. Answers were provided in advance to questions that were likely to be asked either by the staff themselves or by the taxpayers. Despite the government's efforts, insufficient communication with taxpayer organizations and consumer groups damaged the prospects for close cooperation. Passive and active opposition to the introduction of VAT came from many sources. Each interest group had its own reasons for opposing the new tax and each had different reasons. VAT was opposed by labor as regressive. Business in general, particularly small business, opposed the tax compliance costs as being too high. At the Economic Ministers' Meeting, however, in which every major economic policy measure is deliberated, only the minister of commerce and industry opposed the adoption of VAT. He pointed out the likelihood of a substantial increase in the prices of industrial products. Furthermore, the Democratic Republican Party, the ruling party at the time, was not in favor of introducing VAT because the party feared it would weaken support in the upcoming general election. Unhappiness with VAT on the part of the business community was demonstrated by its call to postpone the implementation of VAT immediately before VAT became effective. Some tax administrators also did not support the tax, pointing out the administrative problems of collecting the tax from retailers and the higher cost of collecting VAT than of collecting the taxes it would replace.

The designers of the tax did their work well. Although VAT has gone through a number of changes since its introduction, these have been minor. By 1 January 1984, the VAT law had been amended three times, the VAT presidential decree 15 times, and the VAT ministerial ordinance 12 times, but the basic structure of the tax remained unaltered. The difficulty encountered has been within the bounds of what can be expected on the occasion of any major tax reform.

EFFECTS OF VAT

Since its introduction, VAT has become a major source of revenue in Korea, fulfilling the chief, if tacit, goal of the government. In 1982 VAT yielded 2,094 billion won, or 22 percent of the total tax revenue of the Korean government, national and local, making it by far the single largest tax in Korea (Table 11.3). VAT represents more than 36 percent of the national taxes on goods and services and accounts for approximately 6.5 percent of private consumption.

The central government of Korea relies heavily on taxes on goods and services, which account for more than 68 percent of the total national tax

Table 11.3. National and local tax, 1970–82, and value-added tax yield, 1977–82

Item	1970	1972	1974	1976	1977	1978	1979	1980	1981	1982
Total national and local tax as % of GNP	14.8	13.0	13.9	17.4	17.4	17.9	18.4	19.2	19.3	19.8
Value-added tax										
Amount (10⁹ won)					242	839	1,089	1,471	1,805	2,094
As % of:										
Total national and local tax					8.2	20.4	20.3	22.4	22.1	22.0
Total national tax					9.2	23.0	22.9	25.3	24.9	24.9
Total tax on goods and services					13.5	33.2	33.3	35.8	36.0	36.8
Private consumption					2.2	5.9	6.0	6.4	6.3	6.7
GNP					1.4	3.6	3.7	4.2	4.2	4.4
National tax on goods and services										
Amount (10⁹ won)	223	296	580	1,358	1,793	2,527	3,270	4,104	5,009	5,696
As % of:										
Total national tax	61.1	62.2	63.5	64.9	68.4	69.2	68.7	70.7	69.0	67.8
GNP	8.3	7.3	7.9	10.2	10.5	11.0	11.2	12.0	11.8	11.8

Source: ONTA, ROK, Statistical Yearbook of National Tax (1975, 1980, 1983); MOF, ROK (1983b); BOK, National Income (1982).

revenue (Table 11.3). Though the relative importance of indirect taxes in the Korean tax system has been high, there was no significant change in their importance before and after the introduction of VAT. National taxes on goods and services as a percentage of GNP were 10.2 percent in 1976 and 11 percent in 1978.

The burden of VAT in Korea is still low compared with that in developed industrial countries. VAT has been approximately 4 percent of GNP in recent years. The relatively low overall burden of VAT in Korea can be accounted for by the fact that the ratio of total tax revenue to GNP is below 20 percent in Korea, whereas the figure is well above 30 percent in most advanced countries.

Tax policy has pervasive effects on the economy, influencing the level of economic activity, prices, wages, foreign trade, and the distribution of income and wealth. Adoption of VAT is widely viewed as a move toward a more desirable system of indirect taxation. Because so much has been happening to Korea's fiscal structure, it is difficult to sort out empirically the effects of the introduction of VAT on the economy. To encompass all of these economic effects systematically would require a fully articulated econometric model, which is almost entirely lacking at the moment.

Although the economic effects of VAT are not known with certainty because no systematic analysis has been carried out in Korea so far, our aim here is to summarize whatever evidence is available and to point out policy issues regarding economic effects that were controversial both before and after the introduction of VAT in Korea.

With regard to the economic effects of VAT, we are concerned with four major issues: VAT's effects on the price level, investment, exports, and distribution of the tax burden.

Price Level

In assessing the impact of VAT on the general price level, a conceptual distinction must be made between VAT as an additional tax and as a substitute revenue source. As a new or additional tax, VAT is likely to increase prices, provided there is an accommodating monetary policy. It should be pointed out that although VAT would be reflected in higher prices, this result would be a one-time increase—not a recurrent increase—in the price level unless mismanagement of aggregate demand led to a wage-price spiral.

In the strictly logical sphere, assuming parity in the yield of suppressed taxes and of the new VAT and a perfect market, it may be stated that the substitution of VAT for existing indirect taxes should not have increased the overall price index because the level of public expenditure was not changed nor was the economic nature of taxation, which, in all of these hypotheses, presents the same forward shifting characteristics.

Since VAT in Korea was expected to yield the same amount of revenue as the replaced indirect taxes, direct effects on the general price level were expected to be small, if present at all. Nevertheless, significant changes were expected in the effective tax rates on individual goods and services because the distribution of the replacing and replaced taxes was not identical. There were some fears that the prices of goods on which the tax burdens were reduced would not fall or would fall by less than the prices of goods on which the tax liabilty rose. To the extent that increases in the prices of commodities on which the tax burden increased were more certain than decreases in the prices of commodities on which the tax burden decreased, some increase in price level would occur.

Table 11.4 compares the price changes forecasted with those observed in major industries. It was predicted that the introduction of VAT of a 10 percent rate would lead to an increase in the wholesale price level of 0.155 percent and to a decrease in the consumer price level of 0.537 percent. In the two months after the introduction of VAT, the wholesale price level went up 3.4 percent, of which the implementation of VAT is estimated to have contributed 0.061 percent points.

At the time VAT was introduced, the government estimated that a 13 percent VAT rate would boost consumer prices by 3.4 percent and a 10 percent VAT rate would have no effect on the consumer price index (CPI). During the six- and 12-month periods before the introduction of VAT, the CPI rose by 6.7 percent and 10.1 percent, respectively, compared to increases of 3.9 percent and 14.0 percent in the first six and 12 months, respectively, following the introduction of VAT.

How much of the increase in prices should be attributed to the introduction of VAT is far from clear. However, it can be safely concluded that, due to the tight price controls by the government, the introduction of VAT does

Table 11.4. Predicted and actual change in price levels due to implementation of VAT: 1977 (%)

| Item | Predicted change | | Actual change |
	WPI	CPI	WPI[a]
Agricultural products	0.244	−0.050	0.148
Textile products	−0.439	−0.094	−0.307
Wood products	−0.006	−0.010	0.007
Chemical products	0.136	−0.110	0.053
Ceramics and glass	−0.013	−0.039	0.034
Metal products	0.329	−0.157	0.288
Fuel and electricity	−0.153	−0.029	−0.170
Other	0.057	−0.048	0.008
Total	0.155	−0.537	0.061

Source: MOF, ROK (1980).

a. Actual change within two months of introducing VAT in 1977.

not seem to have had a strong impact on prices, and that most of the increase in prices was attributable to the general inflationary situation in the economy.

In an attempt to meet widespread uncertainty about the price effects of VAT, the Korean government took two steps. First, the government decided to reduce the initially proposed single tax rate from 13 percent to 10 percent just before the introduction of VAT. Second, to prevent use of the new tax as an excuse for firms to raise their prices to consumers, the government imposed strong price controls.

The government had control over the prices charged by monopolies and oligopolies and set ceilings on factory and wholesale prices for 251 goods. A list of pre-July 1977 prices was prepared in order to hold prices to that level immediately before the tax change. The government launched a large-scale campaign to publicize recommended retail prices for a variety of consumer goods. This campaign and the existence of widespread price controls curbed any price increases that could have occurred through uncertainty, increased business margins, and profiteering.

Despite the inflationary condition of the economy, as indicated by the excessive provision of domestic credit and accelerated wage increases, price controls appear to have been successful in dampening the wage-price nexus for inflation (Table 11.5). It is also noteworthy that increases in the general price level were due mainly to a price increase in food products. During the period from the third quarter of 1977 to the last quarter of 1978 food prices went up by 28.7 percent while nonfood prices increased by only 8.4 percent (Table 11.5). This increase in food prices immediately after the introduction of VAT, which was mainly due to crop failures and the increase in government selling prices of rice, led the general public to believe that VAT was the cause of the increase in the general price level. Food products, however, are exempt from VAT.

Broadly speaking, the introduction of VAT does not seem to have had a major impact on the rate of price increases in Korea. The full effects on prices of the implementation of VAT depend not only on the initial impact but also on market interactions, the stage of the business cycle, and other policy measures. This is confirmed by the experiences of other countries that have adopted VAT. According to Alan A. Tait, who analyzed the effects of introducing VAT on the CPI, VAT was not a contributory factor to inflation in 26 out of the 31 countries examined (Tait 1980).

Investment and Savings

Unlike most of the taxes it replaced, VAT does not burden capital goods because consumption-type VAT provides full credit for the tax included in purchases of capital goods. The credit does not subsidize the purchase of capital goods; it simply eliminates the tax that has been imposed on them.

Because investment was taxed under the previous indirect tax system

Table 11.5. Prices, wages, and domestic credit indexes, 1974–80: Three years before and three years after VAT introduction (third quarter, 1977 = 100)

Year	Quarter	CPI	WPI	Index of food prices	Index of nonfood prices	Wage index	Credit index
1974	III	63.6	65.9	54.4	72.1	42.3	45.2
	IV	65.1	68.4	58.4	73.7	47.7	52.4
1975	I	69.7	76.5	65.0	81.8	47.2	59.4
	II	75.4	80.6	71.3	84.9	50.2	62.3
	III	80.3	82.4	74.7	86.1	55.4	66.0
	IV	83.6	84.5	76.6	88.2	60.7	69.3
1976	I	85.3	88.3	80.3	92.2	62.4	72.8
	II	88.2	90.0	83.9	92.9	68.1	76.2
	III	91.5	91.6	86.6	94.0	76.7	78.6
	IV	91.3	93.1	87.6	95.6	82.1	84.3
1977	I	94.2	96.0	91.8	98.0	82.1	87.4
	II	96.9	98.0	95.7	99.3	91.0	92.1
	III	100.0	100.0	100.0	100.0	100.0	100.0
	IV	101.0	101.8	103.9	100.9	108.7	104.3
1978	I	106.5	106.5	113.7	103.3	107.7	115.5
	II	109.9	109.1	119.3	104.4	122.5	127.0
	III	114.7	111.6	124.9	105.4	136.3	136.6
	IV	117.9	114.9	128.7	108.4	149.8	152.1
1979	I	122.9	118.2	131.8	111.8	145.7	162.9
	II	132.6	126.5	136.0	122.2	158.4	171.5
	III	135.7	138.1	136.7	138.8	172.5	185.6
	IV	140.7	142.0	136.5	144.7	188.2	206.2
1980	I	156.1	165.0	153.1	170.1	180.3	226.2
	II	167.4	180.6	167.7	186.3	198.1	241.9
	III	174.9	186.8	178.4	190.8	218.6	261.1

Sources: MOF, ROK (1980); BOK, *Monthly Bulletin* (1981); BOK, *Price Statistics* (1982); BOK, *Quarterly Gross National Product* (1982); Administration of Labour Affairs, ROK (1981).

but was exempted under VAT, investment costs fell accordingly. Support for capital investment by means of VAT refunds is summarized in Table 11.6, which shows that the switch to VAT provided industries such as manufacturing and electricity and gas with substantial benefits. The tax refunds for investment amounted to 18,336 million won for the second half of 1977 and 64,655 million won for all of 1982.

Comparison of the rates of savings and investment in years before the introduction of VAT with those in years since its adoption is not instructive enough to produce any conclusion regarding the effects of VAT on savings

Table 11.6. Support of capital investment through VAT refunds by industry: 1977–82

	July–Dec. 1977		1978		1979		1980		1981		1982	
	Refund (10⁶ won)	Share (%)	Refund (10⁶ won)	Share (%)	Refund (10⁶ won)	Share (%)	Refund (10⁶ won)	Share (%)	Refund (10⁶ won)	Share (%)	Refund (10⁶ won)	Share (%)
Manufacturing	13,449	73.3	34,135	62.1	32,241	58.1	24,045	66.4	23,867	48.2	16,323	25.2
Mining	12	0.1	32	0.0	27	0.0	139	0.4	284	0.6	28	0.0
Construction	418	2.3	1,055	1.9	121	0.2	175	0.5	3,628	7.3	2,159	3.3
Electricity and gas	1,693	9.2	11,502	20.9	18,422	33.2	3,559	9.8	7,734	15.6	30,642	47.4
Wholesale and retail trade	86	0.5	304	0.6	496	0.9	1,377	3.8	1,588	3.2	2,781	4.3
Transport and storage	1,064	5.8	2,142	3.9	739	1.3	1,601	4.4	1,796	3.6	2,384	3.7
Other	1,614	8.8	5,789	10.5	3,422	6.2	5,333	14.7	10,606	21.4	10,338	16.0
Total (A)	18,336	100.0	54,959	100.0	55,468	100.0	36,229	100.0	49,503	100.0	64,655	100.0
Capital investment (B)	2,689,040		7,023,070		9,458,180		11,240,030		12,097,100		14,139,970	
Support ratio (A/B)	0.7		0.8		0.6		0.3		0.4		0.5	

Source: MOF, ROK, internal data.

or investment. Although there is no evidence that investment or savings increased, a questionnaire survey by the government shortly after the adoption of VAT showed that VAT was more conducive to investment than was the old indirect tax regime (MOF, ROK, 1980).

Exports

It is commonly agreed that the introduction of VAT with zero rating on exports has a favorable influence on exports. Zero rating removes any tax paid on goods at any stage because zero-rated goods are fully exempt from any tax when sold, and producers of such goods are entitled to a refund of any tax paid on purchases to produce such goods.

In abstract terms, VAT is neutral with regard to international trade if exports are exempt from payment of tax and imports are subject to the tax. The exported commodity is totally exempt from any taxes, whereas the imported commodity pays a tax equal to that levied on the commodity sold in the domestic market. In actual fact, the neutrality of VAT with regard to international trade is subject to two limitations. The first is the difficulty of verifying the forward shift in the incidence of tax burdens; the second is the technical regulation needed to enforce the neutral characteristic of the tax limit.

Giving greater tax benefits to exporters was one of the stated goals for introducing VAT into Korea. Although this goal is politically appealing, it is logically incorrect. A lot has been said and written about the effects that the adoption of VAT would have on the competitiveness of Korean industry, and subsequently on Korean exports and the balance of payments. To examine the effects of VAT on exports, we have to distinguish between two cases: substitution of direct taxes for VAT and replacement of indirect taxes by VAT. When a country adopts a VAT system as a replacement for direct taxes or with a reduction in direct taxes, it gains a trade advantage because the government can rebate a larger proportion of the tax content of exports and collect VAT on imports. When a country substitutes VAT for indirect taxes, as in Korea, the trade advantage of VAT substitution is negligible because the refund system on export goods is a part of the replaced indirect tax system.

Regardless of which tax VAT replaces, many believe that a VAT rebate, in itself, will expand exports and that a VAT levy will retard imports. This belief might have a positive effect on trade if it encourages businesses to compete more rigorously in international markets. This result would depend on the importance of nonprice considerations in explaining export activity. In a questionnaire survey conducted by the government, a large number of Korean businessmen expressed the view that the new VAT was more favorable to exports than the old indirect taxes (MOF, ROK, 1980).

The effect of VAT on exports can be indirectly investigated by comparing the general characteristics of the new VAT system with those of the previous tax system and by looking at the trend of the indirect tax rebates in supporting exports.

The exact determination of taxes paid under the turnover tax scheme was generally difficult and frequently impossible to calculate. Because the business tax and other indirect taxes were hidden in the price of export goods, they could not be readily rebated although rebates of all indirect taxes were permissible under the law. Because of the cumulative nature of the turnover-type business tax, export goods were exempt only at the final sales stage, and the government had to estimate the border tax adjustment for export rebates on the taxes previously paid in the production and distribution process. The awareness of the problem that it is impossible to calculate the tax content of prices was one of the factors behind the reform of the indirect tax system in Korea.

As it was difficult to determine the amount of taxes included in the price of export goods under the previous indirect tax system, the government had to issue rules prescribing how much tax was buried in the price of each type of export good. The average rate on the credit for export goods was imposed by the government. Therefore, the prescribed average rate was normally either lower or higher than the actual payment. As a result, export prices usually included either a hidden subsidy or a hidden penalty.

The substitution of VAT for the previous indirect tax system has made the determination of taxes paid on exports much easier because the characteristics of a typical VAT can overcome the problem of calculating the taxes paid. This so-called border tax adjustment merely guarantees that both imports and domestically produced goods consumed in Korea bear the same tax and allow Korean exports to enter the world markets free of tax. It should be noted, however, that this border tax adjustment does not stimulate exports but does inhibit imports more than would a comparable turnover tax imposed on sales to Korean consumers.

By examining the trend in the average indirect tax rebate per dollar of exports, one can indirectly estimate the impact on exports of the change in the Korean indirect tax system. Table 11.7 shows that the average tax rebate per dollar of exports has been increasing during the past ten years or so. Though the actual effect may differ from product to product, there was a sharp increase in the average tax rebate per dollar of exports, from 33.56 won per dollar in 1976 to 53.56 won per dollar in 1978. This result shows that the government underestimated the border tax adjustment under the previous tax system. In this sense, the adoption of VAT benefited the export industry.

According to the poll on the new rebating system, a majority of export company officials agreed that the introduction of VAT had a positive effect on the trade competitiveness of their goods (MOF, ROK, 1980). The survey also showed they felt that VAT supported exporters more than the previous tax structure. Though we may conclude that a switch to VAT with zero

Table 11.7. Average annual rebate of indirect taxes per dollar of exports: 1973–82

	Exports (10^6 US $)	Total rebate[a] (10^6 won)	Rebate per dollar (won)
1973	3,225	68,523	21.24
1974	4,460	101,488	22.75
1975	5,081	168,728	33.21
1976	7,715	258,913	33.56
1977	9,687	514,226	53.08
1978	12,711	680,813	53.56
1979	15,055	852,150	56.60
1980	17,505	1,306,584	74.64
1981	21,259	1,748,125	82.23
1982	21,853	1,892,966	86.62

Source: MOF, ROK, internal data.

a. Total rebate under the previous system and VAT, including the special consumption tax.

rating on exports may have made a modest contribution to the improvement of balance of payments in Korea, particularly due to its ease and precision in calculating tax rebates, this contribution should not be overemphasized. Because exchange rates or domestic inflation would soon adjust in response to any initial improvement in the balance of payments, any competitive edge induced by tax substitution would soon dissipate.

Distribution of the Tax Burden

Like other taxes, VAT has distributive properties in that its burden will fall more heavily on some sections of society than on others. Perhaps the most controversial issue when the introduction of VAT was under consideration was its effect on the distribution of tax burdens. The regressivity issue of VAT continues to be a topic for heated debate.

A comprehensive VAT is regressive because lower-income taxpayers consume a higher proportion of their income than do middle- and upper-income taxpayers. A number of studies (Heller 1981; Oh 1982; Han 1982) have been carried out to estimate the distribution of VAT burdens. The results of these estimates are summarized in Table 11.8. Using the household income and expenditure survey, these studies all base the distribution of VAT burdens on consumption patterns and the estimated rate of taxation on each category of consumer goods.

In all these studies (Heller 1981; Oh 1982; Han 1982), VAT is shown to be more or less regressive with respect to income. According to a study by Peter S. Heller (1981), VAT in Korea is regressive, with the burden declining from 5.55 percent of income at the lowest decile to 3.91 percent at the highest. The burden is lower in the farm sector than in the nonfarm sector,

Table 11.8. Effective burdens of VAT on income (%)

Item	Income decile									
	1st	2nd	3rd	4th	5th	6th	7th	8th	9th	10th
Heller										
All households	5.55	5.19	4.19	5.00	4.67	4.84	4.79	4.04	4.11	3.91
Nonfarm households	5.94	5.63	5.82	5.75	5.46	5.38	5.51	5.31	5.02	3.91
Farm households	4.80	4.02	3.42	3.27	3.13	2.89	2.73	2.46	2.22	
Oh										
1976 data	3.62	2.90	2.98	2.94	2.86	2.85	2.76	2.73	2.79	2.42
1978 data	3.56	3.10	3.07	3.05	3.05	2.99	2.91	2.86	2.77	2.60
Han										
Nonfarm households	9.38	7.50	6.70	6.40	5.99	5.69	5.38	5.06	4.67	3.82
Farm households	8.44	5.96	5.14	5.07	4.24	4.18	3.73	3.53	3.17	2.90

Sources: Heller (1981); Oh (1982); Han (1982).

with the relative burden declining at the upper deciles in the farm sector. Whereas Yeon-Cheon Oh's analysis claims that the distribution of VAT burdens is only slightly regressive, Seung-Soo Han's study concludes that regressivity is quite strong (Oh 1982; Han 1982). According to Han's estimate, the effective burden of VAT on income for the highest decile is about 40 percent of that for the lowest decile. The corresponding figure based on Oh's study is around 70 percent.

Not only is the regressivity of VAT more pronounced in Han's study than in Oh's, but the absolute burden of VAT throughout all income classes is also much higher in Han's study than in the study by Oh. Those in the lowest decile pay 9.38 percent of their income as tax according to Han (1982) and 3.56 percent according to Oh (1982). But the people whose incomes are in the top 10 percent are estimated to have tax burdens of 3.82 percent and 2.6 percent of their income in Han's and Oh's analyses, respectively.

A variety of indirect taxes were replaced by VAT and the special consumption tax in Korea. Therefore, it is worth ascertaining whether VAT substitution led to increased or reduced regressivity. As shown in Table 11.9, which summarizes the burdens of domestic indirect taxes before and after the streamlining, the empirical studies done to date yield mixed results.

According to Oh (1982), the distribution of the tax burden by income decile appears on the whole to have become slightly less regressive after the tax reform. Two other studies by Heller (1981) and Han (1982), however, show that regressivity has generally increased. Two explanations can be offered to account for the fact that the distribution of the indirect tax burden changed relatively little in the shift from the pre-VAT to the VAT re-

Table 11.9. Burdens of domestic indirect taxes on income under the pre-VAT and the VAT regimes

Item	Income decile									
	1st	2nd	3rd	4th	5th	6th	7th	8th	9th	10th
Heller										
All households										
Pre-VAT	7.42	7.29	6.30	6.73	6.76	7.14	6.73	6.43	6.22	7.00
VAT	7.81	7.57	6.29	7.15	6.85	7.22	6.80	6.20	6.20	6.85
Nonfarm households										
Pre-VAT	7.64	7.83	8.14	7.57	7.73	7.92	7.73	8.31	7.49	7.00
VAT	8.39	8.40	8.70	8.29	8.07	8.15	8.03	8.38	7.71	6.85
Farm households										
Pre-VAT	6.98	6.25	5.45	5.00	5.02	4.74	4.41	4.37	3.79	
VAT	6.70	5.96	5.18	4.79	4.65	4.35	3.97	3.83	3.30	
Oh										
1976 data										
Pre-VAT	5.93	4.75	4.91	4.79	4.61	4.67	4.51	4.47	4.53	4.12
VAT	4.93	4.07	4.22	4.13	3.98	4.01	3.87	3.82	3.92	3.54
1978 data										
Pre-VAT	5.82	5.15	5.14	5.09	5.07	4.99	4.90	4.81	4.78	4.54
VAT	5.71	4.98	4.97	4.96	4.93	4.85	4.75	4.68	4.62	4.34
Han										
1976	15.70	13.10	12.40	11.90	11.50	11.20	10.80	10.40	9.70	9.10
1978	20.40	15.80	13.80	13.10	12.10	11.40	10.60	9.90	9.00	7.10

Sources: Heller (1981); Oh (1982); Han (1982).

gimes or has become worse over time. First, the VAT system was designed to be quite regressive. Second, the tax rates and tax base of the special consumption tax, which was concurrently introduced to supplement VAT, are insufficient to allow it to play its assigned role. In all the studies reviewed, the burden of the special consumption tax is proportional to income or is even somewhat inversely related to income.

The incidence studies reviewed above vary in their estimates of the distributive effect of VAT itself, and in their comparisons of the distributive effect of VAT and previous indirect taxes. Still, all these studies indicate, as expected, that VAT is regressive and that the replacement of the previous indirect taxes with VAT and the special consumption tax has not lessened the regressivity of overall indirect tax burdens.

Because Korea relies heavily on indirect taxes for its revenue, the regressivity of indirect tax burdens implies that the overall tax burden in Korea is regressive. Therefore, there remains a need for the government to improve the distribution of income by moderating the regressivity of VAT and the indirect tax system in general and by moving toward greater reliance on direct taxes.

CRITICISMS, CURRENT ISSUES, AND LESSONS

Because more than a decade has elapsed since the implementation of VAT in Korea, an interim assessment is possible. VAT in Korea has been working relatively well, in some cases much better than its designers and the taxpayers had anticipated. The number of complaints has been small, though some have been loud. Complaints have been made and will continue to be made about various aspects of the tax structure and the details of its operation. Many of these protests, however, are more in the nature of special interest pleading or general grumbling than attacks on the concept of the tax.

Korean experiences with VAT clearly show the importance of good bookkeeping practices and the implications of the habit of requesting receipts by buyers after each transaction. A precondition for the introduction of VAT was well-established record keeping, which proved to be too demanding and cumbersome for Korean firms, especially small ones accustomed to poor bookkeeping or to keeping no records at all. The practice of bargaining between sellers and buyers to settle prices, which most Koreans take for granted, was a hindrance to the introduction and acceptance of VAT. Other countries planning to adopt VAT should make every effort to establish the system of attaching price tags to retail products.

On almost all counts, VAT in Korea should be considered an improvement over the indirect taxes it replaced. Its base is broader. It permits more precise border tax adjustment. Taxpayers have by now familiarized themselves with VAT. There is no evidence of large-scale tax evasion. Revenue from VAT is large and in line with the calculations based on the volume of private consumption.

Although VAT can and does work in Korea, it is not free from arbitrary elements and controversies. To deal with the annoying problems associated with VAT, a distinction must be made between problems inherent in VAT and those also true of other taxes. By way of conclusion, the major issues currently facing the VAT system in Korea are reviewed to help other countries learn from the Korean experience.

Scope and Coverage of VAT

One recurrent question about the structure of VAT in Korea concerns the possibility of extending VAT to sales that are currently exempt. The widespread use of exemption is founded on the desire to reduce the regressivity of the VAT burden. Needless to say, the extensive use of exemptions reduces the efficiency advantage that might have been gained from a more neutral tax structure.

Exemptions facilitate the administration of VAT. This is true particularly of exemptions for small taxpayers and certain services. It should be borne in mind, however, that excessive exemptions complicate administration because of the difficulty of distinguishing taxable from nontaxable transactions and the resulting need for more detailed records and invoices.

Current issues on the Korean VAT exemption scheme center around two major questions. The first is the very purpose of the VAT exemption, and the second is the possibility of narrowing the scope of the exemption. It is generally understood that exemptions are allowed to reduce the regressivity of the VAT burden. It must be pointed out, however, that the reasons for the exemption scheme in the VAT structure lie not in the reduction of regressivity but in the simplification of administration and compliance.

Moderation of the regressivity could be achieved more effectively through the zero-rating scheme rather than through the exemption scheme. This simple but important point has not caught the attention of VAT designers in Korea and many other countries. Zero-rated supplies are technically taxable but at a low rate; the implication is that VAT charged on inputs relating to them could be reclaimed just as were inputs relating to taxable supplies. Exempt supplies are outside the scope of VAT altogether so there is no question of reclaiming relevant input taxes. Because an exempt transaction bears some VAT, the relief of the tax burden on low-income people should be sought through the application of a zero-rating scheme rather than an exemption scheme for goods and services consumed disproportionally by the poor.

Even under the current exemption scheme, a review of the list of goods and services currently exempted leads one to question the appropriateness of the inclusion of some items on the list. In principle, exemptions from VAT should be limited to basic necessities such as unprocessed foodstuffs and to goods and services the government wishes to exempt for social or cultural reasons.

Several selections on the exemption list have been controversial, including services provided by financial institutions and insurance companies, government-provided goods and services that compete with commercial operations, and independent professional services. On the grounds of tax equity between privately and publicly supplied goods and services and the economic efficiency of preserving the capacity of private firms to compete for business with public agencies, it has been strongly suggested that some commercial activities by semi-governmental bodies should not be exempted.

The exemption of rent, insurance, and financial services means that traders of these outputs have to bear input taxes but cannot reclaim them. They are expected to pass the tax on to their customers. Business users of those services thus have to bear some VAT costs, despite the philosophy of the tax. The major problem with taxing financial services is the difficulty of recalculating the correct tax base. One way to tax the value added of insurance and banking services would be to rely on the direct additive method, that is, adding together their annual wage and salary payments, rental payments, and profit. A tax of 0.5 percent on gross receipts of banking and insurance companies has been imposed in Korea since the beginning of 1982. To determine whether it is desirable to bring these financial institutions within the scope of VAT, one has to consider whether to eliminate the special tax recently imposed or to accept the consequences of imposing a heavier burden on this sector than on others.

Practically all independent professional services, such as those provided by doctors, lawyers, accountants, and architects, are currently exempt. It has been suggested that all these professional services should be taxed. Given the fact that these independent professionals currently pay relatively little tax under the personal income tax, it would seem advisable to make their services subject to taxes unless they can fully shift their tax burdens to their customers. Furthermore, from an equity point of view, it is desirable to adopt a common policy toward all professional services rather than to single out one particular service for exclusion from the exemption.

All in all, exemptions should be held to a minimum not only to keep the VAT base broad but also to minimize administrative problems and distortions in the economy. The neutrality of the tax would be improved if the coverage of services were broadened and if exemptions were replaced by zero ratings. Increased use of zero ratings rather than exemptions would reduce the advantages that large firms have over small ones.

Tax Rate Structure

A single rate of 10 percent has been used in Korea since the introduction of VAT in 1977. If VAT were imposed at a uniform rate on all consumption, it would be regressive when measured against income, because consumption expenditures take a decreasing fraction of personal income as income levels rise. To reduce the tax burden on low-income taxpayers and to inject an element of progressivity into VAT, suggestions have been made to use differentiated multiple rates rather than a single uniform rate.

Experiences with rate differentiation elsewhere do not recommend its use in Korea; the EEC countries have found that such a differentiation complicates administration and compliance and destroys both neutrality and the advantages that uniformity brings. Furthermore, using multiple rates is an inefficient way to achieve redistributive objectives.

The tax rate structure of VAT has a direct influence on its administration and compliance. Many problems arise from the use of multiple rates. First, the rate structure may not be sufficiently defined, leaving products that can fit into more than one category. Second, the categories themselves may be based on criteria for which information is not readily available. Third, multiple rates cost too much for small businesses dealing with a variety of goods, because it is extremely time-consuming for them to account separately for each different category when filling out tax returns. Fourth, multiple rates provide taxpayers with the oppportunity to evade the taxes either through miscalculation or other manipulations.

Given the limitations of record keeping on the part of taxpayers and auditors, it is imperative that the tax be kept simple, and the most important requirement for simplicity is the use of a single rate. If a higher tax burden is desired on certain classes of goods or services, this should be attained by separate levies like the special consumption tax either at the importation or manufacturing level, as is the case now in Korea.

The regressivity of VAT can be moderated, but not eliminated, by special measures like exemptions and differentiated rates. Even if many commodities were zero rated, a significant progressivity or even a substantial decrease in regressivity could not be obtained. A set of distributional goals can be more easily achieved using the available alternative devices.

Participants at the Brookings conference, which reviewed the European experience with VAT, agreed that the use of multiple rates and exemptions complicates administration and compliance and distorts consumption in ways that are unlikely to promote economic efficiency (Aaron 1981). They held that distributional objectives should be pursued with other instruments, notably transfer payments and income taxes. Many of the European countries that have adopted a multiple-rate VAT have been moving to simplify their tax rate structure. The United Kingdom, Belgium, and Ireland have all decreased the number of their VAT rates.

Administrative Problems

The administrative problems posed by VAT have been considerable although administrative efficiency for the VAT system was an important consideration behind its adoption in Korea. All taxable transactions must be fully recorded. Invoices must be issued so that the purchaser can deduct the tax charged on the sale. For some time administration of VAT has been subject to criticism. The administrative aspects of VAT are still controversial, and recent public concern about the VAT system in Korea centers around the issues of administrative efficiency and compliance costs.

The degree of compliance and the cost of administration depend on whether businesses are accustomed to keeping good written records, on the establishment of a modernized distribution system, and on the share of business activity carried out by small establishments. The lack of systematic record keeping in many parts of the Korean economy would make administration difficult and evasion easy even under the best of circumstances. Unless distribution channels through which commodities change hands are modernized and solidly established, there is no way of controlling the illegal transfer of tax invoices to a third party.

VAT is said to be self-enforcing because of how it is usually administered. Korean experience with VAT, however, suggests that the so-called built-in, self-enforcing aspect of the tax, which permits the matching of the tax credits of one taxpayer against the tax payments of another, is illusory or, at least, a much overrated advantage because invoices can be falsified.

The advantages of the invoice method have not been fully realized in practice and are not likely to be fully realized, because of the practical impossibility of checking all invoices on the part of tax collectors and because of efforts to evade the tax on the part of taxpayers. Much evasion occurs through the failure of some parties to report all transactions. There is a measure of self-policing in that evasion by suppliers through the understatement of the tax collected is balanced by the purchasers' interest in ensuring that all tax payments are recorded. Similarly, evasion by purchasers who overstate the taxes they pay runs counter to the interests of suppliers.

It must be stressed that VAT is not a self-enforcing tax. Although taxpayers do have an incentive to request invoices for their purchases to increase their input of tax audit, this incentive is in many instances counterbalanced by the desire to suppress both purchases and sales to avoid not only VAT but also income taxes.

The ability to administer VAT is a function of a large number of factors. One group of factors, which are internal to the VAT system, is the scope of the tax, the degree of its complexity in terms of rate structure, the exemptions, the reporting techniques and procedures, the tax payment procedures, and the treatment of small businesses. Another group of factors, which are external not only to VAT but also to any other kind of tax, includes the degree of literacy, the size of the monetary economy, the adequacy of bookkeeping, the attitudes toward taxation and tax administration, and the efficiency of tax administration services. Administrative difficulties can be overcome when the intrinsic complexity of the tax law is compatible with the external factors mentioned here.

Special Taxpayers

One of the major criticisms of VAT in Korea has been the burden on businesses, particularly on small businesses, to keep books and file returns to the tax authorities in the prescribed format. Taxpayers' records must clearly show not only total sales and the taxes payable but also all purchases and taxes paid. Whereas large and medium-size firms can absorb the accounting and procedural requirements of VAT with relative ease, the problem lies in the size of small businesses. Although the control and audit of special taxpayers may be kept to a minimum, their numbers alone pose problems of registering, filing returns, and collecting taxes that could impede efficient administration of the entire tax system. The cost of managing a large number of special taxpayers must be weighed against the considerations of revenue and equity. If the administrative burden outweighs their revenue potential, it may be better for such special taxpayers to be exempt from VAT.

In 1982, 78 percent of all special taxpayers had annual sales lower than

5 million won, and this group of taxpayers contributed less than 3 percent of total VAT collected. From a purely administrative point of view, exemption of special taxpayers from VAT is attractive in that both administration and compliance would be made easier with no substantial loss in revenue. Some suggest that the authorities should be lenient in applying VAT to small traders. The temptation to move toward more lenient treatment of troublemaking small taxpayers should be resisted, however, because such concessions are costly in terms of government credibility and would have a profound effect on the bookkeeping and accounting practices of all taxpayers, both general and special.

Another important policy issue is the question of how to determine which taxpayers should be considered special or small. Prior to 1988 the dividing limit was total yearly turnover of 24 million won. In 1983 the opposition Democratic Korean Party suggested that the limit be increased to 36 million won per year; the limit was increased to that level in 1988. The increase should have been rejected because the aim of special treatment of small businesses is not to give them more favorable treatment but to provide a simplified system, which approximates the true tax liability without imposing an intolerable burden on either the taxpayer or the tax administration.

Taxpayers are hesitant or reluctant to be categorized as general taxpayers simply because special taxpayers are treated preferentially relative to general taxpayers. The manipulation of sales totals and the disguised closing of businesses are well-known practices. These illegal practices in large part explain the fact that despite the rapid growth of the economy there is no change in the number of special taxpayers as a percentage of total VAT taxpayers.

Coordination of VAT with Direct Taxation

A high degree of coordination between the staff in charge of VAT and those in charge of direct taxes is very important. It is an open secret that in Korea taxpayers cheat on their sales not to evade VAT but to evade personal and corporate income taxes. Operation of VAT resembles that of the income tax more than that of other taxes and an effective VAT system greatly aids income tax administration.

Countries differ in the degree to which they combine administration of their VAT with individual and corporate income taxes. To secure close coordination between them, institutionalization is necessary at the technical level through means such as automatic processing of data obtained through tax returns or audits, the exchange of this information, consultation as to special audit programs, and the design of forms. In any event, close cooperation with the income tax administration is of great importance for strengthening both VAT and the income tax.

One lesson that the Korean experience holds for a country contemplating the adoption of VAT is that implementation of VAT is bound to fall well short of the theoretical ideal. However simple VAT may be in theory, Korean experience makes it clear that it is not simple in practice. It creates a host of special problems that give rise to paperwork and more or less arbitrary distinctions.

POPULATION AND
PUBLIC HEALTH POLICIES

12 Population Policy

by Andrew Mason and Lee-Jay Cho

At the very moment of partition, demographic forces began to exert considerable influence on South Korea's future. Between the end of World War II and the end of the Korean War, over 2 million refugees flooded into the South. Although the influx of refugees brought urban problems to Seoul and other cities where they settled, they also brought a stronger human resource base to the South—valued by a country still threatened from the North and only recently independent of Japanese control after 36 years of occupation. But another demographic force, one less noticed but with far greater long-run implications, also emerged at the end of the Korean War. At the same time that death rates were declining with great rapidity, birth rates reached record heights, pushing the rate of population growth to near 3 percent per year.

The fact that Korea's population was growing far more rapidly than at any previous time was only one of many concerns that occupied Korean policymakers in the early 1950s. Per capita GNP was only US $80, much of the country's physical infrastructure had been destroyed by the war, the development of its human infrastructure had been impeded by Japanese occupation, and domestic saving was so inadequate that there seemed to be little hope for significant economic progress. These problems were more immediate and occupied a much higher place on the national development agenda than did consideration of population policy. Beyond these economic realities, traditional Confucian values emphasizing the importance of the large extended family held sway among Korea's leaders, particularly Syngman Rhee, and discouraged policy dialogue concerned with reducing the rate of population growth.

With the overthrow of the Syngman Rhee regime in 1960, debate on the implications of Korea's population growth and the wisdom of establishing a nationwide program to encourage lower fertility became possible. Park Chung Hee, as a nationalist and Confucian, was reluctant to introduce family planning to Korea. But arguments by Korea's technocrats that rapid population growth would impede Korea's development efforts won the day. In 1961, the Planned Parenthood Federation of Korea was established with the blessing of the government, and the First Five-Year Development Plan (1962–66) established fertility reduction as one of the goals of Korea's national development effort and provided funds through the Ministry of Health and Social Affairs (MOHSA) to establish government-sponsored family planning in Korea.

The concern of the formulators of Korea's early population policy is evident in the demographic situation of Korea today. With a 1985 population estimated at just over 41 million, Korea is one of the most densely populated countries in the world. Even so, its population continues to grow at a rapid pace and will approach 50 million by the year 2000 and, barring a further decline in fertility, will reach 53 million sometime during the twenty-first century (EPB, ROK, 1986). The extent of Korea's population growth is most evident in its enormous urban populations. In 1985 Seoul proper was the home of nearly ten million Koreans; another four million resided in Pusan (W. B. Kim 1986).

The origins of Korea's population growth can be traced to the early 1900s when mortality first began to decline. Population growth, however, did not average 2 percent per year (decadal average) until after the Korean War (Table 12.1). The source of rapid population growth is clear from Figure 12.1—fertility persisted at a high level until the mid-1960s despite a steady decline in mortality.

The speed with which fertility has declined since 1965 is virtually without precedent. Korea's birth rate dropped nearly in half in only two decades, from over 40 births per thousand women to well under 30 per thousand in 1980. Whereas women were typically bearing six children in 1960, they were bearing fewer than three by 1980. The latest available data indicate that total fertility had declined further to two births per women in 1985 (EPB, ROK, 1986). If the further declines targeted in Korea's Sixth Five-Year Development Plan (1987–91) are achieved, the population will peak at 54 million in the year 2023 (EPB, ROK, 1986).

Table 12.1. Population growth: 1900–85

Year	Population (in millions)	Rate of growth
All Korea		
1900	17.1	
1910	17.4	0.2
1920	18.1	0.4
1930	20.4	1.2
1940	23.5	1.4
South Korea		
1949	19.9	
1960	25.0	2.1
1970	32.2	2.5
1980	38.1	1.7
1985	40.4	1.2

Source: Mason (1986b); NBS, EPB, ROK (1987).

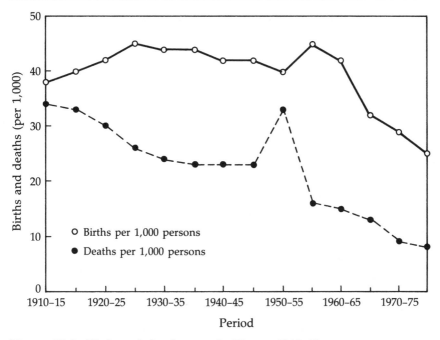

Figure 12.1. Birth and death rates in Korea: 1910–80
Source: Kwon et al. (1975).

Population projections by the Bureau of Statistics are based on the assumption that total fertility will decline further, but more slowly, to reach 1.75 births per woman in 1995 (Table 12.2). Continued improvements in mortality are also anticipated with life expectancy at birth reaching 69.3 years for males and 76.2 years for females by the year 2000. Based on these assumptions the annual rate of population growth will average 1 percent over the next 15 years and the population will reach 48 million in the year 2000.

The reduction in fertility has had far-reaching effects in Korea. Had population growth rates observed during the 1970s prevailed, Korea's population would be more numerous by 20 million in the year 2000. The age distribution of Korea's population has also changed considerably as a consequence of declining fertility. Figure 12.2 shows age pyramids for Korea in 1960, 1980, and projected to the year 2000. As is characteristic of high fertility countries, the 1960 population was relatively young with 42 percent under 15 years of age and only 3 percent 65 or older. By 1980 only one-third and, by 2000 less than one-quarter of the population will be under 15 years of age.

It is, of course, only the number of young that is influenced by Korea's

Table 12.2. Population projections for the Republic of Korea: 1985–2020

Year	Population (in thousands)			Age distribution (%)		
	Total	Male	Female	0–14	15–64	65+
1985	41,056	20,702	20,354	30.6	65.2	4.2
1990	43,601	21,981	21,620	27.2	68.1	4.7
1995	45,962	23,161	22,800	25.2	69.6	5.2
2000	48,017	24,187	23,831	23.1	70.7	6.2
2005	49,710	25,033	24,677	21.3	71.3	7.4
2010	51,028	25,692	25,335	19.8	71.8	8.4
2015	51,963	26,166	25,798	18.6	72.0	9.4
2020	52,473	26,416	26,057	17.6	71.4	11.0

Source: EPB, ROK (1986).

Note: Figures for 1985 are preliminary estimates from 1985 census.

family planning success. In 1980 there were no more than 5 million members in each of the age groups shown in Figure 12.2. In the absence of fertility decline, however, each young cohort would have exceeded the previous one by 10 to 15 percent and the number of children under five years of age could have been twice the number of that age actually living in Korea in 1980.

The way that these demographic changes have, in turn, affected Korea's economy is a matter about which there has been considerable discussion. Although there is disagreement about the effect of demographic factors on education (Schultz 1987; NRC 1986), the rapid expansion of Korea's educational system, already straining existing resources, would surely have been impeded. The decline in childrearing responsibilities among Korean women has been partly responsible for increased labor force participation by women (Bauer and Shin 1986). And a significant portion of the rise in domestic saving rates, so important to continued capital expansion, has been attributed to the decline in the number of young dependents (Mason et al. 1986). All things considered, Korea has achieved its objective of lowered fertility and population growth and this success has complemented other efforts to achieve rapid economic growth.

MAIN FEATURES OF POPULATION POLICY

The formulators of Korea's population policy would no doubt be pleased by the demographic trends outlined above. But the success of Korea's population policy must be judged on the extent to which it was responsible for reduced childbearing. At the very time the government was introducing family planning, Korea was also experiencing rapid changes in child mortality, educational attainment, urbanization, modernization, and standards of living—all factors widely believed to be responsible for fertility decline in today's developing countries. Nonetheless, research described below

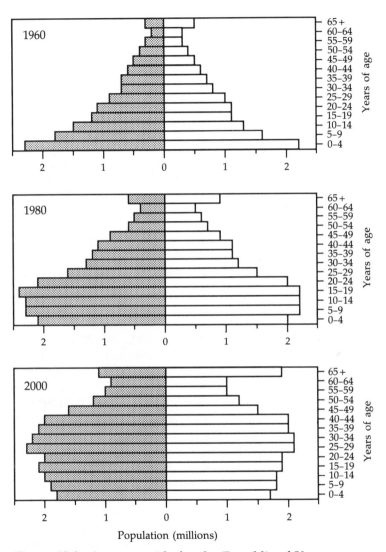

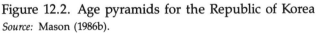

Figure 12.2. Age pyramids for the Republic of Korea
Source: Mason (1986b).

shows that the preponderance of Korea's fertility decline cannot be accounted for by its rapid social and economic development. Rather Korea's family planning program was critical to the reductions in childbearing achieved during the 1960s and 1970s.

Korea first embraced family planning as a national objective in 1961. That year saw the establishment of the Planned Parenthood Federation of Korea (supported by the International Planned Parenthood Federation and private donors), the abrogation of the law prohibiting the import and production of contraceptives, and the adoption of the First Five-Year Development Plan which provided for the establishment of a national family planning program.

Beginning in 1962 the government committed financial resources to family planning through MOHSA. At its inception, the program emphasized the distribution of contraceptive services through established health centers and the provision of family planning information and education through home visits by family planning workers. By 1964 family planning field workers had been assigned to each of 1,473 *myons* (counties) and contraceptive services were being provided to nearly 300,000 men and women. To achieve these gains required a substantial commitment on the part of the government—the program employed over 2,000 workers. The government was aided in its effort through the provision of technical and material assistance from the United States and other countries.

Although the program enjoyed some early successes, it also faced a number of problems. Traditional Korean values were not supportive of efforts to reduce family size with the Confucian emphasis on expanding one's clan and maintaining the family's name over generations. Thus, local leaders and government officials were decidedly mixed in their support of efforts to reduce childbearing. Given the hierarchical nature of Korean society and the pressure to conform, the support of local leaders was critical to program success (L. J. Cho 1971). A second problem was encountered in urban areas. Whereas in rural areas family planning workers could generally gain access to the target population, in urban areas home visits proved to be an ineffective method of promoting contraceptive acceptance and use.

Contraceptive services were provided to nearly 600,000 men and women in 1966, but the family planning program languished somewhat in the late 1960s. Delivery of all three of the methods provided at the time—interuterine devices (IUD), vasectomy, and condoms—declined from 1966 to 1967 and again in 1968.

Several steps were taken to reinvigorate the program in the late 1960s and early 1970s.[1] The political commitment to family planning was strength-

1. Deputy Prime Minister and Minister of Economic Planning Kim Hak Yul's leadership and commitment to population policy are reflected in the major advances in the family planning program during this period.

ened and conveyed more effectively to the provincial administration by involving the Ministry of Home Affairs which established family planning as a high priority program. Beginning in 1968, Mothers' Clubs were established throughout the country. The Mothers' Clubs proved to be an important and effective means by which the importance and value of family planning was communicated throughout rural Korea. In 1968 the pill was introduced and quickly became as popular as the IUD as the method of choice. In 1972 the family planning organization was strengthened by establishing the Bureau of Maternal and Child Health in MOHSA. And in 1973 the legal grounds for induced abortion were liberalized.

Reflecting the strengthening of the program and significant improvements in socioeconomic circumstances in Korea, delivery of contraceptive services recovered beginning in 1969 and grew steadily throughout the early 1970s. By 1973, 36 percent of all women of childbearing age were practicing contraception, and 30 percent had experienced an induced abortion. Total fertility had declined to fewer than four children in 1973 from six children per woman in 1960.

In the 1970s a broad-based approach was taken to improve the performance of the family planning program. First, all segments of society were involved in the family planning movement as part of the New Community Movement. Family planning information was more effectively disseminated in urban areas by actively involving both the public and the private sectors. Medium and large corporations were required to establish family planning programs for their employees. Trade unions were required to provide population education to their members. And the Ministry of Defense provided population education and contraceptive devices to all military personnel.

Second, attention was turned toward the cultural and institutional underpinnings of high fertility. Population education was expanded and introduced into secondary schools and universities. The Ministry of Education revised textbooks and incorporated material on the dangers of rapid population growth into the regular school curriculum. With funding from the United Nations Fund for Population Activities, materials on population were distributed throughout the school system. A variety of incentives and disincentives were established to reinforce small family norms. In 1974 the Ministry of Finance revised the tax codes to allow exemptions for three children only, reduced further to two children in 1977. Expenditures by corporations on family planning services for employees was exempted from corporate income tax, and public housing priority was given to sterilization acceptors with one or two children.

Efforts to attack the social underpinnings of high fertility are particularly well illustrated by the response to son preference. Quantified by the most widely used measure, the Coombs scale, Korea had the strongest preference for sons of any country in one recent study (Arnold and Kuo

1984). Couples with two daughters were twice as likely to bear an additional child as couples with two sons (C. B. Park 1983) and fertility decline leveled off at three children per couple, widely viewed to be a direct consequence of son preference. A two-pronged approach was employed to attack son bias. Efforts were made to raise the status of women by amending family law, including inheritance practices, and the preference for males was attacked directly via public education campaigns.

The nationwide, broad-based effort to reduce fertility culminated in the establishment of the Population Policy Council as part of the Fourth Five-Year Economic and Social Development Plan beginning in 1976. The council was chaired by Deputy Prime Minister and Minister of Economic Planning Nam Duck Woo. Under his leadership the implementation of population policy was the direct responsibility of the vice-ministers of relevant ministries including home affairs, education, finance, transportation, and health and welfare. The central position of the Economic Planning Board (EPB) in population policy considerably strengthened family planning's budgetary clout and its ability to mobilize government resources for family planning efforts.

The strengthened commitment to family planning paid dividends during much of the 1970s. More than 700,000 people received contraceptive services through government-supported programs during 1961–78. Furthermore, an increasing number opted for sterilization rather than temporary measures such as the IUD and pill. By 1979 over half of all women of childbearing age were practicing contraception, and women were averaging around three births apiece.

During the late 1970s and early 1980s, the family planning effort languished. The delivery of all methods of contraception through government programs dropped below delivery in previous years, and the rate of contraceptive practice barely increased between 1979 and 1982. Fertility decline slowed, as well. The reason for the disappointing progress during this period is not altogether clear. It may reflect turmoil in Korea associated with President Park's assassination in 1979 and economic collapse in 1980. Although low fertility is generally associated with an economic downturn, its disruption of the family planning effort may have impeded further decline in fertility.

But at some point in the early 1980s, the family planning effort began to pick up steam. The delivery of contraceptive services through government-supported programs was much more extensive in 1982 and thereafter than in 1981. More important, the method of choice shifted toward sterilization and away from temporary techniques of contraception. In 1982 the number of vasectomies performed exceeded 50,000 and the number of tubectomies performed exceeded 200,000 for the first time. Reflecting these renewed efforts, contraceptive practice increased from 54.5 percent of all women of childbearing age in 1979, to 57.7 percent in 1982, and to 70.4 percent in 1985. In 1984 total fertility reached replacement level—2.1 births per woman—four years before the target date specified in Korea's Fifth Five-Year Development Plan.[2]

In an important sense, the Korean family planning program has accomplished its primary objective. Because women are bearing only two children each, on average, Korea's population will stop growing some time during the twenty-first century. Without further declines in fertility, Korea's population will stabilize at around 60 million. The Sixth Five-Year Development Plan (1987–91) has as its objective further reductions in fertility required to reach zero population growth in the year 2023 at a population of about 53 million. To achieve this goal, contraceptive use is targeted to increase to 76 percent of all women of childbearing age, and fertility is targeted to decline to 1.86 births per woman by 1991 reducing the rate of population growth to only 1 percent by 1993.

As in the past, these objectives will be pursued via an all-encompassing approach to family planning. The potential for intensifying the program through family planning workers in local administrative units, for the most part, has been exhausted. But efforts will be made to improve the quality of contraceptive services and to integrate family planning and programs to promote maternal and child health. Further efforts will be made to foster a social environment that is supportive of small families. Further modifications of family and inheritance laws in favor of women will be aimed at reducing a persistent tendency for childbearing and contraceptive practice to be affected by the gender of surviving children.

KOREA'S FERTILITY DECLINE: DEVELOPMENT OR FAMILY PLANNING?

Korea's family planning program has undeniably provided valuable services to millions of men and women since the early 1960s. But to what extent has the family planning program been responsible for the decline in childbearing? Our review suggests an important contribution, but some would argue that family planning programs did no more than fill a need generated by underlying social and economic change, and that in the absence of government-sponsored family planning, the private sector would have filled the need and childbearing would have declined just as rapidly.

Proponents of this view believe that development is the best or, in a few cases, the only contraceptive. But the evidence presented below based on a recently completed study carried out by the East–West Population Institute, the Nihon University Population Research Institute, and the United Nations Fund for Population Activities (Mason et al. 1986) shows that, at

---

2. Replacement fertility is the level necessary to *eventually* achieve zero population growth; however, even with replacement fertility Korea's population would continue to grow for many decades.

most, social and economic development played a secondary role in reducing Korea's fertility.

The Case for Development

The relationship of fertility to economic development has long been a subject of theoretical speculation and empirical research. Many studies have shown that increased education, especially of women, tends to reduce fertility (Michael 1974; Rosenzweig and Evenson 1977; Cochrane 1979). Urbanization is also recognized as closely related to fertility reduction (Kuznets 1974). In addition, it has been shown that increased child survival leads to fewer births (Ben-Porath 1976; Schultz 1976; Scrimshaw 1978; Trussel and Olsen 1983).

The influence of income on fertility continues to be a matter of dispute. Economic theorists contend that, other things being equal, higher income generally leads to more children (Becker 1960; Becker and Lewis 1973; Willis 1973, but for an alternative view, Easterlin, Pollak, and Wachter 1980). A number of empirical studies appear to support this view, but many others have failed. In any event, the direct effect of income on fertility appears to be small (Schultz 1973; Simon 1974).

Because of the complex interrelationships between demographic change and economic growth, careful assessment of the link between fertility and development is facilitated by employing an econometric model. The model, described in detail in Suits and Mason (1986), consists of a system of equations statistically fitted to data drawn from a cross-section consisting of all nations in the world with labor forces of at least one million workers.

Although the key relationships that compose the model are of interest in themselves, more important is the way they fit together to constitute the structure of economic development and demographic change. Figure 12.3 is a highly schematic representation of this structure. Proceeding from the top left across the figure, we see that per capita GNP affects labor force participation, enrollment, urbanization, the total fertility rate, mean age at childbearing, and, along with improvements in technology, life expectancy at birth. The total fertility rate is also affected by urbanization, child mortality, and educational attainment. Total fertility and mean age at childbearing translate into age-specific fertility rates, whereas life expectancy translates into age-specific survival rates. These combine to determine the rate of increase in population, its size, and its age structure. The age structure of the population, along with past educational attainment, and past school enrollment combine to determine current educational attainment. Next, the figure shows the three key components of economic growth: labor force size (determined by per capita income, school enrollment, and demographic characteristics of the population); labor force quality (determined by educational attainment and population); and investment (determined by the rate of growth of income and the population growth rate). These three factors

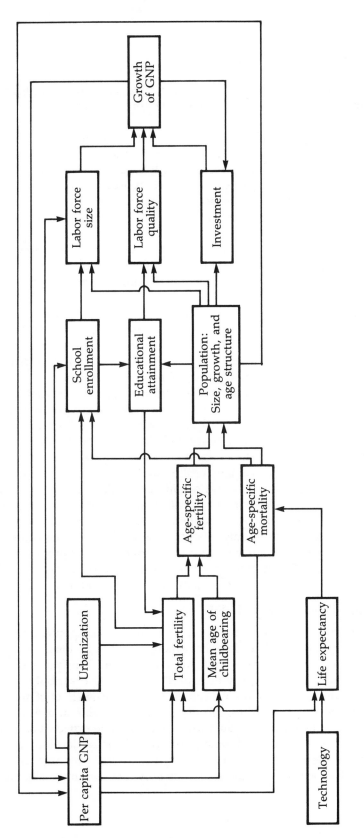

Figure 12.3. Flow chart of Suits and Mason Demographic–Economic Model

combine to determine growth in GNP which, together with population growth carries us back to the left side of the figure with a new level of per capita GNP.

If we begin at the left with per capita income, population, labor force, investment rate, educational endowment, and other characteristics of a modern poor developing nation, we can, with the aid of a computer, work across the figure to determine new conditions to be expected from one year's development. The new conditions become the new starting point for a second year's development, and so on for as many years as we choose to simulate.

The results show the development path to be expected of a nation with an initial per capita GNP equivalent to US $100, of which 20.4 percent is saved and invested. Of the working-age population, 73.4 percent of the men and 36.1 percent of the women are employed. Farming occupies 75.1 percent of the labor force, the remainder is engaged in urban occupations. The total fertility rate is 5.45 births per woman, life expectancy at birth is 41.3 years, and the population growth rate is 1.59 percent per year. Of children of appropriate ages, 78.6 are enrolled in elementary school, 24.5 percent are enrolled in secondary school, and 1.7 percent in college.

From this initial state, a nation whose performance matched that of the world average would grow in 100 years to a developed country with real per capita income approaching $5,000, an increase of about 50 times. Population would grow to more than 5 times the initial level, but fertility would have been cut by more than half. The nation would have gone through a demographic transition from a high fertility, short-lived society to one with low fertility, long life, and slow and declining population growth. Labor force participation by males would have declined steadily in keeping with rising school enrollment and earlier retirement, while that of women would have varied irregularly, with only modest growth under the opposing influences of falling fertility and rising school enrollment. The proportion of the labor force engaged in farming would have fallen to 13 percent, with a corresponding increase in urbanization of the population.

Uses of the Econometric Model

The standard profile depicts a long-run path of income and population that is consistent with observed differences among modern nations. As such, it is interesting in its own right, but, more important, it helps to isolate and analyze the effects of policy measures designed to contribute to development. For example, before we can evaluate the true effect of an official program intended to reduce fertility, we must be able to distinguish what is attributable to the program from what would be expected to occur naturally in the course of development. But the historical development of any one nation departs from that of the standard profile for any number of reasons, of which the official program is only one. An unusually rapid decline in fertility, for example, might be largely the result, not of the official program, but of an unusually rapid rise in income, or an accelerated effort at education.

In the model, fertility is linked to child survival, education, income, urbanization, and religion by an equation statistically fitted to data from the world cross-section of nations as of 1970. The contribution of each factor to fertility decline is calculated by holding all others at their levels as of the beginning of the decade and calculating the change in the total fertility rate associated with the change in the factor in question. As shown in Table 12.3, which gives the decomposition for each of the decades, the importance of each factor varies along the profile. At early stages, education exerts the most pressure on fertility, whereas at later stages increasing income has more impact.

Since the standard profile is derived from a cross-section of countries in the world today, it is important to compare its performance to actual historical experience. Table 12.4 compares recent trends in the crude birth rate for major developing regions of the world. In East Asia and in Latin

Table 12.3. Determinants of fertility decline

Years	Initial fertility (TFR)[a]	Change in fertility	Due to			
			Urbanization	Education	Income	Survival
10–20	5.01	0.30	0.05	0.17	0.04	0.04
50–60	4.00	0.26	0.09	0.04	0.09	0.05
90–100	2.81	0.38	0.02	0.01	0.35	0.01

a. The total fertility rate (TFR) reports the average number of live births were a woman exposed throughout her childbearing years to the schedule of age-specific fertility rates currently in effect.

Table 12.4. Trends in the crude birth rate[a]: Major regions and the standard development profile

Place	Years					Total change
	1955–59	1960–64	1965–70	1970–75	1975–80	
Africa	46	47	46	46	47	−1
Latin America	43	41	39	36	33	10
East Asia	39	33	31	26	22	17
South Asia	44	42	44	41	38	6
Profile	38	37	36	35	34	4

Sources for regional data: United Nations, *Demographic Yearbook* (1978, 1985).

Note: Profile values are for years 0 to 15.

a. The crude birth rate is the number of births per 1,000 persons in a given year.

America the crude birth rate has been declining substantially faster than the standard profile. In South Asia, the rate of decline has been much nearer to that of the profile, whereas there is no evidence of any fertility decline at all among African nations during last 25 years.

Comparison of the Standard Profile with Recent Experience in Korea

The fertility patterns embodied in the profile are those observed worldwide as of 1970, and they are roughly representative of the situation in Korea at that time, as well. The total fertility rate for Korea in 1970 was only 0.2 births per woman higher than predicted from its level of socioeconomic development. Although the observed fertility level of 1970 accords well with international experience, the rate of decline does not. Whereas the model requires 30 years to reduce fertility by one birth per woman, the total fertility rate in Korea from 1960 to 1980 declined at the rate of one birth every five years.

Korea's rapid decline in fertility is widely appreciated by those familiar with that country's demographic experience. Less well understood is why the decline has been so rapid, but two sets of causes can be distinguished. In the first place, model fertility declines in pace with the simulated average rate of economic development, but development in Korea has been more rapid, and the rate of fertility decline has been correspondingly greater. Second, cultural and other forces affecting fertility differ from those in the rest of the world, and these unique features have caused fertility in Korea to decline more rapidly than would have been expected, even given its exceptional rates of economic progress.

Table 12.5 separates the two sets of causes by comparing the total fertility rate recently observed to a corresponding rate calculated based on the standard profile, given urbanization, education, per capita income, and child mortality as of the same years. The rate of decline in the calculated values is an estimate of the contribution of economic growth to fertility reduction, and its difference from the observed decline constitutes an estimate of the contribution of noneconomic factors. The contribution of economic growth is, in turn, decomposed into the 0.03 per year reduction associated with

Table 12.5. The importance of rapid development for fertility decline in Korea

Date	Total fertility rate		Average annual rate of decline		Decline associated with:		
	Actual	Esti-mated	Actual	Esti-mated	Normal growth	Rapid growth	Special factors
1960	6.54	4.60					
1980	2.80	3.54	0.187	0.053	0.030	0.023	0.134

the rate of economic development along the development profile, and a residual attributable to the more rapid development. As the table shows, economic development accounts for only one-quarter of the observed decline in fertility. This leaves a substantial component of fertility decline associated with factors not taken into account in the standard profile.

Evidence from Household Data

The conclusion that rapid development, by itself, has not been sufficient to generate the fertility decline observed in Korea is of sufficient importance to require independent confirmation. Data on 4,050 ever-married women are available from the Korean World Fertility Survey which describe childbearing by women during the early 1970s. Analysis of these data, reported in Koo, Phananiramai, and Mason (1986), substantiates both the basic importance of economic development and the importance of elements outside the development process detailed above.

Analysis of survey data permit age-specific fertility rates for Korean women to be related to development factors one at a time. When age-specific rates are summed over all ages, the result is the corresponding total fertility rate. Fertility rates calculated for women with selected characteristics are shown in Table 12.6. The top three rows show age-specific rates for urban women with average child mortality experience in households where both spouses have primary education. In the first row, however, household income is taken at only 25 percent of the mean for the age-urbanization group. In the second row, income is taken at the mean, and in the third row, at two and one-half times the mean. Comparison of the calculated values shows the effect of income differences, all other things held constant. In similar fashion, other rows of the table permit examination of the difference among women with different educational attainment, residence, or child mortality experience.

As can be seen, fertility declines with rising income. The tenfold increase in income from a level of 25 percent of the group mean to one 2.5 times the mean is associated with a 4 percent drop in the total fertility rate; but among women of ages 35 to 39 fertility declines by 17 percent, and by 30 percent among women of ages 45 to 49.

The total fertility of better-educated households is significantly lower than that of the less well-educated. Education beyond primary school is associated with fertility rates about 10 percent lower than in households with primary-school education only. Households with college-educated spouses, however, display somewhat higher fertility than those with only secondary education, although fertility is still lower than those with only primary education.

Economic Development Versus Other Factors

The standard profile and the survey analysis are both attempts to estimate the contribution of economic development alone to fertility reduction.

Table 12.6. Age-specific fertility rates[a] as calculated from survey data under specified conditions, Korea

	Years of age						Total fertility rate (TFR)
	15–19	20–24	25–29	30–34	35–39	40–44	
Per capita GNP							
.25 × mean	0.12	1.54	1.51	0.89	0.31	0.10	4.47
Mean	0.11	1.54	1.50	0.87	0.30	0.09	4.41
2.5 × mean	0.11	1.54	1.49	0.83	0.26	0.07	4.30
Urbanization							
Urban	0.11	1.54	1.50	0.87	0.30	0.09	4.41
Rural	0.10	1.14	1.45	1.13	0.67	0.34	4.83
Education (both spouses)							
Primary	0.11	1.54	1.50	0.87	0.30	0.09	4.41
Secondary	0.10	1.03	1.55	0.97	0.31	0.08	4.04
College	0.10	1.03	1.69	1.12	0.34	0.08	4.36
Child mortality							
Mean	0.11	1.54	1.50	0.87	0.30	0.09	4.41
.01 below	0.11	1.53	1.50	0.87	0.30	0.09	4.40

Note: Except as indicated, all rates are calculated for urban women in households with average income and child mortality for age-urbanization group, and where neither spouse has more than a primary education.

a. The age-specific fertility rate is the number of births in a given year to women in a certain age group divided by the midyear population of women in that age group.

Comparison of these estimates with recent historical records yields new insight into whether and to what extent the rapid fertility decline observed in Korea involves something beyond economic development.

Table 12.7 presents three sets of estimates of Korea's total fertility rate. The first row contains published estimates for 1970–75 and for 1955–60. The second row contains estimates based on the survey data. For 1970–75, the rates are legitimate estimates of actual total fertility, and any difference from the corresponding estimate in the first row arises solely from differences in estimating procedure and is unrelated to causal factors. For 1955–60, however, the figures in the second row are estimated by carrying back the analysis of the 1970–75 survey data, adjusted to match income, education, urbanization, and percentage of women married in each nation as of 1955–60. The resulting 1955–60 estimates of marital fertility bear the same relationship to income, education, and child mortality as those of 1970–75, so any difference between the two reflects the influence of these factors alone. But any difference between the average historical rate of fertility decline as shown in the first row and the calculated average displayed in

Table 12.7. Comparison of changes in the total fertility rate as estimated
by different procedures: 1955–60 to 1970–75

	1970–75	1955–60	Average annual decline
KIFP estimates	3.9	6.3	–0.16
WFS estimates	4.1	4.9[a]	–0.064
Cross-section	3.9[b]	5.2[c]	–0.086

a. Back projection based on marital fertility equations derived from World Fertility Survey data.

b. 1975.

c. 1960.

KIFP—Korea Institute of Family Planning.

WFS—World Fertility Survey.

the second row is a measure of the extent to which factors other than economic development have played a role in fertility reduction.

The influence of economic development isolated from everything else is also estimated by evaluating the world cross-section relationship at the levels of income, urbanization, education and child mortality observed in 1955–60 and in 1970–75, respectively, and inspecting the difference. The results of these calculations are recorded in the third row.

Despite the great differences in data and methodology, the three estimates of the 1970–75 level of the Korean fertility are quite close. The close agreement of average annual rates of fertility decline within each country as calculated from the survey analysis on the one hand and from the international cross-section on the other confirms that economic development alone was responsible for an annual decline of .06 to .09 births. However, the historical rate of fertility reduction was several times what can fairly be attributed to economic development. One-half of the fertility reduction actually observed during the period 1955–60 to 1970–75 must be ascribed to factors other than development.

Noneconomic Factors in Fertility Reduction

For those who have extensively studied these countries and others like them, neither the remarkable decline in fertility nor its weak relationship to socioeconomic change can be any surprise. Cho, Arnold, and Kwon (1983) summarize current evidence on fertility determinants in Korea by saying:

> . . . economic and social development may be a fundamental cause of fertility transition. However, the family planning program has expedited the process. . . . Cultural factors, [such as] the absence of barriers to ready acceptance of abortion and sterilization, cultural homogeneity in ethnicity, language, and religious tradition, and geographic and political unity, have contributed to rapid fertility transition. The characteristics in turn promote social integration in the form of efficient communication and shared values, norms, and institutions.

A common thread in these discussions is the view that although social and economic development underlies fertility decline, timing and pace are strongly influenced by imperfectly understood diffusion processes that are bound up in the interaction between population policy and cultural factors (Knodel 1977; Freedman 1979; Retherford and Palmore 1983). Furthermore, cogent arguments have been made that change in the family and in the roles of its members is responsible for rapid fertility decline. Caldwell (1976), in particular, points to "Westernization"—which has proceeded largely independently of social and economic development—as the motivating force in the nucleation of families and the decline in the value of children and family size. Ben-Porath (1980) and Willis (1982) point to changes in the family institution more closely linked to social and economic development.

Fertility Decline and Economic Development

No discussion of population policy is complete without consideration of the contribution of fertility decline to economic development. Korea's population policy first began to have a noticeable impact on the structure of the population after 1966. Between 1960 and 1966, the number of dependents (those under 15 or over 65 years of age) per working age adult (those between 15 and 64 years) actually increased from 0.83 to 0.89. But after 1966 the so-called dependency ratio actually declined, falling to 0.71 by 1975 and to 0.53 in 1985. The original framers of Korea's population policy were motivated by the belief that slower population growth and the declining dependency ratio would play a key role in their efforts to achieve rapid economic development. To what extent has this view been supported by subsequent events?

As described more fully elsewhere in this volume, Korea's basic development strategy has been to exploit its comparative advantage, principally a skilled, low-wage labor force, via a policy of vigorous export promotion. In several key ways, demographic change has complemented this development approach. First, because the onset of fertility decline does not affect the size of the working age population for at least 15 years, fertility decline has no immediate adverse impact on the size of the labor force. Moreover, the decline in childrearing responsibilities frees women to participate more fully in the labor force (Bauer and Shin 1986). Thus, labor force growth has been rapid throughout most of the last 25 years. Between 1975 and 1980, for example, the number of workers grew at an annual rate of 2.9 percent.

Korea is now beginning to experience slower growth in the number of workers. Between 1980 and 1984, for example, employment rose at an annual rate of only 1.3 percent. As labor force growth continues to slow and wages rise, Korea will have to continue its shift into industries that are less dependent on low-cost labor.

A second path by which fertility decline has affected Korea's development prospects has been through its impact on education. Korea has expanded its educational system at a rapid pace in the last two decades so that Korean students are unusually well-educated for living in a country with Korea's material standard of living. Fertility decline, by reducing the number of school-age children, has either reduced the fiscal burden of Korea's educational system or allowed the application of more educational resources to each student, or both. One recent study presents evidence that fertility decline in Korea has resulted in higher rates of enrollment, particularly at the secondary level, and greater expenditures per student than would have prevailed under a high fertility regime (Suits and Mason 1986).

Finally, available evidence indicates that fertility decline contributed to the substantial rise in domestic saving in Korea after 1960. In 1962, gross domestic savings amounted to only 3 percent of GNP and the lack of investable funds was considered a key bottleneck to Korea's development efforts. Over the last two decades, however, saving has risen gradually but steadily so that by 1985 gross domestic savings were close to 30 percent of GNP. A number of factors contributed to this rise, but close to one-third of the increase can be attributed to changes in the age structure of the population resulting from fertility decline (Mason 1986a).

CONCLUSIONS

Korea's population policy is of great interest to those trying to formulate, implement, and improve family planning policy in other developing countries. It is of particular interest because Korea represents one of the great success cases of the developing world. In the early 1960s Korean policymakers chose, as their goal, rapid fertility decline to slow population growth. They chose this goal in the belief that it was integral to their efforts to achieve rapid improvements in the material standard of living of the Korean people. It is evident that, 25 years later, these multiple goals—rapid economic growth and slow population growth—have been achieved. But exactly how these achievements are interconnected is less evident.

The evidence presented here demonstrates that much of Korea's fertility decline is a consequence of the modernization and development process to which Korea has been exposed. Child mortality has dropped, education has improved, people have moved to cities, and incomes have risen. As these changes occurred, and occurred with great rapidity, women chose to limit their childbearing. Yet despite the great social and economic changes that Korea has undergone, they are insufficient to account for the speed with which childbearing has declined. The available information indicates that socioeconomic development, in and of itself, accounts for less than half of Korea's fertility decline.

Korea's population policy has facilitated the family planning impact of development by providing contraceptive services to millions of women who have chosen to limit their childbearing over the last 25 years. Just as important, the family planning program has been successful in educating the public about family planning techniques, increasing the availability of services, and influencing attitudes about contraception and childbearing.

We can point to a number of features that have contributed to Korea's family planning success.

1. *Constancy of effort.* From the inception of the family planning program in the early 1960s, Korea has actively pursued its objectives. For the most part, this effort has not been disrupted by outside events or policy reversals.

2. *Broad-based attack.* Korea has not taken a narrow approach to family planning, limiting its efforts to the mere promotion of a "public health" program. Rather, it has mobilized many segments of society—public and private, economic, social, legal, and cultural—to achieve its single-minded purpose of reducing fertility.

3. *Pragmatic approach.* The family planning program has been continually scrutinized and successful approaches were emphasized while failures were abandoned.

4. *High-level support.* The success of family planning has been of interest at the highest levels of government. The political will has been present to mobilize the necessary resources and to sweep away impediments to achieving program objectives wherever they have existed.

Korea's program is not, of course, transplantable in its entirety. There are cultural and social features of Korea that are present to a greater or to a lesser extent in other countries. Nonetheless, Korea's experience does provide some important lessons to those trying to frame and to implement successful population policy in other developing countries of the world.

APPENDIX 12.1
Population Policy Chronology

1961
- Adopted national family planning program policy as a part of economic development plan starting in 1962
- Abrogated the law prohibiting importation and domestic production of contraceptives
- Established the Planned Parenthood Federation of Korea (PPFK) as a nongovernmental voluntary organization
- Adopted family planning slogan "Have few children and bring them up well"

1962
- Started the national family planning program under the jurisdiction of the Ministry of Health and Social Affairs (MOHSA) through the government's health service system
- Established a family planning counseling room and assigned two family planning workers to each of 183 health centers
- Started training programs on vasectomy procedures for family planning workers and for physicians

- Introduced vasectomy, condoms, and jelly into the national program

1963
- Established the Maternal and Child Health (MCH) Division under the Bureau of Public Health, MOHSA
- Assigned two additional family planning senior workers to each of 183 health centers

1964
- Assigned a family planning field worker at each of 1,473 township health subcenters
- Started training program on IUD insertion for physicians and introduced IUD into the national program
- Introduced family planning mobile teams to cover remote areas

1965
- Established Family Planning Survey and Evaluation Team in MOHSA

1966
- Included family planning target system in the national program

1968
- Organized family planning Mothers' Clubs throughout the country

1971
- Established the Korean Institute for Family Planning (KIFP)
- Adopted family planning slogan "Stop at two regardless of sex"

1972
- Strengthened government family planning program organization by establishing the Bureau of MCH in MOHSA

1973
- Promulgated Maternal and Child Health Law providing legal grounds for induced abortion under certain medical conditions or for psychiatric reasons
- Allowed IUD insertion by paramedics

1974
- Initiated special urban family planning projects
- Introduced menstrual regulation service into the national program
- Introduced social support policy measures—income tax exemption for up to three children and population education project

1975
- Started training program for physicians on female laparoscope sterilization procedures
- Established the Korean Association for Voluntary Sterilization (KAVS) as a voluntary organization

1976
- Introduced female sterilization into the national program
- Established the Population Policy Deliberation Committee (PPDC) under the deputy prime minister
- Assigned a male information officer at each of 138 county health centers

1977
- Allowed income tax exemption for up to two children only
- Exempted corporation tax for corporations' expenditures for family planning services to employees
- Revised family law concerning women's property inheritance
- Integrated Mothers' Clubs into Saemaul Women's Association
- Included population education in the high school curriculum

1978
- Gave priority in allotting public housing to sterilization acceptors with one or two children
- Exempted raw materials imported for the manufacture of contraceptives from tariffs
- Adopted family planning slogan "A well-bred girl surpasses ten boys"
- Included population education in the middle school curriculum

1979
- Included population education in the primary school curriculum

1980
- Reduced child delivery charges for sterilization acceptors after second delivery in public hospitals

1981
- Issued 49 innovative policy measures to place great emphasis on social support policies and activation of family planning programs
- Established the Family Health Division in MOHSA to integrate the division of Family Planning and Maternal and Child Health
- Upgraded health workers' status from temporary workers to regular health officials
- Inaugurated the Korea Institute for Population and Health (KIPH) by integrating the Korean Institute of Family Planning and the Korean Health Development Institute

1982
- Reorganized Family Planning Sections of provincial governments making them Family Health Sections covering family planning and maternal and child health services
- Provided sterilization and menstrual regulation services through the medical insurance systems
- Gave priority of livelihood loans for the needy and housing loans to sterilization acceptors with one or two children
- Provided monetary subsidies to low-income sterlization acceptors to compensate for lost wages
- Provided free primary medical services at the health centers for the children up to five years of age of sterilization acceptors with one or two children

- Implemented pilot projects: monetary incentive for sterilization acceptors with one or two children and introduction of new contraceptive methods—the copper-T and foam tablets

1983
- Provided family and education allowances for government employees with up to two children
- Provided medical insurance delivery allowance for the first two deliveries only
- Introduced copper-T into the national program
- Provided IUD services through medical insurance system
- Established family planning evaluation unit at the provincial level and local health centers
- Assigned an additional male information officer to each of 85 city health centers
- Introduced new family planning slogans "Even two are too many" and "Have one child with happiness and love"
- Lowered sterilization age range for women from ages 15–44 to 15–34 years

1984
- Provided mid- and long-term loan priority for public housing to the sterilization acceptors with one child
- Revised regulation banning the employment of female ship crews
- Expanded medical insurance benefit to the parents of married female employees

1985
- Provided free delivery service through the clinics and maternal and child health centers for women who want only one child
- Provided free medical service for children below six years of age and hepatitis vaccination for children below four years of contraceptive acceptors with only one child
- Designated the private pharmacists as "demonstration drug store for family planning counseling"

Source: N. H. Cho (1986).

13 The Health Insurance Scheme

by Chong Kee Park

The record of growth of material wealth in Korea over the past two decades has been impressive. But with its increased living standard and the internal strains that rapid economic growth has generated, Korea is confronted with newly emerging problems in the social sphere. Among these problems are a discrepancy between economic and social development, an imbalance in the distribution of income and wealth among social groups and among different regions, and the various pressures arising from rapid urbanization. These growth-induced phenomena are likely to multiply unless counteracted by specific policies and measures.

During the first 15 years of the nation's five-year development plans, which began in 1962, the nation's scarce resources were devoted mainly to rapid economic growth, whereas social development was given low priority in the allocation of resources. In the pursuit of a "growth first and distribution later" development strategy, the government gave greater priority to industrialization and economic growth in general than to equity and social development.

Not until the Fourth Five-Year Economic and Social Development Plan (1977–81) did the government begin to recognize that economic growth cannot be regarded as satisfactory if rising output and income are not shared by wider segments of the population. The Fourth Plan identified equity as one of the three guiding principles of the plan and promoted social development as one of its basic goals. No previous five-year plan had accorded such eminence to social development. The Fourth Plan, which placed increasing emphasis on development in the social sector, therefore represents a significant departure from the growth-first distribution-later priorities of previous plans. As a result, during the second half of the 1970s Korea began to witness a gradual shift in policy emphasis from rapid industrialization to broader social development.

During the late 1970s, the use of catch phrases such as "the prosperous eighties" and "the welfare state" greatly stimulated expectations of the society as a whole and raised levels of aspiration of the under-served and the underprivileged, in particular. Yet, in the actual allocation of the nation's resources, the social development sector continued to lag behind economic development, and popular expectations in many social development areas remain largely unfulfilled. The social development programs actually adopted and implemented during this plan period covered only limited areas of manpower development, education, and health; and not enough investable resources were provided to support other areas of social development.

It is important to recognize that social development does not take place in a vacuum. Neither the type of social problems we are concerned about nor their ultimate solutions are of a purely social nature. The process of social development is as much affected by economic and political considerations as by social welfare factors. One of the objectives of social development is to provide an opportunity for each member of society to participate in economic and social progress and to attain a decent standard of living. But in Korea an institutional structure is lacking through which a greater number of people could participate equally in the rapidly expanding industrial base of the economy, and this has been one of the causes of the inequitable distribution of developmental benefits.

The predominant policy role of the Korean government in the nation's economic affairs has been widely recognized, and various government economic policies have had important social consequences. Economic policies and measures that the government adopted to accomplish specific economic objectives in the process of rapid growth and industrialization have often served to perpetuate the economic power of the upper stratum of Korean society. The export-oriented, rapid industrialization policy provided relatively greater economic benefits to the entrepreneurial group constituting this upper stratum and relatively fewer benefits to those who were on the outside and had to make their way without benefiting directly from government policies. Undoubtedly, this trend helped bring about greater concentration of the ownership of wealth and restricted the pattern of income distribution in Korea.

Korea's urban-oriented industrialization policies have also caused imbalances in the geographic distribution of the benefits of economic progress, with resultant undesirable social and political consequences. When a largely agricultural country is so rapidly transformed by export-oriented industrialization, it is the cities that will reap the lion's share of the benefits in the short term. Rural people have gained relatively less access than urban dwellers to the social benefits of economic prosperity because the preponderance of investment has been in the industrial sector of the economy. The high rate of return on capital investment in Korea's industrial urban sector has, moreover, made private investment in rural areas less attractive than ever. Although the government has tried to promote rural development, especially through the Saemaul movement (the self-help community program discussed in Chapter 16), rural people still do not have access to the hospitals, schools, and similar benefits that the urban population has come to enjoy during the recent period of rapid industrialization.

Today, as in the past, regional disparities exist in the availability of education, health care, and other services. The concentration of educational institutions and health facilities in urban areas is a factor that does not contribute to the objectives of more equal distribution and, if not corrected, will retard the full development of human resources. It has also created additional pressures on the rural population to intensify the already rapid urbanization that has been taking place in Korea. The recent massive migration of rural people to urban areas was prompted in part by the widening urban–rural differential in the quality of life, and not solely by the availability of jobs.

The primary purposes of this study are to examine the health insurance scheme of 1976 in the light of recent changes in social and economic conditions in Korea, and to identify the lessons that can be learned from the Korean experience with national health insurance. To provide a wider perspective on the historical context in which this policy measure was taken, however, and to assess the major effects of the health program within the broader framework of national policies for socioeconomic development, it will be instructive to outline first some of the other social development programs of the 1960s and 1970s.

OTHER SOCIAL DEVELOPMENT POLICIES

Improvements in social welfare through the early 1970s can be attributed not so much to the planned expansion of social development expenditures, but rather to development strategies and policies that resulted in expanded employment opportunities and to concomitant increased investment in social infrastructure. In contrast to other countries at similar levels of income, Korea has committed a much smaller proportion of government expenditure to health, housing, income security, and other social services. Social development expenditure during 1976–78 (Table 13.1), for example, was given relatively high priority by the governments of Brazil (accounting for 51.5 percent of total government expenditure), Mexico (45.6 percent), Malaysia (33.2 percent), and Turkey (27.6 percent). The lower priorities given to such

Table 13.1. Comparisons of government expenditures on social development, by country: 1976–78 averages (%)

Country	Education	Health	Social security and welfare	Other	Total	Total, excluding education	Per capita GNP, 1978 (US $)
Brazil	6.2	7.2	37.6	0.6	51.5	45.3	1,510
Mexico	19.2	4.2	22.0	0.2	45.6	26.4	1,400
Malaysia	21.7	6.5	2.8	2.1	33.2	11.5	1,150
Turkey	20.1	2.4	2.9	2.3	27.6	7.5	1,250
Korea	15.6	1.5	4.7	0.7	22.5	6.9	1,310
Taiwan	6.4	1.1	12.5		20.0	13.6	1,453

Sources: IMF (1981); IMF (1978–80).

services in Korea (22.5 percent) and Taiwan (20 percent) during the same period can be partly explained by heavier national defense burdens. If education is excluded, however, the magnitude of difference among all these countries is even bigger, ranging from a high of 45.3 percent in Brazil to a low of 6.9 percent in Korea.

The composition of government expenditure in Korea has undergone considerable change since 1961, but public spending on social development has always been less than that on economic development. Moreover, the share of social development in total government expenditure declined from 21.5 percent in 1963 to 20.7 percent in 1980 (Table 13.2). Government support of health and other social development programs has never been substantial in Korea, and the government has left the provision of these services largely to the private sector (Mason et al. 1980).

Housing

Government investment in housing has been low. The public-sector contribution to the nation's housing supply increased gradually after 1965, accounting for an average of about 30 percent during the Fourth Five-Year Development Plan of 1977–81 (KNHC, *Housing Policy Development Research*, 1983:315). Only a small proportion of total public-sector housing investment funds was allocated for low-income housing, however, and government investment in low-income family housing in urban areas has been lagging, especially in view of the rapid urbanization occurring since the mid-1960s. Two major problems retarding development of low-cost housing are the high cost of money and property price escalation spurred by real estate speculation. A third problem is the difficulty of obtaining housing loans. Institutional arrangements are needed to ensure that affordable housing is available to low-income families, possibly through government-guaranteed mortgages at low rates of interest.

Table 13.2. Distribution of government expenditures on economic and social services: Selected years (% of total expenditures)

Item	1963	1968	1975	1980
Social services (total)	21.5	22.7	22.5	20.7
Education	13.4	16.1	14.7	14.9
Health	1.1	0.9	0.6	1.0
Social security and welfare	5.9	4.8	6.3	3.4
Other, including housing	1.1	0.9	0.9	1.4
Economic services	33.1	32.4	33.5	27.7

Source: BOK, *Economic Statistics Yearbook* (1964–81).

Education

During the 1960s and 1970s, the majority of social development expenditure was devoted to education, and only a small fraction was allocated to health, housing, and other social services (Table 13.2). Social development programs, for example, constituted just over one-fifth of government expenditure in 1980, with 14.9 percent of total expenditure going to education and the remaining 5.8 percent going to non-education programs. Despite the preponderance of education in the overall government allocations for social development, public expenditure on education has remained relatively low (about 3 percent of GNP) in recent years. The government share of in-school expenditure (the expenses incurred in the construction and operation of schools) declined from 57 percent in 1971 to 51 percent in 1976, leaving the increased share of the financial burden to private households (KDI 1980a; McGinn et al. 1980). However, even though privately financed education has become increasingly important, government expenditure on education has increased in real terms because the student population remained relatively constant while GNP was growing rapidly during the 1970s.

Pension Programs

Korea's fragmented social security programs originated in the early 1960s. The first social welfare legislation was the Livelihood Protection Law of 1960, which remains in force as the basic legal instrument for present-day public assistance programs for the poor. There are two major groups of persons entitled to receive public assistance under this law: (1) those unable to work (persons 65 years old and over, children under age 18, and the mentally and physically handicapped) and (2) deserted, pregnant women and those regarded as absolutely poor. Eligibility conditions require first that a person in either of the above categories not have a legal guardian (or the legal guardian not be capable of supporting the person) and second that the person's combined income and wealth not exceed a fixed ceiling (set annually by the government).

This law was followed by the Civil Service Pension Law in 1960 and the Military Pension Law in 1963. By a separate law enacted in December 1973, university professors and teachers in private educational institutions were provided with either pension or lump-sum benefits to replace the income loss resulting from old age, disability, and death. The nature and scope of benefits provided under this law are very similar to those provided under the civil servants' pension program, which covers teachers in the public institutions. By the second half of the 1970s, therefore, retirement benefits were available to at least a limited segment of the population comprising civilian officials, military personnel, and the teaching profession. One consequence of the implementation of these three pension laws is that a large portion of government funds allocated annually for social security purposes is automatically committed to former public-sector employees. The remainder is divided among a variety of other social security programs—broadly defined to include social insurance, public assistance, veterans' relief, and social welfare institutions. In 1979, for example, government spending on all social security programs was 328.9 billion won (Table 13.3), which represented a mere 1.1 percent of the 29,357 billion won GNP in that year. Expenditures on the pension schemes and veterans' relief accounted for 45 percent of social security expenditures that year, therefore, only a small fraction of 1 percent of GNP was available for allocation among all other social security programs.

The social security system inherent in Korea's tradition of extended families has tended to deteriorate rapidly in the increasingly urbanized and industrial society of recent decades, and yet it is not being replaced at the same rate with alternative social welfare institutions and systems. The National Welfare Pension Law was originally conceived to fill such a gap. The avowed purpose of this system, as stated by the Ministry of Health and Social Affairs (MOHSA) in the December 1973 draft of the law, was "to contribute to the promotion of the secure life and welfare of the people" by providing protection to workers and their families against loss of earnings resulting from retirement, death, or disability. The National Welfare Pension Law represented the first expression of a changed direction in public social welfare policy and gave promise of being the first step toward the development of a manageable social security system for all Koreans.

The law envisaged a national welfare pension program that would provide four types of benefits to workers in firms with at least 30 employees.

Table 13.3. Estimated social security expenditures: 1979

Item	Amount (10^9 won)	Percentage of total
Social insurance	223.4	67.9
Old-age pension insurance		
Government officials	52.9	16.1
Military personnel	39.6	12.1
Professors and teachers	3.2	1.0
Medical insurance	73.9	22.5
Industrial accident insurance	53.8	16.3
Public assistance	99.7	30.3
Veterans' relief	52.1	15.8
Other public assistance	47.6	14.5
Social welfare institutions	5.8	1.8
Total	328.9	100.0

Source: C. K. Park (1981).

Persons who attained insured status would be entitled to receive retirement benefits for themselves and dependent benefits for their spouses and children. When the insured died, survivor benefits would be paid to the surviving spouse, children, or dependent parents. Benefits would likewise be paid in the event of serious disability. The law also provided for a lump-sum payment to persons not qualified to receive pension benefits. The formula by which these benefits would be calculated is weighted to replace a greater proportion of preretirement earnings for low-income earners than for persons at the upper end of the income scale (C. K. Park 1975).

The National Welfare Pension Law was enacted in December 1973, at a time when the nation's policymakers were already grappling with foreseeable adverse effects of the recent Middle East war and oil shock on the Korean economy. The Presidential Emergency Decree of January 1974, promulgated in the wake of the worldwide energy crisis, postponed the implementation of the newly enacted pension program because the government feared that an attempt to finance this nationwide scheme would exacerbate the economic downturn. Thus, although this was one of the most important and comprehensive of the government's social development initiatives in the early 1970s, the law was not brought into force until 1 January 1988.

Industrial Accident Insurance

As in most other countries, the provision of medical care and the betterment of the financial plight of victims of industrial accidents and occupational diseases received early attention by the Korean government. The Industrial Accident Insurance Law, enacted in November 1963, applies to firms with 16 workers or more. In certain types of hazardous employment, such as mining, chemicals, and plastics, however, the compulsory coverage extends to enterprises with a minimum of only five employees. The benefits provided under this compensation program are broadly classified into medical benefits and cash benefits. The medical benefits provide full medical and hospital care to injured workers until they recover completely. The cash benefits are divided into those for temporary sickness and those for disability. If a temporary injury prevents an employee from working while receiving medical care, the employee receives cash benefits equal to a specified proportion of regular earnings. The second type of cash benefit is provided in cases of permanent disability. Severely disabled workers have a choice of either a pension or a lump-sum payment. The program provides lump-sum payments to less severely disabled persons and also to the survivors of any worker who dies as a result of an industrial accident (Park et al. 1981). The industrial accident insurance program, which has a relatively long history, is generally considered one of the most successfully operated social security branches in Korea.

HEALTH INSURANCE PROGRAM:
ENACTMENT AND IMPLEMENTATION

During the mid-1970s, the government identified health care as a priority area. Better health standards contribute to national economic progress through the improvement of the quality and productivity of the labor force by reducing absenteeism, debility, and disability of individual workers. The high private cost of basic minimal health care, however, works against egalitarian objectives and discriminates against low-income groups. Heavy reliance on private expenditures in areas of basic needs such as health care and compulsory education does not contribute to the elimination of inequalities so long as overall per capita income is still relatively low. A national health care program therefore came to be seen as an essential element of socioeconomic development policy. With the acknowledgment that health care is a basic necessity of life along with food, clothing, and shelter, it became not only one of Korea's most important social issues but also a focal point of the social development component in the Fourth Five-Year Development Plan.

The enactment in 1976 of the medical assistance program for the poor and the national medical insurance scheme for the general population represent the beginnings of a stepped-up evolutionary process of social development in Korea. The primary purpose of the noncontributory medical assistance program that was put into effect in January 1977 is to provide adequate medical care to those without the means to pay. The beneficiaries are the indigent (those who receive public assistance under the Livelihood Protection Law) and persons whose incomes fall below a certain level (identified annually by local government authorities). Under the medical assistance program, recipients are eligible to receive both ambulatory care and hospital treatment free of charge. Low-income persons are also entitled to receive free ambulatory care, but only one-half of their hospitalization costs are paid by the government (and the recipients have to provide reimbursement for the remaining half within three years).

Under the Medical Insurance Law enacted in December 1976, Korea embarked on a nationwide, comprehensive medical insurance program. As stated in the first article of this law, the program was designed to "improve national health and enhance social security by facilitating access to medical care in the event of illness, injury, childbirth, or death." In its coverage and impact, the new law represented the first comprehensive social security program in the nation. Its enactment was thus a landmark in the history of Korea's social legislation. The implementation of this law began in July 1977, and the health insurance program has subsequently played an important role in promoting medical care to more effectively meet the health needs of the working population.

The Medical Insurance Law established a two-part program including (1) a plan requiring employers with at least 500 workers to provide specified medical insurance benefits for their employees and their dependents (Class I), and (2) a voluntary community-based plan providing medical insurance for all others (Class II). In January 1979, complementary legislation extended compulsory insurance coverage to government officials, teachers, and the ancillary staff of private schools. Beginning in January 1980, coverage by this insurance scheme was extended also to dependents of military personnel. Although eligibility under Class I is still available only to the personnel of companies or organizations employing at least the minimum number of persons fixed by government regulation, the legal minimum has been reduced over time so that it covers, for example, companies with as few as 10 employees. All others, including the self-employed and persons working for companies that have fewer than the legal minimum, are grouped under Class II.

The medical insurance law provides broad medical and maternity benefits such as medical examinations, pharmaceutical supplies, surgery, hospitalization, nursing, and ambulance service. The insurance program is administered by the health insurance societies established for the workers in enterprises and industrial parks, and in the case of the self-employed and others (Class II) by the community-based insurance societies set up in county, town, and city administrative districts. The scheme is financed by a fixed percentage (3 to 8 percent) of the payroll, up to a certain ceiling, collected as a premium from the employer. Half of this premium must be charged to the employee. The government contributions to the system are limited to defraying the administrative costs.

Medical care is delivered through purchase of services from existing medical practitioners and facilities. The providers of services are reimbursed (subject to coinsurance) by the insurance societies on the basis of a specified fee for each service rendered. The standard fee schedule for each component of services provided under the medical insurance scheme is set and occasionally adjusted by MOHSA in consultation with the medical profession. As in most other countries with medical insurance schemes where the cost-sharing provision is enforced, patients covered by the insurance program in Korea also share a part of the cost of medical care services. The Medical Insurance Law of 1976 provided that the patient share up to 40 percent of the cost of outpatient care services and up to 30 percent of hospitalization costs.

Institutional Setting

With increasing emphasis on equity and social development, Korea witnessed a major change in concern about the health of the people during the second half of the 1970s. There was a growing awareness among economists and planners of the importance of health care in development strategies for meeting basic needs. The president stressed the importance of expanding the accessibility of health care services to the underprivileged, by stating that health care is the "fourth basic necessity of life" along with food, clothing, and shelter. This change was also manifested in a five-year health sector loan agreement signed between the government of Korea and the United States Agency for International Development in September 1975. One of the major purposes of this agreement was to strengthen the capability of the government to plan, implement, and evaluate a low-cost health care delivery scheme directed primarily toward under-served communities (Park and Yeon 1981).

For the first time, Korea became actively engaged in major planning aimed at improving the organization, delivery, and financing of health care services. A new health development strategy was incorporated in the creation of the National Health Council, the National Health Secretariat in the Korea Development Institute, and the Korea Health Development Institute. The ultimate objective of these sector-planning efforts was to provide access to adequate medical care regardless of income, age, or place of residence. A related objective was the provision of quality health care with reasonable efficiency.

The absence of a well-coordinated mechanism for planning and allocating resources in the health sector attested to the low priority that this sector had been accorded in previous development plans. In the initial stages, the government did not have adequate experience with institutional arrangements, and the public sector would not have been entirely dependable. But because private organizations had been relied upon for the provision of health services for so long, investments of scarce resources were made without an appropriate framework of socioeconomic development goals. A coordinated national health development strategy might have enabled the government to assign priorities to investment projects in accordance with their expected benefits and impact on equity.

At the same time, fragmentation of responsibilities and authority among government ministries and agencies has often resulted in inefficiency and waste of scarce resources in the management of health services in Korea. MOHSA has responsibility for broad health policy coordination throughout the nation. The responsibility for administering programs that substantially affect health, however, are scattered among several other ministries as well. The Ministry of Home Affairs, for instance, is responsible for financing and operating a network of provincial and municipal hospitals and health centers. The Ministry of Education has the administrative responsibility for universities and other institutions training medical professionals and other types of health-care manpower. Finally, the Economic Planning Board (EPB) has the overall responsibility for national development planning and resource allocation.

To provide a coordinating mechanism among the health programs of the various operating agencies, the National Health Council (NHC) was established at the cabinet level in 1976. The membership of this council was composed of the deputy prime minister (concurrently minister of the EPB) as chairman, the minister of health and social affairs as vice-chairman, the minister of home affairs, the minister of education, and three private citizens. The NHC was created to provide an effective forum for policy coordination, resource allocation decisions, and implementation for the health sector. The National Health Secretariat (NHS) was set up within the Korea Development Institute (KDI), which is operated under the aegis of the EPB, to provide inputs and resources to the council for sound planning and operation. The Korea Health Development Institute (KHDI) was also created to develop low-cost health delivery schemes and to engage in microlevel health planning research.

Thus the institutional basis for coordination in health planning and implementation was well established, and the birth of this innovative setup linking three new institutions—NHC, NHS/KDI, and KHDI—was greeted by researchers, health experts, and other interested groups as a highly desirable development in the health field in Korea. However, because of the lower priority given to health issues and problems by policymakers in ministries other than MOHSA, this coordinating mechanism was not fully utilized. Although an initial meeting was held to organize the NHC formally, the council met only twice during the ensuing years and no serious health policy problems were resolved during the meetings. As one observer put it in 1980,

> . . . the present composition of the council seems top heavy for the amount of time that has to be spent on this work. It seems too burdensome for the deputy prime minister and other key ministers . . . Looking at the large task ahead the council may require the full-time service of a distinguished chairman so that the intensive planning exercise can be launched successfully (Clarkson 1980).

Although the NHC has been criticized as being inactive or indifferent in the face of mounting health problems, the system itself has produced some positive results. It provided an opportunity for NHS/KDI economists to participate in a wide range of interdisciplinary research dealing with critical health policy issues and to interact with health researchers from the academic community and medical organizations, as well as with MOHSA officials at the working level. The active involvement of the NHS/KDI in interdisciplinary health research and policy planning has not only facilitated cooperation (which had previously been lacking) between researchers and policymakers, and between economic planners and health planners, but also made significant contributions to the design and implementation of a number of important health policy measures.[1]

---

1. In a study commissioned by the minister of health and social affairs in 1978, for example, the NHS/KDI strongly recommended that local hospitals, run by city and provincial governments as government agencies, be managed by a newly created independent institution under the broad supervision of MOHSA. The study served as a broad basis for extensively reforming city hospitals in Seoul in 1982 (NHS, ROK, 1978).

Health Care Delivery System

The nation's health resources became concentrated in the urban areas because the higher population density and the relative affluence of urban dwellers created a greater effective demand for such services, as compared with the rural sector. It is estimated that in the mid-1970s almost 87 percent of physicians and 90 percent of medical facilities were in urban areas, although only about half of the nation's population resided in those areas (C. K. Park 1979). Furthermore, there was little organized delivery of primary health care services within the system. The expansion of the health delivery system has followed the traditional pattern of emphasizing a high degree of specialization in the training of physicians, thus limiting the number of physicians available for primary care. Not surprisingly, under the growth-first distribution-later philosophy that pervaded the early 1970s, the modern hospitals in urban centers prospered and benefited from the most advanced medical technology available, while primary health care services in the rural areas lagged far behind.

Although innovations of less traditional, low-cost alternative approaches to the delivery of health services to the rural and urban poor have been widely discussed, their use has been substantially limited because of the influence of organizations with vested interests in preserving the traditional methods. There was, however, a growing feeling in the mid-1970s that the climate was suitable for the gradual introduction of these innovative methods. Thus KHDI was created in April 1976 to demonstrate and test these innovative approaches, often referred to as a community-based primary health care system (KDI 1980b).

The basic purpose of the KHDI demonstration project was to improve the delivery capacity of the public rural health system so that it would provide curative as well as preventive and promotional services to at least two-thirds of the rural residents. This system makes maximum use of the new types of health personnel, such as community health practitioners, community health aides, and village health agents, who operate at different levels in the community.

In this connection one of the important tasks assigned to NHS/KDI was to conduct an economic analysis and evaluation of the implementation and outcome of the KHDI demonstration project. Four specific evaluation objectives were: (1) to assess the performance of three new types of health personnel and to study the operation and management of the health care delivery system; (2) to measure the cost-effectiveness of the demonstration projects in three areas and to test for economies of scale; (3) to measure the accessibility to and acceptance of health services by consumers in the three demonstration areas; and (4) to assess the financial, social, and administrative feasibility of replicating nationwide the key features of the health delivery system developed by the KHDI project (Yeon 1981).

Cost and Financing

Throughout the mid-1970s much attention was focused on the rising cost of medical care and its effect on consumers and on the society as a whole. The relative cost of health care was increasing rapidly—due partly to the introduction of advanced medical technology—placing such care beyond the reach of many individuals, especially rural residents and disadvantaged groups in the urban sector. The cost barrier thus emerged as one of the major factors in preventing most people from receiving adequate medical care. The role of the government in financing health care was very limited, and there were no commercial insurance carriers. Direct spending by individual consumers was the major source of financing health services.

Therefore, it was not surprising at the time to find a consensus that a medical insurance scheme would play an important role in overcoming the cost barrier through spreading risks and pooling financial resources, and that it was necessary to introduce such a scheme without further delay. The passage of the Medical Insurance Law in December 1976 was the major accomplishment of the Fourth Five-Year Development Plan so far as social development programs were concerned. The objectives of the law were to raise national health standards and enhance social security coverage by facilitating access to medical care and eliminating the financial hardship of large medical care bills.

One of the most important and often hotly debated issues of the Korean medical insurance scheme has been the method of remuneration. According to the new system, providers of medical services are reimbursed on the basis of a fee-for-service schedule (a specified fee for each service rendered) approved by MOHSA. The schedule uses a point-unit method and is periodically reviewed by the ministry.

Prior to the implementation of the medical insurance system, MOHSA posted a standard fee schedule to be used by the insurance system. The newly adopted point-unit system assigned point values to more than 700 services performed by providers. The new fee schedule lowered the charges for insurance patients by as much as 40 percent of normal charges. In addition, the ministry fixed prices for some 3,000 pharmaceutical items, allowing a margin of only 12 percent over factory prices (C. K. Park 1977). In view of the rapid rise in medical costs at the time, the new government measure was intended to regulate and contain further increases in hospital fees and charges. Immediately after the announcement of the new standard fee schedule by the government, however, the Korean Hospital Association claimed that it could not provide adequate treatment to insured patients at such a low standard fee. It further asserted that the quality of medical care for insured patients might deteriorate and there would be discrimination in favor of patients not covered by insurance. In a stern warning to the medical profession, the ministry countered that providers found to be charging more than the standard fee officially set for insurance patients would be suspended from practice for up to three months (*The Korea Herald*, 19 July 1977).

It was subsequently revealed, however, that after the introduction of the medical insurance system, the utilization rate increased sharply, to the extent that hospitals that had previously had many empty beds were facing shortages of bed space. Physicians who originally protested the 60 percent remuneration suddenly realized that greater use of their services, even at lower rates of remuneration, was resulting in higher total revenues. Consequently, MOHSA was, on several subsequent occasions, able to successfully ward off excessive demands from providers. Realizing that the long-term success of the newly instituted medical insurance system depended, to a great extent, on the support of physicians and the medical industry, MOHSA has sought the cooperation of the Korean Medical Association and the Korean Hospital Association through informal consultation and discussion.

The number of persons covered by various health insurance programs increased steadily, from 3.2 million (or 8.8 percent of the population) in 1977 to 11.4 million (almost 30 percent) by 1981. During the 1977–81 period, a fund of 631 billion won ($927 million at the 1981 exchange rate) was mobilized through the health insurance scheme, and 423 billion won of that amount ($621 million at the 1981 exchange rate) was channeled into organized medical services to improve the health and welfare of the people.

Despite these promising beginnings, the share of government expenditure devoted to health care is and has always been low. Government support of health programs amounted to only 77 billion won in 1980, accounting for merely 1 percent of total government expenditure. In comparison, during the same year the government committed 342 billion won for manufacturing industries and another 120 billion won for air transport (EPB, ROK, *Korea Statistical Yearbook,* 1982). This limited government support of health services reflects the government's approach in general to social services, which have been left largely to the private sector, resulting in unevenness and inequity in distribution (Mason et al. 1980:405).

EFFECTS OF THE
MEDICAL INSURANCE POLICY MEASURE

One of the important advantages of a medical insurance system is that it ensures the flow of funds to the health sector and channels them into organized services. Hence a medical insurance program, even if the coverage is initially limited to a small segment of the population, has the effect of mobilizing additional financial resources for the whole health sector. By facilitating access to health care services, medical insurance can have, over the long run, a favorable effect on the state of health of many workers. Obviously much depends on its scope, on the type of financing mechanism, and on the manner in which the medical benefits are provided.

Since its introduction in July 1977, the medical insurance program has played an important role in promoting the delivery of medical care services to meet more effectively the growing health care needs of the population. Although a latecomer in the field of medical insurance, Korea is one of the few developing countries in which the extension of coverage under the medical insurance scheme has progressed at such a rapid rate.

In July 1977 Korea embarked on a new medical insurance program requiring employers with 500 workers or more to offer medical insurance benefits to their employees and dependents. Provision was also made to include on a voluntary basis firms employing fewer than 500 workers. The automatic coverage requirement was lowered in July 1979 to include firms with at least 300 workers and in January 1981 to include all firms with 100 workers or more. Subsequently government officials, teachers, support staff in private educational institutions, dependents of military personnel, and certain categories of pensioners all became eligible for medical benefits under an act of supplementary legislation.

More than 11.4 million people were entitled to receive medical benefits under various programs of medical insurance in 1981. Nearly 70 percent of this total were dependent family members of insured workers. More than 60 percent of the insured were employed in private industries; the remainder were government officials including public school teachers and professors, and teachers in private educational institutions. The proportion of the total population covered by various medical insurance schemes increased from 8.8 percent in 1977 to 29.5 percent in 1981, an increase of 8.2 million insured in only four years (MOHSA, ROK, 1983).

The extent of population coverage varies considerably, however, from province to province, ranging from a low of less than 15 percent in Cheju, South Chŏlla, and North Ch'ungch'ŏng provinces to 63 percent in Seoul and 31 percent in Pusan. Moreover, though the nation's two largest cities (Seoul and Pusan) contain only about 31 percent of the total population, nearly 57 percent of the persons covered by the medical insurance system are concentrated in those two urban centers. Under the present scheme, in which eligibility extends mainly to Class I employees (i.e., those working for a company or other institution with 10 or more employees), this concentration of medical services in the larger urban areas is virtually unavoidable in the short term. More effort needs to be directed toward extending insurance coverage to the residents of North Ch'ungch'ŏng, South Ch'ungch'ŏng, North Chŏlla, South Chŏlla, and Cheju provinces, where less than 20 percent of the population are insured compared with the national average of 30 percent (Table 13.4).

The scale of medical insurance operations in terms of population coverage has expanded at an exceptionally rapid rate since its introduction in 1977. The growth of the program in both numbers of patients treated and size of benefit payments has also been remarkable.

Table 13.4. Persons covered by the medical insurance system, by province and program: 1981

Province	General population (10³)	Specified occupations (10³)	Total (10³)	% distribution	% of population
Seoul city	4,176	1,269	5,446	47.7	62.8
Pusan city	714	292	1,006	8.8	31.0
Kyŏnggi	796	324	1,120	9.8	21.9
Kangwŏn	258	177	435	3.8	24.1
North Ch'ungch'ŏng	65	142	207	1.8	14.4
South Ch'ungch'ŏng	184	292	476	4.2	15.8
North Chŏlla	189	229	419	3.7	18.2
South Chŏlla	118	394	512	4.5	13.4
North Kyŏngsang	556	454	1,011	8.9	20.1
South Kyŏngsang	478	243	721	6.3	21.1
Cheju	7	47	54	0.5	11.5
Total	7,544	3,863	11,407	100.0	29.5

Source: MOHSA, ROK (1983).

Note: Line and column totals are subject to rounding errors.

The medical insurance system has considerably improved the accessibility to health care services for a wide segment of the populace, resulting in increased use of a greater variety of medical services. The number of treatment cases handled through employee medical insurance societies increased from 884,000 during a six-month period in 1977 to 5.4 million in 1979 and to 14.0 million in 1981. Including government officials and teachers and their dependents (who have been covered by another program administered by the Korea Medical Insurance Corporation since 1979), the total number of treatment cases in 1981 amounted to more than 22.3 million (Federation of Korean Medical Insurance Societies 1983).

The number of treatment cases, however, is largely influenced by changes in the population covered by the medical insurance system. To isolate this effect, Table 13.5 presents the utilization rates for hospitalization and outpatient care, derived by dividing total number of treatment cases by the number of persons covered by medical insurance. As shown in the table, the overall utilization rate (visits per person per year) increased from 0.56 in 1977 to 2.11 in 1981. The level of hospitalization appears to be stabilizing at about 0.05 in recent years, but that of outpatient consultation continues to rise rapidly. Thus the increase in the overall utilization rate largely reflects the increase in the utilization rate for outpatient care.

The growth in the number of persons entitled to medical insurance benefits is reflected in the increased revenues and benefit payments of the

Table 13.5. Medical care utilization rate of persons covered by the medical insurance program: 1977–81 (visits per person per year)

Year	Hospital-ization	Outpatient care	Total
1977	0.030	0.532	0.562
1978	0.038	0.718	0.756
1979	0.052	1.314	1.366
1980	0.057	1.853	1.910
1981	0.055	2.058	2.113

Source: Federation of Korean Medical Insurance Societies (1983).

Note: Figures include medical insurance programs administered by both employee medical insurance societies and the Korea Medical Insurance Corporation.

system, but the disproportionate increase in the latter also reflects sharply increased utilization rates and increased treatment costs since 1977. Expenditures have increased at a much faster rate than revenues, therefore, expenditures as a proportion of revenue rose sharply, from 34.3 percent in 1977 to 76.4 percent by 1981. During the 1978–81 period, revenue grew 5.6 times, from less than 50 billion won in 1978 to almost 275 billion won in 1981. In comparison, expenditures rose 8.3 times, from 25 billion won to 210 billion won over the same period. Expenditures for medical care benefits usually accounts for roughly 90 percent of total expenditures. During the entire period between 1977 and 1981, a total fund of about 631 billion won was mobilized through the medical insurance system, and 423 billion of that amount was channeled into organized medical services to improve the health and welfare of the people (Federation of Korean Medical Insurance Societies 1983).

As mentioned earlier, sharp increases in expenditures can be attributed to increased unit costs as well as increases in utilization rates. Medical care cost per treatment case increased from 8,390 won in 1977 to 11,830 won in 1981, but the increase was attributable for the most part to a sharp increase in the unit cost of hospitalization care. During the 1977–81 period the cost of hospitalization care per case treated more than doubled, while the cost of outpatient care increased by about 35 percent (Federation of Korean Medical Insurance Societies 1983).

As stated in a preamble of the Medical Insurance Law of 1976, the new insurance scheme was introduced to improve the health and welfare of the working class, particularly of people who are unable to pay their mounting medical bills. Accordingly, the contributions to the scheme are linked to salary level, with lower premiums for lower-paid workers. It would be appropriate, therefore, to ask who bears the insurance cost and who benefits most from expenditures of medical insurance schemes. Although it is difficult to ascertain the magnitude of real costs and benefits owing to the brief experience of the medical insurance program and the dearth of data, a recent study by KDI provides some clues as to the redistributive effects of Korea's medical insurance system (Yeon et al. 1983).

Table 13.6 presents the amounts of contributions paid and benefits received per person by monthly salary scale under the 184 separate employee medical insurance societies in 1981. According to this table, members of medical insurance societies who were making on average less than 100,000 won per month paid 31,650 won in contributions in 1981, while receiving 19,600 won in medical benefits. The difference resulted in a benefit/contribution rate of 61.9 percent. By contrast, the rate for employees with average monthly salaries in the range of 100,000–150,000 won per month was higher (66 percent) and higher still (nearly 80 percent) for those in the 200,000–250,000 won salary range. As the table also indicates, the medical insurance societies with a membership earning on average less than 200,000 won per month accounted for about 60 percent of the total number of societies in operation in 1981, and their benefit/contribution rates were much lower than the 74.1 percent average for all employee medical insurance societies. These differences can be partly explained by age structure (younger, healthier workers falling in the lower salary ranges). Those blue-collar workers who have more extended family support, moreover, may be less likely to seek medical treatment in cases of minor illness.

LESSONS OF THE KOREAN EXPERIENCE

The experience of Korea clearly shows that even if rapid growth of the economy is achieved and the overall standard of living is improved, a point is soon reached when it becomes necessary to increase emphasis on social

Table 13.6. Average contribution and benefit per insured person in the Employee Medical Insurance Program, by income level: 1981

Salary range[a] (won)	Distribution of members of insurance societies (%)	Average contribution (won)	Average benefit (won)	Benefit as % of contribution	Dependency rate
< 100,000	2.2	31,650	19,600	61.9	1.58
100,000–150,000	21.8	46,800	31,010	66.2	2.02
150,000–200,000	35.3	62,230	45,920	73.8	2.58
200,000–250,000	27.7	78,750	62,720	79.6	3.32
250,000–300,000	11.4	84,010	64,820	77.2	3.49
> 300,000	1.6	84,790	42,800	50.5	3.35
Total	100.0	65,020	48,180	74.1	2.75

Source: Yeon et al. (1983).

a. Average monthly salary of members of the insurance societies.

development. By then, the growth of inequities in income and wealth, in conjunction with rising aspirations throughout the society, accounts for many of the frictions and instabilities with which social development planning must cope. The government as a dominant force in Korean society is able to influence the ownership of wealth and the pattern of income distribution. This ability could be used to formulate policies leading to more widely based participation in the prosperity that the country has been enjoying. It is also able, to some degree, to establish priorities and set the pace for social development.

Social development is lagging behind the rapid pace of Korea's economic development. Unless the gap is reduced, it will continue to foreshadow social, economic, and political problems of increasing gravity. There is a growing awareness now among economists and planners that the goal of more equal distribution of benefits could be better achieved if more social development policies were enunciated from a broader perspective to parallel and complement economic growth. These policies, translated into well-conceived, concrete programs and services, could then be incorporated into national development plans.

There is a need for a rational health care plan based on the equitable distribution of services and the efficient utilization of resources. In urban areas, low-cost housing and a wide range of environmental improvements are urgently needed. The rapid industrialization of the economy and the aging population, coupled with a disintegration of the traditional extended family system, emphasize the need for an old-age pension system for industrial and other workers in the private sector. At present old-age pension benefits are available only to a small group of the elite—principally government officials, military personnel, teachers, and professors. The modernizing trend in education must be encouraged and technical innovations introduced so that the rapid extension of compulsory education can be accomplished without incurring prohibitive costs.

The government has identified health care as a priority, but government investment in health has been extremely small, and private medical care has been beyond the means of most Koreans. The resulting situation has been further aggravated by a shortage and maldistribution of medical facilities and personnel. The national medical insurance scheme has been a major policy instrument for overcoming the cost barrier, which prevented a substantial number of people from receiving adequate medical care.

The introduction of the medical insurance system was an important milestone in Korea's social development, and it proved to be very popular. Nonetheless, there are inherent weaknesses and shortcomings in the system, particularly in regard to efficiency and equity standards. First, the extent of coverage is grossly inadequate. With only about 30 percent of the population covered by the system, the majority of the low-income groups —i.e., workers employed by marginal firms, self-employed persons, rural community residents—remain unprotected. These groups are more likely to be medically indigent and in much greater need of health care services than those already protected by the system. Although nearly 83 percent of the regularly employed persons in the industrial sector are covered by medical (Class I) insurance, it has been estimated that only about 3 percent of the community residents (Class II insurance) are protected by the medical insurance program. There are also glaring regional disparities in the availability of medical insurance. The proportions of the population entitled to medical insurance benefits vary from only 11 percent in Cheju and 13 percent in South Chŏlla to 63 percent in Seoul.

Another serious shortcoming of the employee medical insurance scheme is the regressive nature of its coinsurance provisions. Under these provisions, the patient pays for 20 percent of hospitalization costs and 30 percent of the costs of outpatient care services. In the case of hospital outpatient care, the patient's share is 50 percent. Although there are justifications for cost sharing, serious questions may be raised as to its ill effects. Since the coinsurance system is based on uniform rates, regardless of income level, it places a heavier relative burden on low-income families. As a consequence, these families may be deterred from seeking needed health services, thereby undermining a major goal of medical insurance, which is to encourage greater use of health care services by the low-income groups.

Korea's medical insurance system has been accumulating surplus funds in substantial amounts. The total revenues of the system have always been greater than the amount it actually spent—for every year since the beginning of the program in July 1977. The accumulated surplus fund for the employee scheme at the end of 1981 amounted to 118.4 billion won (138.6 billion won if the scheme for government officials is also included), roughly equivalent to the total amount expended during 1981. Unless the government deliberately intends to accumulate reserve funds to be used for constructing health facilities for the insured in badly needed areas, there is no justification for accumulating such a huge reserve with contributions collected from a large number of low-income workers. Until now, however, no surplus funds have been used for such purposes.

Sound financial planning and operations are essential if the system is to earn public confidence and popular support. Such planning can be achieved only by more accurate actuarial estimates of the quantity of medical services demanded and received, the level of reimbursement for providers of services, and the amount of administrative expenses. Along with these improvements, serious consideration should be given to the reduction of either the contribution rate or coinsurance rate, particularly for low-income workers who are single. Another alternative would be to improve the level of benefits. A major deficiency in benefits is the limitation of benefit payments to six months for any single diagnosis, which denies relief from the financial burden of prolonged medical care in cases of catastrophic illness.

It is anomalous that a compulsory medical insurance program established by a national law is administered by a large number of relatively small, privately managed insurance societies. Most of the 184 medical insurance societies currently being operated throughout the nation are still too small to take advantage of risk pooling and economies of scale. Many problems and disadvantages are associated with this type of multiple system, as is evident from the experience of Japan. Among these problems are inequalities in contributions and benefits, double standards, and duplication of administration. At this stage of Korea's development, it is critically important to try to avoid the mistakes other countries have made in the past. Because of the potential advantages of economies of scale and of maximum uniformity in coverage, facilities, and internal operation, the centralized management of a medical insurance program is likely to result in lower administrative costs and better control over benefits and coverage. Since the private sector alone does not have adequate experience in this area, centralization in the initial stages would also help to prevent duplication, abuses, and waste and could thus direct scarce health resources to where they are most needed.

All these shortcomings of the medical insurance system need to be resolved. The most urgent need is to speed up the extension of coverage to as large a portion of the populace as available medical facilities and personnel permit. A failure to do so would result in the continued waste of the most basic ingredient in social development—the human resource.

14 The Population Redistribution Plan (1977) and Urbanization Problems

by Lee-Jay Cho and Won Bae Kim

During the past two decades, the spatial distribution of human settlement in Korea has been drastically transformed. Rapid industrialization was accompanied by an enormous upsurge in both the volume and rate of population movement into urban areas. As a result, the proportion of the total population living in urban areas increased from 28 percent in 1960 to 57.2 percent in 1980. Urbanization was both a cause and an effect of rapid industrialization. Although industrialization preceded urbanization in Korea (Table 14.1), the speed of industrialization from 1960 to 1980 was irregular whereas that of urbanization was more or less steady.

The two major problems in Korean urbanization are the persistent primacy of the capital city and regional imbalances. Another feature is the bipolar development of the urban system. For example, in 1980 Seoul and Pusan together accounted for 30.8 percent of the total population and 53.8 percent of the urban population (Table 14.2). Such a pattern of urbanization was partly a result of the government's development strategy, which stressed economies of scale and agglomeration. The effects of several development programs can be identified as factors contributing to the current distribution of population and industries.

First, the Korean government has played an active role in promoting and directing industrialization. The successive five-year development plans, which emphasized growth maximization, can be characterized as "top-down" and "sector-oriented." The spatial dimension of development was ignored. There were few inputs from local and provincial governments into the centralized decision-making process.

Table 14.1. Industrialization and urbanization indexes: 1960–80 (%)

	1960	1966	1970	1975	1980
Nonagricultural employment as a percentage of total employment	20.5	42.1	49.5	51.0	62.2
Rate of change in industrialization		105.4	16.9	3.0	22.0
Urban population as a percentage of total population	28.0	33.6	41.1	48.4	57.2
Rate of change in urbanization		20.0	22.3	17.8	18.2

Source: EPB, ROK, *Population and Housing Census* (1960, 1966, 1970, 1975, 1980).

349

Table 14.2. Urban, rural, and major city population shares: 1960–80

	Population (10³ persons)			Average annual growth rate (%)		
	1960	1970	1980	1960–70	1970–80	1960–80
Urban	6,997 (28.0)	12,953 (41.2)	21,409 (57.2)	6.35	5.15	5.75
Seoul	2,445 (9.8)	5,536 (17.6)	8,364 (22.4)	8.50	4.24	6.35
Pusan	1,164 (4.7)	1,879 (6.0)	3,160 (8.4)	4.89	5.35	5.12
Other cities	3,388 (13.5)	5,538 (17.6)	9,885 (26.4)	5.02	5.98	5.45
Rural	17,992 (72.0)	18,513 (58.8)	15,997 (42.8)	0.27	–1.43	–0.59
Total	24,989	31,466	37,406	2.32	1.75	2.04

Source: EPB, ROK, Population and Housing Census (1960, 1970, 1980).
Note: Percentage shares are shown in parentheses.

Second, Korea's export-oriented industrialization has contributed to the rapid growth of the two largest cities. As international trade increases, most manufacturing industries—which rely heavily on foreign countries for raw materials as well as for markets—have been located near international seaports. Therefore, the Seoul–Inch'ŏn region and the Pusan region with their large ports have played a dominant role in the process of export-oriented industrial expansion. This bipolar development of the Seoul and Pusan regions is evident in the regional distribution of manufacturing employment over the past 15 years (Table 14.3).

Third, public investment decisions have been guided by strong locational predispositions. The allocation of social overhead capital and the establishment of industrial bases, which were primarily governed by national efficiency criterion, favored the economically advanced areas—Seoul and Pusan. After the mid-1970s when growth policy emphasized heavy and chemical industries, an industrial belt took shape along the southeast coast and absorbed a substantial proportion of national employment. The construction of the Kyung-Bu (Seoul–Pusan) Highway also spurred a concentration of development in the large cities along the route. Other regions were relatively neglected and regional imbalances were intensified.

Fourth, despite considerable efforts devoted to rural development, the government's urban-based industrial development policies and programs were a far greater success. Massive rural out-migration occurred in the 1960s and the early 1970s partly because of the urban bias inherent in outward-looking economic development strategies. Notably, the terms of trade between agricultural and manufacturing products was a major cause of the heavy rural out-migration (Renaud 1977).

Table 14.3. Provincial manufacturing employment: 1966–81

Province	1966 Number of workers (10^3)	%	1973 Number of workers (10^3)	%	1981 Number of workers (10^3)	%
Seoul city	180.2	31.8	389.1	33.6	428.0	20.9
Pusan city	102.8	18.1	191.4	16.5	336.0	16.4
Kyŏnggi	51.6	9.1	163.0	14.1	489.5	23.9
Kangwŏn	13.2	2.3	18.8	1.6	19.3	0.9
North Ch'ungch'ŏng	13.7	2.4	25.6	2.2	38.4	1.9
South Ch'ungch'ŏng	33.3	5.9	54.9	4.7	88.5	4.3
North Chŏlla	29.1	5.1	37.5	3.2	55.7	2.7
South Chŏlla	40.0	7.1	49.9	4.3	69.2	3.4
North Kyŏngsang	72.3	12.7	125.6	10.8	272.0	13.3
South Kyŏngsang	30.6	5.3	102.0	8.8	247.9	12.1
Total	566.7	100.0	1,157.8	100.0	2,044.3	100.0

Source: EPB, ROK, *Mining and Manufacturing Survey* (1966, 1973, 1981).

Note: Cheju province is included in South Chŏlla province.

Finally, the government's foremost concern was the industrial sector, whereas basic needs such as health care, housing, and education were left largely to private initiative. This served to increase the disparity between the big cities and other areas in social services. Numerous migrants moved to Seoul or other large cities to take advantage of sociocultural amenities. The concentration of such amenities, especially top-quality universities, attracted highly motivated young people not only from the rural areas but from the small cities as well.

Urban growth in Korea in the 1960s is primarily attributable to the massive influx of migrants from the rural areas, although natural increase contributed more or less equally to urban growth in the 1970s. Most of these migrants went to the cities in pursuit of job opportunities and higher incomes (H. K. Kim 1981; H. S. Lee 1983). Selectivity in terms of age, sex, and education is apparent in this process (L. J. Cho 1974; E. Y. Yu 1978). As a consequence, the age structures of the rural and the urban populations became unbalanced—most significantly, people in the older and younger age brackets remained in rural areas. Educational selectivity is another characteristic in the migration stream. As in many other Asian countries, the more educated a person is the more mobile he is likely to be.

Seoul and Pusan were the centers of this movement. "Step-wise" migration[1] was not frequent in Korea, unlike in many other developing

---

1. "Movement from a rural birthplace first to a local village, then to a small town, and eventually to a major city" (Petersen and Petersen 1986).

countries. A considerable proportion of migrants moved directly to Seoul
from their places of origin (Barringer 1974). Almost two-thirds of all migrants
between 1960 and 1970 moved into the metropolitan areas of Seoul and Pusan and those migrants were the major force underlying the population
implosion that drastically changed the distribution of the Korean population in the 1960s (L. J. Cho 1974). Although the proportion of total migrants
moving to Seoul and Pusan has declined in recent years (36 percent during 1975–80), the annual population growth rate in the two cities still exceeds 5 percent. This trend is likely to continue because of the demographic
multiplier effect. For example, the relative contribution of net migration to
Seoul's population growth was 85.3 percent from 1966 to 1970, while in the
same period the relative contribution of natural increase was 14.7 percent.
However, in the 1970s—particularly during the latter half of the decade—
the relative contribution of natural increase expanded considerably (Table
14.4).

The problems associated with rapid urban growth and the persistent
primacy of Seoul have become major social concerns and policy issues in
Korea. Even though the economic case against the largest cities is not con-
clusive, no one questions the existence of the following acute problems:

- Inadequate supply of infrastructure, housing, and educational facilities;
- Pollution, environmental deterioration, and congestion in metropolitan
  areas;

Table 14.4. Relative contributions of the components of urban growth:
1960–80

Period	Increase in urban population per 1,000 persons	Percentage due to			
		Reclassi- fication	Annex- ation	Net migration	Natural increase
1960–66					
Seoul	1,358	0.0	11.4	57.7	30.8
Total	2,798	8.0	9.3	40.6	42.1
1966–70					
Seoul	1,731			85.3	14.7
Total	3,148			73.1	26.9
1970–75					
Seoul	1,354		1.0	49.7	49.3
Total	3,841	5.0	3.1	48.8	43.1
1975–80					
Seoul	1,477			36.3	63.7
Total	4,638	10.5	4.1	39.7	45.7

Source: EPB, ROK, *Population and Housing Census* (1966, 1970, 1975, 1980).

- Unbalanced regional development with respect to national lands and resource utilization;
- Persistent inequalities among regions and among cities in access to public infrastructure and sociocultural amenities;
- Potential social and political unrest in large cities because of a large concentration of marginal workers and students; and
- National security concerns owing to the large concentration of population and industrial facilities near the border.

There is much disagreement, however, as to whether these problems can be effectively addressed through population redistribution programs. Pollution and congestion, for example, may be more closely related to density and the spatial configuration of cities than to their size. If so, such problems can be more effectively addressed through controlling emissions or regulating the location of polluting industries than through attempts to contain city size (Tolley, Graves, and Gardner 1979). In any event, the Korean government began taking policy initiatives in the late 1960s to grapple with these problems.

MAIN FEATURES OF THE PLAN

Government efforts to achieve balanced spatial development began in the late 1960s. The Ministry of Construction, the Metropolitan Government of Seoul, and the Ministry without Portfolio prepared plans to restrict the amount of in-migration allowed in the capital region. The major instruments of these plans were industrial dispersal, siting new educational and cultural facilities in local areas, and decentralizing some government agencies. In addition, laws were enacted to serve as legal bases for regional planning—notably the Comprehensive National Land Development Planning Law and the City Planning Law. These plans were, however, largely symbolic. Not until the 1970s was the policy dealing with metropolitan concentration actually implemented. In 1971 the First Comprehensive National Physical Development Plan (1972–81) was formulated to direct regional development projects based on the growth-center approach. The plan was not entirely effective in guiding public investment decisions because of its lack of integration with economic development policies, which were largely sector-oriented. The centerpiece of the government's efforts was the Seoul Population Redistribution Plan announced in 1977.

It was recognized even in the 1960s that control over rapid population growth and industrial concentration in Seoul could not be achieved using a piecemeal approach. The need for a comprehensive planning effort was fully understood; consequently, the Population Redistribution Plan was prepared and implemented in 1977. The specific objective of the plan was to divert the projected increase in Seoul's population of 4.3 million people by

1981 to several selected growth centers throughout the country thereby holding the population of Seoul at the then current level of 7 million.

To achieve the planned population distribution, various population measures and programs were adopted regarding industrial location, urban development of five countermagnet metropolitan areas and the southeast coastal industrial belt, and regional distribution of educational institutions. It was even proposed that a new administrative capital be created. The plan was quite comprehensive in the sense that almost every conceivable means and strategy to achieve its objectives was employed.

The plan contained detailed programs for: (1) controlling the expansion or establishment of factories in the capital region and encouraging relocation of existing factories to other regions; (2) the creation of population-absorbing capacity in other designated regions in the southern part of the country; and (3) restricting the expansion of the educational institutions in the capital region and encouraging their redistribution. These programs were to utilize various financial benefits and infrastructure development techniques as incentives and disincentives. The expansion and new development of industries in the capital region were prohibited, whereas industrial development in the designated areas was to be encouraged by every possible means. Differential tax treatment and financial assistance to relocating industries were also included. Detailed educational policies were proposed. The expansion of existing educational institutions and the establishment of new ones was prohibited. Instead, the opening of local campuses of the universities existing in Seoul was encouraged and assisted financially. The transfer of students to Seoul was discouraged and the exchange of professors between Seoul and other regions promoted.

It is in this plan that the importance of service industries was recognized for the first time by including the educational institutions as one of the large employment and population-absorbing sectors in metropolitan areas.

Land-use regulations were to be used to prevent a further concentration of office activities in Seoul. These regulations and other restrictive measures, however, were not strictly enforced and, in effect, were later abandoned when Seoul was chosen as the site for both the 1986 Asian and 1988 World Olympic Games.

The Population Redistribution Plan became inactive around 1980. The plan had been criticized on a few important grounds. First, the target to reduce Seoul's population to 7 million in 1986 from a peak level of 8 million in 1981 was regarded as infeasible. Second, the idea of a new capital was quite controversial. Many doubted the desirability as much as the feasibility of the planned construction of a new capital. The funding problem alone would have jeopardized the plan. In any case, only the restrictive measures, including the tight control over industrial development and expansion of educational institutions in the capital region, were strictly enforced whereas positive development of population-receiving areas, particularly five stronghold urban centers, was either delayed or not effectively implemented for various reasons.

Industrial Location Policies

It was recognized within the circle of government policymakers, even at the early stage of industrialization, that industrial location is an important policy tool in achieving balanced development among regions. Since 1964 the government has tried to restrict the establishment of new industries and the expansion of existing ones in Seoul to curb the rapid concentration of industries and population. Policymakers knew that it would be impossible to stop industrial growth in Seoul, where enormous locational advantages existed at the early stages of economic development, unless incentives to locate elsewhere were created. The Local Industrial Development Law, enacted in 1967, provided the legal basis for governmental assistance in promoting local industrial development through such means as tax exemptions and infrastructure development in designated industrial areas. Nine heavy industrial estates and 24 local industrial estates have been developed by the central and local governments since 1962. The heavy industrial estates were mostly developed along the eastern and southern coastal areas from P'ohang to Yŏch'ŏn.

Land policy measures were adopted to facilitate industrial estate development. The standard price system, one of these measures, was adopted to eliminate speculative land value increases. The government makes a determination of standard prices of land prior to the designation of industrial estate areas. These prices are applied in the compulsory or negotiated purchase of the land for industrial estate development. The cheap land, which is developed for industrial uses, combined with certain tax exemption schemes constitutes an attractive incentive for incoming industrial firms.

The enactment of the Industrial Distribution Law of 1977 opened up a new dimension in industrial location policy. The law authorizes the minister of the Ministry of Commerce and Industry (MCI) to make a comprehensive industry redistribution plan and to classify areas for the purpose of industrial location into three zones: (1) relocation encouragement zone; (2) limitation and coordination zone; and (3) location encouragement zone. The law defines the relocation encouragement zone to be the large cities and surrounding areas with an extremely high concentration of industries and an extremely high growth rate of population. The limitation and coordination zone is defined as the area with a relatively high concentration of industries and high growth of population. Both the relocation encouragement zone and the limitation and coordination zone, therefore, need a restriction of expansion or new establishment of industries. The encouragement zone is the area where the industrial base is presumably weak and where the need to attract industries is strong. The MCI classifies the industries in Seoul into those subject to relocation, and those permitted to stay in the area.

The use of a differential tax scheme and real assistance such as infra-structure development and government loans were major tools for im-plementing industrial decentralization policies.

Recent Plans

In 1980 the major responsibility for planning and implementing popula-tion dispersal policy was transferred from the Ministry without Portfolio to the Ministry of Construction (MOC). The MOC drafted the Second National Land Development Plan (1982–91), which set forth the basic guide-lines for population dispersal, to complement the Fifth Five-Year Develop-ment Plan (1982–86). Both plans were administered by the Economic Planning Board (EPB) and promoted a better integration of population redis-tribution goals with related sectoral plans.

The Second National Land Development Plan is designed to curb ex-cessive population growth in large urban centers and emphasizes balanced national development. The plan has four principal elements:

1. To ensure balanced national development, the country is divided into 28 "integrated regional settlement areas" based on functional economic areas.

2. Potential migrants who are otherwise likely to move to Seoul and Pu-san will be redirected to 15 growth-inducement cities such as Taejŏn, Kwang-ju, and Taegu. To facilitate this redirection of migration, the government will strengthen public administration and management functions in the growth-inducement cities.

3. Underdeveloped areas will receive special attention to bring their lev-els of development up to a national standard.

4. To strengthen interregional socioeconomic interactions, the existing transportation and communications networks will be expanded and new facilities will be built in less developed areas.

THEORETICAL APPROPRIATENESS OF THE PLAN

Migration Policy

The primary objectives of the 1977 plan were to: (1) discourage massive population movement from the countryside into Seoul; (2) divert the fu-ture potential migration flow which would otherwise be directed to Seoul to a few intermediate-size growth centers; (3) disperse development potential away from Seoul to the rest of the country; and (4) attain a more balanced spatial organization of the national economy.

To meet these objectives a "growth center" approach was adopted and five medium-size cities with populations between 200,000 and one million were designated as priority investment urban centers in 1978. These are Taejŏn, Taegu, Masan, Kwangju, and Chŏnju, which happen to be either provincial capitals or industrial complexes. These centers are not "induced" growth centers but "spontaneous" growth centers that had already exhibited rapid population growth due to their strong economies.

The underlying rationale for growth centers is to capitalize on spatial economies of scale and to complete a network of communication and economic flows to capture all systemic effects. It is, however, difficult to justify economically a growth center approach on the basis of spread effects, i.e., benefits to the surrounding areas of a growth center. The idea has the compelling advantage that it implies internally consistent industrial decentralization and migration policies. Growth centers can properly serve as regional centers of in-migration, thus reducing migration flows to the national centers.

Other policy measures set forth in the 1977 plan such as those designed to discourage in-migration to Seoul and to relocate a portion of the existing urban population of Seoul were not only less sound in principle but also often ineffective in practice. These measures are susceptible to the criticism that they work against the well being of the urban poor and potential rural out-migrants. The urban poor would be worse off because they would have to pay extra for either commuting farther or for new housing accommodations if they were willing to make a residential relocation. In theory, rural out-migrants will in all likelihood be better off if they move to urban sectors of any size. Any migration policy aimed at discouraging in-migrants destined for big cities would be contrary to their welfare.

Industrial Location Policy

The manufacturing sector's potential for decentralization and job creation has been well recognized and accordingly the possibility of influencing industrial location has received top priority by policymakers in many developing nations. This emphasis is consistent with the widely accepted theory of an "economic base," which postulates that certain types of manufacturing industries are critical to the growth of a local or regional economy. Furthermore, from the policymaker's viewpoint, manufacturing activities are more amenable to location policies than service activities because the latter are often subject to local markets.

Industrial location policy proposed in the 1977 plan aims at the redistribution of manufacturing employment through the reallocation of capital. Policy instruments for this purpose take two forms: incentives such as financial subsidies and tax concessions, and disincentives like administrative controls and penalties.

The policy of encouraging capital movement between regions is based on the premise that many types of manufacturing activities can be transplanted with relative ease and can operate efficiently in a wide range of alternative locations. Also, it is based on the premise that an adequate level of basic industrial facilities are available everywhere. These assumptions may be correct for the United States and the Western European countries but were not valid for Korea in the 1970s. Basic utilities and support infrastructure are not ubiquitous in Korea. Furthermore, an underdeveloped capital market means very distinctive advantages for firms located in or near the primary metropolitan area—the cost of obtaining financial capital increases with the distance from the primary metropolitan area. In addition, an underdeveloped transport system may focus links to the primary city. Also, the external benefits of locational agglomeration may be disproportionately large in developing economies compared with more developed economies. All of these lead us to suspect the effectiveness of tax concessions and financial subsidies for industrial relocation or capital redistribution.

EFFECTS OF THE POLICY

Rural–Urban Balance

The Korean government implemented various policies in the 1960s and 1970s designed to reduce the rural–urban income gap. These policies certainly improved the farmers' terms of trade, raising them from the low point to which they had fallen in the late 1960s (Table 14.5). On a per capita basis, the rural-to-urban income ratio largely recovered from the dramatic plunge it took in the late 1960s. In 1983 per household rural income was close to per household urban income. The policies did not succeed, however, in significantly reducing the gap in per worker income between rural and urban areas.

Most economic models of migration point to income differentials as the main cause of rural-to-urban migration (Harris and Todaro 1970; Yap 1977). The farmers' terms of trade—the principal determinant of rural income (Adelman and Robinson 1978)—is portrayed as the most important factor for explaining rural-to-urban migration in Korea (Renaud 1977). However, despite an improvement in the farmers' terms of trade and hence in per capita rural income relative to per capita urban income and also in off-farm

Table 14.5. Rural–urban income differentials: 1963–83

Year	1963	1966	1968	1970	1973	1975	1978	1980	1983
Terms of trade	100.7	75.8	81.4	89.6	101.0	100.0	99.2	94.5	84.9
Ratio of rural to urban income									
Per capita	107	75	57	61	80	93	89	76	94
Per worker	43	31	27	31	41	48	u	44	59

Source: EPB, ROK, *Annual Report on the Family Income and Expenditure Survey* (1964–1984); BOK, *Economic Statistics Yearbook* (1964–84); NACF, ROK, *Agriculture Yearbook* (1964–84).
u—unavailable.

employment opportunities, rural-to-urban migration did not decline during 1960–80. In terms of absolute numbers, rural-to-urban migration rose substantially during 1965–70 and then fell slightly during 1970–75 (Table 14.6). The number, however, surged up again during 1975–80. The relative intensity of rural-to-urban migration (migrants divided by rural population) has not decreased either.

This persistent rural-to-urban migration may be due to such structural problems of the rural sector as the small size of landholdings, decreasing labor intensity in the agricultural sector, and unstable rural incomes (J. B. Kim 1979). The uneven distribution of benefits from rural development policies among income groups and among different regions could be another contributing factor to continued rural-to-urban migration (Nam and Ro 1981; Choe and Kim 1985).

Interregional Balance

Regional economic disparities have been one of the major motivations for the national urbanization policy in Korea. In the early 1960s there was a substantial imbalance between the geographical distributions of population and production (Table 14.7). During the same period, "lagging" provinces with a heavy dependence on agriculture remained underdeveloped and their GNP share fell. "Advanced" provinces increased their GNP share and possessed a disproportionate concentration of production capacity. Inter-provincial migration during 1960–80 was largely a process of adaptation to the changing regional structure of production.

Seoul and Pusan were at the receiving end of inter-provincial migration, whereas the other provinces, except Kyŏnggi, were sending out migrants throughout the entire period (EPB, ROK, *Population and Housing Census*, 1966, 1970, 1975, 1980). This inter-provincial migration flow from poor areas

Table 14.6. Rural-to-urban migration

Period	1961–66	1965–70	1970–75	1975–80
(A) Total number of migrants (1,000 persons)	1,422	3,189	3,569	4,887
(B) Rural-to-urban migrants (1,000 persons)	588	1,845	1,754	2,524
Percentage of total migrants (B/A)	40.7	57.8	49.2	51.6
(C) Rural population at beginning of year (1,000 persons)	17,992	19,388	18,506	17,910
Rate of rural-to-urban migration (B/C) (per 1,000 rural population)	32.7	95.1	94.8	140.9

Source: EPB, ROK, *Population and Housing Census* (1960, 1966, 1970, 1975, 1980).

Table 14.7. Provincial shares of production, population, and employment: 1960–80 (%)

Production share[a]	1960	1966	1970	1975	1978
Advanced provinces					
Seoul city	22.7	23.7	27.2	28.5	27.7
Pusan city		7.6	7.9	8.1	8.8
Kyŏnggi	10.9	9.7	10.1	12.2	13.4
Intermediate provinces					
North Kyŏngsang	12.7	13.0	11.4	11.9	11.4
South Kyŏngsang	15.2[b]	9.0	9.9	9.8	11.0
Lagging provinces					
Kangwŏn	6.9	5.2	4.8	4.0	3.9
North Ch'ungch'ŏng	4.4	4.7	4.3	3.9	3.4
South Ch'ungch'ŏng	8.2	8.3	7.8	6.4	6.2
North Chŏlla	7.8	7.1	6.3	5.3	4.9
South Chŏlla	10.6	10.6	9.3	8.5	8.3
Cheju	1.0	1.1	1.0	1.1	1.0
Population share[c]	1960	1966	1970	1975	1980
Advanced provinces					
Seoul city	9.8	13.0	17.6	19.8	22.3
Pusan city	4.6	4.9	6.0	7.1	8.4
Kyŏnggi	11.0	10.6	10.7	11.6	13.2
Intermediate provinces					
North Kyŏngsang	15.4	15.3	14.5	14.0	13.3
South Kyŏngsang	12.1	10.9	9.9	9.5	8.9
Lagging provinces					
Kangwŏn	6.5	6.3	5.9	5.4	4.8
North Ch'ungch'ŏng	5.5	5.3	4.7	4.4	3.8
South Ch'ungch'ŏng	10.1	10.0	9.1	8.5	7.9
North Chŏlla	9.6	8.6	7.7	7.0	6.1
South Chŏlla	14.2	13.9	12.7	11.5	10.1
Cheju	1.1	1.2	1.2	1.2	1.2

to prosperous areas during 1960–80 contributed to a convergence of per capita provincial product, while resulting in an increasing population concentration indicated by the increasing values of the Gini coefficient (Table 14.7). A comparison of the distribution of population and employment among the provinces indicates a less clear trend of convergence in per capita employment opportunities; however, during 1975–80 the deviations between the two distributions were reduced.

The dispersion of educational opportunites, however, must be analyzed not only in terms of quantity but also in terms of quality, considering the substantial gap in educational quality between Seoul and the rest of the nation (Nam and Ro 1981).

Table 14.7. (continued)

Employment share[c]	1960	1966	1970	1975	1980
Advanced provinces					
Seoul city	7.4	11.1	16.0	16.8	20.2
Pusan city		4.3	5.3	6.0	7.7
Kyŏnggi	10.3	10.1	10.3	11.7	12.8
Intermediate provinces					
North Kyŏngsang	15.1	16.1	14.8	14.6	13.7
South Kyŏngsang	16.0[b]	11.1	10.4	10.4	9.9
Lagging provinces					
Kangwŏn	6.4	5.8	6.1	5.4	4.6
North Ch'ungch'ŏng	4.9	5.7	4.9	4.9	4.0
South Ch'ungch'ŏng	9.9	10.1	9.3	9.4	8.4
North Chŏlla	10.5	8.9	8.1	7.6	6.1
South Chŏlla	17.7	15.5	13.6	12.2	11.2
Cheju	1.8	1.4	1.3	1.2	1.3

	1960	1966	1970	1975	1978/80
Sum of absolute differences between population and production distributions	25.8	26.8	23.0	21.2	16.2
Sum of absolute differences between population and employment distributions	10.2	7.0	5.4	8.2	6.8
Index of provincial population concentration[d]	0.272	0.307	0.352	0.385	0.434

a. MOHA, ROK, *Annual Report* (1980); Seoul, The Special City of (1981); BOK, *Regional Income Accounts* (1963).

b. Pusan is included in South Kyŏngsang province.

c. EPB, ROK, *Population and Housing Census* (1960, 1966, 1970, 1975, 1980).

d. The Gini coefficient was used to compute the index.

$$G = \sum_{i=1}^{n} x_i \cdot y_i + 1 - \sum_{i=1}^{n} x_i + 1 \cdot y_i, \, n = 1, \ldots, 11$$

where x_i is area share and y_i is population share.

Intraregional Balance within the Capital Region

Since 1970 the pace of Seoul's population growth has slowed, although it is still higher than the national average. Six satellite cities surrounding Seoul grew very rapidly during the 1970s and the early 1980s (Table 14.8). The suburbanization of Seoul's population began after 1970. The relative decentralization process occurring within the capital region has been praised as a success of population dispersal policies. It should not be confused, however, with a policy success at the national level. The population in the capital region grew very rapidly in the 1970s and in the early 1980s.

The suburbanization of Seoul's population started with the suburbanization of employment. Industrial employment led the process. Other

Table 14.8. Population increase in the capital region: 1960–83 (% growth per annum)

Year	1960–66	1966–70	1970–75	1975–80	1980–83
Capital	4.9	6.3	4.1	3.9	3.6
Seoul	7.6	9.4	4.4	3.9	3.2
Suburban districts[a]	u	6.3	6.1	6.5	5.9
Rest of Kyŏnggi	u	–1.9	0.8	0.0	0.4

Source: Choi and Lee (1985).
a. Suburban districts include the cities of Inch'ŏn, Ŭijŏngbu, Suwon, Songnam, Anyang, and Puch'ŏn, and the counties of Namyangju, Shihŭng, Koyang, Kwangju, and Kimp'o. u—unavailable.

sectors, such as trade and services, were slower in responding to industrial deconcentration. The establishment of a green belt surrounding Seoul in 1971, restrictions on industrial expansion after 1973, and other policy measures undoubtedly contributed to the deconcentration process.

The very slow pace of deconcentration in the nontradeable sectors, however, indicates the relatively strong locational inertia in these sectors compared to the industrial sector. This was a reflection of the superior advantages of Seoul vis-à-vis other cities within the capital region. Seoul's share of office-type employment in the capital region declined by only 3.6 percent between 1970 and 1980, with Seoul retaining 91.2 percent of total office-type employment. In comparison, Seoul's share of total production-related jobs within the capital region dropped from 71.8 percent in 1970 to 60.2 percent in 1980. The government decentralization policy, therefore, had only limited success even at the intraregional scale. Furthermore, the importance of the service sector in Seoul's economy and the difficulties involved in steering service activities away from Seoul imply the unlikelihood of widespread decentralization of Seoul's office employment in the near future (W. Y. Kwon 1981; H. K. Kim 1985).

Urban Size Distribution

During the 1960s Seoul absorbed nearly 52 percent of total urban population growth and about 40 percent of total migration. The proportion of migrants heading toward Seoul of total migrants dropped to 29.5 percent during 1970–75 and to 25.2 percent during 1975–80 (Table 14.9). Other cities became increasingly important as alternative destinations for internal migration in the 1970s. The rapid growth of population in a number of intermediate-size cities (those with populations of between 100 and 500 thousand) helped to reduce the primacy of Seoul and stabilized the city size distribution (Table 14.10; Rondinelli 1985).

The fast-growing intermediate-size cities that doubled their population

Table 14.9. Intercensal migration by area: 1960–80 (10³ persons)

Period	1961–66	1965–70	1970–75	1975–80
In-migration to				
Seoul	675.3	1,182.3	1,053.2	1,232.2
	(46.8)	(37.1)	(29.5)	(25.2)
Pusan	187.2	308.7	376.3	537.9
	(13.0)	(9.7)	(10.5)	(11.0)
Other cities	225.5	1,023.4	1,328.3	2,168.9
	(15.6)	(32.1)	(37.2)	(44.4)
Rural	354.2	674.9	810.9	948.7
	(24.6)	(21.2)	(22.7)	(19.4)
Total	1,442.2	3,189.3	3,568.7	4,887.8
	(100.0)	(100.0)	(100.0)	(100.0)
Out-migration from				
Seoul	121.9	247.9	524.3	696.2
	(8.5)	(7.8)	(14.7)	(14.2)
Pusan	130.7	127.4	169.3	226.0
	(9.1)	(4.0)	(4.7)	(4.6)
Other cities	401.5	672.4	868.2	1,174.2
	(27.8)	(21.1)	(24.3)	(24.0)
Rural	788.2	2,141.6	2,006.9	2,791.4
	(54.7)	(67.1)	(56.2)	(57.1)
Total	1,442.2	3,189.3	3,568.7	4,887.8
	(100.0)	(100.0)	(100.0)	(100.0)

Source: EPB, ROK, *Population and Housing Census*, (1966, 1970, 1975, 1980).
Note: Percentage shares are shown in parentheses.

during the 1970s can be grouped into two types: satellite cities of Seoul enjoying spillover effects from the capital city, and newly industrializing cities that received disproportionate attention from the central government. The first type of city includes Suwon, Anyang, Puch'ŏn, Sŏngnam, and Ŭijŏngbu. P'ohang, Kumi, Ulsan, and Masan belong to the second category.

The economies of these two types of cities differ in some respects. The newly industrializing cities did not, on the whole, experience severe economic distress (measured by an aggregate unemployment rate), whereas the satellite cities of Seoul suffered from high unemployment rates (EPB, ROK, *Population and Housing Census*, 1960, 1970, 1980; MCT, ROK, 1984; EPB, ROK, *Special Labor Force Survey Report*, 1974). The high unemployment rates in the satellite cities of Seoul indicate a supply-induced growth, meaning population growth preceded employment growth. The newly industrializing cities suggest a demand-induced growth where employment growth precedes population growth (W. B. Kim 1985). However, the characteristic common to both type of cities is the large proportion of manufacturing

Table 14.10. City size distribution: 1960–80

Item	City size (10^3 persons)						Total
	Seoul	Over 1,000	500– 1,000	250– 500	100– 250	50– 100	
1960							
Number of cities	1	1	1	2	4	18	27
Population (10^3)	2,445	1,164	675	716	704	1,292	6,997
Percentage of total population	34.9	16.6	9.6	10.2	10.1	18.5	100.0
1970							
Number of cities	1	2	2	2	11	14	32
Population (10^3)	5,525	2,957	1,145	676	1,530	1,096	12,929
Percentage of total population	42.7	22.9	8.9	5.2	11.8	8.5	100.0
1980							
Number of cities	1	3	2	7	21	6	40
Population (10^3)	8,367	5,851	1,379	2,366	3,036	442	21,441
Percentage of total population	39.0	27.3	6.4	11.0	14.2	2.1	100.0
Average annual increase in population (%)							
1960–70	8.5	9.8	5.4	–0.6	8.1	–1.6	6.3
1970–80	4.2	7.1	1.9	13.3	7.1	–8.7	5.2

Source: EPB, ROK, *Population and Housing Census* (1960, 1970, 1980).

employment in their total employment compared with stagnating or slow-growing cities (EPB, ROK, *Population and Housing Census*, 1960, 1970, 1980; MCT, ROK, 1984; EPB, ROK, *Special Labor Force Survey Report*, 1974).

The rapid growth of the newly industrializing cities in the southeast coastal area appears to be directly related to the government's industrialization strategy that emphasized heavy and chemical industries and its concomitant efforts to accommodate key plants in industrial estates and complexes in those cities. In contrast, the stagnating or slow-growing cities are those that were for the most part not included in the central government's social overhead capital investment (K. S. Lee 1982).

CRITICISM AND LESSONS

Korean population redistribution policy in the 1970s was a limited success. Disparities in the level of development remain between the rural and urban areas and between regions. A degree of success, however, can be claimed for employment dispersal within the capital region. But the rapid expansion of population in the satellite cities of Seoul, which are in fact a part of Seoul's economy, resulted in regionwide negative externalities such as congestion, pollution, and higher unemployment, and an increasing demand for regionwide urban services (T. J. Kwon 1983; H .K. Kim 1984; W. B. Kim 1985).

Selective urban growth, for which national economic and sectoral policies are primarily responsible, helped to reduce urban primacy and to stabilize city size distribution in Korea. The rapid growth of intermediate-size cities during the 1970s implies that these cities will have an increasing role in future urban growth (Rondinelli 1985). The relatively weakened role of small-size cities, however, resulting from the underdevelopment of the rural sector, implies that there will be difficulties in integrating the rural economy with the urban economy in the future. A rethinking of the spatial development strategy seems to be necessary for balanced national development.

The selection of manufacturing activities as a key to population distribution policy in Korea seems justifiable. The manufacturing sector, with its rapid growth, provided room for decentralization. However, theoretical justifications such as the higher multiplier effects of manufacturing and locational flexibility are dubious in the Korean case. Heavy and chemical industries are not freely located anywhere. Their location is constrained by site requirements such as good port facilities, transportation convenience, and access to raw materials. Once the investments for heavy and chemical industries are made in particular locations, the locational flexibility of these industries are greatly reduced because of their heavy fixed capital investment. The importance attributed to the multiplier effects of manufacturing activities in a local economy was not warranted (A. J. Kim 1978).

Considering the declining capacity of the industrial sector to generate employment in the future (the manufacturing sector is moving toward a more capital-intensive and skill-intensive structure in Korea), the government's past and current emphasis on industrial decentralization as a key for population redistribution must be modified. The growing importance of the service sector and related office activities should be recognized. Decentralization of business and industrial service activities that are indispensable for manufacturing activities must be considered together with manufacturing decentralization (Clapp and Richardson 1984). However, the dispersal of business and industrial service activities will require much more effort than did dispersal of the manufacturing sector. A narrowly conceived strategy depending heavily on controls and meager incentives, would not succeed in steering those service activities to local areas. Building roads and factories alone will not be enough. Human capital investment is a basic prerequisite for successful dispersion of the business and industrial service activities. In this respect, policy options emphasizing labor (i.e., labor training and labor subsidy schemes) deserve more attention than those encouraging capital movement, which has been the dominant policy approach in Korea and elsewhere (Allen 1979; Townroe 1979).

Policy measures taken in the 1970s in Korea were largely controls. Incentives were not strong enough to bring about the desired level of population dispersal. Controls and regulations have the obvious advantage of a low budgetary cost to the government. However, these controls might incur heavy real costs or unintended side effects, such as the rise in operating costs of the firms relocated to peripheral locations (Choe and Song 1982) and the soaring land prices after the imposition of a greenbelt around Seoul (Mills 1980).

The considerable evidence presented in this chapter suggests that national economic and sectoral policies have had the paramount effect on the urbanization process and spatial transformation in Korea, often overriding the impact of explicit spatial policies. Unfortunately, population redistribution policy in Korea in the 1970s was not integrated with national economic and sectoral policies. An integration and interaction between national economic and sectoral polices, on the one hand, and explicit population distribution polices, on the other hand, has been emphasized for a successful population distribution policy (Renaud 1981; Richardson 1981; Fuchs 1983). This integration can be achieved at the various levels of policy design, evaluation, and implementation. For example, formal requirements can be made within the national government to take account of the spatial effects of some of their sectoral programs that have potentially strong consequences on the distribution of population. Or, the population distribution goal can be added as a constraint in a conventional policy evaluation. At the same time, the impact of explicit spatial policies on national aggregates such as GNP, employment, and income, needs to be estimated to understand the trade-offs between national economic growth and spatial equality. At the level of policy design, for example, the currently separated packages of industrial and locational incentives in a number of Asian countries (Shome and Kee 1977) can be modified into a unified system of incentives differentiated by industry and location.

Frequent changes in policy directions or vacillating commitment to them would be destructive. A consistent policy is essential for both firms and individuals to be convinced that opportunities outside the core region are real and reliable. A firm political commitment also means substantial government investments and concrete development projects. Symbolic gestures and empty rhetoric harm the credibility of the government policies. A policy dependent upon controls focusing on the core region would not solve the problem of concentration. Instead, it would delay or transfer the problem in time and in space because that kind of policy cannot improve the development potential of the periphery, whether it is a rural area or lagging region. To help industrialists and individuals in making their business and residential location choices, the government should develop and publicize a detailed investment schedule for alternative locations outside the core region.

The conceptual separation of the urban sector from the rural sector was an important policy deficiency in Korean population redistribution efforts. Urban policies cannot be formulated and implemented separately from rural policies. The rural-to-urban migration that has been the major force driving rapid urban growth is one indication of the rural–urban linkage. Without simultaneous attention to the urban and rural dimensions of the population concentration problem, any policy would be ineffective. This seems particularly true for nations at the early stage of development with a low level of urbanization. The recently proposed concept of "integrated regional settlement areas" in the Second National Land Development Plan in Korea appears to be appropriate for the consideration of urban and rural sectors as a whole in policy formulation. The concept still views the problem of population distribution from an urban perspective, however, anticipating that "spread effects" will flow outward from the city to the hinterland. Considering the dubious evidence for such a phenomenon in Korea (A. J. Kim 1978) and elsewhere (Salih et al. 1978; Hansen 1981), population redistribution policy should give greater emphasis to rural development so that an increased demand from rural areas for urban goods would enable those small cities and local centers to survive. Without entailing necessary considerations for rural development, a less coordinated strategy of urban development would not guarantee a reduction in the imbalances between rural and urban areas and between different regions.

AGRICULTURAL POLICIES

15 A Positive Grain-Price Policy (1969) and Agricultural Development

by Pal Yong Moon

Until the early 1960s, Korea remained a typical preindustrial country with almost half of its GNP generated by agriculture and the overwhelming portion of its population engaged in farming. But the vigorous industrialization and export drive undertaken in the early 1960s rapidly transformed the agrarian character of the economy. Between 1960 and 1982 the share of agriculture in GNP declined from about 37 percent to 14 percent, and the proportion of rural population declined from 58 percent to less than 25 percent. Expansion in the nonagricultural sector has proceeded far more rapidly than in the agricultural sector. While total GNP expanded at an average annual rate of about 8 percent, the agricultural sector grew at an average of about 3 percent.

Agriculture's declining contribution and slow growth relative to the nonagricultural sector was not, however, the result of unusually poor performance. In fact, Korea's agricultural performance since the early 1960s has exceeded the world average and that of most Asian countries. Korea is probably one of the highest ranking countries in land productivity. Rice yields, for example, were more than double those of most Southeast Asian countries. One of the main reasons for this high land productivity is that Korea had an adequate supply of farm workers relative to its scarce land resources. Korea's land endowment—acreage of cultivatable land per person—is probably one of the smallest in the world.

It is also important to note that the declining contribution of agriculture to overall economic growth is not due to the farmers' failure to respond to various stimuli but rather is basically a result of unfavorable factor endowments. Given the poor land resources and the limited substitutability of capital and labor, it was inevitable that the growth of agriculture would lag behind other sectors.

Despite a declining contribution of agriculture to overall economic growth, the interaction between agricultural and other economic sectors has had important implications for rapid industrialization. The growth of industry has provided increased employment opportunities outside agriculture, thus preventing further fragmentation of existing small-scale farms.[1]

---

1. One estimate indicates that if the population that shifted into the nonagricultural sectors had remained on the farm, the rural areas of Korea would have become much more crowded, and the average farm size by the early 1980s would have been reduced to around 0.5–0.6 hectares—half the current size. The result would certainly have aggravated the difficulty inherent in the marginality of Korean agriculture, because nearly all the problems in the rural sector have their origins in the marginal scale of farming.

Large increases in foreign exchange earnings, mainly from the export of industrial products, made it possible to build fertilizer plants and farm machinery plants as well as to import the requisite technical expertise. The improved foreign exchange earnings also enhanced the nation's ability to obtain more foreign loans to finance various rural development projects for irrigation or other rural infrastructure. Rapid urbanization and industrialization have created a substantial shift in urban consumption patterns toward higher quality foods, which has provided a great incentive for farmers to expand the cultivation of cash crops, instead of concentrating on such mono-grain crops as rice and barley. Thus, Korea's industrialization, urbanization, and export policies have all contributed to the growth of agricultural productivity.

This is not to say, however, that agriculture simply remained as a major beneficiary of industrialization. Instead, it assumed an increasingly important role throughout the process of industrialization. Agriculture continued to provide the main source of income for the rural population and food for the growing and increasingly affluent urban and industrial population. Growing rural demand for farm inputs and consumer goods provided a key stimulus for the expansion of the manufacturing and service industries. Investment in the education of the young rural population, many of whom subsequently migrated to the cities, represents another significant role of agriculture in the process of economic growth. The government policy of maintaining low agricultural prices in the 1950s and 1960s, combined with the massive transfer of surplus farm labor, contributed to keeping urban wages at a relatively low level thereby benefiting the expanding industrial sector.

American grain made available after 1955 under U.S. Public Law 480 provided one of the major props that enabled the Korean government to pursue a low-price policy for staple food grains. The acquisition of grain, excluding rice, for government use became relatively easy under this new aid source. The U.S. farm products imported under this program were wheat, barley, raw cotton, corn, milo, and tallow—of which wheat and barley accounted for about 50 to 60 percent of the total value of imports. The quantity of grain imported was, on the average, equivalent to 8–12 percent of annual domestic grain production during the 1956–65 period. The availability of large quantities of aid grain from the United States that could be purchased with local currency made it possible for Korea to attain more or less balanced food-grain supplies without draining the country's foreign exchange. Although the significant contribution of PL 480 grains to general economic stability has been widely recognized, the availability of aid grain undoubtedly had negative effects on domestic grain production resulting from lower market prices for grain. Another possibility is that the easy availability of free grain may have induced food administrators to overestimate grain shortages, thus creating a disincentive in their attempts to increase domestic production by means of price incentives.

As the economy entered the 1960s and was gradually rehabilitated from its war-wrecked state, there was a strong tendency among policymakers to identify economic growth with industrialization. In both the First Five-Year Economic Development Plan (1962–66) and the Second Plan (1967–71), the major objective was rapid industrial growth. This industry-oriented strategy necessarily required massive investment resources in the non-agricultural sector. It is a widely accepted notion that savings in the rural sector, whether created by voluntary savings of farm surplus or derived through such compulsory measures as land taxes, provide essential sources of investment financing in the initial stage of industrialization.[2] This hardly seems to have been the case in Korea, for there is little evidence that the agricultural sector provided sizeable financial resources for investment in the nonagricultural sectors during the 1950s and 1960s.[3]

Agricultural price policy was a different story. The government's major efforts were directed toward maintaining low prices for staple food grains and preventing wide seasonal price fluctuations, rather than maintaining adequate prices to support farm incomes. Government purchase prices were below market prices in almost every year. Although the rationale for low food prices for urban workers was based on the principle of equitable income distribution, it served primarily to increase industrial profits and capital formation at the expense of farm producers. When the supply of labor was highly elastic, with rural areas overpopulated in the early stages of industrialization, low food prices helped reduce the cost of living in urban areas and made it possible to maintain industrial wages at a level lower than would otherwise have been possible.

The long-lasting adverse terms of trade for farm producers due to the low-price policy further impoverished the already poor rural economy. It also hindered efforts to increase food production and at the same time stimulated rice consumption, resulting in a widening food gap. As long as a large portion of the food grain shortage could be met by local-currency purchases under the U.S. PL 480 program, the food gap itself did not impose a serious burden on the country's foreign exchange position. But once

---

2. In Japan, for example, heavy taxation on farmland served as one of the important transfer mechanisms through which the agricultural sector provided investment resources for the nonagricultural sectors (Hayami 1975:365). In Taiwan, increases in agricultural productivity and the resultant farm surpluses were important sources of investment financing that accelerated the process of industrialization (Hsieh and Lee 1966:2–3).

3. To begin with, there was not much farm surplus in the form of rural savings. Second, the political atmosphere in Korea after World War II was such that it did not permit heavy taxation of the rural sector. In the 1950s farmers in general had a negative cash flow. In the 1960s farmers were able to save a portion of their income, but relatively little of their savings went into the nonagricultural sector. Beginning in the 1970s, Korean farmers achieved substantial cash savings, but varied evidence indicates that most farm savings remained on the farm in the form of farm equipment purchases, housing improvements, and the like. Moreover, the government financial policy was not executed in such a way as to transfer substantial sums of money out of agriculture to other sectors.

the U.S. policy shifted in the late 1960s to cash or credit sales in U.S. dollars, the food grain situation became directly related to the balance-of-payment position.

Faced with the increasing food shortage, the resultant foreign exchange constraints and, at the same time, the growing income disparity between urban and rural households, policymakers were obliged to give serious consideration to expanding food-grain production and to a more equitable income distribution between the agricultural and nonagricultural sectors. In particular, the world food crisis in the early 1970s and soaring grain prices in the world market made it almost inevitable that the government would shift the emphasis in its development strategy toward agriculture. Against this background, the government began in the late 1960s to turn its attention to agriculture, taking the initiative to improve the terms of trade for agricultural products and, at the same time, effecting a two-price system for rice and barley. The level of government investment in the agricultural sector was also substantially increased.

GRAIN-PRICE POLICY

Grain Procurement and Distribution

The combined grain management programs are among the largest nondefense activities of the Korean government. The wide range of government grain programs in Korea reflects a situation of chronic grain deficits in a country where the population is largely dependent on a cereal diet and the belief that direct government action in grain procurement and distribution is necessary to maintain economic stability and ensure a steady flow of grain supplies to consumers. It is also consistent with the belief that it is the government's obligation to provide sufficient supplies of grain to feed the people.

Administration of the grain management programs is the responsibility of the Food Administration Bureau of the Ministry of Agriculture and Fisheries (MAF). The Food Bureau formulates and implements food policies and programs at the national level. There is a Food Division in each provincial and special city government to handle food programs at those levels. Each county (gun) has a Food Administration Section that administers its food programs.

Financial matters are handled by the National Agricultural Cooperatives Federation (NACF), as agent for the Food Bureau. NACF, through its city and county branches and unit cooperatives, disburses funds to pay for grain purchased from farmers. The Agricultural Inspection Office, with provincial, city, and county branches, is in charge of inspecting and grading all grain received from farmers.

The government acquires rice from farmers through various programs at prices set by the government during or after the harvest season. The major acquisition programs include: (1) direct purchase, (2) rice–fertilizer barter, and (3) collection of harvest taxes in kind. Almost all of the rice procured is acquired through direct purchases (Table 15.1). Grains are purchased at government purchasing stations at various localities.

The barter of fertilizer for rice has been the second largest source of government rice supplies. Under that program, farmers obtain fertilizer from NACF by paying the cash equivalent of 40 to 50 percent of the fertilizer cost; the remaining cost is paid by rice delivered after the harvest. Since the government sells fertilizer at a heavily subsidized price, farmers found it more advantageous to purchase fertilizer with cash rather than in exchange for fixed quantities of rice. The rice–fertilizer barter program was discontinued in 1977.

Farmers producing rice crops can pay their land tax in kind or in cash. The average rate is about 6 percent of the harvest. If the total output of the crop is less than 1.4 metric tons, no tax is levied. This exemption applies to about two-thirds of the farmers in Korea.

Table 15.1. Government acquisition of domestic rice and barley: Rice years 1960–82 (10^3 metric tons, polished)

	Rice				Barley
Rice year	Total rice	Direct purchase	Fertilizer barter	Land tax	Direct purchase
1965	183	66	23	94	76
1966	297	58	150	89	152
1967	336	77	155	104	89
1968	286	107	114	64	114
1969	153	21	78	54	203
1970	326	162	101	63	239
1971	346	244	70	32	173
1972	507	405	68	34	382
1973	507	439	35	33	370
1974	480	407	32	41	414
1975	735	657	23	55	520
1976	784	673	42	69	571
1977	1,043	871	81	91	189
1978	1,404	1,316	0	88	485
1979	1,355	1,261	0	94	577
1980	1,301	1,212	0	89	481
1981	546	465	0	81	407
1982	915	840	0	75	415

Source: MAF, ROK, *Agriculture and Fisheries Statistics Yearbook* (1965–82).

Note: The rice year begins with November of the preceding calendar year and extends through October—e.g., rice year 1982 lasts from November 1981 through October 1982.

In addition to the above three programs, the government implemented the rice-lien program which, though not precisely a part of the government acquisition program, was nonetheless an important part of Korean grain policy. That program was analogous in principle to the nonrecourse price-support loans made by the Commodity Credit Corporation in the United States. The government was authorized to provide nonrecourse loans and required to buy rice used as security for the loans whenever the borrowers wished. The program was initiated as one of the measures to prevent a sharp decline in the price of rice during the harvest season. The loan rate ranged from 65 to 90 percent of the government-determined purchase prices. The program was considered quite successful in that it enabled farmers to borrow money on rice after harvest and redeem or sell it later when the price was seasonally higher. With the expanding scale of government direct purchases, the program was discontinued in 1974.

The principal supply programs are for: (1) military use, (2) government institutions, (3) prisoners and detainees, (4) relief, (5) seed grain distribution, (6) grain loans, (7) grain exchange, (8) price stabilization, and (9) contingency or emergency programs. The purpose of "price stabilization" sale of grain is to even out or at least moderate seasonal price fluctuations. Initially the major function of the government grain operation was to supply the armed forces and government institutions, but with the expansion of the operation's scale, the emphasis shifted to stabilizing seasonal grain prices through sales to the grain market.

Grain Pricing

The most important decisions in government grain policy are determination of the amount of grain to be purchased and determination of the price to be paid to farm producers. In both cases, the MAF is responsible for preparing a proposal, which it submits to the five-member Economic Ministers Council for formal approval. In the past, approval was required also from the National Assembly, but since the 1972 "Yushin revolution" this procedure has been discontinued.

In determining purchase prices for grain, a number of formulas can be applied, including: (1) cost of production criteria, (2) price parity ratio, (3) income parity ratio, and (4) international market prices. No one of these formulas or criteria has been used as a single, standard basis for determining government purchase prices for rice and barley. Instead, purchase prices estimated on the basis of these formulas are used as references only. In other words, the method of determining government purchase prices for rice and barley has varied from year to year depending on the prevailing external and internal economic conditions. But in fact, the assessment of overall economic conditions to be reflected in determining purchase prices is largely a matter of judgment and depends much on the viewpoint of the one who makes it.

In the absence of an objective standard formula, therefore, the different government agencies concerned tend to have different opinions on the level of purchase prices that should be paid to farmers. For example, the MAF is tempted to set the purchase price as high as possible with a view to enhancing farm incomes and domestic production of grain, whereas the Economic Planning Board (EPB), whose main concern is to stabilize general price levels, wants to set the price as low as possible. The resistance of the Ministry of Finance is another restraint against higher purchase prices. These differences in viewpoint among agencies—often called the "interministerial purchase price war"—cause a delay almost every year in final determination of purchase prices, resulting in delayed purchases to the detriment of farm producers. Table 15.2 presents the information referred to in determining rice purchase prices and the final prices for selected years.

Two-Price Policy

Widening negative price differentials. Korea's food-grain price policy has tried to achieve a multitude of objectives, many of which are in conflict. The determination of the purchase and selling prices of Korean rice has been closely intertwined with a number of objectives and constraints in the overall development strategy.[4]

Of the many conceivable objectives of the government's agricultural policy, the following six are regarded as having direct relevance in determining price levels:

- reducing foreign exchange expenditures on grain imports;
- stabilizing the general price level;
- reducing government expenditures on its grain operations;
- enhancing farm income;
- increasing incentives for farm producers; and
- improving urban consumer welfare.

Determining which objective should be given the highest priority depends on policymakers' preferences, which may be governed in turn by their perceptions of political, social, and economic conditions. If the government attempts to minimize foreign exchange expenditures on grain imports, both purchase and selling prices must be maintained at a relatively high level to keep aggregate demand and supply in balance with reduced imports. The resulting high prices of grain contribute to high farm income as well

---

4. In a linear programming framework, objectives and constraints are two different concepts. From a policy point of view, however, factors can be viewed as either objectives or constraints. For instance, foreign exchange expenditure on food grain imports can be classified as an objective if the government attempts to reduce spending through policy intervention, or it can be treated as a constraint if the government imposes a certain limit within which a food grain program must be operated.

Table 15.2. Determination procedures of rice purchase price: Selected years, 1965–80 (won/80 kg bag)

Crop year	Information referred to (won)		Criteria adopted (won)		Purchase price (won)	Rate of increase (%)
1965	Agricultural parity ratio (1960=100)	2,987	International price	3,000	3,150	4.9
	Production cost	2,325	Incentive bonus	150		
	International price	3,000				
1970	Agricultural parity ratio (1965=100)	5,881	Agricultural parity ratio	5,881	7,000	35.9
	1965–69 increases in:		Incentive bonus	1,119		
	WPI	5,562				
	CPI	5,738				
	PPFI	5,881				
	Rice farm price	5,675				
1975	Agricultural parity ratio (1975=100)	18,350	Increases in:		19,500	23.7
	1974–75 increase in:		Agricultural parity ratio	18,350		
	Price of nonfood items	17,646	Incentive bonus	1,150		
	WPI	18,329				
	PPFI	17,998				
	Agricultural supply prices	17,982				

	1980	Increase in wholesale price of rice
		45,750
		25.0
Agricultural parity ratio (1977=100)	51,399	
Increase in GNP deflator (1977/1978)	44,100	
1979–80 increase in:		
WPI	49,739	
CPI	47,617	
Wholesale price of rice	45,750	
Production cost	43,920	

Source: Data obtained from Food Bureau, MAF, ROK.

PPFI—Index of prices paid by farmers.

as to high domestic production, but the same prices exert upward pressure on the general price level and raise costs to consumers.

A two-price system for rice and barley—a higher price for farmers and a lower price for urban consumers—was an attempt to resolve this dilemma. The two-price system for barley went into effect beginning with the 1969 summer crop, and for rice beginning in the fall of 1969.

Until 1968 the selling prices for rice were determined by adding intermediate handling costs to the original acquisition prices, resulting in no financial loss due to price differentials. Beginning with the 1969 crop, the selling prices (with the 1971 crop as the sole exception) have been below the costs of acquisition and intermediate handling (Table 15.3). After 1973 the difference between the purchase and selling prices continued to widen, and the government lost 20–35 percent on each bag sold.

In the case of barley, the price differences were even wider (Table 15.4). Government efforts to keep barley selling prices low were motivated by a desire to encourage consumers to substitute barley for rice in their diet. Prior to 1968 the market barley price was maintained at about 65 percent of the rice price. But with the increasing subsidy for barley prices after 1969, the price of barley for urban consumers has been about 50 percent or less than the price of rice.

Deficit in grain operation and inflationary financing. The implementation of the two-price policy caused the costs for the government's grain operations to increase at an accelerating pace. The total accumulated loss incurred by the government in the operation of the Grain Management Fund (GMF) from 1970 to 1982 amounted to 1,235 billion won. The loss due to the price

Table 15.3. Government purchase price versus selling price for rice: Selected years, 1960–82 (won/80 kg bag)

Year	Purchase price (A)	Handling cost (B)	Government's total cost (C = A + B)	Selling price (D)	Government gain or loss (%) [(D−C)/D]
1960	1,059	157	1,216	1,216	0
1964	2,967	346	3,313	3,450	4
1970	7,000	664	7,664	6,500	−18
1971	8,750	738	9,488	9,500	*
1973	11,372	915	12,287	11,264	−9
1974	15,760	1,488	17,248	13,000	−33
1979	36,600	7,126	43,726	32,000	−37
1982	55,970	9,358	65,328	52,280	−25

Source: Data obtained from Food Bureau, MAF, ROK.
* Less than 1 percent.

Table 15.4. Government purchase price versus selling price for barley: Selected years, 1969–82 (won/76.5 kg bag)

Year	Purchase price (A)	Handling cost (B)	Government's total cost (C = A + B)	Selling price (D)	Government gain or loss (%) [(D−C)/D]
1969	3,348	439	3,787	2,750	−38
1970	3,850	548	4,398	3,100	−42
1973	6,993	909	7,902	6,000	−32
1974	6,091	1,412	7,503	8,320	10
1979	22,000	9,618	31,618	10,120	−212
1982	33,780	9,473	43,253	28,000	−54

Source: MAF, ROK, *Agriculture and Fisheries Statistics Yearbook* (1969–82).

subsidy for rice alone represented 48.4 percent of the total (598 billion won); for barley, 44 percent (544 billion won). The loss due to the flour price subsidy during the 1972–76 period, when international wheat prices soared, was 10.4 percent (128 billion won) (Food Bureau, MAF, ROK, unpublished data).

To break down the GMF loss by source of expenditure, 25 percent (305 billion won) of the total loss is attributable to the negative price differentials, whereas 75 percent (930 billion won) resulted from operation and management costs, including interest payments on the borrowed funds. The interest payments on both the long-term borrowings from the Bank of Korea and the Grain Bonds issued represent 50 percent (494 billion won) of the total operating and management costs (Food Bureau, MAF, ROK, unpublished data).

Increasing government intervention in the grain market. The grain market in Korea is characterized today by a dualistic system, combining free-market transactions and government control, although the degree of government control has varied from year to year. The Grain Management Law of 1950 gave the government legal authority for complete regulation of the grain market whenever the government considered it necessary. The purpose of the law was to enable the government to secure sufficient grain from farmers, allowing it to stabilize the national economy by exercising control over grain distribution and consumption through manipulation of government stocks. In 1963 and 1967 the main provisions of the law were reaffirmed and additional authority was given to the government, but the basic direction remained the same. Free-market grain transactions exist only by government sufferance. The government has the authority to import or export grain and can give orders to grain dealers, shippers, and processors, and to hotels and restaurants whenever deemed necessary.

The government directly conducts the procurement, transport, storage, milling, and sale of government-controlled grain. In the early years, the government acquisition program was mainly concerned with rice, but more recently the share of barley has substantially expanded. Whenever the government could not secure sufficient domestic grain, the gap was filled by imports. During the 1950s the market share of government rice was less than 10 percent, but by 1982 had expanded to nearly 50 percent. The government handled almost 90 percent of the barley marketed in 1982.

The primary function of the government grain program during the 1950s was to secure an adequate supply of grain for the armed forces, government institutions (such as the police force and public hospitals), and for other ministries for relief and work programs. Whether intentionally or unintentionally, this procurement action had the effect of providing support for prices at harvest time when grain prices normally fell.

In the 1960s the government expanded the scale of its grain operations through increased purchases from farmers. In addition to the original function of supplying grain for institutional uses, the government began to put emphasis on seasonal price stabilization through direct sales in the market during the nonharvest season, when prices normally rise. These direct sales for seasonal price stabilization accounted for almost 80 percent of the total government grain supply by 1982, reflecting the shift in the government's main concern toward dampening seasonal rises in grain prices. In recent years there has been much criticism of the increasing share of government operations in the grain market and the way in which the government operates the grain program to de-seasonalize rice prices throughout the year.

OTHER AGRICULTURAL POLICIES

Land and Water Resource Development

The development of agricultural water resources has been one of the most intensive projects undertaken since the beginning of the Second Five-Year Development Plan (1967–71). During that period the government emphasized small-scale irrigation projects, such as the construction of small-scale dams, pumping stations, tubewell irrigation, and weirs. But the Third Five-Year Development Plan shifted the emphasis to larger-scale, integrated regional development projects.

The integrated plan for developing the four major river basins that was set out in 1971 included the construction of 13 dams and electric power plants. In addition, afforestation and erosion-control projects on watershed areas of the Han, Kum, Nakdong, and Yongsan Rivers were also undertaken. Projects for developing multipurpose, large-scale farming areas were completed in the Kum River and Pyongtaek Basins, where reservoirs, tidal dikes, water-pumping and draining plants, and canals were constructed. The two tidal dikes completed at Asan and Namyang Bays in 1974 were the biggest water resource development projects in Korean history.

Completion of these projects brought 11,000 hectares (27,200 acres) of land reclaimed from the seabed under cultivation and also irrigated 16,000 hectares (39,500 acres) of existing farmland. Paddy field consolidation projects, initiated in the mid-1960s, continued to be promoted under public financial subsidy with a view to facilitating farm mechanization and increasing farming efficiency. By 1982 the total area of paddy fields rearranged under this program amounted to 400,000 hectares (988,000 acres), or approximately 33 percent of Korea's total paddy lands.

Farm Mechanization

Stimulated by rapid changes in rural conditions, in particular the steady outflow of rural workers coupled with rising rural wages, the government initiated various supportive measures designed to facilitate the introduction of labor-saving farm equipment. As a result, the quantity and variety of farm machinery in use in Korea has increased sharply in recent years.

The government began in 1979 to provide loans for the purchase of mechanized field equipment such as tractors, transplanters, harvesters, and combines. Although this equipment is still in an early stage of diffusion, the numbers are expected to increase rapidly in the years to come (Table 15.5). The levels of farm mechanization attained thus far, however, are not yet high enough to offset the effects of the rural labor shortage to a

Table 15.5. Farm machinery in use: Selected years, 1965–82

Item	1965	1970	1975	1980	1982
Power tiller					
Number (10^3)	1.1	11.8	85.7	289.8	422.0
Farms per machine		206.9	27.8	7.4	4.7
Power sprayer and duster					
Number (10^3)	7.6	45.0	137.7	330.6	403.7
Farms per machine		55.2	17.3	6.5	4.9
Transplanter					
Number (10^3)	0	0	0	11.1	19.7
Farms per machine				194.1	101.3
Harvester					
Number (10^3)	0	0	0	13.7	17.3
Farms per machine				157.3	115.4
Tractor					
Number (10^3)	0	0	0.7	2.7	5.6
Farms per machine					
Combines					
Number (10^3)	0	0	0	1.2	3.5
Farms per machine					

Source: MAF, ROK, *Agriculture and Fisheries Statistics Yearbook* (1965–82).

satisfactory extent. This is because the utilization as well as diffusion of farm machinery has been impeded by the prevailing small-scale, fragmented farming operations and by a lack of adequate physical and economic conditions for mechanization.

Agricultural Credit Policy

A major part of the institutional basis for agricultural credit in Korea was consolidated during the 1960s. Major developments in the agricultural credit field since the early 1970s include the growth of mutual financing through agricultural cooperatives, the strengthening of cooperative lending functions based on the cooperatives' enhanced ability to raise funds on their own, and increased provisions for medium- and long-term development loans.

Mutual financing through basic cooperatives refers to savings and loan arrangements made by economically weak farmers to promote mutual financial help for cooperative members trying to overcome their fund shortages. This mutual financing system was put into practice as part of a program to strengthen the ability of basic cooperatives to become self-funded in conjunction with the enactment of the Credit Union Law in August 1970. The mutual financing system is an extension of traditional cooperative financing practices. It is aimed at pooling small sums of idle funds in rural communities and private capital hitherto used for usurious lending operations. The pool is then utilized for farming loans, thereby facilitating the efforts of basic cooperatives to become financially self-supporting by building up their own financial resources, instead of depending on government help.

To keep pace with the expansion of the physical volume of agricultural credit, institutional improvements have continued in the rural credit system. Such institutional changes include the implementation of a creditworthiness guarantee system for farmers and fishermen that is designed to supplement the limited ability of economically weak farmers and fishermen to provide collateral for their loans. This system was put into effect in 1972 under the Law on Guaranteeing Credit-worthiness of Farmers and Fishermen. NACF administers these funds.

Another major change in the agricultural credit system was the introduction of a farmland mortgage system. The land reform of 1950 made it virtually impossible to mortgage agricultural land, causing confusion and difficulty in the rural credit system for some time. The farmland mortgage system was put into effect in 1970. Farmland may be mortgaged only when the farmer-owner wants to obtain a loan. No one other than an agricultural or fisheries cooperative is authorized to be a mortgagee, and charging advance payments of interest or compound interest on the mortgage loan is prohibited.

In the early 1970s a group lending system was instituted with the aim of improving loans to individual farmers. The new system was designed to make loans to productive organizations, such as crop cultivation teams and farm complexes, with the aim of linking the production and marketing of farm products to agricultural credit. Also, a system of advance announcement of credit availability was put into force, and lending procedures were substantially simplified.

Fertilizer Price Policy

With limited land resources, increasing land productivity is the only means of increasing aggregate farm output. A high rate of fertilizer application is part of the answer. Throughout the 1960s and 1970s, the government made substantial efforts to increase fertilizer use through provision of price subsidies and purchase credits and by means of the rice–fertilizer barter program. As a result, fertilizer consumption in nutrient terms more than doubled during the 1965–80 period, increasing from 393,000 metric tons in 1965 to 800,000 metric tons in 1980, marking an annual average growth rate of 6 percent.

This rapid increase in fertilizer consumption led to the construction of a series of large-scale fertilizer plants. By 1970 the country had not only achieved self-sufficiency in fertilizer supply but was also exporting surplus fertilizer. In 1972 average annual production reached 1,200,000 metric tons of nutrient, exceeding the annual domestic requirement by 400,000 metric tons.

In spite of the surplus produced, the prices paid by farmers, even after subsidizing, are higher than those in the world market. The subsidized price of nitrogen fertilizer is almost double the world market price, and prices of phosphate and potash fertilizers are about 20 percent higher. Such high pricing for domestically produced fertilizer is mainly attributable to the unfavorable terms that were imposed at the time of joint ventures with foreign enterprises in constructing the fertilizer plants. For instance, the Korean government is obliged to procure the entire amount of fertilizer produced at guaranteed profit rates ranging from 15 to 20 percent.

The cumulative deficit in the fertilizer account due to the price subsidy during the 1966–82 period was 570 billion won. If the procurement price actually paid to Hankuk Fertilizer Company were applied to other manufacturers uniformly, 47 percent of the total deficit would accrue to the subsidy for manufacturers and the remaining 53 percent to the subsidy for farmers. If the world price were used as a benchmark price, most of the deficit would accrue to the subsidy for the fertilizer industry.

An interesting study to determine which sector—the fertilizer industry or the farmers—actually benefits from the current fertilizer price policy, estimated the protection rate on the basis of world prices (D. S. Lee 1983). According to the estimates for the 1976–82 period, the protection rate for the Korean fertilizer industry was 68 percent, whereas that for Korean farmers was –18 percent. In the case of urea, the protection rate for the fertilizer industry was 61 percent, but was −51 percent for Korean farmers. These results indicate that the fertilizer industry has benefited from the government price subsidy program. Korean farmers, however, have paid high fertilizer consumption taxes; therefore, it can hardly be said that the Korean fertilizer subsidy program has been implemented in a manner that protects the agricultural sector.

THEORETICAL APPROPRIATENESS OF THE POLICY

Roles Played by Agricultural Prices in Industrialization

Much of the literature on economic development views agricultural development as a precondition for industrialization in the early stages of development. For example, Kuznets (1961) argues that a rise in productivity per worker in agriculture is a precondition of the industrial revolution in any part of the world. Bairoch (1964) also emphasizes that increases in agricultural productivity and growth in demand for agricultural inputs supplied by industry are major forces that give impetus to the process of cumulative economic growth. Since agriculture is by far the largest sector in a traditional economy, it is often assumed that the rural sector not only constitutes a source of capital and labor for industry but also provides the major source of demand for industrial output as well as supplies of industrial raw materials.

Among the various aspects of the interaction between agriculture and other economic sectors, agricultural prices have played one of the most significant roles throughout the process of industrialization. Historically, as part of development policy, agricultural price policy has generally been used negatively. In other words, the terms of trade of agriculture are deliberately depressed with a view to maintaining food prices at a low level and hence sustaining low levels of industrial wages that would otherwise cut into investment in the nonfarm sectors.

The standard explanation of the depressing effect on industrial investment from rising agricultural prices can be traced to Adam Smith and later to W. Arthur Lewis and the basic argument of food as a wage good. Interpreted in terms of price, rising food prices cause upward pressure on money wages, and this in turn causes a squeeze on industrial profits, thereby reducing the incentive and ability to invest by reducing the profits that serve as a major source of investment funds.

A low agricultural price policy has been a common feature of economic policy in the early phases of development in both capitalist and socialist countries, although the institutional mechanisms used in implementation have differed. A variety of evidence to illustrate this effect can be cited from the experiences in the early stages of development of the developed countries.

In the United Kingdom, the whole free-trade movement that came to repeal the Corn Laws in the nineteenth century had the aim of lowering the price of food and raw materials relative to the price of manufactured goods (Tracy 1964). In Russia, the collectivization of agriculture was theoretically endorsed by Lenin and carried out in practice by Stalin to squeeze from the peasantry their whole surplus production at a zero or low price (Kahan 1964). The Japanese story is another illustration. During the early period of economic development, the terms of trade of agriculture were deliberately kept low, and, in addition, agriculture was taxed heavily to finance industrial expansion. The land tax provided about 70 percent of public revenue during the period 1878–1907 and 40 percent during 1908–17. Rents remained at more than half of the rice yield in the earlier period (Okawa and Rosovsky 1960).

In Korea, too, the government's primary efforts were centered on maintaining low prices for food, particularly rice. Because of the role of rice as a wage good, a rise in rice prices was believed to be one of the major causes of an increase in the general price level. Thus, cheap grain played an important role in the early stages of industrialization during the 1950s and 1960s, especially when labor-intensive light industries such as textiles and handicrafts predominated, particularly in the export manufacturing sector.

The process of industrialization cannot rely, however, on a continuous squeeze on agriculture. There is some critical minimum rate of agricultural growth, high or low, without which development efforts will not be able to achieve their general targets, because of the initial dominance of agriculture in income generation, employment, and exports, and because of the dynamic complementarity of agricultural growth and general economic growth. A variety of evidence shows that in many developing countries the minimum rate of agricultural growth consistent with rapid and sustained general growth is quite high and that a continuous negative price policy designed to achieve the goal of industrialization will have a negative effect upon industrialization itself.

There are a number of reasons why a negative agricultural price policy and a stagnant, slow-growing agricultural sector seriously constrain the general rate of growth. First, the rapid increase in population creates an added demand for food that cannot be met under conditions of stagnation or even slow growth. Second, a negative price policy has naturally created disincentives for the increase of farm output, aggravating the food shortage problem as well as causing food prices to soar, which was exactly the opposite of the original purpose of depressing food prices. Third, a negative agricultural price policy can create formidable political difficulties in rural areas, as well as economic ones.

Many countries that once adhered to a negative agricultural price policy as a policy norm began to introduce producer-price support schemes for major crops. The Korean experience offers some of the most dramatic evidence concerning the turn toward a positive price policy.

Price Support Versus Input Subsidization

It is often argued that since the transformation of traditional agriculture is primarily of a technical and organizational nature, this transformation cannot be achieved by high product prices alone. It requires innovation, the absorption of new inputs, the utilization of idle resources, and institutional adjustments. If the policy aim is to accelerate the growth of agricultural output through diffusion of innovations, input subsidization would be a more effective means than product price support.[5]

Krishna (1967) gives several reasons in support of an input-subsidization scheme. If product prices are raised, farmers may or may not invest in improved cultivation methods. They may simply spend the extra income on consumption, resulting in the waste of government expenditure on price supports. If, however, inputs are subsidized, the benefit of government expenditure can be derived by the farmers in proportion to their use of improved inputs. Input subsidization for agriculture will also help keep the prices of food and raw materials low which will benefit the growing industrial sector.

These propositions are valid so far as the same degree of farm producers' response is induced by either scheme. If it does not matter whether the profitability of a product is increased, either by raising the price of the product or by lowering the prices of inputs, the government can use either input subsidies or product price supports to induce a given output response. But there are reasons why ordinary farmers, even in traditional agriculture, are more sensitive to changes in product prices than to input price manipulation.

First, input-price subsidies can cover only the purchased inputs, whereas price support induces an increased use of purchased as well as self-supplied inputs. More specifically, it is possible to subsidize the price of fertilizer, pesticides, farm implements, and irrigation fees, but it is impossible to subsidize family-supplied compost, labor, and land use, which account for a large portion of production costs. Second, most farm producers are concerned with the downward fluctuations in product prices more than with the upward fluctuations in the price of purchased inputs that form a small part of total production costs. Third, input-price subsidization cannot discriminate among products, but product-price supports can be applied selectively to induce increased production of specific products.

In actual policy implementation, however, neither scheme can be a complete substitute for the other. In fact, both are needed as complementary instruments of policy, because farmers become more willing to adopt improved methods of cultivation if the terms of trade for their products become favorable—that is, higher product prices and lower input prices. The

---

5. The theoretical explanations concerning the comparison of the effectiveness of both schemes in this section draw heavily on those given by Krishna (1967:526–28).

improved technology accompanies an increase in productivity of farming resources employed. Thus price incentives have a double effect in increasing agricultural production—fast adoption of improved technology by farm producers and increased use of productive factors, both purchased and non-purchased.

This is the very effect that high grain prices for major food grain and subsidized prices for major farm inputs has brought about in Korea. Since the initiation of economic development plans in the 1960s, the government has put a major emphasis on making the required farm inputs available at heavily subsidized prices. For example, the subsidy component on farm equipment purchases averaged 30 to 50 percent of the purchase prices during most of the 1960s and 1970s. Considering its limited land resources, Korea had to depend on increasing yields per hectare. An important part of the solution was increased use of inputs, such as chemical fertilizer, pesticides, and improved crop varieties as well as the expansion of irrigation facilities. These, combined with high grain prices, contributed to the increase in aggregate production during the 1970s.

Terms of Trade and Labor Productivity

When one appraises whether a certain industry is in a favorable condition or not, relative to other industries, one is apt to judge by the movements of terms of trade. When one does this, one loses sight of an important aspect of price changes, that is, changes in labor productivity. Labor productivity is one of the most important factors (along with price changes) determining supply conditions and incomes. Therefore, in evaluating the relative position of different industries one must not make judgments on the basis of price phenomena alone. To have economic significance, the relative movements of prices must be evaluated by simultaneously taking into consideration the relative changes in labor productivity.

To put this in concrete terms, assuming perfect competition, if labor productivity in a certain industry increases with the adoption of capital-intensive, mass-production methods, the unit cost of production necessarily declines and therefore the product price must decline. If the price does not fall, despite substantial growth of labor productivity, then the price rose relative to other industries. Conversely, if the product price of the industry with stagnant or slow-growing labor productivity does not rise, then that price actually fell relative to that of the fast-growing industry. In short, the rate of change in price is inversely related to the change in labor productivity.

Now let us evaluate the actual movement of the terms of trade in relation to the changes in labor productivity between agriculture and manufacturing in Korea. Table 15.6 compares the differences in both the average annual rate of increase in prices and labor productivity between rice growing and manufacturing for three different periods. For the period 1960–70, the average annual rate of increase in the rice price was 16.5 percent, whereas

Table 15.6. Comparison of the average annual rates of growth in labor
productivity and prices: Rice sector versus manufacturing (%)

Item	1960–70	1970–76	1977–82
Rice price received by farmers (A)	16.5	24.3	18.8
Prices paid by farmers (B)	12.2	19.9	25.0
(A – B)	4.3	4.4	–6.2
Labor productivity in manufacturing (C)	12.6	10.1	11.5
Labor productivity in rice sector (D)	2.2	10.3	4.9
(C – D)	10.4	–0.2	6.6

Sources: Computed from data in MAF, ROK, *Farm Household Economy Survey* (1960–83); EPB, ROK, *Monthly Statistical Review* (1960–82).

that of manufactured goods was 12.2 percent. This means that the prices of rice were at a relatively favorable level for farmers during the 1960s. But when we compare the rate of change in labor productivity, the above judgment may lose ground. Although labor productivity in manufacturing grew at the annual rate of 12.6 percent, that in rice growing increased at a rate of only 2.2 percent.

For the high grain-price period of 1970–76, the picture is completely different. Not only did the price of rice rise at a faster pace (an annual rate of 24.3 percent) compared to that of manufactured goods, but also the annual rate of growth of labor productivity slightly exceeded that in the manufacturing sector. This implies that the terms of trade for rice farming were unprecedentedly favorable in that period. That was the period when the government turned its policy emphasis toward high rice prices and during which the high-yielding rice variety (Tongil) was widely diffused.

After 1976–77 the situation reversed again. The price of rice rose at an annual rate of 18.8 percent, and the price of manufactured goods increased at a rate of 25 percent. Labor productivity in the manufacturing sector far exceeded that in the rice-growing sector. The low growth rate of labor productivity in rice production in this period can be explained by diminishing returns as the yield potential of the new rice variety was substantially exhausted. But the adverse movement of the terms of trade for rice is a reflection of the government's retreat to its old low grain-price policy.

EFFECTS OF THE POLICY MEASURES

Although the Korean economy is basically oriented toward the free-market system, government intervention in the grain market has been continuously intensified over time through price controls as well as demand and supply adjustments. Government intervention has been historically accepted as a given condition, justified on the grounds that undesirable developments that hinder the attainment of policy goals would occur in the grain sector if the determination of grain prices were completely left to market forces.

Which developments should be considered undesirable and what are the policy goals? These are a matter of judgment that depend on the economic conditions of the country concerned. So far as the grain-price policy is concerned, the following policy goals are regarded as relevant: (1) increased food grain production, (2) enhanced farm income, (3) general price stabilization and protection of urban consumers, (4) equitable income distribution, and (5) substitution of barley for rice. The effects of grain-price policy can best be assessed in terms of the degree to which it contributes to achieving the above-stated policy goals.

Effects on Food Grain Production

It has been widely questioned whether farmers engaging in traditional agriculture, where a large portion of their own products are used for family consumption, respond to changes in prices in their production decision making. Some economists have even gone so far as to claim (though never to support the claim empirically) that price responsiveness was reverse, implying that higher output prices result in smaller total output on the basis of the "fixed revenue hypothesis." These views were either abandoned or publicly renounced as a result of extensive research on the price responsiveness of farmers.

Generally, it is said that the extent to which farmers are responsive to external economic conditions varies according to region and to their stages of agricultural development. For example, farmers in relatively more commercialized agriculture or those living close to an urban market are more sensitive to changing market conditions than are those in subsistence farming or those living in remote areas. In Korea, however, where commercial and subsistence farmers coexist side by side in terms of residences and cultivated fields, there is every reason to believe that the behavior of subsistence farmers is influenced by that of commercial farmers.

A change in the relative level of grain prices induces farm producers to change the level of inputs used as well as their allocation among different crops, resulting in changes in aggregate production. The degree of producers' response to price changes is in general measured in terms of price elasticities. The price elasticity of supply measures the willingness as well as the ability of farm producers to adjust to changing price conditions—one of the most important aspects of a dynamic economy.

The price elasticity of supply for rice was estimated by one study to range from 0.2 to 0.3 (Moon 1982). This means that a 10 percent rise in the real price of rice leads to a supply increase of 2 to 3 percent. It is generally accepted that as the yield potential of a crop is exhausted, the price response of output in general slows down. But this does not mean that farmers do not respond in their grain production to changes in relative product prices.

In Korea the overall rate of self-sufficiency in all grain has declined from 80–90 percent in the 1960s to nearly 50–60 percent in the early 1980s, with almost half of the total requirement filled by imports. This rapid decline of the self-sufficiency rate is mainly due to a rapid increase in the importation of feed corn and soybeans. The level of self-sufficiency in rice, however, has been maintained at 95–100 percent despite a continuous increase in demand due to the growth in population and real income. Total rice production increased from 3.5 million metric tons (polished basis) in 1965 to 5.5 million metric tons in 1982, an increase of nearly 60 percent during a period of 17 years. This remarkable increase in production and a stable rate of self-sufficiency for rice are mainly attributable to the high rice-price policy, combined with wide diffusion of a high-yielding rice variety.

Effects on Farm Income

Although the contribution of rice to farm household income varies among farms of different sizes, data show that on average about 57 percent of the total agricultural receipts originated from grain cultivation (MAF, ROK, *Farm Household Economy Survey*, 1982). For farmers with less than 1 hectare, 52 percent of total receipts was contributed by grain; for the farmer cultivating between 1 and 2 hectares, the contribution was 60 percent; for the farmer with more than 2 hectares, grain constituted approximately 65 percent.

According to a recent study applying an econometric technique, a 10 percent rise in the terms of trade for agricultural products results in an increase in agricultural income of farm households by 7 to 8 percent. Regression equations to determine farm income by the recursive method on the basis of 1962–82 data indicate that a 10 percent rise in agricultural labor productivity due to increases in government investments and loans and in educational level is estimated to increase real income by about 5 percent, whereas a 10 percent increase in the agricultural terms of trade raises farm household real income by almost 8 percent (Moon 1982:199–200).

A comparison of incomes of farm households and urban wage earners provides further evidence that the income position of farmers relative to urban wage earners improved during the high grain-price period but declined thereafter when the government policy changed to a low grain-price policy (Table 15.7). This reflects the fact that grain prices, particularly rice prices, are the most critical factor in determining farm household income.

Many economists and public officials argue that farm income should be improved, from the long-run point of view, through increased agricultural productivity instead of subsidizing the prices of agricultural products at government expense. They also claim that the efforts should be directed toward expanding the sources of off-farm income through fostering rural industries.[6] Given the recent trends and various constraints inherent in rural industrialization, however, the predominance of farming activities in determining farm income is destined to continue for quite some time to come.

Table 15.7. Comparison of rural and urban household incom(won)

Year	Farm household (A)	Urban household (B)	
1965	112	113	99.1
1966	130	162	80.2
1967	149	249	59.8
1968	179	286	62.6
1969	217	334	65.0
1970	256	381	67.2
1971	356	452	78.8
1972	429	517	83.0
1973	481	550	87.5
1974	674	645	104.5
1975	873	859	101.6
1976	1,156	1,158	99.8
1977	1,433	1,405	102.0
1978	1,884	1,916	98.3
1979	2,227	2,630	84.7
1980	2,693	3,205	84.0
1981	3,688	3,450	106.9
1982	4,465	4,520	98.8

Sources: MAF, ROK, *Farm Household Economy Survey* (1965–82); EPB, ROK, *Urban Household Living Expenditure Survey* (1965–82).

Effects on General Price Stabilization and Protection of Urban Consumers

In Korea the percentage of income spent on grain is greater than that of any other single item. An increase in the prices of grain, therefore, pushes up the cost of living, causing upward pressure on wages, which in turn drives up the cost of production for manufactured goods and services. The magnitude of this cost-push effect depends largely upon the proportion of grain expenditure in the cost of living. The higher the share of grain in the cost of living for urban workers, the greater the upward pressure on wages will become when grain prices rise. The share of grain in the cost of living for an average urban worker's household was about 19 percent

---

6. When one talks about rural industrialization, he is likely to be concerned with the effects of increasing employment opportunities in rural areas. But one must not overlook the adverse impacts on the overall productivity of agriculture: (1) diversion of farmland into residential and industrial sites, (2) increase in farmland prices, (3) likely overinvestment in farm mechanization due to rise in rural wages, and, most important of all, (4) disincentives for farming due to increasing opportunities for off-farm employment.

in 1975, but it had declined by 1981 to about 11 percent (Table 15.8). It is expected to decline further as real income continues to grow. However, the labor share of income has been maintained at the relatively stable level of 50 percent, that is, other things being equal, a 10 percent rise in grain prices causes an increase of 0.5 percent in the general price level.[7]

The declining share of grain in the cost of living does not mean that changes in grain prices have little or no effect on the prices of other commodities. Contrary to the prevailing concern of public officials, however, the evidence is clear that the cost-push effect of a rise in grain prices has been substantially weakened.

As the economy continues to grow, product lines will become increasingly diversified and the pattern of consumption will undergo a substantial change. As a result, both the variety and volume of nonagricultural goods in the domestic market will increase, while the relative share of grain falls. Therefore, unless there is an extraordinarily sharp rise or fall in the price of grain (say, 30 or 40 percent), maintaining low grain prices will no longer be an effective means of attaining the policy goal of general price stabilization.

Effects on Income Distribution

There are important trade-offs and conflicts among various direct influences and indirect effects of grain-price policy on the real incomes of different income groups. Changes in grain prices, of course, effect a transfer of

Table 15.8. Proportion of grain and rice expenditures in cost of living for urban households and labor income share in manufacturing sector: 1975–81 (%)

Year	Proportion of expenditure		Labor income share
	All grain	Rice	
1975	19.2	17.4	40.8
1976	18.8	17.6	42.6
1977	15.9	14.6	47.6
1978	12.8	11.8	51.2
1979	10.8	10.0	50.3
1980	10.5	10.4	51.0
1981	10.8	9.7	47.5

Sources: EPB, ROK, *Urban Household Living Expenditure Survey* (1975–82); EPB, ROK, *Economic Statistics Yearbook* (1975–82).

---

7. The effect of changes in grain prices on changes in the general price level can be measured in a number of ways. For example, it can be measured by applying the price inverse matrix of the input–output table or by using regression techniques. Considering the quality of the data in the prepared input–output table, however, it is doubtful that such efforts are worthwhile. Furthermore, a straightforward guess/estimate is sufficient for present purposes.

income between the agricultural and nonagricultural sectors of the economy, but what draws our interest is the income distribution between small and large farms within agriculture and between high- and low-income groups in the urban area.

Changes in agricultural prices affect the incomes of individual farms in proportion to their sales of produce. Large farms normally sell a larger portion of what they produce than do small farms. Therefore, the largest effects, both relative and absolute, fall on the largest producers. Some data indicate that farmers with less than 0.5 hectares sold only 21.5 percent of their 1981 rice crop output, the rest being kept for home consumption, whereas those with more than 2 hectares sold 56.2 percent. When the price of rice increases by 10 percent, the real income of the small farm increases by slightly more than 2 percent, whereas the real incomes of large farms rise by 5.2 percent. The difference in absolute terms may be even greater, because the higher percentage increase experienced by large farms is applied to a larger initial income.

These relationships refer to effects of price changes on producers when quantity produced stays constant. In actuality, however, changes in grain price affect rice output, although with some time lag. In general, the farmers with larger holdings market a higher proportion of their production and are more responsive to price changes.

Hence price changes exert a much greater effect on the output of larger than smaller farms, adding further to the disparity. In fact, the smallest farms may be hurt by the price increase. Many farmers with marginal holdings are net purchasers of rice during the off-season when their incomes are earned from off-farm activities. Insofar as they purchase with cash, an increase in rice prices affects them primarily as consumers, causing a decline in real income.

Among urban consumers, a roughly converse situation arises. Agricultural prices affect urban consumers in proportion to the ratio of expenditure on food to their incomes. Generally, lower income urban consumers spend a much higher proportion of their incomes on food grain than do those with higher incomes. According to EPB, ROK, *Urban Household Living Expenditure Survey* (1982) data in Korea, although the top 10 percent in income of urban wage earners spend approximately 1.8 times as much on rice as the lowest 10 percent, they allocate only 4.2 percent of their total living expenditure for rice purchase, compared with 13.3 percent for the lowest-income class. Therefore, a 10 percent rise in the price of rice has the effect of reducing real income only by 0.4 percent for the upper-income group, but reduces the income of the lowest-income group by 1.3 percent.

Thus a high grain-price policy tends to provide benefits primarily to larger farmers and the upper-income class of urban consumers. The majority of small farmers and urban lower-income earners are helped relatively little by a high grain-price policy. On balance, a rise in agricultural prices tends to redistribute income away from low-income urban consumers toward high-income farm producers.

This is not to say, however, that the degree of effect on income distribution must be used as the sole criterion for policy decision in determining grain prices. For Korea, where a chronic food-grain shortage persists and a substantial amount of foreign exchange is spent for grain imports, increasing domestic production of grain and reducing imports is probably more important.

Effects on Substitution of Barley for Rice

A two-price system for barley, which was put into effect beginning with the 1969 crop, was originally designed to induce consumers to substitute barley for rice in their diet. Prior to 1968, the market price had been maintained at a level of more than 65 percent of the rice price; but with the increasing subsidy for barley prices after 1969, the price of barley for urban consumers was lowered to almost 40 percent of the rice price.

Other measures were taken to encourage consumers to substitute barley and other grains for rice. Restaurants were required to serve a mixture of 75 percent rice and 25 percent barley. They were also required to serve noodles and other non-rice food items on Wednesdays and Saturdays. Lunches carried by school children had to contain a similar mixture.

The lower price ratio of barley relative to rice along with various administrative measures was conducive to diversion of consumption away from rice during the early 1970s. An official estimate indicates that the amount of rice saved by this policy was about 600,000 metric tons in 1972. However, as per capita income grew, the average consumer became less responsive to changes in the relative price of barley because of a strong preference for rice. It is doubtful, therefore, that the two-price policy for barley exerted a continuous effect on the marginal rate of substitution between rice and barley. The effort to conserve rice through a price policy and other administrative measures cannot be pursued as a long-run policy.

SOME POLICY RECOMMENDATIONS

Enhancing Agricultural Productivity

Owing to the expanded cultivation of high-yielding varieties and improved farming techniques, promoted by a positive price support program during the 1970s, a remarkable increase has been recorded in aggregate farm output, especially grain production. Nevertheless, overall food-grain supply has been lagging behind overall consumption because of the increase in population and per capita income. Overall self-sufficiency in all grains declined from 93.9 percent in 1965 to 53 percent in 1982, with nearly half of the total requirement filled by imports. Self-sufficiency in rice was nearly attained in the mid-1970s, but then declined to 93 percent in 1982.

The fact that the rice yield in Korea is on the average 10–15 percent lower than that in Japan and is only 70 percent of experimental farm yields suggests, however, that there is potential for achieving yield increases by applying improved technology and building up the production base. In this context, the following policy measures are suggested along with continuous implementation of a positive agricultural price policy.

Farmland development. Since the mid-1960s a significant amount of farmland has been lost to urban expansion and industrial plants. The average annual rate of diversion to nonagricultural uses is estimated at around 8,000 to 10,000 hectares during the 1970s. As industrialization expands, much more farmland is expected to be lost to other uses. Investment opportunities in the expansion of farmland through tideland development and conversion of hilly land into arable land should be intensively investigated. A good beginning has been made in this regard. The Agricultural Development Corporation (ADC) has conducted an extensive survey of the southeast coastline. The results indicate that over 450,000 hectares of sea land has potential for conversion to arable land.

Expansion of irrigation facilities. In Korea more than two-thirds of the total paddy land area is only partially irrigated or rainfed. Moreover, a large portion of paddy land is poorly drained and lacks adequate flood control structures. Also, many of the existing irrigation and drainage systems are obsolete or nearing obsolescence due to lack of repair. It is necessary to launch a massive repair project to recover the original capacity of these facilities. The achievement of higher yields depends upon improvement of irrigation, drainage, and flood control facilities.

Adequate pricing of fertilizer. Recently the government has been planning to totally eliminate the deficit in the Fertilizer Account. If the deficit is to be eliminated by raising selling prices to farmers with the procurement prices for the fertilizer industry remaining unchanged, the selling prices must be increased by 72 percent. If, however, the deficit is to be eliminated by reducing the procurement price paid to the fertilizer industry, then it must be reduced by 32 percent of what is currently being received.

To eliminate the deficit in the Fertilizer Account, the government should direct its efforts toward reducing the cost of fertilizer production, which is substantially higher than world market prices, by taking appropriate measures to enhance the technical and managerial capabilities of the manufacturers. An attempt must also be made to revise the unfair contract with foreign investors in the direction of reducing the quantity obligation in procurement, and at the same time the current marketing and distribution system must be improved so as to reduce marketing costs. Raising fertilizer prices to farmers and maintaining the current level of subsidization for fertilizer manufacturers simply to eliminate the deficit are in no way justifiable.

Expansion of agricultural credit. The primary issue confronting agricultural credit is a need to obtain sufficient funds to meet the rising demand for capital. From a long-range point of view, it is undoubtedly most desirable that the agricultural credit institution expand its funds sufficiently to enable it to operate on a self-supporting basis.

In view of the fact that capital formation within the rural sector still remains at a relatively low level, however, financial support at least for the strategic sector should appropriately be provided by the government.

Furthermore, Korea's traditional rural society has been rapidly transforming into a more commercially oriented one. This period of transition requires an increased supply of medium- and long-term development funds, part of which must inevitably be supplied by the government.

Under the current system, agricultural credit in Korea involves too many types of loans requiring many different procedures and terms. This complexity unnecessarily limits farmers' access to the credit and not only hampers efficient operations of cooperatives but also impairs fairness in providing lending services to farmers. Therefore, the lending methods and terms should be simplified, if not unified, merging those types of loans that are intended for similar purposes.

Expansion of credit for marginal farmers deserves special consideration in Korea. Farm households owning less than 0.5 hectares of arable land still account for more than 30 percent of all farms. Because of their sizeable proportion, these marginal farmers have a fairly substantial bearing on the nation's total agricultural production. Not infrequently, however, these marginal farmers are bypassed in credit provision on grounds that their repayment capability is low due to low productivity and low income.

Given these circumstances, it is both necessary and desirable to establish a special credit system catering exclusively to the needs of marginal farmers. Such a fund, to be operated separately from the regular institutional credit, should be financed with government funds as a part of the social welfare program.

Efficient farm mechanization. Emphasis under the farm mechanization policy has thus far been laid almost exclusively on quantitative aspects. Little or no attention has been given to the need to create conditions favorable to mechanization or to the need to develop systems for ensuring full utilization of machines made available to farmers. Thus, the rate of utilization of machinery purchased by farmers continues to be below par, and in spite of rapid diffusion of farm machinery, the original goal of effectively easing labor shortages during periods of peak agricultural activity has yet to be attained.

In view of the anticipated diffusion in the future of such high-performance implements as tractors, combines, transplanters, and harvesters, the continuation of a simplistic farm mechanization policy of stressing numerical expansion alone would lead to a decline in the rate of utilization of individual implements, almost in inverse proportion to the rate of their diffusion. This would have an adverse impact on the profitability of farming enterprises due to a rise in the unit cost of work. And from the standpoint of the national economy, excessive investments in farm mechanization could result.

Because the current smallholder system in Korea is expected to persist for some time to come, the task of mechanizing Korea's agriculture should be carried out in close association with plans for improving the agrarian structure itself.

Effective farm mechanization can hardly be achieved unless it is pursued simultaneously with renovation of the foundations of farming operations, including the agrarian system and conditions of farmland as well as with development of farm machinery utilization systems suitable to the actual circumstances prevailing in rural communities.

Increased production of livestock and non-cereal products. Rapid economic growth and the subsequent increase in income levels have brought about considerable changes in food consumption patterns. Consumer tastes shifted from carbohydrates to foods containing more protein such as meat and high-protein processed foods. For example, the annual per capita consumption of beef and pork increased nearly threefold, that of chicken five times, and that of milk more than 20 times during the 1965–82 period. The demand for vegetables and fruit also increased rapidly.

To cope with these rapid changes in the pattern of food consumption and the resulting increases in demand for non-cereal foods, higher priority should be given to investment for the expansion of the livestock industry and cash crops.

Improved agricultural marketing. The high rate of income growth and urbanization, combined with the increasing rate of commercialization in rural areas, has created a rapid increase in demand for marketing services. There has been some public and private investment in marketing facilities, but many of those currently in use are inadequate for storage, processing, and distribution. There is an urgent need to upgrade and modernize facilities for marketing farm products and distributing farm inputs.

Elimination of the GMF Deficit

One of the main features of the grain-price policy in Korea is that the financial deficit arising from grain operations has been largely compensated for by inflationary financing. If the deficit were compensated from the general budget account, the effect would be a reduction in budget expenses for other sectors. This was not the case with the grain operation.

Faced with increasing budgetary requirements in nonagricultural sectors, especially for defense purposes, while budgetary sources remain limited, the government has been obliged to rely upon inflationary financing. Most of the deficit has been financed through a long-term overdraft from the central bank and also partly through the issue of short-term grain bonds with a one-year maturity period. The outstanding balance of the long-term borrowing totaled about 1.4 trillion won (approximately US $20 billion) at the end of 1982. Repayment of grain bonds has been financed in turn either by a long-term overdraft or the reissue of grain bonds. Therefore, whichever method is used in financing the GMF deficit, the result is an increase in the money supply.

The GMF deficit accounted for about 22 percent of the total increase in the money supply in 1972 and rose as high as 98 percent in 1975. Thereafter approximately one-fourth of the total increase in the money supply occurred in the grain section (Food Bureau, MAF, ROK, unpublished data; BOK, *Economic Statistics Yearbook,* 1970–82).

Considering the importance of enhancing the socioeconomic status of farmers, who still account for a large proportion of the population, and of protecting consumer welfare, the government grain operation and grain pricing policy must be viewed from a perspective different from that of monetary policy alone. However, the continued reliance on a long-term overdraft from the central bank for financing the grain deficit is definitely inconsistent with a policy goal to achieve fiscal and financial stability.

A net increase in the money supply resulting from the current inflationary financing of the government grain operation is bound to cause upward pressure, with some time-lag, on the general price level.[8] This is because lump-sum funds released at the time of grain acquisition are very likely to be spent immediately by farmers whose cash demand is usually high. For this reason, it is obvious that the two-price policy, though it would temporarily restrain consumer prices, is self-defeating in its purpose of stabilizing the general price level.

An important lesson is that either the grain deficit must be financed from the general account budget, which is noninflationary, or an attempt must be made to eliminate the deficit by narrowing the negative price differentials between government purchase and selling prices. In other words, once the government purchase price is set, the selling prices must cover the costs of transport, handling, storage, administration, and interest.

As long as the government requires grain purchases from farmers, there are two ways to narrow the price differentials: relative reduction in purchase prices or relative increase in selling prices. Whichever method is

---

8. In Japan, the grain deficit arising from the two-price policy for rice is financed by the general account of the national budget. The effect of such financing on the income distribution is exactly opposite to that of financing with an overdraft from the central bank. Financing from the general account means that funds are derived in principle from tax revenue. Inasmuch as a direct tax is concerned, higher tax rates are applied to higher income earners. Therefore, financing the grain deficit from the general account has the effect of transferring income from higher to lower income groups.

chosen, the problem boils down to one of determining purchase prices, high or low. According to the analysis of the effects of grain prices in the foregoing section, a 10 percent rise in the real price of grain would have the positive effects of increasing rice production by 2 to 3 percent and of boosting farm household income by 7 to 8 percent. From the opposite view, the same percentage rise in the real price of grain would result in only a 0.5 percent increase in the general price level and a 1 percent increase in the consumer cost of living. In view of this trade-off relationship, one easily reaches the conclusion that government selling prices must be raised to such a level as to eliminate the grain deficit. It would probably save the government more than it would cost the private sector.

Excessive Government Share in and Shrinkage of the Private Grain Market

With the increased scale of the government grain operation, the volume of nongovernment rice transacted through the wholesale market has drastically declined, in both absolute and relative terms. However, the volume of rice handled directly by retailers in the urban areas has substantially risen. In Seoul, for example, the market share of rice traded through the wholesale market declined from 23.6 percent in 1975 to 3.8 percent in 1981, while the shares of government-controlled rice and that shipped into the city through direct trade between retailers and farm producers increased from 33.4 percent and 37 percent to 52.7 percent and 40.2 percent, respectively, during the same period (Food Bureau, MAF, ROK, unpublished data; Korea Grain Dealers Association, unpublished data). This predominance of grain transactions by poorly financed, marginal-scale retailers who bypass the legally established wholesale market not only impedes efforts to improve the efficiency of grain marketing, but also tends to give rise to various forms of unfair trade. The most desirable form of grain marketing, as far as nongovernment rice is concerned, is one in which grain transactions take place in large volumes through the wholesale market on a competitive basis. The shrinkage of the normal functions of the wholesale market is mainly due to the current government grain management system, which is operated in such a way as to discourage the spontaneous, healthy growth of private grain wholesalers' networks.

Uniform Pricing in Procurement and Selling of Government Grain

The use of a uniform purchase price throughout the rice acquisition period, usually from November through January, has been subject to a number of criticisms. More than 95 percent of government acquisitions are concentrated during this two-month period annually (Table 15.9). Because farmers are paid the same price regardless of when they deliver the grain, they are tempted to dispose of grain as soon as possible, partly because

Table 15.9. Monthly distribution of government rice purchases: 1967–82

Rice year	Total purchase (10^3 MT)	November		December		January	
		Quantity (10^3 MT)	Ratio (%)	Quantity (10^3 MT)	Ratio (%)	Quantity (10^3 MT)	Ratio (%)
1968	286	86	30.2	177	61.8	23	8.0
1969	156	23	15.1	117	75.8	16	9.1
1970	326	86	26.3	210	64.2	30	9.5
1971	365	97	27.1	248	67.6	18	5.3
1972	517	225	45.0	255	50.1	37	4.7
1973	507	76	15.0	238	46.9	193	38.1
1974	480	241	50.2	210	43.8	29	6.0
1975	735	608	82.7	119	16.2	8	1.1
1976	789	571	72.4	201	25.5	17	2.1
1977	1,043	812	77.8	204	19.6	27	2.6
1978	1,404	742	52.9	577	41.1	87	6.0
1979	1,355	967	71.3	346	25.6	42	3.1
1980	1,301	1,194	91.8	100	7.7	7	0.5
1981	546	398	72.9	148	27.1	0	0
1982	915	655	71.6	233	25.4	27	3.0
1983	1,091	687	63.0	340	31.1	64	5.7
Average			63.2		31.5		5.3

Source: Data obtained from Food Bureau, MAF, ROK.

Note: ''Rice year'' refers to the calendar year beginning in January (last two columns). November and December figures are thus from the end of the preceding calendar year.

MT—metric tons.

of lack of adequate storage facilities and partly because of an acute cash demand after the harvest. This practice gives rise to a number of problems.

1. The lack of incentives to retain grain for later sales discourages farmers from investing in storage facilities. And because the acquisition is concentrated into a two-month period, the burden of financing storage falls mostly on the government.

2. The storage of excessively large quantities of government grain often results in deterioration of its quality. This causes a substantial price differential of about 20 to 30 percent between government and nongovernment rice. Taking advantage of this price differential, the intermediate grain dealers are inclined to pursue illicit profit by fraudulently selling repolished government rice as nongovernment rice, though the size of the illegal profit differs, depending on the quality of the government rice.

3. The release of a large amount of funds within a short period of time due to the heavily concentrated acquisition cannot but cause a lump-sum increase in money supply toward the end of each year.

One possible way of improving the acquisition program is to adopt differential pricing for varying months, the price difference being at least large enough to cover the farmers' storage costs. If the government were to raise the purchase price for deliveries in later months, farmers would have an incentive to hold their grain and to distribute their sales more evenly. In addition, there is no particular reason why the purchase program should be limited to only a three-month period each year. Extending the purchase period until March or April in the following year would alleviate budgetary constraints because the government would not require all acquisition funds within such a short period of time. Furthermore, the concentration of purchasing power toward the year-end in rural areas would also be avoided.

Along with the uniform pricing in purchases, the uniform pricing in selling has received no less criticism. Because seasonal stabilization of grain prices is viewed as having an anti-inflationary effect, major emphasis has been placed upon dampening seasonal rises in rice prices. The government customarily uses the change in the WPI to measure price stability. A rise in the price of rice is automatically reflected in this index via its weight (4.6 percent in 1980 as the base year). If the price of rice rises to its seasonal peak (say 20 percent), the WPI automatically rises about 0.9 percent, other prices remaining unchanged. This rise in the WPI is viewed as inflationary by policymakers.

When the market share of government-controlled rice (including imports) was relatively low in the 1960s, the rate of seasonal variation in rice prices ranged from 15 to 25 percent. But with the increased share of government rice, seasonal price fluctuations were substantially dampened, and the range was reduced to 4–9 percent throughout the 1970s and early 1980s (MAF, ROK, *Agriculture and Fisheries Statistics Yearbook*, 1960–82).

The policy of maintaining such a low rate of seasonal variation in market prices causes a number of undesirable effects:

1. Because there is little or no incentive for intermediate grain dealers to invest in storage and other marketing facilities, it is difficult to develop efficient distribution links between farm producers and urban wholesalers. Consequently, a substantial portion of free-market grain is distributed by small, poorly financed retailers who operate in a disorganized and inefficient way.

2. Since grain is available at the same price throughout the year, urban consumers tend to purchase a small quantity sufficient to meet only a few days' needs. Consequently, the government must bear the heavy burden of storing and financing it.

3. The low profit margin rate for handling government grain, usually fixed at 5–6 percent per bag, often causes grain dealers to engage in fraudulent practices such as cheating on quantity as well as selling lower-priced government rice at higher prices, thus impeding the sound development of grain marketing.

To eliminate all these undesirable defects in grain marketing, the government sale price should have a proper rate of seasonal variation, that is, a higher price during the off-season and lower price during or after the harvest season. This practice would induce seasonal variation in the private grain market that is consistent with the wholesalers' costs of holding rice. It is also important that policymakers not view the seasonal pricing policy per se in terms of general price stabilization objectives, and that a seasonally adjusted WPI be used as a stabilization indicator. In short, the current government grain-pricing system must be improved in such a way as to provide the private sector, including farmers and intermediate grain dealers, with greater investment incentives.

16 The Saemaul (New Community) Movement (1971)

by Pal Yong Moon

A fundamental change occurred in the early 1970s in the Korean government's policy toward rural development. The core of this change was the Saemaul (new community) movement begun in the winter of 1971. This government-initiated movement for community development was strongly backed by the late President Park and government agencies at all levels. With government support and assistance, massive-scale investment projects were undertaken for the improvement of physical infrastructure and farm income. Efforts were also directed at influencing rural people's ways of thinking and lifestyle by means of a series of educational campaigns. Rural people were mobilized to participate in community development, the rural infrastructure and environment were greatly improved, and farm-household incomes were substantially increased. In short, during the 1970s the Saemaul movement helped to transform almost every aspect of rural Korea.

After more than a decade of experience, however, the movement is now being criticized mainly because of its top-down authoritarian administration. There is considerable evidence that the authoritarian approach hindered voluntary participation by rural villagers and even led to misallocation of resources.

The general pattern of agricultural development in Western Europe can be described as a continuous process of farming-scale expansion accompanied by technological progress. Progress in agricultural technology enlarges disparities in the productive capabilities of individual farmers within the same rural community. This leads to a disintegration of those classes of farmers with low productive capabilities, enabling the more successful farmers to remain on farms and expand the scale of their farming operations. This in turn facilitates the introduction of advanced technology centered around farm mechanization. The chain of cause and effect has been continuous.

In contrast, Korea's agriculture has long been characterized by small-scale farming, which restricts the adoption of new technology and impedes the improvement of agricultural productivity. This cycle has been constantly repeated. It is hardly an exaggeration to state that virtually all problems confronting Korean agriculture stem from its smallholder nature. Whereas the exodus of rural labor can be considered conducive to the growth of labor productivity through an adoption of new technology such as farm mechanization, the small size of farms and insufficient capital investment impedes such progress.

Since the early 1960s the Korean government has been striving to improve the agrarian structure, but it has been unable to do much to enlarge the scale of farming operations owing to the limited land resources. Farmers who cultivate 1 hectare or less constituted more than one-third of the total number of farm households. The fragmentation of the country's limited cultivatable land is a major constraint on expanding agricultural labor productivity and farm income. Many people have begun to advocate an easing or even a repeal of the 3-hectare ceiling on individual ownership of farmland. Their rationale is to expedite the expansion of individual landholdings by increasing the transferability of land titles. Although the proposed relaxation of the limitation on landownership could pave the way for some farmers to expand the scale of their farming operations, there has been disagreement over the principal reason why farming operations have not expanded thus far—whether it has been the statutory ceiling on individual ownership, the low profitability of farming, or the general economic conditions surrounding Korean agriculture that kept farms small. Over the past two decades the rate of decrease in number of farm households has been much lower than that of the farm population. As a result, the average area of farmland per household has remained almost static at about 1 hectare (Tables 16.1 and 16.2).

The second factor responsible for rural poverty was the persistent negative farm-price policy, particularly affecting major grains. During the 1950s the government's main efforts were directed toward the rehabilitation of the war-wrecked economy and the alleviation of postwar inflation. Policymakers were particularly sensitive to the effects of grain prices on urban wage earners' cost of living and on inflation, so efforts were made

Table 16.1. Cultivated land, rural population, number of farm households, and average farm size: Selected years, 1965–82

Year	Total cultivated land (10^3 ha)	Total rural population (10^3)	Number of farm households (10^3)	Average size of holdings (ha)	Average size of farm family (persons)
1965	2,275	15,812	2,507	0.91	6.3
1970	2,295	14,432	2,484	0.93	5.8
1975	2,240	13,244	2,379	0.94	5.6
1980	2,196	10,831	2,155	1.02	5.1
1982	2,180	9,688	1,996	1.09	5.0

Source: MAF, ROK, Agriculture and Fisheries Statistics Yearbook (1965–82).
ha—hectare (equivalent to 2.47 acres).

Table 16.2. Distribution of farm households by size of holding: Selected years, 1965–82 (%)

Year	\multicolumn{6}{c}{Farm size (hectares)}
	0.5 or less	0.5–1	1–1.5	1.5–2	2–3	3 or more
1965	35.8	31.6	16.5	9.3	5.6	1.2
1970	31.6	34.3	18.5	8.0	5.1	1.5
1975	30.3	36.2	18.9	8.2	4.8	1.6
1980	28.8	35.0	20.6	9.0	5.1	1.5
1982	29.6	37.0	19.9	8.1	4.2	1.2

Source: MAF, ROK, *Agriculture and Fisheries Statistics Yearbook* (1965–82).

to keep grain prices low. Government investment in and loans to agriculture were severely limited owing to the increasing budgetary demand for rehabilitation work and defense. About all that the budget was capable of financing in the agricultural sector was maintenance for existing irrigation facilities and importation of fertilizer. The low farm-price policy was further reinforced by the easy availability of American surplus grain on concessionary terms under the U.S. Public Law (PL) 480 program, begun in 1955.

The low-price policy for major food grains eventually hindered efforts to promote increased domestic food production in the 1960s. The long-lasting adverse terms of trade for farm products further impoverished the already poor rural economy. With the aggravating food shortage, resultant increases in foreign exchange spending on food imports, and the growing income disparity between rural and urban households, the government was obliged to give serious consideration to expanding food-grain production and enhancing the income position of farmers. When a large portion of the food-grain shortage was met by local currency under the PL 480 agreement, the food gap itself did not impose a serious burden on the country's foreign exchange position. But as U.S. aid began to be phased out, food-grain imports caused a substantial drain on the country's foreign exchange reserves.

By the late 1960s rural people became increasingly conscious of the widening standard-of-living gap between urban and rural areas. Since independence, rural voters had tended to support passively whichever regime happened to be in power, despite its pursuit of export-oriented industrialization which favored the urban sector. But over time the situation changed. The government of the late President Park began to perceive evidence of a decline in rural political support. The government's perception of a decline in its political popularity spurred the shift in policy emphasis toward rural development.

Starting with the 1969 crops, the prices at which the government purchased rice and barley were steadily increased with a view to improving the terms of trade for farm producers. The initiation of higher purchase prices for major grains represented a dramatic change in agricultural price policy and was part of a government effort both to stimulate domestic production of food grain and to upgrade farm incomes. Another major shift in policy was the initiation of massive-scale investment in the rural development sphere, which is now generally called the rural Saemaul (New Community) movement.

MAIN FEATURES OF THE SAEMAUL MOVEMENT

Initiation of the Movement

It is generally agreed that the starting point of the Saemaul movement in Korea was related to the disposal of surplus cement. In 1971 cement production far exceeded demand, causing an excessive inventory in the country. After a series of interministerial meetings, a decision was made to use the surplus cement for productive purposes in rural areas.

The government provided, free of charge, 335 bags of cement to each of a total of 33,267 villages during the winter of 1970–71. The recipients were instructed to use the cement only for the purpose of meeting their community's needs as determined by consensus. Local administrations recommended that the cement be used for projects such as: improvement of farm roads, establishment of a sanitary water-supply system, sewage improvements, river-dike repairs, and construction of common wells and public laundry facilities (J. H. Park 1981).

The program was widely welcomed by villagers, who found good uses for the cement, and the results greatly exceeded the expectations of the government officials. Encouraged by the performance of the rural people, the government selected as models 16,600 villages that had responded actively to the cement offer and successfully carried out their projects. In 1972 the government supplied an additional 500 bags of cement together with one ton of steel rods to each of these selected villages.

Further encouraged by this experimentation, the Ministry of Home Affairs (MOHA) conducted a nationwide village survey, classifying all the villages in the country into three categories on the basis of degree of performance and level of development: (1) basic (underdeveloped) village; (2) self-help (developing) village; and (3) self-reliant (developed) village. On the basis of this classification, the government adopted a different approach for each class of village, giving greater assistance to higher-level villages. This was intended to create a sense of competition among villages and to stimulate those in the two lower classes to make more efforts toward advancing to a higher village class. Each village was required to achieve a minimum level of performance prior to advancement in the classification scheme.

Having observed this early experience and success, President Park began to take a keen interest in the program and ordered that it be intensified and extended. He emphasized the importance of identifying and motivating village leaders as well as the need for educating and training them.

Basic Ideology and Contents

According to an official definition used by MOHA, the "Saemaul Undong [movement] is a new community movement in which people cooperate with one another in order to construct better and richer villages, and as a consequence, a richer and stronger nation." In other words, the Saemaul movement is a Korean model of the community development movement with the ultimate goal of developing a strong nation through the elimination of poverty and the construction of a dynamic society. To achieve this goal, leaders of the movement enunciated three strategic objectives: rural enlightenment, social development, and economic development.

Rural enlightenment. The movement sought to enhance rural villagers' willingness to practice self-reliance. It aimed at promoting the spirit of diligence, austerity, thrift, mutual cooperation, and solidarity, which are the moral foundations for the introduction of rural innovation and development. The spirit of self-reliance emphasized the importance of viewing oneself in a correct perspective and solving problems with one's own efforts, thereby encouraging rural people to change deep-rooted fatalistic attitudes. Korean farmers have traditionally adhered to the notion that poverty was their fate—something they could not change by themselves.

Historically, the Korean people were subjected to exploitation by the ruling classes of successive dynasties. More recently, during the Japanese colonial period, they suffered from a painful economic squeeze. The political and socioeconomic systems were such that voluntary participation in community development and cooperative productive activities was not very common.

Moreover, the extended family system, combined with an authoritarian power structure, severely restricted the development of individualism and decision-making abilities. People tended to be dependent upon outside decisions and help. They lacked confidence in themselves and were unable to realize their own potential for improving their lives.

Given these circumstances, spiritual enlightenment was regarded as indispensable to the Saemaul movement as a means of changing people's attitudes. To this end, various training and educational programs were established to augment the physical aspects of the movement.

Social development. The social-development aspects of the Saemaul movement include programs aimed at improving the environment in which villagers live. As rural people have become increasingly conscious of differences between urban and rural living standards, narrowing those differences has received priority in the movement. Social-development programs were of three types: environmental improvements, housing improvements, and public-utility expansion. Each type comprised individual projects. Environmental projects included the establishment of sanitary water-supply systems, improved sewage systems, public bathhouses, village conference halls, public wells, and village laundry yards. Housing-improvement projects included roof improvements, house repairs, and village restructuring. The expansion of rural electrification and the development of communication networks, in particular the installation of public telephones in villages, were also a high priority.

Economic development. The economic-development program had two major components: buildup of the production infrastructure and an income-augmentation program. Included in the infrastructure program were farm-road expansion and small-scale irrigation projects such as construction of weirs, irrigation ponds, and irrigation and drainage canals. Road-improvement projects were undertaken to widen village roads so that farm machinery could pass and to connect village roads to fields and main roads. This program has facilitated farm mechanization and transportation services even in remote areas.

Small-scale irrigation projects led to another important infrastructure improvement fostering agricultural productivity. Much of the existing irrigation and drainage system was obsolete or nearing obsolescence due to lack of repair work over many years. Recovery of the original capacity of these facilities was urgently needed to assist small-scale irrigation.

All these rural infrastructure projects were in the nature of social overhead capital. And as most of the projects were labor-intensive, they could be carried out with indigenous technology. Outside assistance was obtained for only those projects that required technical expertise. Because the work was undertaken during the off-season when labor mobilization was relatively easy, the rate of return on capital was expected to be high.

Included in the income-augmentation program were livestock raising, introduction of cash crops, development of specialized production areas, group farming, and the establishment of Saemaul factories to increase off-farm income sources. The area-specialization project had four types of production: general crops, fruits and vegetables, livestock, and cash crops. After 1977 there were package programs to integrate such projects as infrastructure building, production, establishment of marketing facilities, and farm mechanization. In addition to these income-augmentation projects, the government has provided various kinds of support—financial and technical— for constructing Saemaul factories to increase employment opportunities during the off-season.

Major Developments of the Movement

Initially, the movement's main emphasis was on projects for improving the rural environment, such as piped water-supply systems, sewage improvements, and public wells. From this initial stage emerged an important lesson: that projects should be selected that would contribute immediately to the improvement of villagers' incomes. Although environmental improvements directly benefit the villagers and enhance their hopes for the future, such improvement without accompanying income growth may lead to unfulfilled expectations. Tangible results were needed to promote villagers' adaptability to changing rural conditions and technological progress.

Thus, beginning in the mid-1970s, the emphasis shifted from environment-oriented projects to income-generating ones. The government set a target for increasing average farm income to 1.4 million won (approximately US $3,500) by 1981, the target year concluding the Fourth Five-Year Economic and Social Development Plan. To achieve this goal, income-augmentation projects were introduced and government support was provided in the form of subsidies and credit.

Major income-augmentation projects were regional specialization of crops, livestock raising, group farming and marketing, and wage-earning self-help projects. To implement the projects effectively, especially those involving crop production, villagers were encouraged to organize Saemaul production units for group farming, with every farmer belonging to at least one unit. Rural women were encouraged to organize Saemaul women's clubs and existing 4-H clubs were renamed "Saemaul youth clubs" so that all would participate more actively in the Saemaul movement. A Saemaul credit union was organized in each village with government support to promote the spirit of thrift and saving, and a campaign was launched to induce every farmer to maintain a savings account in the union.

Extensive Participation

The government has widely advocated participation of individuals and groups in the community development movement. Local participation is the major element of community development, distinguishing it from other forms of social and economic policy. The Saemaul movement of Korea is probably unprecedented in its scope of participation.

Having begun with village-centered, environmental improvement projects, the movement rapidly expanded in scope of participation and range of activities. It has been extended to "factory Saemaul," "urban Saemaul," and "school Saemaul."

One can see the Saemaul flag flying beside the national flag and the Saemaul slogan painted at the top of almost every public building throughout Korea. At least once a day there is a television program portraying a success story of the Saemaul movement, accompanied by the Saemaul song. As suggested by cynics, everyone is doing something under the name of

Saemaul. This fact alone indicates how wide participation in the movement has been and how enthusiastically it was launched on a nationwide basis.

An official record compiled by MOHA indicates that more than 36,000 villages have participated in the Saemaul movement every year since 1975. This means that almost every village in Korea—large and small—has been involved in the movement. Participation in rural areas alone has increased from 32 million workdays in 1972, to 117 million workdays in 1975, and 273 million workdays in 1982. Calculated on a per village basis, participation was 923 workdays per village in 1972, 3,160 workdays in 1975, and 7,380 workdays per village in 1982—an almost eightfold increase over a 10-year period. With an average of 60 farm households per village, this implies that the average household was devoting about 123 workdays (or four months) to Saemaul activities in 1982.

The rapid expansion in activities is also indicated by the increasing number of projects undertaken over the period. The projects numbered 320,000 in 1972 and reached a peak of 2,667,000 in 1978—8.3 times as many as in 1972. Since then the number of projects has gradually declined, and a total of 1,080,000 projects were implemented in 1982 (Table 16.3).

The scope of participation is further demonstrated by villagers' contributions of cash, labor, land, and materials. In 1972 investments in Saemaul projects totaled 31.6 billion won, of which rural people contributed 27.3 billion won, or 86.6 percent, while the government's financial assistance amounted to only 3.6 billion won, or 11.3 percent (Table 16.4).

But as the movement has proceeded, the relative shares between the two sources have become reversed, although the absolute amount of

Table 16.3. Scope of participation in the Saemaul movement: 1972–82

Year	Number of villages	Number of workdays (10^3)	Number of projects (10^3)	Number of projects per village	Investment per project (10^3 won)
1972	34,665	32,000	320	14	98
1973	34,665	69,280	1,093	32	88
1974	34,665	106,852	1,099	32	121
1975	36,547	116,880	1,598	44	185
1976	36,547	117,528	887	24	364
1977	36,557	137,198	2,463	67	189
1978	36,257	270,928	2,667	74	237
1979	36,271	242,078	1,788	49	424
1980	36,938	227,856	1,836	51	510
1981	36,792	257,472	1,310	35	537
1982	36,894	272,751	1,080	29	802

Source: MOHA, ROK, *Saemaul Undong* (1972–82).

Table 16.4. Government and village contributions to Saemaul projects: 1972–82

Year	Total investment (10³ won)	Government contribution	Village contribution[a]	Other[b]
		Share of total investment (%)		
1972	31.6	11.3	86.6	2.1
1973	96.1	17.8	80.0	2.2
1974	132.8	23.1	74.4	2.5
1975	295.9	42.1	57.3	0.6
1976	322.7	27.3	70.5	2.2
1977	466.5	29.6	69.7	0.7
1978	634.2	23.0	76.9	0.1
1979	758.2	56.1	43.3	0.6
1980	936.0	u	u	u
1981	702.9	59.2	40.2	0.6
1982	866.6	48.3	34.4	17.3

Source: MOHA, ROK, *Saemaul Undong* (1972–82).

u—data unavailable.

a. Includes loans and credit.

b. Donations from nongovernment organizations.

investment has increased. The proportion of the people's contributions declined to 57.3 percent in 1975 and dropped further to 34.4 percent in 1982. Conversely, the government's share increased to 124 billion won or 42.1 percent in 1975, and again increased to 419 billion won or 48.3 percent in 1982, the rest being donated by various private organizations (Table 16.4). The reason for the shift in relative contributions by villagers and the government is that an increasing number of government-sponsored development activities has been added to the Saemaul category. The amount of investment per project has also increased, from 98,000 won in 1972 to 802,000 won in 1982 (Table 16.3).

Villagers' contributions in the form of labor accounted for 77.2 percent in 1972 but had declined to only 25.2 percent by 1982. Over the decade the major part of villagers' contributions shifted from labor to cash (MOHA, ROK, *Saemaul Undong*, 1972–82).

Training and Education

Early experimentation in implementing projects taught the government an important lesson: leadership is a prerequisite for self-reliant and self-sustaining community development. Village leaders play a crucial role in inducing villagers' participation in the Saemaul movement.

As a result, leadership-training institutions were established, beginning in late 1972. The Saemaul Training Institute was the main training institution at the central level. Under government sponsorship, 14 other central-level and 10 provincial-level training institutions were formed in succession. In addition, various types of informal training programs were provided at the county and village level.

Potential Saemaul leaders were elected from among villagers and offered a special training program that aimed at equipping them with effective leadership skills for becoming agents of change in rural areas. From 1973 onward, as the movement progressed, village women leaders, youth leaders, and county officials were included in the training program. In 1974 social elites and government officials were also included. In 1975 the training program was further expanded to include such classes of social leaders as cabinet members, parliamentarians, religious leaders, university presidents and professors, journalists, corporate leaders, and managers of business corporations.

In training these elites, the government encouraged them to participate positively and to give full support to the basic ideology and strategy of the Saemaul movement. Elites were to receive the training together with village leaders and under the same conditions, regardless of their social status, with a view to bringing them closer to rural situations and fostering the spirit of solidarity. The training included lectures and self-learning through case studies, group discussions, and field work and tours for "learning-by-doing."

The main features of the Saemaul movement can be summarized as follows.

1. The initiative for the movement came from the president and government leadership. All levels of government—central and local—were involved in one way or another, and every rural village was affected by the movement. Such a massive scale of participation and government support is probably unprecedented in the history of community development.

2. The Saemaul movement was designed and implemented around the individual village as the basic unit of community life, characterized by the pursuit of common traditional interests.

3. The movement does not differ much from other community-development efforts in pursuing material betterment of rural society. But it does differ greatly from others in that it has combined education and enlightenment with material goals.

4. The general procedure elsewhere in launching community-development programs has been to adopt an ideology and formulate a plan with objectives and strategies prior to actual implementation. But in the case of the Saemaul movement, action preceded the development of an ideology and appropriate strategies.

5. A wide range of development activities characterize the Saemaul movement. At the central level, almost all of the government's rural-development programs have been organized under the Saemaul label.

Organizational Arrangements and the Planning Process

Owing to the wide range of development activities and the complex nature of the Saemaul movement, it is essential for its programs and projects to be well organized and coordinated. To facilitate program formulation, implementation, and coordination among different projects, government agencies, and regions, a series of councils and consultative bodies was established, linking the central level with the village level.

Among these councils is the Saemaul Undong Central Consultative Council, headed by the minister of home affairs. Its members consist of vice-ministers of other ministries of the central government. Their major responsibility is to make decisions regarding the basic direction of support policies, government financial assistance, and guidelines for program planning at the local level.

At the provincial level is the Provincial Coordinating Committee, with the provincial governor as chairman and its members consisting of the directors of regional offices of such central agencies as the Office of Rural Development, the National Agricultural Cooperatives Federation (NACF), the Agricultural Development Corporation, and the National Livestock Cooperatives Federation. The primary responsibility of this committee is to coordinate among different functional departments of the provincial government and regional agencies the planning and resource allocation for various types of Saemaul projects.

At the county level, the County Saemaul Coordinating Committee has responsibility for promoting and guiding Saemaul projects. Its chairman is the county chief (*gunsoo*), and its members are chiefs of various county-level public offices, including rural agricultural extension, public health, the forestry association, agricultural cooperatives, and livestock cooperatives.

At the *myon* (township) level, the lowest unit of administration, the Myon Saemaul Movement Promotion Committee is responsible for decisions about assistance for the Saemaul village projects. The committee's members include officials and a few Saemaul leaders selected from villages of the *myon*. The committee assumes the crucial function of coordinating various kinds of development activities, in particular the delivery of necessary government support and guidance in project planning and implementation.

The identification of individual projects is the responsibility of village members. Project planning at the village level generally consists of project identification by villagers, design for implementation, and determination of the kind and amount of resources required, including necessary government assistance. The proposed plan is subject to approval by the Village Development Committee, which has 12 members and is chaired by the village chief or Saemaul leader. The committee then submits the plan to the village general meeting for approval by consensus.

The next step is submission to the Myon Promotion Committee, which screens and revises the proposed plans from all villages in the *myon*, taking into consideration available resources and the possibility of government assistance. The selected projects are then submitted to the county chief, who coordinates the proposals from different *myons* in consultation with the County Consultative Council. After going through a similar process of review at the provincial level, all the proposed projects are transmitted to the Central Consultative Council. The council, after compiling all the proposed projects, conducts the final review based on basic policy guidelines from the perspective of national and rural development.

In addition to the consultative bodies at various levels, departments and divisions specializing in Saemaul projects were established within the ministries of the central government to avoid unnecessary duplication and conflict in the planning and implementation process. Such divisions were established in the Ministries of Agriculture and Fisheries, Commerce and Industry, and Education. Within MOHA, the Saemaul Bureau was established to take responsibility for developing overall Saemaul policies and strategies. At all levels of local administration, divisions dealing with the Saemaul projects were established to support and guide Saemaul-related activities at the local level.

Operational Strategy for Government Support

At the national level the government plans a sequence of support, both financial and technical, for the Saemaul movement. It integrates a continuous evaluation of the capacity and performance of individual villages into the process of planning and coordination. The objective of government assistance is not simply to provide direct benefits to rural communities in the form of funds or materials, but also to enable the communities to launch development activities on their own.

Government financial and material support is provided for projects that are beyond the financial capacity of villages. Financial support is given in grants and loans. Efforts are made to supply the funds and materials in a timely manner so that the villages can make the best use of idle labor and other resources.

The government also provides technical support whenever necessary. This technical support includes provision of standard designs for such projects as piped water-supply systems, village hall construction, small bridge construction, and village restructuring; and consultation and training in marketing, management of group action, management skills for the Saemaul credit union, and improved farming methods, such as seedbed preparation, livestock raising, pasture development, and farm-machinery operation.

Technical support for farm activities is provided by rural extension agents. To provide technical services in nonagricultural fields, the Saemaul Technical Service Corps was organized in 1975 under the sponsorship of the

Ministry of Science and Technology. The corps is composed of specialists drawn from various fields, such as engineering, medicine, and food processing. At the local, especially *myon*, level, every official is assigned, in addition to his routine work, to a specific village to promote and guide the Saemaul projects. Police officers are instructed to lend all possible support to the activities of Saemaul leaders.

To maximize the effectiveness of its support measures, the government adopted four general principles of operation. They are:

1. *The best-first principle.* Villages that conduct the most successful Saemaul projects receive government help first. A successful project is defined as one in which villagers display a high degree of willingness, participation, self-help, and cooperative spirit.

2. *The step-wise principle.* As already mentioned, villages are classified into three categories depending on their level of development: basic (underdeveloped), self-help (developing), and self-reliant (developed). Projects are recommended to villages in the different classes according to their size, resource endowment, and physical and socioeconomic condition. Each village is advanced to the next higher class, step-by-step, when the minimum requirement for that class is fulfilled, measured by participation and the villagers' own contributions to project implementation.

3. *The learning-by-doing principle.* Villagers are expected to learn by doing, not merely by talking, through the process of trial and error. Although the process may cause inefficiency or even a waste of resources in the short run, it is expected to lead to greater efficiency in the long run, once experience and self-confidence are gained.

4. *The matching-fund principle.* Government support, particularly financial and material, is provided to villages that mobilize at least half of their total investment requirements in the form of cash or labor (Y. B. Choe 1978).

In addition to these four operational strategies, the government followed four guidelines in selecting and implementing projects. First, projects were selected by the consensus of village members rather than on the judgment of a few influential leaders. The Saemaul leader must try to obtain a consensus, which contributes both to village solidarity and to a democratic way of thinking. Second, projects should provide common benefits to the whole village, not to just a few persons or a small group. Further, projects that contribute to increased productivity and income receive priority. Third, the scale of a project must be based on a realistic assessment of villagers' resources and capabilities, because each village is obligated to contribute half of the total investment. A too ambitious project may discourage villagers' participation and result in the project's abandonment. Fourth, the selection and design of a project should take into consideration the conditions of the village, such as its geographical features, transportation, market access, village traditions, and financial resources.

Investment Patterns

During 1972–82 total investment in Saemaul projects increased 28 times in nominal terms and five times in real prices, while government's investment increased 116 times in nominal terms and 23 times in constant prices (Table 16.4). These investments can be classified as production infrastructure, income augmentation, environmental improvements, rural enlightenment, and urban and factory Saemaul projects.

Investment in production infrastructure, such as the expansion of farm roads and improvement of small-scale irrigation, received 61.8 billion won (or 64.3 percent of the total) in 1973 (Table 16.5). By 1982 the amount had increased to 191 billion won in nominal terms, but the relative share had declined to 22 percent. In the case of income-augmentation projects, the relative share increased from 6.1 percent in 1973 to 43.3 percent in 1982. In contrast, the investment in environmental projects marked a substantial increase in absolute terms, but the relative share remained fairly stable throughout the period (Table 16.5; MOHA, ROK, *Saemaul Undong*, 1972–82).

The investment in education/enlightenment projects, which include training for leaders and establishment of community libraries, increased in both absolute and relative terms. The investment in urban and factory Saemaul projects, which cover improvements in labor-industry relations, improvements in working conditions, and beautification of factory surroundings, remained relatively stable in terms of relative share (Table 16.5).

Table 16.5. Government support by program category: 1973–82

Year	Total investment (10⁹ won)	Share of total investment (%)				
		Production infrastructure	Income augmentation	Environmental improvements	Education/ rural enlightenment	Urban Saemaul projects
1972	31.6	u	u	u	u	u
1973	96.1	64.3	6.1	28.7	0.8	u
1974	132.8	42.5	25.4	21.7	2.4	8.0
1975	295.9	21.5	63.4	10.3	1.6	3.2
1976	322.7	27.9	47.8	20.9	1.8	1.6
1977	466.5	29.1	39.1	23.6	2.2	5.9
1978	634.2	20.6	38.3	38.5	2.0	0.6
1979	758.2	20.9	43.1	32.0	1.0	3.0
1980	936.8	u	u	u	u	u
1981	702.9	15.0	49.9	28.0	2.9	4.3
1982	866.6	22.0	43.3	24.5	4.1	6.1

Source: MOHA, ROK, *Saemaul Undong* (1972–82).
u—data unavailable.

The shift in the pattern of investment, especially from environmental projects to income-generating ones, reflects the changing emphasis in the Saemaul movement.

EFFECTS OF THE SAEMAUL MOVEMENT

It is difficult to make a quantitative assessment of the Saemaul movement's contribution to the rural economy, for two reasons. The movement comprised not only physical aspects of rural community development, but also a wide range of intangible but important aspects such as motivation, attitudinal and behavioral change, and education. In addition, a wide variety of other related projects were undertaken under the label of Saemaul (including even those carried out prior to the Saemaul movement), and one can hardly distinguish the effects of the Saemaul movement from those of other policy measures.

Effects on the Environment

Improvement of the rural living environment is one of the most notable achievements of the movement. The establishment of sanitary water supply systems and improved sewage systems made a substantial contribution to reducing the frequency of water-borne diseases. Prior to the Saemaul movement, most farm households had depended for water for drinking and other purposes on unsanitary village wells, which were located at a distance from most residences. The installation of running-water supply systems has not only provided disease-free water but has also been a great convenience to households.

Housing-improvement projects also contributed substantially to the modernization of the rural environment. In the past, the grey straw-thatched roofs of farm houses were viewed as a symbol of rural poverty and economic stagnation. A straw roof had to be replaced every year, at the cost of considerable labor. Replacement of the straw with tiles and other permanent materials has made it possible for farm families to use the straw for other purposes, such as making straw bags and compost.

Village restructuring projects, consisting of relocation, redevelopment, and partial improvement of villages, have modernized rural villages and raised villagers' confidence in further improvements in their living conditions.

Another important achievement has been the expansion of electrical and communication networks. As of 1971 only about 20 percent of the more than 2 million farm households had electric lighting, while the remaining farmers relied on kerosene lamps. By 1982, however, rural electrification and the installation of a telephone system were almost completed, except in remote mountainous areas and on isolated, small islands. The socioeconomic impact of these projects is quite impressive in rural areas. The projects helped reduce the cultural gap between rural and urban sectors.

Electrification created new consumer demand for home appliances, such as television sets, refrigerators, electric cookers, and electric irons. It also led to the use of electric power for productive purposes, such as the repair of farm machinery. The expansion of communication networks, especially the widespread installation of public telephones, has not only reduced the social distance between villages and cities but also increased the efficiency of transmitting public information, including news about farm products and market conditions.

The construction of village roads, farm feeder roads, and small bridges facilitated farm mechanization, the marketing of farm products, and the mobility of farm inputs.

Effects on Farm Income

With the shift in emphasis from projects designed to improve the living environment to projects designed to boost farm income, two types of projects have received major attention. One is to increase farm income through the introduction of cash crops and livestock raising, area specialization, and group farming and marketing. The other is to increase non-farm income by creating off-farm employment opportunities and wage-earning and self-help projects.

The effects of these projects can be measured by the growth of farm income over time and by a comparison of farm income with the income of the urban wage-earner's household. During the 1965–69 period, when the government's economic policy favored the urban sector, the average annual growth of income for the urban wage earner was 14.6 percent, whereas that for the farm household was only 3.5 percent. During 1970–76 the situation was reversed: farm household income was increasing at an annual rate of 9.5 percent and that of urban wage earners at only 4.6 percent. This was the period in which the high grain-price policy was effected and massive investment projects were implemented under the Saemaul movement. By 1970–82, the rates of income growth for the two sectors were equalized, at 6.6 percent per annum (MAF, ROK, *Farm Household Economy Survey,* 1960–82).

Another indicator of the income effects of the Saemaul movement is found by comparing the income levels of farm and urban wage-earners' households. During the period 1967–70, the average income of farm households averaged between 60 and 70 percent of urban wage earners' income. But since 1974 the gap between the two sectors has substantially narrowed. In some years farm household income even exceeded that of urban households. (See Table 15.7 in Chapter 15 for a comparison of rural and urban household income.) Of course, this improvement in the farm-income position cannot be attributed to the Saemaul movement alone. The high grain-price policy, put into effect two years before the Saemaul movement was launched, also contributed to the improvement of farm income.

Effects on Employment

In the early decades of Korea's development, employment objectives were often treated as a byproduct of economic growth. Today, employment problems are among the central issues to be considered in formulating development strategies. The Saemaul movement is an example of employment-oriented rural development.

Although an accurate estimate of its employment effect is not possible owing to a lack of quantitative information, its positive impact is suggested by the number of workdays that rural people have contributed to various Saemaul projects. Official statistics indicate that 1,858 million workdays of labor were expended in Saemaul projects from 1972 through 1982. Even if this labor contribution was not motivated by wage earnings, its purpose was to produce public goods for the common benefit of all villagers and to enhance the convenience of community life as well as incomes. Therefore, all of the labor participation can be viewed as an employment effect.

But various wage-earning projects were undertaken to absorb the idle labor force during the agricultural off-season. These projects were linked to the improvement of large-scale rural infrastructure and the living environment, such as road construction, development of new land, sewage projects, reforestation, and erosion control. Some 78,000 projects were undertaken that created employment equivalent to 94 million workdays during the 1974–82 period. The government's investment of 226 billion won was paid as wages during the same period (MOHA, ROK, *Saemaul Undong,* 1974–82).

The Saemaul movement has served as an employment-oriented development strategy to absorb large numbers of workers from the rural labor force. It has also alleviated underemployment in farm areas by implementing most projects during the farm off-season.

Effects on Rural Savings

The enhancement of saving propensity in rural areas has been another significant achievement of the Saemaul movement. From its beginning, the movement has emphasized thrift and saving; these virtues have been promoted by an ongoing nationwide savings campaign. Although this saving propensity has been made possible by increased income, a separate assessment is made of it here because of its importance in capital formation in rural areas.

Increases in saving ratio and in the amounts deposited by farmers in the agricultural cooperatives are used as indicators. Throughout the 1960s, when there was neither a high grain-price policy nor the Saemaul movement, farmers were able to save only negligible portions of their incomes. But since 1970 a substantial portion of their income has been saved. The ratio of savings to total income was less than 10 percent during the 1960s but increased to more than 20 percent in the 1970s (Table 16.6). This increase in saving propensity is attributable mainly to an increase in income, but

Table 16.6. Farm saving ratio, average per household: Selected years, 1960–82

Year	Farm income (10³ won)	Farm savings (10³ won)	Saving ratio (%)
1960	45	–0.7	–1.6
1963	83	5	6.0
1965	112	9	8.0
1967	139	11	7.9
1970	256	38	14.8
1973	481	123	25.6
1975	873	227	26.0
1977	1,433	401	28.0
1980	2,693	405	15.0
1981	3,688	803	21.8
1982	4,465	968	21.7

Source: MAF, ROK, *Farm Household Economy Survey* (1960–82).

it is undeniable that the saving campaign under the Saemaul movement helped to accelerate the pace.

In the past, most of the savings were in the form of cash at home because of the lack of modern banking institutions in rural areas. With the establishment of a mutual financing system within the agricultural cooperatives, not only the absolute amount of cash deposits but also the relative share in the total loanable funds have substantially increased (Table 16.7). In 1963 the relative share of farmers' deposits was only 20.6 percent, but it had increased to almost 50 percent by 1980. The saving campaign of the Saemaul movement played a decisive role in inducing farmers to save more and to make deposits in the agricultural cooperatives.

CRITICISM AND LESSONS

From the beginning, the Saemaul movement has been a government-initiated rural-development movement. Initiated by the president and the central government, efforts have been made to mobilize support for the Saemaul programs among all levels of government officials, including even the police and locally based army units. As the movement proceeded, an increasing range of government programs came under the Saemaul umbrella, to the extent that the term "Saemaul" became a synonym for government-sponsored development activities, especially in rural areas. As a determined government policy, implemented through an authoritarian and bureaucratic administrative structure, the movement has undoubtedly affected almost every rural household either by its ideology or through a project.

The Saemaul movement has contributed to the development of the national economy through a series of government investment projects. It has

Table 16.7. Farmers' deposits and relative share in the total loanable funds of agricultural cooperatives: Selected years, 1963–80

Year	Total loanable funds		Farmers' deposits		Funds from other sources[a]	
	Amount (10⁹ won)	Share (%)	Amount (10⁹ won)	Share (%)	Amount (10⁹ won)	Share (%)
1963	27.7	100.0	5.7	20.6	22.0	79.4
1965	44.2	100.0	10.6	24.0	33.6	76.0
1967	73.4	100.0	27.8	37.7	45.6	62.3
1970	192.2	100.0	95.4	49.6	96.8	50.4
1973	313.5	100.0	169.4	54.0	144.1	46.0
1975	615.1	100.0	264.8	43.0	350.3	57.0
1980	2,126.7	100.0	1,052.0	49.5	1,074.7	50.5

Source: NACF, ROK, *Agriculture Yearbook* (1963–80).

a. Includes such sources as government funds, loans from the Bank of Korea, and agricultural credit bond issues.

helped to reduce the income disparity between the urban and farm sectors by boosting farm income. It has fostered a spirit of thrift and saving, thus channeling farm surpluses into banking institutions for continued capital formation in the rural areas. It has contributed to balanced growth between the urban and rural sectors as well as among regions (Whang 1981).

Many people, including government officials and scholars, tend to attribute this successful performance of the Saemaul movement to a strong "top-down" approach, which made it possible to mobilize the massive participation of rural people on the one hand and all levels of administrative agencies on the other. Considering the history of fatalism and economic stagnancy in rural Korea, this top-down approach was an effective way of bringing about change in rural areas. It may have been a necessary step in motivating farmers and mobilizing resources at the village level as well as the bureaucracy at all levels of administration, and it had far-reaching effects throughout the rural areas.

An authoritarian approach could be justified in the initial stage of the movement on economic grounds as well. Rural Koreans did not have sufficient financial and technical resources to improve their own social and economic status. Some kind of inducement mechanism was necessary to stimulate the rural people. Government alone could perform this function and provide momentum as an agent of change.

After more than ten years of experience, however, the question arises whether this top-down authoritarian approach can be effective in administering community-development programs. There are many examples of the authoritarian approach hindering rather than encouraging farmers' voluntary participation and even leading to misallocation of resources in the implementation of projects.

First, at the level of the central government, almost all agricultural and rural-development activities tended to be categorized under the Saemaul label even without direct participation by village farmers. The centralized, authoritarian nature of the government (in particular the fact that it has virtually complete control of local finance) enabled it to exert great pressure on local administrators to produce immediate, dramatic, and concrete results.

At the local levels, officials tended to define the Saemaul movement in terms of the range of directives they received from higher authorities, often with specific targets attached. By and large they did not see themselves as representing or reflecting the opinions, desires, and needs of villagers in their districts. Rather, they tended to be concerned with finding ways of handling pressures from higher units to fulfill predetermined plans and quotas.

In the actual implementation process, therefore, officials at all levels have been concerned with meeting their immediate targets, without giving appropriate attention to the adaptability of programs and without concern for the end product—that is, service to villagers.

In many cases officials of both central and local governments have been too concerned with superficial results. For example, in some projects, resources and efforts were focused on villages close to expressways or railways, while less visible communities were left untouched. This happened especially in housing-improvement and village-restructuring projects. For housing improvement, it was necessary to follow the government design, which was in many cases more suitable for urban-style than farm living. In many village restructuring projects, all the houses were built facing north, which is contrary to custom in Korea, simply because expressways or railways were situated to the north.

Another example concerns the implementation of most Saemaul projects. Middle-echelon administration, including provincial, county, and *myon* offices, have tended simply to convey the higher-echelon administration's instructions to the lower-level administrations without considering local conditions, needs, and the capabilities of local administrators.

A third criticism is that, since individual reputations and promotions depend to a considerable extent on performance in achieving the Saemaul targets determined by higher units, there has been a tendency for the lower level of administration to overstress positive achievements in reporting to superiors. This practice may have led to an inflation of work performance, even to falsification of reports, so that the ordered targets could be fulfilled on paper.

Moreover, because of fierce competition among officials at all levels, for resources and credit for accomplishments, villagers have often been forced to donate, in the name of the Saemaul spirit, their land and labor without being properly compensated. There have been many cases in which excessive bureaucratic zeal in carrying out an assigned task has resulted in widespread resentment among rural people. Such situations have even reminded villagers of compulsory measures during the Japanese colonial period. Examples of this kind of blind execution of instructions from superior administrations are numerous. The planting of a new, high-yielding rice variety (Tongil) presents one of the most conspicuous cases.

With the aim of increasing rice production, the government allotted, through administrative channels, a target of acreage to be planted with the new rice variety. When it was first introduced in the early 1970s, farmers were willing to adopt quotas because of the high yields and favorable prices paid by the government. Market prices for the new rice began to fall because of consumers' strong preference for traditional varieties, and farmers realized that they could make more profit from traditional varieties. Many farmers resisted the quotas, but the government continued to insist that they grow the new variety. This led to severe conflicts between the government and rice farmers. In many cases, local officials destroyed seed beds planted with traditional varieties.

A fourth criticism of the movement is that the hierarchical nature of institutional structures has impeded horizontal coordinating efforts, despite the existence of formally organized consultative bodies at all levels. These bodies exist only in name. Officials tend to be narrowly preoccupied with their own immediate assignments—particularly with visible results.

There are local development headquarters, consisting of rural extension offices, agricultural cooperatives, health centers, forestry associations, and farmland improvement associations. The organizations are all mobilized to participate one way or another in the Saemaul movement. But the lack of horizontal coordination among these organizations has too often resulted in duplicate instructions that only confuse and embarrass rural people.

For instance, on many occasions the administrative authorities have unilaterally determined the types of projects to be implemented and the loan criteria without due consultation with the agricultural cooperatives. This lack of coordination among the related organizations not only reduced the efficiency of credit funds but also impeded the independence of cooperative functions.

A fifth criticism relates to the voluntary participation of villagers, considered to be one of the most crucial factors for the successful implementation of the Saemaul projects. That voluntary participation has been enunciated as a goal of the movement. In practice, however, there was an increasing tendency toward administrative coercion rather than encouraging villagers' voluntary participation and cooperation.

Various organizations have been formed within the villages to promote the Saemaul movement. The Village Development Committee is a typical village-level organization, formed under instructions from MOHA. The chairman of this committee is appointed on government authority, taking on the character of a public administrator. Therefore, the committee tends to channel the administrative orders of the upper-level authorities to the village level, regardless of the interests of the villagers. Under these circumstances, it is almost impossible to expect active participation by the villagers in the decision-making process.

The first lesson of the Saemaul movement is that its style of administration has been obviously inconsistent with the originally enunciated ideology of voluntary participation and cooperation. There is little evidence that the movement itself has promoted a process of planning at the village level or incentives to implement projects voluntarily. Willingness to participate in collective activities has been due in large part to villagers' traditional pattern of cooperative farming, such as labor exchange and joint work for pest control.

The second lesson is that the authoritarian and bureaucratic approach, once considered to be necessary and initially effective, seems to have come to its limit. With the advent of industrialization and urbanization, the rural people have been integrated into the monetary economy, and their educational levels have been enhanced to the extent that they are capable of making their own decisions. Government authorities can no longer expect villagers to submit passively to coercion. The implementation of rural programs depends ultimately on the voluntary efforts of individual farmers as well as on local administration. Planning "from above" must be complemented by planning "from below" for it to be effective.

These lessons imply the need for institutional reform of a fundamental sort as well as for changes in the strategy for rural development. The following suggestions are made in this regard.

1. A new type of administrative system must be sought under which provinces, counties, and *myons* may exercise full administrative functions suitable to their districts. Under the present public administration system, the lower a level is, the more restricted is its autonomy. For local administration, which is most closely related to local development projects and the daily lives of rural people, too little autonomy hinders the implementation of projects suitable to local needs. In the past, some efforts have been made to promote local autonomy to varying degrees, but at present there is virtually no participation by local authorities in the formulation of the policies they are expected to implement. If a system of complete autonomy is not acceptable for political reasons, a system must be devised in which the higher-level administration communicates its intentions to lower-level officials through indirect, rather than direct, involvement. Gradual measures must be taken to devolve work activities, on an individual basis, from planning to execution, to the lower administration.

2. Agricultural cooperatives should reflect farmers' opinions and pressure policymakers accordingly so as to influence the direction of policy. But in reality the agricultural cooperatives in Korea act more as a monopolistic

arm of the government than as a farmers' organization. It is urgent that the nature of agricultural cooperatives be changed so that they can function as true farmers' organizations. The cooperatives' involvement in a wide variety of government development projects should be discontinued. Instead, the selection of projects must be left to each cooperative, based on community requirements. This change will enhance the autonomy of cooperatives' operations and promote farmers' interests in cooperative programs.

3. Korea's rural sector is now in the grip of increasing labor shortages due to a steady outflow of the rural work force to the urban, industrial sector. Such a situation has led, among other things, to sharp rises in rural wages, constituting a major factor in the decline of the profitability of farm production. For this reason, the task of modernizing Korea's agriculture must necessarily be carried out in close association with farm mechanization. Effective farm mechanization can hardly be achieved unless it is pursued simultaneously with renovation of the agrarian system and the condition of farmland, as well as with development of systems for utilizing farm machinery that are suitable to the circumstances prevailing in rural communities.

4. Although the programs of the Saemaul movement have undoubtedly contributed to upgrading overall agricultural productivity, it is questionable whether or not the programs enhanced the profitability of individual farms. There has been a tendency to emphasize the achievement of an aggregate target alone and to neglect the profitability of individual farming activities. Emphasis must be directed toward enhancing individual profitability rather than meeting targets expressed in aggregate terms. Resource endowment, economic worthiness of projects, and the timing of their implementation should all be taken into account. Since the commercialization and monetization of agriculture are proceeding rapidly, market access should receive high priority in project selection.

INDUSTRIAL POLICIES

17 The Heavy and Chemical Industries Promotion Plan (1973–79)

by Suk-Chae Lee

In the course of Korea's highly successful economic development since the 1960s, its economy has confronted many challenges and hardships, but each time, the government has responded with ingenious economic policies. One of the most daring of these policies, and one that is still controversial, is the plan to promote heavy and chemical industries (HCI) launched during the 1970s.

Known informally as the HCI Plan, the plan has been blamed as one of the fundamental causes of the 1979–81 economic setback, during which period the Korean economy faced its worst ordeal. At that time, the government's economic policy was restructured primarily to overcome the problems that had risen in the 1970s from implementation of the HCI Plan. From 1986 to 1988, however, the improved performance of the heavy and chemical industries led to rapid economic growth. The HCI sectors were widely accepted as leading sectors for future growth, and a more positive view of the HCI Plan began to emerge.

With the benefit of hindsight, this chapter reappraises the debate over the appropriateness of having promoted HCI during the 1970s and searches for the lessons to be learned from the HCI Plan. In the next section I outline, briefly introduce, and analyze the characteristics of the HCI Plan. Then I present the reasons for promoting HCI, and, after surveying the major support measures of the HCI Plan, examine the outcome of implementation of the HCI Plan, and review the plan's theoretical appropriateness. Probing the plan's effects on Korean economic development in the subsequent section, I conclude the chapter by drawing the lessons to be learned from the HCI experience.

THE HCI PLAN: CONTENT, AMENDMENTS, AND DISTINGUISHING FEATURES

Korea's HCI Plan had its inception in the first half of 1973; even before 1973, however, HCI-related projects such as the Pohang Iron and Steel Mill and Hyundai Shipyard were under way (Table 17.1). The term "heavy and chemical" was first introduced in the government's Third Five-Year Economic Development Plan (1972–76). This plan, however, was neither an investment plan nor a master plan for promotion of HCI. By contrast, the HCI Plan of June 1973, formally known as the Heavy and Chemical Industries

431

Table 17.1. HCI projects promoted before 1973

Sector	Project name	Size	Building period
Steel and iron	Pohang Steel I	1,030,000 MT	1970–73
	Foundry	200,000 MT	1972–74
	Special steel	60,000 MT	1972–74
Nonferrous metal	Copper, zinc, lead refineries		Planned but not built
Machinery	Heavy machinery factory		1973–74
Shipbuilding	Hyundai shipyard	300,000 MT 5 ships	1972–73
Chemical	Ulsan petrochemical complex		
	Naphtha resolution center	100,000 MT	1968–72
	9 affiliated factories		1968–74

Sources: Figures taken from various HCI documents, compiled and arranged by the author. MT—metric tons.

Promotion Plan, was a comprehensive investment plan that embodied the strong will of the government.

The Original Plan

In his New Year's Address of 12 January 1973, President Park Chung Hee announced his intention to launch the HCI Plan. In May 1973, the Heavy and Chemical Industries Promotion Council, an interministerial committee chaired by the prime minister, was established. And in June 1973, the HCI Plan, requiring a total investment of US $9.6 billion between 1973 and 1981, was formally announced. It was declared a key strategy that would increase Korea's per capita GNP and exports to US $1,000 and $10 billion, respectively, by 1981 (HCI Promotion Council 1973). The corresponding figures for 1972, the year that had just ended when the plan was announced, were a mere $318 for per capita income and only $1.6 billion for exports (EPB, ROK, *Major Statistics*, 1989).

According to the HCI Plan, six industries were designated as "key" industries to be promoted: steel, nonferrous metal, machinery (including automobile), shipbuilding, electronics,[1] and chemical (see Table 17.2 for detailed project plan). There were several basic reasons for designating these six as key industries. First, these industries were expected to make the most

---

1. The heavy and chemical industries, narrowly defined, do not include the electronics industry. However, the electronics industry was one of the core industries slated for promotion in Korea's HCI Plan; therefore, any analysis of the HCI Plan should include the electronics industry.

Table 17.2. Projects included in the HCI promotion plan

Sector	Project name and description	Construction period
Iron and steel	Pohang steel extension (1.03 million MT to 7 million MT)	1979
	Second iron and steel mill (5 million MT)	1976–80
Nonferrous metal	Copper refinery (100,000 MT)	1974–76
	Zinc refinery (80,000 MT)	1975–77
	Lead refinery (50,000 MT)	1979–80
	Aluminum refinery (100,000 MT)	1976–78
Machinery	Changweon machinery industry complex Complex construction	1973–76
	Factory construction	1974–80
	26 material factories	
	39 general machinery factories	
	7 electric instrument factories	
	8 precision instrument factories	
Shipbuilding	Construction of 9 shipyards (2 small, 2 medium, 5 large)	Completed 1981
	Construction of 5 shipyards (2 medium, 3 large)	Completed 1985
Electronics	Gumi electronics complex construction 1st phase	1971–73
	Expansion	1977–81
Chemical	Oil refinery enlargement (860,000 barrels)	1973–81
	Completion of 3 subsidiary factories of Ulsan petrochemical complex	
	Ulsan complex enlargement	
	Naphtha resolution center (100,000 MT to 150,000 MT)	1974
	(300,000 MT to 350,000 MT)	1976
	New affiliated factory construction	
	Yoicheon integrated chemical complex construction	1976–79
	Fertilizer plant construction (7th plant)	1974–75

Sources: Figures taken from various HCI documents, compiled and arranged by the author.

of domestic resources, particularly of Korea's relatively abundant human resources. Second, they would be attractive to foreign investors, so that financing of the projects was expected to be relatively easy. Separate from these six industries, five projects were already under way, with strong government support, to develop special steel, brass, foundry, heavy machinery, and shipbuilding (Hyundai) plants.[2]

The HCI Plan was organized around a few large key projects, including the projects that were already under way. Key projects were expected to induce related investments through linkage effects. In the case of the electronics industry, however, the "key projects" approach was considered untenable, since it would be difficult to identify them; therefore, to induce private businessmen to make investments in these industries, a general incentive system was devised.[3]

It was expected that private enterprises would undertake key projects, except for expansion projects in iron and steel and construction of new chemical fertilizer plants, which would be undertaken by public enterprises. Most of the industries were designed to be developed as future leading export industries, whose share in commodity exports was expected to exceed 50 percent by 1980. Thus, the implication was that HCI's share in manufacturing value added would be increased to more than 50 percent by 1980 as well (HCI Promotion Council 1973).

Amendments to the Plan

After the oil shock of 1973, it was questioned whether the HCI Plan should be implemented, particularly under the conditions of high inflation and lack of foreign exchange reserves resulting from the oil shock. Despite this doubt the original plan was implemented without significant changes.

Nevertheless, the first amendments to the HCI Plan were made in the Fourth Five-Year Economic and Social Development Plan (Fourth Plan), which was finalized in December 1976. In the Fourth Plan, only three sectors' projects were designated to receive continued support: machinery, electronics, and shipbuilding. Several reasons were given for omitting or postponing projects related to the three other original key industries of the HCI Plan of 1973. In the case of steel, the overall supply and demand con-

---

2. As will be discussed in the following subsection, the HCI Plan was an outgrowth of an evolving consensus among Korea's leaders on the need for long-term industrial restructuring. The slant toward heavy industry began to be revealed publicly as early as 1970, and the five projects initiated prior to adoption of the HCI Plan in 1973 represent the beginning of the implementation of a strategy to develop HCI.

3. The incentive system for the electronics industry was composed of the following three elements: (1) a more open policy stance toward inducement of foreign direct investment and technology (e.g., permission for 100 percent foreign ownership); (2) preferential access to financial credit; and (3) provision of large industrial estates, solely for the electronics industry, with the infrastructure provided by the government.

dition dictated that additional construction was not urgent; the nonferrous metal and chemical fertilizer and pulp industries were viewed as lacking comparative advantage (EPB, ROK, *Fourth Plan*, 1975). The revisions of the HCI Plan announced by the Ministry of Trade and Industry following the Fourth Plan were as follows:

- Postponing the fourth expansion of the Pohang Iron and Steel Mill for one year (scheduled to finish in 1982);
- Reducing the scale of the copper smelter (from 100,000 to 80,000 metric tons);
- Dropping the aluminum smelter project;
- Discarding the planned expansion of three chemical fertilizer plants;
- Reducing the scale of the chemical pulp production plant (from 800 to 300 metric tons per day);
- Reducing the number of new shipyards from nine to two.

This amendment of the original HCI Plan, however, did not reflect any weakening of the government's determination to implement the HCI Plan.[4] Rather, it revealed the government's desire to minimize any further revision of the plan under the harsh economic environment caused by the oil shock. Thus, the HCI Plan was faithfully executed until a comprehensive stabilization program was announced in April 1979. By then, however, most of the planned projects had already been either completed or were well under way. Thus, all of the adjustments made thereafter served to ease financial difficulties faced by participants in the HCI program or to salvage sinking ventures.[5]

Distinguishing Features of the HCI Plan

Launching of the HCI Plan might seem like a mere extension or continuation of the government's past approach to industrialization. Even after the liberal reforms of the mid-1960s, Korea continued or strengthened various industrial policy measures, including enactment of industry-specific laws to promote so-called strategic industries such as oil refining, iron and steel production, shipbuilding, and the production of chemical fertilizers and cement. Furthermore, into the 1970s, the government did not hesitate to reveal its intention to build up heavy and chemical industries. And indeed,

---

4. On 28 June 1974, President Park delivered the following remarks in a speech regarding the HCI Plan: "This ambitious HCI Plan once faced severe challenge due to last year's oil shock and consequent worldwide inflation. Some of us suggested that the HCI Plan should be modified substantially considering new economic environments caused by the oil shock. The government, however, continued to implement the HCI Plan with its basic framework intact, and this began to bear fruit." (Office of the President, ROK, 1974).

5. For a full discussion of adjustment policies, see H. S. Chung (1985).

this constituted one of the central themes of the Third Five-Year Economic Development Plan (EPB, ROK, *Third Plan*, 1971).

The HCI Plan distinguishes itself from past approaches and plans, however, in several important respects. First, no past plans were as comprehensive in terms of the coverage of HCI projects, nor were they as ambitious. The past plans, covering five-year periods, set direction of industrial structure but fell short of singling out industrial projects that must be undertaken. The HCI Plan, however, covered a ten-year period and was composed of detailed, project-wise investment programs along with timetables for their construction. This leads to the second distinguishing aspect of the HCI Plan.

The past plans were far from being imperative plans,[6] though they strongly influenced resource mobilization and patterns of resource allocation. The HCI Plan, by contrast, was designed from the very beginning as an imperative plan, representing the government's strong will to complete each of the planned investment programs on schedule.

Because of the great size and the uncertainty of the business prospects of HCI projects, only the large business groups were qualified to take on such projects. They were extremely reluctant to participate in HCI programs, however. Thus the government had to handpick private investors for the key projects and coerce them into undertaking the projects by using the carrot-and-stick method. It accorded various incentives to those undertaking HCI projects, details of which are presented later on in the chapter.

Korea's resource endowment and level of economic development, however, made it highly unlikely that planned investments in the HCI sectors could be realized merely by stimulating private initiatives through incentives or by relying on the market mechanism. This brings us to the third distinguishing feature of the HCI Plan.

In the early 1970s, Korea clearly lacked financial resources, technically able manpower, and business experience, all of which are vital for the successful construction and operation of HCI sectors. This led the government to take a key project-oriented approach in implementing the HCI Plan. In this approach, the government would initially construct one or two large-scale plants in each targeted industry, usually in the form of final or intermediate assembly plants, and thereafter establish a business foothold in those projects. Through this approach, the planners expected to secure at least a minimum market size for related projects such as parts and components, in turn triggering chain investment activities by small and medium-size firms. In a sense, it was a top-down rather than a bottom-up approach to industrial restructuring.

---

6. An imperative plan, in contrast to an indicative plan where only broad objectives and strategies are provided, is quite detailed. The programs in the imperative plan are expected to be executed meticulously.

An additional characteristic of the HCI Plan was the collective accommodation of related projects in large industrial parks. Typical examples of such industrial parks were Changwon Park for the machinery industry and Yeochon Park for the petrochemical industry. This approach was expected to result in savings of infrastructure costs and mitigate pollution problems.

The ambitious scope, imperative nature, and key-project approach of the HCI Plan worked together to affect deeply the course and speed of Korea's economic development. The next section reviews the reasons why the government conceived such an ambitious plan.

BACKGROUND OF THE HCI DRIVE

Changes in both international and domestic conditions prompted Korea's decision to promote HCI. Internationally, Koreans faced a shift in U.S. foreign policy toward Asia and a potential change in Korea's comparative advantage due to economic development in other Asian nations. Domestically, Korea's successful construction of light industries as well as lessons from late-industrialized countries gave planners confidence that Korea should indeed construct its own HCI sector.[7] The following subsections describe in detail the circumstances and logic behind Korea's decision to promote HCI.

Concern for National Security

The advent of the Nixon administration signaled a rapid evolution in U.S. Far Eastern policy. Announced in Guam on July 1969, the Nixon Doctrine asserted that, barring a threat from a major military power, the defense of each Asian nation—both conventional and strategic—lay in the individual nation itself.

The Nixon Doctrine was intended to address the U.S. intervention in Vietnam, and it implied a decreased direct American role in Asia in the wake of worsening Sino-Soviet relations due to the Cultural Revolution in China. The withdrawal of American troops from Vietnam, therefore, signified the prospect of Washington's decision to withdraw its troops from Korea as well. The issue of U.S. troop withdrawal from Korea was decided in the spring of 1970, and the first phase of withdrawal was completed by March 1971.

Thus, under the rapidly changing conditions in Asia, President Park Chung Hee decided to adopt a policy of self-defense to ensure the national security of Korea. Such a policy required an economy centered on defense industries and supported by the development of HCI.

---

7. Most of these arguments are found in World Bank (1986:38–39). Some of them, on the other hand, reflect the author's personal observation as a participant in economic policy decision making since 1970.

Limitations of Light Industry-Led Growth

Several concerns with the limitations of light industry-led growth further convinced Korea's leaders of the necessity of constructing the HCI sector. First, import restrictions began to be put on Korean light industry exports by the United States and other developed countries in the late 1960s, and thus it was feared that the world market for light industrial products might not expand very rapidly.[8] Second, expectations of increased light industry product exports in the world market from less developed countries (LDCs) such as the People's Republic of China signaled that Korea's comparative advantage in light industry would be eroded. Third, Korea would not be able to overcome its trade deficit and consequent foreign debt burden as long as it continued to rely on foreign capital goods and intermediate materials to produce light industry export products.

Through development of HCI, Korea hoped to overcome the limitations of light industry-led industrialization. Moreover, the government gained substantial confidence in promoting HCI after completing the Pohang Integrated Iron and Steel Mill and the Hyundai Shipyard.

Confidence in Constructing HCI

Despite overwhelming skepticism on the part of economists, including those on the World Bank staff, toward the idea of Korea's building a large-scale iron and steel mill, President Park pushed the project, which carried much of his personal prestige. The mill's first machine was installed at Pohang in April 1970, with financial and technological support from Japan. During the month of July 1973, the firm produced more than 100,000 tons of steel; eventually it produced one million tons of steel annually. By 1974, the project was considered a great success because it produced quality steel products at internationally competitive prices.[9]

In the private sector, the Hyundai Group constructed a large-scale modern shipyard in 1972 with support from European business circles.

---

8. One example of why Korea's leaders were pessimistic about the prospects for light industrial exports is found in the Korea–United States Synthetic Textile Fiber Agreement signed in 1971. The Korean government and business circles were shocked when they received less favorable treatment in synthetic textile trade from the United States than that received by Japan. The Koreans had expected special treatment from the United States because: (1) the textile industry was vital to Korea's economy, as indicated in its 40 percent share of total Korean exports in 1970; (2) Korean textiles posed no threat as their market share in the United States was only 2 percent; (3) Korea fought alongside the United States in Vietnam; and (4) Korea was still a very poor country.

9. The price competitiveness of the Pohang Mill at its initial stage stems partly from government assistance in the form of infrastructure provided and discounted utility costs. However, most of its competitive strength came from the low cost of construction, state-of-the-art facilities, and the increase in capital costs after the first oil shock. (For a detailed discussion, see Amsden 1989:chap. 12. Amsden (1989:chap. 11) also includes a description of the success of Hyundai shipyard.)

Again, it became an instant success because it could compete in the world market.

The government concluded that these successes did not occur by accident but were the natural outcomes of a combination of bold risk-taking and careful utilization of changing domestic and international economic conditions. The economic conditions considered favorable to Korea's drive to build HCI were as follows:

First, Korea enjoyed the advantage of an abundant, well-trained work force and relatively low wage rates compared to the advanced countries, which were experiencing manpower shortages, workers' avoidance of heavy-labor jobs, and high wage rates.

Second, Korea could start with state-of-the-art facilities, and thereby acquire comparative advantage against advanced countries having relatively old facilities. This had been verified by the success of Korean steel mill and shipyard projects.[10]

Third, Korea could attract sufficient amounts of foreign capital for the HCI projects, given the country's credit rating in the international financial market.

Fourth, as a result of Korea's successful promotion of light industry, the critical market size for the HCI products could be secured domestically with "temporary" protective measures, thereby resolving the marketing problem, which was so crucial to success of the HCI Plan.

Fifth, Korea's businessmen as well as government officials were experienced in running industrial businesses for the world market, and could play a pivotal role in promoting HCI sectors as new export industries.

In addition to these favorable economic conditions, Korea had the benefit of the Japanese model, which could serve as a rationale for the HCI Plan in many respects. As a latecomer, Japan had relied heavily on foreign technology and equipment in its HCI development efforts. Yet, in the 1960s, Japan developed a world-class steel industry, and in the early 1970s the nation deeply penetrated the world's steel, machinery, electronics, and automobile markets, surpassing the United States and Europe in competitiveness. These accomplishments, which were pay-offs to its early efforts to build up HCI, enabled Japan to become a fully developed nation. Therefore, in order for Korea to catapult into the ranks of advanced nations, the government felt that development of HCI was the only available choice, and that there was little reason why Korea could not repeat the Japanese success.

---

10. The competition between the industrial countries and the deep economic recession after the oil shock of 1974 allowed Korea to gain easy access to the most modern technologies in the development of its HCI sector. Though some countries were reluctant to transfer advanced technology to potential competitors, there were always some countries that were willing to do so.

POLICY MEASURES TO PROMOTE THE HCI PLAN

To execute the HCI Plan, the government devised a new incentive system and readjusted the way it managed economic development. The most pronounced aspect of this change was a shift away from its previous development strategy, which had been characterized by export-oriented industrialization guided by market forces. Under the previous strategy, which was successfully implemented from the early 1960s to the early 1970s, most of the industrial projects were undertaken by private initiatives, and the government played only a supporting role. Exceptions were limited to strategic industries such as iron and steel, fertilizer, and oil refining.[11] After examining the development management and incentive systems of the 1960s and early 1970s, I will discuss how they were modified by the HCI Plan.

Development Management and Incentive Systems Prior to the HCI Drive

Even before the implementation of the HCI Plan, the technocrats who played the central role in formulating medium-term economic development plans sometimes had a hard time accommodating some of the big projects that were conceived by the president and thrust into their planning framework. Examples of such projects were the Pohang Integrated Iron and Steel Mill, the Seoul–Pusan Highway, and the Soyang Multipurpose Dam. These projects were introduced one by one, however, so the basic macro-framework charted by medium-term planners did not have to be discarded and the foundation of the incentive system did not have to be modified. These projects usually reflected an entrepreneurial spirit that was at odds with the technocrats' rational approach. They turned out to be successful and provided various external economies. Thus, the thrusting of big projects by political leaders into development plans often reinforced the rational approach of technocrats.[12]

The incentive regime of the period before the HCI Plan can be summarized as follows. First, various incentives, including preferential loan facilities and tax credits were targeted to foster export activities and export sectors in general rather than key industries. Second, the exchange rate was frequently adjusted to reflect the won's real scarcity value. Third, imports of the raw materials, intermediate goods, and capital equipment that were needed for exports were kept free of tariff and non-tariff barriers.

Thus, under this incentive regime, export-related activities and export industries were not discriminated against as compared to import-substi-

---

11. For a detailed analysis of Korea's development strategies and industrial policies during this period, see World Bank (1986:29–38).

12. This argument again represents the author's personal observation as a staff member of the Economic Planning Board from 1970 through 1984.

tuting activities or industries. Indeed the World Bank (1986:44) noted that the maintenance of an incentive regime with little sectoral bias was a remarkable aspect of Korea's development strategy.

The government attempted to reduce fragmentation and repression of the financial market even in its financial policies, by setting the real interest rates positive. Also, the trade regime was scheduled to be more open, as shown by the policy shift from a positive to a negative system in announcing the lists of importable items.[13]

With these development management systems and incentive regimes, which prevailed from the early 1960s to the early 1970s, however, promotion of the HCI Plan seemed very difficult. Thus, a powerful promotion body was set up in the Presidential Office, and modifications both in the existing development management system and the incentive regime began to be made.

New Development Management and Incentive Systems

With the announcement of the ambitious HCI Plan as an imperative plan, the Third Five-Year Development Plan, which had been formulated in 1971 to provide the basic macro-framework for economic management for 1972 through 1976, was effectively superseded. The simultaneous launching of numerous large-scale projects that required huge outlays of resources was simply impossible within the Third Plan's resource allocation framework.

As described earlier, most of the projects in the HCI Plan were to be undertaken by private enterprises. The private sector, however, considered business prospects for HCI to be uncertain and resource requirements for the projects to be beyond their capacity. Therefore it was difficult for the government to induce even the biggest enterprises to participate in the HCI programs without some kind of coercion plus sufficient incentives.[14] This situation led to the birth of a new incentive regime and the modification of the development management system. The main focus of the new incentive regime was on channeling resources into the targeted industries and thus securing their markets. To this end, financial and trade policies had to be changed and shifts in fiscal preferences also had to be made. Among these, the change in financial policy had the greatest impact on the industrial incentive structure.

To secure an adequate flow of financial resources into HCI and to lessen the risks involved, the government had to control the entire credit system and give preferential access at greatly subsidized rates to targeted industries. To do so, it established a special fund called the National Investment

---

13. For a review of financial reform, see McKinnon (1973:105–111) or Cole and Park (1983). For trade policies during this period, see World Bank (1986:32–37) or Krueger (1979:82–130).

14. A typical method of coercing was to convey to the concerned businessman President Park's wish to see the businessman's participation in the HCI Plan's projects.

Fund (NIF), which was funded by the government and financial institutions. Because the size of NIF was insufficient to cover the financial needs of the entire HCI Plan, the government decreed that a portion of commercial bank lending should be allocated to HCI projects as well.

Since a lower interest rate would reduce the risks involved in undertaking HCI ventures, the government discontinued the high interest-rate policy of the 1960s. Throughout the 1970s, the real interest rate remained negative (Table 17.3); this, in turn, created an excess demand for bank credit. Under these circumstances, credit rationing by the government became the eventual rule of the game, and governmental intervention in and influence on real resource allocation expanded continuously (World Bank 1986:39).

The liberalization of the trade regime that had been pursued since 1967 was reversed, and the government restricted imports of intermediate goods and of equipment needed to produce export goods. Such imports had hitherto faced no trade barriers.

In its fiscal policy, the government increased the budget for construction of HCI-related infrastructure. Large-scale industrial parks were constructed to accommodate HCI factories. And, with government funding, education and training systems were overhauled to produce engineers and skilled workers. Science and technology research institutes were also established to develop the technology needed for HCI.

The eventual consequence of these efforts was the transformation of a privately led market economy into a government-controlled one, in which the market mechanism was largely replaced by an imperative plan for the promotion of HCI.

Table 17.3. Real interest rates in the 1970s

Year	General loan rate	GNP deflator	Real interest rate
1972	15.5	16.3	−0.8
1973	15.5	12.1	3.4
1974	15.5	30.4	−14.9
1975	15.5	24.6	−9.1
1976	17.0 to 18.0	21.0	−4.0 to −3.0
1977	15.0 to 19.0	15.9	−0.9 to 3.1
1978	18.5 to 19.0	21.6	−3.1 to −2.6
1979	18.5 to 19.0	20.0	−1.5 to −1.0
1980	19.5 to 24.0	25.3	−5.8 to −1.3
1981	16.5 to 17.0	15.4	1.1 to 1.6

Source: BOK, Economic Statistics Yearbook (1974–82).

Note: Real interest rate = general loan rate − GNP deflator.

The following subsection briefly analyzes the actual implementation of the incentive system for the execution of the HCI Plan.

Actual Implementation of the Incentive System

Establishment of the HCI Promotion Council. As noted earlier, the HCI Promotion Council, with the prime minister as its chairman and the related ministers as its members, was set up to promote the HCI Plan. President Park wanted a closer control over the plan, however, and this led to the appointment of a senior economic secretary to the president solely in charge of the plan. The secretary was supported by a special task force whose formal status was the secretariat of the council. The senior economic secretary and the task force then made up the core organization that was empowered to implement the HCI Plan, under the supreme power of the president.

This organization had many functions, from choosing the enterprises that would participate in HCI programs, to developing incentives to induce participation and clearing obstacles to the execution of the plan.

The National Investment Fund and HCI's financial support. The initial funding of the NIF was only about 70 billion won—more than one-half of which was contributed by the banking sector. The size of the NIF grew rapidly, however, and by 1979 equaled 540 billion won. Although this growth was partly financed by contributions from forced savings schemes (the National Savings Association and National Life Insurance), the banking sector continued to provide the lion's share of funding for the NIF (Table 17.4).

The HCI sector was not the sole recipient of NIF financing. During the initial two years of the NIF, only about one-half of its funds was lent to HCI. Beginning in 1976, however, the proportion of lending by the NIF to HCI rose sharply and accounted for three-quarters of new lending. About 14 to 25 percent of NIF funds were lent in the form of credits for buyers of HCI products—both at home and abroad (Table 17.5).

The NIF was not, however, large enough to finance the execution of the HCI Plan alone. The banking sector, therefore, had to extend a large portion of their new lending to HCI. The share of incremental lending to HCI by the whole banking sector more than doubled from 32.2 percent in 1974 to 65.8 percent in 1975. Although this ratio dropped slightly after 1975, bank lending to HCI still accounted for more than 56 percent of incremental lending throughout the second half of the 1970s (Table 17.6).

Between 1975 and 1978, HCI sectors enjoyed borrowing costs that were 25 percent below those of other sectors. Terms of the loans made for HCI projects were also favorable: repayment periods were long (eight to ten years), and interest rates charged were, on average, 5 percentage points lower than the general loan rate. This difference in borrowing costs, however, disappeared during the HCI adjustment period of 1979–81 (Table 17.7).

Table 174. Financing sources of the National Investment Fund (NIF) (10^8 won; %)

Fund source	1974	1975	1976	1977	1978	1979	1980	1981
National Savings Association	88	113	121	170	264	390	418	480
	(12.4)	(10.6)	(6.4)	(8.0)	(5.9)	(7.2)	(10.3)	(7.1)
Public funds	115	168	254	453	546	644	914	755
	(16.2)	(15.7)	(13.4)	(21.4)	(12.2)	(11.9)	(22.5)	(11.2)
Postal savings and National Life Insurance	100	150	185	−21	0	0	0	−243
	(14.1)	(14.0)	(9.8)	(−1.0)	0	0	0	(−3.6)
Banking institutions	369	535	1,024	1,004	2,000	2,572	1,025	2,774
	(52.1)	(50.0)	(54.2)	(47.4)	(44.6)	(47.6)	(25.2)	(41.2)
Insurance companies	26	74	122	181	241	163	240	207
	(3.7)	(6.9)	(6.4)	(8.5)	(5.4)	(3.0)	(5.9)	(3.1)
Balance from previous years and redemption	10	30	184	331	1,436	1,636	1,471	2,760
	(1.4)	(2.8)	(9.7)	(15.6)	(32.0)	(30.3)	(36.2)	(41.0)
Total	708	1,070	1,890	2,118	4,487	5,405	4,068	6,734
	(100.0)	(100.0)	(100.0)	(100.0)	(100.0)	(100.0)	(100.0)	(100.0)

Source: BOK, Overview of the NIF (1989).

Note: Figures in parentheses represent the percentage share of each financing source in NIF funding.

Table 17.5. Allocation of NIF financing by sector: 1974–82 (current 10⁹ won)

Description	1974	1975	1976	1977	1978	1979	1980	1981
HCI	34.4	54.3	100.7	135.3	251.3	302.2	266.7	333.0
Facility loan	30.7	49.0	80.9	109.9	216.7	267.7	225.7	269.2
Credit for domestic machinery purchase	3.7	5.3	19.8	25.4	34.6	34.5	41.0	63.8
Electricity	17.0	43.2	40.0	40.0	102.0	100.0	120.0	160.0
Financing for exports on credit	0	3.0	10.0	30.0	29.7	30.0	30.0	75.0
Rural sector[a]	11.3	18.7	27.4	13.7	19.1	25.2	21.7	38.7
Total	62.7	119.1	178.1	219.0	402.1	457.4	438.4	606.7

Source: BOK, *Overview of the NIF* (1989).

NIF—National Investment Fund.

a. Includes financing for rural factories, promoted as "Saemaul Factories," and agricultural productivity enhancement projects.

Table 17.6. Incremental credit allocation by the deposit-money banks and the Korea Development Bank (%)

Industry	1973	1974	1975	1976	1977	1978	1979	1980	1981	1982	1983
(A) Food and beverage	8.9	14.5	8.9	3.5	3.2	2.8	2.5	3.4	6.0	7.2	8.7
(B) Textile and appliance	42.2	34.8	12.9	34.9	26.6	23.4	18.5	17.4	20.1	10.9	14.0
(C) Wood and furniture	7.1	7.6	-8.2	1.2	1.4	4.9	2.8	2.9	4.9	4.8	4.7
(D) Paper and printing	4.8	5.6	2.3	3.9	2.5	4.6	6.2	6.0	5.2	4.1	7.3
(E) Chemical, petroleum, and coal	7.6	11.6	25.3	17.3	16.0	16.1	14.1	19.6	16.1	15.3	15.6
(F) Nonmetal mineral products	3.3	4.2	8.1	2.1	4.7	7.2	5.5	5.6	6.2	2.0	4.7
(G) Basic metal	12.3	7.0	8.9	18.9	12.3	12.2	14.6	10.4	16.3	17.3	4.7
(H) Fabricated metal and equipment	15.8	13.6	31.6	19.7	32.4	27.4	29.7	29.8	20.2	35.9	38.0
(I) Other manufacturing	-1.0	1.1	10.3	-1.5	0.9	1.5	6.1	4.9	5.0	2.8	2.3
Total	100.0	100.0	100.0	100.0	100.0	100.0	100.0	100.0	100.0	100.0	100.0
Heavy industry	35.6	32.2	65.8	60.0	60.7	55.7	58.4	59.8	52.5	68.4	58.3
Light industry	64.4	67.8	34.2	40.0	39.3	44.3	41.6	40.2	47.5	31.6	41.7

Sources: World Bank (1986); BOK, Economic Statistics Yearbook (1985); BOK, National Income (1985).

Note: The figures are the shares allocated to each industry of the net credit increases of deposit-money banks and the Korea Development Bank. The HCI sector includes (E), (G), (H), and light industry includes (A), (B), (C), (D), (F), and (I).

Table 17.7. Commercial bank borrowing costs for HCI projects (%)

Year	Discount rate on commercial bills	Interest rate on equipment loans for HCI projects
1970	24.30	12.00
1971	23.00	12.00
1972	17.79	11.17
1973	15.50	10.00
1974	15.50	10.00
1975	15.29	12.00
1976	16.33	12.42
1977	17.25	13.00
1978	18.02	14.17
1979	18.75	15.00
1980	23.33	20.50
1981	19.50	18.00
1982	12.38	12.75
1983	10.00	10.00

Sources: BOK, *Economic Statistics Yearbook* (1970–85).

Tax incentives and other financial adjustments. To support the HCI Plan, the government instituted tax incentives and adjusted financial parameters in favor of HCI sectors. A major support measure for the HCI Plan was the Tax Exemption and Reduction Law of 1975, which offered a variety of tax incentives including tax holidays, investment tax credits, and accelerated depreciation to participants in HCI programs. As a result, the marginal effective corporate tax rate for program participants was between 15 and 20 percent, whereas the rate was between 48 and 52 percent for non-HCI firms (Table 17.8).

Meanwhile, export industries suffered a decline in competitiveness due to elimination or reduction of tax exemptions and other subsidies. Furthermore, as a result of the government's expansion of the money supply and fixing the exchange rate in order to contain inflationary pressure, the real value of the won rose, which lowered the competitiveness of Korea's export sector (World Bank 1986:42–44).

Modifications of trade policy and limitations on domestic competition. Implementation of the HCI Plan required a reversal of the government's trade policy, from export promotion to import substitution. This required instituting import restrictions and rolling back tariff exemptions on imports of certain items in order to encourage the purchase of products from domestic HCI companies.

Table 17.8. Effective marginal tax rate of HCI (%)

Year	Petro-chemicals	Basic metals	Fabricated metals and equipment	HCI (average)	Non-HCI[a]
1972	29.5	24.8	28.8	27.7	29.8
1973	33.6	30.8	36.1	33.5	38.6
1974	33.8	33.7	22.3	29.9	37.7
1975	16.9	12.4	18.3	15.9	52.1
1976	19.1	11.9	21.3	17.5	49.5
1977	19.3	11.9	21.3	17.5	49.5
1978	18.2	11.0	21.6	16.9	48.4
1979	21.6	10.6	22.7	18.3	48.5
1980	17.2	15.0	22.8	18.3	48.5
1981	19.5	16.4	26.0	20.6	51.1

Source: Kwack (1985:63–70).

a. The average of food and beverages, textiles and apparel, wood and furniture, paper and printing, nonmetallic mineral products, and other manufacturing.

The so-called Limited Tariff Drawback system, for instance, placed tariffs on imported items needed by Korean exporters. And establishment of domestic content requirements for industrial facilities further helped to increase turnover for firms participating in the HCI Plan. Moreover, higher investment tax credits were granted to businesses purchasing domestically produced machines, and in most cases high business entry barriers were imposed.

Cultivation of technical manpower. Construction and development of the HCI sectors would require a great amount of skilled manpower. It was estimated that the demand for skilled manpower in 1982 was 750,000, a six-fold increase from 127,000 in 1971.[15]

To meet the demand, several efforts were made. First, the government increased the enrollment capacities of science and engineering colleges, expanding the total capacity from 26,000 in 1973 to 58,000 in 1980. At the same time, the total enrollment in technical high schools doubled, and enrollment in technical junior colleges increased more than fivefold between 1973 and 1980. In the same period, the government established 22 vocational training centers, which produced 12,000 technicians per year.

The government also established six research institutes for science and technology, especially for the machinery, chemistry, and electronics sectors.

---

15. Expansion of technical manpower and promotion of science and technology had also been among the key objectives of the Third Five-Year Economic Development Plan.

Furthermore, it rapidly increased research and development expenditures. From 1974 to 1979, the amount financed by the government was 306 billion won, representing 54.5 percent of total R & D expenditure in the Korean economy (EPB, ROK, *Major Statistics*, 1989).

Construction of industrial complexes and other government support. Construction of industrial complexes was undertaken to save overall infrastructure costs, to realize operating efficiencies resulting from forward and backward linkage effects, and to minimize and control pollution produced by the chemical, nonferrous metal, and other industries. Between the announcement of the plan in 1973 and 1979, nine complexes were constructed.

HCI-related factories were placed at different locations based on their characteristics. For example, a steel industry complex was placed in Pohang, the nonferrous metal industry in Kunsan, the electronics industry in Kumi, the machinery industry in Changwon, the shipping industry in Ulsan, Ok-po, and Chukdo, and the chemical industry in Ulsan and Yeochon.

Besides these industrial complexes, the government supported major HCI projects through direct investment or subsidized NIF credits, or both. Because iron, steel, and fertilizer were essential to the development of the manufacturing and agricultural sectors, the government made direct investments in them through the Pohang Iron and Steel Company (POSCO) and the Korea General Chemical Corporation.

From 1974 through 1981, government spending on HCI projects amounted to 893 billion won, representing 3.0 percent of the total economic development budget (Table 17.9). Of that total, direct investment in major projects amounted to 466 billion won; construction of industrial complexes, 344 billion won; and interest rate subsidies, 211 billion won (Table 17.10).

Nevertheless, HCI's share of expenditures in relation to the total of all economic development expenditures showed no substantial increase. The government made large investments (relative to the economic development budget) in POSCO and the Korea General Chemical Corporation even before the announcement of the HCI Plan in 1973, and this explains the lack of a substantial increase in the ratio of HCI expenditures to total economic development expenditures.

OUTCOME

The basic framework of the HCI Plan, as described earlier, remained intact despite cancellation or postponement of some HCI programs. Even the first oil shock and the consequent adverse world economic environment could not shake the government's determination to fulfill the goals of the HCI Plan. Thus, by 1975, with its new incentive system, the plan had gained an irreversible momentum.

At that time, most of the big business groups in Korea were scrambling for a ride on the HCI bandwagon expecting to reap huge benefits from the

Table 17.9. Trends in size of government budget support for HCI programs: 1970–81 (10⁹ won; %)

Year	Total central government budget (A)	Budget for economic development expenditures (B)	Budgetary support for HCI (C)	Percentage of total budget devoted to HCI support (C/A)	Percentage of economic development expenditures devoted to HCI support (C/B)
1970	446.3	121.8	17.2	3.9	14.1
1971	555.3	153.0	29.4	5.3	19.2
1972	709.3	209.0	80.6	11.4	38.6
1973	659.7	143.5	13.6	2.1	9.5
1974	1,038.3	222.8	40.6	3.9	18.2
1975	1,586.9	397.0	80.8	5.1	20.4
1976	2,258.5	576.5	123.0	5.4	21.3
1977	2,744.6	654.7	91.3	3.3	13.9
1978	3,517.0	716.1	137.0	3.9	19.1
1979	4,905.7	1,431.9	93.2	1.9	6.5
1980	6,118.2	1,338.8	222.0	3.6	16.6
1981	8,040.0	1,493.9	104.8	1.3	7.0

Source: Figures from EPB, ROK, *Budget Summary* (1970–81), compiled and arranged by the author.

Note: General account basis.

new incentive system rather than from profitability of the ventures. Such eagerness on the part of Korea's major business groups enabled the HCI investment plan to be implemented successfully, and between 1977 and 1979 investments in HCI accounted for more than 75 percent of all investments in manufacturing (Table 17.11).

The policy goal of making Korea's industrial structure more sophisticated was also generally successful, at least from the HCI Plan's perspective. Such sophistication was generally considered identical to raising the share of HCI in total value added and in exports of manufactured goods. The plan targeted the share of HCI to exceed 50 percent by 1980. Though there was a slight delay in this timetable, the share of HCI in manufacturing value added and exports indeed had surpassed the 50 percent benchmark by the early 1980s (Table 17.12). It is noteworthy that the HCI Plan was successfully executed and produced at least the targeted statistical results.

Despite the statistical success, most of the HCI projects suffered from extremely low capacity utilization (Table 17.13) resulting in consequent financial difficulties for Korea's major business groups by 1979. The difficulties

Table 17.10. Allocation of government budget for HCI programs: 1970–81 (10⁶ won; %)

Year	Industrial complexes		Government investments in HCI		Subsidies for interest rate		Total	
	Value	Share	Value	Share	Value	Share	Value	Share
1970	6,825	39.8	7,130	41.6	3,198	18.6	17,153	100.0
1971	5,295	18.0	19,758	67.2	4,360	14.8	29,413	100.0
1972	4,476	5.6	71,957	89.2	4,205	5.2	80,638	100.0
1973	3,823	28.0	8,177	59.9	1,640	12.0	13,640	100.0
1974	23,846	58.7	11,657	28.7	5,088	12.5	40,591	100.0
1975	30,081	37.2	40,476	50.1	10,221	12.7	80,778	100.0
1976	42,884	34.9	67,000	54.5	13,070	10.6	122,954	100.0
1977	44,869	49.1	25,000	27.4	21,437	23.5	91,306	100.0
1978	47,735	34.9	63,815	46.6	25,406	18.6	136,956	100.0
1979	44,323	47.5	0	0	48,898	52.5	93,221	100.0
1980	52,183	23.5	133,571	60.2	36,259	16.3	222,013	100.0
1981	37,297	35.6	17,260	16.5	50,228	47.9	104,785	100.0
1974–81	323,218	36.2	358,779	40.2	210,607	23.6	892,604	100.0
1970–81	343,637	33.3	465,801	45.1	224,010	21.7	1,033,448	100.0

Source: Figures from EPB, ROK, Budget Summary (1970–81), compiled and arranged by the author.
Note: General account basis.

Table 17.11. Facility investment in the manufacturing sector (10⁹ won)

	All industries	Manufacturing (A)	HCI (B)	Percentage of facility investment in HCI (B/A)
1973–74	1,054	707	434	61.4
1975	1,098	621	481	77.5
1976	1,279	838	622	74.2
1977	2,026	1,380	1,040	75.4
1978	3,125	2,148	1,719	80.0
1979	3,734	2,469	1,870	75.7
Average				75.5

Source: Korea Development Bank (1984).

Table 17.12. Structural change in manufacturing (% share)

	Value added				Export			
	1970	1975	1980	1983	1970	1975	1980	1983
Light industry	64.0	55.5	48.6	46.1	81.8	66.1	52.4	43.5
HCI	36.0	44.5	51.4	53.9	18.2	33.9	47.6	56.5
Total	100.0	100.0	100.0	100.0	100.0	100.0	100.0	100.0

Source: Compiled by the Ministry of Trade and Industry, ROK, using data from BOK, *Input-Output Tables* (1985).

Table 17.13. Capacity utilization in HCI (%)

Industry	1976	1977	1978	1979	1980
Chemical	91.9	98.1	110.4	95.4	80.3
Basic metals	78.6	81.1	88.1	81.0	71.3
Fabricated metals and machinery	61.0	57.1	61.7	62.6	53.1

Source: Compiled by the Ministry of Trade and Industry, ROK.

Note: "As of 1980 Korean urea production costs were five times as high as U.S. and Canadian costs, and ten times as high as Middle Eastern costs. Thus substantial capacity had to be scrapped. Utilization of automobiles had fallen to about one-third of capacity. The Changwon machinery complex's huge foundry shops were operated at only a fraction of capacity" (World Bank 1986).

became more severe when a new economic policymaking team formed in early 1979 began to tighten the money supply, which had been previously loosened in the wake of implementing the HCI Plan. The tight monetary policy and the severe world economic recession that followed the second oil shock, among other factors, worked together to transform the difficulties into a crisis.

In 1980, Korea experienced its worst economic crisis since the end of the Korean War. Its growth rate plunged to –3.7 percent, while the inflation rate soared to 39 percent in terms of the wholesale price index and the balance-of-payments deficit climbed to approximately 9 percent of GNP (Table 17.14). Though the assassination of President Park and the ensuing political and social turmoil on the eve of the second oil shock undoubtedly contributed to these results, the financial crisis faced by Korea's major business groups and the weakening competitiveness of Korea's light industries were considered the fundamental causes of the disasterous economic conditions.

When the second oil shock took place, Korea was poorly prepared to weather the consequent adverse world economic environment. Most new investments in the second half of the 1970s had been made in the form of HCI projects, very often at the expense of light industries. Also, various economic parameters worked against not only these light industries but against exporting activities in general as well. (A detailed analysis of this situation will be made below.)

In addition, Korea still lacked the basic conditions required for successful operation of HCI businesses even by the end of the 1970s. These conditions include having enough scientists and skilled manpower, as well as experience in marketing HCI products. Moreover, the leaders of HCI businesses failed to realize the importance of upgrading their technology and productivity, a vital requirement, in the long run, for the successful

Table 17.14. Economic circumstances surrounding the 1980 economic crisis

Economic indicators	1978	1979	1980	1981
Economic growth rate (%)	9.8	7.2	–3.7	5.9
Price increase rate (%)				
WPI	11.8	18.6	39.0	20.4
CPI	14.5	18.2	28.7	21.4
Current account deficit (10^6 US $)	10.9	41.5	53.2	46.5
Foreign debt (10^6 US $)	148.7	205.0	273.7	324.9
Oil price ($/barrel)	13.1	18.0	30.9	34.5
International interest rate (Asian dollar rate)	12.0	14.8	18.1	13.9

Source: EPB, ROK, *Major Statistics* (1990).

operation of the HCI businesses. This problem could arise because the benefits accorded to the participants of the HCI program under the new incentive regime were large enough to guarantee profitability even without state-of-the-art technology and productivity.

The unpreparedness of Korea's major business groups to run the HCI businesses and the financial crisis that they faced worked together to convince the new government's top decision makers, who took power in 1980, that most of the newly built HCI projects were de facto white elephants. Their pessimistic view of the future prospects of HCI was hardened by the realization that, due to high real oil prices, most of Korea's basic petrochemical businesses could not compete with their counterparts in natural-gas-producing countries.

These developments led the new government to launch a wide range of economic reforms to salvage the future of the Korean economy. Its first step toward reform was focused on relieving Korea's major business groups of their financial difficulties, most of which were caused by their participation in the HCI programs. Thus, major heavy electrical equipment producers (Hyosung, Kolon, and Ssangyong) were merged in 1980 and were granted monopoly status. Automobile producers were required to specialize: Hyundai and Daewoo in passenger cars, Kia in trucks, and Dong-A in specialty vehicles. Hyundai Heavy Machinery Company was nationalized, but it was ultimately broken into smaller firms that were handed over to the management of Samsung, Lucky-Goldstar, and the Korea Electric Power Company (KEPCO). In addition, the fertilizer industry was merged and its capacity reduced (World Bank 1986:50; H. S. Chung 1985).

At the same time, price stabilization, rather than growth, was accorded top priority, and industrial policy shifted its focus away from industry-specific policies toward a functional approach. Under this new industrial policy, the incentive regime was reorganized to give R & D activities and the training of engineers and skilled workers tax incentives and financial support irrespective of industry. Also, the wide dispersal of effective protection rates among industries was narrowed. As a result, exporting activities and export sectors—both light and HCI sectors—came to enjoy at least neutral treatment compared to the import-substituting activities of HCI. The government also shifted its role away from making investment decisions toward coordinating industrial policy and promoting small and medium-size firms while encouraging science and technology development efforts.

Along with adjusting its own role, the government lifted various market-entry barriers in order to promote competition. It believed that only through competition would Korean enterprises regain their competitiveness in the world market, and that this, in turn, was the only way to put the economy back on a rapid growth track. It was this spirit that promoted the rapid liberalization of the trade regime and enactment of a new fair trade law

(EPB, ROK, *Fifth Plan*, 1981).

Despite these painful structural adjustment efforts, general performance of the HCI sectors remained sluggish until 1984. According to a Bank of Korea survey (BOK, *Comparative Advantage of Korean Industries*, 1985), for example, the competitive position of HCI, measured in terms of revealed comparative advantage (RCA) indices, still remained very weak, as shown by RCA indices of below 100 for all HCI sectors except shipbuilding, iron and steel products, and cement for 1982. Even in the case of the electronics industry, the RCA barely exceeded 100 (Table 17.15).

Dramatic changes have occurred, however, since 1986. The changes were foreseen even before then, with the electronics and petrochemical industries taking off in 1983. The petrochemical industries, whose outlook was particularly gloomy because of high real oil prices,[16] experienced a sudden swing of fortune as real oil prices began to drop, contrary to the expectations of many economists. The turning point for HCI sectors as a whole, however, arrived in early 1986, with the "three lows"—low oil prices, low

Table 17.15. Trends in RCA indices by commodity

Commodity	1970	1975	1980	1982
Chemical products	8.3	12.3	18.1	17.5
Rubber products	56.6	181.7	279.1	142.7
Shipbuilding	18.0	99.6	278.7	666.6
Fertilizer	155.3	0.1	265.6	154.5
Cement	130.8	261.4	234.3	239.0
Pottery and china	11.4	73.6	209.9	184.9
Watches	3.5	164.2	157.2	109.4
Iron and steel	25.4	61.7	154.4	174.4
Electronic equipment	74.6	107.8	134.8	108.7
Glass products	16.1	32.3	29.8	38.8
Railroad vehicles	0.0	117.3	87.4	94.3
Automobiles	1.9	18.5	18.2	16.0
Machinery	6.8	9.1	12.8	11.1
Nonferrous metals	14.2	2.6	12.9	16.1
Precision instruments, etc.	21.2	24.5	30.0	21.5
Average	37.5	78.0	128.5	133.9

Source: BOK, *Comparative Advantage of Korean Industries* (1985).

RCA—Revealed comparative advantage.

16. Even in 1986, the World Bank's outlook for Korea's petrochemical industry was very dark (see World Bank 1986:46).

world interest rates, and low value of the U.S. dollar (which in turn reflected a substantial depreciation of the Korean won versus the Japanese yen and the deutsche mark). Since then, the vast, empty sites of Changwon and Yeochon industrial parks, which had come to symbolize the wastefulness and recklessness of the HCI Plan, have been fully occupied by new business projects.

The phenomenal increase in HCI activities and investments, as witnessed by the change in the industrial parks, was helped tremendously by the success of car exports to America. It not only induced a continuation of new investments into the steel and auto parts and components industries but also improved the overall image of Korean manufactured products. It was at this time that Korea's leading business groups began to secure a beachhead into high-tech electronics sectors such as videotape recorders, microchips, and computers. As the following table indicates, the double-digit economic growth since 1986 was clearly led by the exports of and investments into the HCI products (Table 17.16). Furthermore, the success of HCI sectors contributed greatly to the achievement of the long-cherished goal of attaining a balance-of-payments surplus by leading the rise in exports, on the one hand, and by replacing domestic supply for hitherto

Table 17.16. Trends in major indicators in the manufacturing sector (% increase)

Indicators	1980	1982	1984	1986	1988	Average 1986–88
Manufacturing growth rate	−0.7	6.7	17.3	18.4	13.0	16.5
HCI	−2.9	8.9	20.4	20.9	17.0	20.2
Others	1.4	4.4	13.6	15.0	7.1	11.4
Total employment in manufacturing	−4.6	6.1	2.5	9.2	5.7	10.0
Full-time employment	−3.6	3.5	3.4	3.6	0.7	3.4
HCI	−4.5	6.0	6.4	5.9	3.1	5.7
Others	−2.7	1.1	0.2	1.0	−2.3	0.7
Manufacturing exports (current)	17.6	3.7	20.2	15.1	30.1	27.0
HCI	25.2	14.6	24.1	5.5	36.8	25.7
Others	11.7	−6.1	15.1	29.3	21.9	38.9
Manufacturing fixed investment	−28.7	3.7	37.1	25.1	14.0	25.3
HCI	−20.1	2.2	49.6	43.9	12.1	27.6
Others	−43.0	6.4	17.9	−13.5	18.9	20.3

Sources: BOK, *National Income* (1985–89); Ministry of Labor, ROK, *Monthly Labor Statistics* (1981–89). Fixed investment by sector was calculated by the Research Department, Bank of Korea.

imported industrial intermediate inputs, on the other.

Further success of the HCI Plan can be seen in the performance of the petrochemical and steel industries. The petrochemical industry, which became a new star of the Korean economy, continued to support the production and expansion of Korean exports by providing a stable supply of petrochemical products even in the midst of worldwide shortage. The steel industry also played a key role in sustaining the competitiveness of Korea's manufactured exports by serving domestic industrial activities even when the world's demand for steel outstripped its supply. In addition, the success of HCI generated a lion's share of productive job opportunities, thereby ending Korea's labor surplus (Table 17.16).

Currently the Korean economy's future depends on the performance of HCI sectors, since Korea has transformed its industrial structure away from one led by labor-intensive light industries to one led by skill-intensive HCI sectors. This new status of HCI sectors, therefore, suggests a positive, though cautious, evaluation of the HCI Plan. In the following sections, I will look at the plan's theoretical appropriateness and its impact on Korea's long-term economic development.

THEORETICAL APPROPRIATENESS

Theoretical Issues of the HCI Plan

We should understand both the objectives of the HCI Plan and the logic behind it in order to test its theoretical validity. Unlike most Latin American nations, which have promoted industrialization by import-substitution while ignoring the benefits of the international division of labor, Korea with its HCI Plan aimed to gain the long-term benefits of international trade from the very beginning. Thus, industries such as electronics, automobile, shipbuilding, and machinery constituted the core of the plan. It was believed that Korea would have dynamic comparative advantage in these rapidly expanding, technology-intensive industries.

Projects targeted by the government under the HCI Plan also included producer-goods sectors such as chemicals, nonferrous metals, and steel, which the government believed should be promoted for reasons other than merely to gain dynamic comparative advantage. In addition to developing these industries as a prerequisite to the promotion of defense industries, it was conceived as a way to ease the balance-of-payments deficit by substituting domestically produced goods for imports; they would also serve as cushions in case of worldwide shortage. The HCI planners thought that even these industries could gain a competitive edge, if they were built in the optimum scale with state-of-the-art facilities. However, the basic rationale behind the plan for these producer-goods industries stems not from efficiency but from noneconomic considerations.

If investment decisions had been left solely to private initiatives or market forces, neither investments into nor an international competitive edge in these industries would have been possible. This was the reason for developing the HCI Plan and the incentive system for implementation of the plan.

Considering the objectives of and the logic behind the HCI Plan, we can narrow the focus of the plan's theoretical validity to two issues. The first issue is related to sectoral resource allocation, which has favored HCI sectors in order to attain a desirable industrial structure even at the expense of light industries. The second relates to how to secure desired resource allocation. Specifically, the issue is whether the government should systematically select investment projects and intervene in the market to realize the planned resource allocation, or whether it should let private initiatives and market forces determine investment allocation.

Theories Supporting the HCI Plan and Its Implementation Method

The Soviet economist Fel'dman, whose works were introduced to the West by Domar, shows in his two-sector model that, in the case of a developing country like the Soviet Union, allocation of greater resources into the capital-goods sector would not only accelerate the economic growth rate but also ensure a greater consumption level in the long run (Domar 1957:223–61). The Indian economist Mahalonobis (1953/54) reached the same conclusion (Bhagwati and Chakravaty 1969). The development strategy advocated by Fel'dman and Mahalonobis was adopted in Joseph Stalin's development plans for the Soviet Union and in India's First Five-Year Economic Development Plan.

Galenson and Leibenstein, the postwar development economists, insisted that developing countries should invest in capital-intensive industries to maximize future income stream. Their theory rests on the assumption that capital-intensive industries have relatively high profit margins, which would effect a rise in the savings rate and thus lead to an increased growth rate (Galenson and Leibenstein 1955). If we assume that HCI sectors are capital-intensive, then we can interpret their argument to be in support of the HCI Plan.

Many studies that use historical analysis also support this strategic emphasis on capital-goods industries. From the development experiences of advanced countries, Hoffman (1958) showed that as an economy develops, the weight of the capital-goods sector, and therefore the share of HCI, increases. Also, Gerschenkron (1962) pointed out that the "late-industrialized countries" of Europe concentrated on the promotion of capital-goods industry rather than on the consumption-goods industry. Nakamura, a Japanese economist, also indicated that Japan's postwar economic success was helped largely by the nation's HCI sectors, which were built at the government's initiative since the late 1930s in preparation for the Second World War (Nakamura and Grace 1985:56–57).

A different theoretical approach was taken by development economists such as Rosenstein-Rodan, Hirschman, and Chenery, who advocated that the developing countries should allocate their resources to sectors with technological or dynamic external economies. Chenery (1961), in particular, suggested that the neoclassical resource allocation theory should be modified to emphasize dynamic comparative advantage. These theories support the HCI Plan's strategy of promoting the electronics, machinery, automobile, and shipbuilding industries, since the reasons for promoting these industries rest on the principles of dynamic comparative advantage and externality.

The second point, that industrialization of a developing country should be led by government instead of market forces, has also been supported by the postwar economists' analysis of the experiences of "late-industrialized" countries. A detailed explanation of the experiences of the "latecomers" will not be made in this chapter, as they have been well documented in Gerschenkron (1962).

Similar prescriptions were offered by the development economists who were active after World War II. It is well known that they cited industrialization as the surest way to economic development for underdeveloped countries. They also believed that industrialization efforts in the developing countries were hampered by constraints such as shortage of entrepreneurs and savings, distortions arising from the existence of externalities on a wide range of market prices, and segmentation of domestic markets. Thus, they argued that without deliberate, intensive, and guided governmental effort, developing countries would not achieve industrialization (Sen 1983; Rosenstein-Rodan 1984).

These theories, in combination with a pessimistic attitude toward export of industrial products, gave birth to the Latin American-style development strategy, which denies resource allocation by market forces. Even Asian countries under the influence of the above theory (with the exception of Hong Kong and Singapore, both of which adopted a development strategy of making the most of the benefits of the international division of labor) considered a development plan supported by strong government leadership to be essential to achieving industrialization.

Empirical Evidence and Counterarguments

I have examined a variety of historical evidence and development theories supporting the logic behind Korea's HCI Plan. Yet the empirical evidence of postwar development efforts shows clearly that these theories, in many cases, failed to deliver on their promises. Failure was particularly pronounced when a nation failed to exploit the benefits of the international division of labor. The experiences of the Soviet Union and India are examples of such cases. Their development performances have shown that emphasizing the capital-goods sector while ignoring the benefits of the international division of labor impairs a nation's long-term economic competitiveness and fails to increase national output.

Such failures appear inevitable because the great obstacles to the development of underdeveloped countries were the lack of savings and foreign exchange. Nevertheless, these nations sacrificed profitable and foreign exchange-earning light industries and therefore experienced an inadequate supply of foreign exchange. In addition, their use of expensive but poor quality machines and inferior intermediate goods produced by domestic heavy industries undermined the international competitiveness of their light industries.

Such apparent failures notwithstanding, the infant industry argument, which considers dynamic comparative advantage and various externalities, is still deemed reasonable by even the most conservative economists, though there remains some disagreement on the method of promotion. The real issue, therefore, does not lie in selecting the industries for promotion, but in charting the role of government and the kind of incentive system that needs to be established.

In this respect, Harberler (1964) represents one extreme, opposing any kind of activist government role, whereas the World Bank takes a more practical view. In his counterargument to Chenery's assertion that neoclassical resource allocation theory should be modified, Harberler (1964) once insisted that no kind of government planning could be superior to the functioning of the market mechanism and that government could not supersede the role of private entrepreneurs. Evaluating the postwar development efforts of LDCs, the World Bank (1983:41) concluded that the best way to achieve continued economic growth is to maintain a price system reflecting relative scarcity (see also World Bank 1987). In other words, even if a government takes an active role in developing its economy, it should not distort or shrink the market function but encourage the market function and pursue the benefits of the international division of labor.

Conclusion

In light of the above discussion, one should criticize the HCI Plan not for its sectoral choice but for the validity of the government's role and the cost Korea paid to achieve the plan's target. Even in this regard, one must note that there are abundant cases that make it inappropriate to criticize the HCI Plan solely on the basis of theoretical norms of static neoclassical economics.

The trend until the 1970s, for instance, was to promote infant industries and to accept an active role for government to that end. Both Germany and Japan completed their industrialization successfully, with approaches that differed from static neoclassical economics, and caught up to the United States, Great Britain, and France (Gerschenkron 1962; Nakamura and Grace

1985; Morishima 1982). Such cases indicate that the development processes in the real world are much more complex than might be judged by pure economic theory.[17]

Nevertheless, harsh criticism of the HCI Plan continued in the early 1980s. The criticism centered on the misallocation of resources that resulted from its "pick the winner" approach and its deliberate ignoring of market forces. The incentive regime designed to support the plan's implementation was another target of criticism, on the grounds that it distorted market prices and induced economic behavior that damaged Korea's economic growth potential. Since much of the criticism has centered on the cost of the HCI Plan (J. H. Yu 1989), let us review its costs as well as its benefits to the economy.

EFFECTS ON KOREA'S ECONOMIC DEVELOPMENT

There are two contrasting views of the impact of the HCI Plan on Korea's economic development. A critical view, which emerged out of the economic crisis of 1980, is now widely accepted because it has been supported by rigorous economic analysis. This view has recently been challenged by another view that came to the fore after the HCI's successful performance during the mid-1980s. This second view, however, lacks the support of systematic analysis based on empirical or theoretical evidence. In this section, I will assess the validity of both views after briefly reviewing their arguments. In the assessment, due attention will be given to fundamental differences between the theoretical and the real world.

The Critical Viewpoint

The critical view can be summarized as follows: First, contrary to the logic underlying the HCI Plan, the plan's execution led to misallocation of resources, thereby weakening the Korean economy's growth potential. Second, the process of implementation of the HCI Plan distorted various market prices. The distortion caused a sharp drop in the domestic savings rate and a proliferation of undesirable business behaviors, and, above all, discouraged export activities. Third, implementation of the overambitious plan was responsible for the rapid inflation of the late 1970s and early 1980s. Fourth, the plan led to excessive concentration of economic power and an uneven distribution of wealth and income. Fifth, some of the HCI Plan's pet projects have put great strains on Korea's resources while producing poor results. For example, projects such as Okpo Shipyard and Hankook Heavy Machinery Company are still unprofitable. Sixth, the recent success of various HCI sectors stems in fact from the revival of private initiative

---

17. Even in the United States the opinion that reliance on market mechanisms and macroeconomic policy alone will not reverse the declining industrial competitiveness and power of the American economy is gaining adherents (see Dertouzos 1989:46–50). Aggressive industrial strategies and an increased government role in the economy are advocated by Prestowitz (1988).

and market function that resulted from the painful structural adjustment efforts of the 1980s. I will elaborate further on these criticisms below.

Misallocation of resources. Given the factor endowments and the economic constraints of the 1970s, the critics continue, Korea should have allocated its capital and foreign exchange to labor-intensive, foreign-exchange-earning sectors and should have reduced its dependence on foreign energy. Under the HCI Plan, however, most of Korea's scarce capital and foreign exchange was preempted by capital-intensive and high energy-consuming sectors such as petrochemicals and copper smelting.

This misallocation of resources not only deprived Korea's most competitive sectors, light industries, of opportunities to expand and renovate their production capacities but also raised Korea's incremental capital–output ratio (ICOR) far above that of most other developing countries as well as above its historic pattern (Table 17.17). Moreover, Korea's energy dependence rose sharply[18] despite an uncertain world oil situation, thereby weakening the nation's ability to weather another worldwide oil crisis. Thus, the sudden decline in its economic growth and its bulging balance-of-payments deficit since the second half of 1979 were expected consequences of the implementation of the plan.

Table 17.17. International comparison of incremental capital–output ratios (ICORs)

Country	1960–70	1970–80
Argentina	4.6	9.0
Brazil	3.5	3.2
Greece	3.5	5.5
Hong Kong	2.4	2.2
Korea	1.8	3.6
Philippines	3.9	4.3
Portugal	3.3	3.7
Singapore	2.5	4.0
Thailand	2.7	3.5
Yugoslavia	5.5	5.4
Average	3.4	4.4

Source: World Bank (1986).

18. When measured by total energy consumption per $1,000 of gross domestic product, this argument is not substantiated, as the figure declined slightly from 0.68 in 1973 to 0.64 in 1978. There is, however, an obvious trend of increasing dependence on oil as the share of oil in total energy consumption rose sharply from 54 percent in 1973 to 63 percent by 1979.

Distortion of the pricing system and its adverse effects on the economy. As we have seen earlier, the execution of the HCI Plan necessitated the distortion of various economic parameters including the interest rate, exchange rate, and effective protection rates among industries. The negative interest rate entailed an implicit subsidy to capital, encouraging the adoption of capital-intensive technology and thus further raising Korea's overall ICOR; on the other hand, it also resulted in a lower domestic savings rate by penalizing savings.[19] The declining domestic savings rate drove the economy to depend further on foreign debt, and the increased debt service burden weakened Korea's growth potential. In addition, the intentional channeling of subsidized loans into favored HCI sectors enabled Korean businesses to remain profitable without their making the all-out effort to improve productivity and technology that is vital to the development of HCI.

To meet the overambitious goals of the HCI Plan, the Korean government had to rely on an excessive growth in the supply of money, and this fueled inflationary pressures.[20] As a major policy tool to curb this inflationary pressure, the government held the nominal exchange rate constant. This, in turn, resulted in appreciation of the real exchange rate throughout the second half of the 1970s (Table 17.18), causing a wide range of export industries to experience a significant erosion in competitiveness.

At the same time, a drift toward a more protective trade regime, which was introduced to secure markets for HCI products, caused a wide dispersion of effective protection rates (EPRs) among industries by the late 1970s. The economy's target sectors were offered high EPRs, whereas traditionally important exporters were offered very unfavorable, in some cases negative, rates (Table 17.19). By the late 1970s, this drift, in combination with the appreciation of the real exchange rate, had substantially narrowed the margin of incentives that favored exports.[21]

The overwhelming support that the HCI Plan offered to "key" industries, on the other hand, drove businesses to expend their energies on making inroads into HCI programs rather than on producing efficiently or on building export markets. For these reasons, the economic crisis that occurred after the second oil shock was not at all surprising.

---

19. Beginning in 1976, the domestic savings rate began to rise sharply reaching a level of 29 percent of GNP by 1978. The rate then dropped to 22 percent in 1979 and stayed at that level during 1979–81. The sharp drop may in large part be due to a decline in real income caused by the deterioration of Korea's terms of trade after the second oil shock. Korean planners, however, tended to attribute the decline in the domestic savings rate to negative real interest rates (EPB, ROK, *Fifth Plan*, 1981).

20. During 1974–79 M_2 grew by 30.9 percent and M_1 increased by 26.4 percent annually. The annual average GNP deflator was 22.7 percent during the period. The actual causes of the excessive growth of the money supply during this period are quite complicated, but the inflow of foreign earnings from overseas construction activities was considered a prime cause of the high monetary growth rate since 1976.

21. For an analysis of the effects on trade-related activities of the policies to promote the HCI Plan, see World Bank (1986:42–44).

Table 17.18. Exchange rates during the 1970s (won per US $)

Year	Nominal rate	Real effective rate
1971	373.3	84.69
1972	398.9	92.29
1973	397.5	104.45
1974	484.0	89.56
1975	484.0	90.24
1976	484.0	83.88
1977	484.0	83.56
1978	484.0	85.60
1979	484.0	78.99
1980	659.9	81.29
1981	700.5	79.02

Source: Jwa (1988).

Note: Calculated using the real effective exchange rate during the period from 3 April 1985 through 2 April 1986 as a base (100).

Table 17.19. Effective protection rates by sector (% of value added)

Sector	1968	1978	1982
Agriculture	18.5	57.1	74.3
Mining	4.0	−1.5	−1.7
Manufacturing	−1.4	31.7	28.2
Food	−18.2	−44.0	−48.4
Beverages, tobacco	−19.3	33.4	15.0
Construction materials	−11.5	11.8	51.1
Intermediate I	−25.5	37.6	61.9
Intermediate II	26.1	20.6	39.6
Nondurable consumer goods	−10.5	67.4	42.4
Durable consumer goods	64.4	242.9	52.5
Machinery	44.2	44.2	31.3
Transport equipment	163.5	326.6	123.9

Source: World Bank (1986). For original data see KDI (1982:187–210).

Note:

Intermediate I—Industrial inputs requiring raw processing, such as yarn, naphtha, fuel, etc.

Intermediate II—More processed industrial inputs such as textiles, paper, petrochemcial products, and steel products.

Inflation and the HCI Plan. Simultaneous construction of a multitude of HCI projects necessitated a rapid expansion of the money supply, as explained earlier. At the same time, the projects triggered a rapid rise in wages during the late 1970s[22] because they required a large number of engineers and skilled workers despite the short supply of qualified personnel in Korea. The inflationary pressure, which continued to rise as the HCI Plan was being executed, was contained by direct government price controls and by appreciation of the real exchange rate. In 1980, however, containment measures failed, and the inflation rate exploded out of control.

The high inflation rate discouraged domestic savings as well as business activities designed to improve both technology and productivity. It was also responsible for the weakening of Korea's export competitiveness. These factors worked against Korea's economic development.

The HCI Plan and concentration of economic power. The large scale of HCI projects as well as the huge risks involved prompted the participation of Korea's big business groups in the HCI Plan. They were subsidized with government-directed policy loans and provided with many newly built industrial sites. Thus big businesses were able to accumulate wealth rapidly and take over many smaller firms. During this period a few of Korea's big business groups grew extremely fast, mostly at the expense of small and medium-size firms.[23]

Both the financial subsidies to big business and the high effective protection rate favoring them widened wage disparities between big and smaller firms. At the same time, employment opportunities in the big firms were relatively shrinking. Therefore, income distribution deteriorated during the second half of the 1970s.[24]

Poor performance of some HCI programs. Despite structural adjustment efforts and financial support provided to the HCI projects, the Okpo Shipyard and Hankook Heavy Machinery continued to rely heavily on the government's debt relief programs; they still show no sign of becoming

---

22. For three consecutive years beginning in 1976, real wages grew on average by 18.5 percent per annum while labor productivity rose by only 10 percent. The growth rate of the real wage was far higher than the historical trend of about 6 to 8 percent.

23. SaKong (1980) showed that the share of value added by conglomerates in gross domestic product more than doubled during the 1970s. The share of the top ten conglomerates was 5 percent in 1973 but rose to 10.9 percent in 1978. K. Lee (1990:28) computed the conglomerates' share in manufacturing sales, and showed that the degree of concentration was accelerating even after 1978, when the share of the top ten conglomerates was 22 percent, and reached its peak in 1982, when the share of the top ten conglomerates in manufacturing was 30.2 percent.

24. Estimates of Korea's size distribution of income show that income distribution deteriorated sharply during the first half of the 1970s, but remained virtually unchanged in the second half of the decade. In the second half of the 1970s, however, the people became more acutely aware of the inequality in income distribution. This might be explained by the

viable businesses.[25] These projects were directly conceived by the government and received the bulk of the economic resources. According to critics, these unsuccessful projects demonstrate once again how costly the HCI Plan was.

Challenges to the current success of the HCI projects. It is true that today most of the HCI sectors are performing well, and that they acted as the engine of Korea's rapid economic growth during the 1980s. A careful examination, however, would refute any claim that the success can be solely attributed to the HCI drive.

The electronics and automobile industries, which have been most successful, are not products of the HCI Plan. Instead, they have been left to the play of private initiatives and given little financial help from the government. This is verified by the electronics industry's relatively stagnant performance during the second half of the 1970s. Furthermore, some of the most successful projects were conceived and started in the 1980s, for instance, microchips, computer-related firms, and Hyundai's new Pony Excel automobile project.

Therefore, paradoxically, the current successes of HCI projects strengthen the claim that the "pick the winner" policy of the government, which was the core of the HCI Plan, does not work in a complex economy like that of Korea.

The Positive Viewpoint

Even while acknowledging the adverse effects of the HCI Plan on Korea's economic development, those with a positive view toward the HCI Plan

---

deterioration of wealth distribution caused by the sharp increases in real estate prices and the increased concentration of economic power that occurred during this period. The following table shows the income shares (in percent) of the 20 percent of the population with the highest incomes compared with the share of the 40 percent of the population with the lowest incomes.

Income group	Percentage share of total income		
	1970	1976	1980
Top 20 percent	41.6	45.3	45.4
Bottom 40 percent	19.6	16.9	16.1

Note: The figures for 1976 and 1980 are not really comparable since the former was estimated by Choo (1979) and the latter by the Bureau of Statistics of the EPB (EPB, ROK, *Social Indicators*, 1982).

25. The Korean government had to take a debt-relief measure for the Okpo Shipyard Company in 1989. The relief measure consisted of exemption from the interest rate burden and extension of the amortization period for the firm's debt to Korea Development Bank. Deciding how to salvage the sinking Hankook Heavy Machinery Company, on the other hand, involved a long debate. After futile efforts to privatize Hankook, it was decided to maintain it as a public enterprise with an additional capital subscription of 100 billion won by KEPCO and the Korea Development Bank. The firm was also made the exclusive supplier of electricity-related facilities and plants.

assert that attention must be paid to the following points.[26]

First, considering its changing pattern of comparative advantage, Korea had no alternative but to build up HCI sectors, and the policy goals set by the HCI Plan could not be challenged.

Second, the huge cost involved in implementing the HCI Plan has been more than paid off by the recent successes of the HCI projects and by external economies generated by the plan. The external economies include the pecuniary external economy, or linkage effects, as witnessed by the booming investment activities related to the HCI projects such as parts and components for both the automobile and the machinery industries. In addition, a wide range of Korea's industries benefited from having a stable domestic supply of petrochemical products and iron and steel products during the world shortage of these items during the mid-1980s' economic boom.

Moreover, the HCI Plan helped that industrial boom by producing large numbers of scientists, engineers, and skilled workers through its manpower and technology programs. Since such programs take time to bear fruit, the early start of the HCI Plan was able to do away with the shortage in human resources and technology at the right time by expanding the supply of engineers and skilled workers (Table 17.20).

Third, given the nature of HCI sectors and the difficulties involved in building them, a nation can hardly expect to build a sophisticated industrial structure simply by responding to price signals. Price signals usually do not carry information about the future, especially in developing economies. Even if they do, reacting to price signals alone is not a promising

Table 17.20. Supply of engineers and skilled technical workers (100 persons)

Category of worker	1973	1975	1979	1980	1982
Graduates of technical high schools	273	332	553	591	640
Graduates of engineering junior colleges[a]	1.6	0.3	0.4	319	328
Graduates of university departments of engineering	65	72	113	136	206
Trainee graduates of public training centers	12	30	127	150	157

Sources: Ministry of Education, ROK, *Education Statistics Yearbook* (1975–85); Ministry of Labor, ROK, *Labor Statistics Yearbook* (1975–85).

a. The junior college system was not firmly established until 1979; therefore, the number of graduates before and after 1979 are not really comparable.

26. A written, well-documented argument in defense of the HCI Plan does not seem to exist. Therefore, most of the arguments introduced here represent widely scattered individual opinions including those of Korea's businessmen and people from the Ministry of Trade and Industry.

approach to building up the HCI sectors, which usually require a long gestation period and specialized business experience—both of which can be secured only through first-hand experience—as well as skilled manpower.

Because of the volatility of the current world economic climate and because the major competitors in HCI sectors are advanced countries, developing countries can capture the world HCI markets only through preinvestment and the trial-and-error method. In other words, to be successful in building up an industrial base for HCI, one must be ready to penetrate established markets. Such penetration is possible only when a crack occurs in the established markets, and to be able to take advantage of such a situation requires years of careful preparation.

In the Korean experience, market cracks usually occurred unexpectedly, as in the cases of microchips, automobiles, and petrochemicals. The markets for these products became available to Korean suppliers given conflicts and failures in the advanced countries' policies or sudden changes in the world economic environment. Markets for the automobile industry, for instance, opened up when Japan shifted its marketing strategy away from cheap, small cars toward bigger, more expensive cars in the wake of the stronger yen and because of trade friction with the United States. Markets for petrochemical products opened up when real oil prices dropped sharply and natural-gas-using petrochemical products lost their competitiveness while the advanced countries failed to expand their facilities.

Examples are endless, and the message is clear. Developing countries must be prepared to seize opportunities if they want to secure a beachhead in the world HCI, and simply responding to price signals does not lead to such preparedness. In addition, past experiences of late-industrialized countries such as Germany, Japan, and Italy point to the importance of being prepared.

Fourth, the positive view contends that some of the criticisms directed at the HCI Plan have been misleading or misdirected, though not totally mistaken. For example, the high capital–output ratio suggested as a cost of the HCI Plan would be lower if the ratio is calculated after HCI projects are fully operational. As for the appreciation of the real exchange rate and the high inflation rate of 1979–81, overseas construction activities and government policy mistakes of the period, rather than the HCI Plan, should take more of the blame. Earnings from overseas construction activities, for instance, disguised the balance-of-payments situation and led to both the overvaluation of the won and rapid expansion of the domestic money supply.[27]

---

27. In 1977 Korea recorded, for the first time, a current account surplus of US $25 million, mainly due to earnings from overseas construction activities. Because of this surplus, monetary policy faced severe disarray; to fix this, appreciation of the Korean won was seriously discussed among policymakers. This phenomena could be construed as a typical Dutch disease.

In sum, the positive view holds that the critics have overemphasized the costs of the HCI Plan while ignoring its dynamic benefits to Korea's economic development.

Assessment of the Two Viewpoints

Despite all of these positive aspects of the HCI Plan, one cannot deny that it was very costly and that many of its objectives might have been achieved with less cost (World Bank 1986:46–48). Yet questions linger.

Could Korea have successfully developed its electronics, automobile, iron and steel, and petrochemical industries if investment decisions had been left to market forces alone or if there had been no active government support for those industries, as was indicated in World Bank (1986:45–48)? Why did the "late-industrialized" countries take different routes in the "catching-up" process from those of the front-runners and achieve great success? Given that economic development in the real world requires a quantum leap to be successful, that the development process is characterized by indivisibility or discontinuity or a process of making the best use of external economies, that market information is imperfect or short-sighted (or even when it is not, and that the opportunities to capture the world market are volatile or short-lived), it seems extremely naive and irresponsible for policymakers of developing countries to denounce totally the HCI Plan.

In the real world, no country and no economic system is free of errors. But there are two kinds of errors. The first occurs as a result of doing nothing, and the second, as a result of doing something. If successful economic development results from aggressively seizing opportunities and taking bold risks, particularly for the presently developing countries, then doing something is certainly better than doing nothing. Being active, for instance, enabled Korea's automobile and electronics industries to seize the opportunity to enter the world market.

This, however, does not imply that doing something is always good. As will be indicated in the concluding section, for such an activism to be successful, economic conditions must also work in its favor. Beyond that, when economic conditions dictate it, a government should be able to dismantle or reform the incentive regime that has supported such an activism. In the Korean case, the incentive regime built for the HCI Plan was dismantled only because a new government, free of past commitments, came to power. Otherwise, such a reform would have been impossible, since any incentive regime carries its own political momentum, thus making existing regimes very hard to change, let alone reform. In this regard, Korea's good fortune in having a change of leadership transformed a potential disaster into a brilliant success.

LESSONS AND CONCLUSION

In drawing lessons from Korea's experience with the HCI Plan, we need to take a careful look at the case of India in the 1950s, which provided a marked contrast to Korea's success in the 1980s with construction of HCI while building up rapid growth momentum.

India sought rapid economic growth by directing its resources into its HCI sectors in the early 1950s, but the results were unsuccessful.[28] Korea, by contrast, overcame the initial costs and strains caused by the HCI Plan and is now back on a rapid growth track, mainly led by the booming HCI sectors. What differences account for such contrasting consequences?

First, Korea, unlike India, launched its HCI drive with the goal of participating in the international division of labor. Thus, the top architects of the HCI Plan always strived to achieve competitiveness in HCI.

Second, Korea had a solid light industrial base, which continued to earn valuable foreign exchange and to provide employment opportunities in the economy despite the HCI Plan's unfavorable effect on competitiveness.

Third, while the HCI Plan was being vigorously executed, Korea had a well-educated and motivated industrial labor force.[29] And the abundance of engineers and skilled workers that resulted from the HCI Plan's manpower training measures greatly helped to resurrect the Korean economy in the 1980s.

Fourth, Korea's entrepreneurs were vigorous and experienced in competing in the world market. Thus, when they were freed of regulations and forced to seek survival on their own, they took innovative, bold measures to vitalize the HCI projects.[30]

Fifth, the Korean government was pragmatic and bold enough to reform the entire incentive and economic management regime when circumstances dictated it. The reforms of the early 1980s, for example, contained inflation and encouraged exports while raising domestic savings beyond the amount required for domestic investment. The rising savings rate and the development of financial markets gave further impetus to the success of HCI projects.

Sixth, the Korean economy benefited tremendously from a favorable world economic environment characterized by low interest rates, low oil

---

28. India's development experience since its independence was described as one of few success stories by Higgins (1968:653–77). India, however, has the lowest recorded per capita GNP growth rate, and it still remains one of the poorest nations in the world.

29. Gerschenkron (1962) noted that one of the major bottlenecks of developing countries' economic development is lack of a qualified labor force in industrial work; he argued that LDCs are not labor-abundant economies but labor-scarce ones.

30. Hyundai Motor Company and Samsung IC Company are typical examples of successes due to bold entrepreneurship. Until 1982, Hyundai was still considered unsuccessful, but it survived successfully after it collaborated with a Japanese firm. Samsung IC grew into a worldwide firm after the deregulation of business activities by the government.

prices, and above all, a realignment of exchange rates in Korea's favor.

These differences show how risky and difficult it is for developing countries to take such bold measures as those required by the HCI Plan. If a developing country lacks the right combination of elements to make its HCI drive work, then the country is well advised to look for another development strategy. Considering the difficulties, therefore, the most recommended development strategy for a government to pursue in order to successfully develop its economy may not be a drastic one like the HCI Plan, but rather a more stable one as suggested by the World Bank (1983:41):

> To bring performance into line with potential, governments must play a central role in ensuring, first, a stable macroeconomic environment, by adopting sustainable monetary, fiscal, and foreign exchange policies; second, a system of incentives that encourages resources to be allocated efficiently and used optimally; and third, a pattern of growth in which benefits are widely shared.

ACKNOWLEDGMENTS

I am grateful to Dr. Keum Chung-Yeon (Ministry of Finance), Mr. Chang Seok-Jun (Economic Planning Board), and Mr. Chung Joon-Seok (Ministry of Trade and Industry) for their assistance and comments. Most of the basic facts, figures, and government documents related to the HCI Plan were provided by them. I am also grateful to Mr. Chung Hong-Shik (Office of the President) for his comments and assistance in supplying valuable documents on HCI. Mr. Chung was in charge of HCI projects for over ten years at Chong-Wa-Dae. I must express my thanks to Ms. Sarah Serafim, Ms. Anne Stewart, and other reviewers for their valuable comments and good editing.

18 Policy Measures to Reduce Industrial Concentration and Concentration of Economic Power

by Kyung Tae Lee

The Korean economy experienced remarkably rapid growth throughout the 1960s and 1970s, with the exception of a few sluggish periods resulting from internal and external disturbances. The average annual growth rate of real GNP was 8.5 percent in the 1960s and 8.1 percent in the 1970s. The quantitative expansion of the aggregate economy was accompanied by drastic qualitative changes in industrial structure, market organization, and openness of the economy. Among these changes, the increasing concentration of market power on macro, industrial, and commodity levels is of special interest.

In 1972 the Korean legislature passed a law aimed at encouraging family-owned big enterprises to go public by selling some minimum portion of their equities in the open stock market. In 1974 the late President Park issued a special presidential decree, generally called the "May 29th measure," to improve the financial structure of the big business groups by forcing them to go public and to regulate more stringently the volume of credit available to them. These two measures and the "September 27th measure" in 1980 represent government policies to curb excessive concentration of economic power in the hands of the small group of conglomerates.

Policies to regulate monopoly-oligopoly and unfair trade in individual industries or commodity markets were implemented in accordance with the Price Stability and Fair Trade Law and the Antitrust and Fair Trade Law, which were put into effect in 1976 and 1981, respectively. These antitrust measures were taken for securing the rules of the game in the capitalist economy in order to accommodate an official policy change toward freer competition instead of government-controlled operation of the economy.

ECONOMIC BACKGROUND OF THE POLICY MEASURES[1]

Industrial Concentration in the Manufacturing Sector

The high growth rate of the aggregate economy in the 1970s was led primarily by the manufacturing sector. During the period 1970-77, manufacturing

---

1. Much of this section is directly quoted from or draws upon Lee and Suh (1981).

grew at an annual average rate of 18.1 percent, compared with 9.8 percent for the economy as a whole, 4.1 percent for the primary sector, and 9.0 percent for social overhead capital and other services. As a consequence, the share of the manufacturing sector in GNP increased from 17.9 percent to 29.2 percent during the same period, while that of the primary sector decreased from 30.2 percent to 20.8 percent (Lee and Suh 1981). The number of employees in the manufacturing sector rose 2.2 times. Real value added in the same sector rose 4.0 times, while the number of firms increased by only 11.1 percent (SaKong 1980). This indicates that the expansion of the manufacturing sector was achieved mainly by the enlargement of existing firms rather than the establishment of new ones.

An overall concentration ratio is used to measure the degree of concentration in the entire manufacturing sector, without further disaggregation into subsectors. Table 18.1 shows the percentages of employment, gross output, and value added in the manufacturing sector accounted for by the top 50 firms and top 100 firms in 1970 and 1977. The top 100 firms accounted for 44.6 percent of total manufacturing shipments in 1970 and 38.9 percent in 1977. These firms' share also declined similarly in terms of value added.

Although the large firms' share declined somewhat during the period, it is apparent that production was highly concentrated in an extremely small group of firms, since the 100 firms represented only 0.41 and 0.37 percent of the total numbers of firms in 1970 and 1977, respectively.

Furthermore, since more than half of the 100 firms belonged to the 30 largest conglomerates, real concentration of economic power was even more serious (Table 18.2).

The industrial concentration ratio measures the market organization of the individual industry. The ratios in Table 18.3 are based on the percentage shares of shipments of the three largest firms in 213 individual industries. A comparison of 1970 and 1977 data reveals a general decline in industrial concentration—the number of industries in which the concentration ratio of the top three firms exceeded 60 percent decreased from 105 to 94, and the share of shipments of these industries also decreased from 52.8 to 41.1 percent. Despite this trend, the fact that highly concentrated industries shipped more than 40 percent of the total indicates a significant degree of concentration.

Table 18.1. Overall concentration ratios for manufacturing: 1970 and 1977 (%)

| Year | Top 50 firms | | | Top 100 firms | | |
	Employ-ment	Ship-ments	Value added	Employ-ment	Ship-ments	Value added
1970	10.8	33.8	38.6	18.2	44.6	48.1
1977	11.1	29.4	28.2	16.2	38.9	36.8

Source: Lee and Suh (1981).

Table 18.2. Distribution of large firms: 1977

Category of firm	Employment				Shipments			
	Top 50 firms		Top 100 firms		Top 50 firms		Top 100 firms	
	Number of firms	Share (%)	Number of firms	Share (%)	Number of firms	Share (%)	Number of firms	Share (%)
Member of top 30 conglomerates	28	63.9	47	56.3	34	61.7	53	56.8
Other private firms	20	31.0	50	39.5	12	11.3	43	22.1
State-owned	2	5.0	3	4.2	4	27.0	4	21.1
Total	50	100.0	100	100.0	50	100.0	100	100.0

Source: Lee and Suh (1981).

Table 18.3. Number of manufacturing industries and share of shipments by class of industrial concentration ratio: 1970 and 1977

Class of the concentration ratio of top three firms (%)	Number of industries		Share in total shipments (%)	
	1970	1977	1970	1977
80 to 100	58	49	24.3	27.5
60 to <80	47	45	28.5	13.6
40 to <60	56	64	22.4	31.0
20 to <40	39	41	16.0	18.6
0 to <20	13	14	8.8	9.3

Source: Lee and Suh (1981).

The average concentration ratios for the manufacturing sector given in Table 18.4 are either the weighted or the simple averages of the concentration ratios of 213 individual industries measured in terms of shipments. The table shows both weighted and simple average concentration ratios for the three largest firms in the manufacturing sector in 1970 and 1977. The sector is divided into two broad groups—producer goods and consumer goods—and the latter group is further broken down by durable and nondurable consumer-goods industries. Several interesting points can be observed. First, the average concentration ratio of strongly monopolized industries declined while that of weakly monopolized ones increased. Second, the concentration ratio of the producer-goods industries declined, while that of consumer-goods industries, particularly nondurables, showed an increase. This was possibly because the government's big push to develop heavy and chemical industries during the period induced more entries of new firms into the producer-goods industries, whereas the nondurable consumer-goods industries were already mature. Thus the exercise of stronger monopoly power by big firms in the consumer-goods industries through product differentiation or advertising could be practiced more easily. In addition, different market orientations might be important: for instance, producer-goods industries are more export-oriented whereas nondurable consumer-goods industries are more domestic-market oriented. Third, the weighted average concentration ratio for all industries in the manufacturing sector stayed almost unchanged during the period. At the absolute level, the three big firms in 1977 accounted for 57 percent of all shipments in the manufacturing sector, which indicates considerable concentration in this sector.

Commodity markets are classified into four different categories or types: monopoly, duopoly, oligopoly, and competitive market. The generalized criteria for classification are:

Monopoly: $CR_1 \geq 80\%$, $S_1/S_2 > 10.0\%$

Duopoly: $CR_2 \geq 80\%$, $S_1/S_2 < 5.0\%$, $S_3 < 5.0\%$
Oligopoly: $CR_3 \geq 60\%$ (except monopoly and duopoly)
Competitive market: $CR_3 < 60\%$

where CR is the share of cumulated shipments by the top i-number firms in the relevant commodity market, and S is the share of the ith firm in the relevant commodity market.

The commodity market was highly concentrated and almost invariant between 1970 and 1977. In 1977 the monopoly and oligopoly markets produced 83.7 percent of commodities (1,766 of the total 2,109 items) and accounted for 61.2 percent of total shipments. Another observation is that large commodity markets are less monopolized than the smaller ones. In 1977 almost 40 percent of the commodities in the markets of more than 10 billion won transactions were produced in the competitive markets, whereas only 4 percent were produced in the competitive markets of less than 1 billion won. This is consistent with the theoretical prediction that large markets provide increased opportunities for competition through easier entry of new firms and fewer incentives for leading firms to maintain monopoly power (Lee and Suh 1981).

Computing the share of the three largest firms provides us with a measure of the absolute level of industrial concentration, but it captures neither the relative market power of these three firms nor their effects on the character of market organization. The degree of asymmetry between the top two firms measured by the ratio of their shipments is shown in Table 18.5. Industries with lower concentration ratios have a noticeably lower degree of asymmetry; that is, there is less difference in market power between the top two firms in more competitive industries. For example, among 14 industries with concentration ratios of less than 20 percent in 1977, 11 had a degree of asymmetry less than 1.5 and none greater than 2.5. On the other hand, among 48 industries with a concentration ratio of more than 80 percent, 26 had degrees of asymmetry larger than 2.5. This implies that potential competition between the top two rival firms in the duopoly-oligopoly market is quite limited.

Conglomerates *(Jaebul)*

Thus far the discussion of market concentration has been based on the individual firm as a unit of measurement, not taking into account whether an individual firm is an independent entity in terms of ownership or a member of a large business group in which firms are interrelated through ownership or management or both. If numerous large firms belong to a few conglomerates *(jaebul)*, the actual concentration becomes more serious than the concentration ratio alone might indicate. Conglomerates in Korea have been expanding rapidly both in the numbers of their subsidiaries and the shares of their production in the aggregate economy. Between 1974 and 1980 the number of firms in the entire industrial sector belonging to the 30

Table 18.4. Weighted or simple average concentration ratios for the manufacturing sector: 1970 and 1977

| Type of industry | Weighted average of shipments[a] | | | | | | | | | | Simple average concentration ratio of shipments | | |
| | CR₃ < 60%[b] | | | CR₃ ≥ 60%[b] | | | All industries | | | | | | |
	Number of industries	1970 (%)	1977 (%)	Number of industries	1970 (%)	1977 (%)	Number of industries	1970 (%)	1977 (%)	Change (%)	1970 (%)	1977 (%)	Change (%)
Capital goods	57	37.1	42.8	61	86.2	71.4	118	62.7	59.6	-3.1	63.5	57.7	-5.8
Consumer goods	51	35.4	39.6	44	81.8	74.4	95	53.2	52.8	-0.4	59.2	58.4	-0.8
Durables	29	36.0	39.8	20	83.0	53.0	49	45.3	43.5	-1.8	58.8	54.0	-4.8
Nondurables	22	34.9	39.2	24	81.5	87.1	46	57.8	62.6	4.8	59.6	63.3	3.7
All industries	108	36.2	41.2	105	84.6	72.2	213	58.5	57.0	-1.5	61.6	58.0	-3.6

Source: Lee and Suh (1981).
a. Weighted by shipments.
b. Industries in which the concentration ratio of the top three firms was less (or more) than 60 percent in 1970.

Table 18.5. Degree of asymmetry between the two largest firms: 1970 and 1977 (number of industries)

Degree of asymmetry	CR_3											
	0 to <20%		20 to <40%		40 to <60%		60 to <80%		80 to 100%		Total	
	1970	1977	1970	1977	1970	1977	1970	1977	1970	1977	1970	1977
1.0 to <1.5	7	11	19	25	21	25	14	12	10	11	71	84
1.5 to <2.0	1	1	9	5	12	13	11	6	10	10	43	35
2.0 to <2.5	2	2	6	3	7	3	4	9	6	1	25	18
2.5 to <3.0			6	1	7	6	3	2	5	3	15	12
3.0 to <4.0			1	2	3	5	4	2	2	2	10	11
4.0 to <5.0			2	1	3	4	2	7	4	3	11	15
5.0+			1	2	3	6	8	3	17	18	29	29
Total	10	14	44	39	56	62	46	41	54	48	204	204

Source: Lee and Suh (1981).

Note: CR_3 is a concentration ratio of the three largest firms. Degree of asymmetry is a ratio of the shipments of the top two firms.

largest conglomerates increased from 304 to 608 (Table 18.6). Considering only the manufacturing sector, in 1980 these 30 conglomerates owned 327 firms, comprising 23.7 percent of total manufacturing employees and 34.7 percent of total manufacturing production (Table 18.7). In particular, the five largest conglomerates were the predominant force, accounting for 15.7 percent of total shipments, 14.5 percent of value-added products, and 9.1 percent of employment in the manufacturing sector for 1977. Tables 18.8 and 18.9 show other aspects of economic power concentration among large conglomerates.

Table 18.6. Number of firms owned by 30 largest conglomerates: 1974–80 (entire industrial sector)

1974	Firm integration during 1975–79					1980
	New	Purchase	Merger	Joint venture	Disposi- tion (–)	
304	152	173	13	17	38	608

Source: Lee and Suh (1981).

Table 18.7. Market power of the 30 largest conglomerates: 1977–80 (manufacturing sector)

Year	Number of member firms	Employment		Shipments	
		Persons (10^3)	Share (%)	Value (10^9 won)	Share (%)
1977	239	410	20.5	496	32.0
1978	290	487	22.2	732	34.5
1979	348	536	24.4	917	35.0
1980	327	497	23.7	1,244	34.7

Source: EPB, ROK, Tasks for earlier settlement of the antitrust system (1983).

Table 18.8. Conglomerates' share of fixed capital and value added in manufacturing: 1977 and 1980

	Fixed capital		Value added	
	1977	1980	1977	1980
Manufacturing value[a] (10^9 won)	3,936.7	12,862.3	5,604.0	11,863.2
Share of top 5 conglomerates (%)	10.9	16.7	14.5	13.8
Share of top 30 conglomerates (%)	33.6	36.9	31.4	31.3

Source: EPB, ROK, Proceedings of the Industrial and Technological Policy Advisory Meeting (1983).

a. In current prices.

Table 18.9. Conglomerates' share in technology imports: 1962–80 (number of cases)

Category of conglomerate	Total technology imports (A)	Imports by top 12 conglomerates (B)	(B/A)
Oil refineries and chemicals	306	59	19.3
Electronic and electrical equipment	326	114	35.0
Machinery	512	221	43.2
Total	1,144	394	34.4

Source: EPB,ROK, Proceedings of the Industrial and Technological Policy Advisory Meeting (1983).

The market power of conglomerates at the industry or commodity market level are shown in Table 18.10. According to this table, a single conglomerate occupies more than 60 percent of the market share in 14.5 percent of total commodity items (140 out of 968 items). This may indicate that the market power of conglomerates is not visibly significant, but the measurement of market power by market position has a different implication. The top 30 conglomerates hold the largest market share for 314 commodities (23.4 percent), and they are either the first, second, or third largest suppliers in 595 commodity markets (61.5 percent). All in all, conglomerates in Korea are characterized by a high degree of aggregate market concentration, persistent expansion through mergers, and considerable market power in individual commodity markets.

Causes and Effects of Concentration

In a sense, the high concentration of economic power in Korea on industrial and macro levels is a natural consequence of economic conditions and government policies in the country. Economies of scale and the small size of the domestic market provide leading firms with a considerable advantage because of their ability to exploit lower costs stemming from large capacity. Any new entrant faces serious risks in attempting to penetrate a market already dominated by another firm. Moreover, government policies were inclined to promote and encourage such concentration in the early stage of economic development.

It is well known that Korea vigorously pursued import substitution and then export promotion by combining foreign capital and technology with domestic labor. In the design process, more capital-intensive technologies embodied in large-scale production units were preferred on the basis of economies of scale and the resulting cost advantage in international competition. Large firms were also advantageous in terms of technological

Table 18.10. Market power of the 30 largest manufacturing conglomerates: 1977

Rank[a]	Number of commodities shipped	Number of commodities by market share					Number of commodities by order of market share				Weighted average market share
		0 to <20%	20 to <40%	40 to <60%	60 to <80%	80 to 100%	1st	2nd	3rd	Total	
1	111	52	26	17	7	9	46	23	7	76	23.8
2	42	23	8	5	2	4	16	4	6	26	24.2
3	69	43	12	6	2	6	18	11	10	39	14.5
4	94	65	10	9	3	7	21	20	12	53	12.5
5	40	21	8	1	6	4	18	6	1	25	22.5
6	26	14	1	1		10	11	5	7	23	15.1
7	23	13	5	2	1	2	8	5		13	14.3
8	22	13	4	1	1	3	8	2		10	32.0
9	36	30	3	1	1	1	4	8	5	17	8.8
10	35	26	3	3		3	8	4	3	15	9.8
11	28	14	6	2	1	5	10	4	3	17	15.3
12	48	27	5	4	3	9	22	11	6	39	22.4
13	28	16	7	2	1	2	9	6	4	19	25.1
14	21	12	4	2	1	2	6	4	2	12	14.1
15	18	13	2	1		2	3	5	2	10	13.1
16	33	22	5	3	2	1	8	6	6	20	11.4
17	25	15	6			4	7	8	2	17	11.7
18	28	18	1	3	2	4	10	2	3	15	16.6
19	20	14	5	1			8	3	1	12	24.1
20	38	25	4	5	4		10	5	6	21	7.4

21	48	25	3	8	4	8	21	6	4	31	15.7
22	9	6	2		1		2	3	2	7	18.5
23	11	6	2	2	1		5	1	1	7	13.1
24	14	6	5	3			6	3	1	10	27.0
25	5	2		2		1	3			3	46.9
26	20	12	6	1		1	3	8	4	15	9.0
27	8	6	1	1			1	1	3	5	11.6
28	24	11	5	5	2	1	10	6	3	19	23.2
29	24	22	1		1		2	2	2	6	7.2
30	20	9	3	3		5	10	2	1	13	8.1
Total	968	581	153	94	45	95	314	174	107	595

Source: Lee and Suh (1981).

a. Conglomerates are ranked by size of total shipments.

innovation and capital accumulation. Thus from the very beginning, industrial concentration in Korea was initiated rather than left to evolve by means of mergers or integration among firms as has been generally observed in the history of economic development of other industrialized countries.

The excessive expansion of a large business group or conglomerate can possibly be explained by the circular political-economic process. Economic size means economic power and influence on the government's resource-allocation decisions (Jones 1980). Although access to government decision makers was necessary, the government was expected to be very selective in deciding to undertake a big project because of its commitment to economic growth (SaKong 1981). In this regard, large business groups with managerial ability and experience, talented manpower, and capital-mobilizing capabilities were better positioned to take part in the allocation of scarce resources, particularly in the heavy and chemical industries. Purchases or mergers of existing firms by a conglomerate played a greater role than the establishment of new firms within conglomerates (Table 18.6). This suggests that conglomerates allocate much of their monopoly profits, bank credits, and surplus resources for the acquisition of existing firms in the industrial sector. Although manufacturing and construction are the major sectors in which the conglomerates have invested, they have nonetheless diversified into other sectors, including transportation, communications, and finance, among others (Table 18.11).

Increasing criticism has been raised about industrial concentration and its negative effects on resource allocation, income distribution, macroeconomic stability, and sociopolitical imbalances.

Table 18.11. Value-added share of conglomerates by sector: 1978 (%)

| Sector | Number of conglomerates | | | |
	Top 5	Top 10	Top 20	Top 46
Agriculture, forestry, fisheries	0.14	0.10	0.14	0.12
Mining	0.88	0.66	0.62	0.51
Manufacturing	54.05	51.31	56.55	59.91
Construction	17.54	24.74	20.77	19.85
Electricity, water, and sanitary services	0.11	0.08	0.07	0.05
Transportation and communication	9.90	9.24	7.92	6.69
Wholesale and retail trade	4.11	3.26	4.58	4.05
Finance and insurance	9.53	7.52	6.45	6.34
Pure services	3.74	3.10	2.90	2.48
Total	100.00	100.00	100.00	100.00

Source: SaKong (1980).

Concentration and economic efficiency. Theory predicts that optimum resource allocation is fulfilled when factor and commodity markets are in perfect competition. Monopoly and oligopoly firms produce less than optimum levels of output at prices that are higher than marginal costs, thereby creating monopoly profits. Resources are used in less productive areas causing net losses in economic welfare. In addition to these static efficiency considerations, dynamic impacts of concentration on economic growth deserve due attention. Korea's economic growth has been mainly attributed to the increase in the factor inputs of labor and capital. The abundant supply of cheap skilled and unskilled labor and the subequilibrium real interest rate provided a competitive edge in the export market for labor-intensive goods such as textiles, plywood, wigs, and home electronics. But as the economic structure shifted to more capital-intensive, technology-oriented industries, export promotion by mere increases in factor inputs had reached its limit.

An increase in total factor productivity through technological innovation and managerial improvement is imperative to provide a better competitive edge to Korean export goods in terms of price and quality. There are conflicting arguments as to whether atomistic firms in a perfectly competitive market or big firms in a monopoly-oligopoly market are more favorable to innovation. But there is no doubt that big firms whose monopoly positions are protected by legal and administrative barriers have little, if any, incentive to devote scarce resources to create changes needed to place themselves in a superior competitive position vis-à-vis their rivals. Their monopoly rent is a windfall profit earned by external institutions rather than through innovations in quality and marketing techniques. This description is typical of the situation in which the economic activities of Korea's enterprises are molded. In this context, there is a growing body of opinion that market mechanisms designed to enhance competition and new entries should be introduced.

Concentration and income distribution. It is frequently asserted that the high level of concentration was one important cause of the deterioration of equitable distribution in the 1970s as measured by the Gini coefficient. This may be true but there are few empirical studies to support or contradict such an assertion. Jones (1980) argued that even if the government were to tax away the entire distributed earnings of the large conglomerates and reallocate them to the population as a whole, the redistributional effect would be negligible. On *a priori* grounds the distributional effect of concentration is determined by factors other than the degree of concentration itself.

As an example, ownership patterns and efficiency considerations are important. If ownership is not separated by stock dispersion and if dynamic inefficiencies are created by industrial and aggregate concentrations, the adverse effect on income distribution will be magnified. In this context, Korea's high concentration of ownership among a few business families and inefficiencies caused by a highly monopolized market structure should have worsened income distribution.

Concentration and inflation. On *a priori* grounds it can be hypothesized that monopolized industries have higher inflation than competitive ones. Three factors underlie these assumptions: the monopoly firm has discretionary control over the price of its output, whereas the competitive one is a price taker; the monopoly firm uses its control power to maximize profit margin over the cost (mark-up pricing theory); and the monopoly firm is able to transfer more of a given change in cost conditions to the output price than are competitive firms. Table 18.12 shows that monopoly-oligopoly commodities experience much higher price rises than competitive ones. The sample period covers the sharp price rise of crude oil during the second oil crisis. This may have generated higher price increases for monopoly-oligopoly commodities since these commodities are more sensitive to input price changes. Thus the interpretation that price rise differentials are indicative of market power should be accepted with some caution. Kyuuck Lee (1977:135–40) performed multiple regression analysis using the price equations in which labor cost, material cost, and concentration ratio are explanatory variables. In the test results, the concentration ratio had a positive and significant relationship with price rise.

Concentration and sectoral disequilibrium. The domination by big firms over market structure is manifest in the serious imbalance between small/medium-size firms and big firms. As shown in Table 18.13, the growth rate of the output of small and medium-size firms was significantly lower than the average growth rate of the economy throughout the 1960s and 1970s. The lower growth rate resulted in the relatively inconspicuous posi-

Table 18.12. Comparison of price increases between monopoly-oligopoly and competitive commodities: 1973–75 (%)

Commodity type	January 1973–74	January 1974–75	January 1973–75
Monopoly-oligopoly (31 sample commodities)	23.7	72.3	113.2
Competitive (19 sample commodities)	18.3	28.2	51.7
Total (50 sample commodities)	21.3	53.7	86.5
Wholesale price rise[a]	21.2	45.5	74.9

Source: K. Lee (1977).

a. Added by the author.

tion of small and medium-size firms in output, employment, and bank loans (Table 18.14). In 1981 Korea's small and medium-size firms shared 51.1 percent of total employment, 32.3 percent of gross output, and 45.2 percent of bank loans, compared with 71.5, 52.7, and 61.1 percent, respectively, in the case of Japan.

Behind the numerical indicator lies the structural problem of a deficient complementarity between small firms and big ones. Their production lines are not efficiently linked. Instead of a harmonious interdependent relationship between the big firms which have large-scale assembly lines and the small firms that supply parts, large firms often undertake the entire production process by themselves. Moreover, conglomerates often diversify into areas where small firms could operate more efficiently.

Concentration and flexibility of economic power. As was said, economic power embeds the political influence by which big businesses are able to exploit the benefits of government intervention in credit rationing, taxation, foreign exchange control, and distribution of economic rents. This implies

Table 18.13. Sectoral growth rates in Korea: 1962–81 (% per annum)

Years	GNP	Manufacturing	Small and medium-size firms
1962–66	7.8	13.5	2.8
1967–71	10.5	22.5	4.2
1972–76	10.1	26.2	16.1
1962–79	9.3	26.6	11.0
1980	–6.2	–1.1	–8.3
1981	7.1	6.8	14.5

Source: EPB, ROK, *Economic Statistics Yearbook* (1971, 1981, 1982); EPB, ROK, *Survey Report of Mining and Manufacturing Statistics* (1971, 1981, 1982).

Table 18.14. Shares of employees, gross products, value added, and bank loans among small and medium-size firms in Korea, Japan, and Taiwan: 1981 (%)

Item	Korea	Japan	Taiwan
Small and medium-size firms as a percentage of total firms	96.0	99.2	u
Employees	51.1	71.5	68.2
Gross product	32.3	52.7	u
Value-added product	34.8	57.1	50.4
Bank loans	45.2	61.1	u

Source: EPB, ROK, Tasks for earlier settlement of the antitrust system (1983).
u—unavailable.

that government intervention worsens market imperfection rather than improves it.

Big business groups also use their economic and political power to protect their own interests from macro- and micro-level economic policies. For example, they have expressed strong objections to the policies of import liberalization, tight credit, price controls, and fair trade, which are essentially designed to increase the efficiency and equity of the overall economy at the cost of certain sectors of the economy.

Considering the serious imbalance of power among interest groups (e.g., large versus small businesses, producers versus consumers), the lobbying efforts of big conglomerates often cause government policies to tilt toward excessive protection of their interests. A typical example is the long-delayed government regulation over conglomerate diversification by merging firms in different industries and by purchasing real estate for purely speculative purposes.

Concentration and market-oriented economic policy. In the 1960s and early 1970s, Korea pursued government-led economic growth. Resource mobilization and allocation were undertaken through direct and indirect government intervention in a wide range of economic activities. As the absolute size of the economy grew and its structure became increasingly complicated, the appropriateness and feasibility of government-led economic growth declined correspondingly.

The private sector came to possess more competent managerial talent and gained better access to market and technological information than the government. In contrast, the government encountered increasing difficulties in collecting the vast amount of information required for efficient intervention. For this reason, deregulation and a greater role for the market mechanism have been emphasized since the late 1970s. But that market mechanism presupposes a set of rules of the game that ensure competition on an equal basis. Industrial and business concentration is conducive to the abuse of market power, which nullifies the otherwise advantageous operation of the private sector.

MAIN FEATURES OF THE POLICY MEASURES

Policies Toward Industrial Concentration

The Price Stability and Fair Trade Law, 1976. The Price Stability and Fair Trade Law was enacted in March 1976. Its important provisions are as follows:

1. The government is authorized to set price ceilings for goods and services when needed for economic stability.

2. Monopoly and oligopoly businesses are obliged to declare their product prices to relevant government ministries, which then examine the validity of those prices.

3. The government is authorized to control the supply conditions of goods when the prices of goods increase sharply due to supply shortages. The measures may include administrative decrees to control production plans, shipments, exports, imports, transport and storage, and improvement of the distribution system.

4. Monopoly-oligopoly firms are prohibited from engaging in unfair trade practices, such as discrimination against certain customers, unfair procedures to compel a rival's customers to make transactions with the firm, false or misleading advertising, and hoarding or cornering in pursuit of excessive profits.

5. Monopoly-oligopoly firms are prohibited from attempting to restrict competition by fixing, maintaining, and raising output prices; by imposing restrictive conditions on commodity sales, service provisions, and payments; by restricting production, sales, and shipment of goods and services; and by restricting sales of output to certain customers or geographic regions.

6. As an exception to the provisions in item 5 above, cartels are permitted to rationalize industrial structure on a selective basis.

The purpose of the law was twofold: to regulate certain prices directly and to control unfair trade practices. Direct price regulation was introduced to curb inflationary pressure caused by monopoly power. Control of unfair trade was pursued mainly by regulating market performance rather than by improving market structure.

To be designated as a monopoly-oligopoly firm, firms must satisfy the following criteria: (1) a 30 percent or greater market share; (2) a 20 percent or greater share in a market where the three largest firms produce more than 60 percent of the total; and (3) substantial monopoly power in a commodity market essential to the national economy. Using these criteria, the Korean government annually designates monopoly-oligopoly commodities, the prices of which must be reported to the government for evaluation. The number of designated monopoly-oligopolgy commodities ranged between 148 and 157 between 1976 and 1979 (EPB, ROK, Policy proposals for improving the antitrust system, 1981).

The government also designates certain commodities whose ceiling prices are subject to official approval. The number of commodities with a government-set price ceiling declined from 251 in 1977, to 19 in 1978, and to two in 1979. The government's efforts against unfair trade practices between 1976 and 1979 resulted in 80 indictments, six corrective orders, and three warnings (EPB, ROK, Policy proposals, 1981).

The Antitrust and Fair Trade Law, 1981. Several shortcomings of the Price Stability and Fair Trade Law enacted in 1976 were revealed in the course of its implementation. Direct regulation of prices may have price-stabilizing effects in the short run, but only at the risk of creating black markets, double prices (open market and black market prices), disincentives for capital investment, and resultant supply shortages in the long run. Determining what constituted normal profit also necessitated estimating production costs, which was a difficult burden for the government.

Another critical drawback of the law was that it did not attempt to regulate such monopolizing behavior as mergers and interlocking directorships. Hence the law could not contribute to making the market structure more competitive. Such behaviors are, however, explicitly restricted by the Antitrust and Fair Trade Law that was enacted in April 1981.

The new law also prescribes the regulation of monopoly-oligopoly commodity prices, although this regulation is somewhat different from the old system of *ex ante* and direct price control. The important provisions of the new law are as follows:

1. A market-dominating firm is prohibited from using its market power in an "inappropriate manner" to: determine, maintain, or change commodity prices; control the volume of sales; interfere in the affairs of other firms; add new capacity or expand existing capacity for the purpose of blocking entry of a rival firm or excluding rival firms from a certain business area; collude in raising the prices of homogeneous or similar commodities; or engage in other activities that substantially reduce competition or impede consumer welfare. The term "inappropriate manner" is defined as the case in which the price fluctuates excessively in light of supply and demand, or cost conditions in the market; the case in which the profit rate of the market-dominating firm is very high; or the case in which the marketing expenses of the market dominator are abnormally high. By definition, a market dominator has to have annual transactions exceeding 30 billion won as a supplier in the commodity or service market in which either a single firm's market share exceeds 50 percent, or the combined market shares of the three biggest firms exceed 70 percent.

2. Business combinations through the purchase of equities, interlocking directorships, mergers, transfers of all or important parts of the business activities of other firms, or the establishment of new firms are prohibited if they substantially reduce competition in certain business areas. Exceptions can be granted by government permission in cases where such combinations are required for industrial rationalization or to strengthen international competitiveness. This antitrust provision is applicable to a firm whose paid-in capital is more than 1 billion won, or whose total assets are valued at more than 5 billion won.

3. Cartels are prohibited if they substantially reduce competition. But exceptions are acknowledged when the firms concerned can prove that a cartel is necessary in order to survive a depression or rationalize their industrial structure.

4. The following unfair trade practices are proscribed: improper discrimination among customers; improper trading to exclude rival competitors;

enticing or forcing a competitor's customers to make transactions with one-self; using an advantageous position in an improper manner when dealing with one's customers; dealing with one's customers on conditions that restrict their business activities improperly; false or misleading advertising; and misrepresentation of the quality or quantity of a commodity.

5. Business organizations are prohibited from engaging in the following activities: limiting competition substantially in certain business areas by engaging in practices proscribed in item 4 above; restricting the current or future number of competitors; restricting the business activities of a member firm improperly; and forcing a member firm to engage in unfair trade proscribed in item 4 above or resale price cartels proscribed in item 6 below. Business organizations are defined as business interest groups consisting of more than two mutually independent business entities in manufacturing, wholesale and retail, transportation and storage, construction, or other personal services.

6. An individual firm or a business organization is prohibited from making international contracts or arrangements involving improper cartels or unfair trade. An international contract or arrangement covers foreign loans, joint investment, import of technology, and long-term import contracts for commodities and services.

7. The 1981 law established a five-member Fair Trade Commission in the Economic Planning Board (EPB) to deliberate and decide on important matters relating to the implementation of the law. (For a discussion of its functions, see "Institutional Setting for the Antitrust Policy" below.)

Since antitrust policy in Korea is still in a developing stage, emphasis is placed on the consolidation of operational institutions and increasing the public's understanding of the issues. Moreover, substantial efforts have been made to develop the administrative capability to supervise and correct collusive and unfair trade practices.

During 1981–83, 195 firms were designated as market dominators and placed under extensive supervision by the fair trade authorities with regard to pricing and improper use of their market power. Corrective measures were taken in the two cases of mergers attempted by means of purchasing equity. A cement industry sales cartel that had lasted more than ten years was dissolved. A total of 780 business organizations were supervised with regard to possible competition-restricting activities, and 41 of these were ordered to revise their articles of association that stipulated collusive pricing, production and shipment allotments among members, and restrictions on new capacity and expansion of existing capacity.

Additional measures were taken to provide a solid environment for fair trade. Twelve typical unfair trade patterns were identified and subjected to extensive supervision, including dumping, improper refusal of transactions, and improper enticement of customers. To promote competition in price and quality, restrictions were imposed on the value of gifts accompanying sales and on the frequency and duration of such sales, while discount sales in a single store were limited to 90 days per year. Fact-finding investigations were carried out in the food, medicine, cosmetic, clothing, footwear, and real estate sectors to gather information on labeling and advertising of price, quality, ingredients, and place of origin. Based on these investigations, 70 firms were warned about false or misleading labeling and advertising. Measures to improve unfair trade in construction subcontracting include prohibitions against delayed payments and improper determination of construction costs and against delayed payments and improper determination by assembling firms regarding the prices of commodities delivered by the producers of parts. Violations were found in ten firms engaged in highway and subway construction and 17 firms in the manufacturing sector; all of these were corrected. Finally, retail price fixing by cosmetics producers was gradually curtailed, from 14 kinds of cosmetics labeled with a uniform retail price in 1981 to only five in 1983.

The number of corrective measures taken by type of violation is tabulated in Tables 18.15 and 18.16. The tables show that a major effort has been made to improve market behavior by regulating such unfair trade practices as false advertising and improper transactions in subcontracting.

Policies Restricting Aggregate Concentration

Our discussion of policies toward aggregate concentration is centered on policies affecting conglomerates because the majority of the biggest 100 or 200 firms are affiliated with one conglomerate or another. Government efforts to restrict both the excessive accumulation of wealth in the hands of a small number of conglomerates and the unrestrained use of that wealth have a longer history than that of the antitrust policies discussed above.

In June 1961 the military government enacted a special law, aimed at punishing the plutocrats who had accumulated wealth in an improper way, and nationalized the commercial banks. This legislation reflected the new government's determination to sweep away the old injustices and wrong-

Table 18.15. Number of corrective measures taken against antitrust violations: 1981-83

Type of violation	1981	1982	1983	Total
Merger	0	2	0	2
Competition restrictions	5	8	5	18
Unfair trade	16	25	24	65
International contracts	80	162	130	372
Total	101	197	159	457

Source: EPB, ROK, Tasks for earlier settlement of the antitrust system (1983).

doings that had been committed in the process of wealth accumulation after the country's liberation in 1945. It was also in response to the general public's criticisms that many of the big businesses had been created through political connections and were thus responsible for much of the corruption and favoritism that had prevailed in the previous decade.

Thereafter there were no explicit anticonglomerate policies until 1974. The government's growth-oriented economic policies emphasized export promotion as an engine of growth and promoted big businesses. In May 1974, however, a measure that reflected a policy change from an implicit promotion to a balanced control of conglomerates was taken.

May 29th (1974) measure. The focal point of the measure enacted on 29 May 1974 was to induce big businesses to go public by providing incentives and disincentives in bank credit, tax, and foreign exchange policies. As mentioned, conglomerates in Korea accomplished rapid growth largely through easy access to bank credit and foreign exchange, which in turn worsened their financial positions.

Policies to open the big businesses to the public and develop the equity and bond markets had been attempted before the May 29th measure. These were embodied in the Capital Market Development Law enacted in 1968 and the Law for the Promotion of Going Public enacted in 1972. Neither of these laws was very successful in promoting the opening of large family corporations, mainly because of the passive or uncooperative response of the private firms. The new measure in 1974 introduced some compulsory clauses and stronger incentives for the opening of closed corporations to augment the preceding laws.

Table 18.16. Number of corrective measures taken against fair trade violations: 1981–83

Type of violation	1981	1982	1983[a]	Total
Improper refusal of transactions	2	0	1	3
False advertising	6	12	10	28
Excessive gifts	1	5	2	8
Abnormal discounted sales	1	2	1	4
Sales price fixing	1	2	5	8
Sales area fixing	3	1	0	4
Unfair subcontracting	1	2	4	7
Enforcement of transactions	1	1	1	3
Total	16	25	24	65

Source: EPB, ROK, Tasks for earlier settlement of the antitrust system (1983).

Note: This table is the disaggregated contents of the unfair trade category listed in Table 18.15.

a. January through September.

The May 29th measure had two objectives. The first was to separate ownership and management by opening family-owned businesses to the public. The purpose of opening up family corporations was twofold: to return profits to society by paying dividends to a wider range of equity holders, and to modernize management by enabling professional managers to undertake important roles in business administration. The second objective was to improve the financial structure of the conglomerates and to correct the credit allocation mechanism that was tilted toward big businesses.

Both objectives were important from the viewpoint of conglomerate policy. The open-market sales of equity shares was a necessary, although insufficient, condition for decentralizing decision making and for bringing about a wider distribution of conglomerate income. At the same time, more stringent loan management would decelerate the rapid expansion of conglomerates that had been purchasing other firms and expanding existing capacity mainly with borrowed capital. The May 29th measure was initiated by an administrative order from the Office of the President and followed up by a series of implementation measures.

The major objectives of the May 29, 1974, Special Order of the President were:

- more active enforcement of laws promoting the opening of large family corporations;
- improvement of the financial structure of big businesses;
- realization by firm owners of their social obligations and responsibility to bring competent professional managers into their business operations; and
- development of the heavy and chemical industries with maximum efficiency to meet international competition.

To improve the firms' financial structure, excessive domestic and foreign currency borrowing needed to be corrected, particularly in those firms that were passive about going public. Moreover, a firm's management system should be transformed from the closed family type to an open public type, and a balanced relationship developed between ownership and management.

To accomplish the above objectives, the presidential order stipulated that appropriate ministries should implement the following measures:

1. Financial, foreign exchange, and tax policies should give preferential treatment to open corporations established by competent entrepreneurs.

2. A centralized information management system should be adopted to facilitate analysis of the overall situation regarding loans, other financial transactions, and tax payments of the individual big businesses or the big business groups and their major shareholders who receive large domestic and foreign loans.

3. An excessive allocation of domestic and foreign loans to big businesses (particularly those that do not go public) should be corrected by strengthening the loan management system.

4. Finally, when a businessman with a high debt-ratio plans to start a new venture, he should be guided to finance part of the required capital by selling a portion of his existing firms and equities.

The Banks' Agreement on Credit Management of Big Businesses, enacted on 13 July 1974, was based on the Government Policy Concerning Financial Credit and Concentration of Ownership announced by the Ministry of Finance on 30 May 1974. It stipulated specific guidelines and criteria for improving the financial structure of big business groups. All business groups whose total outstanding loans exceeded 5 billion won were subjected to strict credit management by the banks. These groups were categorized into "A" and "B" groupings according to debt ratio. An "A" business group was required to submit a stringent plan for improving its financial structure, which contained a scheme for going public by selling equities in the open market, as well as a scheme for repayment of debts by selling the equities of large shareholders and affiliated firms and real estate holdings not actually used for business purposes. Business groups were also put under severe restrictions for new foreign capital borrowing, investment in new ventures, and purchases of real estate.

Finally, the Credit Management Agreement by Major Banks was intended to centralize all information concerning the financial transactions of each big business within its major bank. Big businesses generally conducted financial transactions with as many banks as possible to maximize credit mobilization. The lack of understanding of the integrated financial position of an individual firm or a big business group made it extremely difficult for the authorities to supervise actual executions of the financial improvement plan submitted by that firm. Under this agreement, a major bank of the business group was made responsible for guiding the group's business management, establishing the ceilings on working-capital lending, coordinating joint lending with other banks, and supervising the execution of the financial improvement plan submitted.

From July 1974 through December 1977, the execution of the financial improvement plans submitted by the pertinent business groups was strongly promoted by the major banks and the Banks Supervisory Board within the central bank. Table 18.17 outlines the accomplishments of the plans submitted and shows that the only ones falling short of the planned objectives were the numbers of businesses going public and the disposition of nonbusiness real estate holdings.

September 27th (1980) measure. The Korean economy faced its most serious challenges after the second oil crisis in 1979. Worldwide recession reduced foreign demand for Korea's export goods, and the double-digit

Table 18.17. Accomplishments of the Financial Structure Improvement Plan: 1974–77[a]

Type of accomplishment	Planned (A)	Actual (B)	(B/A) (%)
Going public (number of firms)	146	90	61.6
Mergers (number of firms)	50	61	122.0
Capital increases (10^9 won)	168.7	443.4	262.8
Sales of equities by major shareholders (10^9 won)	66.6	68.8	103.4
Disposition of subsidiaries (number of firms)	38	40	105.2
Disposition of nonbusiness real estate holdings (10^3 *pyung*)[b]	7,149	3,819	53.4

Source: MOF, ROK (1979a).

a. From 1 July 1974 through 31 December 1977.

b. 1 *pyung* = 0.65 square meters.

interest rate imposed a heavy burden on debt service. To make things worse, the political chaos after the assassination of President Park created uncertainties for private sector businesses.

On 27 September 1980, newly elected President Chun announced an important policy aimed at strengthening the efficiency and competitiveness of private businesses, particularly big businesses. The policy stressed that the sluggishness of the domestic economy was at least partially attributable to the critical problems created by big businesses—for example, the big businesses' excessive investment in real estate for purely speculative purposes, their disorderly diversification into a wide range of industries instead of specializing in their principal industries, and their excessive business expenditures.

Such critical problems were so deeply rooted in Korean entrepreneurial behavior that economic recovery was considered unattainable without a drastic change that would lead to rational and efficient management. Only by drastically changing attitudes and behavior could the social responsibilities and obligations of big businesses be fulfilled satisfactorily. This would in turn contribute to improving the unfavorable public opinions regarding the behavior of big businesses.

The September 27th measure was designed to accomplish four principal objectives: disposition of nonbusiness real estate owned by big business; disposition of peripheral firms affiliated with conglomerates; auditing of incorporated companies' accounts by outside auditors; and rationalization of the tax system to improve the financial structure of big businesses. The first two are directly related to the issues of business concentration and therefore a more detailed description of them is given below.

Any firm affiliated with a conglomerate whose total bank credit exceeds 20 billion won or any individual firm whose total bank credits exceed 10 billion won is obligated to report all of its real estate holdings to its principal bank. Land and other real estate not actually classified for business use should be sold and the proceeds used to repay the firm's bank loans. If the real estate is not sold in the open market, a public enterprise such as the Land Development Corporation or the Housing Corporation may purchase it, by making payment in bonds.

One of the characteristics of conglomerates in Korea is that they have many firms in a wide range of industries. Diversification of a conglomerate's resources into many unrelated business areas inevitably results in sluggish managerial and technological innovations because an innovation would more likely result from a concentration of its resources in certain specialized areas. To deal with the 20 largest conglomerates in terms of the number of affiliated firms, the September 27th measure laid down the following principles for the disposal of peripheral firms.

1. The 20 conglomerates should voluntarily choose the principal type of industry most suitable to their respective managerial and technical capabilities.

2. The conglomerates should dispose of all firms other than the main ones engaged in the principal type of industry.

3. The proceeds from the sales of these peripheral firms should be used to improve the financial structure of the main firms.

4. First priority should be given to the sale of small and medium-size firms.

5. All these plans should be formulated and implemented on the basis of voluntary cooperation by the conglomerates. The government's role should be limited to coordinating and adjusting the plans from the viewpoint of macroeconomic efficiency. If necessary, the government may also provide financial and tax incentives to support these plans.

6. If voluntary implementation of a plan proves to be unsatisfactory within a certain period of time, the government can consider punitive measures.

The amount of nonbusiness real estate and the number of firms sold by the big businesses up to the end of February 1983 were substantial. According to the data prepared by the Ministry of Finance for the National Assembly in 1980, about 77.8 percent of the planned target was met in the disposal of land and other real estate; the 240 billion won revenue was used to repay financial debts. During the same period, the 20 largest conglomerates disposed of 122 of their peripheral firms out of a planned total of 166. More detailed data prepared by the Federation of Korean Industries (1983), however, reveal that although 95 firms were disposed of by February 1982, in fact 32 of them had been disposed of prior to the September 27th measure and 26 others were merely reclassified as nonsubsidiaries of conglomerates (Table 18.18). These data indicate that some caution is necessary in

Table 18.18. Disposition of subsidiaries by conglomerates: February 1982 (number of firms)

Type of disposal	Planned	Actual
Sale	58	16
Merger	43	17
Dissolution	7	4
Reclassification[a]	26	26
Previously disposed of[b]	32	32
Total	166	95

Source: Federation of Korean Industries (1983).

a. Reclassified as nonsubsidiaries.

b. Disposed of prior to the September 27th (1980) measure.

evaluating the true performance of the scheme in the disposal of peripheral firms.

THEORETICAL APPROPRIATENESS

In a perfectly competitive market structure, Pareto optimality conditions are satisfied and social welfare is maximized in the sense that nobody's utility can be increased without reducing the utility of somebody else. The stringent conditions of perfect competition are hardly ever met in the real world. If Pareto optimality conditions are unsatisfied in several parts of the economy, a public policy to restore them in a particular part of the economy—a second-best solution—does not necessarily increase the total welfare of the overall economy. Whether or not such partial competitive solutions are in fact optimal will depend on the particular situation and on the nature of the constraints present in the economic system. Although this argument is appealing on theoretical grounds, its use as a guideline for actual policymaking poses many difficulties because the social welfare function and supply-demand elasticities for each commodity should first be ascertained to identify the cases where antitrust policy increases total welfare.

Accordingly, actual antitrust policy is guided by the concept of effective competition, which does not require all the rigorous conditions of perfect competition but preserves the merits of perfect competition on more realistic grounds. Effective competition is said to prevail when the following conditions are fulfilled: (1) a considerable number of suppliers and demanders exist in a commodity market; (2) an individual supplier or demander does not possess market power strong enough to manipulate the market price; (3) there is no collusive agreement among transactors; and (4) new entry is not limited by noneconomic forces such as administrative and legal restrictions or by deliberate intervention by existing rival firms.

The Antitrust and Fair Trade Law of 1981 was aimed at improving market structure and behavior, bringing them closer to effective competition. By banning mergers and other monopolizing business combinations and by establishing strict guidelines to rule out unfair trade and other competition-reducing behavior, the law is expected to increase consumer welfare, allocative efficiency, and distributional equity. It is also expected to contribute to economic growth by providing increased incentives for managerial and technological innovation because firms whose monopoly-oligopoly positions are secure have little, if any, motivation to allocate scarce resources for innovative activities. These dynamic aspects of antitrust policy are more important than static efficiency considerations in the context of a developing economy like Korea. In the early stages, Korea's economic growth was based on combining foreign capital and technology with abundant domestic labor, producing unskilled labor-intensive products to export to developed countries. But as Korea's comparative advantage shifts to skilled-labor and technology-intensive products, innovative entrepreneurship is urgently required for continuous economic growth. The reward and punishment system inherent in the competitive market mechanism should be given a relevant institutional backing so that it can freely operate to render incentives for higher profits by applying new technology and cost-saving and efficient production methods, rather than by supranormal price increases using monopoly power.

There is a strong argument that a big business is more capable than a smaller one of making research and development investments and in managing the ensuing technical changes, and hence antitrust regulations based on bigness are ill-suited to Korea's present needs. Research and development investments in high technology require human and financial resources that a small business can seldom mobilize. Antitrust policy in Korea adequately addresses this point. It does not attempt to split a big firm into several smaller ones through divestiture. It only prohibits business combinations that substantially reduce competition. Even in that case, a merger or other type of business combination essential for industry rationalization and stronger international competitiveness is permitted.

FORMULATION AND IMPLEMENTATION

Long-Delayed Enactment of the Antitrust Law

Antitrust legislation was first discussed by government authorities in 1963. Not until 13 years later was a law finally enacted, suggesting a sharp conflict of interests among government, private business, and consumer groups.

A scandal arose in 1963 involving wheat, sugar, and cement. The producers of these necessities— all big firms wielding considerable monopoly power—were earning enormous excess profits by selling their products at prices much higher than the ceiling prices set by the government. Moreover, they were accused of evading taxes by underreporting sales revenues. Faced with strong public criticism of the collusive market manipulations by the monopoly and oligopoly firms, in 1964 the EPB drafted an antitrust bill that focused on the regulation of unfair cartel activities.

Private businesses adamantly opposed the enactment of such a law on various grounds. First, since economies of scale should be utilized fully to secure competitiveness in the export market, they were concerned that monopoly-oligopoly regulations based solely on the criterion of production capacity would decelerate the growth of production scale. Second, the biggest plants, which are built with foreign loans, lead to monopolization from the start. An antimonopoly policy in this situation might hinder foreign borrowing. Third, the demerits of monopoly-oligopoly can be sufficiently taken care of by price control. Other antimonopoly policies would only dampen the motivation to engage in business activities. It was thus argued that such policies were premature. In the end, the draft of the antitrust bill was shelved even before it reached the legislature.

In 1966 the government drafted another, slightly revised bill and submitted it to the legislature. Once again, strong objections from business circles played a major role in preventing its passage.

In 1968 President Park ordered the deputy prime minister to draw up an antitrust bill and have it passed by the legislature. The order reflected strong public criticism concerning the excess profits enjoyed by monopolistic firms. Bad feelings were sparked with the public when a legislative inspection uncovered a smuggling scandal involving a large automobile manufacturer. The EPB proceeded more cautiously this time, consulting all relevant organizations, including the ruling party. The bill was discussed in public hearings before it was submitted to the legislature. Surprisingly, it failed to pass, presumably blocked by the powerful business lobby.

In 1971 the government again submitted the bill to the legislature, and once again it was abandoned. By this time many academics and consumer groups had begun to doubt the willingness of the government to pass any antitrust legislation.

In 1975 the antitrust bill was finally enacted into law. It is difficult to explain why the bill was passed at that particular time. The protracted debate had, however, gained a momentum of its own. Moreover, private businesses became passive in opposing the bill after benefiting enormously from the government's August 3rd measure of 1972.

Policies restricting business concentration did not encounter strong opposition from the big business groups. Although private business circles did not welcome the May 29th measure when it was announced in 1974, they accepted the policy recognizing that sound financial structure and equity dispersion of big businesses were essential for long-term economic growth. Because of considerable anxiety about the possible constraining impacts of the measures, they repeatedly asked the government to take a cautious, flexible, and realistic attitude in the implementation of the measure. In response, the government emphasized that the measure should be beneficial to private businesses in the long run, and the government listened closely to their suggestions and recommendations concerning the technical aspects of the measure.

Business circles were seemingly more cooperative with regard to the September 27th measure in 1980. On the day following the announcement of the measure, they organized a committee called the Commission on Consolidating the Constitution of Business Enterprises. This prompt response can be attributed to the following factors. First, the government repeatedly emphasized that the measure should be carried out through the initiatives of the business itself. Second, the business circles felt uneasy about mounting public criticism pertaining to the excessive concentration of economic power, real estate investment by big businesses, and significant imbalances between big and small firms. They recognized that the bad public image of big business—right or wrong—was too serious to be ignored. They thus had to do something about it on their own.

Tension still exists between the government and private business regarding the scope and degree of actual implementation of the antitrust law. Government officials often complain about the lack of cooperation from private business when they gather data to analyze antitrust behavior. Recently the Federation of Korean Industries—an interest group for big business—recommended that the enforcement of the law be eased. In particular, the criteria for designating market-dominating firms should be loosened to reflect realities in individual industries.

Institutional Setting for the Antitrust Policy

The institutional framework for the implementation of antitrust policy has a three-tiered structure. The minister of the EPB is in charge of final decisions concerning the enforcement of the law and violations against it. The Fair Trade Commission deliberates upon and resolves the important issues before the minister announces his final decision. The Fair Trade Bureau within the EPB is a secretariat that is in charge of investigating violations, drafting legal and administrative ordinances, and other operational procedures.

The Fair Trade Commission, which undertakes the very important functions of deliberation and resolution, is comprised of five members (including the chairman), three of whom are permanent. The members are appointed by the president on the recommendation of the minister of the EPB who may himself serve as commission chairman. The term of membership is three years and members cannot serve more than two consecutive terms. Members cannot be dismissed against their will unless they are convicted of a crime or are unable to carry out their duties because of chronic illness.

The commission deliberates and makes decisions on the following important issues: (1) enactment or revision of the law in areas such as antitrust policy, designation of exemptions from the antitrust law, and legal restrictions on competition; (2) designation of market-dominating firms, unfair trade activities, and criteria defining improper international contracts; (3) corrective measures on violations of the antitrust law; (4) orders requiring market-dominating firms to pay penalties for abusive pricing behavior; (5) lawsuits to nullify a business combination or the establishment of a new firm; (6) processing appeals from businesses that have been charged with violating the antitrust law; and (7) other matters that may be submitted to the commission by the minister of the EPB.

Violations of the antitrust law are handled according to the following procedures:

1. *Recognition:* A violation is recognized either by government authorities or through a report by an outsider or a concerned party.

2. *Investigation:* The case is investigated by an inspector of the Fair Trade Bureau under the EPB. The inspector is authorized to make inquiries among persons involved in the case, collect necessary data and other materials, and conduct on-the-spot investigations if necessary.

3. *Post-investigation development:* The minister of the EPB has three options for discretionary action once an investigation has been completed. He can disregard the case if he decides the charge is minor; he can suggest that the firm either discontinue activities deemed to be in violation of the law or take corrective measures with the consent of the victims if this is more desirable; or he can present the case to the Fair Trade Commission for consideration. In the latter instance, the commission deliberates on the case following a quasi-judicial procedure, after which it either dismisses the case, suggests corrective measures to the violator, or files a suit in the courts.

EFFECTS, CURRENT ISSUES, AND LESSONS

A more elaborate evaluation of the effects of the antitrust policy on the market structure would include a comparison of the degree of industrial concentration before and after the implementation of the antitrust law in 1981, and an identification of the various factors contributing to this difference between the two periods. The market structure showed slight improvement during the period 1977-85. The market share of the competitive firms increased from 17.1 percent to 22.3 percent in terms of number of commodities, and from 26.1 percent to 37.8 percent in terms of shipments. But as of 1985, the market share of monopolgy-oligopoly firms remained high at 77.7 percent in terms of number of commodities and 62.2 percent in terms of shipments (Table 18.19). The number of market-dominating firms and commodities designated by the government show continuous upward

Table 18.19. Trends in market concentration: 1977 and 1985

	Monopoly		Oligopoly		Competitive		Total	
	1977	1985	1977	1985	1977	1985	1977	1985
Number of commodities	475	534	807	1,421	264	561	1,546	2,516
Share of commodities (%)	30.7	21.2	52.2	56.5	17.1	22.3	100.0	100.0
Share of shipments (%)	12.7	9.4	61.2	52.8	26.1	37.8	100.0	100.0

Source: K. Lee (1988).

trends, increasing from 48 commodities of 87 firms in 1982, to 58 commodities of 107 firms in 1983, and to 71 commodities of 136 firms in 1984.

Another possible method of evaluation is to look into the specific actions of the government to improve the market structure. Two types of government action can be considered in this regard: the enforcement of divestiture by existing monopoly-oligopoly firms, and the prohibition of attempted mergers. Since the antitrust law took effect in 1981, no actions have been taken in the first category and only two attempted mergers have been prevented. Thus it can be concluded that the antitrust policy did not have a significant effect on improving the market structure or on making it more competitive.

The antitrust policy nonetheless has had obvious effects on market behavior and performance. Besides these specific actions, the antitrust policy also contributes to improving market behavior and performance by infusing a new consciousness about the importance of enhanced competition into the minds of both producers and consumers. Producers are increasingly aware that the pursuit of excess profits through monopoly pricing, collusive marketing, and other unfair trading practices cannot continue without the risk of substantial penalties.

Consumers are becoming more intensely cognizant of their rights of protection against the abuse of monopolistic market power. This awareness is reflected in the significant increase in charges brought by consumers against violations of the fair trade laws, from 7,365 in 1980 to 21,727 in 1982.

One of the issues yet to be settled is the balance between economies of scale and a competitive market structure. As the economic structure moves toward more capital- and technology-intensive heavy industries, the minimum efficient scales in technological and managerial terms tend to increase, thus inevitably leading to monopolistic-oligopolistic market structure given the small domestic market. Import liberalization fits into this situation, augmenting actual and potential competition by increasing the number of actual and potential substitutes in a given commodity market.

In 1983 the Korean government announced a gradual but ambitious plan to liberalize imports by removing quantitative restrictions on 80.4 percent of total tradable items in 1983, increasing to 95.2 percent in 1988. However, the import liberalization ratio for monopolistic-oligopolistic commodities is much lower than that for the competitive ones. As of 1983 almost 80.4 percent of all tradable commodities were liberalized from quantitative restrictions and the average tariff rate was 23.7 percent. In contrast, only 37.5 percent of the commodities produced by the monopoly-oligopoly firms were import-liberalized from quantitative restrictions and the average tariff rate on such commodities was 41.5 percent. The stated rationale for this difference is that many of the monopolized commodities are either strategically important or produced by infant industries. Critics insist, however, that many of the monopolized commodities are protected largely because their producers wield strong influence upon government trade policy. Competition with foreign goods should be an important instrument for attaining a more atomistic market structure in a small economy like Korea's. To maximize protection efforts, the protection given to an infant industry should be minimized and its duration should be specified in advance.

Barriers against new entries still remain to a considerable extent. Restrictions on the establishment of new plants and on the expansion of existing ones are embodied in various administrative decrees and practices on the grounds of industrial policy. Although the antitrust law requires *ex ante* consultation regarding legislative attempts to restrict competition, the lack of specific operational criteria impedes full-fledged application of the law. Such consultation could be invigorated by means of closer coordination among government agencies.

The current antitrust law regulates manufacturing, wholesale and retail services, transportation and storage, construction, food services, and lodgings. Other industries such as the banking and nonbanking financial institutions, insurance companies, and real estate services are not subject to regulation by the antitrust law. The fair trade authorities insist that these sectors should be made subject to the antitrust law. They argue that, because these sectors are so closely related to everyday life, consumer protection could be affected seriously if they are not regulated. Also, if the flow of funds through financial intermediaries is distorted by discriminatory or collusive lending behavior, competition in the real sector of the economy will be distorted accordingly. Other opinions are opposed to or cautious about regulating these sectors (particularly the financial sector) within the same framework as the real sector. It is often argued that financial intermediation plays too important a role in the economy to be entrusted to free-market mechanisms.

One thing to be considered in this discussion is the privatization of commercial banks. As government-held shares of the commercial banks are sold to private shareholders, the management will eventually be taken over by the big businesses that own the majority of the equities. The increasing discretionary power of the private stock owners might lead to abusive market power or discriminatory lending behavior, which would impose serious constraints upon competition in the real sector.

In spite of government measures, such as the May 29th and September 27th measures, the situation concerning the degree of economic power concentration has hardly improved. The shares of output (value added) produced by the five largest and the 20 largest conglomerates have increased steadily since 1973 (Table 18.20). The number of subsidiary firms belonging to the 30 largest conglomerates also increased from 327 in 1980 to 481 in 1982. The share of bank lending to conglomerates in total financial credit remained at a very high level—in October 1982 the five largest conglomerates held 20.3 percent of total bank loans and 26.4 percent of total bank credits (Table 18.21).

A new development in recent years is the participation by conglomerates in the ownership of commercial banks. In 1982 the government decided to denationalize the banks by selling state-owned shares in the open stock market to remove bureaucratic intervention in the purely financial operations of the banking system. As anticipated, the conglomerates purchased a major portion of the shares offered. As of October 1982, 37 percent of the commercial banks' total capital was accounted for by the 20 largest

Table 18.20. Value-added share in GDP of the five largest and the 20 largest conglomerates: 1973–81 (%)

Category of conglomerates	1973	1975	1978	1981
5 largest	3.5	4.7	8.1	8.7
20 largest	9.1	9.8	14.0	15.5

Source: EPB, ROK, Proceedings of the Industrial and Technological Policy Advisory Meeting (1983).

Table 18.21. Shares of bank loans and credits granted to the five largest and 30 largest conglomerates in totals, as of October 1982

Category of conglomerates	Bank loans		Bank credit[a]	
	Amount (10^9 won)	Share (%)	Amount (10^9 won)	Share (%)
5 largest	4,118	20.3	10,764	26.4
30 largest	7,811	38.6	20,832	51.2

Source: EPB, ROK, Proceedings of the Industrial and Technological Policy Advisory Meeting (1983).

a. Bank credit is the sum of bank loans and guarantees.

conglomerates. Among them, three super-conglomerates held enough shares to control the management of some commercial banks (Table 18.22).

This combination of industrial and financial capital increases the possibility that the allocation of credit will worsen. Conglomerates with high bank equity holdings may tend to favor their subsidiary firms by giving them easier access to scarce credit. It is too early to derive any empirical conclusion on this matter since the new, large shareholders are not yet allowed to control the actual management of the banks. The government has also taken measures to prevent any further concentration of bank lending to conglomerates.

Economic power concentration within a small group of conglomerates is one of the most serious issues in today's economy, drawing wide attention and provoking heated discussions. Economic and political power sometimes go hand in hand, affecting the government's decisions on resource allocation. The imbalance between large conglomerates and small and medium industries also reduces the overall efficiency of the Korean economy. Misunderstanding and distrust by the public of the economic and social functions of conglomerates will be detrimental to the continuous growth of a capitalist economy. The conglomerates account for the dominant portion of Korea's GNP and labor force. Mutual cooperation and understanding between big business groups and consumers is therefore indispensable for the political and economic stability of Korea.

It may not be fair to ask the conglomerates to assume full responsibility for their bad public image. The public should acknowledge the following facts: first, the primary objective of a private enterprise is profit maximization; second, the excessive expansion of the conglomerates has been induced or encouraged by growth-oriented government policy; and finally, the conglomerates have made significant contributions to Korea's economic development over the past two and a half decades. It is widely believed that better integrated measures should be taken to regulate the negative side effects of conglomerate growth. Individual policies relating to antitrust law, credit management, taxation, securities markets, and industry in general should be coordinated to maximize their effects and to make them consistent with other economic policy objectives such as capital accumulation

Table 18.22. Bank equity holdings of three super-conglomerates, as of October 1982

Conglomerate	Percentage held
A	29.8% of the total equities of 3 banks
B	30.5% of the total equities of 2 banks
C	23.5% of the total equities of 2 banks

Source: EPB, ROK, Proceedings of the Industrial and Technological Policy Advisory Meeting (1983).

and export promotion. Two important areas toward which this integrated policy should be directed are discussed below.

Conglomerate Diversification

Table 18.23 shows the distribution of conglomerate business activities in Korea. The top 30 conglomerates are engaged in an almost comprehensive range of industries, among which manufacturing, construction, and international trading are predominant.

Table 18.24 presents the distribution of the fixed capital stock of the top five and the top 30 conglomerates in the manufacturing sector. Their production lines cover labor-intensive textiles, capital-intensive chemical and nonferrous metal industries, and technology-intensive machinery and electronics. The top five conglomerates have invested more heavily in machinery and electronics than the smaller conglomerates. There is no doubt that their diversification has gone beyond the optimum level that can be explained

Table 18.23. Sectoral distribution of total assets, own capital, and employment of the top 30 conglomerates: 1980 (%)

Item	Manufacturing	Construction	Trade	Transportation and storage	Finance	Tourism
Total assets	46.3	15.2	15.8	10.7	7.5	0.6
Own capital	53.6	15.0	8.2	12.1	4.3	2.2
Employment	56.3	20.6	9.0	8.1	2.3	0.4

Source: EPB, ROK, Proceedings of the Industrial and Technological Policy Advisory Meeting (1983).

Table 18.24. Distribution of conglomerates' fixed capital stock in manufacturing: 1980 (%)

Category	Food and textiles	Chemicals and nonferrous metals	Machinery and electronics
5 largest conglomerates	10.3	31.6	58.1 (47.5)[a]
30 largest conglomerates	23.0	30.3	46.6 (37.6)[a]
Total manufacturing	27.5	27.0	45.5 (24.8)[a]

Source: EPB, ROK, Proceedings of the Industrial and Technological Policy Advisory Meeting (1983).
a. Machinery only.

by risk-pooling or the utilization of surplus resources in a closely related business area. One way of interpreting this phenomenon is to regard it as the natural consequence of the conglomerates' attempts to eventually diversify into newly emerging industries. But a more plausible view is simply that conglomerates take part in almost all industries whose profit outlooks are promising.

The dispersion of human and material resources across a wide range of unrelated industries is detrimental to technological innovation, which is carried out more efficiently by specialization in certain areas. With a given amount of resources, it would be much more beneficial for the economy to invest in research and development rather than in expanding the superficial size of the conglomerates by purchasing other firms and real estate.

Excessive diversification by the conglomerates constricts the maneuverability of small and medium-size firms, which are placed in a strikingly disadvantageous position relative to the big firms. This is clearly illustrated by comparing Korea to Japan and Taiwan (Table 18.14).

The conglomerates often establish their own small and medium-size firms to supply parts and materials to their own member firms. Table 18.25 compares the paid-in capital and value added of the member firms of three conglomerates with those of independent small and medium-size firms. The former clearly hold a superior position to the latter.

In an attempt to curb the increasing diversification of the conglomerates, the May 29th (1974), September 27th (1980), and other measures were implemented but without much success. One reason for the unsatisfactory result may be the existence of too many legal loopholes. As a typical example, a large firm with a high debt ratio can be exempted from stringent credit controls when a bank loan is judged essential to export promotion. It is not difficult to imagine that many firms have been exploiting this escape route to the maximum extent. It must also be recognized that the govern-

Table 18.25. Paid-in capital, fixed capital stock, and value added of small and medium-size firms, conglomerate members compared to independents: 1980 (10^8 won)

Category	Paid-in capital	Fixed capital stock	Value added
Member firm (averages of top 3 conglomerates) (A)	11.3	25.3	15.7
Independent firm (average of all firms) (B)	0.3	1.1	1.2
Ratio (A/B) (%)	37.7	23.0	13.0

Source: EPB, ROK, Proceedings of the Industrial and Technological Policy Advisory Meeting (1983).

ment was not ready to sacrifice its other policy objectives such as rapid export-led economic growth even in the short run. Government financial policy cannot be so stringent that it prevents consideration of discrete situations. However, effective implementation of anti-diversification policy could be achieved if the commercial banks were required to take greater responsibility and exercise sound judgment in allocating credit.

In addition to the role of credit management, antitrust law can be an effective instrument for restricting diversification. The current antitrust law cannot readily regulate a business combination between diverse industries because the effects of such combinations on competition in specific business areas are dubious. The competition-reducing effects of these kinds of business combinations need to be defined in a broader sense to encompass the stronger economic influences on the behavior of other firms through access to political decision making, monopolistic power in labor and credit markets, and the supply of intermediate goods, rather than defining by a static criterion applicable to the same commodity market.

Industrial policy should also be directed toward curbing a certain kind of diversification. In the past, a large-scale new venture or a firm with a default risk was almost always entrusted by the government to a conglomerate on the grounds that other business entities lacked the capital and managerial ability to undertake the task. This policy can hardly be justified when it is considered that the conglomerates depend upon additional bank loans for the required capital. Independent small and medium-size firms should receive stronger protection from conglomerates' intrusions by designating some industrial sectors as areas exclusively for small and medium-size firms.

Ownership and Management Patterns of Conglomerates

In Korea a conglomerate's member firms are controlled directly by a centralized management system whose top echelon consists of a small number of owner-managers. These owner-managers are in many cases family members of the founder of the conglomerate. Two unique characteristics are derived: first, a conglomerate is itself an independent entity that can mobilize all the human and nonhuman resources of the member firms in a highly coherent manner; second, its ownership and management are monopolized by a handful of the founder's family members. (This is very similar to the pre-World War II stage of development of the Japanese *zaibatsu*. See SaKong and Jones 1981:290–92.) These characteristics reinforce the real concentration of economic power that creates a barrier to maintaining harmonious relationships with other interest groups in the society.

To separate ownership from management, the first thing to be done is to lower the minimum portion of the total equities that can be held by oligopolistic shareholders of a single family. When that is accomplished, professional managers should replace the owner-managers in the actual operation of the conglomerates.

According to widespread opinion, it may be too late to control the conglomerates because their enormous power has already exceeded the limit within which some type of equilibrium could be achieved by means of market mechanism checks and balances. This is why strong political will on the part of the government is required to solve this long-avoided problem of the Korean economy.

19 Promotion Measures for General Trading Companies (1975)

by Sung-Hwan Jo

Korea's general trading companies (GTCs) were not the natural outcome of the evolution and expansion of Korea's export-oriented trading firms—they were artificially created by government decree in 1975. It is, therefore, appropriate to review the economic background and circumstances that led to the government's decision to create GTCs rather than to focus our attention on the firm-specific aspects of the internationalization of Korean business enterprises.

Changes in the international economic environment after the 1973-74 oil shock were extremely detrimental to prospects for a continuous expansion of Korea's exports. Overseas demand for labor-intensive industrial exports from developing economies fell sharply due mainly to the oil shock-related stagflation in the developed countries—Korea's major export markets—and to the growing neo-protectionism against industrial exports. On the domestic front, general price inflation and increases in wages for unskilled and semi-skilled workers since 1973 had weakened the international competitiveness of Korea's industrial exports.

However, because the government's drive for export expansion had been intensified by a strong incentive system and profit earnings from export activities had begun to rise, the number of export-oriented trading firms increased tremendously—from 816 in 1970 to 1,842 in 1975. Notwithstanding the increasing number of establishments, the average size of exporting firms remained relatively small. The average value of exports per firm increased from US $10.2 million in 1970 to US $27.6 million in 1975. Furthermore, an increasing number of processing firms began to expand their activities into export trading (forward linkage), while many trading firms began to expand their activities into processing (backward linkage). Thus, export trading was overcrowded with small and mid-size traders, leading to cutthroat competition in overseas export markets.

In addition, after President Park forcibly carried out the politically controversial constitutional amendment in 1972 that virtually guaranteed his continued rule, Park and his government viewed export-oriented economic growth and prosperity as the most effective means of pacifying political discontent among the Korean people. The "export target of US $10 billion" was a politically attractive goal, and the government made an all-out effort to attain this quantitative target.

In short, faced with the changed external and internal circumstances and out of political necessity, the government took a series of measures to expand exports that included the creation of the GTC system, which was designed to increase economies of scale and functional specialization in the overcrowded and fragmented export trading sector.

MAIN FEATURES OF THE POLICY MEASURES

Korea's GTCs, following more or less the Japanese model of general trading companies (*shogogaisha*), were designed to cope with problems affecting Korea's export trading activities, including: (1) declining export market demand due to worldwide recession and rising protectionism; (2) lack of a functional division of labor between export traders and export manufacturers and among export traders; and (3) excessive competition among small-scale exporters. The government expected the GTCs to:

- Strengthen on-site export marketing activities by using their networks of overseas branches to reach out to final consumers in existing export markets and develop new markets through the diversification of products and regions

- Act as "windows" (or representatives) for small and medium-size export processing enterprises by taking care of all aspects of their export trade, thereby promoting the functional division of labor between export trader and producer

- Reduce excessive competition and dumping in overseas markets, particularly among small and medium-size exporters, through economies of scale and the functional specialization to be gained from the GTCs' worldwide network of branches and information sources, and their massive supply capacity

By appointing the trading subsidiaries of large business groups to the status of GTCs, the government hoped to use the limited resources or funds for subsidies more effectively among a small number of oligopolistic trading firms rather than stretching its resources among a large and increasing number of small and financially weak exporters.

Requirements for GTC Designation

Against the economic background and the government objectives reviewed above, the Ministry of Commerce and Industry established, by decree, a set of formal requirements for qualification of the GTCs. In 1975 these requirements were: (1) minimum capitalization of 1 billion won, and a minimum value of exports per year of more than US $50 million; (2) exports of each of at least seven items valued at more than US $500 thousand; (3) annual exports worth more than US $1 million to each of ten or more countries; and (4) encouraging public ownership of GTCs through stock issue.

Minimum requirements for capitalization and value of exports were increased, respectively, from 1 billion won and US $50 million in 1975 to 1.5 billion won and US $100 million in 1976, and further to 2 billion won and US $150 million in 1977. Such increasing minimum requirements were meant to encourage economies of scale in GTC operations and to strengthen their market power in export trading.

The requirement for exports of at least seven items valued at US $500 thousand or more was designed to promote product diversification. This requirement was especially suited to large business groups (Korea's conglomerates) with multiple product lines, and triggered a wave of takeovers of small enterprises by larger business groups.

The requirement for exports worth more than US $1 million to each of ten or more countries was designed to indirectly induce new market development and regional diversification of exports. The minimum number of overseas branches for each GTC was not specified in the list of formal requirements, though the expansion of overseas branch networks subsequently was encouraged in the process of providing government incentives and assistance to the GTCs.

The requirement for going public through stock issues was in part politically motivated to justify government loans, subsidies, and other forms of public support and in part to encourage the development of Korea's stock market.

Because the GTCs were created by the government as a byproduct of its export drive rather than through the natural evolution and growth of export-oriented Korean firms, the government came to specify minimum export targets, capitalization requirements, number of export items, number of overseas branch offices, and extent of public share ownership for each GTC. From 1975 to 1977, the minimum requirements for amount of exports, product diversification, and regional specialization were again increased. These requirements soon proved too tough for the GTCs to meet, and led them to take the myopic approach of mere quantitative maximization of exports to the point of disregarding long-run profit potentials. In 1978 the requirements for number of export items, number of countries, and capitalization were greatly relaxed. Later, the formal requirements for achieving and maintaining GTC status were also eased. These modifications were considered necessary because the first and second oil shocks had created an unfavorable international business environment that increasingly deteriorated the export performance and profitability of GTCs. The formal requirements for GTC status were again revised in January 1981 (Table 19.1).

In 1978 the requirement for a minimum level of capitalization was abolished. The various requirements for specific minimum amounts of exports were replaced with the requirement that a GTC's exports be at least

Table 19.1. Minimum requirements for designation as a GTC

Period of qualification
  Before[a]:   Annual requalification required at the beginning of each year
  Current[b]: Qualification effective as long as it is not cancelled by the
             government

Minimum requirements
  Export
    Before: 2 percent or more of the country's total commodity exports
    Current: Same
  Number of overseas branches:
    Before: 20 or more
    Current: Requirement abolished
  Number of export items worth more than US $1 million
    Before: 5 or more
    Current: Requirement abolished
  Form of ownership
    Before: Public share ownership
    Current: Same

Conditions for cancellation of GTC status
1. Failure to meet the minimum requirements for two consecutive years
2. Engaging in unlawful and unfair practices in domestic and overseas trading
   activities
3. Mismanagement and financial insolvency

a. Prior to January 1981.
b. After January 1981.

2 percent of the country's total commodity exports. This meant that GTC
export requirements would be automatically escalated by the annual growth
of exports.

In 1977 the requirements for regional diversification of exports for GTCs
included: (1) exports over US $1 million to each of more than 20 countries;
(2) at least 20 overseas branches; and (3) a specific minimum value of exports and minimum number of overseas branches for new export markets
in the Middle East, Latin America, and Africa. Of these three requirements,
items 1 and 3 were abolished in 1981. Therefore, one of the major functions originally envisaged for GTCs, namely, the development of new export
markets, was no longer subjected to government control. This development
opened up the possibility of increasing export concentration in existing export markets—the United States, Japan, and Western Europe.

The requirements for product diversification were also relaxed. In 1977
a GTC was required to export ten items, each with a value of more than
US $1 million. In 1978 this was reduced to five items and the requirement

was abolished altogether in 1981. This implies that any trading company exporting a single item comprising 2 percent of the value of the country's total commodity exports could achieve GTC status.

Such a major relaxation in the requirements for GTC status once again pushed to the forefront the quantitative export maximization of a small number of commodities going to the existing export markets of the developed countries, while denigrating the initial objectives of product and regional diversification.

Incentives

The incentives given to the GTCs can be considered as the "rights" (or benefits) that counterbalanced the "obligations" (or costs) of meeting the requirements for GTC designation. These incentives are reviewed in terms of international trade, administrative, financial, and foreign exchange aspects (BOK, *Present State of General Trading Companies, 1977*).

Trade and administrative incentives. GTCs are given preferential treatment in international bidding. They have access to membership in various trade and export associations because the government has eased membership eligibility requirements for GTCs and allows them to pay reduced membership fees. GTCs also enjoy easy access to the import of raw materials.

Financial incentives. GTCs are given preference in obtaining bank loans within the limit of their past export performance for a specific period. In addition, local trade credit is allowed for the GTC's domestic purchase of finished products within the limits of one-third of the firm's export records for the previous year. In this connection GTCs are permitted to issue a "local" letter of credit to local suppliers without receiving a "master" letter of credit from foreign importers, and to use the local letter of credit as collateral for loans for financing domestic purchases. This privilege accorded exclusively to GTCs was designed to permit them to accumulate a stock of exportable products in anticipation of actual demand.

Foreign exchange incentives. Overseas branches of GTCs are awarded Class-A status, and parent companies can dispatch up to ten persons to each of their overseas branch offices. But this privilege is accorded to all other trading companies with large annual volumes of exports (US $10 million or more). Overseas branch offices of GTCs can repeatedly use a letter of credit guaranteed by a home-country bank in obtaining loans from overseas banks for working capital and in opening letters of credit for importing from the home country without obtaining a new letter of credit for each new loan. However, this revolving utilization of the guaranteed letter of credit, within the upper limit of the amount guaranteed, is not confined to the branch offices of the GTCs alone. The same system is widely available to many other classes of trading companies as well.

Other incentives. Although the upper limit of business funds that can be accumulated by overseas branch offices of non-GTCs is set at US $300 thousand, GTC branch offices are exempt from such an upper limit. Other incentives are given to all exporters, but the benefits from those incentives are bound to be greater for the GTCs because of the volume of their exports.

Direct incentives for tax savings include the return of value-added taxes on purchases and the exemption of business income tax up to 24 percent of the increase in capital. Indirect benefits can be accrued in the form of interest savings from the deferred payment of corporation taxes authorized for such company reserves as market development funds, reserve funds for export losses, reserve funds for overseas direct investments, and reserve funds for price changes. GTCs can lower their interest costs by making deferred installment payments for taxes on these special reserves.

Unlike other trading companies, GTCs are allowed to hold regular consultation meetings with other GTCs to discuss various issues of common interest, exchange information, and prepare their collective recommendations for presentation to the government authorities. The collective opinions and policy recommendations of the GTCs have greater influence on government agencies than do those of other business associations. GTC status enhances an individual firm's public image and its credibility in personnel recruitment, as well as its effectiveness in dealing with the government and in international and local business dealings.

Most of the government incentives discussed above are provided not only for GTCs but also for other trading companies. Preferential treatment in international bidding, the privilege to issue a local letter of credit and gain access to trade credit based on that letter of credit, and the flexible upper limits on overseas business funds accumulated in branch offices are the exclusive incentives offered to the GTCs.

THEORETICAL APPROPRIATENESS

Before examining the outcome of interactions between government incentive policies and GTCs' performance, it is appropriate to ask the following questions: (1) Is the government policy of fostering the development of GTCs appropriate considering the nation's economic and social goals? (2) Are the policy measures for GTC promotion appropriate for the attainment of the stated objectives?

The first question is directly related to Korea's basic strategy of economic development. At issue is whether the collective social gain from the economic efficiency achieved in concentrating export trading activities into the hands of a small number of large business groups is greater than the social gain—creative dynamism, social harmony, and equitable distribution—that the free entry into export trading by a number of small and medium-size enterprises could bring. Is the attainment of efficiency and relative stability in export activities more important than equity in income distribution and employment generation? These are the kinds of questions that should have been considered in the government's decision to create GTCs. Because of its continuous efforts to promote the GTCs, it appears that the government has put more emphasis on economic efficiency than on social equity.

The second question asks whether the policy *means* adopted by the government to support the growth of the GTCs are appropriate to the attainment of the policy *objective* of sustained export growth through product and regional diversification. This question can be considered in two stages. One is whether the policy decision to promote the GTCs would have been better than the absence of such a policy or the policy of nonintervention, and another is whether the particular policy measures actually adopted are better than alternative measures to attain the stated objectives in creating GTCs. At this stage the following preliminary observations are offered:

1. The government's decision to create GTCs out of the existing large business groups (Korean conglomerates) clearly reveals the Park government's view that economic efficiency was a higher priority than social equity as a development objective.

2. Because the formal requirements for achieving and maintaining GTC status have been relaxed gradually, particularly in connection with product and regional diversification objectives, and because most of the export incentives were provided not only for the GTCs but also for all other exporters, two points can be made. First, the special incentives for the GTCs were not much greater than those enjoyed by all other exporters. The government could have promoted the GTCs or similar entities through informal administrative discretion under the general package of export incentives. Second, the tough requirement for quantitative export targets (or quotas) and the subsequent abolishment of the formal requirements for product and regional diversification only led to the short-run quantitative maximization of a limited number of industrial exports to the established developed-country markets at the expense of developing long-run export profit incentives, product diversification, and new markets.

IMPLEMENTATION AND EFFECTS: INTERACTIONS BETWEEN THE GOVERNMENT AND GTCS

Because of the government's active export drive and the business groups' positive responses to government incentives, the relative position of the GTCs in total export activities increased rapidly over a short period of time. Five business groups' trading firms—Samsung, Daewoo, Ssangyong, Kukje, and Hanil—were registered as GTCs in 1975, the initial year of the decree. Six more trading companies—Hyosung, Bando, Sunkyong, Samwha, Kunho, and the government-owned Koryo Trading Company that specialized in exports from small and medium-scale producers—were designated GTCs in 1976. Hyundai joined the group in 1977. The number of GTCs in subsequent years has been fairly stable at around ten to 12, with one or two joining and others dropping out.

Share of Exports

Over the period 1975–82, the share of GTCs in total commodity exports increased rapidly, from 13 percent in 1975 to 48 percent in 1982. The share of the small and medium producer-exporters declined from 36 percent in 1978 to 22 percent in 1982. The share of large-scale producers also shows a gradual decline from 36 percent in 1978 to 30 percent in 1982. The share of Japanese GTCs operating in Korea remained quite stable at a level of about 10 percent (Table 19.2).

The rapid decline in the export share of the small and medium industries can be attributed to several factors: (1) a relative decline in competitiveness of the industries; (2) the shift from direct export by small and medium industries to indirect export through the GTCs as the unfavorable external conditions developed after the oil shocks; and (3) the tendency of actual exports by these industries to be understated in the export statistics as these industries "transferred" (sold), for a premium, part of their export records to the GTCs, which were sometimes eager to inflate their own export performance to maintain GTC status.

The relative decline in the share of the non-GTC large-scale producers in total commodity exports mainly reflects the growing tendency of large business groups to export their products through their own GTCs and the corresponding decline in the share of exports by large-scale producers with no GTCs of their own. The Japanese GTCs have been quite active in export and import activities ever since they started operations in Korea.

Table 19.2. Share of exports by type of firm: 1975–82 (%)

Year	Korean GTCs	Large-scale export producers	Small-scale export producers	Total	Japanese GTCs
1975	13.3	u	u	100.0	u
1976	17.2	u	u	100.0	u
1977	21.7	u	u	100.0	12.1
1978	27.0	36.6	36.4	100.0	10.2
1979	33.9	37.4	28.7	100.0	10.4
1980	41.0	33.4	25.6	100.0	10.0
1981	42.9	u	u	100.0	10.0
1982	48.2	29.5	22.3	100.0	10.0

Source: Korean Traders Association and the Korean Association of Small and Medium Industries, internal reference materials.

u—unavailable.

GTCs came to dominate Korea's international business activities mainly through three routes:

First, compared with other trading companies, GTCs are well positioned to facilitate export activities, obtain market information, and identify business opportunities using their extensive networks of branch offices and overseas subsidiaries.

Second, GTCs have made efforts to develop and expand exports of heavy and chemical industrial products manufactured by the subsidiaries of their own business groups. GTCs are not only under pressure from the government to diversify their export products and markets—they are compelled to explore and expand new export markets for the heavy and chemical industry products that their own subsidiaries produce. The scale of the newly erected plants and equipment in some heavy and chemical industries (HCIs) has been far larger than current domestic demand warrants; only by expanding overseas markets can the underutilization of productive capacity be remedied. GTCs have been particularly active in expanding the exports of ships, iron and steel, chemical fertilizer, electric machinery, and other chemicals to the new export markets of developing regions. HCI exports arranged by GTCs increased from 39.8 percent of total HCI exports in 1979 to 57.6 percent in 1981 (Table 19.3). The growth rate of HCI exports arranged through the GTCs for this three-year period was 126.9 percent, far surpassing the 56.9 percent growth rate of Korea's total exports for the same period.

Third, GTCs have increased their share in total commodity exports by acting as export agents and representatives for small and medium-size industrial producers. GTCs not only act as export agents for small and medium-size export processing firms but in some cases also participated in equity investment. GTCs even provided these smaller firms with management assistance, operational funds, and raw materials. In 1976 about 21 percent of exports supplied by small and medium-size industries were arranged by the GTCs. The share increased to 32 percent in 1979.

The relationship between the GTCs as exporters and the small and medium industry producers as subcontractors has not been well coordinated and developed to take full advantage of the potential complementarity. In some cases, the conflict of interests and the lack of mutual trust impeded the natural development of linkages between the large exporters (the GTCs) and small industry producers.

Major Characteristics of Korean GTCs

Although it is true that the GTCs were created by the government as an expedient approach to its export drive, it cannot be overlooked that the formation and growth of the GTCs have been closely linked with the formation and growth of the country's unique "business groups" (conglomerates), which have exerted a pervasive influence over every facet of business activity in the past quarter century. Korea's business conglomerates are

Table 19.3. Share of GTCs' exports by type of product: 1979 and 1981
(US $ 10⁶)

Type of product	Total exports (A)	Exports by GTCs (B)	Percentage of exports by GTCs of total exports (B/A)
Primary			
1979	1,485	213	14.3
1981	1,484	72	4.9
Growth rate 1979–81 (%)	–0.1	–19.2	na
Light industrial			
1979	7,509	2,475	33.0
1981	9,998	3,346	33.5
Growth rate 1979–81 (%)	33.1	35.2	na
HCI products			
1979	6,062	2,415	39.8
1981	9,510	5,480	57.6
Growth rate 1979–81 (%)	56.9	126.9	na
Total products			
1979	15,056	5,103	33.9
1981	20,992	8,898	42.4
Growth rate 1979–81 (%)	39.4	77.2	na

Source: Korean Traders Association, internal reference materials.
na—not applicable.

characterized by: (1) their strong propensity to follow the government's policy lead; (2) their external orientation through export expansion; and (3) their drive toward all-inclusive business diversification through takeovers and mergers.

During the primary import-substitution period, business firms actively participated in government-initiated industrial development projects by taking full advantage of the strong industrial incentives and protectionism. In this stage of early industrialization, they gained entrepreneurial and industrial experience and consolidated their base for industrial growth. As government development policy shifted from inward-looking to outward-looking industrial development, incentives were mainly given for export activities. Business firms rapidly followed the government's lead by expanding labor-intensive, export-oriented industrial activities. In the process of ever-expanding, export-oriented growth, certain business firms grew into all-inclusive giant conglomerates. From 1973, when the government began to place top priority on the promotion of HCIs, these business groups joined the government in developing HCIs while still maintaining their existing export-oriented industrial activities (Jo 1984). As a result, *each* of about ten business groups now has diverse business lines across all industries. The Samsung group, for instance, has been involved in diverse business lines including foreign trade, textiles and clothing, electronics, shipbuilding, heavy engineering, petrochemicals, food processing, construction, news media, tourism and hotels, insurance, nonbanking finance, department stores, and overseas joint ventures. The Hyundai group has numerous subsidiaries in civil engineering, export and import, automobile assembly, construction, cement, shipbuilding, industrial machinery, electric generators, marine engineering, gas, and nonbanking finance. The Daewoo group, starting from textile exports, has expanded into leather products, exportable sundry goods of all kinds, insurance, machinery, automobile assembly, construction, shipbuilding, and overseas joint ventures.

The business groups' strong propensity to follow the government's policy shift, their all-pervasive business lines, and their strong export orientation could have resulted in the formation and growth of the GTCs or similar entities even without explicit government policy measures.

The unique feature of Korea's GTCs can be thus characterized by the following points: (1) the GTCs as a group or system are receptive instruments of the government's export-oriented policy; (2) they are almost exclusively externally oriented to the point of neglecting domestic trading activities; and (3) they act as "windows" for their own business groups by exporting the diverse products produced by their own subsidiaries in many industries. In this connection it is instructive to compare the main differences in orientation and function between the Korean and the Japanese GTCs (T. S. Cho 1983: vol. 1).

Comparison of Korean and Japanese GTCs

Japanese GTCs are not engaged in manufacturing activities themselves but specialize in a variety of trading activities, including domestic commerce (50 percent of total sales), export (20 percent), and import (20 percent) activities and also in facilitating trade among Third World countries (10 percent). Korean GTCs are engaged in manufacturing as well as export trading.

Japanese GTCs are profit-oriented, taking advantage of differences in selling and buying prices of commodities between countries (between Japan and foreign countries as well as between Third World countries). In addition to dealing with many kinds of products, they have, from the early stages of Japan's economic development, played an important role in international technology markets. Korean GTCs put top priority on exports of products from their own plants and subsidiaries of their own business groups, and consider exports for other producers to be of secondary importance. They import materials and technology merely to meet their own internal and intra-business group needs.

There is a basic difference between Japanese and Korean GTCs in their relationship with small and medium-size industries. Japanese GTCs have played a pivotal role in developing small and medium-size firms into strong, well-coordinated supply bases for exports by providing them with financial loans, managerial and technical assistance, market information, and steady supplies of imported raw materials. They are also instrumental in industrial restructuring and development of new industries in response to the changing overseas demand (Kohama and Yamazawa 1982).

The unique relationship between the Japanese GTCs and small and medium producers can be characterized as follows:

1. Financing for small and medium-size export industries in Japan is channeled mainly through the GTCs; the banking institutions are not directly involved. The GTCs are in an excellent position to assess the financial needs, credit-worthiness, and profit potential of the export industries because of their close working relationship (Yamazawa 1979).

2. Because Japanese GTCs are not directly engaged in manufacturing, they do not compete with small and medium producers and, therefore, take a neutral attitude toward all producers. Furthermore, the small and medium producers have no reason to fear being taken over by GTCs. Therefore, their own long-run interests coincide with the demands made by the GTCs for managerial improvement and product development (C. Y. Lee 1984).

The relationship between GTCs and small and medium export producers in Korea is not as complementary as the Japanese case, mainly for the following reasons:

1. Because under Korea's export incentive system all exporters, including the GTCs, have access to export financing and other benefits from the government, the GTCs are partly in competition with small and medium export producers for the same source of government support.

2. Because the GTCs are engaged in many areas of export processing, they are in direct competition with small and medium export producers. To the extent of overlapping activities and competition, the potential for systematic coordination between the two is weakened.

3. Mutual trust in the business community in Korea is not yet strong enough to bring about a stable and well-coordinated relationship between the large and the small firms.

Whereas Japanese GTCs have been dealing with relatively capital- and technology-intensive products and are rapidly shifting emphasis toward higher quality, more expensive consumer durables and producer goods, Korean GTCs are still dealing with unskilled and semiskilled labor-intensive, low-priced products. Japan is competing in the international markets on the basis of quality and technology, whereas Korea is competing on the basis of quantity and low unit price. Accordingly, Korean GTCs tend to put emphasis on mass production and mass distribution to reduce unit costs.

Export marketing strategy, therefore, tends to differ between the two countries' GTCs.

CRITICISMS AND LESSONS

There is no doubt that the formation and growth of GTCs in Korea have made a great contribution to the *quantitative* expansion of Korea's industrial exports. They have been particularly instrumental in increasing the share of HCI exports. Although the quantitative expansion has been attained, quality improvement and product and regional diversification of exports have left much to be desired.

Export marketing activities have been improved through the expansion of the GTCs' overseas branch offices; the market information scanning function of these offices has been strengthened and a large pool of marketing personnel with international expertise has been created.

The performance of the GTCs as the specialized trade agents for export producers has produced somewhat mixed results, mainly because of the dual nature of the GTCs as both exporters and producers. The GTCs as producers have been in competition with other exporters and have created conflicts of interest and mutual distrust between the two groups.

The government's encouragement of scale expansion of the GTCs has resulted in mergers and takeovers of export producers and excessive competition among GTCs, as well as between the GTCs and export producers. This phenomenon has resulted in excessive concentration of economic and market power of large business groups, leading to socio-political tension. Too much emphasis placed on efficiency through scale economies by a small number of large business groups in export and production has resulted in too little attention paid to economic equity and social justice.

Because both the GTCs and other exporters have been competing for export incentives, the social cost of the unbalanced allocation of loanable funds in favor of the GTCs and the manufacturing sector and tax revenue losses due to exemptions have been excessive.

Criticisms

The main fault with the government's policy of promoting the formation and growth of GTCs lies in its strategy of economic development via export growth that emphasizes the expansion of a few conglomerates in the name of efficiency at the expense of economic equity and social justice. When a small number of large business groups dominate industry, their GTCs cannot be expected to be neutral in promoting the exports of other export producers. The GTCs are primarily export windows for the "department store-type" operations of their own groups, and as export processors tend to suppress rather than assist other export producers. The separation between exporting and producing is an essential precondition if GTCs are expected to equitably serve all exporters. Such a separation of functions is unlikely to take place unless the concentrated economic power in the hands of a small number of large business groups is broken up and their ownership widely dispersed through a rather radical policy shift.

The near total dependence of the GTCs on export trade and their lack of a domestic trade base is one of the main sources of the instability in the GTCs' earnings and profits. Their profit position is vulnerable to fluctuations in international markets, and their risks associated with the export of heavy industrial products are great because exports of these kinds involve long-term trade credit and deferred payments of a large magnitude. The existence of a reliable domestic market for the GTCs would serve as a cushion in stabilizing earnings.

The government's preoccupation with the attainment of the quantity target of exports assigned to the GTCs has produced many undesirable side effects: (1) the purchase at a premium by the GTCs of the export records amassed by small and medium export producers; (2) a short-run quantity maximization of exports at the expense of long-run profits; (3) deterioration in the quality of exported goods; and (4) excessive competition among the GTCs in overseas export markets.

Although they are expanding and diversifying exports, the GTCs are still weak in import markets. A strong position in the import markets would be a potential source of earnings for GTCs, ultimately reducing the unit cost of Korea's exports, which depend on imports of raw materials, components, and equipment.

Lessons

There is a limit to what the government can do in export promotion. The government cannot just impose an institution like the GTCs by decree and incentive schemes to promote industrial exports. Judging from the relative performance of Korea's GTCs in recent years, it can be said that Korean exporters' networks of overseas branch offices and their marketing activities would have evolved to the same extent even without an explicit government push for creating the GTCs while maintaining the existing general export incentive schemes.

If a small number of large business groups are increasingly predominant in almost all industries and are competing with a large number of small-scale producers in many areas, the GTC of a particular business group will become merely the "super" export department (or the export window) of all the subsidiaries of that particular group. It would tend, therefore, to compete with, rather than to complement, the small and medium export producers. In other words, the GTCs cannot become neutral and honest brokers of exports for other producers and therefore cannot line up small and medium industries under them for well-coordinated export promotion because of conflicts of interest, fear of takeovers and mergers, and a general feeling of mutual distrust. In short, the extreme concentration of manufacturing and economic power that currently exists in Korea—centered in the very companies that have been designated as GTCs—precludes the sound development of GTCs as impartial specialized exporters, along the lines of the Japanese GTCs.

The stability of the profit earnings and viability of the GTCs requires a strong base in domestic- and import-market transactions, in addition to export expansion and diversification. The diversification of sources of earnings in export, import, and domestic trade is a condition for survival and sound growth of the GTCs.

If economic and business conditions are not ripe for the sound development of the GTCs as specialized exporters and importers, a less ambitious but more sensible alternative to GTCs would be the development of an export-import trading agency out of a group of export producers, large and small, operating in the same industry, or in a group of related industries. Such an agency, acting as an industry-wide association of export producers, would specialize in trading functions and would thus act as manufacturers' representatives in both export and import markets.

20 Promotion Measures for Construction Service Exports to the Middle East (1975)

by Chung Hoon Lee

One of Korea's outstanding economic achievements during the past three decades is the phenomenal growth in exports of construction services to the Middle East. Although Korea has been exporting construction services since 1965, only since 1973 have they been exported to the Middle East. That year Sam Hwan Corporation obtained a contract from Saudi Arabia to build a highway for $24,059,000. After 1975 the value and number of overseas construction contracts obtained by Korean companies from the Middle East grew rapidly, reaching a figure in excess of $12 billion and involving 72 contracts in 1981. Over the eight-year period from 1974 through 1981, Korea obtained construction contracts from Middle East countries worth approximately $41 billion—94.4 percent of the country's total overseas construction service exports during the period. Given the modest beginning of $24 million in 1973, which accounted for only 5.7 percent of total overseas construction service exports for the 1965–73 period, the $41 billion attests to the accomplishment achieved by the Korean construction industry in only eight years (Table 20.1).

What were the effects on the Korean economy of these overseas construction service exports? The exports brought in scarce foreign exchange—directly through the remittance of wages and profits, and indirectly through the export of machinery, equipment, and materials related to overseas construction projects. The increase in foreign exchange earnings in turn increased the domestic money supply, which, along with the increase in national income, had a multitude of effects on the domestic economy. To determine how important these effects were requires building a fully specified, general equilibrium model of the economy, but such a task is beyond the scope of this chapter.

It is possible, however, to gain a sense of the importance of construction service exports by comparing them with merchandise exports. For the nine-year period from 1965 through 1973, the value of merchandise exports was approximately $8.6 billion whereas the value of construction service exports to the Middle East was only about $24 million, a mere 0.3 percent of merchandise exports. For the eight-year period from 1974 through 1981, however, the value of construction service exports to the Middle East increased to 44 percent of the value of merchandise exports, which had risen to $94

Table 20.1. Exports of overseas construction services (10^3 US \$)[a]

Year	Destination Middle East	Southeast Asia	All others	Total
1965–73	24,059	300,363	98,288	422,710
	(5.7)	(71.1)	(23.3)	(100.0)
1974	88,813	145,048	26,711	260,572
1975	751,210	42,513	20,973	814,696
1976	2,429,112	34,631	37,996	2,501,739
1977	3,387,000	119,273	9,963	3,516,236
1978	7,982,393	91,041	71,588	8,145,022
1979	5,958,383	378,010	14,943	6,351,336
1980	7,819,404	408,996	30,974	8,259,374
1981	12,670,601	838,200	172,203	13,681,004
1974–81	41,086,916	2,057,712	385,351	43,529,979
	(94.4)	(4.7)	(0.9)	(100.0)
1965–81	41,110,975	2,358,075	483,639	43,952,689
	(93.5)	(5.4)	(1.1)	(100.0)

Source: Adapted from Overseas Construction Association of Korea (1984: tables 1-7 and 1-9).

Note: Percentages are shown in parentheses.

a. In terms of the value of contracts.

billion. Construction service exports had become a major component of Korea's external trade.

While there are numerous issues of interest relating to overseas construction service exports, the main focus of this chapter will be on the policy measures that the Korean government took to promote these exports. In December 1975 the government established the Overseas Construction Promotion Act and thereby began taking active measures to promote construction service exports. How effective were the measures? What effects did they have on the Korean economy? These are some of the questions that I will attempt to answer in this chapter.

BACKGROUND

Excess Capacity for the Export of Construction Services[1]

By the early 1970s the Korean construction industry, which had reached the international standard in terms of technology and management know-how, was suffering from excess capacity. It was, therefore, more than ready

---

1. The discussion of the history of the Korean construction industry is based on Overseas Construction Association of Korea (1984).

to seize the opportunity when some of the OPEC countries began spending part of their huge oil revenues on construction projects. How then did the construction industry of Korea, a country in the process of industrialization, acquire technology and management know-how on a par with the international standard? And what is the reason for its excess capacity in the early 1970s?

At the time of liberation from Japanese colonialism in 1945, the Korean construction industry consisted of only two firms. However, the industry grew rapidly during the Korean War owing to the demand for construction of military facilities by the United States Army. Thereafter, the construction industry continued to expand as the Korean government gave priority to the reconstruction of infrastructure and factories that had been destroyed during the war. In 1957 the industry entered a new stage when the U.S. government started building up its military strength in Korea, and the U.S. Army thus placed orders for large-scale construction projects.

As the U.S. Army contracted with Korean companies to build harbor facilities, airfields, roads, bridges, barracks, warehouses, and fortifications, the number of construction companies increased to 1,700 by the end of the 1950s. These were the kinds of projects that many of the Korean companies would not have had the experience of building if the U.S. Army had not been in Korea. By undertaking these construction projects, they acquired the experience of handling large projects, which they could later utilize in the Middle East.

Doing business with the U.S. Army meant that Korean construction companies had to draw blueprints and write contracts in English in the manner acceptable to the U.S. Army. By being forced to carry out business at the level practiced in an advanced industrialized country, these companies acquired an advanced level of technology and management know-how. This type of technology transfer occurs in a country when an external military force from a technologically more advanced country is present.[2] Another requirement for doing business with the U.S. Army was that Korean companies had to use imported heavy machinery and equipment. The use of this sophisticated equipment must certainly have resulted in a capital–labor ratio inappropriate to the factor prices prevailing in Korea. However, when these companies went abroad to carry out massive construction projects, they were already experienced in the use of sophisticated machinery and equipment.

There are two other factors, in addition to the experience of doing business with the U.S. Army in Korea, that contributed to the modernization of the construction industry. One is the construction experience gained in

---

2. Spencer (1965) found that the Japanese acquired technology from the U.S. Army stationed in Japan. He found the same process, albeit less strong, operating in Korea.

Vietnam during the second half of the 1960s when Korean companies undertook construction projects for both the U.S. Army and the Korean Army.

The other contributing factor is that, beginning in 1962, Korea launched its program to industrialize the economy and began building highways, refineries, cement factories, fertilizer plants, high-rise housing complexes, and a subway system. Many of these massive projects were financed by international development organizations ($115.6 million during the 1961–66 period and $810.8 million during the 1967–71 period). As a condition of the loans, the lending organizations imposed a much higher standard on the construction projects than that normally practiced in Korea. As a result Korean companies involved in these projects had to improve their technology and management know-how for all phases of construction.

By the early 1970s the construction industry had thus acquired advanced technology and management know-how and had gained experience in carrying out massive construction projects in foreign countries using sophisticated machinery and equipment; that is, it had accumulated both the human and nonhuman capital necessary for undertaking overseas construction projects. Furthermore, the industry found itself in the early 1970s with excess capacity in both human and nonhuman capital.

By the end of the Second Five-Year Economic Development Plan (1967–71), the initial phase of Korea's industrialization had ended, and much of the basic infrastructure (social overhead capital) had been built. During the 1970–74 period, fixed capital formation (excluding transport equipment, machinery, and other equipment) grew at an average annual rate of only 6 percent in contrast with 30 percent during the 1964–69 period (Table 20.2). Furthermore, Korea began the withdrawal of its troops from Vietnam in December 1971, thus bringing an end to war-related construction projects in Vietnam. Although Korean firms had undertaken some construction projects in countries other than Korea and Vietnam (Hyundai Construction Company had a contract to build a highway in Thailand in 1965), the impetus to search for new markets for construction services came with the shrinking of opportunities at home and in Vietnam in the early 1970s.

The First Oil Crisis and the Demand for Overseas Construction Services

The first oil crisis of 1973 brought huge increases in oil revenues for the oil-producing Middle East countries. Intent on economic development but lacking in necessary human resources, these countries had to rely on foreign companies and workers to build their physical capital. Starting in 1974 there was a tremendous increase in the demand for construction services in the Middle East. Korean firms, well-equipped with modern technology and management know-how and suffering from excess capacity, were ready to seize the opportunity.

Table 20.2. Gross domestic capital formation and its rate of growth

Year	Gross domestic capital formation at 1970 constant prices (10^9 won)	Rate of growth (%)
1964	109.35	
1965	139.10	27
1966	174.63	26
1967	204.95	17
1968	295.79	44
1969	396.82	34
1970	416.57	5
1971	406.91	-2
1972	386.98	-5
1973	505.19	31
1974	514.99	2

Source: BOK, *Economic Statistics Yearbook* (1977: table 141).

Note: The figures in the table refer only to gross domestic capital formation in dwellings, nonresidential buildings, and other construction and works, excluding transport equipment, machinery, and other equipment.

An effect of the oil crisis, seen from Korea's point of view, was a drastic change in the composition of demand for its exports. The oil crisis brought about a transfer of income primarily from the industrialized countries to the OPEC countries. Korea's exports to the former had been mostly labor-intensive manufactured products, and the income transfer and the world recession subsequent to the oil crisis dampened the growth of Korea's merchandise exports to these countries. The income transfer, however, led to an increase in the demand for construction services, which are labor-intensive, in the oil-rich Middle East countries. Many developing countries could not adjust to the changing composition in their external demand—from commodities and manufactured products to construction services—but Korea, for the reasons mentioned above, was in a position to respond readily to the changing external demand.

The Middle East war of October 1973 and the attendant oil crisis brought home to Korea its extreme vulnerability to external developments. The total cost of petroleum imports alone rose from $313 million in 1973 to $1,055 million in 1975. The oil price increases caused a 19 percent deterioration in Korea's net barter terms of trade in 1974 and during 1975 it deteriorated by a further 10 percent. The related deep recession in the United States and Japan, Korea's major trade partners, caused a sharp 3 percent decline in the real export growth rate in 1974. The current account deficit, which had declined from $848 million in 1971 to $31 million in 1973, shot up to a staggering figure of about $2 billion in 1974 and 1975. Under these circumstances, the Korean government saw salvation for the economy in the export of construction services to the Middle East.

Since 1975 the Korean government has taken various measures to promote the "advance to the Middle East." Here we have classified these measures into three categories: legislative, administrative and diplomatic, and other supportive measures. (For a more detailed discussion of the policy measures, see H. J. Kim 1982.)

MAIN FEATURES OF THE POLICY MEASURES

Legislative Measures

The Overseas Construction Promotion Act was promulgated in December 1975, exactly two years after the contract for the first construction project in the Middle East was signed by a Korean company. Since then it has been amended three times. The stated objective of the act is to support and manage the export of construction services and thereby strengthen the international competitiveness of the Korean construction industry. It specifies the administrative requirements for licenses and permits, and describes measures for promoting the export of construction services.

The act requires that a construction company be licensed by the Ministry of Construction (MOC) before it may engage in overseas construction business. The stated purposes of the requirement are to enhance the professionalism of the construction industry, thereby improving its level of technical competence, and to strengthen the international competitiveness of the industry by granting licenses only to those firms meeting the necessary standards.

The act also requires that a licensed company obtain from the MOC a permit to bid for a construction project. This is to prevent disorderly competition among Korean companies for the same construction project, but it has in fact given the MOC the authority to ration the right to make bids for construction projects.

In the name of strengthening the international competitiveness of the construction industry, the act empowers the minister of the MOC to encourage formation of joint ventures among Korean companies when warranted by the size of a project. The minister may also restrict some firms to the status of subcontracting. Such subcontracting is to be made only with Korean companies that have obtained overseas construction contracts. The purpose is again to reduce the number of Korean companies bidding for the same project. For the same purpose, the minister may also designate the countries or regions in which certain companies can compete.

Institutional Reforms

Until 1973 Korea had had little contact with and was largely ignorant about the Middle East. To remedy that situation, the government created in January 1976 the Institute of Middle East Affairs as an information and guidance center concerned with the study of markets in the Middle East. The institute played an active role in gathering and compiling political, diplomatic, and economic information on the countries in the region, analyzing and evaluating that data, and distributing the results of its analyses, fact finding, and projections to interested government agencies and business firms. As the institute successfully carried out its mission, it expanded the scope of its functions to other regions of the world and in January 1977 became the Korean International Economic Institute.

Another institution established by the government in January 1976 was the Commission on Middle East Economic Cooperation. The commission, which is composed of the prime minister and several ministers, is the highest policymaking body in the government on matters relating to the export of construction services to the Middle East. To support the commission's work and to implement its decisions, a standing working committee chaired by the vice minister of the Economic Planning Board (EPB) was also established. In February 1976 the Office of Middle East Economic Cooperation was created within the EPB, and the offices dealing with overseas construction service exports in the MOC were expanded. The establishment of new commissions and offices and the expansion of existing offices were made for the purpose of formulating policies, coordinating the functions of various government agencies, and streamlining administrative procedures.

To strengthen its relationship with Middle East countries, the government created many channels for diplomatic exchange. It established bilateral economic cooperation commissions with Saudi Arabia and Iran. It also began exchanging ambassadors with many countries in the region, increasing the number of embassies in the region from five in 1975 to 12 in 1981.

Other Supportive Measures

To promote construction service exports, the government has provided various forms of assistance to companies engaged in overseas construction projects. One form of assistance is the provision of bond services by government-controlled banks. Once an overseas construction project receives a contract permit from the government, a commercial bank is obliged, according to the Overseas Construction Promotion Act of 31 December 1975, to issue a financial guarantee on behalf of the company against performance default to the foreign contractee. However, as construction projects grew larger and larger in scale, Korean commercial banks became hesitant to post bonding (e.g., bid bonds, performance bonds, advanced payment bonds) for overseas construction projects worth more than $50 million. Accordingly, on 3 December 1976, the Deliberation Council of Economic Ministers decided to enforce a system of joint guarantees among commercial banks. On 30 December 1977, the bank law was revised to increase the limit of guarantees to up to 20 times of a bank's equity capital. This limit, however, can be increased by a resolution of the Monetary Board.

Because the export of construction services has been mostly to the Middle East and other developing countries, there are risks of loss resulting from foreign exchange control, war, or abrogation of contracts. To reduce this risk the government provides insurance on such losses, thus encouraging the export of construction services to these countries.

A more direct subsidy to construction service exports is provided in the form of a lower tax rate. In December 1975 the corporate income tax on income earned from overseas construction service exports was reduced by 50 percent. This subsidy, however, was reduced in 1982 by a government measure, which exempts from tax only 2 percent of the foreign exchange thus earned.

While subsidizing overseas construction service exports with these and other supportive measures, the government also has taken measures to control certain financial practices of the construction companies. One measure, which has had a significant effect on Korea's money supply and on macroeconomic stability, is the requirement that 80 percent of employees' wages, denominated in dollars, be paid in Korea and that the companies may keep only up to 3 percent of its foreign exchange earnings on site, the rest being remitted within 30 days. As will be discussed later, this requirement led to a significant improvement in official foreign exchange holdings but at the same time had various ill effects on the economy.

THEORETICAL APPROPRIATENESS

As discussed in the preceding section, the government has taken various measures to promote construction service exports since 1975. A question that follows, then, is how appropriate were these measures to the objectives of the government. We need to consider two sets of objectives. One is the explicit, proximate objective of expanding overseas construction service exports, and the other, implicit but ultimate, involves macroeconomic objectives such as reducing the balance-of-payments deficit, increasing national income, reducing unemployment, maintaining economic stability, and bringing about an equitable distribution of income. Therefore, discussion of the theoretical appropriateness of the policy measures must be undertaken with the criteria of the two sets of objectives.

In analyzing the theoretical appropriateness of the measures, we will look into only the *theoretical* appropriateness in the sense that if the measures had any effect it would be as intended. It is possible that, although qualitatively correct, the measures may have had no significant quantitative effect.

Appropriateness to Promoting Construction Service Exports

Although the Overseas Construction Promotion Act was designed to promote the export of construction services, its immediate effect was to impose regulation over the construction industry with its system of licenses and permits. A question to be asked, therefore, is how is it possible to promote the exports by controlling which companies can bid for contracts.

By granting licenses only to those companies that are "qualified," the government has assumed the role of screening the qualified from the unqualified bidders, which otherwise would have been undertaken by the party offering the contract. If the latter trusts the "seal of approval" of the Korean government, it would save the cost of screening. The cost of screening construction services is high because information on the performance of a particular construction company is obtained by the potential buyer of the service through the experience of using it. That is, construction services are analogous to what are called "experience goods" for which the brand name or reputation is important in conveying information on their characteristics.[3] Thus, in competition with companies such as Bechtel of the United States, Korean companies would have had a disadvantage without the government's seal of approval. Of course, a license is only as good as the credibility of the licensor.

Another reason licensing may possibly increase exports of construction services is the external effect. Within Korea the failure of one construction company to complete its project under the contract will not adversely affect the entire construction services. Buyers of construction services would have no alternative to using domestic construction companies because of the high barriers to entry by foreign construction companies.

In the world market for construction services, however, the adverse effect of a Korean firm's failure to perform under a contract will not be confined to the firm itself. The credibility of the entire Korean construction industry may be damaged by the action of that one company. In the world of imperfect information, stereotyping is a way of economizing on information costs, and the government may be justified in attempting to maintain a good "image" for the Korean construction industry abroad. It should be added, however, that with the accumulation of experience in using Korean firms the buyers of construction services would acquire information on the qualifications of individual Korean firms and thus would be less swayed by stereotype information. Thus, the argument in favor of licensing because it reduces the buyers' screening costs and because of the

---

3. See Nelson (1974) for the difference in informational characteristics between "experience goods" and "search goods."

external effect seems to be valid only for a short period after Korean firms began to move to the Middle East.

Finally, by limiting the number of Korean companies bidding for the same contract, the government has attempted to reduce competition among Korean companies. Actually, limiting the number makes sense only when they would be the lowest bidders compared with their foreign competitors. Then, by reducing competition, a Korean company would be getting the contract at terms more favorable than would be the case if competition were not abated. For Korea what matters is that a Korean company, whichever it may be, gets the contract at the most favorable terms. If Korean companies as a group are not the lowest bidders, then by limiting the number of potential bidders the government increases the risk of Korea not getting the contract. Thus, unless the government has prior information on how Korean companies would behave as a group, limiting the number of companies bidding for a contract may not be in the country's interest.

The institutional reforms may be regarded as an investment in social overhead capital, and in that sense they have been productive in promoting the export of construction services. There are, however, two issues that need to be addressed. The first is that some of the administrative measures were productive only because the Korean economy was very much a government-directed economy. The government intervened extensively in and regulated the economy. Given the multitude of agencies and bureaus dealing with the construction industry and overseas construction service exports, administrative measures for coordinating the agencies and bureaus became a necessity. Their coordination for a common objective was probably productive, but we must ask first of all whether the existence of these agencies and bureaus could be justified in terms of economic efficiency or even equity. If the economy had been basically more of a free market economy, the only measure needed to promote the export of construction services might have been a subsidy to exporters.

The second issue is whether or not a research institute such as the Institute of Middle East Affairs should be publicly funded. Because what is being produced by the institute is in the nature of a public good, the government's action can be justified in terms of efficient allocation of resources. There is, however, the question of whether the research carried out at the institute is relevant to the promotion of exports. The implicit assumption in the argument for the public provision of a public good is that it is a good and not a "nongood." The fact, however, is that the output of such a research institute may not be useful to construction companies, although in the opinion of the government it is. Given the possibility that what is being produced by the institute is a mixed bag of relevant and irrelevant information, we may argue that an alternative arrangement, a market solution, may be better. A construction company may produce information internally or hire a consulting firm to provide the necessary information. This arrangement leads to socially suboptimal production of information, but it will bring about the production of information that the construction company would find useful.

The other supportive measures such as bond service, insurance, and lower tax rates, mentioned in the preceding section are subsidies to the exporters of construction services, and as such they promote exports.

The foreign exchange control measures requiring the payment of 80 percent of wages in Korea and remission of 97 percent of foreign exchange earnings within 30 days would have a disincentive effect on exports of construction services. If firms and workers were free to place dollars wherever they wanted and free to bring them to Korea whenever they wanted, they would have chosen the place and time to maximize their gains from interest arbitrage and exchange rate speculation. By preventing them from doing so, their income and profit were less than if no exchange control existed. Obviously, the government wanted to maximize the amount of remittances and prevent capital flight, even at the expense of possibly reduced exports of construction services.

Appropriateness to Macroeconomic Objectives

Even though the policy measures were theoretically appropriate to the objective of expanding the export of construction services, were they also appropriate to macroeconomic objectives such as reducing the balance-of-payments deficit, increasing national income, reducing unemployment, maintaining economic stability, and bringing about an equitable distribution of income? Or to put it differently, could the government achieve all or at least some of these objectives by promoting the export of construction services? The answer to this question depends crucially on whether the economy had an unlimited or a limited supply of labor. Even though the policy measures were appropriate to an economy with an unlimited supply of labor, they might have become inappropriate once the economy no longer had an unlimited supply of labor. Thus, the policy measures, once appropriate, might have become inappropriate as the underlying condition of the economy changed.

The oil crisis of 1973 was a traumatic experience for Korea, which relies entirely on imported oil and is heavily dependent on the world market for the export of its manufactured products. The oil crisis had in fact the effect of "scissors" on the Korean economy in the sense that it was being squeezed by the high price of oil on the one hand and the sagging world demand for its manufactured exports on the other. The looming current account deficit and the unemployment problem called for some immediate action, and the government found its answer in the promotion of construction service exports to the Middle East.

Given the initial condition of labor surplus and excess capacity in the construction industry, the expansion of construction service exports had all salutary effects on the economy. With unemployed resources in the economy, the policy measures brought about the foreign trade multiplier effect on the economy. The current account improved immediately and, of course, the unemployment rate went down with the export of construction services.

It seems, however, that even before the government took measures in 1975 to promote construction service exports, the private sector had already responded well to the opportunities in the Middle East. That is, equilibrating adjustments had been going on in the economy even without government measures. Their effects, therefore, were to bring about the recovery from the effects of the oil crisis and the consequent recession in the world economy sooner than would have been the case otherwise.

Beginning in the late 1970s, the condition of labor surplus no longer existed in the Korean economy. In fact Bai (1982) argues that the Korean economy passed the Lewisian turning point from unlimited to limited labor supply around 1975. Whatever the exact time of the turning point may have been, the economy no longer suffered from the problem of surplus labor in the late 1970s, and in such an economy the effects of the policy measures cannot be analyzed simply in terms of the foreign trade multiplier effect. Now the expansion of construction service exports resulting from the policy measures was made less with unemployed resources and more at the expense of the tradable and the nontradable goods sectors of the economy. The question, therefore, becomes why should the government promote the expansion of one sector—construction service exports—at the expense of other sectors in the economy?

Two reasons can be suggested as justifications for the government's action. One is the argument that the construction industry was in the infant stage of development and thus could not compete with those of developed countries without the government's support. The evidence, however, does not seem to support this argument. As mentioned, some Korean firms were already doing business abroad and even in the Middle East when the government began taking measures to promote construction service exports. These firms did not have the most sophisticated technology and management know-how, but what they had was probably quite adequate for construction projects in the Middle East. That is, although they may have been incapable of undertaking the most technologically sophisticated construction projects in the world, Korean firms may have had a competitive edge in the projects being built in the Middle East.

The other reason is the external effect. That is, firms operating abroad acquire technology they would not at home, and the technology thus acquired becomes diffused among firms in Korea. But, as argued above, Korean firms already had technology quite adequate for projects in the Middle East, and it is unlikely that there was any transfer of technology to them in the Middle East from firms in developed countries.

In sum, the policy measures promoting construction service exports were probably appropriate for a couple of years after 1975 when Korea had a labor-surplus economy. They became inappropriate, however, when the economy no longer suffered from surplus labor. By then the overseas construction service sector had already expanded too much and painful contractionary adjustments had to be made.

FORMULATION AND IMPLEMENTATION PROCESSES

Since its enactment in December 1975, the Overseas Construction Promotion Act has been amended three times. The act is augmented by five presidential decrees and five MOC administrative rules. How were they formulated and implemented? What was the interaction, if there was any, between government and business? These are difficult questions to answer because the processes of policy formulation and implementation as practiced in Korea are not open processes observed by and reported to the public.

In their study of the role of government in Korea's economic development, Jones and SaKong (1980) argue that the executive branch overwhelmingly dominated the formulation and execution of policy. They argue, furthermore, that President Park was the ultimate power, both in substance and formality, making major decisions and settling disputes. In an important case such as the export of construction services to the Middle East, there is no reason to expect an exception to the rule.

According to Doe (1984), President Park summoned the heads of the *jaebul* (family-based industrial conglomerates) sometime in 1975 to a meeting where he personally urged them to look for business opportunities in the Middle East. He recognized that a potentially huge market for construction service exports existed in the region and thought that Korea should exploit the opportunities. One reason for his keen interest in the Middle East was, according to Doe, that President Park was deeply worried about the huge current account deficits resulting from the high cost of oil imports.

Doe also says that within the government there was some opposition by the Ministry of Finance to providing supportive measures for the export of construction services. The opposition was on the grounds that the measures would lead to dumping of construction services and weakening of the financial health of the banks providing bond services. However, because of the president's strong interest in promoting these exports, the Ministry of Finance did not prevail. In fact, once President Park's view on this matter was known, the export of construction services was said to have become a sacred cow and no one dared to oppose supporting the exports.

Jones and SaKong (1980) point out that for Korea short-term policy formulation was made quickly without studying problems in depth and without taking into account all possible ramifications of policy. However, they argue that the government monitored the results continuously, adjusting policy as necessary to achieve the desired outcome. Such a practice seemed to have been applied to the Overseas Construction Promotion Act to a certain extent, as demonstrated by the amendments and new decrees and rules. An example of the government's ability to monitor and adjust policy is the institution of the requirement that firms obtain permits to bid for a contract. According to Doe (1984), it was a practice of Korean firms to retain local agents to assist them in getting contracts. Competition among Korean firms for the services of an agent was so keen that certain local rules governing the relation between principal and agent were violated with the consequence of imprisonment of certain Korean businessmen. The requirement for permits was a result of such cases.

Although Jones and SaKong (1980) argue that the government monitored the results of policy, making appropriate adjustments when necessary, it seems that regarding some basic principles—such as the promotion of exports of construction services and how not to promote them—the government did not demonstrate much flexibility and openness. As argued in the preceding section, the policy measures promoting construction service exports may have become inappropriate by the late 1970s. There was, however, no attempt (as far as we are aware of) to terminate the policy measures.

It is difficult to say how much influence the *jaebul* had on policy formulation. If they had a strong influence, they would have tried to limit the number of construction companies licensed to go to the Middle East. Although the government maintains a licensing system, it does not seem to have used it to erect barriers to entry in favor of the *jaebul*. At the end of 1976 there were 73 companies licensed to undertake overseas construction business. The number then increased to 121 in 1977 and to 132 in 1979. Of these 132 companies at least 100 were not *jaebul*. If the family-owned conglomerates had had strong influence on government policy formulation, it is unlikely that so many non-*jaebul* companies would have competed with them in the Middle East.

EFFECTS OF THE POLICY MEASURES

What were the effects of the policy measures? To answer this question, we first need to know what the economy would have been like in the absence of the policy measures. Only by comparing this counterfactual economy with the actual economy can we say what the effects were. To make such a comparison is a rather formidable task, theoretically and because of data requirements, and is beyond the scope of this chapter. I will instead carry out a less rigorous analysis without the aid of a formal model of the economy. The analysis first involves an investigation of the effects of construction service exports on the balance of payments, employment, economic stability, and the structure of the economy. I will then attempt to answer how the policy measures might have influenced these effects.

Effects of Construction Service Exports

Effect on the balance of payments. The importance of construction service exports in Korea's balance of payments is clearly demonstrated in Table 20.3, where I compare net receipts from construction service exports with oil imports during 1977–82. Net revenues from construction service exports—revenues minus on-site purchase expenses for foreign machinery, equipment, and materials and other expenditures made locally—ranged from 24.1 percent of oil imports in 1980 to 46.8 percent in 1978. For the six-year period total net revenues were equal to 33.1 percent of oil imports, which amounted to more than $25 billion. What the figures show is that Korea was able to pay for one-third of its oil imports directly by exporting labor services to the Middle East. Many other developing countries borrowed externally or increased their merchandise exports to pay for oil imports. Borrowing

Table 20.3. Effects of construction service exports on the balance of payments (10^6 US $)

Item	1977	1978	1979	1980	1981	1982
(1) Net revenue from overseas construction service exports[a]	618	1,024	1,396	1,355	1,738	2,257
(2) Oil imports[b]	1,926	2,187	3,100	5,633	6,371	6,097
(3) [(1)/(2)] (in %)	32.1	46.8	45.0	24.1	27.3	37.0
(4) Exports of machinery, equipment, and materials related to construction service exports[c]	452	942	389	498	422	492
(5) Induced imports[d] [(4) multiplied by 0.64]	289	603	249	319	270	315
(6) Net exports [(4) – (5)]	163	339	140	179	152	177
(7) Net revenue from service and merchandise exports [(1) + (6)]	781	1,363	1,536	1,534	1,890	2,434
(8) Percentage of oil imports paid for with net revenue from service and merchandise exports [(7)/(2)]	41	62	50	27	30	40

a. From Overseas Construction Association of Korea (1984: table 4-1).

b. From Overseas Construction Association of Korea (1984: table 4-2).

c. From Overseas Construction Association of Korea (1984: table 4-5).

d. 0.64 is the marginal propensity to import of the merchandise exports related to construction service exports.

abroad, of course, simply meant the postponement of the burden of oil imports, and financing the imports with increased exports of merchandise meant for some countries a terms-of-trade deterioration, increasing the burden of oil imports. Korea was fortunate in being able to pay for a third of its oil imports by exporting labor services to the Middle East, where burgeoning oil revenues had increased the demand for labor.

The export of construction services led to exports of machinery, equipment, and materials related to overseas construction projects. The export of construction services also brought about increases in imports, first through the spending effect of net oil revenues remitted to Korea, and second through the linkage effect arising from the export of machinery, equipment, and materials. The latter required the import of raw materials and intermediate products.

Using an input–output analysis, B. H. Park (1983) estimated the imports induced by merchandise exports to the Middle East for 1973 through 1980. His estimates of the ratio of imports to exports range from 62.1 percent to 66.4 percent with a simple average of 64 percent. If I assume as a first approximation that this ratio also applies to merchandise exports related to total overseas construction service exports and not just to those related to the exports to the Middle East, the value of induced imports during 1977–82 amounts to more than $2 billion (Table 20.3, item (5)). The value of net merchandise exports during 1977–82 resulting from the export of overseas construction services would then be about $1.1 billion (Table 20.3, item (6)), which indicates that the latter had a positive effect on the balance of trade. The estimates range from $140 million in 1979 to $339 million in 1978. The effect of overseas construction service exports on the current account is as shown in item (7) of Table 20.3.

The figures in item (7) may be regarded as a rough measure of the direct and indirect effects of construction service exports on the balance of payments. As an indicator of their importance for the economy, I divided the figures by the cost of oil imports in item (2). As reported in item (8), the result ranges from 27 percent in 1980 to 62 percent in 1978, and for the six-year period the total net revenues from construction service exports paid for 38 percent of oil imports.

Until recently Korea had a large external debt. In 1982, for instance, its total outstanding debt was $37.3 billion and debt-service payments (amortization and interest payments) were $5.9 billion. Korea's ability to earn foreign exchange to meet debt-service was, therefore, a matter of great importance. One measure commonly used to evaluate a country's capacity to service external debt is the debt-service ratio. This is the proportion of foreign exchange earnings from merchandise and service exports used to meet debt-service payments.

As a rough measure of the importance of construction service exports to the Korean economy, I calculated the debt-service ratio that would have

Table 20.4. External debt service

Item	1977	1978	1979	1980	1981
(1) Debt service (10³ US$)[a]	1,557.2	2,391.0	3,173.3	4,233.7	5,635.4
(2) Exports of merchandise and services (10³ US$)[b]	13,073.5	17,160.7	19,530.7	22,577.3	27,504.4
(3) Debt-service ratio [(1)/(2)] (%)	12	14	16	19	20
(4) Net revenue from exports of construction services and related merchandise (10³ US$)[c]	781	1,363	1,536	1,534	1,890
(5) Counterfactual debt-service ratio {(1)/[(2) − (4)]} (%)	13	15	18	20	22

a. From I. C. Kim (1983b: table 2).

b. From BOK, *Economic Statistics Yearbook* (1982: table 122).

c. From Table 20.3.

existed if there were no construction service exports and related merchandise exports, and compared it with the actual debt-service ratio. As shown in Table 20.4, the actual debt-service ratio was 12 percent in 1977, steadily increasing to 20 percent in 1981. The counterfactual debt-service ratio is, however, 13 percent for 1977, increasing to 22 percent in 1981. That is, it appears that the debt-service ratio would have been 1 to 2 percentage points higher if there were no construction service and related merchandise exports. A debt-service ratio exceeding 20 percent is regarded as undesirable; without construction service exports, Korea would have reached that point in 1981.[4]

Effect on employment and the real wage rate. The export of construction services had direct and indirect effects on employment. Workers were sent overseas on construction projects, and they numbered up to 171,170 in 1982. Employment opportunities also were created in industries manufacturing machinery, equipment, and materials exported to construction projects abroad. The estimated induced employment effect increased from 30,000 jobs in 1977 to 132,000 in 1982 (Table 20.5, item (2)). Adding the number of workers thus employed in domestic industries to the number of workers

4. See J. Lee (1983) for a discussion of various debt indicators. Obviously, for Table 20.4 I made the assumption that external debt would have been the same whether or not Korea had exported construction services. This is a rather extreme assumption and the figures on the table should be viewed as a benchmark for comparison.

Table 20.5. Effect of construction service exports on employment

Item	1977	1978	1979	1980	1981	1982
(1) Workers employed in overseas construction projects	45,725	84,964	105,696	131,137	163,088	171,170
(2) Induced employment[a]	30,000	114,000	99,000	102,000	125,000	132,000
(3) [(1) + (2)]	75,725	198,964	204,696	233,137	288,088	303,170
(4) Total labor force (10^3)	13,440	13,932	14,206	14,454	14,710	15,080
(5) [(3)/(4)] (%)	0.6	1.4	1.4	1.6	2.0	2.0
(6) Unemployment rate (%)	3.8	3.2	3.8	5.2	4.5	4.4
(7) Change in real wage rate[b] (%)	17.1	17.3	10.1	–4.5	–3.4	u

Source: Adapted from Overseas Construction Association of Korea (1984: table 4–6).

a. Workers employed in the manufacture of merchandise exported to overseas construction projects.

b. From R. Y. Park (1983: table 7).

u—unavailable.

sent abroad provides the total effect on employment of the export of construction services. This total employment effect constituted 0.6 percent of the total labor force in 1977 and increased to 2.0 percent in 1982.

The employment-creating effect of construction service exports shown in Table 20.5 is based on the highly unlikely assumption that those employed in overseas construction projects and in the related industries at home would have been unemployed otherwise. The other extreme assumption is that the employment created by the export of construction services was entirely at the expense of employment in other sectors of the economy. The truth probably lies somewhere between these two extreme cases.

It is likely that the magnitude of the employment-creating effect depended on the general state of the economy. As shown in Table 20.5, the real wage rate increased significantly in 1977, 1978, and 1979 but decreased by 4.5 percent in 1980 and by 3.4 percent in 1981. It seems reasonable to conclude then that during the years when the real wage rate was increasing, the overseas demand for labor was competing with the domestic demand for labor, and consequently there was some "crowding-out" effect on the labor market. It is, however, unlikely that overseas demand for labor was competing with domestic demand in 1980 and 1981 when the real wage rate was in fact falling in absolute terms. In those years there probably was no crowding-out effect and the figures shown in item (3) of Table 20.5 may be net additions to employment. In terms of the unemployment rate, then, one could argue that for 1977, 1978, and 1979 the unemployment rate without construction service exports might have been slightly higher than those shown in item (5); but for 1980 and 1981 it would have been more like 6.8 percent (5.2 percent + 1.6 percent) and 6.5 percent (4.5 percent + 2.0 percent), respectively. For these years the Middle East may be said to have served as a residual market for Korea's unemployed labor.

Effect on economic stability. One of the charges made against construction companies in the popular press is that they have invested huge profits earned from overseas construction projects in real estate, thus starting and fueling speculation in the real estate market. These companies also took over other established companies.

The proximate cause for real estate acquisition and the takeover of other companies is no doubt the profits earned from the overseas construction projects. Another source of funds was advance payments on contracts, which until recently amounted to 20 percent of the contract value. The argument that construction companies are responsible for the speculation, however, misses the point. The fact that they had funds to invest in real estate does not mean that they would have done so if other opportunities for investment existed. They had limited choices imposed by the government, and the blame for real estate speculation and other adverse effects must be laid on the government. There are several reasons for assigning the blame to the government.

First, the government has required that construction companies remit all but 3 percent of their foreign exchange receipts to Korea. Once remitted, they were converted into won, thus increasing the funds available for investment or speculation. Because some of the foreign exchange receipts were advance payments, which were eventually spent abroad as well as at home as the construction projects proceeded, they could have been allowed to be kept abroad. Profits earned by the companies also could have been invested in foreign assets instead of being brought back as foreign exchange earnings. Thus, if there were less restrictive exchange control, some of the foreign exchange receipts would have been kept abroad and consequently less would have been converted into won for domestic circulation—official foreign exchange reserves would have been less and private foreign capital outflow would have been larger. Given the alleged obsessive, daily concern shown over the amount of foreign exchange reserves by President Park after the first oil crisis, it is doubtful if anyone could then have persuaded the government to relax exchange control. In any case, according to B. H. Park's (1983) estimate, the money supply attributable to the exports to the Middle East increased at an average annual rate of 343 percent during the 1971–80 period, whereas the total money supply increased at an average annual rate of 28.4 percent. It seems that, given the record of real estate speculation, the government failed to ask what the companies were going to do with these large sums of money, which were increasing at a rapid rate.

Second, the government controlled interest rates on deposits at financial institutions and kept them artificially low.[5] Time or savings deposits could not, therefore, compete with real estate for funds from the Middle East.

Another problem with the repressed financial system was that the government could not use standard sterilization policy to offset the increase in money supply resulting from foreign exchange earnings remitted from the Middle East. If the government could sell bonds in the open market to offset the increase in money supply, the construction companies and the public would have had less liquid government bonds instead of money. But the sale of bonds would have increased interest rates, which the government controlled.

Even though a sterilization policy could not have been pursued in such a setting, the government could have allowed the construction companies to purchase nontransferable, long-term bonds from the central bank, preferably with staggered maturity. This would have prevented the sudden increase in money supply and would have been less onerous than outright taxation. This scheme should have been applied only to profits and not to advance payments, which the companies should have been free to place at home or abroad.

Third, as discussed before, remittance of 80 percent of wage payments was required. Workers and their families would not have found time or savings deposits any more attractive than did the construction companies. Furthermore, the income elasticity of demand for houses was high for people who did not own homes.

While the demand for houses increased at a rapid rate, their supply could not respond as rapidly. The factors of production required for construction were the factors that had been and were being exported to the Middle East. With the increasing demand for houses but with the lagging supply of houses, prices of houses inevitably had to rise.

Given the regime of financial repression, the government should have sold housing bonds to the workers and their families with five- to ten-year maturities. The government should have been able to predict that the Middle East construction boom could not go on forever. The companies and their workers would have to come back home sooner or later, and they would have been the resources that could be used to build houses. In other words, the demand for houses could have been postponed with the issue

---

5. For a thorough discussion of Korea's financial system and policies, see Cole and Park (1983).

of housing bonds until the supply could meet the demand at prices that would not start housing speculation.

Another cause for instability is the requirement that workers be paid in the amount specified in terms of the U.S. dollar. Table 20.6 reports the index wage payments, both in the won and the dollar. Beginning with 100 in 1976, the wage payment reached an index of 145.9 in dollars in 1982. That is, in six years wage payments increased by 45.9 percent, measured in terms of dollars. But the payment, when remitted and converted into won, increased by 116.5 percent during the same period. The difference is due to the won devaluations in 1980, 1981, and 1982. Therefore, the workers gained from current devaluation in those three years. The money supply increased further, and the increase in their nominal wage rate could not have had a stabilizing effect on the domestic wage rate.

Effect on the structure of the economy. The problems that the Korean economy has had in adjusting to the inflow of earnings from the Middle East are similar to those experienced by countries that have the "Dutch disease" or "booming sector" economic problem (Corden 1982). It refers to the adverse effect on traditional manufacturing industries of an oil or gas field discovery. The discovery leads to a higher real exchange rate than otherwise and, as a consequence, resources move out of the traditional manufacturing sector and its exports decline.

In Korea there was no discovery of an oil or gas field but instead the discovery of a booming market for labor services. Thus resources moved abroad instead of moving to a booming sector within the economy, but still

Table 20.6. Wage index of production workers employed by Korean overseas construction companies[a]

Year	U.S. dollar index	Won index[b]
1976	100	100
1977	120	120
1978	132	132
1979	141	141
1980	145	173
1981	146	203
1982	146	217

Source: Adapted from R. Y. Park (1983: table 8).

a. Basic pay plus fringe benefits.

b. Exchange rates:
      1976–79: $1 = 485 won
    March 1980: $1 = 580 won
    March 1981: $1 = 674 won
    March 1982: $1 = 720 won

moved away from the tradable goods sector (mostly manufacturing) and the nontradable goods sector (such as housing).

There was a further shift of resources out of the tradable goods sector. With the income remitted from the Middle East and with a positive income elasticity of demand for nontradable goods, there was an excess demand for them at constant prices. Their prices thus rose relative to the prices of tradable goods, which were largely determined in the rest of the world. This increase in the relative price of nontradable goods shifted resources away from the tradable goods sector to the nontradable goods sector (C. H. Lee 1986).

To demonstrate empirically how much relative contraction the tradable goods sector has experienced is a difficult task requiring a counterfactual model of the Korean economy. However, a crude measure of the relative contraction may be seen by comparing the 1972–78 period, when merchandise exports in Korea grew at an average annual rate of 43.4 percent, with the 1979–81 period when they grew by only 17.6 percent (IMF 1983). During the latter period, Taiwan's exports grew at an average annual rate of 20.8 percent (Director of Intelligence, U.S., 1983). Although there may be other reasons for the higher growth rate of Taiwan's exports, the higher rate is consistent with the hypothesis that Taiwan's tradable goods sector did not experience a relative contraction because Taiwan did not export construction services.

Effects of the Policy Measures

What were the effects of the policy measures promoting construction service exports on the balance of payments, employment and the real wage rate, economic stability, and the structure of the economy? To the extent that the measures were successful in promoting exports of construction services, the effects on the economy discussed previously were greater than they would have been in the absence of the measures.

By bringing about an overexpansion of construction service exports, the government hurt the export of manufactured products and fueled a speculative boom in the real estate market, given its policy of financial repression. Moreover, with the contracting demand for construction services in the Middle East, the overexpansion burdened the country with a problem of retrenchment greater than would have occurred otherwise. The booming sector was no longer booming, and resources had to move back to the tradable and the nontradable goods sectors. The necessary adjustment would have been less if the overseas construction service exports had not overexpanded.

As already discussed, the policy measures were probably appropriate during the early years of construction service exports to the Middle East. However, they should have been discontinued late in the 1970s when they were no longer appropriate to an economy that had passed the Lewisian turning point.

CRITICISMS AND LESSONS

Since 1975 the Korean government has undertaken various measures to promote exports of construction services. At the time when the Overseas Construction Promotion Act was established, the Korean economy had just experienced the first oil crisis and was staggering under the weight of the high cost of oil imports. Moreover, it suffered from the weakening demand for merchandise exports resulting from a worldwide recession. The export of construction services helped to reduce the excess capacity in construction as well as in manufacturing industries.

However, further expansion beyond the point where unemployed resources could be absorbed brought about some adverse effects on the economy. Even without the further expansion induced by government subsidies, exports of construction services would have created problems of adjustment for the rest of the economy. Obviously, these problems, referred to as the "Dutch disease," were intensified by the measures that had promoted the exports. The government instead should have devised measures to cope with the problems arising in a booming sector economy rather than making them worse by fueling the boom.

The adjustment process would have been less costly if the government had not pursued the policy of financial repression. One consequence of the policy was the underdevelopment of the capital market, and as a result the market could not accommodate with any degree of stability the sudden influx of large sums of money. Given the state of the market, the government should have controlled the growth in money supply by adopting measures such as those discussed in the preceding section.

The policy of promoting exports of construction services, formulated in the atmosphere of a crisis, probably became inappropriate by 1978. Jones and SaKong (1980) claim that in Korea short-term policy was continuously monitored and adjusted when necessary, and as a result problems that might not have been foreseen in the process of quick formulation of policy were corrected in time or their effect on the economy was mitigated. Their claim, however, depends on the condition that the government had the ability and resources to monitor continuously and had the political will to make necessary adjustments even in opposition of the established constituency of the policy. For some policies, this condition may have existed but for others it may not. It seems that for a complex issue such as the export of construction services, in which the *jaebul* have had a big stake, the government probably had neither the ability and resources to monitor nor the political will to make necessary adjustments. A hastily formulated short-term policy, once appropriate, thus became a long-term policy kept on regardless of its appropriateness.

PART III
CULTURE, EDUCATION, AND SOCIAL CHANGE

21 Ethical and Social Influences of Confucianism

by Lee-Jay Cho

This study treats the subject of economic development in a somewhat unorthodox way, based on the premise that an understanding of development policies requires an examination of many factors outside the discipline of pure economics. Government economists do not simply sit together, discuss their facts and research findings, and make policy decisions. Their formulation of policies is a far more complex, political process, and a fundamental understanding of this process must give due consideration to the society in which it operates. This chapter has been included to give the reader a sense of how Koreans behave, what they value, and how they relate among themselves and to their leaders. Rigorous analysis is not applied here to topics such as the role of culture and values in development, national sensitivities and priorities, and the ways in which Korean leaders manage the government and the public. Yet, after accounting for the quantifiable variables, these factors have undeniably influenced the direction of Korean economic development discussed earlier in this volume. It is hoped that a simplistic overview and the brief anecdotes and illustrations cited will give the reader a better perspective on the cultural dimensions of modernization and will perhaps stimulate further research in this area.

A principal reason for the increasing interest in the relationship between Confucianism[1] and the economy is the rapid development achieved during the past three decades by the countries that have been strongly influenced by Confucianism and other East Asian cultural influences. How do we account for the rapid economic development in Japan, Korea, Taiwan, Hong Kong, and Singapore, all of which are poorly endowed with natural resources for economic growth? Human capital formation has undeniably been a major contributing factor, and in this regard exploring the influence of Confucian ethics and values on contemporary approaches to problem solving is an intriguing exercise.

The literature on Korea contains numerous references to Confucianism as an impediment to reforms and development. The ways in which Confucianism has been interpreted and applied by governments and societies have

---

1. The term Confucianism is used here to refer to the popular value system of China, Korea, and Japan, which is derived from the synthesis of the traditional cultural values espoused by Confucius and his followers and subsequently influenced by elements of Taoism, Legalism, Mohism, and even Buddhism, and in the case of Korea and Japan, by Shamanism.

probably been inhibiting factors for development under certain circumstances.[2] It would be wrong, however, to depict Confucianism only as a barrier to development, just as it would be wrong to claim that it is solely responsible for recent economic achievements in East Asia. Our purpose is to examine not the elements that inhibit but those that promote human capital formation, thereby exerting a positive influence on rapid economic development. This is not an exhaustive study of Confucianism in economic development but an examination of some positive elements of Confucian ethical values based on "humanity, righteousness, and frugality" that have clearly contributed to economic growth in Korea and neighboring countries.

CONFUCIAN VALUES AND ETHICS

Throughout history Korea has been dominated by Chinese culture, which has predominated among the nations of East Asia. For several millenia China was a feudal state, in which Confucian values and ethics, mixed with Taoism and later with Buddhism, played the paramount role in shaping not only the form of government but also the ways in which people relate to their leaders, peers, and families.

Up to about the sixth century, the predominant influences in Korean society were Confucianism and Taoism (Rutt 1972). Beginning in the sixth century, Buddhism also exerted a significant influence over Korean cultural values. The Buddhist doctrines of benevolence and *samsara* (the cycle of rebirths), intermingled with the traditional values of Confucianism, provided the core of Korea's cultural values for a period of about a thousand years, from the era of the Three Kingdoms (A.D. 57–668) and the united Silla dynasty to the end of the Koryŏ dynasty in the late fourteenth century. At the beginning of the Yi dynasty (1392–1910), however, Confucianism became the predominant state ideology of Korea, and Buddhist influence receded. During the succeeding five centuries, Confucianism played the predominant role in social, political, and all other spheres of Korean society. The traditional cultural values that have exerted the longest and most lasting influence on the Korean pattern of modernization are therefore deep-rooted in Confucianism.

Traditional Chinese philosophy is based on Confucianism, which is not a religion but the prevailing ethics and values that evolved over thousands of years. Confucius, who lived in the late sixth century B.C., summarized and synthesized these ethics and values, giving them a form that became known as Confucianism. The teachings of Confucius were expanded upon

---

2. Palais (1975:22), for example, cites "Confucian dogma" as one of three features of the old political order contributing to the failure of reforms in Korea more than a hundred years ago. The same author (1975:19) notes, however, the ambivalence of Korean leaders in sometimes upholding and sometimes ignoring Confucian doctrine, to suit their own purposes or convenience.

further by Mencius (380–289 B.C.), a Chinese philosopher whose influence in defining orthodox Confucianism was second only to Confucius.

The main axis of Confucian political philosophy is formed by the concepts of *chung* (harmony between the leadership and the masses) and *hsiao* (filial piety). The principal relationships upon which emphasis is placed are those between the ultimate ruler and his people, between parents and their children, and between peers. The latter, horizontal relationships are maintained through trust and friendship. With respect to the first two, however, harmony is maintained by stipulating that the relationship between the masses and the ruler is like that between children and their parents. Hence, filial piety is the basis for harmony within the family as well as the state. The emphasis on family and communal relationships and collectivism contrasts with the Western emphasis on individualism. Filial piety is the "generalizing principle" in defining relationships within the group.[3]

The energizing force in working out and implementing these relationships is the emphasis placed on harmony, learning, and diligence. A constant learning process is the ideal, where unceasing efforts are made to achieve perfection. From the earliest times, the Chinese classics placed emphasis on being prepared for hard times and hard work, but also on being prepared to take advantage of opportunities. This is already evident in the earliest Chinese poetry, as illustrated in the following passage quoted from writings dating from about B.C. 1100–1200 (Legge 1959):

> It is said in the *Book of Poetry*,
>   "Before the heavens were dark with rain,
>   I gathered the bark from the roots of the mulberry trees,
>   And wove it closely to form the window and door of my nest."
>
> People of Tse have a saying,
>   "A man may have wisdom and discernment,
>   but that is not like embracing the favorable opportunity.
>   A man may have fine farm implements,
>   but what use are they if the planting season has passed?"

The notions of preparedness, illustrated by the parable of the bird that must prepare itself for the coming storm, existed long before and were reinforced by the codification of such ethics by Confucius. The emphasis on preparedness is redoubled in the second quotation, in which the farmer not only must prepare for physical work (with his tools) but must also be ready to seize his opportunities (the farming season). Preparedness is a quality that has been cherished by the Chinese for thousands of years.

---

3. As Max Weber distinguished, "whereas Puritan rationalism has sought to exercise rational control over the world, Confucian rationalism is an attempt to accommodate oneself to the world in a rational manner" (Morishima 1982:2).

The Confucian classics also stress diligence as an important quality, typified by the admonition in the *Zhong Yong* (Lyall and King 1927) on striving constantly to attain the golden mean—a center course of moderation that avoids all extremes. The diligent scholar is encouraged to engage in a constant process of reexamination and to seek the truth through facts. Emphasis is also placed on learning for the purpose of application. This in turn encourages adaptability, flexibility, and pragmatism.

Confucius is said to represent the "complete concert" of the three ideal types of sages that are described in the writings of Mencius (Legge 1959:812–17). One type of sage is an incorruptible purist, another undertakes even the most difficult public-service task in pursuit of the common good, and the third is the sage of "harmony," who accepts even the most humble position and responsibilities. According to Mencius, the second type of sage took upon himself the heavy charge of empire, regarding the people's sorrows and burdens as his own. These qualities, if properly inculcated in modern leaders, are well suited to economic leaders and to others who have to deal with the problems of government and society.

Confucianism teaches that human relationships are increasingly refined through the process of learning and acquiring knowledge. Education also served as the primary vehicle for advancement in imperial China. For these reasons, the Chinese emphasis on education—which is also an emphasis on diligence—has been handed down over the centuries, serving to enhance traditional respect for intellectual achievement and public service and the modern emphasis on higher education.

According to Max Weber, the Protestant ethic contributed to Western industrial development as the driving force for capital formation through hard work, frugality, and saving. The accumulation of wealth was considered a measure of success and an indication of "good" behavior. An interesting parallel can be drawn with the Chinese ethic of diligence, hard work, and thrift. The Chinese measures of success were attaining high government office and accumulating wealth, but it was also important for the successful individual's ancestors to "see" his achievements. Ancestor worship, which Koreans shared in common with the Chinese, was based on the belief in the continuing existence of a person's spirit after death. When someone gained an honorable title or achieved some other success, it was customary to visit the family tombs and "report" to the ancestors in the presence of other relatives and friends. Although the beliefs and rituals differ fundamentally, the actual driving forces of the Protestant ethic and the Confucian ethic are similar.

Neo-Confucianism, which was articulated by Sung dynasty (906–1279) scholars led by Zhou Dwan Yi and Zhu Xi, was a reaction against and attack on the then-prevailing Buddhism. Although it incorporated some Buddhist elements, it emphasized the revival of the original Confucian values (Fu 1985: vol. 2). The basic concept was respect for "heavenly order" and the "oneness" of the universe and of human existence. Accordingly, human nature is the same as the nature of the universe. This movement's notion of violating heavenly order is illustrated in a statement—attributed to the two Cheng scholar-brothers and based on the "abstract" Confucian tenet of "internal self-respect, external righteousness"—that starvation is a minor matter when compared to a loss of propriety, which is a serious human event. Neo-Confucianism as practiced during the Sung dynasty was a conservative philosophy that defended feudalism and served as a weapon against the "New Policies" proposed by Wang An-Shih (1021–1086), a writer and statesman whose proposed administrative and economic reforms were designed to break up powerful groups and the landlords.

Neo-Confucianism was imported to Korea over a period of several centuries, beginning in the late Koryŏ dynasty (fourteenth century) and extending into the early Yi dynasty (established in 1392). Unlike in China, Neo-Confucianism in Korea provided the early Yi dynasty with a basis for major reforms, and it served as a powerful weapon against the rich and powerful, the landlords, and the corruption that prevailed under the later Koryŏ dynasty when Buddhism was the predominant religion.

The Korean version of Neo-Confucianism was codified principally by Yi T'oegye (also known as Yi Huang) and Yi Yulgok, who also elaborated on the elements of pragmatism implicit in the Confucian tradition. Yi T'oegye called for reforms in government and for more efficient agricultural production through better irrigation and improved technology. He also wanted to expand the private school network and was an advocate of higher education for the Korean population (Tsukuba University 1986).

Korean Confucianism during the centuries after Yi T'oegye's life evolved into a more orthodox, conservative school that emphasized propriety and rituals, thereby preserving the class structure and reflecting the deteriorating distribution of wealth and power. It became so orthodox that, at certain times during the Yi dynasty, the Korean royal family and government officials became perhaps more "abstract" Confucian than their Chinese counterparts. This trend is reflected in the respect paid by the Korean government to the Chinese emperor as the Son of Heaven and to China as the center of the world, and in the fact that Korea was depicted, in communications to China, as "a small, distant country." Over the centuries, official Korean Confucianism became increasingly ritualistic and impractical and served to defend the existing order favoring the rich and powerful.

In the seventeenth and eighteenth centuries, Korean scholars on a mission to Beijing came into contact with and were impressed by Catholic missionaries who were trying to gain influence among potential converts by introducing Western science, mathematics, and astronomy. They also were influenced by adherents of the pragmatic school of political economy that had been established in the eleventh century by a small group of

Confucian scholars including Xue Ji Xuan. In China, however, this pragmatic school had never had significant influence (Fu 1985: vol. 2).

In the eighteenth century, some of Yi Yulgok's followers started the "practical" school (Shilhak) in Korea. The practical school (which called itself the Political Economy School) advocated a minimum of ritual and formalities and concentrated instead on the practical elements of Confucianism in combination with Western science, focusing on agriculture, industry, commerce, and empiricism (Historical Association of Korea 1973; H. H. Kim 1979). During the first half of the eighteenth century, the principal goals of the school were agrarian land reform and organizational reform in government and other institutions.[4] The adherents of the practical school were labelled as "heretics" because they deviated from orthodoxy, and they were also accused of importing undesirable Western influences from the Catholic missionaries in China.

During the second half of the century, the emphasis of the practical school (under the new name of Utilitarian Economy School) shifted to commerce, industry, trade, science, technology, skills, and strong national defense. In the first half of the nineteenth century, when the school was facing conservative government control and oppression, it turned to more scholastic pursuits. Renamed the "school for seeking truth through facts," it focused its attention on the validation of the Confucian classics through facts and empirical data.

Orthodox Confucianism prevailed until the end of the Yi dynasty, and the practical school never succeeded in gaining official acceptance.[5] The philosophy underlying subsequent modernization movements, however, is based on some of the practical school's more important ideas, which include agrarian reform, social harmony, equitable distribution of wealth, and the promotion of industry, trade, science, and technology. The leaders of the modernization movement who promoted efforts to open the country at the turn of the present century had either received a Japanese education or were Japanese influenced. Despite their efforts at modernization, however, this movement was cut short by Japan's expansion into the peninsula, which ended with Korea becoming a colony of Japan. Only during the second half of the twentieth century were leaders such as President Park Chung Hee able to put into practice on a massive scale some of these practical values inherent in Confucian ethics.

---

4. Chung Nak Yong is considered a representative scholar who synthesized the philosophy of the practical school. Some other scholars worthy of mention are Yu Hyung Won, Yi Yik, and Park Ji Won.

5. In this regard, Dr. Ki-Jun Rhee, former chairman of the Korea Development Institute, argues that *yang ming shue*, which emphasizes the unity of knowledge and practice, was introduced to Japan and made an important contribution to the Meiji revolution, whereas this idea was not adopted in Korea (personal communication from Dr. Rhee).

CONFUCIAN SOCIAL ORDER
AND AUTHORITARIANISM

Ascriptive society holds that kings will be kings, scholars will be scholars, and peasants will be peasants. The basic bifurcation of society into the people who are trained to govern and those who are governed is implicit in the writings of Mencius, who observed that "those who work their minds rule the people, and those who perform physical labor are governed by the former" (Legge 1959). The idea of virtuous government as prescribed by Confucianism is so widely accepted by the majority of the populace in China, Japan, and Korea that the positive role of government has been taken for granted. An important characteristic of the policymaking process common to China, Japan, and Korea is the acceptance by the masses, both historically and today, of the role of intellectuals in policymaking. For a long time to come, the general public in all three countries will continue to accept leadership by intellectuals, and indeed the public expects intellectuals to play such a role. In contrast to Western-style public opinion, the public perspective with Confucian influence is based on the traditional respect shown to persons with superior intellectual ability. In this regard, Chinese, Japanese, and Koreans differ in a fundamental way from Westerners because they expect the government to play an important role in society and in industry. The public freely accepts the Japanese government's use of "administrative guidance" *(gyosei shido)* and the Korean government's "government instructions" *(chungboo chishi)* when intervening directly in industrial affairs. The Japanese and Korean public accept this terminology itself in a way that Westerners find difficult to comprehend. Government-business relations in Korea have been characterized by strong leadership from a government that did not hesitate to intervene directly with markets by means of commands and discretionary measures. The government assumed the role of senior partner in partnership with business. The acceptance of the role of junior partner on the part of large private enterprises was in part by necessity and in part cultural.

The Chinese, Japanese, and Koreans still place great value on entering the civil service and thereby participating in decision-making processes. In China the competitive scholarly examination system for entry into the civil service was introduced during the Han dynasty in the second century B.C. Similar systems evolved in Korea (in the tenth century A.D.) and Japan (during the past century) that were instrumental in institutionalizing the hierarchical arrangement of personnel in formal organizations. The concept of hierarchy has been firmly entrenched in Chinese social philosophy for so many centuries that it is difficult to conceive how the concept of egalitarianism might take root in this society. This constraint is likewise felt in Korea and Japan.

The corollary of this hierarchical perspective is the formation of a uniform personality trait that inclines toward authoritarianism. The mitigating factor for the individual in China and Korea was the tradition of allowing appeals against government officials whenever an injustice was committed. From a wider historical perspective, however, the lack of any sufficient countervailing force among the Chinese has occasionally brought about political situations in which the existing political forces were eclipsed, making way for entirely new successors. Under such situations where total collapse was deemed essential (notably changes in dynasties), it would have been difficult to accommodate powerful countervailing forces. This is manifested in human behavior observed in the Chinese cultural setting, with its holistic or once-and-for-all predisposition, typified by the old saying: "Mow down everything uniformly with a single, trenchant sweep of the sword blade."

To appreciate the extent to which the values of uniformity and harmony have influenced human behavior—and hence political behavior and policies—it is essential to grasp the underlying propulsion towards uniformity. One important implication emerging from these considerations is that, even if a policy is not itself exceptionally good, people will nonetheless follow it through, all acting together. Ultimately, the results of their efforts in terms of overall development may not be bad. It is also true, however, that such national authoritarian personality traits and the lack of countervailing forces can bring about a disastrous outcome.

Ever conscious of this tradition, Chinese leaders have strived to achieve harmony and consensus by means of absolute statements and prescriptions. It helps to explain why an absolute majority of Mao Zedong's followers agreed with whatever he preached about economic reform in the 1950s and why an absolute majority likewise agreed with whatever Deng Xiaoping preached about economic reform in the early 1980s. Fairbank (1986:298) succinctly depicts its impact on China's efforts at postwar development:

> Underlying this situation was another inherited factor, the docility of the Chinese peasantry, who were remarkably inured to following the dictates of authority because it represented the peace and order on which their livelihood depended. The vision of the leadership could be imparted to the populace because in the early 1950s the CCP [Chinese Communist Party] and the Chinese people generally still felt united in a common cause of building up China. The people trusted Chairman Mao. This at once opened the door to utopianism and illusion because the party cadres, drawn increasingly from the upper ranks of the peasantry, were fervently ready to go along, follow the leader, and bring the masses with them. Thus the local obedience to the state and party authority, plus the personal charisma of Mao Tse-tung, could create situations of mass hysteria where people worked around the clock and abandoned established ways, almost like anarchists seeking freedom from all constraints.

One example is the period of the Great Leap Forward, when everyone in China was following the commands of a single leader and moving together harmoniously and cohesively—but toward economic disaster. The same follow-the-leader behavioral patterns help to account for Japanese conduct during World War II. Such cultural traits are stronger than ideology, and the Chinese have struggled in vain to overcome them. Similar tendencies are observable in Korea also.

The Confucian ethic was modified in Japan through the process of dissemination, the political realities in that country, and the introduction of Western rationalism during the Meiji era. The Japanese placed more emphasis than the Chinese on loyalty (to one's immediate superior and, through the hierarchy of society, especially to the ultimate ruler). For most of Japanese history, the military has played the greater role in government, leaving only the imperial court itself with a tradition of civilian administration. In Sung-dynasty China, by constrast, the civilian bureaucracy was elevated above the military under the slogan *zhong wen ching wu* ("emphasis on the civilian side, de-emphasis on the military"). Korea, too, was controlled primarily by a civilian bureaucracy during the Yi dynasty.

The Confucianism practiced in China, Korea, and Japan (as outlined by Morishima 1982:4–9) emphasized in varying degrees the qualities of loyalty, filial piety, benevolence, faith, and bravery. The significant differences are that the Koreans shared their emphasis on the latter three qualities with China, whereas Japan (which gave no special place to benevolence) shared only the qualities of faith and bravery with its neighbors. These differences in emphasis highlight a distinct difference in philosophy. From very early in their history, the Japanese placed the strongest emphasis on loyalty, subordinating even filial piety to loyalty to the state and, moreover, giving no special consideration to benevolence (*ren*, which was a central concept in Chinese Confucianism) and moral obligations and concern for family, relatives, and friends. Hence Morishima concludes that, whereas the Confucianism of the Chinese and Koreans "is one in which benevolence is of central importance, Japanese Confucianism is loyalty-centered Confucianism" (Morishima 1982:8–9). Loyalty is given a preeminent place by the Japanese because social hierarchy is far more intensive in Japanese society. In Japan, loyalty to the ultimate ruler took precedence even over filial piety.

According to Dr. Ki-Jun Rhee, who translated Michio Morishima's book *Why Has Japan 'Succeeded'?* into Korean, the Chinese interpreted the term *chung* as a form of loyalty in which the subject serves his ruler with the greatest sincerity based on his conscience, whereas the Japanese interpreted it as loyalty that is absolute, to the extent that the subject may even have to sacrifice his own life for the ruler. For this reason, whenever a conflict arose in Japan between *chung* (loyalty to the ruler) and *hsiao* (filial piety), the Japanese had to opt for *chung*.

In Korea and China, on the other hand, there was greater emphasis on *ren* (benevolence), which Confucius regarded as the foundation of social morality, deriving from the natural affinities that exist among members of a family.

Confucian philosophy places particular emphasis on family and extended-family harmony. If one's parents have committed some wrong act, it is the filial duty of the child neither to accuse them nor to report them to the authorities, but to persuade them not to repeat the act. This is illustrated in the following quotation (Legge 1959) from the *Analects* of Confucius:

> The Duke of Sheh informed Confucius, saying "Among us here are those who may be styled upright in their conduct. If the father have stolen a sheep, they will bear witness to the act."

> Confucius said, "Among us, in our part of the country, those who are upright are different from this. The father conceals the misconduct of the son, and the son conceals the misconduct of the father. Uprightness is to be found in this."

The latter attitude still prevails in China and Korea. The Japanese emphasis upon loyalty (to higher authority) and the Western concept of the social-contract society both run counter to it.

In terms of extended family relationships, the fact that it is your duty to "look after your relatives" has rendered it extremely difficult for China and Korea, in particular, to introduce rational, fair, and objective planning and to implement state policies. The Chinese, despite the introduction of socialist principles and communism, supposedly based on scientific arguments, have never managed to suppress the cultural values that foster nepotism. This is a barrier that the Koreans likewise have not entirely overcome. Since it may derive from certain national personality traits, it will be useful to look specifically at the evolution of authoritarian tendencies in society in this context.

One aspect of authoritarian behavior derives from the Confucian concept of the family. The values, obligations, and loyalty prescribed within the family system extend to all types of social groups—political organizations, government, schools, and factories. The head of the household not only provides moral leadership and the family's livelihood, but also provides leadership in all other respects. He is not, however, omniscient. He does make mistakes, and as a result, many families suffer. Although good ideas may be available among the lower echelons of the family, they are effectively silenced under authoritarianism.

A hierarchical system contributes to better efficiency in communications. Such a system can be characterized, within a given group of people, by lines of communication radiating out from the leader to his numerous subordinates. Each individual is thus linked into the system strictly through his leader (see Leavitt 1958). In Korea and Japan, such hierarchical systems have considerable merit in terms of management and production efficiency. Under such a system, people are willing to perform in a collective setting without questioning their leader, whom they regard as better educated and more experienced than themselves.

The democratic counterpart stands out in sharp contrast. Under the democratic system, the lines of communication are more complex, forming a network not only between leader and subordinate but also among the subordinates. Everyone supposedly provides input into decision making. The amount of communication in the democratic effort is greater, hence there is greater satisfaction for the individuals. But this type of system is the less efficient of the two models in terms of time and energy required to reach a decision, since much time and energy have to be expended on arriving at a consensus.

The arguments put forward by Mancur Olson (1982) are especially relevant in this regard. Rigidities and barriers established by labor unions in some countries have inhibited technology transfer, efficiency in allocating manpower, and development of the organizational structure necessary for increasing productivity. Fewer social rigidities may make faster economic growth possible (as in Texas or postwar Japan), whereas greater rigidities resulting from the necessity to generate sufficient consensus in a democratic system (as in the northeastern United States with its long-established labor unions) may slow growth. That is, being too democratic may dampen economic growth.

Korean businesses were almost totally free of labor unions during the initial stage of rapid economic development. There were, of course, many genuine grievances and accusations of "exploitation." The lack of labor organizations also meant that there was no institutionalized forum for expressing workers' interests. Korean corporations nonetheless had the advantage of greater flexibility in organizing and utilizing their manpower.

Each of the models has its relative advantages. Production teams in Japan have a certain democratic aspect in the sense that the supervisor shares with the members of his work unit the information on objectives and scope of the work assigned to them. He does so in the same way that an elder brother tells his younger brothers or a head-of-household tells family members why, for the common good, a certain task must be performed. The hierarchical system prevails among Koreans and Japanese, because of their attachment to hierarchy and harmony. They tend to prefer the hierarchical model, in spite of its disadvantage in providing less satisfaction to the individual, because they prefer to listen to an older or better-educated person.

The tendency to follow and learn from the "wise" leader has supplied the Japanese with a valuable productivity edge, which is enhanced by the readiness of Japanese to subordinate themselves in a collective activity for the common good, each working in harmony with the others toward a common goal. Koreans have retained something of this spirit. Although in certain situations one could persuade Westerners to pull together and work in the same fashion, the concept is not deeply ingrained in their character and philosophy. Westerners will not almost instinctively subordinate themselves within a hierarchy to deal with each and every collective activity. In *The Zero-Sum Solution* Thurow (1985) suggests that Americans can benefit by emulating useful East Asian traits. But his views are not realistic, because it would be difficult if not impossible for Westerners to duplicate the learning process that helps to shape such culture-laden behavior.

In Japan, the selection of the leader (and equally important the changing of leadership) is founded on the premise that most individuals will be satisfied with the person chosen. Japan has a longer history of formalization of industrial organization than Korea, and therefore the selection of leaders has been institutionalized in Japan under the influence of the Confucian ideal of sharing together as a group both the benefits and the burdens of any undertaking. This idea is illustrated by Mencius (Legge 1959:479):

> When a ruler rejoices in the joy of his people, they also rejoice in his joy. When he grieves at the sorrow of his people, they also grieve at his sorrow. A sympathy of joy will pervade the empire. A sympathy of sorrow will do the same. In such a state of things, it cannot be but that the ruler attain to the imperial dignity.

Within the context of a work unit, the Japanese pay close attention to their criteria for promotion; universal observance of the accepted rules makes it difficult for someone to be promoted haphazardly. In Korea, this selection process has not been entirely institutionalized, in that the peer group evaluation process has not yet taken root. The founder-owner of a business is able without much consultation to appoint or replace leaders at any level. In this context, the feudal values of looking after one's extended family and friends and complying with the favors requested by powerful government officials have been more extensive in Korea than in Japan. In the absence of strong labor unions in Korea (up until 1987), the erosion of the rational recruitment process in the selection of leaders was more pervasive than in Japan. Conflict arises when a leader does not turn out to be entirely capable and fails to make wise decisions, while still expecting the respect and obedience of others. If the leader of a production unit, for example, makes many mistakes, the output of his unit will suffer; its productivity will probably be lower than its democratic-model counterpart. The lack of institutionalizing the selection of leaders therefore puts Koreans at risk of being saddled with two negative features—both the lack of satisfaction inherent in the hierarchical model and the inefficiency inherent in the too-democratic one.

Authoritarian behavior is most prevalent in Korean business enterprises, including the medium- and large-scale conglomerates. The owner-head of a thriving Korean company, by virtue of his successful past endeavors, establishes himself in an authoritarian position comparable to that of a head of household. At the same time, the executives (in the case of a large corporation) consciously build up their leader beyond life size, partly with the rationale that his contacts among equally high elites in government and business will ultimately help the corporation to prosper. The chief himself encourages the construction of this facade, not only for the personal satisfaction of being depicted as a hero but also for leading the corporation (a surrogate big family) toward further economic success.

The management system in the corporate world, in contrast to that in politics and government, is far more authoritarian when an owner-founder heads the company. Once the corporate hero has been created and is perceived as such, the forum for the discussion of independent ideas ceases to exist. In the process, it becomes increasingly rare for subordinates to make critical evaluations of projects and policy decisions. Subordinates will not offer objections or even raise questions that might displease the hero. The hero, in turn, does not want to hear anything that might call his wisdom and abilities into question or that might detract from the aura of his past accomplishments. Eventually, rational evaluation of the owner-head's performance becomes almost impossible.

By never disagreeing with the leader or proposing alternatives, the executives cannot then play their proper role. In the Korean corporation, decisions thus become strictly personal ones, revolving around a single personality. This can be dangerous, especially when a single, overconfident chief makes a decision solely on a whim, while his executives hesitate to confront him with any rational analysis. Even in an efficient business organization, therefore, at some stage of development the undesirable facets of the authoritarian family system come into play. Later efforts to perpetuate earlier successes draw the corporation into rivalry with competitors and into risky ventures that may be economically unsound (such as acquiring nuclear electric power reactors for reasons of prestige). If a competitor has launched a new enterprise, the chief may want to follow suit immediately, to maintain at least parity with the competitor. The executives acquiesce, because they want to preserve the image of their corporation, even though it has been inflated beyond life size and beyond their resources to uphold. The economic consequences will not be discussed in advance and will probably be covered up once they become manifest, likewise to maintain the image.

Another negative aspect of the family authoritarian system is that heads of corporations want to bequeath not only ownership but also leadership to their sons, brothers, cousins, and relatives by marriage, who may not be equally dynamic or even fully qualified. The consequences may not be so serious in the case of small and medium-size businesses. But can such a procedure be justified by a conglomerate? Especially if the corporation's debt to the government is a large percentage of the entire business? One positive advantage is that a succession of brilliant leaders can stimulate the greatest possible advances for the corporation, particularly because personal trust and loyalty are highly valued within the corporation, as they are within the family. But objective, rational management is difficult to introduce when there are less capable heirs expecting to assume not only the chief's powers but also his undisputed authoritarian role.

One positive outcome is risk-taking and the willingness to use venture capital. The confidence built up in the hero will induce him to take greater risks. (One example of this is the highway project between Seoul and Pusan, undertaken by Hyundai and other major Korean construction companies despite the opposition from the World Bank and other consultants.) This tendency has had many positive effects, and Koreans are fortunate that their ventures have proved successful so frequently in the past.

This tendency is also partly a reflection of the division of the country into north and south. The constant awareness that Koreans must be forever alert vis-à-vis belligerent North Korea and prepared to defend themselves—harking back to Confucian admonitions concerning preparedness—has prompted business to be more alert and to take greater risks. South Koreans are motivated to surpass the North, even if this means taking greater risks in order to widen the development gap between North and South. This motive apparently surmounts the uncertainty from the danger of renewed war. Although the perspective is a short-term one, taking greater risks to achieve the desired development gap within a short span of time, it is reinforced by the conviction that, if the economy is strengthened as a result, the South Koreans will be even more capable of defending themselves.

Koreans have not yet developed rational, regularized procedures for making decisions in either public or private institutions. Koreans need to rationalize their family authoritarian notions—which promote diligence and hard work—extending collective harmony, loyalty, respect with proper incentives to industrial and government organizations and institutionalizing them more fully, so that major institutions will become genuinely surrogate families drawing upon all these strengths.

In contrast, the Japanese have achieved greater success in rationalizing and adjusting their authoritarian tendencies—a process that was hastened during the postwar years under the American military government in Japan. To understand the broad linkages as well as differences in the modern Japanese and Korean experiences, it will be useful to examine, in the following chapter, some of the salient features of the educational systems, both traditional and modern, that have evolved in the two countries.

22 The Educational System

by Lee-Jay Cho and Kennon Breazeale

The modern educational system in Korea is a new creation built gradually by a nationwide effort since the time of liberation in 1945 and based partly on infrastructure developed during the Japanese colonial period.[1] The national policy to make primary education universally available at the public expense was enacted into law in the late 1940s. Subsequently, however, much of the educational infrastructure was destroyed in the Korean War, and not until the mid-1950s was the government able to implement its basic plan for education.

Resources were concentrated most heavily at first on making free primary education available. It was premature to debate the quality and direction of education until the basic goals of the late 1940s were met—that is, to make education available to all children eligible to enroll. In the case of primary schools (ages 6–11), the objective was to make six years of schooling universally available at public expense. For middle and high school enrollment (ages 12–14 and 15–17, respectively), eligibility was to be determined by examination, and the continuation of schooling at these levels was at the parents' expense.

The early post-liberation achievements are impressive, and primary education was rapidly made available to the vast majority of Korean children during the 1950s. An estimated 71 percent of eligible children in 1952 were attending primary schools—which managed to continue operations despite the ravages of war. At the same time, 19 percent of eligible children were continuing to middle school and 12 percent to high school (UNESCO 1954:32). The traditional value placed on education by even poor villagers in South Korea provided a strong impetus to support the government's ambitious program. A United Nations mission (UNESCO 1954:21) investigating education during the Korean War reported

> . . . a burning desire on the part of parents for their children's education today, a condition which is rather difficult to match in other countries. The greater part of the expenses of construction and repair of school buildings and of teachers' salaries comes from the parents' pockets directly, and many go without food in order to see that their children go to school.

---

1. The authors wish to express sincere appreciation to former minister of education, Professor Kyo Ho Rhee, and to Drs. Jae Souk Sohn and Sung-Yeal Koo for reviewing an earlier draft of this chapter and providing valuable insights and suggestions.

The implementation of the government's six-year plan for compulsory primary education was delayed until the war ended. It began in 1954 and was virtually completed in 1959, when 96 percent of school-age children entered elementary schools (Ministry of Education, ROK, 1986:26).

The expansion in the number of elementary teachers started from a large base—nearly 20,000 teachers in 1945, more than trebling within 15 years and doubling again within the next 20 years. Even more important, the average number of students per teacher has shown a progressive and substantial decline (Table 22.1).

The rapid increase in the number of primary school teachers was facilitated by the existing infrastructure. The graduates of teachers' colleges, high schools, and even middle schools were able to find employment as teachers in the lower levels of the school system. The most difficult task in the early years of the republic, however, was to provide adequate training for teachers at higher levels, particularly in the virtual absence of qualified professors at the tertiary level. Far more than a generation was needed for prospective teachers from each successive graduating cohort to find their niches in the school system, thereby gradually raising the quality of instruction to the desired standard.

The need for a new educational philosophy was already evident during the Korean War (UNESCO 1954:29). Yet the sheer size of the infrastructure required—especially the reconstruction of the educational physical plant lost in the war—took the largest share of available resources in the late 1950s.

Table 22.1. Numbers of students and teachers: Selected years, 1945–85

Item	1945	1960	1970	1980	1985
Elementary schools					
Students	1,366,024	3,622,685	5,749,301	5,658,002	4,856,752
Teachers	19,729	61,605	101,095	119,064	126,785
Ratio[a]	69.2	58.8	56.9	47.5	38.3
Middle schools					
Students	80,828	528,593	1,318,808	2,471,997	2,782,173
Teachers	1,186	13,053	31,207	54,858	69,553
Ratio[a]	68.2	40.5	42.3	45.1	40.0
High schools					
Students	40,217[b]	273,434	590,382	1,696,792	2,152,802
Teachers	1,720[b]	9,627	19,854	50,948	69,546
Ratio[a]	23.4	28.4	29.7	33.3	31.0

Source: Ministry of Education, ROK (1986:27).

a. Average number of students per teacher.

b. Data for 1951.

Government policies in the 1960s and 1970s relied on existing human resources as a basic input in the push toward development, but it was difficult to overcome the constraints on the expansion of public secondary education, particularly lack of funding and trained teachers. By the end of the 1960s, however, the goals in primary education were realized. During the 1970s, educational opportunities at the secondary level were greatly expanded, although enrollment in middle and high schools continued to be voluntary and parents still had to pay the costs. Larger and larger proportions of primary graduates continued from primary into middle school and from middle school into high school (see Table 22.1). In the mid-1980s middle school enrollment was approaching 100 percent, and high school enrollment had surpassed 75 percent (UNESCO 1988:54). The fundamental goals pursued since liberation had long since been achieved, and universal, compulsory education even at the high-school level had become foreseeable. By this time the nation's think tanks were reassessing the hard-won accomplishments of the postwar period. The educational reforms to be undertaken during the coming years will determine to a large extent the quality of the Korean workforce that will lead the nation into the next century and meet the new challenges of high-technology industries and increased internationalization of trade and services.

Although the chronological period covered by this book does not encompass new policy directions for schools and universities, the gradual change in availability and quality of education from World War II to the present has been vital to the successful implementation of many economic policy measures. The rapid economic growth of the nation during this period can thus be better appreciated through an understanding of the dynamics of change in education that are responsible for the quality of the modern workforce.

CONFUCIAN EDUCATION
AND THE VALUE OF LEARNING

Despite the linguistic and ethnic homogeneity of the modern nation, the Korean language did not take its rightful place as the first language of scholarship until after liberation in 1945. By tradition, learning and scholarship were equated with the study of the Confucian classics. Only a small proportion of Korean men from wealthy families had the means and leisure time to learn the tens of thousands of Chinese characters necessary to read and understand ancient texts. Chinese was the language of scholarship, and the Chinese classics had a revered position (not unlike Latin in the West, which was still the first language in English schools as late as the eighteenth century). The examination texts for entrance into the Korean civil service were in Chinese. There were no social barriers to gaining an education in the Confucian classics, but the prerequisite of devoting years of rigorous study to the task excluded virtually all but the sons of the well-to-do, and women had no place at all in this tradition.

State civil service examinations on the Confucian model were introduced to Korea during the Koryŏ dynasty (918–1392). The strengthening of this examination system, particularly under the Yi dynasty (1392–1910), nurtured the growth of Korean scholarship and educational institutions. A Confucian university, four official schools in the capital, and official schools in provincial capitals became the great centers of learning for Koreans. Private schools also played an important role in the development of scholarship, as did private tutoring provided by individual scholars across the land. The outstanding intellectual achievement of the early Yi period was the Korean script—a scientific phonetic system institutionalized in 1446 by the scholarly King Sejong.

In theory the civil service examinations were open to all men at all levels of Korean society. Stressing the Confucian values placed upon literature as well as upon creativity, these examinations required not only a deep understanding of classical literature but also the ability to compose poetry and to write to a high standard. In the past, even an illiterate peasant if he was not of the servant class would urge his children to study hard and obtain knowledge, in hopes of improving their situation in life through the examination system. As a result, traditional Korean culture placed great emphasis upon the education of children.

In actual practice, however, as Korean society became more stratified and as the delineation of class boundaries became rigid, the examinations tended to become increasingly exclusive and available only to the members of the upper class (yangban) who possessed the wealth and leisure requisite to high-quality education. The landed classes were able to generate sufficient resources to pay for the tuition necessary to prepare their children for the civil service examinations in the capital city. Rich upper-class families could support such an education for all their children. But among the typical rural gentry, only the eldest son was given the privilege—possibly as much as 20 years of instruction—and the opportunity to go to Kaesŏng (the Koryŏ capital) and later to Seoul (the Yi capital) for the examinations. Ordinary farmers, by contrast, found it virtually impossible to afford the cost of a tutor. Although the opportunity to enter the civil service was effectively restricted during much of this half-millenium of state Confucianism, the most lasting value contributed to Korean society by Confucian ethics was the emphasis on the value of learning.

TRADITIONAL EDUCATION IN THE KOREAN LANGUAGE

In parallel with the limited numbers of Confucian literati, an indigenous literary movement spread throughout the country from the fifteenth century onward. This movement was made possible by the invention of a phonetic writing system (called *han'gŭl*) in the mid-fifteenth century. The simple characters of the han'gŭl alphabet (24 in modern usage) were expressly designed by King Sejong and his court scholars to enable Koreans of even humble means to obtain for the first time a reading and writing knowledge of their own spoken language. Easily learned within a matter of weeks or less, han'gŭl was the vehicle for Korea's folk literature—read largely by women and children—which became widespread after the invention of moveable printing type in the fifteenth century. The spread of printed han'gŭl nurtured the tradition of literacy and an abiding enthusiasm for reading among women and children, unlike other Confucian countries, thus making education a goal of the highest importance for everyone, including poverty-ridden farmers (Oliver 1956:720). Han'gŭl never gained respectability, however, in the view of Korea's traditional scholars, who scorned the use of the vernacular and banned the use of han'gŭl in the schools as being too easy to learn and too commonplace for a serious scholar. For these reasons, up to the end of the monarchy in 1910, Korea had two exclusive types of education: one in Chinese for the privileged minority and the second in the vernacular available to the masses.

ORIGINS OF MODERN EDUCATION

Modern concepts of education based primarily on the use of the Korean language were first introduced into Korea during the 1880s by Protestant missionaries. Their schools, which used Korean-language texts written in the easy-to-learn han'gŭl script, initially attracted the interest of very few Koreans, and enrollment in substantial numbers did not take place until the 1920s (Fisher 1928:5–6). A series of government reforms were initiated in 1894 to create a primary school system, some high schools, and a normal college, but early in the twentieth century, as Japanese influence became predominant in Korea, education was still available only to the well-to-do (Adams 1956:19, 22). In the meantime, Korea's traditional suzerain (China) was eliminated as a rival for influence in Korea after the Sino-Japanese war of 1894, and Russia likewise was eliminated as a potential rival after the 1904–1905 Russo-Japanese war. In 1905 Korea became a protectorate of Japan, and during the next five years a dual system of education (Korean schools for Koreans, Japanese schools for Japanese residing in Korea) was instituted. This dual system was retained when Korea was annexed to Japan in 1910, and it remained in force until 1938 (Adams 1956:24).

The concept of universal primary education was introduced to Korea during the period of Japanese rule from 1910 to 1945 (J. C. Chung 1985). The colonial government provided an increasing proportion of school-age children with minimal primary schooling, supplemented by a program of vocational education. The educational system was intended, however, to train a subservient workforce of subjects loyal to Japan and capable of filling the growing number of menial and low-paying jobs for the benefit of the

Table 22.2. Registered students in Korea by type of school: Selected years, 1910–37 (10^3 students)

Type of school	1910	1919	1930	1937
Primary schools (years 1–6)				
for Japanese	15.5	42.8	67.4	89.8
for Koreans	20.1	89.3	450.5	901.2
Middle schools (years 7–12)				
for Japanese	0.2	2.0	5.8	7.8
for Koreans and Japanese	0.8	3.2	11.1	15.6
High schools for girls				
for Japanese	0.5	1.9	8.3	11.9
for Koreans	0.4	0.7	4.4	7.1
Teachers' seminaries	0.0	0.0	1.3	3.8
Industrial schools	1.1	4.5	15.3	26.6
Colleges	0.4	0.9	2.5	4.0
University preparatory schools	0.0	0.0	0.3	0.4
University	0.0	0.0	0.6	0.5
Nonstandardized schools[a]	71.8	39.2	47.5	142.6
Total[b]	110.8	184.5	614.4	1,211.4

Source: UNESCO (1954:23).

a. Includes short-course elementary schools.

b. Column totals are subject to rounding errors.

imperial economy. Numerous schools were built, and the enrollment of Korean children increased dramatically. The major accomplishment of this period was at the level of primary education (Table 22.2). Toward the end of Japanese rule, only about 5 percent of Korean children were able to continue to the secondary level (UNESCO 1954:23). For the handful of Koreans who gained entrance to universities, the choice of subjects was severely restricted—mainly law, classical literature, and medicine—and bereft of any content that might help to prepare a Korean for a leadership role.

Despite the shortcomings of the system, Korea gained at least some basic educational infrastructure under Japanese rule. The increasing availability of education brought about improvements in skills and the quality of labor, thereby contributing to the development of the economy. As a proportion of the entire Korean population in 1939, there were places for 5.52 percent at the primary level, 0.13 percent at the secondary level, and 0.12 percent in vocational schools. At higher levels, virtually no places were available to Koreans. About 27 Koreans per 100,000 population were receiving education at the tertiary level (including teachers' colleges), whereas less than one Korean per 100,000 population gained admission to a university (UNES-CO 1954:24).

The state educational system was supplemented by an extensive network of Protestant mission schools, mostly at the primary level. In the mid-1920s these Christian schools were providing primary education to more than 37,000 pupils who attended the more than 750 mission schools that met government standards. A further 13,000 pupils got at least some minimal instruction from the more than 300 one-room mission schools (Fisher 1928:2). The missions also operated two Christian colleges for men, two theological seminaries, Ewha College for Women, and a medical college.

By 1935 about 128,000 Koreans were completing elementary-school education annually, and the high schools were producing an additional 11,000 graduates (Suh 1978:152). The decade and a half preceding the Pacific war brought dramatic changes in school enrollments at all levels. In 1925 only 12.3 percent of Korean children in the age range of 6–12 were enrolled in school; by 1940 this figure had reached 32.7 percent. During the same period, the percentage of children in the age range of 13–18 rose from 0.8 percent to 2.4 percent, and the percentage of Korean youths pursuing advanced education (those in the 19–24 age range) rose from 0.06 percent to 0.17 percent (Cho et al. 1971:563).

Higher education was confined, as before, to children from well-to-do families and families that worked for the Japanese administration. Conservative Koreans equated Japanese-style education not only with the foreign invaders of their land but also with unwanted Western influences. Japanese-style education in many ways did not fit the Korean national identity and cultural values. Many Koreans regarded this kind of education as unacceptable in the context of traditional Korean values and aspirations for national independence and thus wanted to avoid it. Yet, there was no alternative. The entire body of Korean literature and the use of the Korean language itself were officially banned from 1938 to 1945, even in the primary schools where they had previously been permitted. Hence the whole generation of young Koreans educated prior to liberation in 1945 were arbitrarily cut off from traditional Korean sources of knowledge. The people of this same generation, once educated, were also denied the full benefits of their learning, because scores of thousands of Japanese civil servants came to the peninsula to staff the expanding modern bureaucracy, thereby preempting potential Korean candidates.

Although Japanese-style education was a cultural shock for the Koreans and deemed undesirable in the short term, it did bring rapid, positive change to Korea. It provided even the ordinary people with some exposure to modern education. It was accompanied by much-needed modern foreign technology, which the isolationist Yi dynasty had adamantly denied itself. The people born during the first three decades of the twentieth century are the first generation of Koreans to have received a modern, albeit

Japanese, education. Significantly, they became the technocrats who contributed to economic and social development from the beginning of the Republic of Korea in 1948. President Park Chung Hee was a typical product of this type of education, having attended a Japanese-run primary school and a Japanese-run normal school in Korea, a Japanese military school in Manchuria, and ultimately a military academy in Japan.

EDUCATION AFTER LIBERATION, 1945–50

The development of education in modern, independent Korea was not a process of reconstructing and modernizing an existing philosophy or institution. At the time of liberation, Koreans had been isolated from their traditional educational system by three and a half decades of foreign rule. The task facing Korean educators was not one of rebuilding and modernizing an existing system but to create appropriate institutions from the ground upward. Scarce resources therefore had to be concentrated on creating a system that was appropriate to the nation's level of economic and social development at that time, not looking back to the heritage of the past but forward to the needs of the country. Perhaps most important, for the first time Koreans were in a position to use education in the pursuit of their own political, social, and economic goals.

After the Japanese were repatriated at the end of World War II, virtually all remaining inhabitants regarded themselves as ethnically Korean. Their homogeneity precluded potentially divisive identification in linguistic, racial, ethnic, or other cultural terms. The postwar nation likewise did not inherit a culture-bound class system. (It can be argued, moreover, that Japanese tradition permitted less social mobility than Korean, because the Confucian examination system was not used in pre-Meiji Japan.) These factors helped to ensure greater mobility and have long-term implications in many areas of social, economic, and political activity.

The most serious shortage was teachers. Judging from 1938 data, the departing Japanese represented about 40 percent of all primary school teachers, 80 percent of all high school teachers, and 70 percent of college and university teachers (UNESCO 1954:24). The same data show that, on the eve of war, only about 300 Koreans were employed as teachers at the secondary level and higher in both the northern and southern regions of the country. At the war's end, the shortage of teachers was acute, and no teachers' training facilities existed. The only solution was to adopt a demand-first, quality-later policy by inducting thousands of persons with inadequate teaching qualifications into the system at all levels.

Even the qualified and experienced teachers, however, were not entirely suited for the task ahead of them, because almost all of them were products of the Japanese educational system. Under Japanese rule, the Japanese language was the sole medium of instruction at the secondary level and above, and the curriculum was the same as in Japan itself. The primary schools for Korean children, on the other hand, used the Korean language and the han'gŭl script as the medium of instruction, and a little Korean history and cultural content were permitted until shortly before the world war. The goal laid down in the 1922 education law, however, was to increase proficiency in the "national" (i.e., Japanese) language by expanding instruction in Japanese at the primary level and eventually eliminating the use of the Korean language altogether. In 1938 all Korean aspects of the schools were suppressed, and the school system became uniformly Japanese. All uses of han'gŭl were banned, and students were forbidden to speak Korean either inside or outside the schools.

Unlike some postcolonial Asian nations that moved gradually to indigenize the educational systems they inherited, by phasing out the curricula and language of the colonial power, Koreans suddenly discarded the entire existing system because it was Japanese and began to build anew. Japanese textbooks were discarded because both the language and content were unsuitable for independent Korea. All textbooks at every level had to be written. The entire content of education had to be created from 1945 onward at every level from primary school to university. The buildings emerged from World War II undamaged, but the infrastructure had to be vastly expanded to make primary education universally available. In 1945 there were no Korean textbooks for any level of education, no facilities for writing or printing books in han'gŭl, and no precedents for a curriculum to meet the aspirations of an independent people.

Important tools for modern education had nonetheless been preserved throughout the war by members of the Han'gŭl Society, which was originally established to compile a complete Korean dictionary and which continued its work underground after 1938. The society's text on standardized spelling published in 1933 was used as a basis for postwar Korean grammar books. A six-volume dictionary had almost been completed by 1945, although its publication was delayed for many years—first by the lack of paper and printing facilities, then by the Korean War (in which most copies of the first edition were destroyed), and later by a lack of funds to complete the printing and to prepare supplementary volumes of badly needed technical and scientific terminology (UNESCO 1954:121, 124).

THE KOREAN WAR AND POSTWAR ACHIEVEMENTS

Although much of the educational infrastructure was destroyed during the first year of the Korean War, an extraordinary effort was made to keep the educational system in operation. Many schools (such as those in Seoul) were temporarily moved to safer sites. By 1952 about 60 percent of classrooms had been destroyed or badly damaged, or were temporarily requisitioned for other uses, and more than 80 percent of equipment, books, and furniture were lost (UNESCO 1954:119). Yet schools continued to function—in tents or even in the open air when the weather permitted.

Education, like the economy, had to be almost entirely reconstructed when the war ended. The United Nations' aid mission for reconstruction was assisted in postwar educational planning by a team from the United Nations Educational, Scientific and Cultural Organization (UNESCO). Many of the UNESCO recommendations were not carried out, but this mission more than any other set the stage for the types and amounts of educational aid to Korea during the mid and late 1950s (Adams 1956:226).

As the nation approached the goal of universal, free primary education, the demand for further education at the middle- and high-school level was greater than the number of places available. Although substantial progress was made in expanding the number of higher level schools and universities, as well as in developing vocational education and educational research, the increase in student numbers was limited by selection through examination for entry into middle school. In 1969, after this barrier was removed, there was a sudden increase in middle-school enrollment. In terms of sheer numbers, this bold move succeeded within a decade in raising the proportion of primary-school graduates continuing into middle school from less than 60 percent in 1969 to more than 90 percent in 1979 (Jayasuriya 1980:59–60). By the mid-1980s middle-school education, although not compulsory or free, had become universally available.

From the educators' point of view, however, this sudden change adversely affected the quality of education. To cope with the serious shortage of classrooms, some schools operated two or three teaching shifts per day. For the first time, teachers in public secondary schools had to give instruction not just to the best students but also to those with lesser ability. The government's intention was to bring about a democratic reform by abolishing an elitist principle inherited from the distant past, but the quality of education inevitably suffered in the short term.

The ratio of students per teacher is one measure of quality in education. There has been a progressive improvement in the ratio at the primary level ever since liberation (Table 22.1). The ratio for high schools has fluctuated within a reasonable range since the 1960s. At the middle-school level, however, the ratio showed a substantial improvement up to the 1960s, worsened in the 1970s, and reverted to the 1960s levels only in the mid-1980s, reflecting a major change in middle-school enrollment that began at the end of the 1960s. The impact on the high schools, by contrast, was partly exacerbated through the expansion of vocational instruction at the secondary school level, and by 1979 about 40 percent of all new high school students were being channeled into vocational education (Jayasuriya 1980:61).

REFORMS FOR THE 1990s AND BEYOND

A presidential commission was established in 1985 to examine potential reforms in the national educational system and to formulate policy measures to ensure higher quality education. The need for a better educated workforce to sustain the pace of national development to the end of the century and beyond is reflected in the broad composition of the commission, which included not only educators and other civil servants but also economists, industrial leaders, scientists, and professionals in social affairs. The initial recommendations of the Presidential Commission for Educational Reform were outlined in *Strategies for Educational Reform*, published by the commission in 1986. A complementary study carried out by the Korean Educational Development Institute (KEDI) underscored the lack of flexibility in the present system to meet the nation's changing educational needs (UNESCO 1988:49). The final report of the commission, containing its comprehensive reform proposals, was completed in 1988. It placed particular stress on improvement in the quality of education and emphasized that the maintenance and further development of Korea's international competitiveness in economic, technical, political, and other spheres can be achieved only through maximum development of human resources (Sohn 1988).

During the past few decades, a well-educated workforce has been regarded as an important asset for achieving rapid economic growth. The work of the presidential commission and KEDI indicate, however, that a major shift in educational philosophy is imperative and that the availability of higher quality education must itself be a goal of the development process. Although nearly all primary graduates were already continuing to middle school in the mid-1980s, education at this level was not compulsory and parents still had to pay for a portion of the costs. One researcher (K. K. Lee 1986:12), noting that there is no distinction between urban and rural or rich and poor in the desire for more educational opportunities, poignantly describes the continuing plight of poorer rural parents:

> Education is considered to be the main means for social mobility and the ladder for promotion in the workplace. In rural areas, parents sell their rice fields to pay for the education of their children. Yet when a child has finished college, he will not go back to the farm and his parents' house. Still, parents want to send all their children to college. When the economic conditions of the family are too poor to support them all, the eldest son is sent to college; the other sons complete middle school and the daughters complete primary school. This division of children's education reflects property division in the past.

The government has now announced that education at the middle-school level will be made compulsory on an incremental basis, concentrating first on the lesser-developed rural areas that are lagging behind in educational opportunities and afterward bringing the urban schools formally within the compulsory system. Meanwhile, the trend of enrollment at the high-school level (already more than 75 percent) is expected to exceed 86 percent by the turn of the century, thus laying the foundation for universal, free high-school education (UNESCO 1988:54–55).

The most important aspect of the presidential commission's recommendations is to improve the quality and scope of education at the primary and secondary levels to ensure that the workforce can maintain a competitive edge in the world marketplaces of the coming decades. In this context, the commission proposes to improve foreign language instruction and to add international affairs to the curriculum to create greater awareness and understanding of political, economic, and social issues that shape the world (Sohn 1988).

The KEDI study highlights the potential role of education as an agent for social change and an instrument through which the welfare of ordinary people can be improved. It also concludes that education should have a complementary relationship with the political process, economic and social affairs, and national culture, because problems in education derive from these and other aspects of life. Both studies acknowledge that, as the percentages of enrollment in all age brackets increase, the greatest problem facing educators will be to maintain and improve standards of education (UNESCO 1988:50, 56). In this regard, it is instructive to examine some of the problems associated with raising standards, which are in part a legacy of the pre- and postwar era.

LESSONS FROM THE
MODERN EDUCATION EXPERIENCE

Cultural Identity Conflict

For Koreans, the cultural orientation of prewar curricula was the most distasteful aspect of the Japanese educational system. It was designed for Japanese children, fostered the Japanese national identity, and strove to instill Japanese nationalistic values in the students. Its enforcement in Korea produced a conflict in identity for Korean children, who had no alternative to schools in which they had to speak the Japanese language and act as though they were Japanese, while always conscious that they were not.

Because of their cultural identity, Koreans resisted the attempt to press them into a Japanese mold of collective behavior. The Japanese, in their collective activities, placed great emphasis on adhering to norms. Koreans, in contrast, did not hesitate to deviate to a certain extent from expected norms. Even under Japanese tutelage, Koreans did not train themselves to act together cooperatively as the Japanese do. The fact that Koreans tended to cause more disruption than the Japanese reflects also the enforced loss of old Korean values (which in terms of harmony-seeking were actually similar to the Japanese). Ultimately, the Japanese-style educational system, imposed upon the entire first generation of Koreans to benefit from universal education, prevented the evolution of strong Korean traits based on Korea's own culture and national identity.

This experience with Japanese-style education made Koreans more individualistic than the Japanese. Koreans took advantage of the educational opportunities offered to them, but with the idea of personal gain and advancement rather than of transforming themselves into the uniform products for which the Japanese educational system was designed. Koreans who were fortunate enough to possess both the intellectual ability and the financial means to continue their education at the professional-school and university level tended to specialize in medicine or law, thus becoming physicians or filling the lower administrative and judicial positions in the civil service.

The individualistic character of the Korean working class is illustrated in a prewar attitude toward compensation for labor. In the Japanese view at that time, a group of Japanese laborers could be paid regular monthly wages and could be relied upon to work together at a certain level of efficiency in carrying out a particular job. The Japanese thought that Koreans, in contrast, would work slowly and less efficiently if paid regular monthly wages. At the same time, the Japanese felt that Koreans would in fact work faster than their Japanese counterparts to complete a particular job if paid piece-rates for each task performed. In other words, the Japanese were good at working collectively at a pace determined by the group, but with no individual trying to outshine his peers, whereas each Korean was working as an individual for the rewards of his labor. This attitude toward labor became intensified as a result of the Japanese-type educational system. It helps to explain why Koreans of the present day are fiercely competitive, excelling over other nationalities, for instance, in the implementation of overseas construction contracts. If given proper incentives to finish quickly, Korean laborers are willing to work long hours without complicated labor-union restrictions.

Placed in the right situation, Koreans will strive to outperform anyone, even under nearly impossible odds. One author (Griffis 1897:42–43) depicts this important character trait as reflected in records of warfare ranging across thirteen centuries. He begins by describing the Chinese rout of a Korean army in the seventh century:

> After so crushing a loss in men and material, one might expect instant surrender of the besieged city. So far from this, the garrison redoubled the energy of their defense. In this we see a striking trait of the Korean military character . . . . Chinese, Japanese, French, and Americans have experienced the fact and marvelled thereat. It is that the Koreans are poor soldiers in the open field . . . . But put the same men behind walls, bring them to bay, and the timid stag amazes the hounds. Their whole nature seems reinforced. They are more than brave. Their courage is sublime. They fight to the last man, and fling themselves on the bare steel when the foe clears the parapet.

Korean individualism was reinforced by a trait that might be called a "sabotage complex," originating in the period of Japanese rule. Korean students, constrained within a Japanese educational system tailored to the Japanese national identity, funneled their energies into subversive channels. Unable to act openly against the system, they developed a tendency to sabotage the process by which they were being Japanized, thereby partly defeating the purposes of the system itself. Although the original common target was the Japanese, these behavioral characteristics became strongly ingrained in a whole generation of Koreans educated by the Japanese and inevitably persisted even after liberation in 1945. They were, moreover, passed on to the succeeding generation—their later sabotage objectives shifting from one Korean leader to another. This type of behavior, because of its origins in a repressive system, has unfortunately taken a destructive rather than a creative form; several generations may be required to correct it, possibly by diverting and absorbing the energies derived from this sabotage tendency into positive political change.

Experiences of the Han'gŭl Generation

After the departure of the Japanese at the end of World War II, the public desire for greater educational opportunities resulted in unprecedented expansion. The modern curriculum had to be both practical and Korean in concept, reversing the process of distortion that began with the proselytizing of Western missionary schools followed by decades of suppression of traditional Korean values by the Japanese-administered schools. At the time of liberation, virtually everyone wanted to gain more and more education at higher and higher levels. Koreans willingly invested as much as they could afford to provide their children with a good education. Investment in universal education significantly improved the quality of the modern Korean workforce, thus paving the way to rapid economic development in the 1960s and 1970s. The new workers of the two decades immediately after World War II were the first generation exposed to the post-Japanese system of general education.

The Koreans who received their education immediately after World War II are frequently called the "han'gŭl generation." They learned relatively few Chinese characters and were the first generation of Koreans to receive a formal education through the medium of the han'gŭl phonetic system of writing. The Korean educators of this period tried to emulate the achievements of their Japanese counterparts in terms of inculcating nationalism, and thus the content of postwar Korean education was strongly nationalistic. Unlike the Japanese, however, the Koreans do not have a long tradition of modern education. In formulating its policies, the Korean government was selective and sometimes inconsistent.

Official policy concerning the writing system, for example, was reversed several times. Although the Korean language was restored as the medium of instruction after 1945, Korean nationalist sentiments were misguided in insisting that only the han'gŭl system of writing should be taught in public schools. Immediately after the war, an attempt was made to eliminate Chinese characters because they were regarded, incorrectly, as a lingering influence of Japanese- and Chinese-style education. In fact, Chinese characters have always served as an integral part of Korean literary tradition, with the partial exception of folk literature.

Some Koreans still argue that Chinese characters can be eliminated altogether, but to do so would be disadvantageous in various ways. The use of select Chinese characters in combination with the han'gŭl script offers numerous attractions, and even today few Koreans would willingly abandon the thousand or more characters that are still taught and in common everyday use. Although any Korean word can be written in the Korean script, it is often more practical to substitute a Chinese character to indicate a precise or complex meaning. The configuration of a Chinese character can enable the reader to recognize a precise meaning or concept that is less efficiently conveyed by the phonetic equivalent. (Chinese characters thus have the advantage of distinguishing between two words that are pronounced identically but could not be differentiated in han'gŭl script except when read in context.) Precise or elaborate meanings conveyed visually by the configuration of a Chinese character cannot be conveyed by a simple phonetic rendering of the spoken word. Hence Chinese (or Koreans), when a meaning comes into question, generally write the character so that the listener can see it, rather than explain the meaning verbally. From a modern perspective, moreover, familiarity with Chinese characters provides potentially valuable training to facilitate trade and communications with the Chinese and Japanese in the future, since schoolchildren in all three countries learn many of the same characters in common.

Han'gŭl was reinstated as the official written language in 1945. Under the education laws enacted by the Republic of Korea, primary schools were expected to teach only the han'gŭl script; secondary schools were required to use han'gŭl textbooks but also to teach 1,000 Chinese characters. In practice, this limitation on the use of Chinese characters was too severe, since newspapers and even official documents in the early 1950s continued to use a larger number of Chinese characters. By the time of the Korean War, most secondary schools found it necessary to teach more than 2,000 Chinese characters so that students could read newspapers and official statements (UNESCO 1954:18). Officially, the total number of required characters remains about 1,000, but well-educated Koreans take pride in learning many more. The debate about the use of Chinese characters has thus continued, and the question is not yet fully resolved.

Most of the Korean educators of the han'gŭl generation had to be recruited from among the Koreans who had received a Japanese-type education. They were the "individualists" who went through the alienation phase under

Japanese administration. Their individualist tendencies were fostered by Japanese-style education, in which they experienced national and cultural alienation, in terms of both the curriculum and the regimentation of their training. They did not on the whole become a disciplined group, and they could not shed the behavioral characteristics that they had acquired from their educational experiences under the Japanese. Most of them were not the best possible teachers, and they passed their undesirable behavioral characteristics to the next generation.

At the university level, most Korean academics during the Japanese colonial period were graduates of the best imperial universities in Japan. At that time, however, very few Koreans attained the rank of professor. After liberation, the existing corps of first-class Korean academics was too small to meet the needs of the numerous new colleges and universities that sprang up throughout the country. To fill the dramatically increasing number of faculty positions, the new institutions had to recruit Koreans who had only modest academic credentials obtained from lower-ranked Japanese institutions. Because of the serious shortage at this level, the government had to draw also upon the existing pool of high-school instructors, who would not normally qualify for university-level teaching. The shifting of many qualified educators away from the secondary schools may have caused both higher and secondary education to suffer from lack of teachers properly trained for their respective levels.

The climate created by the post-Pacific war educators lingered on after the Korean War, in the form of slovenly teaching habits, lack of creativity, and lack of discipline. The students were eager and capable, but the instructors were not equal to the task of providing quality education. The han'gŭl generation also seemed less disciplined than the Japanese in terms of collective behavior. Although the first generation of teachers in independent Korea were unable to provide high quality education, there were at least sufficient numbers of them to meet existing numerical demand. The government, needing every available teacher, had to employ many whose work habits were poor and who possessed only limited qualifications. These were the foundations on which modern Korean education had to be built.

As the demand for education grew, the supply of teachers could not catch up with the boom, particularly in terms of quality. Today, perhaps too many educational opportunities are available, although not yet enough of the highest quality. Competition for entry to the prestigious schools and universities is fierce, often requiring long hours of private tutoring beyond the standard curricula and sometimes leaving teenagers with an inadequate four or five hours each night for sleep. There is pressure on parents, too, for reasons of social prestige, which in turn puts a grave strain on students to gain admission to a particular institution, to get a diploma, and to continue their university education through graduate school.

The diploma itself came to be regarded as the only goal of education, because the diploma seemed to be the key to a successful career. Unfortunately, some students, including very bright ones, did not value education for its own sake and cared only about the coveted diploma. How they got it—whether by cheating or other means—did not concern them. As a result, discipline eroded in Korean universities. Pure scholarship requires persistence and hard work, without expectation of special remuneration. Once their ties with the old scholarly traditions were severed, Koreans were never retrained to appreciate this kind of discipline. Many among the scholarly community, once they receive their degrees, neither continue to carry out research nor pursue knowledge for its own sake—except insofar as such activities may be required to preserve their positions or livelihoods.

American Influences

Korea, unlike Japan, had to overcome many basic obstacles in building a modern educational system and later in improving standards. Even before World War II, the Japanese successfully harnessed the positive features of traditional Japanese education for useful purposes in economic development. Korea, however, did not follow the same pattern after liberation. Immediately after the war, there was no modern Korean-style educational system on which to build, and Koreans therefore had to search for their own model.

Public education in Korea benefited in material terms from U.S. foreign aid after the Korean War, although the imposition of American educational philosophy was resisted. The American effort had three educational policy goals: democratization, decentralization of administration, and the creation of coeducational classes to improve the status of women. These basic objectives were never met: democratization was not achieved, Korean education remains hierarchical, and educational administration has become more centralized. Coeducational classes were never accepted beyond the primary level (AID, U.S., 1985). This attempt to induce policy changes reflects a lack of cross-cultural perception and understanding. Korean cultural traits proved resistant to the somewhat evangelistic posturing behind the American offer of aid. The Korean government accepted the material assistance but did not use the funds to carry out improvements in ways that the American donors intended.

The 1960s witnessed the first massive flow of Korean students to the United States and Europe for higher education. Successive age cohorts among them have returned home to help build better quality higher education. Although the period of exposure has been much shorter, the Koreans have in many ways become much more Americanized than the Japanese. This tendency is partly a result of the intensity and suddenness of exposure by Koreans to American values and education during the past quarter century, in contrast to the more gradual, century-long Japanese experience, which was characterized by extensive exposure to many Western nations.

Koreans have always had an exaggerated expectation of the people who have studied in a country that is more advanced than Korea. Great respect was traditionally given to Korean scholars who journeyed to China, which was once regarded as the source of advanced learning. Upon their return home, these scholars were treated as though they knew everything. They were presumed to be more knowledgeable than people educated in Korea, wiser, and better teachers. In more recent times, new graduates returning from the United States were greeted with similar traditional esteem. The period of the late 1950s onward saw the beginnings of the influx of American-trained Ph.D.s into the Korean bureaucracy. American-trained economists played an important role in introducing new skills and rationalizing the development process. They were able to play a major role in Korea, in contrast to their counterparts in Japan, because of the absence of a sufficient number of indigenously trained Korean bureaucrats. (Immediately after the Korean War, however, there were still a few older Korean bureaucrats trained in the Japanese tradition who were formulating economic policy.)

The newly returned graduates thus filled an important gap. They were promoted with astonishing rapidity to senior posts, without passing through the essential stages of institutional training or gaining experience at various levels of the bureaucracy. Because of their unique positions, their roles may have exceeded realistic limits beyond which, in several ways, they tended to become dysfunctional. Thus the 1960s and 1970s might be characterized as an important stage of the learning process, one result of which was a complementary combination of indigenous elitist bureaucrats, on the one hand, working together with Western-trained technical bureaucrats, on the other.[2]

Because of the scarcity of Ph.D.s in the late 1950s, anyone with a doctorate in economics was held almost in awe—as though he knew everything about the economy. The new degree holders returning to Korea were expected, moreover, to be able to perform immediately as skilled experts. Their degrees were, however, only certifications of analytical ability and training within a specific discipline, and their university studies alone could not have prepared them to deal with the broad range of problems faced by policymakers in the real world. In some cases, the theoretical aspects of their American-university training may have been irrelevant to the Korean economic setting. Upon their return to Korea, rather than acting with modesty and prudence, most of them yielded to the pressure and temptations. Their broad recommendations and suggestions then became the bases of economic policy.

---

2. Two examples are Mr. Jong-Yum Kim, who received a Japanese-style education and was promoted through the bureaucracy in Korea to become minister of commerce and trade, minister of finance, and President Park's chief of staff, and Dr. Duk-Woo Nam, former prime minister and minister of finance, who received graduate training in economics in the United States.

During the 1960s and 1970s, the increasing number of American-trained economists played a major role in formulating development policy for Korea. They popularized general Western economics knowledge in Korea, thereby contributing to rational planning. They were the communicators of Western economic thinking, rational planning, ideas of market economy, and analytical tools. They played a positive role by serving as a bridge to communicate concepts and techniques for analyzing the economic situation of Korea. One positive outcome is that they were well prepared to interact with Americans and to promote better mutual understanding, which was especially important because American assistance had played a major role in the Korean economy since the 1950s. The American-educated economists were also exposed to (although not necessarily experienced in) the American way of managing an economy. But the perceptions of such economists frequently fell short of the mark in their understanding of Korean conditions, traditional values, and behavioral characteristics relevant to economic development, when compared with the indigenous bureaucrats who had remained more closely in touch with local conditions.

By contrast, the Japanese postwar miracle of economic development was led basically by a school of elite bureaucrats (Nobusuke Kishi and others). In retrospect, as Chalmers Johnson (1982) indicates, these elitists bureaucrats were insightful and consistent over a longer time frame in nurturing consistent development policies. No American-trained Ph.D. was directly involved in formulating important Japanese development policies within the Economic Planning Ministry or the Ministry of International Trade and Industry (MITI). Most of the Japanese with American Ph.D.s were filtered instead into Japanese universities, where their work as researchers and advisers contributed only indirectly to the bureaucrats' thinking.

Korea did not have enough elite bureaucrats who had received the type of training that their Japanese counterparts possessed. Indigenously educated bureaucrats were helpful in assessing local situations, whereas those who received their doctorates in the West were not trained to grasp the traditional aspects of the economy and society. They tended to develop policies based instead on their technical training from Western literature—in essence, a textbook treatment of economic policies. For example, the implementation of a value-added tax (VAT) system worked well in Europe. Korean bureaucrats with a sense of traditional behavior and institutional arrangements were opposed to the adoption of a VAT system in Korea. But some Korean economists with American training were fascinated by the European sucess with VAT and persuaded the government to introduce this tax system in Korea. In spite of their compelling arguments and persuasive theory, the Korean experiment turned out to be a costly lesson, because of the failure to take into consideration the way Koreans behave in consonance with their expectations, habits, and customs. Given sufficient time, Korean behavioral norms could be modified to accommodate the VAT system, but such radical change cannot be brought about rapidly.

In some ways, the recent generation of highly skilled graduates returning from the West can be compared with their predecessors who were products of the Japanese educational system. In the post-Korean War period, because of the predominant role that Americans played in military and economic assistance, which the Koreans appreciated, it seems in retrospect that Koreans were too ready to accept things American, including American-style education and its content. Only later did Koreans see that American-style education is not the all-encompassing panacea that they once imagined and that it does not completely fit the traditional Korean value system. The tendency at present is to look back and search for an amalgamation of both traditional Sino-Korean and contemporary Western-technological education.

CONCLUDING REMARKS

The potential for rapid expansion of education in Korea already existed at the time of liberation in 1945. Japanese rule provided not only a legacy of basic infrastructure but also modern concepts, the more important of which were the goal of making schooling universally available and modern curricula and teaching methods to train the workforce to carry out national economic objectives. The Japanese use of education to enforce social change, however, had several negative consequences, fostering a sense of alienation, stimulating the sabotage complex, and distorting traditional Korean values that did not fit the Japanese mold. Nevertheless, rapid advances after liberation were facilitated by the positive Korean outlook concerning educational opportunities—most notably the high value placed on education at every level of Korean society, the Confucian concepts that predominated among the majority of the population, and the tradition of learning based on Chinese characters and held in common with the rest of East Asia. Teachers were held in high esteem. Koreans were very receptive to education as a means of personal advancement, and the learning process was facilitated also by the discipline inherent in the hierarchical nature of society, with its emphasis on respect for elders.

The modern educational system provided the nation's workforce from 1945 to the 1980s with essential basic skills, which industry utilized as one of the driving forces for economic expansion and industrialization. Future development, however, especially in high-technology industries and in trade and services based on medium and high technology, will rely on higher standards of teaching, increasing technological sophistication in educational curricula, and a more disciplined labor force. The greatest task for Korean educators as the nation enters the 1990s is to achieve rapid improvements in the quality of education, particularly at the secondary and tertiary levels. Such advances are vital if the generation of Korean youth entering the labor market at the turn of the century are to be adequately prepared to meet the intensified international competition from other advanced industrialized economies.

23 Changes in the Social Structure

by Lee-Jay Cho and Kennon Breazeale

The social structure of Korea has undergone disruptive changes during the past two to three generations, particularly as a result of subjection to colonial rule, two major wars, and political turmoil under the six successive republics. By the early 1940s, Korea had ceased to be the "land of the morning calm" where farmers tilled their fields while the class of landed gentry (*yangban*) provided community and national leadership and served as the repository of traditional values. Large numbers of Koreans were mobilized by Japan for the war effort, and in Korea itself the number of factory workers more than doubled within a few years—from 0.27 million in 1939 to 0.55 million in 1943 (H. Choi 1971:291). The economic infrastructure of the peninsula was relatively undamaged at the end of World War II but was later destroyed during the Korean War. Thus, unlike most other countries occupied during and immediately after World War II, Korea's economic rehabilitation was delayed for almost a decade. The entire period from the time of liberation was, however, one of rapid social change.

POPULATION MOVEMENTS

Geographic Mobility

There is a long history of northward migration by Korean farmers in search of farmland in Manchuria, but the era of large-scale population movement out of the peninsula coincides with the years of Japanese colonization from 1910 to 1945. Manchuria continued to attract most of the emigrants until about 1920, when the tide of emigration shifted to Japan (Table 23.1). The number of emigrants to Manchuria continued to increase, however, and reached an unprecedented level in the 1930s when Japan was attempting to develop the resources of the puppet state established in 1932.

These emigration statistics, although only approximations, demonstrate clearly the magnitude of Korean emigration during this period. On the eve of World War II, large numbers of Koreans were residing outside the peninsula: about 778,000 in Manchuria and 730,000 in Japan in 1937 (H. Choi 1971:275). The emigrants to Japan were largely from the agricultural south, where the population loss was more noticeable than in the industrial north. During the war, the Koreans who were sent to Japan for the war effort constituted a substantial proportion of the "emigrants." Between 1940 and 1945 about 630,000 people, representing 2.5 percent of the entire Korean population, moved to Japan. Subsequent emigration from Korea has not been significant.

Table 23.1. Net Korean migration to Japan and Manchuria: 1910–40

| Years | Net Korean migration to | | |
	Manchuria	Japan	Both areas
1910–15	150,000	1,000	151,000
1916–20	174,600	34,000	208,600
1921–25	24,200	138,300	162,500
1926–30	101,400	200,300	301,700
1931–35	175,500	262,400	437,900
1936–40	565,200	456,500	1,021,700

Source: Kwon et al. (1975).

Table 23.2. Estimates of migration into South Korea: 1945–49

| Place of origin | Data source | | |
	Ministry of Foreign Affairs	Ministry of Health	Survey of Man-power Resources
Japan	1,117,819	1,407,255	936,000
North Korea	648,784	456,404	209,000
Manchuria	317,327	382,348	212,000
Rest of China	72,848	78,442	42,000
Other places	32,864	157,916	481,000
Total	2,189,642	2,482,365	1,880,000

Source: C. C. Yun (1974:126).

After the occupation of the peninsula in 1945 by Soviet and American troops, above and below the 38th parallel, many people moved south across the artificial dividing line, and most Koreans residing outside the country tried to return. Although no accurate records were maintained during this turbulent period, official estimates of migration to South Korea between 1945 and 1949 range from 1.9 to 2.5 million (Table 23.2). Comparisons of prewar and postwar census data suggest that the total number of immigrants to South Korea during 1945–49 was in the range of 1.7–1.8 million (Kwon et al. 1975:33). About 1.0–1.4 million of these came from Japan alone, mostly returning to their areas of origin in the three southern provinces, but settling in urban rather than rural areas. The total number of returnees from Manchuria may never be known, but as many as 400,000 of them resettled in South Korea by 1949. (For further details, see Kwon et al. 1975:29–36 and Taeuber and Barclay 1950.)

The social and economic dislocation of this period was exacerbated by wartime casualties, two waves of migration between the North and South, and internal migration within South Korea alone. Estimates of those who moved south across the military occupation line during 1945–49 range from 150,000 to 740,000 (Kwon et al. 1975:33; Table 23.2). The great majority of the migrants from the North settled either in Seoul or simply moved across the line and into the rural areas of the two northern provinces of South Korea. During the Korean War (1950–53), the entire peninsula was affected by the attacks and counterattacks deep into both North and South Korea, although at the end of the war the country remained divided at the original arbitrary occupation line. The toll taken by the war in South Korea included more than 760,000 civilians and more than 200,000 military personnel killed, missing, or abducted and never returned, plus nearly 230,000 civilians and more than 100,000 military personnel wounded (Table 23.3). In addition, 16 nations deployed troops to aid South Korea. The U.S. military alone suffered nearly 33,750 dead and 103,300 wounded among the 0.5 million U.S. soldiers who fought in the war (Department of Defense, U.S., 1989). During the Korean War, it is estimated that nearly 650,000 people from the North moved to South Korea, and nearly 290,000 moved from the South to the North (Kwon et al. 1975:35–36).

Urbanization and the Emergence of a Middle Class

Seoul was the destination for 45 percent of all migrants from North Korea during 1945–49. About 48 percent of the refugees from the North during the Korean War crowded into the cities. During 1950–53 about 44 percent of the urbanward refugees from the North moved into Seoul. More than a third settled initially in Pusan, which became the provisional wartime capital. When the national administrative functions were transferred back to Seoul during the second half of the 1950s, however, these refugees likewise tended to move to the Seoul area (Kwon et al. 1975:36–37).

Because the wartime destruction affected almost every part of the peninsula, the period up to 1953 and several years beyond was one of

Table 23.3. South Korean casualties during the Korean War: 1950–53

Category	Civilian			Military
	Male	Female	Total	
Killed in fighting	166,104	78,559	244,663	29,494
Executed	97,680	31,256	128,936	—[a]
Wounded	168,849	60,776	229,625	101,097
Taken prisoner to North Korea and not returned	78,377	6,155	84,532	65,601
Missing	253,271	49,941	303,212	105,672
Total	764,281	226,687	990,968	301,864

Source: C. C. Yun (1974:126).

a. Combined with "killed in fighting."

deprivation and hardship for the majority of the populace, who had to turn to any means available to survive and provide bare necessities for their families. A large proportion of the people involved in the massive migrations into and within Korea from 1945 to 1953 were uprooted from their previous occupational niches, and the only choice for most was to eke out a living in an urban area. The Seoul metropolitan area, which had fewer than 1 million inhabitants in 1945, absorbed within the first decade after liberation more displaced persons than its original population. The populations of the capital and other cities in the South thus swelled suddenly, not as a result of industrialization and economic growth but because of wartime chaos and movements of refugees.

Comparative census data show the growing tendency among South Koreans to change their place of residence after the two wars. The South had very low interprovincial migration rates prior to World War II, but the volume of movement away from native provinces increased substantially in the postwar period. Three-quarters of the internal migration was urbanward, predominantly to the two independent metropolitan areas. Seoul (a metropolitan area since 1945) acquired 51 percent of its population through in-migration from the provinces by 1960 and 56 percent by 1966; Pusan (a metropolitan area since 1966) likewise had a high rate of in-migration. At the same time, almost all of the nine provinces were experiencing a net loss of population. Hence the increase of the South Korean population during the 1960s was absorbed largely by the two metropolitan areas and, to a lesser extent, by smaller cities (L. J. Cho 1973:25–33).

Although the speed of industrialization between 1960 and 1985 was rapid but irregular, that of urbanization was steady. The proportion of the total population residing in urban areas increased from 28 percent in 1960 to 65 percent in 1985. By 1985 the population of Seoul reached 9.6 million and accounted for more than 36 percent of the nation's urban population. Between the end of World War II and 1985, the population of Pusan grew from 200,000 to 3.5 million, accounting for an additional 13 percent of the total urban population (EPB, ROK, *Census Report*, 1985:22, 34).

The quality of life in rural areas did not improve after the Korean War, largely because of rapid population growth and increased agricultural density. The pressure on the land was already apparent under colonial rule (average landholding per farm declining by about 12 percent between 1918 and 1936), and although the number of independent farm households remained steady (at just over 0.5 million during 1914–40), representing roughly one-fifth of all households, the proportion of tenant farming had increased to more than half of all households by 1940 (H. Choi 1971:264–65). After the Korean War, rural poverty resulted in another massive influx into the cities.

Because of the desperate economic conditions, there was a strong desire at both individual and collective levels to find any means available in urban areas to overcome poverty. The urbanward migrants crowded into the slums of Seoul and Pusan, where the need to survive fostered an increase in unskilled and semi-skilled employment, such as unskilled construction workers, street vendors, tailors, cooks, and drivers. Later, the rapidly expanding economy, centered mainly on urban areas, attracted increasing numbers of in-migrants from rural areas, and consequently the proportion of the populace engaged in agriculture dwindled.

The gradual inundation of original city dwellers by refugees and other in-migrants brought about important changes in attitudes and self-perception. At the end of the Korean War, the middle class was a very small proportion of the populace—mainly teachers, merchants, lawyers, physicians, government officials, and other educated people. Only a few individuals—notably great landowners and some entrepreneurs—were actually rich, and the vast majority of the populace regarded themselves as poor. This perception was overturned, however, by the relative prosperity and expanding educational opportunities in the 1960s and 1970s. Rapid urbanization exposed an increasing number of rural people to urban occupational opportunities, such as services, sales, and small business. With the economic take-off of the 1960s, most city dwellers were able to find occupational niches. Shacks and shabby shops were replaced by substantial and prosperous-looking buildings, as Seoul's former refugee slums (such as Itaewan, Haebangchon or "Liberation Village," Mok-dong, Oksoo-dong, Eungbong-dong, Sanggye-dong, and Jungkye-dong) were transformed into middle-class districts. Objective statistical indicators during the past several decades reveal a substantial change in the proportion of the population perceiving themselves as middle class—from about 20 percent in 1960 to 30 percent in 1970 and 48 percent in 1980 (D. S. Hong 1980). By 1987, according to a survey published by the newspaper *Dong-a Ilbo*, the number had reached 65 percent. This increase and the emergence of the middle class as the predominant segment of society reflect the effects of rapid economic development on incomes and occupational diversification.

SOCIAL DEVELOPMENT

Social Mobility

Political turmoil and geographical mobility helped to bring about radical changes in social mobility patterns. The cities became melting pots of people from different regions. While some of the poor were growing richer, however, some of the rich were sliding into poverty. Some of the wealthiest Koreans of the 1945–50 period may now be among the poorest, and none of the ten richest Koreans of that period are among the top ten today. Similarly, none of the top ten businessmen from these interwar years would rank among the top 50 today. The patterns of mobility in the Korean business community can thus be characterized as unprecedentedly dynamic.

Lack of education, moreover, no longer seems to be a major barrier to economic mobility, since the owners of today's large business conglomerates received much lower levels of education than the military elite or the nation's bureaucrats.

Meanwhile, the position of the landlord class in the social hierarchy, especially in economic terms, practically ceased to exist. Most former landlords gained possession of their property through inheritance and enjoyed the benefits of rental income. They capitalized on the status accompanying their positions as board members and managed to build positions for themselves in the industrial corporations. After the implementation of land reform, some rich landlords used the compensation received for their land to start businesses and engage in other entrepreneurial activities. Some of the landed class with the biggest landholdings were able to maintain their status in the social hierarchy because of benefits accruing from earlier investments in private educational institutions (such as building schools and universities). The majority of the former landowners, however, joined the ranks of the middle class, and some even became impoverished. Regardless of economic status, most of them could afford to provide an education for their children, thereby enabling their descendants to find places in the universities, other educational institutions, and the major professions.

The rate of social mobility in Korean society has been higher than in other developing countries in recent decades (D. S. Hong 1980:59-99). Rapid social change and turmoil have eroded class boundaries and given the Korean people the idea that the self-perpetuating class is an institution of the past. The fact that anyone with resources, energy, and luck now has the opportunity to climb the social ladder has contributed greatly to the emergence of a strong egalitarian ideology among the masses.

Culture and Values

Large-scale geographic mobility has been accompanied by a dilution of traditional values. As people have moved away from their ancestral lands and parents and have become increasingly profit oriented, they have become less concerned with perpetuating the rituals and customs that reinforce traditional values and passing them on to the next generation.

Two distinctive features of religious organization in Korea are the low level of professed religious affiliation and the tendency to blur the lines of demarcation between major religions. One analysis of 1983 data (I. H. Yun 1985) showed that fewer than 40 percent of the population categorized themselves under a specific religion—that is, 18.9 percent (7.5 million people) were Buddhist, 13.5 percent (5.3 million people) were Protestant, and 4.0 percent (1.6 million people) were Catholic. The analysis showed further that, after a pattern of steady growth during 1971–81, there was a decrease in the numbers of both Buddhists and Protestants between 1981 and 1983. The decline was especially sharp in the case of Buddhists, probably reflecting a change in self-categorization. Some persons may have upheld a set of values drawn variously from Buddhism, Christianity, and Confucianism, formerly declaring themselves under one group but later preferring to place themselves in no specific category. (This factor, which is basically one of definition, does not apply to Catholics, who registered a slow but steady increase in number throughout the period measured.)

The recent alienation from traditional culture has been accompanied by a dilution of the individual discipline that was once typical of the cohesive village community. Urbanization and economic development have been so rapid that the villagers have not had sufficient time to make the necessary social and other adjustments to "urbanism as a way of life." Korean cities, unlike those of Japan, have thus become concentrations of villagers and refugees. The time span of at least a generation will be required for those new city dwellers to make themselves an integral part of the cities and urban life.

At least five broad patterns can be discerned among the changes in individual values since the time of Korean independence. At the end of World War II, everyone's attention was concentrated on patriotism toward the nation in the wake of liberation from colonialism. By the end of the Korean War, however, attitudes had changed, and people placed greater weight on wealth, status, and political power. The attitude that only the end, and not the means, was important led to an erosion in traditional moral values. The 1960s witnessed the recovery of traditional moral values and heightened economic values. During this time, people tended to attach greater value to national development, patriotism, diligence, self-reliance, improved standards of living, and a happy (preferably small or nuclear) family. In the 1970s there was less emphasis on diligence and wealth but greater value was placed on social welfare and a happier life. This period witnessed the emergence of ordinary, nonmaterial aspects of happiness: individualism, equality, social justice, and human rights. The 1970s also witnessed the reemergence of strong family values and respect toward elders. In the 1980s, the trend turned once again toward wealth, but with less emphasis than before on patriotism and national development, as people grew more concerned about health and the pleasures of life. The overall trend indicates that the younger generation of the 1980s exhibits a greater degree of individualism than the older postwar generation and has experienced a transition from family and clan consciousness to a wider social consciousness (Cha 1985).

Student Radicalism

Students have always played a political role by expressing discontent and pressing for political change in the East Asian countries, and student groups have often been hotbeds of radical thought. The 1960 student protests in Korea against corruption and dictatorship helped to overthrow the regime of Syngman Rhee. Later in the 1960s Korean students organized massive demonstrations to protest the normalization of relations with Japan (just as Japanese students protested violently in the 1950s against the Japan–U.S. security treaty). Massive student demonstrations in 1986 and 1987 called for democratic reform and an end to the military regime under President Chun. (During the past few years, students in China likewise have called for more democratic freedoms and a relaxation of the prevailing communist ideology.) Student rioting and occupation of university buildings in 1988 seems to have taken an even more violent turn, reflecting a more radical ideology that is anti-establishment, anti-capitalist, and anti-American; in its opposition to rapid economic development and international trade dependence, it is also to some extent anti-development. (For an academic approach to dependency issues affecting Korean development, see K. D. Kim 1987.) An intriguing facet of student radicalism is the effort to heighten nationalist sentiments by demanding the unification of North and South Korea at any cost. It is instructive to examine this radicalization from the perspective of the contrasting experiences of successive generations of Korean society.

Student radicalism is related in some ways to the demographic transition, reflecting the change from high to low fertility levels and from poverty to prosperity. A common pattern can be discerned in societies that have undergone extended periods of depression followed by relative prosperity. In the United States, for example, the fertility rate was low during the depression of the 1930s and the war of the early 1940s. Postwar economic prosperity was accompanied by a baby boom, and the parents who suffered during the depression and war years were anxious to provide their children with everything that they had never been able to afford for themselves. But in lavishing upon their children all the necessities of life, a good education, and other luxuries, they brought up the new generation in the absence of want. As the generation of the baby boom approached adulthood—a more numerous generation, reflecting the rise in fertility and consequent population increase—many of them were not inculcated with the older generation's values such as respect for authority and hard work. The anti-establishment protests of the 1960s and 1970s were thus partly a reflection of the markedly different conditions prevailing during the formative years of the two generations—hence the tendency to oppose or reject whatever their parents had established or believed. This phenomenon is also apparent among the radicalized Japanese students of the 1950s who had not experienced the economic difficulties and war of their parents' generation.

In China a double reversal of a similar behavioral pattern can be discerned. Some of the elderly generation among China's leaders came from the landed class and, in their youth, had heated arguments with their parents over the perpetuation of feudalism, the exploitation of land rights, and the misery of their tenants. That generation a half century ago sought a solution in the absolute equality implicit in communist philosophy. The children of today's leaders, on the other hand, have grown up in the absence of war and have not suffered the deprivations that their parents did. In Chinese cities at least, standards of living have improved greatly in recent years. And yet the extreme poverty of the majority of the population increasingly stands out in contrast to the better standards of living enjoyed by urban dwellers and by farmers with access to nonstate markets. The dinner-table debate in the leaders' homes has thus shifted in the opposite direction, and many younger Chinese now declare that the older generation has failed to modernize China and has left it one of the world's poorer countries.

The radicalization of Korean students can be better understood in the context of this behavioral pattern of action and reaction by successive generations against the values of their parents' generation. In Korea and China alike, authoritarianism and the traditional ideal of collective work served to motivate people, to help them overcome poverty, and to promote development. But as people grow richer, the desire for more individual freedom emerges. Because of this inherent conflict, a certain amount of political and economic change becomes inevitable. If a regime becomes so rigid and entrenched that it does not respond to these generational changes, then further radicalization and conflict likewise seem inevitable.

REGIONAL POLARIZATION

One interesting phenomenon, despite massive movements of people from rural to urban areas and from one province to another, is the persistence of regional or provincial differentiation. The sharpest geographical and political division is between two traditional rival regions—Kyŏngsang and Chŏlla. This conflict is deeply imbedded in Korean history and can be traced back to the struggles during the first millenium A.D. between the two kingdoms of Silla (modern Kyŏngsang) and Paekje (modern Chŏlla)—from which Silla emerged the victor. The interprovincial conflicts were brought into increasingly sharper focus by 1950–53 wartime conditions, post-Korean War industrialization, and the presidential election campaign of 1971.[1]

The southeastern part of the country is divided into North Kyŏngsang (which includes Taegu, the nation's third largest city), and South Kyŏngsang (which until 1966 included Pusan, Korea's second largest city). Kyŏngsang has the largest population of any part of the country, and its people have played a predominant role in national politics, business, and the military since the military coup of 1961. All nine army chiefs of staff between

---

1. Kim Dae Jung, an opposition leader from Chŏlla, lost the 1971 presidential election to Park Chung Hee (a Kyŏngsang native) by a small margin.

1966 and 1985, for example, were of Kyŏngsang origin, as were Presidents Park, Chun, and Roh. Among the heads of the leading conglomerates, those of Kyŏngsang origin would certainly constitute a majority. The Kyŏngsang region not only has two of the largest Korean cities but also has industrialized much faster than the two neighboring Chŏlla provinces, which constitute the southwestern extremity of the peninsula. Although Chŏlla's two main cities (Kwangju and Chunju) have become important industrial centers, Chŏlla was unable to maintain parity with Kyŏngsang in its shares of political and military leadership. This was partly because Chŏlla was geographically outside the mainline transportation network developed under Japanese rule and remained mostly agricultural. It was also partly a result of the fortunes of war.

Given the infrastructure that existed at the time of liberation (most notably the Japanese-built harbor facilities and the Pusan–Seoul rail line), scarce capital was obviously better invested in the regions around Seoul and Pusan. President Park Chung Hee, himself a native of Kyŏngsang, made an effort to develop the Chŏlla region during the 1960s, but the philosophy of "growth first, distribution later" in this context reflects the undeniable fact that, for lack of capital and resources, all parts of the country could not undergo economic growth simultaneously or at equal rates. For the long-term benefit of the country as a whole, investment had to be concentrated first on the best economic assets, although in the short term this uneven growth pattern inevitably resulted in income differentials between the rapidly developing southeast and the more slowly developing southwest. In 1970 per capita incomes were 85,000 won for Kyŏngsang and 59,000 won for Chŏlla (when the national average was 70,000 won), compared to 8,400 won and 7,500 won, respectively, in 1960 (when the national average was 9,500 won) (Hong and Cho 1986). The persistence of these differentials between the two provinces is amazing in some ways, particularly since economic development has provided mass communications and an elaborate transportation system, making the country much "smaller" than it was prior to the Korean War in terms of interactions. These differentials were manifested in the 1987 presidential and parliamentary elections, in which the people of Chŏlla denounced the apparent economic and political discrimination by the governments of the past quarter century against Chŏlla and in favor of Kyŏngsang. To expedite the initial stage of economic development, however, such regional imbalance was probably unavoidable in the short term.

During the Korean War, the initial offensive from the North in 1950 pushed the South Korean forces into a relatively small perimeter in the southeast, including Pusan (which became the provisional capital) and Taegu. Although a counter-offensive moved the front line north beyond Seoul later the same year, a renewed North Korean offensive shifted it back into the south by early 1951. At the very beginning of the war, therefore, the two Chŏlla provinces became occupied territory. For security reasons, anyone from Chŏlla or other provinces overrun by the enemy came under close scrutiny because of the danger of enemy infiltration among the civilian populace.

The emergency conditions necessitated an unparalleled expansion of the military academy, which had to rapidly provide commissions to meet the need for more officers to conduct the war. The members of Class 10 were commissioned immediately after their entry in July 1950, and the academy was then closed temporarily. Subsequent officer trainees were recruited, given a month's training, and transferred to the army's training school. The regular four-year training program resumed only in early 1952, when the academy was reopened in Chinhae, a naval base near Pusan.

During the next few years recruitment in the army was apparently concentrated among young men from the surrounding Kyŏngsang area, and entrants to the reopened academy were drawn from both this area and the enlisted ranks. It was almost impossible for men living in enemy-occupied areas to reach Pusan, and the security clearance required of each entrant excluded virtually everyone outside Kyŏngsang. Security clearances likewise excluded prospective university students from those areas. People from the other provinces lost out by default, because of the geographic and strategic position of Kyŏngsang during a brief period of rapid expansion of military personnel. The effects of these wartime conditions are still being felt, manifested during the 1980s by increasing tension in the two Chŏlla provinces during the presidency of Chun Doo Hwan (1981–87) and the 1987 election campaign of President Roh Tae Woo, both of Kyŏngsang origin and commissioned with Class 11—the first regular graduates after the academy was reopened in the Kyŏngsang area.

POSTWAR INSTITUTIONAL CHANGES

Status of the Military

Immediately after liberation, particularly in the South, a career in the military was not regarded with high esteem. This perception was shaped by Chinese cultural influences over recent centuries. Soldiers were looked down upon, whereas the literati-cum-officials were granted high professional prestige, arising from Confucian values and emphasis on scholarship but disdain for military prowess.

The military elite of the post-Korean War period and of today were drawn mostly from the agricultural and the urban working classes. Military officers are likely to be the sons of farmers, shopkeepers, or blue-collar workers. Many of the early entrants into the military after national liberation in 1945 had served in the Japanese army as enlisted men or as student conscripts. The ranks of the armed forces were expanded by refugees from North Korea who were not successful in finding stable occupations in the South. In addition, some who joined the new Korean military service had gone through the regular selection process in the Japanese military academy and had served as officers. Park Chung Hee, for example, served as an officer in Japan's Manchurian Army.

The outbreak of the Korean War necessitated a dramatic expansion of the Korean armed forces. All those in uniform before the war (competent or not) who survived the war were propelled up the social ladder. This was an unprecedented opportunity for upward social mobility and for gaining access to leadership positions in society. Such a phenomenon would never have occurred had the war not broken out. It is reflected in the educational attainment of today's military elite, who have achieved a level of education comparable to that of the civil service or almost any other sector of Korean society outside academia.

Among the Korean government elite, there appears to be a value congruence between those who have a military background and those who do not (Hong and Cho 1986). The political party elite with a military background tend to hold an attitude similar to that of the professional military elite. The military elite, moreover, share much in common with owners of small businesses in their perceptions of economic development and social harmony. The military elite are more progressive in their views regarding policies for redistribution of income than are corporate executives and owners of large businesses. Over the period of great upheaval and change after independence, Koreans have become more egalitarian-minded about the distribution of wealth. This is an important perceptional change that accompanied social change during the Park period.

Legacy of the Colonial Legal System

The executive branch of the independent government of Korea was patterned on the structure that existed during the Japanese colonial period, although it was modified and enlarged to suit the needs of the newly liberated nation. Many of the bureaucrats who served the Japanese administration were promoted and continued in government service when the First Republic was established. With the exception of the top leadership, therefore, the executive branch experienced no clear break with the past. For this reason, the workings of the colonial bureaucracy—including attitudes, values, and practices—were perpetuated to some extent after independence.

The judicial branch likewise was based on the system instituted during the colonial period, including both a law code patterned after continental European law and a legal profession trained at Keijo Imperial University in Seoul or universities in Japan. In theory, the Korean legal system and laws from the First Republic onward were designed to serve and protect the people. In practice, however, Korean lawyers and judges helped to perpetuate the colonial concept that the legal system served primarily as a means of exercising control over the population. Not surprisingly, therefore, many people continued to believe, even after the representative system of government was established, that laws were formulated to serve the elite rather than the ordinary citizen. This perception did not foster a sense of respect for the legal system, and people tended to avoid compliance if they could do so without personal risk. Although a more rational attitude has gradually evolved, the perceptions ingrained during the colonial period still linger, and lack of respect for the law still contributes to inadequate enforcement (Yang 1985). Many people fail to perceive the civil code as an instrument that helps to guarantee their rights, and they regard legal action as an embarrassment to family honor and social status. Because of this aversion to litigation, there is a tendency to pursue out-of-court settlements, which in turn reinforces the lack of confidence in and respect for the legal system.

Rise of the Labor Movement

Although Korea has a long tradition of labor unions, the labor movement was shaped by the conditions under which it evolved during the period of Japanese colonialism from 1910 to 1945. Neither before nor after independence did appropriate institutions evolve to accommodate the resolution of conflict between labor and management, and in some ways the legacy of the colonial period still lingers.

Two major features of the Korean labor movement bear the imprint of the colonial period. Under Japanese rule, the workers were all Korean whereas management was mostly Japanese. The more defiance demonstrated by labor leaders against Japanese management, the more patriotic they appeared to their fellow Koreans. Such circumstances precluded any system of compromise—which was equated with "collaboration" and portrayed as a betrayal of the rank-and-file Korean workers. Under these circumstances, the labor movement developed a political and anti-colonial orientation rather than concentrating primarily on negotiations for increased pay and improved working conditions. Hence the process of institutionalization to achieve Western-style, business-like trade unionism was stifled by circumstances that also nurtured a tradition of violence as the principal recourse in resolving conflict.

After the Korean War, the government formulated an elaborate program of labor legislation. The laws that were enacted in the mid-1950s, however, were not a response to labor-management needs but were designed instead to counterbalance North Korean propaganda. (In essence, when the communist government began publicizing North Korea as a laborers' paradise, Syngman Rhee's government enacted new laws designed to show that labor conditions in the South were even better.) Because industry and government alike could not afford to provide all workers simultaneously with an attractive package of benefits, it was obvious to labor leaders that the statutory requirements were merely window dressing. Furthermore, the absence of an institutionalized labor movement in Korea itself forced the lawmakers to look elsewhere for precedents and models. Their draft legislation was thus copied largely from labor laws recently enacted in Japan, which in turn were based on American models of the postwar Allied occupation period.

The Japanese did not find such models to be entirely appropriate for conditions in Japan, and they did not enforce all legal stipulations to the letter of the law.

The unfortunate consequence of these contradictions is that, from the outset, all concerned parties simply disregarded the Korean labor laws. Employers could not afford to provide all the benefits and did not abide by the law. Labor leaders, on the other hand, could not get the government to enforce the law. This cycle of delinquincy-by-default prevented the growth of any sense of mutual obligations among the three parties and established a behavioral pattern that has persisted up to the present.

The colonial tradition of violence and confrontation as the principal alternative to compromise likewise persists and is particularly noticeable in recurrent crowd behavior that shows no regard for rules or order. The curtailment of individual political rights during the 1970s and 1980s, moreover, exacerbated the pent-up feelings of the younger generation at a time of dramatic rise in the level of education, increased international communications, and greater awareness of labor- and political-rights activities in other countries. Amidst these rapid changes, the labor movement was muted most of the time, although there were occasional explosive outbursts—such as the violence that erupted in the last year of the Park administration.

With the political liberalization that began in 1987, the relationship between labor and management began to change dramatically. Up to this time, labor disruptions were relatively rare in Korea, whereas during a two-month period alone in 1987 there were 3,300 recorded labor disputes (all wildcat strikes). Unless there is a major political reversal, the labor movement will continue to emerge as a major factor in politics and the economy. Many years will be needed, however, for the three parties concerned—government, management, and the unions—to develop institutional arrangements for conducting peaceful negotiations and procedures for settling labor disputes, thereby achieving the genuine objectives of a labor union: material benefits for the rank and file, participatory satisfaction of members, institutional constraints, and a respect for law and order.

Viewed from the present time, it may be instructive to ponder whether the rapid industrialization and rapid growth accomplished by the Park regime were worth the restriction of public participation and civil liberties. When material benefits must be considered together with social and political costs, how should the national ledgers of rapid industrialization and rapid growth be balanced? Although the costs of economic development are by no means negligible, should not economic development be imperative, when it is the sole alternative for eliminating extreme poverty? For those who wish to study what to emulate and what to avoid by drawing comparisons from the past, the experiences of Korea provide a useful perspective on the question of whether political development can or should be postponed under certain circumstances.

PART IV
EPILOGUE

24 Political, Economic, and Social Developments in the 1980s

by Lee-Jay Cho and Yoon Hyung Kim

RETROSPECTIVE ON THE PARK ERA

The two decades of political stability that President Park Chung Hee maintained through his dexterous political skill and firm leadership, paved the way for rapid economic growth in Korea. The Park government took rapid economic growth and the elimination of absolute poverty as its major goals and assumed the role that many political economists attribute to the capitalist developmental state.[1] Government played an increasingly active role in managing the economy, beginning with the launching of the First Five-Year Economic Development Plan and nationalization of all commercial banks in 1961. To overcome rural poverty and motivate the rural people to participate in improving their situation, the government launched the Saemaul (new community) movement, which aimed at rapid rural development and transformation. President Park also fostered the development of a strong, efficient, and effective economic bureaucracy, enhancing its capabilities in formulating and implementing policies reflecting the government's active role in the economy. Institutions and legal systems were forged to facilitate the implementation of the developmental priorities of the government. In these ways, the government laid the foundation for subsequent economic growth.

During the rapid international changes of the 1970s, in particular the U.S. initiative in developing a political and economic relationship with China and the possibility of a U.S. troop withdrawal from Korea, President Park's strong and effective government led Korea not only in dealing effectively with national security issues but also in readjusting the structure of the entire Korean economy to achieve long-term goals.

The government's basic purpose in intervening in the management of the economy at that time was to create the infrastructure needed for self-defense by accelerating the development of heavy industry. Under the Heavy and Chemical Industries Promotion Plan, announced in 1973, the new industrial strategy was to restructure Korean industry by shifting

---

1. The "capitalist developmental state" exists when the state leads economic development—"when it mobilizes and allocates capital, when it licenses or subcontracts its projects to private entrepreneurs, and when it plays the predominant role in controlling the organization of workers. . . . Korea since 1961 is a prime example" (Johnson 1989).

manufacturing output and exports away from light manufactured goods toward more sophisticated and high value-added industrial goods. The government chose to emphasize the heavy and chemical industries not only because of national defense concerns but also in anticipation of the industrial transition from the prevailing labor-intensive types of production to capital-intensive industries.

The government's heavy-handed intervention in the big push for heavy and chemical industrialization has frequently been criticized for creating overcapacity (particularly in machinery and shipbuilding) and causing a sectoral imbalance in investment. Although the Heavy and Chemical Industry Promotion Plan was on the whole consistent with Korea's drive for greater competitiveness and emerging advantage in international markets, the pace was too rapid. The plan was also criticized for its excessive cost. The development plan for the heavy and chemical industries, which absorbed a large percentage of the nation's financial resources, essentially replaced market tests for performance with bureaucratic judgment.

The late 1970s can be characterized as a tumultuous period of rough-riding and risk-taking for the government. The biggest risk was the push for heavy and chemical industrialization, which could have had serious repercussions on the national economy if the destabilizing factors had not been managed properly. Inflationary pressure had built up during the earlier expansionary response to the oil shock of 1973–74, and it was accelerated during the second half of the 1970s by the massive injections of capital in the heavy and chemical industries and the increase in the money supply resulting from the sudden influx of foreign exchange earnings from the Middle East. The introduction of a value-added tax system in 1977 exacerbated the already serious inflationary pressure, because it necessitated an across-the-board adjustment of the entire price structure. The weakening of export competitiveness, inflationary distortions in resource allocation, and growing frustration among workers (who were increasingly aware of the widening disparity in the distribution of wealth and income) pointed to chronic inflation as a principal force undermining economic health. It became clear that sustained economic growth would be difficult unless inflation was curbed. In April 1979 the government announced the Comprehensive Stabilization Program to control aggregate demand through restrictive fiscal and monetary management and investment adjustment in the heavy and chemical industries.

The single most destabilizing factor for Korea was the assassination of President Park in October 1979, which sent shock waves through government, the business community, and the general public. The shock was so great that, for the first time in almost two decades, the Korean economy recorded a negative growth rate (−3.7 percent) in the following year. Although the economy quickly regained its high growth rate, the assassination marked the end of almost two decades of unprecedented political stability under strong political leadership.

President Choi Kyu Hah, who automatically succeeded to the presidency under the existing *Yushin* constitution, did not demonstrate the strong leadership needed in early 1980 to restore political stability and to direct and manage the national economy. The consequences for the economy were disastrous and the morale of the business community and general public ebbed to its lowest point. The situation was worsened by large-scale student demonstrations and disorder.

President Park had built up the nation's military capabilities to face external aggression, but he had not developed institutional arrangements to ensure a smooth and peaceful succession in the leadership. Thus, when the nation abruptly became leaderless in late 1979, the military was in the strongest position to fill the power vacuum and had a further advantage because of its role in maintaining law and order. General Chun Doo Hwan became the most powerful leader within the military after the December Twelfth (1979) Incident (also known as the "Night of the Generals"). At that time, the younger officers who were allied to General Chun (then chief of the military security command) and his classmates consolidated their power. On 18 May 1980 full martial law was declared and the military assumed control of national administration.[2] President Choi subsequently resigned.

General Chun was elected to serve for the remainder of the current presidential term, as stipulated under the constitution, by the National Reunification Assembly (which was created in the latter part of the Park regime). In June 1980 the military government established the National Security Council, which was expanded in August 1980 into an interim legislative body to draft a new constitution. The new constitution, ushering in the Fifth Republic, was approved by a plebiscite conducted under martial law in October. A new election law instituted the electoral college system for the selection of the president and also limited the president to a single, seven-year term. The presidential election was held in December 1980, and Chun was elected. A new National Assembly was elected in March 1981.

---

2. In addition to imposing martial law, the Korean authorities arrested opposition political leaders and closed the universities. These actions led to massive protests in the city of Kwangju, which is located in the home province (Chŏlla) of opposition leader Kim Dae Jung. These protests, characterized as riots during the Chun regime, were recently described as prodemocracy demonstrations by President Roh Tae Woo. After the protesters gained control of the city the military instituted a siege and finally mounted a full-scale assault. By the time the military regained control of the city on 27 May 1980, 190 civilians had been killed.

The Kwangju tragedy remains a major issue in Korean politics, exacerbating regional tensions between Chŏlla and Kyŏngsang provinces. A special committee on investigation of the Kwangju incident was formed in the National Assembly in June 1989 and President Roh has called for early implementation of measures to compensate the families of those killed during the military suppression of the civil uprising.

RETROSPECTIVE ON THE FIFTH REPUBLIC, 1980–87

The Just Society

From the outset, a reformist and puritanical stance was adopted by the younger military officers who were the principal architects of the Fifth Republic and the advocates of a "Just Society." The first step in the realization of this goal was to retire a number of politicians belonging to both the progovernment majority and the opposition parties, because the government considered them to be obstacles to forming a new society. Also as part of the "purification" drive, the Chun regime purged nearly 8,000 civil servants in July 1980.[3] The puritanical tendencies were strengthened by the elimination of part of the news media and the consolidation of newspaper and broadcasting companies under state control, with the official aim of remolding the news media into a "more desirable, ethical, and healthy" industry.[4] In its efforts to "purify" Korean society, the Chun government also sent so-called troublemakers (gangsters, hoodlums, armed robbers, rapists, pimps, and other chronic lawbreakers) to the Samchong re-education camps, with the goals of training the individuals to be useful citizens and instilling greater social discipline in general.[5]

By 1982 a certain distance had developed between the more puritan-minded young officers and the older cohort headed by President Chun. The gap between the opposing views widened as a result of the "Lady Chang scandal" over financial maneuvering in which relatives of the president's wife were implicated. Ultimately, disagreements about ethics in running the government culminated in the departure of the younger cohort from the center of political power. Their major objection was the involvement of the president's relatives in financial dealings and government affairs. In 1982 President Chun consolidated his political power and established his own political base.

---

3. After the establishment of the Sixth Republic, the government of President Roh Tae Woo began to re-examine its predecessor's actions during this period and has, for example, offered a formal apology and a pledge of monetary compensation to thousands of former civil servants who were dismissed in the 1980 purge.

4. In November 1990 a Seoul lawcourt ordered Munhwa Broadcasting Corporation, the only private broadcasting company in Korea, to return some of its shares to their original owners, who were stripped of their holdings by the Defense Security Command Investigators in the forced media merger of 1980. This is the first instance in which the judiciary has ruled that the military intelligence authorities' acts, committed in the course of the 1980 media merger, were a "serious breach of the Constitution and law" (*The Korea Times*, 2 November 1990; *The Korea Herald*, 2 November 1990).

5. The criteria for designating "troublemakers" were arbitrary and some innocent people were sent to the camps. There were instances of mismanagement of the camps and abuses of inmates' human rights—including wrongful death and torture. President Roh has promised to restore honor and provide compensation to the innocent victims of the Samchong camps.

In the succeeding years, the younger cohort and their puritanical orientation had a decreasing influence, and the president did not eliminate the practices that they strongly cautioned against. In spite of their objections, for example, the president's younger brother continued in his position as head of the Saemaul movement. During the Sixth Republic he was charged with illegally mobilizing political contributions through the Saemaul movement, which was intended to be a pure and clean rural development organization operated on a voluntary basis. He was convicted and is still serving a 13-year prison sentence.

Although a good military leader, and very able in mobilizing and taking care of his troops, President Chun was not endowed with the political acumen and vision that came naturally to President Park. His lack of experience in politics helped to perpetuate the authoritarian features of the Park regime, while differing from it in important ways. One factor that ultimately contributed to his political downfall was his "taking care of" and mismanagement of his relatives. A second was his arbitrary use of power while lacking any long-term political vision or philosophy of government. He conveyed the image of a nice and personable man. But he did not appreciate or understand the fundamental meanings and consequences of power.

The tight monitoring of political contributions from the business community in the initial stage of the Chun administration represents a change that is not fully recognized by the general public. During the time of President Park Chung Hee, the channel of political contributions was decentralized. President Park distanced himself personally and left the task of gathering and managing such funds to the political leaders and senior government officials serving him. To combat this system, which made certain parts of the bureaucracy and some politicians amenable to corruption, the younger puritanical cohort instituted a monitoring system early in the Chun administration, as part of the movement toward clean government. The system monitored the business community's political contributions to and financial dealings with higher levels of the executive branch (including cabinet members) and with senior politicians in the legislature. The president himself concentrated most of these financial dealings at the very top of the administration, sometimes acting through his close associates and frequently also his relatives. Thus the president and his relatives eventually bore the full brunt of the assault on corruption.[6] There were no major leakages of contributions to the cabinet and senior politicians who, under Chun's watchful eye, were thus spared from involvement in corruption scandals. In this sense, some progress may have been achieved in institutionalizing a system to resist major corruption in the middle and lower echelons.

---

6. After leaving office former President Chun Doo Hwan apologized to the nation for the abuses and failings of his administration and went into seclusion at Pakdam Temple in September 1988.

Contributions to Economic Development

With his vision of the "Just Society," President Chun established his own goal of making "My Country, an Advanced Country." He placed great emphasis on mobilizing competent technocrats and academics to promote development. The 1980s represent a period of economic stabilization and liberalization for Korea, with the government still maintaining high growth. From the economic modernization perspective, the achievements of the Fifth Republic were substantial. The positive contributions that can be credited to the Fifth Republic can be assessed under the following three major areas related to economic development.

Economic progress. Despite the rocky start in the 1980–81 period of severe recession, the economic performance of Korea in the 1980s has been excellent. When the Chun regime came to power, the Korean economy was beset by the strains and structural imbalances created by the heavy and chemical industry drive of the 1970s and the second oil crisis. There were strong inflationary pressures, rapidly rising unit labor costs, a negative real interest rate, and sectoral bias in incentives. These internal imbalances were aggravated by the second oil crisis, the surge in international interest rates, and the onset of the international recession.

This confluence of events, coupled with poor harvests and the domestic political uncertainties caused by the assassination of President Park, brought the Korean economy to a state of crisis in early 1980. Consequently, during 1980 the Korean economy experienced, for the first time in modern economic history, a negative real growth rate (−3.7 percent), which was accompanied by a 39-percent jump in the wholesale price index and a current account deficit that reached 9.4 percent ($5.3 billion) of GNP (Table 24.1).

Given these circumstances, the Chun government embarked on stabilization and structural adjustment as its overriding objectives in economic policy. The macroeconomic policies followed were essentially a strong implementation of the restrictive monetary, fiscal austerity, and wage control policies initiated by the Park government in 1979. President Chun's political leadership and commitment to the stabilization policy successfully eradicated the chronic high inflation from which the country had suffered since the start of modernization and that had seriously undermined the country's growth potential, particularly in the latter part of the 1970s. The inflation rate declined sharply from 39.0 percent in 1980 to 4.6 percent in 1982 and remained at less than 1.0 percent during 1983–87. The current account deficit declined to $1.6 billion in 1983 and further to $1.4 billion in 1984. In the meantime, the GNP growth rate averaged 9.7 percent during 1982–84. In 1985 a sharp fall-off in export growth caused by the international recession led to a reduced GNP growth rate of 7.0 percent (Table 24.1).

In addition to the stabilization program, the Chun government in 1981–82

Table 24.1. Major indicators of the Korean economy: 1979–89

	1979	1980	1981	1982	1983	1984	1985	1986	1987	1988	1989
GNP growth rate (%)	7.2	-3.7	5.9	7.2	12.6	9.3	7.0	12.9	12.9	12.4	6.7[a]
Per capita GNP (US $)	1,644	1,592	1,734	1,824	2,002	2,158	2,194	2,505	3,110	4,127	4,968[a]
Current account balance (10^9 US $)	-4.2	-5.3	-4.7	-2.7	-1.6	-1.4	-0.9	4.6	9.9	14.2	5.1
Inflation rate (%)											
Wholesale prices	18.6	39.0	20.4	4.6	0.2	0.7	0.9	-1.5	0.5	2.7	1.5
Consumer prices	18.2	28.7	21.6	7.1	3.4	2.3	2.5	2.8	3.0	7.1	5.7
GNP deflator	19.6	24.0	16.9	7.1	5.0	3.9	4.2	2.7	3.4	5.9	4.7
Wages	28.3	23.4	20.7	15.8	11.0	8.7	9.2	8.2	10.1	15.5	21.1
Expansion of money supply[b] (%)											
Narrowly defined (M_1)	20.7	16.3	4.6	45.6	17.0	0.5	10.8	16.6	14.7	20.2	17.9
Broadly defined (M_2)	24.6	26.9	25.0	27.0	15.2	7.7	15.6	18.4	19.1	21.5	19.8
Interest rates[b] (%)											
One-year time deposits	18.6	19.5	16.2	8.0	8.0	10.0	10.0	10.0	10.0	10.0	10.0
General loans (one-year)	19.0	20.0	17.0	10.0	10.0	10.0–11.5	10.0–11.5	10.0–11.5	10.0–11.5	11.0–13.0	10.0–12.5
Exchange rate (won/US $)	484.0	659.9	700.5	748.8	795.5	827.4	890.2	861.4	792.3	684.1	679.6
Gini coefficent[c]	0.373	0.389	u	u	u	u	0.345	u	u	0.336	u

Sources: BOK, *Economic Statistics Yearbook* (1990); EPB, ROK, *Major Statistics* (1990).

a. Preliminary.
b. Year-end.
c. For all families. The Gini coefficient is a measure of inequality in income distribution. The ratio may vary between 0 (no inequality) and 1 (complete inequality).
u–unavailable.

undertook major structural adjustment programs that a democratic government would have found difficult to implement. These economic reforms were aimed at dismantling the regulations that were constraining the capacity of the Korean economy to adjust to the new external and internal environments. As a first step toward financial liberalization, the Chun administration started denationalizing commercial banks in 1981 by disinvesting the government's share. By 1983 the government turned all nationwide city banks over to private ownership and reduced its control over day-to-day operations. To promote competition among banks, two new nationwide commercial banks—joint ventures with foreign banks—were authorized. Perhaps the most important part of the financial reform was the rearrangement of the interest rate structure. Although the monetary authorities still maintain interest-rate ceilings on bank deposits and loans, the real rate of interest has been kept positive since 1981. The autonomy and the efficiency of the banking industry, however, have been limited by the bailouts of depressed industries and the accumulated substantial amounts of nonperforming assets (loans) of nationwide commercial banks.

To improve industrial efficiency, a fundamental policy reform was instituted which aimed at reducing the government's direction of and control over investment decision making and at increasing the industry's exposure to market forces and external competition. The Fair Trade Law was promulgated in 1981 to guard against anticompetitive mergers, unfair advertising, and restrictive trade practices. The Chun government bypassed competitive solutions in most of its restructuring operations. Nevertheless, there were justifications for some of the interventions, because financial distress was so widespread that it threatened the viability of the commercial banks as a group. Most significant, the government began to reverse its past preference for large, heavy-industry firms by reserving credit for small and medium-size firms. Thus industrial policy became more neutral.

Finally, the Chun government committed itself to reforming the import regime, so that by 1986 it would reach the level of liberalization achieved by industrialized countries, and to overhauling the import-tariff schedule to reduce both the average level and the spread of tariff rates. The Tariff Reform Act, promulgated in 1984, included phased general reductions in tariff levels and charges, aimed at creating greater uniformity in tariff rates.

Restrained macroeconomic policies, combined with major structural reforms on the supply side, enabled Korea not only to achieve price stability and industrial efficiency but also to be well-positioned to take advantage in the first quarter of 1986 of an exceptionally favorable sequence of developments in the world economy. These events included the steep decline in oil prices, the decline in international interest rates, the sharp depreciation of the U.S. dollar relative to the Japanese yen, and enhanced OECD growth prospects.

All of these developments made it easier for Korea to achieve a balance-of-payments surplus and a high GNP growth rate without exceeding its targets for external debt acquisition and inflation. The decline in the price of oil helped Korea directly by reducing its import bill and indirectly by sparking a higher rate of world economic growth and trade. The decline in interest rates also improved Korea's balance of payments by reducing debt-service payments. These two developments also made it easier to maintain price stability. Finally, the effective devaluation of the won relative to the yen, resulting from the dollar depreciation, enhanced Korea's export prospects, especially in the United States and the European Economic Community, where Korea competes actively with Japan in such important product lines as automobiles, electronic goods, and iron and steel products.

The Korean economy as it entered 1986 started to revitalize, thanks to favorable external conditions and the legacy of strong structural reforms. During the three-year period 1986–88, Korea managed to post very respectable real growth rates, with GNP increments averaging 12.7 percent annually. The current account balance has been in surplus since 1986. As a result, in 1988 GNP exceeded $170 billion, and per capita GNP reached $4,127. The current account surplus amounted to $4.6 billion in 1986 and increased to $9.9 billion in 1987. It further increased to $14.2 billion in 1988 (Table 24.1), due mostly to export expansion and the inflow of foreign currency from the Seoul Olympic Games.

Korea is now faced, however, with various social and economic problems that are the unfortunate byproducts of rapid industrialization and unbalanced modernization. For example, income and wealth distribution, which were quite equitable by world standards in the early 1970s, has deteriorated in recent years; economic policy decision making is now concentrated around highly centralized political power; economic power is highly concentrated in a small number of major corporations; many banks have become financially insolvent; and the relationship between management and labor has turned acrimonious.

One feature created by the restructuring exercise of the 1980s is the problem of "moral hazard." The active government role resulted in a reduction in incentives for taking tough private adjustment decisions. In some cases, firms persisted in borrowing rather than take the hard decisions required to reduce capacity and numbers of employees. Anticipating a government rescue, weak firms postponed adjustment, hoping that their shares in some eventual merger or cartel arranged by the government would represent an improvement over the immediate prospects for scaling down or accepting a private merger proposal. Despite these shortcomings, the government of the Fifth Republic succeeding in remolding business and industry along the lines of a more "modern" industrial structure through its trade liberalization policy and changes in incentives.

Promotion of science and technology. The government's intervention in the promotion of technology is reflected in the establishment of institutions for scientific training and for basic and applied research. There has been a remarkable increase in research and development investment since 1981. Under a "technology drive" policy, investment in science and technology increased from 0.9 percent of GNP in 1981 to 2.2 percent in 1987, and roughly 40 percent of public expenditure on science and technology was channeled to general research and to create and operate special research centers in areas such as energy, resources, machinery, electronics, telecommunications, and chemicals (Ministry of Science and Technology, ROK, 1987). In line with this policy shift, more efforts are being made to improve the research capabilities of universities.

To broaden and intensify the support for research and development activities aimed at industrial innovation, the government began in 1980 to offer tax and financial incentives to the corporate sector. The commercial tax law was revised in 1981 and 1982 to encourage the private sector to promote science and technology. Among the tax incentives for private firms were a 10 percent tax credit on research and development expenditures, a local tax exemption on the purchase of real estate for a research establishment, income tax exemptions for foreign technicians, a tariff reduction on goods imported for research and development, and a lower special consumption tax on products representing new technology. As a result, the number of research centers in the private sector multiplied almost sixfold, from 53 in 1981 to 290 in 1987. Investment in the corporate sector, which was 120 billion won in 1981, increased by a factor of 4.8 by 1985. The development of science and technology was further expedited by the establishment of a national project in 1982 to fund public as well as private-sector joint research and development activities (Ministry of Science and Technology, ROK, 1987).

A long-term plan for the development of science and technology through the year 2000 was launched during the Fifth Republic. The primary emphasis of the plan, which calls for increasing investment in science and technology up to 3.1 percent of GNP by the year 2000, is the development and mobilization of manpower, which involves investment in education and training in basic and applied science and technology within the country. A major effort has been made to recruit highly trained scientists and technicians from abroad, especially from the United States and Western Europe.

The plan is designed to improve the structure and management of research institutions as a means of developing a better system of research. Industry is encouraged to concentrate on industrial technology to improve product quality, increase productivity, and develop more innovative products. Just as President Park contributed in the 1970s to generating the export-oriented mood, President Chun contributed in the 1980s to generating the technology-minded mood. The big corporations are encouraged to develop and invest in their own scientific and technological research activities. The government also offers subsidies to encourage small and medium-size firms to pool their resources and establish applied technology research centers for their mutual benefit.

As a foundation for advancing to the next stage of economic development, Korea must create this scientific research infrastructure and highly trained manpower. The government's plan places great emphasis on "catching up" with more advanced countries at the cutting edge of modern technology, including electronics, genetic engineering, high-tech chemistry, and automation. The government is also trying to promote greater corporate interaction with industries in the United States and other countries. Korean corporations are urged to establish research centers, engage in joint research, and increase their investment in joint ventures in the United States and other advanced countries, and to attract advanced foreign technology to Korea. Such activities contribute to identifying the most advantageous niches that a country the size of Korea can occupy in the international markets. Basic research provides the necessary underpinning for cutting-edge technological development. But Korea does not have to be a leader in all areas of research. To prosper, it is necessary only to gain timely access to profitable applications or to specialize in something that maintains good terms of trade with countries that have such access or are already research leaders.

Education and welfare programs. Investment in education continued to expand under the Fifth Republic. In the high schools the ratio of students to teachers improved from 45:1 in 1979 to 36:1 in 1987. During the same period, high school enrollment rose from 81 percent to 92 percent, and the number of college and university students trebled from 330,000 to 990,000 (Kang 1989).

Among the significant welfare accomplishments are the compulsory medical insurance system (which applies to both urban and rural areas) and the minimum wage legislation of 1987. Also, a pension system was established in 1988 as part of a larger social security scheme, which is applicable to all firms with 30 or more employees. Infrastructure for rural development was substantially expanded through the construction of houses and roads and the provision of piped water to rural residents. Rural areas have also been provided with greater telephone services, and it is now possible to make a direct-dial international telephone call from almost any village in the country.

Some recent social indicators reflect continued success in combating rural poverty. Between 1980 and 1987 the national average per capita daily intake of protein increased by 50 percent. Between 1980 and 1985, the proportion of Korean households possessing a refrigerator rose from 39 percent to 70 percent and those equipped with a telephone increased from 22 percent to 50 percent. Income distribution, as measured by the Gini coefficient, has shown a gradual improvement from the late 1970s to the mid-1980s, and real annual wage increases of about 7 percent kept up with growth in productivity until the end of the Fifth Republic (Kang 1989).

The latter half of the 1970s saw an increase in public dissatisfaction, even though absolute poverty had been overcome, because of the deterioration in income distribution and the worsening of differentials in regional development. During the 1980s the Chun government responded by increasing investment in social development and making a major effort to achieve more balanced economic growth throughout the country. Between 1982 and 1986, benefiting in part from price stability, the government made at least a slight improvement in income distribution. To bring about a major improvement, however, some drastic institutional reforms would probably have been necessary.

Diminishing Regional Tensions

Prior to the 1970s, when China initiated its open-door policy and began experimenting with the market economy, no progress was made in diminishing mutual hostility between Korea and China. Two international incidents brought the changing relationship between the two countries to the general public's attention and improved the Chinese leadership's image of Korea. The first was the 1983 hijacking of a Chinese airliner, which was forced to land in Korea. The Korean government's considerate treatment of the passengers and the informal intergovernment cooperation that was necessary for their return helped to dampen Chinese hostility toward the government in Seoul. The Chinese perception was further changed by Korea's cooperative response in 1985 when a Chinese torpedo boat entered Korean waters, was briefly detained by the Korean authorities, and was returned with its crew to China.

During the 1980s, much effort was made through business and quiet diplomacy to open and widen the avenues of communication. A notable result was China's decision to send a team to the Seoul Olympics in 1988. Meanwhile, unofficial trade between the two countries has gradually expanded through indirect channels and reached $3.1 billion in 1988. Relations with the Soviet Union have also developed rapidly since the Seoul Olympics, and high-level officials, politicians, and businessmen from Korea have visited the U.S.S.R. in increasing numbers. On 30 September 1990 the Republic of Korea and the Soviet Union announced the immediate establishment of full diplomatic relations.

The international political climate has changed remarkably through the expansion of cultural exchange, international athletics, and other nonpolitical relations. There has been a dramatic increase in trade activities between Korea and her two superpower neighbors, which in turn has contributed to a reduction of political tensions in the region. Economic activities with China were not affected by the June 1989 Tiananmen Square incident and are likely to increase steadily. The development of a substantive economic relationship between Korea and her powerful neighbors is creating a more peaceful mood and helping to ease the tension that persists between North and South Korea.

If these trends continue, the Korean economy will be in a strong position to benefit from further development of economic ties across East Asia. One difficulty is that the policy of the South Korean government toward China, North Korea, and the Soviet Union has been neither well-coordinated nor based on careful economic and political analysis. Many Korean moves relating to these three countries were made in the context of short-term, domestic political gains. In the future, Korea can promote mutually beneficial relations only through a dependable long-term strategy that is consonant with Korea's development in the international context as an economic and political partner.

PERSPECTIVE ON THE SIXTH REPUBLIC: THE 1988 OLYMPICS AND BEYOND

Extraordinary amounts of time and resources were lavished by President Chun and other leaders of the Fifth Republic on the effort to make possible the Seoul Olympic Games in October 1988. Viewing this event partly as a vehicle for exhibiting Korea to the international community as an advanced country, the nation's leaders took great national pride in planning for the games.

The circumstances preceding the games were very fortunate for Korea. The economy was doing extremely well during the years immediately before the games. The government was therefore able to afford the vast expenditure necessary not only for the athletic facilities but also to improve the infrastructure of major Korean cities, thereby accommodating an unusually large amount of travel and tourism both at home and from abroad. Five persons, including President Chun, were the architects and political engineers of the Seoul Olympics. It is ironic that, for political reasons, none of them was able to participate in the opening ceremonies.

Toward the end of the Fifth Republic, student demonstrations over the issue of political legitimacy became more intense and numerous. Massive protests took place in June 1987 in opposition to the president's plan to choose his own successor. On 29 June 1987, a sweeping plan of action for political democratization was announced by the head of the Democratic Justice Party, Mr. Roh Tae Woo, who was not only a presidential candidate but also a close friend, fellow classmate, and subordinate of President Chun. The president reluctantly agreed to these demands, haggling between the government party and the opposition over proposals for a parliamentary system was stopped, and a new constitution was drafted. The new constitution provides for the direct election of the president, who is limited to a single five-year term, and for the election of National Assembly members under the "small election district" system (one member per election district, rather than multiple members per region as before).

In relinquishing his power in a peaceful transition President Chun took an important step. Although a historic event for Korea, it is unlikely to be appreciated as such by Westerners accustomed to rigorous mechanisms for changes of administration and succession to political power. Syngman Rhee was forced out of office in 1960 by student agitation; the Chang Myon government was removed by a military coup in 1961; Park Chung Hee was assassinated in 1979; and Choi Kyu Hah resigned in 1980 under conditions of political instability and pressure from the military. Although compelled to do so under the political circumstances at the time, Chun Doo Hwan is the only leader who served his term and left office according to the provisions of the constitution.

Roh emerged the victor in the fall 1987 presidential election, which marked the beginning of the Sixth Republic, although with only 36 percent of the vote and a slim margin over two of his rivals. He thus became a minority president representing a minority of the popular vote. A potentially more serious problem for the new administration, however, is the regional pattern of voting. The 1987 election dramatized strong emotional and regional appeal of the candidates, as did the April 1988 elections for the National Assembly, when the government party lost its majority, further polarizing the regional differences.

Kim Dae Jung's Peace Democracratic Party got 100 percent of the seats in his home area (Chŏlla). Kim Young Sam's Democratic Party garnered most of the seats in the Pusan Metropolitan Area and neighboring South Kyŏngsang province. Kim Jong Pil's New Republican Party got most of their seats in the leader's home province of South Ch'ungch'ŏng. And the government party got most of their seats from President Roh's home area and the outskirts of the Seoul Metropolitan Area. The absence of a mandate from a cross section of the nation undermines the government's legislative basis for asserting strong political leadership and implementing national development policies.

The Sixth Republic inherited many unresolved problems from the preceding administration. The principal leaders of the Fifth Republic (including former President Chun) were accused of corruption, misuse of power, and extortion of contributions to establish what was perceived to be Chun's own foundation and research institute. Most of the former president's family and relatives were indicted and have received jail sentences, and Chun's personal property (including his house) has been surrendered. A National Assembly hearing on the misconduct of Fifth Republic leaders was in session until the last hour of 1989 but was not able to reach a clear-cut conclusion.

A serious political issue that has persisted into the Sixth Republic is the May 1980 Kwangju incident, in which the military was sent to deal with a prodemocracy demonstration. Some of the protesters had armed themselves, and more than 190 demonstrators were killed in a clash with the army. The responsibility for this incident is still unresolved.

Meanwhile, workers and students have taken to the streets, demanding higher wages and greater democracy. Korean labor unions are organized to an extent unimaginable in Western countries and even cover scientific and technical research institutes. The unions have informed most large and medium-size corporations that they will join in wildcat strikes, which have become a daily routine in the Sixth Republic. The government has been unable to deal with the 25 percent average wage increase demanded by the labor unions. Korean wages are growing much more rapidly than those of their competitors, implying that Korea is losing competitiveness in the international marketplace.

The trade balance began to deteriorate in 1989, and after the middle of the year the monthly balance became negative again. Although the trade and the current account balances for the entire year will still be positive, the magnitude will be much less than in 1988. This deterioration is due mostly to the government's inability to hold wage increases below productivity increases, with the consequent loss of international competitiveness and loss of time due to strikes. Low morale among workers has brought about laxity in production and deliveries. The business community, moreover, has drastically reduced investment, which is the key to increased productivity in subsequent years. In November 1989 the Economic Planning Board declared the current situation an "economic crisis" and planned to take drastic action, starting with the lowering of interest rates.

Despite the spiraling wage increases that are the result of succumbing to union demands, income distribution may not have improved, because of the exorbitant real estate price increases that have ominously affected the pattern of wealth distribution. During the past couple of years, real estate prices have doubled almost yearly in the Seoul metropolitan area, which offsets any gains in wage increases. The increase in the value of land and real estate has thus become a major economic, social, and political issue. Various options for legislation concerning land utilization are under consideration. Based on the "communal concept" of land, the intention is to discourage business conglomerates from speculating in real estate by establishing criteria to identify idle land and taxing it more heavily than land in productive use. In addition, the government may determine that 200 *pyung* (661 square meters or 7,117 square feet) is a reasonable limit for residential use in metropolitan areas. If a plot of residential land exceeds this limit, the portion above 200 *pyung* would bear a form of luxury tax set at a much higher rate. The tax proposals have aroused much controversy.

They are supported by the majority of the population—i.e., those with modest or no land holdings—but corporations and other big landowners are strongly opposed and argue that such laws would violate the basic constitutional right of property ownership.

The government has likewise been unable to deal with student demands. Violent demonstrations have taken place at most universities, accompanied by destruction of university property and equipment. In the span of two years following the end of the Fifth Republic, there was a change of president in virtually every university and college in the country. The lack of discipline among students in the aftermath of chaotic rioting and demonstrations may have a serious effect on the quality of education, which it is essential to improve if Korea is to maintain its competitive edge in the next stage of development of the capital- and technology-intensive economy.

The Sixth Republic began with a great vision of a democratic society. But the rapid swing from authoritarian government to political stalement without clear leadership has produced some negative consequences: the decline in discipline in factories and other places of work, work stoppages and strikes, student demonstrations, seizure of university buildings and influence over university management, the deterioration in law and order, and the increased incidence of rape, violent robbery, and other crimes. As a result, the morale of the middle class and business community has been sinking.

The formulation and implementation of economic policies to solve current problems are rendered all the more difficult by the precarious political situation. Since the opposition parties won a majority of the seats in the 1988 National Assembly elections, the government has been unable to implement effective leadership in economic affairs, and it is becoming clear that Korea will face very difficult economic problems in the next few years. Koreans may have to learn the difficult lessons of a pluralistic, democratic society—its strengths and weaknesses and its costs and benefits—the hard way. It is likely that the Korean electorate, after several years of the current precarious and economically costly political situation will opt for a more stable government and party structure.

In early 1990 the government party and two of the opposition parties led by Kim Young Sam and Kim Jong Pil announced a merger to form the new People's Democratic Liberal Party. This alliance constitutes a majority in the legislature and has managed to convey at least the appearance of moving toward a political solution. The big question in the short term, however, is whether the existing parties can integrate smoothly and effectively to provide stable leadership. Many obstacles must be overcome to create a viable political entity from this merger. The parties are characterized by very different interests, objectives, and personalities and have experienced different patterns of party history and intraparty struggles for leadership and power. Some of Kim Young Sam's followers opted to resign from his party rather than join the alliance. Such factors do not bode well for achieving the political stability required for continued healthy economic performance.

In the long term, however, the vitality, flexibility and hard work of the Koreans will overcome the transitional difficulties facing the country today. Creative and effective leadership will be essential to bring about the institutional changes and reforms required to synergize the hard working labor force and the vitality of entrepreneurs and business leaders toward sustained economic growth and more equitable distribution of the benefits of development. Korea will then emerge as a far stronger economic force in East Asia and the Pacific.

References

Boldface numbers in square brackets after dates of publication represent the chapters in which the referenced works are cited.

Aaron, Henry J. (ed.). 1981. **[11]** *The Value-Added Tax: Lessons from Europe.* Washington, D.C.: Brookings Institution.

Adams, Donald K. 1956. **[22]** Education in Korea, 1945–1955. Unpublished Ph.D. dissertation, University of Connecticut.

Adelman, Irma, and Sherman Robinson. 1978. **[14]** *Income Distribution Policy in Developing Countries: A Case Study of Korea.* Stanford: Published for the World Bank by Stanford University Press.

Administration of Labour Affairs, Republic of Korea (ROK). 1981. **[11]** *Report on Monthly Labour Survey* (June). Seoul.

Agency for International Development (AID), United States (U.S.). 1985. **[1,2,22]** *Foreign Aid and the Development of the Republic of Korea: The Effectiveness of Concessional Assistance.* AID Evaluation Special Study No. 42. Washington.

Allen, Kevin. 1979. **[14]** *Balanced National Growth.* Lexington, Mass.: Lexington Books.

Amsden, Alice H. 1989. **[17]** *Asia's Next Giant: South Korea and Late Industrialization.* New York: Oxford University Press.

Arnold, Fred, and Eddie C. Y. Kuo. 1984. **[12]** The value of daughters and sons: A comparative study of the gender preferences of parents. *Journal of Comparative Family Studies* 15 (Summer):299–318.

Bahl, Roy W., Chuk Kyo Kim, and Chong Kee Park. 1986. **[10]** *Public Finances During the Korean Modernization Process.* Studies in the Modernization of the Republic of Korea, 1945–75. Cambridge, Mass.: Council on East Asian Studies, Harvard University.

Bai, Moo-Ki. 1982. **[20]** The turning point in the Korean economy. *Developing Economies* 20(2):117–40.

Bairoch, P. 1964. **[15]** *Revolution industrielle et sous-developpement.* Paris: n.p.

Balassa, Bela. 1971. **[5]** Industrial policies in Taiwan and Korea. *Weltwirtschaftliches Archiv* 106.

Balassa, Bela, and Associates. 1982. **[5]** *Development Strategies in Semi-Industrial Economies.* Baltimore: Published for the World Bank by Johns Hopkins University Press.

Ban, Sung Hwan, Pal Yong Moon, and Dwight H. Perkins. 1980. **[4]** *Rural Development in Korea, 1945–1975.* Studies in the Modernization of the Republic of Korea, 1945–1975. Cambridge, Mass.: Council on East Asian Studies, Harvard University.

Bank of Korea (BOK). 1960–86, 1990. **[Preface,3,4,5,6,8,9,10,13,14,15,17,20,24]** *Economic Statistics Yearbook.* Annual. Seoul.

621

Bank of Korea (BOK). 1963. **[14]** *Regional Income Accounts, 1962.* Seoul.

Bank of Korea (BOK). 1967. **[6]** *A Survey on Business Finance and the Unorganized Money Market for the First Quarter of 1967.* Seoul.

Bank of Korea (BOK). 1970, 1975, 1978, 1985. **[8,17]** *Input–Output Tables.* Annual. Seoul.

Bank of Korea (BOK). 1973. **[7]** *Report on the Results of the August 3, 1972, Presidential Emergency Decree.* Seoul.

Bank of Korea (BOK). 1974–82, 1985–89. **[3,4,6,7,10,11,17]** *National Income in Korea.* Seoul.

Bank of Korea (BOK). 1977. **[19]** *The Present State of General Trading Companies and Measures Toward Strengthening Their Functions* (in Korean). Seoul.

Bank of Korea (BOK). 1980. **[7]** *Flow of Funds Accounts in Korea.* Annual. Seoul.

Bank of Korea (BOK). 1981. **[7]** *Financial Statements Analysis for 1980.* Seoul.

Bank of Korea (BOK). 1981. **[11]** *Monthly Bulletin* (June). Seoul.

Bank of Korea (BOK). 1982. **[11]** *Price Statistics Summary.* Seoul.

Bank of Korea (BOK). 1982. **[11]** *Quarterly Gross National Product.* Seoul.

Bank of Korea (BOK). 1983. **[3]** *Financial System in Korea.* Seoul.

Bank of Korea (BOK). 1985. **[17]** *The Comparative Advantage of Korean Industries and the Direction of Restructuring* (in Korean). Research Paper 85-15. Seoul.

Bank of Korea (BOK). 1989. **[17]** *Overview of the National Investment Fund* (in Korean). Seoul.

Barringer, Herbert R. 1974. **[14]** Rural–urban migration and social mobility: Studies of three Korean cities. Paper presented at the ILCORK (International Liaison Committee for Research on Korea) Conference, Korea.

Bauer, John, and Young-Soo Shin. 1986. **[12]** Prospects for the Korean labor force. Unpublished paper.

Becker, Gary S. 1960. **[12]** An economic analysis of fertility. In Universities–National Bureau for Economic Research (ed.), *Demographic and Economic Change in Developed Countries.* Princeton: Princeton University Press.

Becker, Gary S., and H. Gregg Lewis. 1973. **[12]** Interaction between quantity and quality of children. *Journal of Political Economy* 81 (March/April): S279–S288.

Ben-Porath, Yoram. 1976. **[12]** Fertility response to child mortality: Micro data from Israel. *Journal of Political Economy* 84 (August): 163–78.

Ben-Porath, Yoram. 1980. **[12]** The F-connection: Families, friends, and firms and the organization of exchange. *Population and Development Review* 6 (March):1–30.

Bhagwati, J. N., and S. Chakravaty. 1969. **[17]** Contributions to Indian economic analysis: A survey. *American Economic Review* 59 (supp. to no. 4).

Bittker, Boris I. 1980. **[10]** Equity, efficiency, and income tax theory. In Henry J. Aaron and Michael J. Boskin (eds.), *The Economics of Taxation.* Washington, D.C.: Brookings Institution.

Bottomley, Anthony. 1963. [6] The premium for risk as a determinant of interest rates in underdeveloped rural areas. *Quarterly Journal of Economics* (November):637–47.

Brown, Gilbert T. 1973. [5,6,10] *Korean Pricing Policies and Economic Development in the 1960s.* Baltimore: Johns Hopkins University Press.

Caldwell, John C. 1976. [12] Toward a restatement of demographic transition theory. *Population and Development Review* 3 and 4 (September/December): 321–66.

Census and Statistics Department, Hong Kong. 1977–83. [9] *Hong Kong Monthly Digest of Statistics.*

Cha, Chae-ho. 1985. [23] Kach'igwan ui pyonhwa (Changes in value system). *Sasang kwa chongch'aek* 2(4):154–73.

Chan, Wing-tsit. 1979. [2] Chinese philosophy. In *Encyclopaedia Britannica, Macropaedia,* vol. 4. Chicago: Encyclopaedia Britannica, Inc.

Chenery, Hollis B. 1961. [17] Comparative advantage and development policy. *American Economic Review* 51 (March):18–51.

Chenery, Hollis B., S. Shishido, and T. Watanabe. 1962. [5] The pattern of Japanese growth, 1914–1954. *Econometrica* 30.

Cho, Ki-Jun, Yun-Gun Lee, Bong-Chul Yoo, and Young Mo Kim. 1971. [22] *Ilje ha ui minjok sang whal sa* (A history of national life during the Japanese colonial period). Seoul: Minjung Seogan.

Cho, Ki-Zun. 1977. [1] *Studies in the History of Korean Capitalist Development.* Seoul: Hanguk.

Cho, Lee-Jay. 1971. [12] The level of fertility and mortality in a Korean rural community. In Minoru Tachi and Min Muramatsu (eds.), *Population Problems in the Pacific: New Dimensions in Pacific Demography.* Tokyo: Convenors of the Congress Symposium No. 1, Eleventh Pacific Science Congress.

Cho, Lee-Jay. 1973. [23] *The Demographic Situation in the Republic of Korea.* Papers of the East–West Population Institute, No. 29. Honolulu: East–West Center.

Cho, Lee-Jay. 1974. [14] Demographic aspects of urbanization in Korea. *Journal of East–West Studies* 3(1):123–38.

Cho, Lee-Jay. 1984. [2] Population dynamics and policy in the People's Republic of China. In Marvin E. Wolfgang (ed.), *The Annals of the American Academy of Political and Social Science* 476:111–27.

Cho, Lee-Jay, Fred Arnold, and Tai Hwan Kwon. 1983. [12] *The Determinants of Fertility in the Republic of Korea.* Committee on Population and Demography, Report No. 14. Washington, D.C.: National Academy Press.

Cho, Lee-Jay, and Janis Y. Togashi. 1985. [2] Industrial transition and demographic dynamics of the Asia–Pacific region. In *Proceedings of the International Symposium on the Role of the Asia–Pacific Region in World Economic Development, December 17–20, 1984.* Tokyo: College of Economics, Nihon University.

Cho, Nam Hoon. 1986. [12] Population policy in Korea. Paper presented at Seminar on Population and Economic Development in Korea, Population Research

Center, Dong-A University, and East-West Population Institute, June 30–July 3, Pusan, Korea.

Cho, T. S. 1983. [19] *General Trading Companies in South Korea* (in Korean). Vols. 1 and 2. Seoul: Bubmurn-sa.

Choe, Sang Chuel, and Jong Kee Kim. 1985. [14] Rural industrial policy in Korea: Past experiences and new approach. Unpublished manuscript.

Choe, Sang Chuel, and Byung Nak Song. 1982. [14] *An Evaluation of Industrial Location Policies for Urban Deconcentration in the Seoul Region.* World Bank Discussion Paper UDD-7. Washington, D.C.: World Bank.

Choe, Y. B. 1978. [16] *The Korean Model of Rural Saemaul Undong: Its Structure, Strategy and Performance.* Korea Rural Economics Institute Working Paper No. 4. Seoul.

Choi, Hochin. 1971. [23] *The Economic History of Korea: From the Earliest Times to 1945.* Seoul: The Freedom Library.

Choi, Jin Ho, and Tae Il Lee. 1985. [14] Attributes of metropolitan suburbanization in the Seoul Capital Region and their policy implications. Paper read at the Korea–U.S. Seminar on Urban/Regional/Transportation Development Planning.

Choo, H. C. 1979. [17] Estimates of size distribution of income and causes of changes (in Korean). *Korea Development Review* (March).

Chung, Hong-Shik. 1985. [17] A study on the adjustment of HCI in Korea (in Korean). Unpublished M.A. thesis, Yonsei University.

Chung, Jae-Chul. 1985. [22] *Iljeui dae hanguk sikminji kyoyuk jungchaeksa* (History of Japanese education policy in Korea). Seoul: Ilji-Sa.

Clapp, John M., and Harry W. Richardson. 1984. [14] Technological change in information-processing industries and regional income differentials in developing countries. *International Regional Science Review* 9(3):241–56.

Clarkson, Graham. 1980. [13] *Health Care Services in Korea with Particular Emphasis on the Medical Insurance Program.* Seoul: Korea Development Institute.

Cochrane, Susan Hill. 1979. [12] *Fertility and Education: What Do We Really Know?* World Bank Staff Occasional Papers, No. 26. Baltimore: Johns Hopkins University Press.

Cole, David C., and Princeton N. Lyman. 1971. [10] *Korean Development: The Interplay of Politics and Economics.* Cambridge, Mass.: Harvard University Press.

Cole, David C., and Yung Chul Park. 1983. [3,4,6,7,8,17,20] *Financial Development in Korea, 1945–78.* Studies in the Modernization of the Republic of Korea, 1945–75. Cambridge, Mass.: Council on East Asian Studies, Harvard University.

Corden, W. Max. 1982. [20] *Booming Sector and Dutch Disease Economics.* Working Paper No. 079. Canberra: Faculty of Economics and Research School of Social Sciences, Australian National University.

Council for Economic Planning and Development, Executive Yuan, Taiwan. 1980, 1983. [9] *Industry of Free China.* Monthly. Taipei.

Das Gupta, Jyotirindra. 1978. [2] A season of Caesars: Emergency regimes and development politics in Asia. *Asian Survey* 18(4):315–49.

Department of Defense, United States (U.S.). 1989. [23] *Defense 89 Almanac.* Washington, D.C.

Department of Statistics, Singapore. 1980, 1983. [9] *Yearbook of Statistics.* Singapore.

Dertouzos, Michael L. 1989. [17] *Made in America: Regaining the Productive Edge.* Cambridge, Mass.: MIT Press.

Director of Intelligence, United States (U.S.). 1983. [20] *Handbook of Statistics, 1983.* Washington, D.C.

Directorate General of the Budget, Accounting and Statistics, Executive Yuan, Taiwan. 1977–80. [9] *Monthly Bulletin of Statistics.* Taipei.

Directorate General of the Budget, Accounting and Statistics, Executive Yuan, Taiwan. 1977–83. [9] *Quarterly National Economic Trends, Taiwan Area.* Taipei.

Doe, Joon Ho. 1984. [20] Overseas construction: Its myth and fiction (in Korean). *Monthly Korea* (February):83–104.

Domar, Evsey D. 1957. [17] *Essays in the Theory of Economic Growth.* New York: Oxford University Press.

Easterlin, Richard A., Robert A. Pollak, and Michael L. Wachter. 1980. [12] Toward a more general model of fertility determination: Endogenous preferences and natural fertility. In Richard A. Easterlin (ed.), *Population and Economic Change in Developing Countries.* Chicago: The University of Chicago Press.

Economic Commission for Asia and the Far East (ECAFE). 1962. [6] Measures for mobilization of domestic savings. *ECAFE Bulletin* (December):22.

Economic Planning Board (EPB), Republic of Korea (ROK). 1960–82. [15] *Monthly Statistical Review.* Seoul.

Economic Planning Board (EPB), Republic of Korea (ROK). 1960, 1966, 1970, 1975, 1980. [14] *Population and Housing Census.* Seoul.

Economic Planning Board (EPB), Republic of Korea (ROK). 1964–84. [9,14] *Annual Report on the Family Income and Expenditure Survey.* Annual. Seoul.

Economic Planning Board (EPB), Republic of Korea (ROK). 1965–82. [15] *Urban Household Living Expenditure Survey.* Annual. Seoul.

Economic Planning Board (EPB), Republic of Korea (ROK). 1966, 1973, 1981. [14] *Mining and Manufacturing Survey.* Seoul.

Economic Planning Board (EPB), Republic of Korea (ROK). 1970–81. [17] *Budget Summary.* Annual. Seoul.

Economic Planning Board (EPB), Republic of Korea (ROK). 1971. [17] *The Third Five-Year Economic Development Plan.* Seoul.

Economic Planning Board (EPB), Republic of Korea (ROK). 1971, 1975–82. [15,18] *Economic Statistics Yearbook.* Annual. Seoul.

Economic Planning Board (EPB), Republic of Korea (ROK). 1971, 1981, 1982. [18] *Survey Report of Mining and Manufacturing Statistics.* Seoul.

Economic Planning Board (EPB), Republic of Korea (ROK). 1974. [14] *Special Labor Force Survey Report.* Seoul.

Economic Planning Board (EPB), Republic of Korea (ROK). 1975. [17] *The Fourth Five-Year Economic Development Plan.* Seoul.

Economic Planning Board (EPB), Republic of Korea (ROK). 1980. [8] *Handbook of Korean Economy.* Seoul.

Economic Planning Board (EPB), Republic of Korea (ROK). 1981. [17] *The Fifth Five-Year Economic and Social Development Plan.* Seoul.

Economic Planning Board (EPB), Republic of Korea (ROK). 1981. [18] Policy proposals for improving the antitrust system (in Korean). Unpublished paper.

Economic Planning Board (EPB), Republic of Korea (ROK). 1982. [13] *Korea Statistical Yearbook.* Seoul.

Economic Planning Board (EPB), Republic of Korea (ROK). 1982. [9,17] *Social Indicators in Korea.* Seoul.

Economic Planning Board (EPB), Republic of Korea (ROK). 1982–83, 1989–90. [4,5,10,17,24] *Major Statistics of Korean Economy.* Seoul.

Economic Planning Board (EPB), Republic of Korea (ROK). 1983. [18] Proceedings of the Industrial and Technological Policy Advisory Meeting for the Revision of the Fifth Five-Year Plan (in Korean). Unpublished paper.

Economic Planning Board (EPB), Republic of Korea (ROK). 1983. [18] Tasks for earlier settlement of the antitrust system (in Korean). Unpublished paper.

Economic Planning Board (EPB), Republic of Korea (ROK). 1985. [7] *Budget Summary, 1983* (in Korean). Seoul.

Economic Planning Board (EPB), Republic of Korea (ROK). 1985. [23] *Census Report for 1985.* Seoul.

Economic Planning Board (EPB), Republic of Korea (ROK). 1986. [12] *Population Projections Based on 1985 Census Results.* Seoul.

Fairbank, John King. 1986. [21] *The Great Chinese Revolution, 1800–1985.* New York: Harper and Row.

Federation of Korean Industries. 1983. [18] *Thirty-Year History of the Federation of Korean Industries* (in Korean). Seoul.

Federation of Korean Medical Insurance Societies. 1983. [13] *Medical Care Security System in Korea.* Seoul.

Fisher, James E. 1928. [22] *Democracy and Mission Education in Korea.* New York: Bureau of Publications, Teachers College, Columbia University.

Frank, Charles R., Jr., Kwang Suk Kim, and Larry E. Westphal. 1975. [5] *Foreign Trade Regimes and Economic Development: South Korea.* New York: National Bureau of Economic Research.

Freedman, Ronald. 1979. [12] Theories of fertility decline: A reappraisal. In Philip M. Hauser (ed.), *World Population and Development: Challenges and Prospects.* Syracuse: Syracuse University Press.

Fu, Luo Cheng. 1985. [21] *History of China* (in Chinese). Taipei: Da Zhungquo Tushu Gongshe.

Fuchs, Roland J. 1983. **[14]** *Population Distribution Policies in Asia and the Pacific: Current Status and Future Prospects*. Papers of the East–West Population Institute, No. 83. Honolulu: East–West Center.

Galenson, W., and H. Leibenstein. 1955. **[17]** Investment criteria, productivity, and economic development. *Quarterly Journal of Economics* 69 (August):343–70.

Gerschenkron, Alexander. 1962. **[17]** *Economic Backwardness in Historical Perspective*. Cambridge, Mass.: Belknap Press of Harvard University Press.

Griffis, William Elliot. 1897. **[1,22]** *Corea, The Hermit Nation*. New York: Charles Scribner's Sons.

Gurley, John G., Hugh T. Patrick, and Edward S. Shaw. 1965. **[6]** *The Financial Structure of Korea*. Seoul: United States Operations Mission/Korea.

Gurley, John G., and Edward S. Shaw. 1955. **[6]** Financial aspects of economic development. *American Economic Review* (September):515–38.

Gurley, John G., and Edward S. Shaw. 1956. **[6]** Financial intermediaries and the saving–investment process. *Journal of Finance* (May):257–76.

Gurley, John G., and Edward S. Shaw. 1967. **[6]** Financial structure and economic development. *Economic Development and Cultural Change* (April):257–68.

Han, Seung-Soo. 1982. **[11]** *Empirical Analysis of the Tax Burden in Korea and Theoretical Analysis of Optimal Tax Burden*. Seoul: Korea Economic Research Institute.

Hansen, Niles. 1981. **[14]** A review and evaluation of attempts to direct migrants to smaller and intermediate-sized cities. In *Population Distribution Policies in Development Planning*. New York: United Nations.

Harberler, G. 1964. **[17]** An assessment of the current relevance of the theory of comparative advantage to agricultural production and trade. *International Journal of Agrarian Affairs*.

Harris, John R., and Michael P. Todaro. 1970. **[14]** Migration, unemployment and development: A two-sector analysis. *American Economic Review* 60(1):126–42.

Hayami, Yujiro. 1975. **[15]** Japan's rice policy in historical perspective. *Food Research Institute Studies* 14:4. Stanford, Calif.: Stanford University.

Heavy and Chemical Industries (HCI) Promotion Council. 1973. **[17]** *The HCI Promotion Plan* (in Korean). Seoul.

Heller, Peter S. 1981. **[11]** Testing the impact of value-added and global income tax reforms on Korean tax incidence in 1976: An input–output and sensitivity analysis. *IMF Staff Papers* 28 (June):375–410.

Henderson, Gregory. 1968. **[1]** *Korea, The Politics of the Vortex*. Cambridge, Mass.: Harvard University Press.

Higgins, Benjamin H. 1968. **[17]** *Economic Development: Problems, Principles, and Policies*. 2nd ed. New York: Norton & Company.

Historical Association of Korea (eds.). 1973. **[21]** *Studies of the Practical School of Confucianism in Korea* (in Korean). Seoul: Ilchokak.

Hoffmann, Walther G. 1958. **[17]** *The Growth of Industrial Economies*. Manchester: Manchester University Press.

Hong, Doo-Seung. 1980. [23] Social stratification and social values in contemporary Korea. Ph.D. dissertation, University of Chicago.

Hong, Doo-Seung, and Lee-Jay Cho. 1986. [23] Development and equity as perceived by the Korean military and business elites. Paper presented at the Eleventh World Congress of Sociology, 18–23 August 1986, New Delhi.

Hong, In Kie. 1974. [10] *Recent Changes in the Tax Structure of Korea.* Korea Development Institute Monograph 7405. Seoul.

Hong, Wontack. 1980. [3] *Trade Distortions and Employment Growth in Korea.* Seoul: KDI Press.

Hsieh, Sen-chung, and T. H. Lee. 1966. [15] *Agricultural Development and Its Contribution to Economic Growth in Taiwan: Input–Output and Productivity Analysis of Taiwan Agricultural Development.* Economic Digest Series, No. 17. Taipei: Chinese–American Joint Commission on Rural Reconstruction.

Ichimura, Shinichi. 1985. [2] Comments on the Korean economic policy case studies. Memorandum.

International Monetary Fund (IMF). 1978–80. [13] *Government Finance Statistics Yearbook.* Annual. Washington, D.C.

International Monetary Fund (IMF). 1981–83. [9,13,20] *International Financial Statistics Yearbook.* Annual. Washington, D.C.

Irvine, Reed J., and Robert F. Emery. 1966. [6] *Interest Rates as an Anti-Inflationary Instrument in Taiwan.* Washington, D.C.: Board of Governors of the Federal Reserve System.

Jain, K. F. 1965. [6] Some aspects of interest rate policy for economic growth. *The Indian Economic Journal* (July–September):29–40.

Jayasuriya, J. E. 1980. [22] *Education in Korea: A Third World Success Story.* Colombo: Associated Educational Publishers.

Jo, S. H. 1984. [19] Industrial growth and international expansion of the South Korean economy (1955–80). Honolulu: East–West Center. Mimeo.

Johnson, Chalmers. 1982. [3,22] *MITI and the Japanese Miracle: The Growth of Industrial Policy, 1925–1975.* Stanford, Calif.: Stanford University Press.

Johnson, Chalmers. 1989. [24] South Korean democratization: The role of economic development. *The Pacific Review* 2(1).

Johnson, Robert H. 1972. [10] The role of fiscal policies in the Third Five-Year Development Plan. In Sung-Hwan Jo and Seong-Yawng Park (eds.), *Basic Documents and Selected Papers of Korea's Third Five-Year Economic Development Plan (1972–1976).* Seoul: Sogan University.

Jones, Leroy P. 1980. [18] *Jae-Bul and the Concentration of Economic Power in Korean Development: Issues, Evidence and Alternatives.* Consultant Paper Series, No. 12. Seoul: Korea Development Institute.

Jones, Leroy P., and Il SaKong. 1980. [7,20] *Government, Business, and Entrepreneurship in Economic Development: The Korean Case.* Studies in the Modernization of the Republic of Korea, 1945–1975. Cambridge, Mass.: Council on East Asian Studies, Harvard University.

Jwa, Sung-Hee. 1988. [17] *Korea's Exchange Rate Policy—System Effects and Issues*. KDI Working Paper 8802. Seoul: Korea Development Institute.

Kahan, A. 1964. [15] The collective farm system in Russia: Some aspects of its contribution to Soviet economic development. In Carl K. Eicher and Lawrence W. Witt (eds.), *Agriculture in Economic Development*. New York: McGraw-Hill.

Kang, Bong-Kyun. 1989. [24] Equity issues in the process of democratization. for the Project of the Future Economic and Social Modernization of Korea (in Korean). Seoul: Economic Planning Board. Mimeo.

Kim, An-Jae. 1978. [14] Industrialization and growth pole development in Korea: A case study of the Ulsan Industrial Complex. In Fu-chen Lo and Kamal Salih (eds.), *Growth Pole Strategy and Regional Development Policy: Asian Experiences and Alternative Approaches*. New York: Published for the United Nations Centre for Regional Development by Pergamon Press.

Kim, Byungkuk. 1965. [3] *Central Banking Experiment in a Developing Economy: Case Study of Korea*. Seoul: Korean Research Center.

Kim, Han Hsik. 1979. [21] *The Political Thought of the Practical School of Confucianism in Korea* (in Korean). Seoul: Ilchisa.

Kim, Hee Joo. 1982. [20] *Korea's Advance to the Middle East and Her Supportive Measures* (in Korean). Seoul: Korea Institute for Industrial Economics and Technology.

Kim, Hyung Kook. 1981. [14] Social factors of migration from rural to urban areas with special reference to developing countries: The case of Korea. *Social Indicators Research* 10(1):29–74.

Kim, Hyung Kook. 1984. [14] Regional development policy response in a rapidly growing economy: The case of the Republic of Korea. In Ed. B. Prantilla (ed.), *Regional Development Problems and Policy Responses in Five Asian and Pacific Countries*. Nagoya: United Nations Centre for Regional Development.

Kim, Hyung Kook. 1985. [14] Theories of national spatial development (in Korean). Seoul: n.p.

Kim, In Chul. 1983a. [7] Economics of external indebtedness and Korea's foreign debt management (in Korean). *Korea Development Review* 5:96–124.

Kim, In Chul. 1983b. [8,20] Models of external debt and Korea's management of external debt (in Korean). *Korea Development Research* (Fall):96–124.

Kim, Joo-Hoon. 1987. [8] External debt and the growth of the Korean economy. Unpublished Ph.D. dissertation, University of Hawaii.

Kim, Joon Bo. 1979. [14] Korean economy and wage structure (in Korean). Seoul: n.p.

Kim, Kwang Suk. 1972. [7] The effect of the August 3rd emergency measures on bank loan rates and business profitability. In *Studies on Stabilization and Growth Policy*. Seoul: Korea Development Institute.

Kim, Kwang Suk. 1977. [7] The causes and effects of inflation. In C. K. Kim (ed.), *Planning Model and Macroeconomic Policy Issues*. Seoul: Korea Development Institute.

Kim, Kwang Suk, and Michael Roemer. 1979. **[5]** *Growth and Structural Transformation. Studies in the Modernization of the Republic of Korea, 1945–1975.* Cambridge: Council on East Asian Studies, Harvard University.

Kim, Kwang Suk, and Larry E. Westphal. 1976. **[5]** *Foreign Exchange and Trade Policy in Korea* (in Korean). Seoul: KDI Press.

Kim, Kyong-Dong. 1987. **[23]** *Dependency Issues in Korean Development: Comparative Perspectives.* Seoul: Seoul National University Press.

Kim, Suyong. 1980. **[4]** *Trade Policy and Price Changes in Korea.* Korea Institute for Industrial Economics and Technology (KIET) Research Series No. 4. Seoul.

Kim, Wan-Soon. 1972. **[7]** The effect of accelerated depreciation allowances on fixed investment (in Korean). In *Studies on Stabilization and Growth Policy.* Seoul: Korea Development Institute.

Kim, Wan-Soon. 1977. **[7]** The equalizing effect of financial transfers: A study of intergovernmental fiscal relations (in Korean). In C. K. Kim (ed.), *Planning Model and Macroeconomic Policy Issues.* Seoul: Korea Development Institute.

Kim, Won Bae. 1985. **[14]** Urban unemployment in Korea. Paper presented at Korea–U.S. Seminar on Urban/Regional/Transportation Development Planning and Environmental Management, 18–24 August 1985, Seoul, Korea.

Kim, Won Bae. 1986. **[12]** Urbanization and urban growth in Korea. Paper presented at the Seminar on Population and Economic Development in Korea, Population Research Center, Dong-A University, and East–West Population Institute, June 30–July 3, Pusan, Korea.

Kim, Yoon Hyung. 1983. **[8]** Rational and effective use of energy in Korea's industrialization. *Energy, The International Journal* 8(1):107–12.

Kim, Yoon Hyung, and Kirk R. Smith (eds.). 1989. **[8]** *Electricity in Economic Development: The Experience of Northeast Asia.* Westport, Conn.: Greenwood Press.

Knodel, John. 1977. **[12]** Family limitation and the fertility transition: Evidence from the age patterns of fertility in Europe and Asia. *Population Reports* 31:219–49.

Kohama, H., and I. Yamazawa. 1982. **[19]** *General Trading Companies and Expansion of Foreign Trade: A Comparative Study of Korea, Thailand and Japan.* Tokyo: International Development Center of Japan.

Koo, Sung Yeal, Mathana Phananiramai, and Andrew Mason. 1986. **[12]** Fertility decline: How important is economic development? In Andrew Mason and Daniel B. Suits (eds.), Population growth and economic development: Lessons from the Pacific Basin. Unpublished manuscript.

Korea Development Bank. 1984. **[17]** *Facility Investment Trend* (in Korean). Seoul.

Korea Development Institute (KDI). 1979. **[9]** *Korea's Income Distribution and Determining Factors.* Vol. 1. Seoul.

Korea Development Institute (KDI). 1980a. **[13]** *Development Strategy and Policy Priorities for the Fifth Five-Year Development Plan.* Seoul.

Korea Development Institute (KDI). 1980b. **[13]** *Overview and Evaluation of KHDI Health Projects.* Seoul.

Korea Development Institute (KDI). 1981. [9] *Collected Materials for the Economic Stabilization Measures.* Seoul.

Korea Development Institute (KDI). 1982. [17] *Basic Issues of Industrial Policies and Direction of Revision of the Incentive Regime* (in Korean). Research Report 82-09. Seoul.

Korea National Housing Corporation (KNHC). 1980, 1983. [7,9] *Handbook of Housing Statistics.* Seoul.

Korea National Housing Corporation (KNHC). 1983. [13] *Housing Policy Development Research.* Seoul.

Korean Economic Development Institute (KEDI). 1967. [6] *Analysis of Capital Costs— Selected Industrial Establishments.* Seoul.

Krishna, Raj. 1967. [15] Agricultural price policy and economic development. In Herman M. Southworth and Bruce F. Johnston (eds.), *Agricultural Development and Economic Growth.* Ithaca: Cornell University Press.

Krueger, Anne O. 1979. [17] *The Developmental Role of the Foreign Sector and Aid.* Studies in the Modernization of the Republic of Korea. Cambridge, Mass.: Council on East Asian Studies, Harvard University.

Kuznets, Simon. 1961. [15] Economic growth and the contribution of agriculture: Notes on measurements. *International Journal of Agrarian Affairs.*

Kuznets, Simon. 1974. [12] Rural–urban differences in fertility: An international comparison. *Proceedings of the American Philosophical Society* 118(1) (February):1–29.

Kwack, Tae Weon. 1985. [17] *Depreciation System and Capital Gains Tax* (in Korean). Seoul: Korea Development Institute.

Kwon, Tae Joon. 1983. [14] Population concentration in the Capital region: Problems and policies (in Korean). *Journal of Population Studies* 24:2–11.

Kwon, Tai Hwan, Hae Young Lee, Yunshik Chang, and Eui-Young Yu. 1975. [12,23] *The Population of Korea.* Seoul: The Population and Development Studies Center, Seoul National University.

Kwon, Won Yong. 1981. [14] A study of the economic impact of industrial relocation. *Urban Studies* 18:73–90.

Leavitt, Harold J. 1958. [21] Some effects of certain communications patterns on group performance. In Eleanor E. Maccoby, Theodore M. Newcomb, and Eugene L. Hartley (eds.), *Readings in Social Psychology.* New York: Holt.

Lee, Chung H. 1986. [20] Migration abroad for temporary employment and its effects on the country of origin. *Journal of International Economic Integration* 1(2):132–48.

Lee, C. Y. 1984. [19] *Foreign Trade Development and General Trading Companies in South Korea* (in Korean). Seoul: Korean Economic Research Institute.

Lee, Doo-Sung. 1983. [15] A study of the effects of fertilizer price policy in Korea. Unpublished master's thesis, Konkuk University.

Lee, Han Soon. 1983. [14] Changing pattern of Korean internal migration: 1960–1980 (in Korean). *Journal of Population Studies* 24:124–43.

Lee, Jungsoo. 1983. [20] The external debt-servicing capacity of Asian developing countries. *Asian Development Review* 1(2):66–82.

Lee, Ki-Suk. 1982. [14] The impact of national development strategies and industrialization on rapid urbanization of Korea. In Victor F. S. Sit and Koichi Mera (eds.), *Urbanization and National Development in Asia: A Comparative Study.* Hong Kong: University of Hong Kong; Tsukuba, Japan: University of Tsukuba.

Lee, Kwang-kyu. 1986. [22] Confucian tradition in the contemporary Korean family. In Walter H. Slote (ed.), *The Psycho-Cultural Dynamics of the Confucian Family: Past and Present.* Seoul: International Cultural Society of Korea.

Lee, Kyuuck. 1977. [18] *Market Structure and Monopoly-Oligopoly Regulation* (in Korean). Seoul: Korea Development Institute.

Lee, Kyuuck. 1988. [18] *Economic Power Concentration and Fair Trade Policy* (in Korean). Seoul: Korea Development Institute.

Lee, Kyuuck. 1990. [17] *Business Groups and Economic Power* (in Korean). Seoul: Korea Development Institute.

Lee, Kyuuck, and Jin-Kyo Suh. 1981. [18] *Analysis of Industrial Concentration in the Korean Manufacturing Industries* (in Korean). Seoul: Korea Development Institute.

Legge, James, translator. 1959. [21] *The Four Books: The Great Learning, The Doctrine of the Mean, Confucian Analects, and the Works of Mencius.* Chinese text with English translation and notes by James Legge. Taipei: The Culture Book Company.

Little, Ian M. D., Tibor Scitovsky, and Maurice F. Scott. 1970. [5] *Industry and Trade in Some Developing Countries: A Comparative Study.* Published for the Development Centre of the Organisation for Economic Co-operation and Development. London: Oxford University Press.

Lyall, Leonard A., and Chien-Kun King, translators. 1927. [21] *The Chung Yung, or the Centre, the Common.* London: Longmans.

Mahalanobis, P. C. 1953/54. [17] Some observations on the process of growth of national income. *Sankhya* (December):307–12.

Mason, Andrew. 1986a. [12] Demographic change and the saving rate. In Andrew Mason and Daniel B. Suits (eds.), Population growth and economic development: Lessons from the Pacific Basin. Unpublished manuscript.

Mason, Andrew. 1986b. [12] *Demographic Prospects in the Republic of Korea: Population, Households, and Education to the Year 2000.* Working Papers of the East–West Population Institute, No. 43. Honolulu: East–West Center.

Mason, Andrew, Daniel B. Suits, Sung-Yeal Koo, Naohiro Ogawa, Mathana Phananiramai, and Hananto Sigit. 1986. [12] *Population Growth and Economic Development: Lessons from Selected Asian Countries.* Policy Development Studies, No. 10. New York: United Nations Fund for Population Activities.

Mason, Edward S., Mahn Je Kim, Dwight H. Perkins, Kwang Suk Kim, David C. Cole, Leroy Jones, Il SaKong, Donald R. Snodgrass, and Noel F. McGinn. 1980. [2,5,10,13] *The Economic and Social Modernization of the Republic of Korea.* Studies in the Modernization of the Republic of Korea, 1945–1975. Cambridge, Mass.: Council on East Asian Studies, Harvard University.

McGinn, Noel F., Donald S. Snodgrass, Yung Bong Kim, Shin-Bok Kim, and Que-Young Kim. 1980. [13] *Education and Development in Korea*. Studies in the Modernization of the Republic of Korea, 1945–1975. Cambridge, Mass.: Council on East Asian Studies, Harvard University.

McKinnon, Ronald I. 1967. [5] Tariff and commodity tax reform in Korea: Some specific suggestions. Unpublished paper prepared for USAID/Korea.

McKinnon, Ronald I. 1973. [3,7,17] *Money and Capital in Economic Development*. Washington, D.C.: Brookings Institution.

McKinnon, Ronald I. 1976. [7] Saving propensities and the Korean monetary reform in retrospect. In Ronald I. McKinnon (ed.), *Money and Finance in Economic Growth and Development, Essays in Honor of Edward S. Shaw*. New York: Marrcel Dekker.

Meade, Edward Grant. 1951. [1] *American Military Government in Korea*. New York: King's Crown Press.

Michael, Robert T. 1974. [12] Education and the derived demand for children. *Journal of Political Economy* 82 (March/April):S128–S167.

Mills, Edwin S. 1980. [14] *Procedures for Allocation of Land in Korea*. KDI Consultant Paper No. 6. Seoul: Korea Development Institute.

Mills, Edwin S., and Byungnak Song. 1979. [4] *Urbanization and Urban Problems*. Studies in the Modernization of the Republic of Korea, 1945–1975. Cambridge, Mass.: Council on East Asian Studies, Harvard University.

Min, Byoung Kyun. 1976. [7] Financial restrictions in Korea, 1965–1974. Unpublished Ph.D. dissertation, University of Hawaii.

Ministry of Agriculture and Fisheries (MAF), Republic of Korea (ROK). 1960–82. [15,16] *Agriculture and Fisheries Statistics Yearbook*. Annual. Seoul.

Ministry of Agriculture and Fisheries (MAF), Republic of Korea (ROK). 1960–83. [15,16] *Farm Household Economy Survey*. Annual. Seoul.

Ministry of Commerce and Industry (MCI), Republic of Korea (ROK). 1967–83. [5] *Semi-Annual (or Annual) Trade Programs—Public Notices*. Seoul.

Ministry of Commerce and Trade (MCT), Republic of Korea (ROK). 1984. [14] *Status of Industrial Estates*. Seoul.

Ministry of Education, Republic of Korea (ROK). 1975–85. [17] *Education Statistics Yearbook*. Seoul.

Ministry of Education, Republic of Korea (ROK). 1986. [22] *Education in Korea, 1985–1986*. Seoul.

Ministry of Finance (MOF), Republic of Korea (ROK). 1967. [10] *The White Paper on Tax Reform* (in Korean). Seoul.

Ministry of Finance (MOF), Republic of Korea (ROK). 1972. [10] *An Outline of the 1971 Tax System Reform* (in Korean). Seoul.

Ministry of Finance (MOF), Republic of Korea (ROK). 1975a. [10] *Defense Tax Law* (in Korean). Seoul.

Ministry of Finance (MOF), Republic of Korea (ROK). 1975b. **[10]** *Summary of Revised Tax Laws* (in Korean). Seoul.

Ministry of Finance (MOF), Republic of Korea (ROK). 1977. **[10]** *Value-Added Tax* (in Korean). Seoul.

Ministry of Finance (MOF), Republic of Korea (ROK). 1978. **[5]** *Thirty Years History of Public Finance and Banking in Korea* (in Korean). Seoul.

Ministry of Finance (MOF), Republic of Korea (ROK). 1979a. **[18]** The financial policies of Korea (in Korean). Unpublished paper. Seoul.

Ministry of Finance (MOF), Republic of Korea (ROK). 1979b. **[10]** *History of the Korean Tax System* (in Korean). Seoul.

Ministry of Finance (MOF), Republic of Korea (ROK). 1980. **[11]** *Survey and Report on the Value-Added Tax.* Seoul.

Ministry of Finance (MOF), Republic of Korea (ROK). 1983a. **[11]** *Major Statistics on Indirect National Taxes.* Seoul.

Ministry of Finance (MOF), Republic of Korea (ROK). 1983b. **[11]** *Summary of Financial Implementation for FY 1982.* Seoul.

Ministry of Health and Social Affairs (MOHSA), Republic of Korea (ROK). 1983. **[13]** *Yearbook of Health and Social Statistics.* Seoul.

Ministry of Home Affairs (MOHA), Republic of Korea (ROK). 1972–82. **[16]** *Saemaul Undong: From Its Beginning Until Today.* Annual. Seoul.

Ministry of Home Affairs (MOHA), Republic of Korea (ROK). 1980. **[14]** *Annual Report of Gross Regional Product.* Annual. Seoul.

Ministry of Labor, Republic of Korea (ROK). 1975–85. **[17]** *Labor Statistics Yearbook.* Seoul.

Ministry of Labor, Republic of Korea (ROK). 1981–89. **[17]** *Monthly Labor Statistics.* Seoul.

Ministry of Science and Technology, Republic of Korea (ROK). 1987. **[24]** *Twenty Years' History of Science and Technology Administration* (in Korean). Seoul.

Moon, Pal Yong. 1982. **[15]** *Modern Agricultural Economics.* Seoul: Sonjin Co.

Morishima, Michio. 1982. **[17,21]** *Why Has Japan 'Succeeded'? Western Technology and the Japanese Ethos.* Cambridge: Cambridge University Press.

Musgrave, Richard A. 1959. **[10]** *The Theory of Public Finance: A Study in Public Finance.* New York: McGraw-Hill.

Musgrave, Richard A. 1967. **[10]** Suggestions for the 1967 tax reform. Unpublished paper submitted to the Ministry of Finance, Republic of Korea.

Nakamura, Takafusa, and Bernard R. G. Grace. 1985. **[17]** *Economic Development of Modern Japan.* Tokyo: Ministry of Foreign Affairs.

Nam, Chong Hyon. 1981. **[5]** Trade, industrial policies and the structure of protection in Korea. In Wontack Hong and Laurence B. Krause (eds.), *Trade and Growth of the Advanced Developing Countries in the Pacific Basin.* Seoul: KDI Press.

Nam, Duck-Woo, and Kong-Kyun Ro. 1981. [14] Population research and population policy in Korea in the 1970s. *Population and Development Review* 7(4):651–69.

Nam, Sang-Woo. 1981. [4] Cost and monetary factors in inflation (in Korean). *Korea Development Review* (Winter). Seoul.

Nam, Sang-Woo. 1982. [9] A study of the appropriate measure of money in Korea (in Korean). *Korea Development Review* (June). Seoul.

National Agricultural Cooperatives Federation (NACF), Republic of Korea (ROK). 1963–84. [14,16] *Agriculture Yearbook*. Annual. Seoul.

National Bureau of Statistics (NBS), Economic Planning Board (EPB), Republic of Korea (ROK). 1987. [12] *1985 Population and Housing Census Report*. Vol. I, *Whole Country*. Seoul.

National Health Secretariat (NHS), Republic of Korea (ROK). 1978. [13] *Reform Measures for City and Provincial Hospitals*. Report submitted to the Ministry of Health and Social Affairs. Seoul: Korea Development Institute.

National Research Council (NRC), United States. 1986. [12] *Population Growth and Economic Development: Policy Questions*. Washington, D.C.: National Academy of Sciences Press.

Naya, Seiji, D. H. Kim, and W. James. 1984. [8] External shocks and policy responses: The Asian experience. *Asian Development Review* 2(1):1–22.

Nelson, Paul. 1974. [20] Advertising as information. *Journal of Political Economy* 82(4):729–54.

Office of National Tax Administration (ONTA), Republic of Korea (ROK). 1960, 1967–68, 1974–75, 1980, 1982–83. [10,11] *Statistical Yearbook of National Tax*. Annual. Seoul.

Office of National Tax Administration (ONTA), Republic of Korea (ROK). 1967. [10] *An Outline of Korean Taxation*. Seoul.

Office of the President, Republic of Korea (ROK). 1974. [17] *President's Speech Collection* (in Korean). Vol. 5. Seoul.

Oh, Yeon-Cheon. 1982. [11] An evaluation of the tax reform for a value-added tax in Korea with special reference to distribution of the tax burden, administrative efficiency, and export. Unpublished doctoral dissertation, New York University.

Okawa, Kazusi, and H. Rosovsky. 1960. [15] The role of agriculture in modern Japanese economic development. *Journal of Economic Development and Cultural Change* 9:2.

Oliver, Robert T. 1954. [1] *Syngman Rhee: The Man Behind the Myth*. New York: Dodd Mead and Company.

Oliver, Robert T. 1956. [22] Psychological warfare in Korea—Old and new. *Vital Speeches* (September):718–20.

Oliver, Robert T. 1978. [1] *Syngman Rhee and American Involvement in Korea, 1942–1960: A Personal Narrative*. Seoul: Panmun Book Company.

Olson, Mancur. 1982. [21] *The Rise and Decline of Nations: Economic Growth, Stagflation, and Social Rigidities*. New Haven, Conn.: Yale University Press.

Overseas Construction Association of Korea. 1984. [20] *White Paper on Overseas Construction* (in Korean). Seoul.

Palais, James B. 1975. [1,21] *Politics and Policy in Traditional Korea*. Cambridge, Mass.: Harvard University Press.

Park, Byung Ho. 1983. [20] Economic consequences of the Middle East advance (in Korean). In *Overseas Migration of Koreans*. Seoul: Institute of Population and Development, Seoul National University.

Park, Chai Bin. 1983. [12] Preference for sons, family size, and sex ratio: An empirical study in Korea. *Demography* 20 (August):333–52.

Park, Chong Kee. 1970. [10] An analysis of income elasticity of the tax yield in Korea. Doctoral dissertation, George Washington University.

Park, Chong Kee. 1975. [13] *Social Security in Korea: An Approach to Socio-Economic Development*. Seoul: Korea Development Institute.

Park, Chong Kee. 1977. [13] *Financing Health Care Services in Korea*. Seoul: Korea Development Institute.

Park, Chong Kee. 1978. [10] *Taxation and Economic Development in Korea*. Korea Modernization Study Series No. 13. Seoul: Korea Development Institute.

Park, Chong Kee. 1979. [13] *Health Care Financing and Medical Insurance in Korea* (in Korean). Seoul: Korea Development Institute.

Park, Chong Kee. 1981. [13] Economic growth and major issues of social security in Korea (in Korean). *Korea Development Research* (Spring).

Park, Chong Kee, and Ha Choeng Yeon. 1981. [13] Recent developments in the health care system of Korea. *International Social Security Review* 2:151–67.

Park, Chong Kee, Sang Mok Suh, Ha Cheong Yeon, Chai Sung Min, and Dong Hyun Kim. 1981. [13] *Research Report on the Improvement of the Social Security System in Korea* (in Korean). Report prepared at the request of the deputy prime minister and minister of the Economic Planning Board. Seoul: Korea Development Institute.

Park, Chung Hee. 1963. [2] *The Country, the Revolution and I*. Seoul: n.p.

Park, J. H. 1981. [16] Process of Saemaul Undong project implementation in Korea. In Lee Man Gap (ed.), *Toward a New Community*. Seoul: Institute of Saemaul Undong Studies, Seoul National University.

Park, Rae Yung. 1983. [20] Effects of labor service exports to the Middle East on the domestic labor market of Korea (in Korean). In *Overseas Migration of Koreans*. Seoul: Institute of Population and Development, Seoul National University.

Patrick, Hugh T. 1966. [6] Financial development and economic growth in underdeveloped countries. *Economic Development and Cultural Change* (January).

Petersen, William, and Renee Petersen. 1986. [14] *Dictionary of Demography: Terms, Concepts, and Institutions*. Vol. 1. New York: Greenwood Press.

Prestowitz, Clyde V. 1988. [17] *Trading Places: How We Allowed Japan to Take the Lead*. New York: Basic Books.

Renaud, Bertrand. 1977. **[14]** *Economic Fluctuations and Speed of Urbanization: A Case Study of Korea, 1955–1975.* World Bank Staff Paper No. 270. Washington, D.C.: World Bank.

Renaud, Bertrand. 1981. **[14]** *National Urbanization Policy in Developing Countries.* New York: Published for the World Bank by Oxford University Press.

Republic of Korea (ROK), Government of. 1966. **[6]** *The Second Five-Year Economic Development Plan, 1967–1971.* Seoul.

Republic of Korea (ROK), Government of. 1976. **[11]** Value-added tax law, 22 December.

Retherford, Robert D., and James A. Palmore. 1983. **[12]** Diffusion processes affecting fertility regulation. In Rodolfo A. Bulatao and Ronald D. Lee (eds.), *Determinants of Fertility in Developing Countries.* New York: Academic Press.

Richardson, Harry W. 1981. **[14]** National urban development strategies in developing countries. *Urban Studies* 18:267–83.

Rondinelli, Dennis A. 1985. **[14]** Land development policy in South Korea. *Geographical Review* 74(4):426–40.

Rosenstein-Rodan, Paul N. 1984. **[17]** Natura facit saltum: Analysis of the disequilibrium growth process. In Gerald M. Meier and Dudley Seers (eds.), *Pioneers in Development.* New York: Published for the World Bank by Oxford University Press.

Rosenzweig, Mark, and Robert Evenson. 1977. **[12]** Fertility, schooling, and the economic contribution of children in rural India: An econometric analysis. *Econometrica* 45 (July):1065–1079.

Rutt, Richard. 1972. **[21]** *James Scarth Gale and His History of the Korean People.* Seoul: Royal Asiatic Society (Korea Branch) and Taewon Publishing Company.

SaKong, Il. 1980. **[3,17,18]** Economic growth and the concentration of economic power (in Korean). *Korea Development Review* (Spring).

SaKong, Il. 1981. **[18]** Economic development and the role of government (in Korean). *Korea Development Review* (Spring).

SaKong, Il, and Leroy P. Jones. 1981. **[18]** *Economic Development and the Role of Government and Entrepreneur.* Seoul: Korea Development Institute.

Salih, Kamal, Phisit Pakkasem, Ed. B. Prantilla, and Sugijanto Soegijoko. 1978. **[14]** Decentralization policy, growth pole approach and resouce frontier development: A synthesis of the response in four Southeast Asian countries. In Fu-chen Lo and Kamal Salih (eds.), *Growth Pole Strategy and Regional Development Policy: Asian Experiences and Alternative Approaches.* New York: Published for the United Nations Centre for Regional Development by Pergamon Press.

Schultz, T. Paul. 1973. **[12]** Explanation of birth rate changes over space and time: A study of Taiwan. *Journal of Political Economy* 81 (March/April):S238–S274.

Schultz, T. Paul. 1976. **[12]** Interrelationships between mortality and fertility. In Ronald G. Ridker (ed.), *Population and Development: The Search for Selective Interventions.* Baltimore: Johns Hopkins University Press.

Schultz, T. Paul. 1987. **[12]** School expenditures and enrollment, 1960–1980: The effects of income, prices, and population growth. In D. Gale Johnson and Ronald

D. Lee (eds.), *Population Growth & Economic Development: Issues and Evidence*. Madison: University of Wisconsin Press.

Scrimshaw, Susan C. M. 1978. [12] Infant mortality and behavior in regulation of family size. *Population and Development Review* 4 (September).

Sen, A. 1983. [17] Development: Which way now? *The Economic Journal* 93 (December):745–62.

Seoul, The Special City of. 1981. [14] *Annual Account of City Income, 1980*.

Shaw, Edward S. 1973. [3,7] *Financial Deepening in Economic Development*. London: Oxford University Press.

Shome, Parthasarathi, and Woo Sik Kee. 1977. [14] Tax incentives in selected Asian countries: A comparative study. *The Philippine Review of Business and Economics* 14(2):105–22.

Simon, Julian L. 1974. [12] *The Effects of Income on Fertility*. Chapel Hill: Carolina Population Center.

Sohn, Jae Souk. 1988. [22] Korea's educational reform proposal and international education. Unpublished discussion paper distributed at the East-West Center, Honolulu.

Song, Heehyon. 1972. [7] Quarterly economic growth and price movements (in Korean). In *Studies on Stabilization and Growth Policy*. Seoul: Korea Development Institute.

Spencer, David. 1965. [20] An external military presence, technological transfer, and structural change. *Kyklos*, Fasc. 3, 451–74.

Suh, Sang-Chul. 1978. [1,22] *Growth and Structural Changes in the Korean Economy, 1910–1940*. Cambridge, Mass.: Harvard University Press.

Suits, Daniel B., and Andrew Mason. 1986. [12] Description of demographic-economic model. In Andrew Mason and Daniel B. Suits (eds.), Population growth and economic development: Lessons from the Pacific Basin. Unpublished manuscript.

Syrquin, Moshe. 1976. [5] Sources of industrial growth and structural change. Unpublished paper, World Bank, Washington, D.C.

Taeuber, Irene B., and George Barclay. 1950. [23] Korea and the Koreans in the Northeast Asian region. *Population Index* 16(4):278–97.

Tait, Alan A. 1980. [11] *Is the Introduction of a Value-Added Tax Inflationary?* IMF Fiscal Affairs Department, Paper No. DM/80/75, November 3. Washington, D.C.

Tait, Alan A., Angelo E. Faria, and Peter S. Heller. 1979. [10] *Korea: Taxes in the 1980s*. Washington, D.C.: International Monetary Fund.

Thurow, Lester C. 1985. [21] *The Zero-Sum Solution: Building a World-Class American Economy*. New York: Simon and Schuster.

Tolley, George S., Phillip E. Graves, and John L. Gardner. 1979. [14] *Urban Growth Policy in a Market Economy*. New York: Academic Press.

Townroe, Peter M. 1979. [14] Employment decentralisation: policy instruments for large cities in LDCs. *Progress in Planning* 10:85–154.

Tracy, Michael. 1964. [15] *Agriculture in Western Europe*. London: Jonathan Cape.

Trussell, James, and Randall Olsen. 1983. [12] Evaluation of the Olsen Technique for estimating the fertility response to child mortality. *Demography* 20 (August):391–406.

Tsukuba University, Foundation for the Promotion of International Science (Tsukuba Daigaku Kokusai Kayaku Shinto Zaidan). 1986. [21] *The Eighth International Conference on the T'oegye School of Neo-Confucianism, August 27–29, 1985* (in English and Japanese). Tokyo: Toyo Shoin.

Tun Wai, U. 1956. [6] Interest rates in the organized money markets of underdeveloped countries. *IMF Staff Papers* (August):249–78.

United Nations. 1977–83. [9] *Monthly Bulletin of Statistics*. New York.

United Nations. 1978, 1985. [12] *Demographic Yearbook*. New York.

United Nations Educational, Social, and Scientific Organization (UNESCO). 1954. [22] *Rebuilding Education in the Republic of Korea: Report of the UNESCO-UNKRA Educational Planning Mission to Korea*. Paris: UNESCO.

United Nations Educational, Social, and Scientific Organization (UNESCO). 1988. [22] *Education in Asia and the Pacific: Reviews, Reports and Notes*. Bangkok: UNESCO Principal Regional Office for Asia and the Pacific.

Westphal, Larry E., and Kwang Suk Kim. 1977. [5] *Industrial Policy and Development in Korea*. World Bank Staff Working Paper No. 263. Washington, D.C.: World Bank.

Westphal, Larry E., and Kwang Suk Kim. 1982. [5] Korea. In Bela Balassa and Associates (eds.), *Development Strategies in Semi-Industrial Economies*. Baltimore: Johns Hopkins University Press.

Whang, In-Joung. 1981. [16] *Management of Rural Change in Korea: The Saemaul Undong*. Institute of Social Sciences, Korean Studies Series No. 5. Seoul: Seoul National University Press.

Willis, Robert J. 1973. [12] A new approach to the economic theory of fertility. *Journal of Political Economy* 81 (March/April):S14–S69.

Willis, Robert J. 1982. [12] The direction of intergenerational transfers and demographic transition: The Caldwell Hypothesis reexamined. In Yoram Ben-Porath (ed.), *Income Distribution and the Family*. A special issue of *Population and Development Review* 8:207–34.

World Bank. 1978–83, 1987. [9,17] *World Development Report*. New York: Oxford University Press.

World Bank. 1986. [17] *Korea: Managing the Industrial Transition*. Vol. I. Washington, D.C.: The World Bank.

Yamazawa, I. 1979. [19] General trading companies and trade expansion (in Japanese). *Keizai-kabu-Kenkyu* (Hitotsuha-shi University Research Annals).

Yang, Sung-du. 1985. [23] Sahoe pyonhwa wa pop ui sik ui pyonhwa (Social change and attitudes toward law). *Sasang kwa chongch'aek* 2(4):122–32.

Yap, Lorene Y. L. 1977. [14] The attraction of cities: A review of the migration literature. *Journal of Development Economics* 4:239–64.

Yeon, Ha Choeng. 1981. [13] *Primary Health Care in Korea: An Approach to Evaluation*. Seoul: Korea Development Institute.

Yeon, Ha Choeng, Chong Kee Park, Chai Sung Min, Chong Duk Hong, Jai Yong Park, Il Soon Kim, Dal Sun Hahn, and Hak Yung Kim. 1983. [13] *Policy Issues and the Future Development of Medical Insurance in Korea* (in Korean). Seoul: Korea Development Institute.

Yu, Eui Young. 1978. [14] Internal migration and urbanization. In H. Y. Lee and Tae Hwan Kwon (eds.), *Korean Society: Population and Development*. Vol. I. Seoul: Seoul National University Press.

Yu, Jung-Ho. 1989. [17] The Korean experience with an industrial targeting policy. Seoul: Korea Development Institute. Mimeo.

Yun, Chong-Chu. 1974. [23] *Inguhak* (A study of population). Seoul: Hanol Mungo.

Yun, I-hum. 1985. [23] Munhwa pyondong kwa ta chonggyo sanghwang ui munje (Cultural change and religious patterns). *Sasang kwa chongch'aek* 2(4):199–214.

Index

THE EAST-WEST CENTER is a public, nonprofit educational institution established in Hawaii in 1960 by the United States Congress with a mandate "to promote better relations and understanding among the nations of Asia, the Pacific, and the United States through cooperative study, training, and research."

Some 2,000 research fellows, graduate students and professionals in business and government each year work with the Center's international staff on major Asia-Pacific issues relating to population, economic and trade policies, resources and development, the environment, culture and communication, and international relations. Since 1960, more than 25,000 men and women from the region have participated in the Center's cooperative programs.

Principal funding for the Center comes from the United States Congress. Support also comes from more than 20 Asian and Pacific governments, as well as private agencies and corporations. The Center has an international board of governors.